The Editor

A NORTON CRITICAL EDITION

BEN JONSON'S PLAYS AND MASQUES

Authoritative Texts of
VOLPONE • EPICOENE • THE ALCHEMIST
THE MASQUE OF BLACKNESS •
MERCURY VINDICATED FROM THE
ALCHEMISTS AT COURT • PLEASURE
RECONCILED TO VIRTUE

Contexts

Backgrounds and Sources

Criticism

SECOND EDITION

Edited by

RICHARD HARP
UNIVERSITY OF NEVADA, LAS VEGAS

First Edition edited by
ROBERT M. ADAMS
LATE OF THE UNIVERSITY OF CALIFORNIA, LOS ANGELES

W • W • NORTON & COMPANY • *New York* • *London*

Copyright © 2001 by W. W. Norton & Company, Inc.

The text of this book is composed in Electra
with the display set in Bernhard Modern.
Composition by PennSet, Inc.
Manufacturing by Courier Companies
Book design by Antonina Krass.

Library of Congress Cataloging-in-Publication Data

Jonson, Ben, 1573?–1637.
   [Selections. 2000]
   Ben Jonson's plays and masques : authoritative texts of Volpone, Epicoene, The
alchemist, The masque of blackness, Mercury vindicated from the alchemists at
court, Pleasure reconciled to virtue : contexts, criticism.—2nd ed. / edited by
Richard Harp.
      p. cm.— (A Norton critical edition)
   "First edition by Robert M. Adams."
   Includes bibliographical references.

ISBN 0-393-97638-6 (pbk.)

   1. Jonson, Ben, 1573?–1637—Dramatic works. 2. Masques—History and
criticism. I. Harp, Richard. II.Title.

PR2602 .A3 2000
822'.3—dc21
                                               00-060906

W. W. Norton & Company, Inc., 500 Fifth Avenue, New York, N.Y. 10110
www.wwnorton.com

W. W. Norton & Company Ltd., 10 Coptic Street, London WC1A 1PU

1 2 3 4 5 6 7 8 9 0

Contents

Preface

Ben Jonson wrote nineteen plays and had an assistant's hand in several others; he was the author of twenty-four masques and entertainments. To represent in reasonable compass the scope of his work for the stage and the court, one must select. The first choices are not at all difficult, since everyone agrees that his twin masterpieces for the stage are *Volpone* and *The Alchemist*, both in verse. *Epicoene*, in prose, is our third choice; it has a beautifully articulated plot and a set of characters whose manners and motives are relatively easy to grasp. In fact it is close kin to the sort of gentlemanly comedy that would come into full fashion at the Restoration —easy and fluent in its wit, full of the spirit of play, but tough too (as Jonson could always be tough) in its judgment of moral and social values.

Jonson's masques and courtly entertainments, as they have come down to us, vary enormously in size and "seriousness," depending on the social occasion that called them forth. They might help to welcome a distinguished visitor to a country house, to celebrate a wedding or a birthday, or to enliven the Christmas season at court, when merry-making and feasting were traditional. The persons participating might be of the very highest rank under the king, or of somewhat lower status; the amount of money spent might be slight or enormous. For the great court masques, in which the richest ladies in the land vied to outdo one another, thousands of pounds might be invested in costumes, musicians, and stage-machinery; and for such occasions, the poet as well might feel impelled to outdo himself.

The plays and masques selected for this volume can be supplemented, for the poetry and critical prose, by Hugh MacLean's Norton Critical Edition of *Ben Jonson and the Cavalier Poets*; and from there, the devotee of Ben is invited to move on to the *Complete Works* edited by Herford and Simpson in a classic 11-volume edition. Our texts here have been modernized for greater accessibility, but checked against the old-spelling versions of Herford and Simpson, according to principles outlined in the Note on the Text. The background materials contain hints toward Jonson's structure of esthetic values and glimpses of his informal personality; the appended critical essays provide a cross section of modern views as they relate particularly to the materials of this collection.

This edition of *Ben Jonson's Plays and Masques* retains the three dramatic masterpieces printed in the first edition, *Volpone* (1606), *Epicoene* (1609), and *The Alchemist* (1610). Nearly all of that edition's notes have been retained as well, although a considerable number of new ones have been added to make the plays even more accessible to students. Jonson's comedy is rich in plot, character, and language, and the latter demands as much annotation as space allows without making the page too forbidding for the reader. Two masques from the first edition are also here, *Mercury Vindicated from the Alchemists at Court* (1615) and *Pleasure Reconciled to Virtue* (1618), along with the new *The Masque of Blackness* (1605), Jonson's first masque and one that deals with issues of interest to our own culture.

A new section on "Backgrounds and Sources" has been added to this edition. Clear and coherent sources for many of Jonson's plays are lacking, but for *Volpone* and *The Alchemist*, at least, there are certain obvious texts that helped to shape the dramatist's vision. Aesop's fable of the fox and the crow is the seed from which grew the abundance of *Volpone*, and the subsequent incarnations and adaptations of this fable are here represented in selections from the medieval bestiary, William Caxton's *Reynard the Fox*, Chaucer's "The Nun's Priest's Tale," and La Fontaine's "The Fox and the Crow." This last, of course, was published after Jonson died but is included here as representing the most famous short version of the fable in later literary history. Ancient satires on legacy hunting that were useful to Jonson's portrayal of his greedy birds of prey are represented in the selection from Horace's *Satires*. Sources for *The Alchemist* included here are Erasmus's famous dialogue on alchemy, first published in 1524, and some selections from Stanton J. Linden's book on the history of alchemy in English literature.

Nine new critical essays, most representing scholarship and interpretations of the past twenty years, are included in this edition. Those by Robert Evans and Leah S. Marcus relate Jonson's work to personalities and issues of his time, a frequent emphasis in current Renaissance scholarship. Interest in the masques has grown considerably since the publication of the first edition; that interest is reflected here in the article by Marcus as well as in those by John Mulryan on *Pleasure Reconciled to Virtue* and by Stephen Orgel and D. S. Gordon on *The Masque of Blackness*. Issues of religion and the theater in *The Alchemist* are considered in essays by Richard Harp and Ian Donaldson; Robert Watson discusses the ways in which Jonson "parodies" previous dramatic conventions in *Epicoene*, and Anne Barton examines the use of names in the three plays. The classic seventeenth-century "Examen" by John Dryden of *Epicoene* is reprinted in this edition, as are the important articles by Jonas A. Barish and Edward B. Partridge on *Volpone* and *The Alchemist*, respectively. The bibliography has been considerably enlarged.

Jonson was one of the few important writers of the early seventeenth century to offer detailed literary criticism, and many of his comments will be found in the section "Jonson on His Work." His remarkably frank *Conversations with William Drummond of Hawthornden* is given in modernized English. The great impact he had on his contemporaries is further illustrated in the subsection "Contemporary Readers on Jonson." Much like his famous predecessor Thomas More, Jonson was a man for all seasons, and his work, in its variety and depth, and his person, magisterial and commanding yet always in touch with "life's common way," can be seen in much of its fullness in this volume.

The Staging of Jonson's Plays and Masques

The plays in this volume which were mounted on the stage were exhibited to paying audiences in theaters of two different sorts. *Volpone* and *The Alchemist* were staged, in 1606 and 1610 respectively, by the King's Men at the Globe Theater on the Bankside: this was a public theater. *Epicoene* was first acted in 1609 by the Children of the Queen's Revels, at the Whitefriars Theater; this was a private theater. The masques were not staged for a paying audience at all; each had a single performance in a large assembly-room at court, which served a number of functions besides theatrical display. All these circumstances call for a bit of explanation.

The King's Men were the oldest and most successful company of actors in London; under several earlier titles, they had been active since 1572, taking the name of the King's Men at the accession of James in 1603. Though they were nominally "his" men, and occasionally by particular request put on a play at court, the King actually had very little to do with them. They took his name and were under his protection largely because, years before, when actors were mainly strolling players and so liable to the laws against vagabonds, a custom had sprung up among them of claiming to be some nobleman's servants. But by now the King's Men were substantial citizens. They owned their own theater, in which the principal players held shares; they had a library of plays which they had already performed and could mount from time to time as a venture promised profit; they had an assortment of props and costumes. Shakespeare was of their number, and they produced most of his plays; for example, between 1606 and 1610, they put on *Antony and Cleopatra* and *King Lear*. It was a good time, obviously, to be an actor; and with plays like these to sink their teeth into, the King's Men were a practiced repertory company. Both Jonson's plays at the Globe were resounding successes, and *Volpone* was repeated twice the following year, when the King's Men went visiting to Oxford and Cambridge.

Working in their own open-air theater, the Globe, the King's Men had a large raised stage facing a substantial auditorium, without, however, any sort of artificial lighting or any proscenium curtain. Plays were performed in the afternoon, and in both *Volpone* and *The Alchemist* Jonson is careful (far beyond the wont of his contemporaries) to confine the time of the action to a single day: thus the sun would be setting in stage time just as it was in real time. A full house would have consisted of about two thousand spectators, running the social gamut, from lords and knights who sat in boxes or on chairs at the side of the stage, down to the lowest-priced admissions, the "groundlings," who had standing room in what we would call the "orchestra" and they called the "pit." As the play began, there being no special way to signal that the action had started, the actors onstage had to assert themselves over the audience noise—hence the noisy quarrel with which *The Alchemist* begins, and the audacious blasphemies with which Volpone unveils his gold-hoard and performs devotions before it.

Because the stage protruded quite far out into the "pit" or "ground," a good deal of the action onstage must have been essentially "in the round," as we now say. Looking out over the upturned faces of the groundlings (just about the level of his feet), the actor would face three tiers of boxes. The audience, as they looked back at him, would see him against a wall or backdrop, which might be of one story or two; over his head would be a small roof or hut, covering the central part of the stage. Characters entered and exited through doors set in the rear wall: probably there were two of them, though some stage directions seem to imply three—the third might be a door in a screen placed onstage for the occasion. In the center of the rear wall there was often a hanging or curtain, which could be raised or drawn aside, as when Volpone uncovers his gold-hoard. Behind the wall (and invisible, of course, to the audience) was the "tiring room," in which the actors donned or changed their costumes. (During the performance of *The Alchemist*, it must have been a frantic place.) As for the roofed hut overhead, it served in the first place to keep brief rain showers off the actors—the groundlings got wet, but serious storms cancelled the show entirely—and it may also have had acoustical advantages. Besides, the hut may have had a second story, from which Celia, for example, could flutter her handkerchief coyly to "Scoto" atop his platform erected on the main stage.

Perhaps too much has been made of the plainness of the Elizabethan stage, its lack of scenic props—Puritan moralists of the day were apt to complain of its excessive and gaudy decoration. None of Jonson's plays call for palatial luxury or elaborate visual effects, but the rudiments of scenic differentiation were clearly available; the officers of the Scrutineo must have sat on some sort of raised bench, perhaps behind a desk; when the laboratory blows up in *The Alchemist*, it would be a very poor stage manager who couldn't contrive, in addition to crashing noises on tin sheets and a couple of gunshots offstage, a puff of smoke through the door leading to the laboratory. The well-known producer Philip

Henslowe has left us an inventory of the props available on March, 1598, in his theater, the Rose. They include such sizable items as numerous trees, a chariot, a little altar, "the cloth of the Sun & the Moon," dragons, lions, a rainbow, a good deal of armor, "the City of Rome," plus lesser items like cloaks, visors, crowns, and so forth. One wouldn't need much more than a fair selection of this stuff to make as much of Venice or London as Jonson's two plays were likely to require.

In some respects, the Elizabethans had more appetite for stage realism than we give them credit for. Battles might indeed be represented by "armies" of a few actors on a side, clad in tin armor and waving wooden swords; but in formal duels (like that in Act V of *Hamlet*), the audience clearly wanted a good show, the playwright drew out the scene to give them one, and it is very likely that at the height of the struggle a little bladder of pig's blood, hidden under the actor's outer garments, was punctured to procure a gory climax. Thunder was simulated by rolling a cannonball down a wooden trough, and boys touched off flashes of powder to suggest lightning. Rain on a roof was represented by pouring peas from a height onto a tin plate, and sailors just rescued from drowning in *The Tempest* were instructed to come onstage dripping wet. But Jonson, as we've said, was notably conservative about using these scenic devices: both *Volpone* and *The Alchemist* require very little stage machinery. Perhaps a screen pushed onstage could represent the door through which Lovewit parleys with Jeremy, and Bonario could be shoved, like Dapper, behind the hanging till it was time for him to interrupt the action onstage.

Though some plays were much more successful than others, it is not clear how, or even if, the more successful playwright was more largely rewarded. Publication of a play was not automatic, nor did publication imply (in those days before copyright and royalties) reward for the author. Jonson was the object of much ridicule when in 1616 he published his *Works*. English authors were not supposed to have "Works"; the word was applied only to Latin authors, whose works were called "Opera." In any case, during his last years when he was sick and poor, Jonson got some help from the King, some from the government of London city, and some from loyal patrons, but from those who had published his books and produced his plays he got nothing at all.

On the stage of the Globe, female parts were of course taken by boys; not till after the Restoration (1660) did actresses appear on the English stage. Because boys lost their clean chins and soprano voices in the natural course of time, their stage careers were relatively short, and skillful ones were not in large supply. In the plays done for the King's Men, Jonson makes use of a few female characters, whereas in *Epicoene*, which was acted by and written for a company of boys, male and female characters are about equally balanced.

Where did these boys in the company known as "Children of the

Queen's Revels" come from? Historically, they had begun as a boys' choir, selected and trained for the musical delight of the court; under certain circumstances and during certain periods, boys could even be impressed (that is, forcibly removed from their parents) for service in the choir. Gradually they began putting on plays; then they largely ceased to sing (much to the distress of their parents, who often shared middle-class prejudices against actors, and thought they were being forced into a vagabond, ne'er-do-well existence); and by the turn of the century they were a regularly established theatrical company. Shakespeare speaks of them with ill-concealed bitterness in the second act of *Hamlet*:

> but there is, sir, an eyrie [nest] of children, little eyases [eaglets], that cry out on the top of the question and are most tyrannically clapped for it; these are now the fashion, and so berattle the common stages—so they call them—that many wearing rapiers are afraid of goose-quills [pens], and dare scarce come hither.

The children's companies did not act at the Globe, across the river in the suburbs, but in "private" theaters within the city limits. These were smaller houses, roofed in so they were more available during the winter months, using artificial lighting, and on the whole attracting a more select audience than the raffish crowd that attended the Globe. The best known of them were a pair constructed in old abbey buildings lying between Fleet Street and the river Thames: from the monks who used to inhabit them, they were known as Blackfriars (Dominicans) and Whitefriars (Carmelites)—but it was many years since friars of any shade had occupied the buildings. They were used for storage depots and record offices, rented out to storekeepers, and adapted to playhouses. The relation of the "private" to the "public" theaters was not altogether antagonistic; for example, the Burbage family, who took the lead in building the Globe and its predecessor (known simply as The Theater) also built the Blackfriars Theater, and the King's Men sometimes played there. Perhaps they also recruited from the children's company; for these boys were not by any means fringe performers. They had excellent coaching, and by all accounts they were trained professionals; several, we know, went on to adult careers on the stage. Before *Epicoene*, they had staged several of Jonson's earlier plays (*Cynthia's Revels, The Case Is Altered*); other playwrights wrote for them, and plays of their performance were just as likely to make the author's reputation, and earn him money, as any others.

Whatever the theater in which they were staged, or the company producing them, Elizabethan plays did not generally have long consecutive runs because the supply of available spectators was not very large. When everyone who wanted to had seen the play, the script was placed in the company's library of reserve scripts, where it would be available in case a revival was called for or a road company wanted to take it on tour. When they were unusually successful in London, like *Volpone*, plays might be performed in the universities, and they sometimes went out into the provinces (especially when the plague grew hot in London) to be performed in inn yards and the main halls of country houses. If he could interest a publisher, the author might get his play printed. The seventeenth-century stage represented one of the few ways to make money by writing, but nobody, not even the prolific and popular Shakespeare, got really rich at it; and Jonson died destitute.

The masque as it flourished in England in the early seventeenth century was a brief artistic growth, ephemeral if not exotic. There had been very primitive court-entertainments as early as the late thirteenth and early fourteenth centuries; they were called "mummings" or "disguisings." Early in the sixteenth century, they started to be called "masks" or "masques"; there may have been a Continental influence, but its extent is not clear. Sometimes the participants wore false faces, sometimes not; they generally figured or represented an imaginary personage or an abstraction. Masques reached a climax of complexity and beauty under James I, and withered under the chill blasts of Puritanism, disappearing for all-but-good with the outbreak of the Civil Wars in 1640.*

Because they were written by many different authors under a great variety of circumstances, because they had no classical precedents to follow, nor any critical canons to observe, masques took many diverse forms. They were, after all, not literary forms so much as courtly entertainments; poets and men of letters got involved with them only by the side door, as it were, and incidentally. The first and most important element of the masque was the practice of dressing up and showing off. Already this distinguishes them sharply from stage plays, where the actors, though they wear costumes and assume characters not their own, are precisely *not* showing off, *not* calling attention to their own qualities, *not* involving themselves in their own persons with the audience. Masques are analogies if not allegories, deliberately fantastic and unrealistic in their mode, so that they can more accurately mirror the ideals of a courtly audience. They grow out of three other courtly ceremonies, the *tournament*, the *pageant*, and the *triumph*, each of which is related to the others.

As tournaments ceased to consist of real or mock battles, they took on a kind of allegorical or didactic structure. The ladies were labeled Truth, Modesty, Virtue, etc.; the knights, Honor, Temperance, Fortitude, etc. The triumphant knight got to dance with the lady of his choice; each was complimented, and both joined to present their compliments to the person in whose honor the tournament, gradually being

---

* A few small exceptions must be made for later works like Dryden's *Secular Masque* (1700), which deliberately revived for a momentary occasion a form that was essentially dead.

converted to a pageant, was being held. All the participants wore their finest and fanciest costumes: they carried out some minimal instructive action, for they were all amateur actors, and not up to complex emotions or elaborate speeches. Dancing was a natural consequence of the choosing of partners, and music accompanied, inevitably, the dance. The whole structure led toward the presentation of the supreme compliment to the most important person present. And then the audience was called on to mingle with the masquers in a way that the playhouses would have found socially unthinkable and physically impossible. The final dance circled around the central luminary of the occasion; everyone took part in it because no one was present who was not part of the court, and everyone in the court was bound, by ties of loyalty and reverence, to its supreme figure. In this way the tournament-become-pageant easily melted into the pageant-become-triumph. Dignitaries visiting at country houses, monarchs on tour or celebrating a birthday, princes being crowned or princesses getting married, all could easily be made the centers of a festive event in which they were welcomed, reverenced, felicitated—in a word, flattered. By our rough democratic standards the flattery often appears fulsome; in the seventeenth century, within the narrow circles of the court, it was an expression of normal good manners and social propriety. One called King James the fountain of honor and the wellspring of nobility or one described Queen Anne as the paragon of feminine beauty, on the same principle that, nowadays, one tells a Hollywood actor that his latest film is "sensational," or an actress that she's looking "divine."

Words, it is important to recall, were only one element in a masque; and though Ben Jonson ultimately made them equal partners, they never over-balanced their fellow-ingredients, music, dance, and spectacle. There was a lot of singing and dancing in every masque; professional composers wrote the melodies, instrumentalists were hired, and good voices were picked for the singing parts. The masquers were ladies and gentlemen of the court, that is, of the idle rich class. As they commonly dressed with great elegance in everyday life, when they dressed up for a masque they were bound to indulge in high fantasy and extravagant costuming. The masque was an occasion for the ladies in particular to show off, and some masques had much the character of a fashion show. Participation in them was very expensive; indeed, its cost was one of the limiting and exclusive features of the form. Finally, the masques generally called for the introduction of elaborate and costly "machinery." Even though the anticipated run of a masque was for only one night, the sets were much more elaborate and expensive than those of the playhouses. Inigo Jones, the great architect and designer of the age, had brought back from his Italian travels ideas for perspective sets, which produced the illusion of three dimensions. One had to have rather a sophisticated eye to understand this principle. Most Englishmen had seen very little of the art of the Renaissance; their eyes didn't readily compose a set of receding flats—that is painted canvas backdrops—into a deep landscape. And because a perspective stage has to be looked at fairly straight on, to produce its effect, perspectives couldn't be used on the Elizabethan stage. Most of the audience in the Globe would have seen sets as we know them from an impossibly acute angle, and some would have seen them, actually, from behind. But the masque focused so closely on one figure in the audience that perspectives could be used, and the King at least could enjoy them.

In addition, the masques made liberal use of onstage scenery. Mountains opened up into caves, witches' dens turned abruptly into the House of Fame. Generally, these effects were achieved by machines that actually rotated, their operation perhaps concealed by a puff of smoke. Sometimes characters or groups of musicians could be made to appear in moving chariots, or individuals could be made to descend from the sky, dangling on cords run over pulleys and worked by stagehands in the wings. New and surprising effects were much in demand; in the matter of stage machinery, the masques were far in advance of the playhouses. Engineers, painters, musicians, choreographers, poets, and stage designers made up a sizable troop of artists; a really ambitious masque, like *The Masque of Queens*, cost the royal treasury over £3,000, not to speak of the sums that the masquers themselves spent on their costumes. Money equivalents are extremely hard to estimate, but in those days a hundred pounds a year was comfort, a thousand pounds a nice fortune, and three thousand pounds for a single evening's entertainment inconceivable extravagance.

Being essentially so lofty and aristocratic a form, the masque inevitably required material for contrast and relief, and this led Jonson, with his strong theatrical sense, to develop anti-masques. These were simply counter-figures, either grotesque or comic, who appeared in the first part of the show: gentry, of course, never took these parts. They might be pygmies, satyrs, witches, Irishmen, alchemists; like Vices in the old morality plays, they were half-comic antagonists of the Virtues, macabre, funny, or actively sinister, they performed their antics and displayed their characters onstage for a while, until (inevitably) the forces of Virtue appeared and triumphed over them. In some ways they are like the villains of stage plays, but without intrigue or motivation. The conflict is heraldic, not dramatic; good appears, declaring itself, and the figures of evil withdraw like the shades of night when the sun rises.

The masque was thus a deliberately limited and exclusive form; though some masques were performed at country houses and under domestic circumstances (i.e., as family festivals), the great majority were performed at court, where vast halls, gorgeously attired courtiers, fine ladies, musical and artistic talent, and immense sums of money could be woven into a short-lived but stunning theatrical complex. But these various elements were not easily reconciled. Like the court itself, where "favor" was sought with ferocious intensity, the masques easily became occasions for jealous resentment. Jonson quarrelled with Chapman over assignments; and after a short period of fruitful collaboration, he quarrelled bitterly and permanently with Inigo Jones, the architect and scene designer, who had contributed largely to Jonson's first masques.

Jones (1573–1652) was a remarkable man. Though born in humble circumstances, he was pensioned in his late twenties by William Herbert, third earl of Pembroke, to travel in Italy and study the works of painting and architecture, as well as the classical ruins, to be found there. The experience was not lost on Jones: he not only learned a great deal about the art of building in the neo-classical mode, he developed a taste for the painting of the Italian Renaissance such as few Englishmen possessed, and investigated the arts of theatrical design and scenic representation. One of the chief influences on his thinking was the Italian architect Andrea Palladio (1518–80), whose book on architecture he annotated and translated; and one of Palladio's outstanding achievements was the Teatro Olimpico in Vicenza, which certainly helped to make Jones what he was, the foremost scenic artist in England. His quarrel with Jonson, which became open warfare in the 1620s, was stirred more, it would seem, by personal than by artistic differences. The two men were strong, outspoken, even truculent characters; their collaboration ended in a welter of recriminations. In any event, Jones's real career was in architecture; and in the last part of his life, when masques had fallen out of fashion, and Jonson himself was old and neglected, Inigo Jones continued to carry on a busy career as builder and designer of stately homes and public edifices.

Because only a few aristocrats got to see them performed, masques naturally aroused a good deal of curiosity in the public at large; Jonson was proud of his part in them, and put forth the text of several in tiny quarto pamphlets. But even with their stage directions, masques were never long enough to constitute a proper volume, and most of Jonson's are known simply from their appearance in the several folio editions of his Works (1616, 1640). * * *[1]

ROBERT M. ADAMS

---

1. Jonson's first masque was *The Masque of Blackness*, which was written for Queen Anne and performed at Whitehall Palace in the Old Banqueting House in 1605, and Jones was his collaborator for the scenic design. In it Jones introduced for the first time in England an illusionistic stage setting, a product of his Italian travels, which depended for its effectiveness upon the spectators applying the laws of perspective to the rich scene in front of them. Scenery played no part in regular theatrical productions of the time and not all the audience could appreciate the dynamic interrelationships between the various pieces on the busy stage. It might be easier for modern viewers, however, who are used to such scenery, and Jonson gives us a very detailed picture of Jones's design. Some of the notes that Jonson supplied to his text are included in brackets in the annotations [Editor].

A Note on the Texts

By the standards of his day, Jonson was a meticulous corrector of proof, and he had ample opportunity to correct most of the texts reprinted here. *Volpone*, printed as a separate quarto in 1607, and *The Alchemist*, similarly printed in 1612, were included in two folio editions of Jonson's *Works* published during his lifetime (1616, 1631), as well as the post-humous folio of 1640. *Epicoene*, first published in the folio of 1616, was reprinted as a separate quarto in 1620, as well as in the *Works* of 1631 and 1640. *The Masque of Blackness* was published with its sequel *The Masque of Beauty* in a quarto edition in 1608 and also in the folios of 1616 and 1640. *Mercury Vindicated* was first printed in the 1616 folio, and *Pleasure Reconciled to Virtue* in the 1640 folio. In the absence of positive evidence to the contrary, the authority of anything appearing in the 1640 *Works* is very good, for though Jonson never read proof on it, the editors had full access to his papers. The most careful and accurate reprint of all these texts is that of C. H. Herford, and Percy and Evelyn Simpson, in their classic eleven-volume edition of the *Works* (Oxford, 1925–52).

To make a proper text for modern students, however, Jonson's page has to be considerably altered. A lot of extra *e*'s have dropped off words like "selfe" and "heire"; *u* has set itself up as a separate letter from *v*, so that words like "enuie" and "deuill" look odd; *i* and *j* have similarly parted ways, so that "iuyce," "iest," and "iustice" are also strange; and Jonson's system of colloquial contractions has grown obsolete, so that forms like "I'am," "do's," "I'le," and "ha's" disturb the eye, though the intent is clear. Besides, some words have changed form with the years. Jonson is constant in spelling "window" as "windore," and "ostrich" as "estrich"; and his system of punctuation often does not agree with modern conventions. He or his printer uses an occasional ampersand (&) for "and"; he prints numbers ("a 1000 crowns") where we would spell out the word; he capitalizes and italicizes much more freely, and erratically, than we do. In these respects and a few others, like removing the extra *u* from "humour," "honour," etc., the text has been silently restyled in order to render it as accessible as possible to a modern American reader. Seventeenth-century texts had very few stage directions and made few scene divisions; for ease in following the action and referring to specific passages of the text, the editors have copied or

modified these pieces of apparatus, as first introduced by Jonson's major
19th-century editor, William Gifford.

Textual Notes: Major Variants

Volpone

IV,v,43	1616 *substitutes* goodness *for* virtue
IV,v,130	1616 *substitutes* catholic *for* Christian
V,iv,55	1616 *substitutes* fitted *for* apted

The Alchemist

I,i,48	1616 *substitutes* Death on me! *for* God's will!
I,ii,56	1616 *substitutes* Xenophon *for* Testament
I,ii,135	1616 *substitutes* Jove *for* Gad
II,ii,58–	1616 *adds* They will do it best,
59	Best of all others.
III,i,2–5	1616 *substitutes*

And such rebukes we of the separation
Must bear with willing shoulders as the trials
Sent forth to tempt our frailties.
for 1612
And such rebukes th' elect must bear with patience;
They are the exercises of the spirit,
And sent to tempt our frailties.

V,iii,44	1616 *substitutes* Come forth you seed of sulphur, sons of fire

for 1612 Come forth you seed of vipers, sons of Belial

V,v,23–24	1616 *substitutes*

They are the vessels
Of pride, lust, and the cart
for 1612
They are the vessels
Of shame and of dishonor

V,v,99	1616 *substitutes* Idol *for* Nimrod

Epicoene

The basic text of this play is that reproduced in the Folio of 1616. The
Quarto of 1620 is a careless reprint of this original text, and the Folio
of 1640 also reproduces it, faithfully copying the consequences of an
accident that occurred in the course of the 1616 printing. One large
tray (form) of type was apparently spilled on the floor after a number
of examples had been printed; it was picked up and put together, very
carelessly, by someone about the print shop, and more copies of the

1616 folio were then printed off, containing about 280 changes from the original, correct version. It was one of these careless copies that was used as the basis for the 1640 Folio. The present editor has not thought it necessary to record these variants, or the other unimportant variants introduced by 1620 and 1640.

The Texts of
THE PLAYS AND MASQUES

Volpone

or
The Fox

The Persons of the Play[1]

VOLPONE, *a magnifico*
MOSCA, *his parasite*
VOLTORE, *an advocate*
CORBACCIO, *an old gentleman*
CORVINO, *a merchant*
BONARIO, *son to Corbaccio*
SIR POLITIC WOULD-BE, *a knight*
PEREGRINE, *a gentleman traveller*
NANO, *a dwarf*
CASTRONE, *an eunuch*
ANDROGYNO, *an hermaphrodite*

GREGE (*or Mob*)

COMMANDATORI, *officers of justice*
MERCATORI, *three merchants*
AVOCATORI, *four magistrates*
NOTARIO, *the register*

LADY WOULD-BE, SIR POLITIC'S *Wife*
CELIA, CORVINO'S *Wife*
SERVITORI, *Servants, two* WAITING-WOMEN, *&c.*

1. Most of the names are Italian, and in that language many of them signify animals. Volpone: "fox." "Magnifico" is not a formal title; it simply means "gentleman." Mosca: "fly." The figure of the parasite implies scavenging, as well as fawning dependence. The client-patron relationship in Rome fostered parasitical dependents, and Jonson saw similar figures, not only around the English court, but around the big moneymen of London City. Voltore: "vulture." Corbaccio: "raven." Corvino: "crow." Bonario: "good-natured." Sir Politic Would-be: In the seventeenth century the word "politic" carried overtones of devious and subtle calculation; his name spells out Sir Politic's character, and in its abbreviation ("Pol") suggests further the parrot he is. Peregrine: in English a falcon, but the word also associates with "pilgrim," i.e., "traveller." Nano: "dwarf." Castrone: "gelding." Androgyno: from the Greek, "man-woman," i.e., "hermaphrodite." Grege: from the Latin, "mob" or "crowd." Commandatori: a not very distinguished title of honor; Jonson assigns them a function akin to sergeants or marshals of a court. Mercatori: "merchants." Avocatori: properly, in Italian, "prosecutors"; Jonson makes them judges. Notario: "recorder." Celia: literally, "heavenly."

THE SCENE: *VENICE*

The Argument[2]

Volpone, childless, rich, feigns sick, despairs,
Offers his state to hopes of several heirs,
Lies languishing; his parasite receives
Presents of all, assures, deludes; then weaves
Other cross plots, which ope themselves, are told.
New tricks for safety are sought; they thrive: when bold,
Each tempts the other again, and all are sold.[3]

Prologue

Now, luck yet send us, and a little wit
    Will serve to make our play hit;
According to the palates of the season
    Here is rhyme, not empty of reason.
This we were bid to credit from our poet,   5
    Whose true scope, if you would know it,
In all his poems still hath been this measure,
    To mix profit with your pleasure;[4]
And not as some, whose throats their envy failing,
    Cry hoarsely, All he writes is railing;[5]   10
And when his plays come forth, think they can flout them,
    With saying, he was a year about them.
To these there needs no lie,[6] but this his creature,
    Which was two months since no feature;
And though he dares give them five lives to mend it,   15
    'Tis known, five weeks fully penned it,
From his own hand, without a co-adjutor,
    Novice, journey-man,[7] or tutor.
Yet thus much I can give you as a token
    Of his play's worth, no eggs are broken,   20
Nor quaking custards with fierce teeth affrighted,[8]
    Wherewith your rout[9] are so delighted;

---

2. A capsule summary of the plot. The first letter of each line forms an acrostic of the title.
3. Deceived.
4. That the task of the poet is to mix profit with pleasure was an idea dating back to Horace's *Art of Poetry* (ca. 19 B.C.E.), lines 343–44.
5. Abuse, invective.
6. Denial.
7. Piece-worker, apprentice, or assistant.
8. Comic routines—thrown eggs or custard pies—had popular success on the low Elizabethan stage. A giant custard pie was also served at city feasts inaugurating the Lord Mayor; sometimes an attendant fool jumped into it.
9. Mob, common herd.

Nor *hales he in a gull*[1] *old ends reciting,*
   To stop gaps in his loose writing;
With such a deal of monstrous and forced action,   25
   As might make Bedlam[2] *a faction:*
Nor made he his play for jests stolen from each table,
   But makes jests to fit his fable;
And so presents quick comedy refined,
   As best critics have designed;   30
The laws of time, place, persons he observeth,[3]
   From no needful rule he swerveth.
All gall and copperas from his ink he draineth,
   Only a little salt remaineth,[4]
Wherewith he'll rub your cheeks, till, red with laughter,   35
   They shall look fresh a week after.

Act I

ACT I   SCENE 1. *A ROOM IN* VOLPONE'S *HOUSE*

[*Enter* VOLPONE *and* MOSCA.]
VOLPONE. Good morning to the day; and next, my gold!
   Open the shrine,[1] that I may see my saint.
      [MOSCA *withdraws the curtain, and discovers piles of gold,*
      plate, jewels, &c.]
   Hail the world's soul, and mine! More glad than is
   The teeming earth to see the longed-for sun
   Peep through the horns of the celestial ram,[2]   5
   Am I, to view thy splendor darkening his;
   That lying here, amongst my other hoards,
   Show'st like a flame by night, or like the day
   Struck out of chaos, when all darkness fled

1. Buffoon. Elizabethans were fond of wise saws and ancient adages ("old ends") and often put into plays characters who recited them.
2. Bethlehem Hospital, the madhouse.
3. The so-called Aristotelian unities, actually imposed as prescripts by the Italian Renaissance critics Castelvetro and Scaliger, placed limits of time (should take place within twenty-four hours) and place (should reflect possibilities of genuine travel in the world) on dramatic action; the limitation on persons (should be appropriate to setting and genre) was less strict.
4. Gall and copperas (i.e., green vitriol) are traditional ingredients of ink; both are corrosive and bitter to the taste. Salt, though not an ingredient of ink, is a classical metaphor for wit, that which gives flavor to speech or writing.
1. Though there was no proscenium curtain such as rises on a modern play, in the Elizabethan theater there was a small curtained inner area, and that is what Mosca unveils. By "the world's soul and mine" Volpone means the soul of the universe and his own immortal essence, both identified with gold.
2. The sun peeps through the horns of the constellation "Ram" in the zodiac about the middle of April; cf. Chaucer at the opening of the *Canterbury Tales* (lines 5–8): "When Zephyrus eek with his sweete breeth / Inspired hath in every holt and heeth / The tendre croppes, and the yonge sonne / Hath in the Ram his halve cours yronne."

Unto the center. O thou son of Sol,[3]   10
But brighter than thy father, let me kiss,
With adoration, thee, and every relic
Of sacred treasure in this blessèd room.
Well did wise poets, by thy glorious name,
Title that age which they would have the best;[4]   15
Thou being the best of things, and far transcending
All style of joy, in children, parents, friends,
Or any other waking dream on earth.
Thy looks when they to Venus did ascribe,
They should have given her twenty thousand Cupids;[5]   20
Such are thy beauties and our loves! Dear saint,
Riches, the dumb god, that givest all men tongues,
That canst do nought, and yet mak'st men do all things;
The price of souls; even hell, with thee to boot,
Is made worth heaven. Thou art virtue, fame,   25
Honor and all things else. Who can get thee,
He shall be noble, valiant, honest, wise—
MOSCA. And what he will, sir. Riches are in fortune
A greater good than wisdom is in nature.
VOLPONE. True, my belovèd Mosca. Yet I glory   30
More in the cunning purchase[6] of my wealth
Than in the glad possession, since I gain
No common way; I use no trade, no venture;
I wound no earth with plough-shares, fat no beasts
To feed the shambles;[7] have no mills for iron,   35
Oil, corn, or men, to grind them into powder;[8]
I blow no subtle glass, expose no ships
To threat'nings of the furrow-facèd sea;
I turn no moneys[9] in the public bank,

---

3. The circle of a gold coin is compared to the created cosmos, i.e., the world with sun, moon, and stars, created by God in Genesis 1. When the sun illumined the outer universe, darkness "fled to the center," i.e., to hell, underground. Gold is said to be "the son of Sol" (the sun) because in Renaissance lore, the fertilizing rays of the sun, penetrating the ground, were responsible for developing the "seeds of gold" naturally found there.
4. The "Golden Age" was the first and best of the four classical ages; the others were the ages of silver, bronze, and iron.
5. Lines 16–20 are translated from a fragment of Euripides (ca. 485–406 B.C.E.); Seneca (ca. 4 B.C.E.–65 C.E.) tells us that when they were pronounced onstage, the audience was so indignant that it would allow the play to continue only after Euripides provided assurance that the speakers would be badly punished in the course of the play. A traditional epithet of Venus is "golden"; Volpone, however, is not satisfied with her minting a single golden boy; he wants a lot of them.
6. Acquisition.
7. Slaughterhouse.
8. As Jonson wrote, household industries were just starting to be converted, in a few places, to factory industries run by water power. Glass was a Venetian specialty, in Jonson's day as now, but in England it was just starting to be used for glazing.
9. Take no interest. Banking and money-lending were more important in Venice, where long voyages were common mercantile practice, than in England.

Nor usure private.

MOSCA.   No, sir, nor devour   40
Soft prodigals. You shall have some will swallow
A melting heir as glibly as your Dutch
Will pills of butter, and ne'er purge[1] for it;
Tear forth the fathers of poor families
Out of their beds, and coffin them alive   45
In some kind clasping prison, where their bones
May be forth-coming, when the flesh is rotten.
But your sweet nature doth abhor these courses;
You loathe the widow's or the orphan's tears
Should wash your pavements, or their piteous cries   50
Ring in your roofs, and beat the air for vengeance.

VOLPONE. Right, Mosca; I do loathe it.

MOSCA.   And besides, sir,
You are not like the thresher that doth stand
With a huge flail, watching a heap of corn,
And, hungry, dares not taste the smallest grain,   55
But feeds on mallows, and such bitter herbs;
Nor like the merchant, who hath filled his vaults
With Romagnía, and rich Candian wines,
Yet drinks the lees of Lombard's vinegar.[2]
You will lie not in straw, whilst moths and worms   60
Feed on your sumptuous hangings and soft beds.
You know the use of riches, and dare give now
From that bright heap, to me, your poor observer,
Or to your dwarf, or your hermaphrodite,
Your eunuch, or what other household trifle   65
Your pleasure allows maintenance. —

VOLPONE.   Hold thee, Mosca, [*Gives
him money.*]
Take of my hand; thou strik'st on truth in all,
And they are envious term thee parasite.
Call forth my dwarf, my eunuch, and my fool,
And let them make me sport. [*Exit* MOSCA.] What should I do,   70
But cocker up[3] my genius, and live free
To all delights my fortune calls me to?
I have no wife, no parent, child, ally,

1. Suffer indigestion. Many jokes were made in the seventeenth century on the Dutch appetite for butter. Loan sharks swallowed up heirs by lending them money at exorbitant rates against their future inheritance.
2. Romagnía was a sweet wine from Greece; Candian is wine from Crete (Candia). During the Renaissance good wine was thought to come from the eastern Mediterranean, or else from Spain (sack and canary). French and Italian wines ("Lombard's vinegar") were not much appreciated, and the "lees" (dregs) were of course the worst part of any bottle.
3. Pamper, indulge.

To give my substance to, but whom I make
Must be my heir; and this makes men observe me.   75
This draws new clients daily to my house,
Women and men of every sex and age,
That bring me presents, send me plate, coin, jewels,
With hope that when I die (which they expect
Each greedy minute) it shall then return   80
Ten-fold upon them; whilst some, covetous
Above the rest, seek to engross me whole,[4]
And counter-work the one unto the other,
Contend in gifts, as they would seem in love.
All which I suffer, playing with their hopes,   85
And am content to coin them into profit,
And look upon their kindness, and take more,
And look on that; still bearing them in hand,
Letting the cherry knock against their lips,
And draw it by their mouths, and back again.[5]—How now!   90

ACT I   SCENE 2

[*Enter* MOSCA *with* NANO, ANDROGYNO, *and* CASTRONE.]
NANO. *Now, room for fresh gamesters, who do will you to know,*
They do bring you neither play nor university show;
And therefore do entreat you, that whatsoever they rehearse,
May not fare a whit the worse, for the false pace of the verse.[6]
If you wonder at this, you will wonder more ere we pass,   5
For know, here[7] *is enclosed the soul of Pythagoras,*
That juggler divine, as hereafter shall follow;
Which soul, fast and loose, sir, came first from Apollo,
And was breathed into Æthalides,[8] *Mercurius his son,*
Where it had the gift to remember all that ever was done.   10
From thence it fled forth, and made quick transmigration
To goldy-locked Euphorbus,[9] *who was killed in good fashion,*
At the siege of old Troy, by the cuckold of Sparta.

---

4. An engrosser bought up an entire crop of grain, held it for hard times, then sold it at exorbitant prices.
5. "Chop-cherry" is a country game in which a cherry hung from a string is dangled before a player who tries to catch it with his or her teeth.
6. This little interlude tells us something about the tastes of the man for whom it is performed. The loose, jog-trot meter that the characters recite is reminiscent of the vices who, in the old morality plays, were buffoonish figures of evil.
7. He points at Androgyno. The Greek philosopher Pythagoras (ca. 580–500 B.C.E.) put forward the doctrine of transmigration of souls, and fantastic lineages were a frequent comic exercise in the Renaissance. Nano's comic story is copied from the life of Pythagoras, by Diogenes Laertius.
8. Herald of the Argonauts.
9. Trojan hero, killed by Menelaus, "the cuckold of Sparta"; Pythagoras specifically claimed to have been Euphorbus, and to recall the event.

Hermotimus was next (I find it in my charta)[1]
To whom it did pass, where no sooner it was missing,   15
  But with one Pyrrhus of Delos it learned to go a fishing;
And thence did it enter the sophist of Greece.
  From Pythagore, she went into a beautiful piece,
Hight Aspasia, the meretrix;[2] and the next toss of her
  Was again of a whore, she became a philosopher,   20
Crates the cynic,[3] as itself doth relate it:
  Since kings, knights, and beggars, knaves, lords, and fools gat it,
Besides ox and ass, camel, mule, goat, and brock,[4]
  In all which it hath spoke, as in the cobbler's cock.
But I come not here to discourse of that matter,   25
  Or his one, two, or three, or his great oath, BY QUATER!
His musics, his trigon, his golden thigh,[5]
  Or his telling how elements shift; but I
Would ask, how of late thou hast suffered translation,
  And shifted thy coat in these days of reformation.   30
ANDROGYNO. Like one of the reformed, a fool, as you see,
  Counting all old doctrine[6] heresy.
NANO. But not on thine own forbid meats hast thou ventured?
ANDROGYNO. On fish, when first a Carthusian I entered.[7]
NANO. Why, then thy dogmatical silence hath left thee?   35
ANDROGYNO. Of that an obstreperous lawyer bereft me.[8]
NANO. O wonderful change, when sir lawyer forsook thee!
  For Pythagore's sake, what body then took thee?
ANDROGYNO. A good dull mule.
NANO.   And how! By that means
  Thou wert brought to allow of the eating of beans?[9]   40
ANDROGYNO. Yes.

---

1. Hermotimus is indeed mentioned in Nano's "charts," i.e., the text of Diogenes Laertius, but hardly anywhere else. Pyrrhus of Delos is an equally obscure figure, a fisherman mentioned only in Diogenes. The "sophist of Greece" is Pythagoras himself.
2. Whore; but Aspasia was simply the mistress of Pericles (ca. 495–429 B.C.E.), Athenian statesman.
3. Crates was a philosopher of the Cynic school, a follower of Diogenes who professed a particularly bitter brand of skepticism.
4. Badger. The Greek satirist Lucian's (ca. 125–ca. 200) comic dialogue, "Gallus, or the Cock," which reproduces much of this material about Pythagoras, is a dialogue between a cobbler and a chicken.
5. Pythagorean theories about music and numerology, the Pythagorean theorem about right triangles, and the myth that Pythagoras had a golden thigh are glanced at here. A trigon is a triangle; the oath "by Quarter" (four) is reported in Plutarch, On the Sayings of the Philosophers.
6. Catholic and Anglo-Catholic theology; "the reformed": recent Puritan reformers, not those of sixteenth-century reformation.
7. As a Carthusian monk (a particularly strict order), he learned to eat fish, which as a Pythagorean was forbidden to him.
8. Having taken a vow of silence as a Carthusian, he became a lawyer and learned to blabber.
9. Pythagoras forbade the eating of beans. All these prohibitions and special observances were supposed to have occult or mystical meaning.

NANO.   *But from the mule into whom didst thou pass?*
ANDROGYNO. *Into a very strange beast, by some writers called an ass;*
By others, a precise,[1] pure, illuminate brother,   ❦
    Of those devour flesh, and sometimes one another;
And will drop you forth a libel, or a sanctified lie,   45
    Betwixt every spoonful of a nativity pie.[2]
NANO. *Now quit thee, for heaven, of that profane nation,*
    And gently report thy next transmigration.
ANDROGYNO. *To the same that I am.*
NANO.   *A creature of delight,*
    And, what is more than a fool, an hermaphrodite![3]   50
Now, prithee, sweet soul, in all thy variation,
    Which body wouldst thou choose, to keep up thy station?
ANDROGYNO. *Troth, this I am in, even here would I tarry.*
NANO. *Cause here the delight of each sex thou canst vary?*
ANDROGYNO. *Alas, those pleasures be stale and forsaken;*   55
    No, 'tis your fool wherewith I am so taken,
The only one creature that I can call blessed;[4]
    For all other form I have proved most distressed.
NANO. *Spoke true, as thou wert in Pythagoras still.*
    This learned opinion we celebrate will,   60
Fellow eunuch, as behooves us, with all our wit and art,
    To dignify that whereof ourselves are so great and special a part.
VOLPONE. Now, very, very pretty! Mosca, this
    Was thy invention?
MOSCA.   If it please my patron,
    Not else.
VOLPONE. It doth, good Mosca.
MOSCA.   Then it was, sir.   65
        [NANO *and* CASTRONE *sing.[5]*]
            Fools, they are the only nation
            Worth men's envy or admiration;
            Free from care or sorrow-taking,
            Selves and others merry making,
            All they speak or do is sterling.[6]   70
            Your fool he is your great man's darling,

---

1. Adhering to a literalistic interpretation of the law. All the adjectives in this line would be understood as pointing at the Puritans, to whom Jonson had a standing aversion.
2. The Puritans did not like the old word "Christmas" because it included the "idolatrous" word "mass," so they began using the neutral word "Nativity," which Jonson here derides.
3. One who is, anatomically, both a man and a woman; derived from the Greek mythological character Hermaphroditus, who was the son of Hermes and Aphrodite.
4. Jonson is drawing here on one of the wellsprings of Renaissance thought, Erasmus's (1466?–1536) mock-oration, *The Praise of Folly*, published in 1511, which was spoken by Dame Folly in praise of herself.
5. The song is a patchwork of passages from Erasmus.
6. Of good value; originally, a "sterling" was an English silver penny.

And your ladies' sport and pleasure;
Tongue and bauble[7] are his treasure.
E'en his face begetteth laughter,
And he speaks truth free from slaughter; 75
He's the grace of every feast,
And sometimes the chiefest guest;
Hath his trencher[8] and his stool.
When wit waits upon the fool,
　O, who would not be
　　He, he, he? [*Knocking without.*] 80

VOLPONE. Who's that? Away! [*Exeunt* NANO *and* CASTRONE.]
　Look, Mosca.
MOSCA. Fool, begone! [*Exit* ANDROGYNO.] 'Tis signor Voltore, the
　advocate;
　I know him by his knock.
VOLPONE. 　　　　　Fetch me my gown,
　My furs, and night-caps; say, my couch is changing, 85
　And let him entertain himself awhile
　Without i' the gallery. [*Exit* MOSCA.] Now, now my clients
　Begin their visitation! Vulture, kite,
　Raven, and gor-crow, all my birds of prey,[9]
　That think me turning carcass, now they come; 90
　I am not for them yet.
　　　　[*Re-enter* MOSCA, *with the gown, &c.*]
　　　　　　　How now? The news?
MOSCA. A piece of plate,[1] sir.
VOLPONE. 　　　　　Of what bigness?
MOSCA. 　　　　　　　　Huge,
　Massy, and antique, with your name inscribed,
　And arms engraven.
VOLPONE. 　　　Good! And not a fox
　Stretched on the earth, with fine delusive sleights 95
　Mocking a gaping crow?[2] Ha, Mosca!
MOSCA. 　　　　　　　Sharp, sir.
VOLPONE. Give me my furs. [*Puts on his sick dress.*]
　　　　　　Why dost thou laugh so, man?
MOSCA. I cannot choose, sir, when I apprehend
　What thoughts he has without now, as he walks:—

---

7. Fool's baton or stick.
8. Dish.
9. Volpone foresees his visitors precisely in the order they come: Lady Politic is the kite, Corvino the gor-crow ("gor": filth). They are not, however, birds of prey, but all carrion-eaters.
1. A solid silver platter. In those days, when banks were uncertain and display important, families often put much of their wealth in massive silver dinnerware.
2. Volpone imagines an allegorical device, taken from one of Aesop's fables, engraved on the piece of plate. See p. 367.

That this might be the last gift he should give;   100
That this would fetch you; if you died to-day,
And gave him all, what he should be tomorrow;
What large return would come of all his ventures;
How he should worshipped be, and reverenced;
Ride with his furs and foot-cloths;³ waited on   105
By herds of fools and clients; have clear way
Made for his mule, as lettered as himself;
Be called the great and learned advocate:
And then concludes, there's nought impossible.
VOLPONE. Yes, to be learned, Mosca.
MOSCA.   O, no; rich   110
Implies it. Hood an ass with reverend purple,
So you can hide his two ambitious ears,
And he shall pass for a cathedral doctor.⁴
VOLPONE. My caps, my caps, good Mosca. Fetch him in.
MOSCA. Stay, sir; your ointment for your eyes.
VOLPONE.   That's true;   115
Dispatch, dispatch.⁵ I long to have possession
Of my new present.
MOSCA.   That, and thousands more,
I hope to see you lord of.
VOLPONE.   Thanks, kind Mosca.
MOSCA. And that, when I am lost in blended dust,
And hundred such as I am, in succession—   120
VOLPONE. Nay, that were too much, Mosca.
MOSCA.   You shall live,
Still, to delude these harpies.⁶
VOLPONE.   Loving Mosca!
'Tis well. My pillow now, and let him enter.   [Exit MOSCA.]
Now, my feigned cough, my phthisic,⁷ and my gout,
My apoplexy, palsy, and catarrhs,   125
Help, with your forcèd functions, this my posture,
Wherein, this three year, I have milked their hopes.
He comes; I hear him—Uh! [coughing] Uh! Uh! Uh! O—

---

3. Ornate tapestries, laid upon the beast, not his rider; the furs would be for the lawyer.
4. The power of money to make the stupid wise, the ugly beautiful, etc., had been a satiric commonplace since antiquity. "Cathedral doctor": a doctor of theology.
5. Hurry.
6. Predatory birds with the faces of women in Greek mythology.
7. "Phthisic": various throat or lung diseases; "gout": inflammation of the joints; "apoplexy": loss of blood supply to the brain, as in a stroke; "palsy": shaking or trembling; "catarrhs": discharge of mucus from the nose or throat.

ACT I   SCENE 3

[*Enter* MOSCA, *introducing* VOLTORE *with a piece of plate.*]
MOSCA. You still are what you were, sir. Only you,
  Of all the rest, are he commands his love,
  And you do wisely to preserve it thus,
  With early visitation, and kind notes
  Of your good meaning to him, which, I know,   5
  Cannot but come most grateful. Patron! Sir!
  Here's signor Voltore is come—
VOLPONE.   [*faintly*] What say you?
MOSCA. Sir, signor Voltore is come this morning
  To visit you.
VOLPONE.   I thank him.
MOSCA.   And hath brought
  A piece of antique plate, bought of St. Mark,[8]   10
  With which he here presents you.
VOLPONE.   He is welcome.
  Pray him to come more often.
MOSCA.   Yes.
VOLTORE.   What says he?
MOSCA. He thanks you, and desires you see him often.
VOLPONE. Mosca.
MOSCA.   My patron!
VOLPONE.   Bring him near, where is he?
  I long to feel his hand.
MOSCA.   The plate is here, sir.   15
VOLTORE. How fare you, sir?
VOLPONE.   I thank you, signor Voltore;
  Where is the plate? Mine eyes are bad.
VOLTORE.   [*putting it into his hands*] I'm sorry,
  To see you still thus weak.
MOSCA.   [*aside*] That he's not weaker.
VOLPONE. You are too munificent.
VOLTORE.   No, sir; would to heaven,
  I could as well give health to you, as that plate!   20
VOLPONE. You give, sir, what you can; I thank you. Your love
  Hath taste in this, and shall not be unanswered;
  I pray you see me often.
VOLTORE.   Yes, I shall, sir.
VOLPONE. Be not far from me.
MOSCA.   Do you observe that, sir?
VOLPONE. Hearken unto me still; it will concern you.   25

_____
8. I.e., bought in St. Mark's square, the central plaza of Venice.

MOSCA. You are a happy man, sir; know your good.
VOLPONE. I cannot now last long—
MOSCA.   You are his heir, sir.
VOLTORE. Am I?
VOLPONE.   I feel me going; Uh! uh! uh! uh!
  I'm sailing to my port, Uh! uh! uh! uh!
  And I am glad I am so near my haven.   30
MOSCA. Alas, kind gentleman! Well, we must all go—
VOLTORE. But, Mosca—
MOSCA.   Age will conquer.
VOLTORE.   'Pray thee, hear me:
  Am I inscribed his heir for certain?
MOSCA.   Are you!
  I do beseech you, sir, you will vouchsafe
  To write me in your family.[9] All my hopes   35
  Depend upon your worship. I am lost,
  Except the rising sun do shine on me.
VOLTORE. It shall both shine, and warm thee, Mosca.
MOSCA.   Sir,
  I am a man, that hath not done your love
  All the worst offices.[1] Here I wear your keys,   40
  See all your coffers and your caskets locked,
  Keep the poor inventory of your jewels,
  Your plate and moneys; am your steward, sir,
  Husband[2] your goods here.
VOLTORE.   But am I sole heir?
MOSCA. Without a partner, sir; confirmed this morning.   45
  The wax is warm yet, and the ink scarce dry
  Upon the parchment.
VOLTORE.   Happy, happy, me!
  By what good chance, sweet Mosca?
MOSCA.   Your desert, sir;
  I know no second cause.
VOLTORE.   Thy modesty
  Is loath to know it; well, we shall requite it.   50
MOSCA. He ever liked your course, sir; that first took him.
  I oft have heard him say, how he admired
  Men of your large profession, that could speak
  To every cause, and things mere contraries,
  Till they were hoarse again, yet all be law;   55
  That, with most quick agility, could turn,

9. Inscribe me on the list of your servants.
1. Services.
2. Safeguard.

And return; make knots, and undo them;
Give forkèd counsel;[3] take provoking gold
On either hand, and put it up. These men,
He knew, would thrive with their humility.   60
And, for his part, he thought he should be blessed
To have his heir of such a suffering spirit,
So wise, so grave, of so perplexed a tongue,
And loud withal, that would not wag, nor scarce
Lie still, without a fee; when every word   65
Your worship but lets fall, is a sequin[4]—
                                        [*Knocking without.*]
Who's that? One knocks; I would not have you seen, sir.
And yet—pretend you came, and went in haste;
I'll fashion an excuse—and, gentle sir,
When you do come to swim in golden lard,   70
Up to the arms in honey, that your chin
Is born up stiff, with fatness of the flood,
Think on your vassal; but remember me:
I have not been your worst of clients.
VOLTORE.   Mosca—
MOSCA. When will you have your inventory brought, sir?   75
Or see a copy of the will? [*Knocking again.*] Anon![5]
I'll bring them to you, sir. Away, be gone;
Put business in your face.   [*Exit* VOLTORE.]
VOLPONE.   [*springing up*] Excellent Mosca!
Come hither, let me kiss thee.
MOSCA.   Keep you still, sir.
Here is Corbaccio.
VOLPONE.   Set the plate away.   80
The vulture's gone, and the old raven's come.

ACT I   SCENE 4

MOSCA. Betake you to your silence and your sleep.
[*Puts the plate away.*] Stand there and multiply. Now shall we see
A wretch who is indeed more impotent
Than this can feign to be; yet hopes to hop
Over his grave. [*Enter* CORBACCIO.] Signor Corbaccio!   5
You're very welcome, sir.
CORBACCIO.   How does your patron?
MOSCA. Troth, as he did, sir; no amends.

3. Ambiguous, ambivalent advice. This ironic praise of lawyers is probably from Cornelius
   Agrippa's influential book *On the Uncertainty and Vanity of the Sciences and Arts* (1531).
4. Zecchino, a gold coin.
5. Said in response to a sharp rap at the door; a modern Mosca would say, "Coming!"

CORBACCIO.   What! Mends he?
MOSCA. No, sir, he's rather worse.
CORBACCIO.   That's well. Where is he?
MOSCA. Upon his couch, sir, newly fallen asleep.
CORBACCIO. Does he sleep well?
MOSCA.   No wink, sir, all this night.   10
     Nor yesterday; but slumbers.[6]
CORBACCIO.   Good! He should take
     Some counsel of physicians. I have brought him
     An opiate here, from mine own doctor.
MOSCA. He will not hear of drugs.
CORBACCIO.   Why? I myself
     Stood by while it was made, saw all the ingredients,   15
     And know it cannot but most gently work.
     My life for his, 'tis but to make him sleep.
VOLPONE. [aside] Ay, his last sleep, if he would take it.
MOSCA.   Sir,
     He has no faith in physic.
CORBACCIO.   Say you, say you?
MOSCA. He has no faith in physic. He does think   20
     Most of your doctors are the greater danger,
     And worse disease, t'escape. I often have
     Heard him protest, that your physician
     Should never be his heir.
CORBACCIO.   Not I his heir?
MOSCA. Not your physician, sir.
CORBACCIO.   O, no, no, no,   25
     I do not mean it.
MOSCA.   No, sir, nor their fees
     He cannot brook; he says, they flay a man,
     Before they kill him.
CORBACCIO.   Right, I do conceive you.
MOSCA. And then they do it by experiment;
     For which the law not only doth absolve them,   30
     But gives them great reward; and he is loath
     To hire his death, so.
CORBACCIO.   It is true, they kill
     With as much license as a judge.
MOSCA.   Nay, more;
     For he but kills, sir, where the law condemns,
     And these can kill him too.
CORBACCIO.   Ay, or me,   35
     Or any man. How does his apoplex?

6. Catnaps.

Is that strong on him still?
MOSCA.   Most violent.
His speech is broken, and his eyes are set,
His face drawn longer than 'twas wont—
CORBACCIO.   How! How!
Stronger than he was wont?
MOSCA.   No, sir: his face   40
Drawn longer than 'twas wont.
CORBACCIO.   O, good!
MOSCA.   His mouth
Is ever gaping, and his eyelids hang.
CORBACCIO.   Good.
MOSCA. A freezing numbness stiffens all his joints,
And makes the color of his flesh like lead.
CORBACCIO.   'Tis good.
MOSCA. His pulse beats slow and dull.
CORBACCIO.   Good symptoms still.   45
MOSCA. And from his brain—
CORBACCIO.   Ha? how? Not from his brain?
MOSCA. Yes, sir, and from his brain—
CORBACCIO.   I conceive you; good.
MOSCA. Flows a cold sweat, with a continual rheum,
Forth the resolvèd corners of his eyes.
CORBACCIO. Is't possible? Yet I am better, ha!   50
How does he, with the swimming of his head?
MOSCA. O, sir, 'tis past the scotomy;[7] he now
Hath lost his feeling, and hath left to snort.
You hardly can perceive him, that he breathes.
CORBACCIO. Excellent, excellent! Sure I shall outlast him!   55
This makes me young again, a score of years.
MOSCA. I was a coming for you, sir.
CORBACCIO.   Has he made his will?
What has he given me?
MOSCA.   No, sir.
CORBACCIO.   Nothing? Ha!
MOSCA. He has not made his will, sir.
CORBACCIO.   Oh, oh, oh!
What then did Voltore, the lawyer, here?   60
MOSCA. He smelt a carcass, sir, when he but heard
My master was about his testament;
As I did urge him to it for your good.
CORBACCIO. He came unto him, did he? I thought so.
MOSCA. Yes, and presented him this piece of plate.   65

_____

7. Dizziness, with dimness of sight; "resolvèd": loosened.

CORBACCIO. To be his heir?
MOSCA.   I do not know, sir.
CORBACCIO.   True,
  I know it too.
MOSCA. [aside] By your own scale, sir.[8]
CORBACCIO.   Well,
  I shall prevent him, yet. See, Mosca, look,
  Here, I have brought a bag of bright sequins,
  Will quite weigh down his plate.
MOSCA.   [taking the bag] Yea, marry, sir.   70
  This is true physic, this your sacred medicine;
  No talk of opiates, to this great elixir![9]
CORBACCIO. 'Tis aurum palpabile,[1] if not potabile.
MOSCA. It shall be ministered to him, in his bowl.
CORBACCIO. Ay, do, do, do.
MOSCA.   Most blessèd cordial!   75
  This will recover him.
CORBACCIO.   Yes, do, do, do.
MOSCA. I think it were not best, sir.
CORBACCIO.   What?
MOSCA.   To recover him.
CORBACCIO. O, no, no, no; by no means.
MOSCA.   Why, sir, this
  Will work some strange effect, if he but feel it.
CORBACCIO. 'Tis true, therefore forbear; I'll take my venture.   80
  Give me it again.
MOSCA.   At no hand; pardon me.
  You shall not do yourself that wrong, sir. I
  Will so advise you, you shall have it all.
CORBACCIO.   How?
MOSCA. All, sir, 'tis your right, your own; no man
  Can claim a part; 'tis yours without a rival,   85
  Decreed by destiny.
CORBACCIO.   How? How, good Mosca?
MOSCA. I'll tell you, sir. This fit he shall recover—
CORBACCIO. I do conceive you.
MOSCA.   And, on first advantage
  Of his gained sense, will I re-importune him
  Unto the making of his testament.   90
  And show him this.   [Pointing to the money.]

---

8. The phrase seems to imply, "You think so because that's the sort of creature you are yourself."
9. No comparison of sedatives ("opiates") to this great medicine is possible. The elixir was supposed to be the supreme, universal medicine, capable of prolonging life indefinitely as well as of transforming baser metals to gold.
1. Palpable, material gold; aurum potabile, or drinkable gold, was the elixir.

CORBACCIO.   Good, good.
MOSCA.   'Tis better yet,
  If you will hear, sir.
CORBACCIO.   Yes, with all my heart.
MOSCA. Now, would I counsel you, make home with speed;
  There, frame a will, whereto you shall inscribe
  My master your sole heir.
CORBACCIO.   And disinherit   95
  My son?
MOSCA.   Oh, sir, the better: for that color
  Shall make it much more taking.[2]
CORBACCIO.   O, but color?
MOSCA. This will, sir, you shall send it unto me.
  Now, when I come to enforce, as I will do,
  Your cares, your watchings, and your many prayers,   100
  Your more than many gifts, your this day's present,
  And last, produce your will; where, without thought,
  Or least regard unto your proper issue,
  A son so brave and highly meriting,
  The stream of your diverted love hath thrown you   105
  Upon my master, and made him your heir:
  He cannot be so stupid, or stone-dead,
  But out of conscience, and mere gratitude—
CORBACCIO. He must pronounce me his?
MOSCA.   'Tis true.
CORBACCIO.   This plot.
  Did I think on before.
MOSCA.   I do believe it.   110
CORBACCIO. Do you not believe it?
MOSCA.   Yes, sir.
CORBACCIO.   Mine own project.
MOSCA. Which, when he hath done, sir—
CORBACCIO.   Published me his heir?
MOSCA. And you so certain to survive him—
CORBACCIO.   Ay.
MOSCA. Being so lusty a man—
CORBACCIO.   'Tis true.
MOSCA.   Yes, sir—
CORBACCIO. I thought on that too. See, how he should be   115
  The very organ to express my thoughts!
MOSCA. You have not only done yourself a good—
CORBACCIO. But multiplied it on my son?
MOSCA.   'Tis right, sir.

---

2. That circumstance or appearance ("color") will make the trick more effective.

CORBACCIO. Still, my invention.
MOSCA.   'Las, sir! Heaven knows,
    It hath been all my study, all my care   120
    (I e'en grow gray withal), how to work things—
CORBACCIO. I do conceive, sweet Mosca.
MOSCA.   You are he,
    For whom I labor, here.
CORBACCIO.   Ay, do, do, do:
    I'll straight about it.   [Going.]
MOSCA.   Rook go with you, raven![3]
CORBACCIO. I know thee honest.
MOSCA.   [aside] You do lie, sir!
CORBACCIO.   And—   125
MOSCA. Your knowledge is not better than your ears, sir.
CORBACCIO. I do not doubt, to be a father to thee.
MOSCA. Nor I to gull my brother of his blessing.[4]
CORBACCIO. I may have my youth restored to me, why not?
MOSCA. Your worship is a precious ass!
CORBACCIO.   What sayest thou?   130
MOSCA. I do desire your worship to make haste, sir.
CORBACCIO. 'Tis done, 'tis done; I go.   [Exit.]
VOLPONE.   [leaping from his couch] O, I shall burst!
    Let out my sides, let out my sides—
MOSCA.   Contain
    Your flux of laughter, sir; you know this hope
    Is such a bait, it covers any hook.   135
VOLPONE. O, but thy working, and thy placing it!
    I cannot hold; good rascal, let me kiss thee:
    I never knew thee in so rare a humor.
MOSCA. Alas, sir, I but do as I am taught;
    Follow your grave instructions; give them words;   140
    Pour oil into their ears, and send them hence.
VOLPONE. 'Tis true, 'tis true. What a rare punishment
    Is avarice to itself![5]
MOSCA.   Ay, with our help, sir.
VOLPONE. So many cares, so many maladies,
    So many fears attending an old age,   145
    Yea, death so often called on, as no wish
    Can be more frequent with them, their limbs faint,
    Their senses dull, their seeing, hearing, going,
    All dead before them; yea, their very teeth,

3. The rook is a common crowlike bird, raucous and thievish, but Mosca is playing on a secondary meaning—cheat or deception: "May you be deceived, you raven!"
4. Jacob robbed Esau of his blessing by impersonating him before blind old Isaac (Genesis 27).
5. Seneca, Epistle 115, par. 16.

Their instruments of eating, failing them: 150
Yet this is reckoned life! Nay, here was one,
Is now gone home, that wishes to live longer!
Feels not his gout, nor palsy; feigns himself
Younger by scores of years, flatters his age
With confident belying it, hopes he may,   155
With charms, like Æson,[6] have his youth restored;
And with these thoughts so battens, as if fate
Would be as easily cheated on, as he,
And all turns air! [*Knocking within.*] Who's that there, now? A
    third!
MOSCA. Close, to your couch again; I hear his voice.   160
    It is Corvino, our spruce merchant.
VOLPONE.   [*lies down as before*] Dead.[7]
MOSCA. Another bout, sir, with your eyes. [*Anointing them.*]
                              —Who's there?

ACT I   SCENE 5

    [*Enter* CORVINO.]
    Signor Corvino! Come most wished for! O,
    How happy were you, if you knew it, now!
CORVINO. Why? What? Wherein?
MOSCA.   The tardy hour is come, sir.
CORVINO. He is not dead?
MOSCA.   Not dead, sir, but as good:
    He knows no man.
CORVINO.   How shall I do then?
MOSCA.   Why, sir?   5
CORVINO. I have brought him here a pearl.
MOSCA.   Perhaps he has
    So much remembrance left, as to know you, sir.
    He still calls on you; nothing but your name
    Is in his mouth. Is your pearl orient,[8] sir?
CORVINO. Venice was never owner of the like.   10
VOLPONE. [*faintly*] Signor Corvino!
MOSCA.   Hark.
VOLPONE.   Signor Corvino!
MOSCA. He calls you; step and give it him.—He's here, sir,
    And he has brought you a rich pearl.
CORVINO.   How do you, sir?

6. In Greek mythology, Aeson, Jason's father, was restored to life by the charms of Medea the
   witch.
7. I.e., "Pretend that I'm dead." The "bout . . . with your eyes" is a dose of gummy medicine.
8. Lustrous.

Tell him, it doubles the twelfth carat.[9]

MOSCA.   Sir,
He cannot understand, his hearing's gone;   15
And yet it comforts him to see you—

CORVINO.   Say,
I have a diamond for him, too.

MOSCA.   Best show it, sir;
Put it into his hand; 'tis only there
He apprehends:[1] he has his feeling, yet.
See how he grasps it!

CORVINO.   'Las, good gentleman!   20
How pitiful the sight is!

MOSCA.   Tut! Forget, sir.
The weeping of an heir should still be laughter
Under a visor.[2]

CORVINO.   Why, am I his heir?

MOSCA. Sir, I am sworn, I may not show the will
Till he be dead; but here has been Corbaccio,   25
Here has been Voltore, here were others too,
I cannot number 'em, they were so many,
All gaping here for legacies; but I,
Taking the vantage of his naming you,
Signor Corvino, Signor Corvino, took   30
Paper, and pen, and ink, and there I asked him,
Whom he would have his heir? Corvino. Who
Should be executor? Corvino. And,
To any question he was silent to,
I still interpreted the nods he made,   35
Through weakness, for consent; and sent home th' others,
Nothing bequeathed them, but to cry and curse.

CORVINO. O, my dear Mosca! [They embrace.] Does he not per-
    ceive us?

MOSCA. No more than a blind harper. He knows no man,
No face of friend, nor name of any servant,   40
Who 'twas that fed him last, or gave him drink;
Not those he hath begotten, or brought up,
Can he remember.

CORVINO.   Has he children?

MOSCA.   Bastards,
Some dozen, or more, that he begot on beggars,

---

9. Weighs 24 carats, or more than a third of an ounce—a huge pearl. "Twenty-four-carat" has
   other overtones, as a measure of perfect purity in gold.
1. In English, "apprehends" means "to understand intellectually," but the root Latin sense is
   "to grasp physically."
2. An heir should look sad by way of concealing his jubilation.

Gypsies, and Jews, and black-moors, when he was drunk.   45
Knew you not that, sir? 'Tis the common fable,
The dwarf, the fool, the eunuch, are all his;
He's the true father of his family,
In all save me; but he has given them nothing.
CORVINO. That's well, that's well! Art sure he does not hear us?   50
MOSCA. Sure, sir! Why, look you, credit your own sense.
                                        [*Shouts in* VOLPONE's *ear.*]
The pox approach, and add to your diseases,
If it would send you hence the sooner, sir.
For your incontinence, it hath deserved it
Throughly and throughly, and the plague to boot!—   55
You may come near, sir—Would you would once close
Those filthy eyes of yours, that flow with slime,
Like two frog-pits; and those same hanging cheeks,
Covered with hide instead of skin—Nay, help, sir—
That look like frozen dish-clouts set on end!   60
CORVINO. Or like an old smoked wall, on which the rain
Ran down in streaks!
MOSCA.   Excellent, sir! Speak out.
You may be louder yet; a culverin[3]
Discharged in his ear would hardly bore it.
CORVINO. His nose is like a common sewer, still running.   65
MOSCA. 'Tis good! And what his mouth?
CORVINO.   A very draught.[4]
MOSCA. O, stop it up—
CORVINO.   By no means.
MOSCA.   'Pray you, let me:
Faith I could stifle him rarely with a pillow,
As well as any woman that should keep him.[5]
CORVINO. Do as you will; but I'll be gone.
MOSCA.   Be so;   70
It is your presence makes him last so long.
CORVINO. I pray you, use no violence.
MOSCA.   No, sir! Why?
Why should you be thus scrupulous, pray you, sir?
CORVINO. Nay, at your discretion.
MOSCA.   Well, good sir, be gone.
CORVINO. I will not trouble him now to take my pearl?   75
MOSCA. Puh! Nor your diamond. What a needless care
Is this afflicts you? Is not all here yours?

3. Horse-pistol.
4. Cesspool.
5. "I could smother him as well as a nurse."

Am not I here? Whom you have made your creature?
That owe my being to you?
CORVINO.   Grateful Mosca!
Thou art my friend, my fellow, my companion,   80
My partner, and shalt share in all my fortunes.
MOSCA. Excepting one.
CORVINO.   What's that?
MOSCA.   Your gallant wife, sir.—
                                    [*Exit* CORVINO.]
Now is he gone: we had no other means
To shoot him hence, but this.
VOLPONE.   My divine Mosca!
Thou hast today outgone thyself. [*Knocking within.*]—Who's
    there?   85
I will be troubled with no more. Prepare
Me music, dances, banquets, all delights;
The Turk is not more sensual in his pleasures,
Than will Volpone. [*Exit* MOSCA.] Let me see; a pearl!
A diamond! Plate! Sequins! Good morning's purchase.   90
Why, this is better than rob churches,[6] yet;
Or fat,[7] by eating, once a month, a man—[*Enter* MOSCA.]
Who is't?
MOSCA.   The beauteous Lady Would-be, sir,
Wife to the English knight, Sir Politic Would-be
(This is the style, sir, is directed me),[8]   95
Hath sent to know how you have slept tonight,
And if you would be visited?
VOLPONE.   Not now:
Some three hours hence—
MOSCA.   I told the squire so much.
VOLPONE. When I am high with mirth and wine, then, then.
'Fore heaven, I wonder at the desperate valor   100
Of the bold English, that they dare let loose
Their wives to all encounters!
MOSCA.   Sir, this knight
Had not his name for nothing, he is *politic*,[9]
And knows, howe'er his wife affect strange airs,
She hath not yet the face to be dishonest.[1]   105
But had she Signor Corvino's wife's face—
VOLPONE. Has she so rare a face?

---

6. I.e., easy money.
7. Here, Volpone is talking about growing "fat" (rich) by charging exorbitant interest rates.
8. I.e., "this is the way I've been told to announce her."
9. Devious, subtle.
1. "She's not beautiful enough to be unchaste."

MOSCA.   O, sir, the wonder,
  The blazing star of Italy! A wench
  Of the first year! A beauty ripe as harvest![2]
  Whose skin is whiter than a swan all over,   110
  Than silver, snow, or lilies! A soft lip,
  Would tempt you to eternity of kissing!
  And flesh that melteth in the touch to blood!
  Bright as your gold, and lovely as your gold!
VOLPONE. Why had not I known this before?
MOSCA.   Alas, sir,   115
  Myself but yesterday discovered it.
VOLPONE. How might I see her?
MOSCA.   O, not possible;
  She's kept as warily as is your gold;
  Never does come abroad, never takes air,
  But at a window. All her looks are sweet,   120
  As the first grapes or cherries, and are watched
  As near as they are.
VOLPONE.   I must see her.
MOSCA.   Sir,
  There is a guard of ten spies thick upon her,
  All his whole household; each of which is set
  Upon his fellow, and have all their charge,   125
  When he goes out, when he comes in, examined.
VOLPONE. I will go see her, though but at her window.
MOSCA. In some disguise, then.
VOLPONE.   That is true; I must
  Maintain mine own shape[3] still the same; we'll think.

                                      [Exeunt.]

Act II

ACT II   SCENE 1. *ST. MARK'S PLACE, BEFORE* CORVINO'S *HOUSE*

[*Enter* SIR POLITIC WOULD-BE, *and* PEREGRINE.]
SIR POLITIC. Sir, to a wise man, all the world's his soil.
  It is not Italy, nor France, nor Europe,
  That must bound me, if my fates call me forth.
  Yet, I protest, it is no salt[4] desire
  Of seeing countries, shifting a religion,   5
  Nor any disaffection to the state

2. A blazing star is literally a comet, hence a heavenly object of special attention. "A wench of the first year" seems to be a metaphor from wine-making, implying that the first crop of grapes makes the best wine.
3. My own disguise as an invalid.
4. Wanton, frivolous.

Where I was bred, and unto which I owe
My dearest plots,[5] hath brought me out; much less,
That idle, antique, stale, gray-headed project
Of knowing men's minds and manners, with Ulysses![6]   10
But a peculiar humor of my wife's,
Laid for this height of Venice, to observe,
To quote, to learn the language, and so forth.—
I hope you travel, sir, with license?[7]
PEREGRINE.   Yes.
SIR POLITIC. I dare the safelier converse—How long, sir,   15
Since you left England?
PEREGRINE.   Seven weeks.
SIR POLITIC.   So lately!
You have not been with my lord ambassador?
PEREGRINE. Not yet, sir.
SIR POLITIC.   Pray you, what news, sir, vents our
    climate?[8]
I heard last night a most strange thing reported
By some of my lord's followers, and I long   20
To hear how 'twill be seconded.
PEREGRINE.   What was't, sir?
SIR POLITIC. Marry, sir, of a raven that should build
In a ship royal of the king's.[9]
PEREGRINE.   This fellow,
Does he gull me,[1] trow? Or is gulled?—Your name, sir?
SIR POLITIC. My name is Politic Would-be.
PEREGRINE.   [aside] O, that speaks[2] him.—   25
A knight, sir?
SIR POLITIC.   A poor knight, sir.
PEREGRINE.   Your lady
Lies here in Venice, for intelligence
Of tires and fashions and behavior
Among the courtesans?[3] The fine Lady Would-be?
SIR POLITIC. Yes, sir; the spider and the bee, oft-times   30
Suck from one flower.
PEREGRINE.   Good Sir Politic,

---

5. Projects, notions.
6. Ulysses (Homer says) knew the minds of many men and saw many cities. The "humor" (fancy)
   of Sir Politic's wife was exactly calculated, he thinks, to bring her to Venice.
7. Special permission to travel abroad.
8. I.e., "What news does our climate (country) give off?"
9. A raven is a bird of ill omen.
1. To "gull" is constantly used in the sense of to fool or deceive; "trow?": do you think?
2. Identifies his character.
3. Attires, costumes. Venetian prostitutes were for hundreds of years reputed to be the most
   desirable in Europe, perhaps because Pietro Aretino advertised them so flatteringly in his
   pornographic poems.

I cry you mercy; I have heard much of you.
'Tis true, sir, of your raven.
SIR POLITIC.   On your knowledge?
PEREGRINE. Yes, and your lion's whelping in the Tower.[4]
SIR POLITIC. Another whelp!
PEREGRINE.   Another, sir.
SIR POLITIC.   Now, heaven!   35
What prodigies be these? The fires at Berwick![5]
And the new star! These things concurring, strange
And full of omen! Saw you those meteors?
PEREGRINE. I did, sir.
SIR POLITIC.   Fearful! Pray you, sir, confirm me,
Were there three porpoises seen above the bridge,   40
As they give out?[6]
PEREGRINE.   Six, and a sturgeon, sir.
SIR POLITIC. I am astonished.
PEREGRINE.   Nay, sir, be not so;
I'll tell you a greater prodigy than these.
SIR POLITIC. What should these things portend?
PEREGRINE.   The very day
(Let me be sure) that I put forth from London,   45
There was a whale discovered in the river,
As high as Woolwich, that had waited there,
Few know how many months, for the subversion
Of the Stade fleet.[7]
SIR POLITIC.   Is't possible? Believe it,
'Twas either sent from Spain, or the Archduke's: 50
Spinola's whale, upon my life, my credit![8]
Will they not leave these projects? Worthy sir,
Some other news.
PEREGRINE.   Faith, Stone the fool is dead,
And they do lack a tavern fool extremely.
SIR POLITIC. Is Mas' Stone dead?[9]
PEREGRINE.   He's dead, sir; why, I hope   55

---

4. Lions were in fact kept caged in the Tower of London, and cubs were whelped from time to time. Most of the events to which Sir Politic alludes had in fact occurred shortly before the time of the play's first production and would have been familiar to the audience.
5. A new star appeared in October 1604, and the aurora borealis over Berwick in January 1605 was said to resemble armies of men fighting in the sky.
6. It was unusual for deep-sea creatures to venture up the Thames, past London Bridge.
7. The English Merchant Adventurer's fleet was at Stade (formerly Stode), a port northwest of Hamburg, Germany. How a whale in the Thames could subvert it is not very clear.
8. Sir Politic's suggestions about the origin of the whale all involve Spain, the enemy of England. It comes either from Spain itself; or from the Archduke Albert, ruler of the Spanish Netherlands in the name of the Spanish king Philip II; or from Ambrosio Spinola, general of the Spanish armies in Holland.
9. Stone the fool was an actual figure, about whom various anecdotes survive. "Mas' ": short for master, the common denomination of fools and boys.

You thought him not immortal?—O, this knight,
Were he well known, would be a precious thing
To fit our English stage. He that should write
But such a fellow, should be thought to feign
Extremely, if not maliciously.
SIR POLITIC.   Stone dead!   60
PEREGRINE. Dead. Lord! how deeply, sir, you apprehend it!
He was no kinsman to you?
SIR POLITIC.   That I know of.
Well! That same fellow was an unknown fool.
PEREGRINE. And yet you knew him, it seems?
SIR POLITIC.   I did so. Sir,
I knew him one of the most dangerous heads   65
Living within the state, and so I held him.
PEREGRINE. Indeed, sir?
SIR POLITIC.   While he lived, in action.
He has received weekly intelligence,
Upon my knowledge, out of the Low Countries,
For all parts of the world, in cabbages;[1]   70
And those dispensed again to ambassadors,
In oranges, musk-melons, apricots,
Lemons, pome-citrons, and such-like; sometimes
In Colchester oysters, and your Selsey cockles.[2]
PEREGRINE. You make me wonder.
SIR POLITIC.   Sir, upon my knowledge.   75
Nay, I've observed him, at your public ordinary,[3]
Take his advertisement from a traveler
(A concealed statesman) in a trencher of meat;
And instantly, before the meal was done,
Convey an answer in a tooth-pick.
PEREGRINE.   Strange!   80
How could this be, sir?
SIR POLITIC.   Why, the meat was cut
So like his character, and so laid, as he
Must easily read the cipher.
PEREGRINE.   I have heard,
He could not read, sir.
SIR POLITIC.   So 'twas given out,
In polity,[4] by those that did employ him: 85
But he could read, and had your languages,

---

1. Cabbages were a recent importation from Holland.
2. "Pomecitrons" we would call simply "citrons," or limes. The oysters and cockles specified
   were the best shellfish to be had in England and were often served to royalty.
3. Common tavern. "Advertisement": secret message, tip.
4. For political reasons, as part of his cover story.

And to't,[5] as sound a noddle—
PEREGRINE.   I have heard, sir,
That your baboons were spies, and that they were
A kind of subtle nation near to China.
SIR POLITIC. Ay, ay, your Mamaluchi.[6] Faith, they had   90
Their hand in a French plot or two; but they
Were so extremely given to women, as
They made discovery of all; yet I
Had my advices here, on Wednesday last,
From one of their own coat, they were returned,   95
Made their relations, as the fashion is,
And now stand fair for fresh employment.
PEREGRINE.   [aside] 'Heart!
This Sir Politic will be ignorant of nothing.
—It seems, sir, you know all.
SIR POLITIC.   Not all, sir; but
I have some general notions. I do love   100
To note and to observe; though I live out,
Free from the active torrent, yet I'd mark
The currents and the passages of things,
For mine own private use; and know the ebbs
And flows of state.
PEREGRINE.   Believe it, sir, I hold   105
Myself in no small tie unto my fortunes,
For casting me thus luckily upon you,
Whose knowledge, if your bounty equal it,
May do me great assistance, in instruction
For my behavior, and my bearing, which   110
Is yet so rude and raw.
SIR POLITIC.   Why? Came you forth
Empty of rules for travel?
PEREGRINE.   Faith, I had
Some common ones, from out that vulgar grammar,
Which he that cried Italian to me,[7] taught me.
SIR POLITIC. Why this it is that spoils all our brave bloods,   115
Trusting our hopeful gentry unto pedants,
Fellows of outside, and mere bark.[8] You seem
To be a gentleman of ingenuous[9] race:
I not profess it, but my fate hath been

---

5. In addition.
6. Mamaluchi is the Italian form of *mamelukes*, a group of slaves and warriors originally from Circassia, in Asia Minor, who held or controlled the throne of Egypt for many years.
7. Trained me in the pronunciation of Italian.
8. Superficial and ignorant teachers.
9. Noble.

To be where I have been consulted with,   120
In this high kind, touching some great men's sons,
Persons of blood and honor.—
PEREGRINE. [seeing people approach] Who be these, sir?

ACT II   SCENE 2

[Enter MOSCA and NANO disguised, followed by persons with
materials for erecting a stage.]
MOSCA. Under that window, there 't must be. The same.
SIR POLITIC. Fellows, to mount a bank. Did your instructor
In the dear tongues, never discourse to you
Of the Italian mountebanks?[1]
PEREGRINE.   Yes, sir.
SIR POLITIC.   Why,
Here you shall see one.
PEREGRINE.   They are quacksalvers,   5
Fellows that live by venting oils and drugs?[2]
SIR POLITIC. Was that the character he gave you of them?
PEREGRINE. As I remember.
SIR POLITIC.   Pity his ignorance.
They are the only knowing men of Europe!
Great general scholars, excellent physicians,   10
Most admired statesmen, professed favorites,
And cabinet counselors to the greatest princes;
The only languaged men[3] of all the world!
PEREGRINE. And I have heard they are most lewd impostors;
Made all of terms and shreds; no less beliers   15
Of great men's favors, than their own vile medicines;
Which they will utter upon monstrous oaths,
Selling that drug for two-pence, ere they part,
Which they have valued at twelve crowns before.
SIR POLITIC. Sir, calumnies are answered best with silence.   20
Yourself shall judge—Who is it mounts, my friends?
MOSCA. Scoto of Mantua, sir.[4]
SIR POLITIC.   Is't he? Nay, then
I'll proudly promise, sir, you shall behold

1. The word "mountebank" comes from the Italian montambanco, meaning "to mount the bench"; other terms for the same fellow are saltimbanco and charlatan. Montebanks were a mixture of public entertainer and patent-medicine salesman who gave a very considerable semidramatic, improvised performance before delivering their pitch.
2. "Venting": vending; "quacksalvers": quacks.
3. The best of talkers.
4. Scoto of Mantua was a real person, a juggler, magician, and performer at legerdemain; he actually visited England and performed before Queen Elizabeth, about a quarter of a century before Volpone had its first performance.

Another man than has been phant'sied[5] to you.
I wonder yet that he should mount his bank, 25
Here in this nook, that has been wont t'appear
In face of the Piazza!—Here he comes.
[*Enter* VOLPONE *disguised as a mountebank and followed by*
a crowd of people.]
VOLPONE. [*to* NANO] Mount, zany.[6]
MOB.   Follow, follow, follow, follow,
follow!
SIR POLITIC. See how the people follow him! He's a man
May write ten thousand crowns in bank here. Note, 30
[VOLPONE *mounts the stage.*]
Mark but his gesture: I do use to observe
The state he keeps in getting up.
PEREGRINE.   'Tis worth it, sir.
VOLPONE. *Most noble gentlemen, and my worthy patrons! It may*
seem strange, that I, your Scoto Mantuano, who was ever wont to
fix my bank in face of the public Piazza, near the shelter of the 35
Portico to the Procuratia,[7] *should now, after eight months' absence*
from this illustrious city of Venice, humbly retire myself into an
obscure nook of the Piazza.
SIR POLITIC. Did not I now object the same?
PEREGRINE.   Peace, sir.
VOLPONE. *Let me tell you: I am not, as your Lombard proverb saith,* 40
cold on my feet;[8] *or content to part with my commodities at a*
cheaper rate, than I accustomed; look not for it. Nor that the
calumnious reports of that impudent detractor, and shame to our
profession (Alessandro Buttone, I mean), who gave out, in public,
I was condemned a sforzato *to the galleys, for poisoning the car-* 45
dinal Bembo's—[9] *cook, hath at all attached, much less dejected*
me. No, no, worthy gentlemen; to tell you true, I cannot endure
to see the rabble of these ground ciarlitani,[1] *that spread their*
cloaks on the pavement, as if they meant to do feats of activity,

---

5. Described.
6. Zany: from the Italian name Giovanni; a generic term for a fool, clown, performer. The
   speech of the crowd is intended to mimic a confused hubbub.
7. The arcade along the north side of Piazza San Marco, where the Procurators, the highest
   government officials, resided. Jonson takes great pains to make his Venetian details specific
   and accurate.
8. This is an Italian proverb, "Haver freddo a 'piedi," meaning "to be so hard up that one has
   to sell one's goods at a loss."
9. Alessandro Buttone is an imaginary rival who has dreamed up a slander against Scoto—but
   the tale is most unlikely since Cardinal Bembo died in 1547, more than fifty years before the
   play is supposed to be taking place. A *sforzato* is a galley slave; the dash before "cook" is
   supposed to indicate that the title of cook is just a euphemism.
1. Ground *ciarlatani*, or charlatans, put on their acts and sold their nostrums at street level.

and then come in lamely, with their moldy tales out of Boccaccio,[2]   50
like stale Tabarin, the fabulist: some of them discoursing their
travels, and of their tedious captivity in the Turks' galley, when,
indeed, were the truth known, they were the Christians' galleys,
where very temperately they ate bread, and drunk water, as a
wholesome penance, enjoined them by their confessors, for base   55
pilferies.[3]

SIR POLITIC. Note but his bearing, and contempt of these.

VOLPONE. *These turdy-facy-nasty-paty-lousy-fartical rogues, with one*
poor groat's-worth of unprepared antimony, finely wrapped up in
several scartoccios,[4] *are able, very well, to kill their twenty a week,*   60
and play; yet, these meager, starved spirits, who have half-stopped
the organs of their minds with earthy oppilations,[5] *want not their*
favorers among your shrivelled salad-eating artisans, who are over-
joyed that they may have their half-p'orth of physic; though it
purge them into another world, it makes no matter.   65

SIR POLITIC. Excellent! Have you heard better language, sir?

VOLPONE. *Well, let them go. And, gentlemen, honorable gentlemen,*
know, that for this time, our bank, being thus removed from the
clamors of the canaglia[6] *shall be the scene of pleasure and delight;*
for I have nothing to sell, little or nothing to sell.   70

SIR POLITIC. I told you, sir, his end.

PEREGRINE.   You did so, sir.

VOLPONE. *I protest, I, and my six servants, are not able to make of*
this precious liquor, so fast as it is fetched away from my lodging
by gentlemen of your city; strangers of the terra firma;[7] *worshipful*
merchants; ay, and senators too: who, ever since my arrival, have   75
detained me to their uses, by their splendidous liberalities. And
worthily; for, what avails your rich man to have his magazines
stuffed with moscadelli,[8] *or of the purest grape, when his physi-*
cians prescribe him, on pain of death, to drink nothing but water
cocted[9] *with aniseeds? O, health! health! The blessing of the rich!*   80
The riches of the poor! Who can buy thee at too dear a rate, since
there is no enjoying this world without thee? Be not then so

---

2. Boccaccio told in the *Decameron* (ca. 1350) a great many popular stories; as he lived in the
   fourteenth century, the tales were "moldy" by the seventeenth. Like Scoto, Tabarine was an
   actual Italian comedian of the time who performed in France (not, so far as we know, in
   England) during the 1570s.
3. Venetian galleys required many oars, often operated by captive Turks or condemned criminals,
   who were chained to the bench, fed miserable food, and whipped mercilessly.
4. Antimony was the basis of most common emetics; *scartoccios* were little paper envelopes in
   which drugs were placed.
5. Obstructions.
6. The common mob.
7. *Terra firma* is still the Venetian term for land across the lagoon, the mainland.
8. Muscadel or muscatel is wine made from certain grapes, in Italian *moscatini*, that seem to
   have the perfume of musk; "magazines": storehouses.
9. Flavored.

sparing of your purses, honorable gentlemen, as to abridge the
natural course of life—
PEREGRINE. You see his end.
SIR POLITIC.   Ay, is't not good?   85
VOLPONE. *For, when a humid flux, or catarrh, by the mutability of*
    air, falls from your head into an arm or shoulder, or any other
    part; take you a ducat, or your sequin of gold, and apply to the
    place affected: see what good effect it can work.[1] *No, no, 'tis this*
    blessed unguento, *this rare extraction, that hath only power to*   90
disperse all malignant humours, that proceed either of hot, cold,
    moist, or windy causes—
PEREGRINE. I would he had put in dry too.[2]
SIR POLITIC.   'Pray you, observe.
VOLPONE. *To fortify the most indigest and crude stomach, ay, were*
    it of one that, through extreme weakness, vomited blood, applying   95
    only a warm napkin to the place, after the unction and fricace;[3]
    —for the vertigine *in the head, putting but a drop into your*
    nostrils, likewise behind the ears; a most sovereign and approved
    remedy: the mal caduco, *cramps, convulsions, paralyses, epilep-*
    sies, tremor cordia, *retired nerves, ill vapors of the spleen, stop-*   100
    pings of the liver, the stone, the strangury, hernia ventosa, *ilica*
    passio; *stops a* dysenteria *immediately; easeth the torsion of the*
    small guts, and cures melancholia hypocondriaca,[4] *being taken*
    and applied, according to my printed receipt. [Pointing to his bill
    and his vial.] *For, this is the physician, this the medicine; this*   105
    counsels, this cures; this gives the direction, this works the effect;
    and, in sum, both together may be termed an abstract of the
    theoric and practic[5] *in the Æsculapian art. 'Twill cost you eight*
    crowns. And, Zan Fritada,[6] *prithee sing a verse extempore in*
    honor of it.   110
SIR POLITIC. How do you like him, sir?
PEREGRINE.   Most strangely, I!
SIR POLITIC. Is not his language rare?
PEREGRINE.   But alchemy,[7]
I never heard the like; or Broughton's books.

1. I.e., money won't cure your cold when you catch it (but his "blessed unguent"—ointment—
will).
2. Of the four "humours," or ingredients of a balanced human complexion, "Scoto" has left out
one, as Peregrine drily observes.
3. Anointing and massage; "vertigine": vertigo, dizziness.
4. "melancholia hypocondriaca" is severe depression. The other ailments are *mal caduco*: falling
sickness, epilepsy; *tremor cordia*: palpitations of the heart; strangury: painful urination; *hernia
ventosa*: gassy hernia; *iliaca passio*: cramps of the small intestine.
5. Theory and practice. The Aesculapian art: medicine (from Aesculapius, Greek god of
medicine).
6. Literally, "Johnny Omelet," obviously one of the mountebank's stooges.
7. Except for alchemy. Jonson had no use for books of Hugh Broughton (1549–1612), a Puritan
divine and rabbinical scholar.

[NANO *sings.*]
    Had old Hippocrates, or Galen,[8]
    That to their books put med'cines all in,   115
    But known this secret, they had never
    (Of which they will be guilty ever)
    Been murderers of so much paper,
    Or wasted many a hurtless taper;
    No Indian drug had e'er been famed,   120
    Tobacco, sassafras not named;
    Ne yet, of guacum[9] *one small stick, sir,*
    Nor Raymond Lully's great elixir.
    Ne had been known the Danish Gonswart,
    Or Paracelsus, with his long sword.[1]   125
PEREGRINE. All this, yet, will not do; eight crowns is high.
VOLPONE. No more. *Gentlemen, if I had but time to discourse to you the miraculous effects of this my oil, surnamed* oglio del Scoto;[2] *with the countless catalogue of those I have cured of the aforesaid, and many more diseases; the patents and privileges of* 130 *all the princes and commonwealths of Christendom; or but the depositions of those that appeared on my part, before the signory of the Sanita*[3] *and most learned College of Physicians; where I was authorized, upon notice taken of the admirable virtues of my medicaments, and mine own excellency in matter of rare and* 135 *unknown secrets, not only to disperse them publicly in this famous city, but in all the territories, that happily joy under the government of the most pious and magnificent states of Italy. But may some other gallant fellow say, 'O, there be divers that make profession to have as good, and as experimented receipts as yours.'* 140 *Indeed, very many have essayed, like apes, in imitation of that which is really and essentially in me, to make of this oil; bestowed great cost in furnaces, stills, alembics,*[4] *continual fires, and preparation of the ingredients, (as indeed there goes to it six hundred several simples,*[5] *besides some quantity of human fat, for the con-* 145 *glutination, which we buy of the anatomists) but, when these practitioners come to the last decoction, blow, blow, puff, puff,*

---

8. Famous doctors of the Classical world.
9. Modern guaiacum, obtained from the bark of a South American tree.
1. Raymond Lully or Lull was a Spanish mystic philosopher of the thirteenth century who claimed to have discovered the elixir (see p. 18, note 9). "The Danish Gonswart": not identified; Paracelsus, the famous German doctor of the sixteenth century, had a famous sword in the handle of which he kept, according to legend, familiar spirits, and according to history, medications and herbs.
2. Scoto's oil.
3. The Board of Medical Examiners in Venice.
4. Distilleries, retorts.
5. Herbs; "conglutination": coherence, sticking together.

and all flies in fumo:[6] *ha, ha, ha! Poor wretches, I rather pity
their folly and indiscretion, than their loss of time and money; for
those may be recovered by industry: but to be a fool born, is a* 150
disease incurable.

For myself, *I always from my youth have endeavored to get the
rarest secrets, and book them, either in exchange, or for money: I
spared nor cost nor labor, where anything was worthy to be
learned. And, gentlemen, honorable gentlemen; I will undertake,* 155
*by virtue of chemical art, out of the honorable hat that covers
your head, to extract the four elements; that is to say, the fire, air,
water, and earth, and return you your felt without burn or stain.
For, whilst others have been at the balloo,[7] I have been at my
book; and am now past the craggy paths of study, and come to* 160
the flowery plains of honor and reputation.

SIR POLITIC. I do assure you, sir, that is his aim.

VOLPONE. *But to our price—*

PEREGRINE.   And that withal, sir Pol.

VOLPONE. *You all know, honorable gentlemen, I never valued this*
ampulla, or vial, at less than eight crowns; but for this time, I am 165
*content to be deprived of it for six: six crowns is the price, and
less in courtesy I know you cannot offer me; take it or leave it,
howsoever, both it and I am at your service. I ask you not as the
value of the thing, for then I should demand of you a thousand
crowns; so the cardinals Montalto, Farnese, the great duke of* 170
*Tuscany, my gossip[8] with divers other princes, have given me; but
I despise money. Only to show my affection to you, honorable
gentlemen, and your illustrious state here, I have neglected the
messages of these princes, mine own offices, framed my journey
hither, only to present you with the fruits of my travels.* [To 175
NANO.]—*Tune your voices once more to the touch of your instruments, and give the honorable assembly some delightful recreation.*

PEREGRINE. What monstrous and most painful circumstance
Is here, to get some three or four *gazettes,*[9]
Some three-pence in the whole! For that 'twill come to. 180

[NANO *sings.*]
       You that would last long, list to my song,
       Make no more coil,[1] but buy of this oil.

---

6. In smoke; "decoction": boiling down.
7. Balloon, ball—i.e., while others have been diverting themselves with ball games.
8. Literally, "godparent"; here, "my friend." Cardinal Montalto became Pope Sixtus V in 1585;
   Alessandro Farnese had become Pope Paul III in 1534; "the great duke of Tuscany" was
   Cosimo de Medici.
9. The smallest Venetian coins, worth less than an English penny.
1. Stir, fuss.

Would you be ever fair and young?
Stout of teeth, and strong of tongue?
Tart of palate? Quick of ear?   185
Sharp of sight? Of nostril clear?
Moist of hand and light of foot?
Or, I will come nearer to't,
Would you live free from all diseases?
Do the act your mistress pleases,   190
Yet fright all aches from your bones?
Here's a medicine for the nones.[2]

VOLPONE. Well, I am in a humor at this time to make a present of
the small quantity my coffer contains; to the rich in courtesy, and
to the poor for God's sake. Wherefore, now mark: I asked you six   195
crowns; and six crowns, at other times, you have paid me; you
shall not give me six crowns, nor five, nor four, nor three, nor two,
nor one; nor half a ducat; no, nor a mocenigo.[3] Sixpence it will
cost you, or six hundred pound—expect no lower price, for, by the
banner of my front, I will not bate a bagatine,[4]—that I will have, 200
only, a pledge of your loves, to carry something from amongst you,
to show I am not contemned by you. Therefore, now, toss your
handkerchiefs, cheerfully, cheerfully,[5] and be advertised, that the
first heroic spirit that deigns to grace me with a handkerchief, I
will give it a little remembrance of something, beside, shall please   205
it better, than if I had presented it with a double pistolet.[6]

PEREGRINE. Will you be that heroic spark, sir Pol?

    [CELIA at a window above, throws down her handkerchief.]
O, see! The window has prevented[7] you.

VOLPONE. Lady, I kiss your bounty; and for this timely grace you
have done your poor Scoto of Mantua, I will return you, over and   210
above my oil, a secret of that high and inestimable nature, shall
make you for ever enamored on that minute, wherein your eye
first descended on so mean, yet not altogether to be despised, an
object. Here is a powder concealed in this paper, of which, if I
should speak to the worth, nine thousand volumes were but as   215
one page, that page as a line, that line as a word; so short is this
pilgrimage of man (which some call life) to the expressing of it.
Would I reflect on the price? Why, the whole world were but as

---

2. For the occasion.
3. A Venetian coin, worth about nine English pennies.
4. A tiny coin; "bate": lower.
5. When business was brisk at the mountebank's stand, customers sometimes knotted their money
   in a handkerchief or glove and tossed it on stage; the money was taken out, replaced with
   the medicine, and the handkerchief tossed back to the purchaser.
6. A double pistolet was a Spanish coin of some value, worth a little less than an English pound.
7. Forestalled, anticipated.

an empire, that empire as a province, that province as a bank,
that bank as a private purse to the purchase of it. I will only tell 220
you: it is the powder that made Venus a goddess (given her by
Apollo), that kept her perpetually young, cleared her wrinkles,
firmed her gums, filled her skin, colored her hair; from her derived
to Helen, and at the sack of Troy unfortunately lost; till now, in
this our age, it was as happily recovered, by a studious antiquary, 225
out of some ruins of Asia, who sent a moiety[8] of it to the court of
France (but much sophisticated) wherewith the ladies there now
color their hair. The rest, at this present, remains with me; ex-
tracted to a quintessence, so that, wherever it but touches, in youth
it perpetually preserves, in age restores the complexion; seats your 230
teeth, did they dance like virginal jacks,[9] firm as a wall; makes
them white as ivory, that were black as——

ACT II   SCENE 3

[*Enter* CORVINO.]

CORVINO. Spite o' the devil, and my shame! Come down here;
   Come down; [*To* VOLPONE.]—No house but mine to make
   your scene?
   Signor Flaminio,[1] will you down, sir? Down?
   What, is my wife your Franciscina, sir?
   No windows on the whole Piazza here, 5
   To make your properties, but mine? But mine? [*Beats away*
   VOLPONE, NANO, *&c.*]
   Heart! Ere to-morrow I shall be new christened,
   And called the *Pantalone di Besogniosi,*[2]
   About the town.
PEREGRINE.   What should this mean, Sir Pol?
SIR POLITIC. Some trick of state, believe it; I will home. 10
PEREGRINE. It may be some design on you.
SIR POLITIC.   I know not.
   I'll stand upon my guard.
PEREGRINE.   It is your best, sir.
SIR POLITIC. This three weeks, all my advices, all my letters,
   They have been intercepted.
PEREGRINE   Indeed, sir!
   Best have a care.

---

8. Fraction; "sophisticated": refined, purified.
9. The quills that pluck the strings of a harpsichord ("virginal").
1. Signor Flaminio was Flaminio Scala, a Venetian comic actor of the day; Franciscina is an always-available serving girl in popular Italian comedy (*commedia dell'arte*).
2. Pantaloon of the Paupers. Pantaloon, in the tradition of *commedia dell'arte*, is a doddering old fool in perpetual terror of being cuckolded.

SIR POLITIC.   Nay, so I will.
PEREGRINE.   This knight,   15
I may not lose him, for my mirth, till night.   [*Exeunt.*]

ACT II   SCENE 4. *A ROOM IN* VOLPONE'*S HOUSE*

[*Enter* VOLPONE *and* MOSCA.]
VOLPONE. O, I am wounded!
MOSCA.   Where, sir?
VOLPONE.   Not without;
Those blows were nothing; I could bear them ever.
But angry Cupid, bolting from her eyes,
Hath shot himself into me like a flame,
Where now he flings about his burning heat,   5
As in a furnace an ambitious[3] fire,
Whose vent is stopped. The fight is all within me.
I cannot live, except thou help me, Mosca;
My liver melts, and I, without the hope
Of some soft air, from her refreshing breath,   10
Am but a heap of cinders.
MOSCA.   'Las, good sir!
Would you had never seen her.
VOLPONE.   Nay, would thou
Hadst never told me of her.
MOSCA.   Sir, 'tis true;
I do confess I was unfortunate,
And you unhappy: but I'm bound in conscience,   15
No less than duty, to effect my best
To your release of torment, and I will, sir.
VOLPONE. Dear Mosca, shall I hope?
MOSCA.   Sir, more than dear,
I will not bid you to despair of aught
Within a human compass.
VOLPONE.   O, there spoke   20
My better angel. Mosca, take my keys,
Gold, plate, and jewels, all's at thy devotion;[4]
Employ them how thou wilt; nay, coin me too,
So thou, in this, but crown my longings. Mosca?
MOSCA. Use but your patience.
VOLPONE.   So I have.
MOSCA.   I doubt not   25
To bring success to your desires.

---

3. Aspiring, growing. Most of Volpone's erotic torments are of the sort popularized 300 years before by Francesco Petrarch (1304–1374), Italian poet.
4. At your service.

VOLPONE.   Nay, then,
  I not repent me of my late disguise.
MOSCA. If you can horn[5] him, sir, you need not.
VOLPONE.   True:
  Besides, I never meant him for my heir.—
  Is not the color of my beard and eyebrows   30
  To make me known?
MOSCA.   No jot.
VOLPONE.   I did it well.
MOSCA. So well, would I could follow you in mine,
  With half the happiness!—And yet I would
  Escape your epilogue.[6]
VOLPONE.   But were they gulled
  With a belief that I was Scoto?
MOSCA.   Sir,   35
  Scoto himself could hardly have distinguished!
  I have not time to flatter you now, we'll part:
  And as I prosper, so applaud my art.   [*Exeunt.*]

ACT II   SCENE 5. *A ROOM IN* CORVINO'S *HOUSE*

  [*Enter* CORVINO, *sword in his hand, dragging in* CELIA.]
CORVINO. Death of mine honor, with the city's fool!
  A juggling, tooth-drawing, prating mountebank!
  And at a public window! Where, whilst he,
  With his strained action, and his dole[7] of faces,
  To his drug-lecture draws your itching ears,   5
  A crew of old, unmarried, noted lechers,
  Stood leering up like satyrs: and you smile
  Most graciously, and fan your favors forth,
  To give your hot spectators satisfaction!
  What, was your mountebank their call?[8] Their whistle?   10
  Or were you enamored on his copper rings,
  His saffron jewel, with the toad-stone in't?
  Or his embroidered suit, with the cope-stitch,
  Made of a hearse cloth?[9] Or his old tilt-feather?
  Or his starched beard? Well! You shall have him, yes!   15
  He shall come home, and minister unto you
  The fricace for the mother.[1] Or, let me see,

5. Cuckold, that is, make his wife unfaithful to him.
6. Avoid the beating you got.
7. Guile, trickery; the suggestion is of false faces or masks.
8. "Did you arrange the appearance of Scoto deliberately to draw a crowd?"
9. Copper rings and toad-stone jewelry are Corvino's sneers at the cheap and flashy dress of the mountebank, whose suit (he imagines) is made of coarse brown burlap ("hearse-cloth") prettied up with embroidery.
1. Massage for the womb.

I think you'd rather mount;[2] would you not mount?
Why, if you'll mount, you may; yes, truly, you may:
And so you may be seen, down to the foot.   20
Get you a cittern,[3] Lady Vanity,
And be a dealer with the virtuous man;
Make one: I'll but protest myself a cuckold,
And save your dowry.[4] I'm a Dutchman, I!
For if you thought me an Italian,   25
You would be damned, ere you did this, you whore!
Thou'dst tremble to imagine that the murder
Of father, mother, brother, all thy race,
Should follow, as the subject of my justice.
CELIA. Good sir, have patience.
CORVINO.   What couldst thou propose   30
Less to thyself, than in this heat of wrath,
And stung with my dishonor, I should strike
This steel into thee, with as many stabs,
As thou wert gazed upon with goatish eyes?
CELIA. Alas, sir, be appeased! I could not think   35
My being at the window should more now
Move your impatience, than at other times.
CORVINO. No? Not to seek and entertain a parley
With a known knave, before a multitude?
You were an actor with your handkerchief,   40
Which he most sweetly kissed in the receipt,
And might, no doubt, return it with a letter,
And 'point the place where you might meet; your sister's,
Your mother's, or your aunt's might serve the turn.
CELIA. Why, dear sir, when do I make these excuses,   45
Or ever stir abroad, but to the church?
And that so seldom—
CORVINO.   Well, it shall be less;
And thy restraint before was liberty
To what I now decree: and therefore mark me.
First, I will have this bawdy light dammed up;[5]   50
And till't be done, some two or three yards off,
I'll chalk a line, o'er which if thou but chance
To set thy desperate foot, more hell, more horror,
More wild remorseless rage shall seize on thee,

2. I.e., both on the man and on the stage.
3. A kind of guitar, with which she could set up with the mountebank as whore and pimp
   ("dealer"). "Lady Vanity" is a stock figure out of the old morality plays.
4. In the event of her infidelity, Celia's dowry would be forfeited to her husband. "I'm a Dutchman": the stolidity, not to say complacency, of Dutch men was a common theme of satire—
   Italians, on the other hand, were reputed to be fiercely jealous.
5. I.e., brick up the window.

Than on a conjuror, that had heedless left   55
His circle's safety ere his devil was laid.[6]
Then here's a lock which I will hang upon thee,
And, now I think on't, I will keep thee backwards;
Thy lodging shall be backwards; thy walks backwards;
Thy prospect, all be backwards; and no pleasure   60
That thou shalt know but backwards. Nay, since you force
My honest nature, know, it is your own,
Being too open, makes me use you thus.
Since you will not contain your subtle nostrils
In a sweet room, but they must snuff the air   65
Of rank and sweatly passengers. [*Knocking within.*]—One
    knocks.
Away, and be not seen, pain of thy life;
Nor look toward the window: if thou dost—
Nay, stay, hear this: let me not prosper, whore,
But I will make thee an anatomy,[7]   70
Dissect thee mine own self, and read a lecture
Upon thee to the city, and in public.
Away!—[*Exit* CELIA.] Who's there? [*Enter* SERVANT.]
SERVANT.   'Tis signor Mosca, sir.

ACT II   SCENE 6

CORVINO. Let him come in. [*Exit* SERVANT.] His master's dead:
    there's yet
Some good to help the bad. [*Enter* MOSCA.] My Mosca,
    welcome!
I guess your news.
MOSCA.   I fear you cannot, sir.
CORVINO. Is't not his death?
MOSCA.   Rather the contrary.
CORVINO. Not his recovery?
MOSCA.   Yes, sir.
CORVINO.   .   I am cursed,   5
I am bewitched, my crosses meet to vex me.
How? How? How? How?
MOSCA.   Why, sir, with Scoto's oil!
Corbaccio and Voltore brought of it,
Whilst I was busy in an inner room——
CORVINO. Death! That damned mountebank! But for the law   10
Now, I could kill the rascal: it cannot be

---

6. When a magician raised the devil, he was well advised to draw around himself a magic circle,
   over which the devil could not step.
7. A skeleton hung up in a medical laboratory for demonstration purposes.

His oil should have that virtue.[8] Have not I
Known him a common rogue, come fiddling in
To the *osteria*,[9] with a tumbling whore,
And, when he has done all his forced tricks, been glad   15
Of a poor spoonful of dead wine, with flies in't?
It cannot be. All his ingredients
Are a sheep's gall, a roasted bitch's marrow,
Some few sod earwigs,[1] pounded caterpillars,
A little capon's grease, and fasting spittle: 20
I know them to a dram.
MOSCA.   I know not, sir;
But some on't, there, they poured into his ears,
Some in his nostrils, and recovered him,
Applying but the fricace.[2]
CORVINO.   Pox o' that fricace!
MOSCA. And since, to seem the more officious   25
And flattering of his health, there, they have had,
At extreme fees, the college of physicians
Consulting on him, how they might restore him;
Where one would have a cataplasm[3] of spices,
Another a flayed ape clapped to his breast,   30
A third would have it a dog, a fourth an oil,
With wild cats' skins; at last, they all resolved
That, to preserve him, was no other means,
But some young woman must be straight sought out,
Lusty, and full of juice, to sleep by him;   35
And to this service, most unhappily,
And most unwillingly, am I now employed,
Which here I thought to pre-acquaint you with,
For your advice, since it concerns you most,
Because I would not do that thing might cross   40
Your ends, on whom I have my whole dependence, sir.
Yet, if I do it not, they may delate[4]
My slackness to my patron, work me out
Of his opinion; and there all your hopes,
Ventures, or whatsoever, are all frustrate!   45
I do but tell you, sir. Besides, they are all
Now striving, who shall first present him; therefore—
I could entreat you, briefly conclude somewhat;

---

8. Efficacy.
9. Tavern (Italian).
1. Boiled insects; "capon": castrated male chicken, fattened for eating; "fasting spittle": as it
implies, spit taken from a hungry man.
2. I.e., all they had to do was rub it in.
3. A medicated, usually heated cloth applied to sores.
4. Denounce, complain of.

Prevent[5] them if you can.

CORVINO.   Death to my hopes,
This is my villainous fortune! Best to hire   50
Some common courtesan.

MOSCA.   Ay, I thought on that, sir;
But they are all so subtle, full of art,
And age again doting and flexible,
So as—I cannot tell—we may, perchance,
Light on a quean[6] may cheat us all.

CORVINO.   'Tis true.   55

MOSCA. No, no: it must be one that has no tricks, sir,
Some simple thing, a creature made unto it;
Some wench you may command. Have you no kinswoman?
God's so—Think, think, think, think, think, think, think, sir.
One o' the doctors offered there his daughter.   60

CORVINO. How!

MOSCA.   Yes, Signor Lupo,[7] the physician.

CORVINO. His daughter!

MOSCA.   And a virgin, sir. Why, alas,
He knows the state of 's body, what it is;
That nought can warm his blood, sir, but a fever;
Nor any incantation raise his spirit: 65
A long forgetfulness hath seized that part.
Besides, sir, who shall know it? Some one or two—

CORVINO. I pray thee give me leave. [*Walks aside.*] If any man
But I had had this luck—The thing in itself,
I know, is nothing—Wherefore should not I   70
As well command my blood and my affections,
As this dull doctor? In the point of honor,
The cases are all one of wife and daughter.

MOSCA. [*aside*] I hear him coming.

CORVINO.   She shall do't: 'tis done.
Slight! If this doctor, who is not engaged,   75
Unless 't be for his counsel, which is nothing,
Offer his daughter, what should I, that am
So deeply in? I will prevent him. Wretch!
Covetous wretch![8]—Mosca, I have determined.

MOSCA. How, sir?

CORVINO.   We'll make all sure. The party you wot[9] of   80
Shall be mine own wife, Mosca.

5. Forestall.
6. Prostitute.
7. Doctor Wolf.
8. The words are spoken by Corvino to himself about himself.
9. Know.

MOSCA. Sir, the thing,
But that I would not seem to counsel you,
I should have motioned[1] to you, at the first.
And, make your count, you have cut all their throats.
Why, 'tis directly taking a possession! 85
And in his next fit, we may let him go.
'Tis but to pull the pillow from his head,
And he is throttled: it had been done before,
But for your scrupulous doubts.
CORVINO. Ay, a plague on't,
My conscience fools my wit! Well, I'll be brief, 90
And so be thou, lest they should be before us.
Go home, prepare him, tell him with what zeal
And willingness I do it; swear it was
On the first hearing, as thou mayst do truly,
Mine own free motion.
MOSCA. Sir, I warrant you, 95
I'll so possess him with it, that the rest
Of his starved clients shall be banished all,
And only you received. But come not, sir,
Until I send, for I have something else
To ripen for your good; you must not know it. 100
CORVINO. But do not you forget to send now.
MOSCA. Fear not. [*Exit* MOSCA.]

ACT II   SCENE 7

CORVINO. Where are you, wife? My Celia! Wife!
[*Enter* CELIA, *weeping.*]
What, blubbering?
Come, dry those tears. I think thou thought'st me in earnest?
Ha! By this light I talked so but to try thee.
Methinks the lightness of the occasion
Should have confirmed thee.[2] Come, I am not jealous. 5
CELIA. No?
CORVINO. Faith I am not, I, nor never was;
It is a poor unprofitable humor.
Do not I know, if women have a will,
They'll do 'gainst all the watches of the world,
And that the fiercest spies are tamed with gold?[3] 10
Tut, I am confident in thee, thou shalt see't;
And see, I'll give thee cause too, to believe it.

---

1. Suggested; "make your count": depend on it.
2. You should have seen I was joking because the occasion was so trivial.
3. Immemorial commonplaces on the lust and treachery of women.

Come, kiss me. Go, and make thee ready straight,
In all thy best attire, thy choicest jewels,
Put them all on, and, with them, thy best looks: 15
We are invited to a solemn feast
At old Volpone's, where it shall appear
How far I am free from jealousy or fear.   [*Exeunt.*]

Act III

ACT III   SCENE 1. *A STREET*

[*Enter* MOSCA.]
MOSCA. I fear I shall begin to grow in love
With my dear self, and my most prosperous parts,
They do so spring and burgeon;[4] I can feel
A whimsy in my blood. I know not how,
Success hath made me wanton. I could skip   5
Out of my skin, now, like a subtle snake,
I am so limber. O! your parasite[5]
Is a most precious thing, dropped from above,
Not bred 'mongst clods and clodpoles, here on earth.
I muse the mystery[6] was not made a science,   10
It is so liberally professed! Almost
All the wise world is little else, in nature,
But parasites or sub-parasites. And, yet,
I mean not those that have your bare town-art,
To know who's fit to feed them; have no house,   15
No family, no care, and therefore mold
Tales for men's ears, to bait[7] that sense; or get
Kitchen-invention, and some stale receipts
To please the belly, and the groin; nor those,
With their court dog-tricks, that can fawn and fleer,   20
Make their revenue out of legs and faces,[8]
Echo my lord, and lick away a moth.[9]
But your fine elegant rascal, that can rise,
And stoop, almost together, like an arrow;
Shoot through the air as nimbly as a star;   25
Turn short as doth a swallow; and be here,

---

4. Grow.
5. The Roman comedies of Terence and Plautus, with which Jonson was thoroughly familiar, swarm with parasites; the very idea of the relationship was repugnant to his sturdy, Stoic independence of spirit.
6. Craft. Mosca is playing on the idea of the liberal arts and sciences.
7. The parasite who talks for a living "baits" (teases, gratifies) the sense of hearing; others gratify the bellies and groins of their patrons.
8. Scrapings and looks of admiration.
9. I.e., from his clothes.

And there, and here, and yonder, all at once;
Present to any humor, all occasion;
And change a visor[1] swifter than a thought!
This is the creature had the art born with him; 30
Toils not to learn it, but doth practice it
Out of most excellent nature: and such sparks
Are the true parasites, others but their zanies.

ACT III   SCENE 2

[*Enter* BONARIO.]
MOSCA. Who's this? Bonario, old Corbaccio's son?
The person I was bound to seek.—Fair sir,
You are happily met.
BONARIO.   That cannot be by thee.
MOSCA. Why, sir?
BONARIO.   Nay, pray thee know thy way, and leave me:
I would be loath to interchange discourse   5
With such a mate as thou art.
MOSCA.   Courteous sir,
Scorn not my poverty.
BONARIO.   Not I, by heaven;
But thou shalt give me leave to hate thy baseness.
MOSCA. Baseness!
BONARIO.   Ay; answer me, is not thy sloth
Sufficient argument? Thy flattery?   10
Thy means of feeding?
MOSCA.   Heaven be good to me!
These imputations are too common, sir,
And easily stuck on virtue when she's poor.
You are unequal to me, and howe'er
Your sentence may be righteous, yet you are not,   15
That, ere you know me, thus proceed in censure:
St. Mark bear witness 'gainst you, 'tis inhuman. [*Weeps.*]
BONARIO. [*aside*] What! Does he weep! The sign is soft and
    good;
I do repent me that I was so harsh.
MOSCA. 'Tis true that, swayed by a strong necessity,   20
I am enforced to eat my careful bread
With too much obsequy;[2] 'tis true, beside,
That I am fain to spin mine own poor raiment

---

1. The mask of his expression.
2. Flattery, obsequiousness.

Out of my mere observance,[3] being not born
To a free fortune: but that I have done   25
Base offices, in rending friends asunder,
Dividing families, betraying counsels,
Whispering false lies, or mining men with praises,
Trained their credulity with perjuries,
Corrupted chastity, or am in love   30
With mine own tender ease, but would not rather
Prove the most rugged, and laborious course,
That might redeem my present estimation,
Let me here perish, in all hope of goodness.

BONARIO. [*aside*] This cannot be a personated[4] passion.—   35
I was to blame, so to mistake thy nature;
Prithee forgive me and speak out thy business.

MOSCA. Sir, it concerns you; and though I may seem,
At first to make a main offense in manners,
And in my gratitude unto my master;   40
Yet, for the pure love, which I bear all right,
And hatred of the wrong, I must reveal it.
This very hour your father is in purpose
To disinherit you—

BONARIO.   How!

MOSCA.   And thrust you forth,
As a mere stranger to his blood; 'tis true, sir.   45
The work no way engageth me, but, as
I claim an interest in the general state
Of goodness and true virtue, which I hear
T'abound in you; and, for which mere respect,
Without a second aim, sir, I have done it.   50

BONARIO. This tale hath lost thee much of the late trust
Thou hadst with me; it is impossible.
I know not how to lend it any thought,
My father should be so unnatural.

MOSCA. It is a confidence that well becomes   55
Your piety; and formed, no doubt, it is
From your own simple innocence: which makes
Your wrong more monstrous and abhorred. But, sir,
I now will tell you more. This very minute,
It is, or will be doing; and, if you   60
Shall be but pleased to go with me, I'll bring you,
I dare not say where you shall see, but where

---

3. Service.
4. Contrived, false.

Your ear shall be a witness of the deed;
Hear yourself written bastard, and professed
The common issue of the earth.[5]
BONARIO.   I'm 'mazed.   65
MOSCA. Sir, if I do it not, draw your just sword,
And score your vengeance on my front and face;
Mark me your villain: you have too much wrong,
And I do suffer for you, sir. My heart
Weeps blood in anguish—
BONARIO.   Lead; I follow thee.   [Exeunt.]   70

ACT III   SCENE 3. A ROOM IN VOLPONE'S HOUSE

[Enter VOLPONE.]
VOLPONE. Mosca stays long, methinks. Bring forth your sports,
And help to make the wretched time more sweet.
[Enter NANO, ANDROGYNO, and CASTRONE.]
NANO. Dwarf, fool, and eunuch, well met here we be.
A question it were now, whether of us three,
Being all the known delicates[6] of a rich man,   5
In pleasing him, claim the precedency can?
CASTRONE. I claim for myself.
ANDROGYNO.   And so doth the fool.
NANO. 'Tis foolish indeed: let me set you both to school.
First for your dwarf, he's little and witty,
And every thing, as it is little, is pretty;   10
Else why do men say to a creature of my shape,
So soon as they see him, 'It's a pretty little ape'?
And why a pretty ape, but for pleasing imitation
Of greater men's actions, in a ridiculous fashion?
Beside, this feat[7] body of mine doth not crave   15
Half the meat, drink, and cloth, one of your bulks will have.
Admit your fool's face be the mother of laughter,
Yet, for his brain, it must always come after:
And though that do feed him, it's a pitiful case,
His body is beholding to such a bad face. [Knocking within.]   20
VOLPONE. Who's there? My couch! Away! Look, Nano, see!
                    [Exeunt ANDROGYNO and CASTRONE.]
Give me my caps, first—go, enquire. [Exit NANO.] Now, Cupid
Send it be Mosca, and with fair return!
NANO. [within] It is the beauteous madam—
VOLPONE.   Would-be—is it?

5. A man without a recognized father was known to the Romans as a *filius terrae*, "son of earth."
6. Favorites.
7. Trim.

NANO. The same.

VOLPONE.   Now torment on me! Squire her in;   25
    For she will enter, or dwell here forever:
    Nay quickly. [*Retires to his couch.*]—That my fit were past! I
      fear
    A second hell too, that my loathing this
    Will quite expel my appetite to the other:[8]
    Would she were taking now her tedious leave.   30
    Lord, how it threats me what I am to suffer!

ACT III   SCENE 4

      [*Enter* NANO *with* LADY POLITIC WOULD-BE.]

LADY POLITIC. I thank you, good sir. 'Pray you signify
    Unto your patron, I am here. This band
    Shows not my neck enough. I trouble you, sir.
    Let me request you, bid one of my women
    Come hither to me. In good faith, I am dressed   5
    Most favorably to-day. It is no matter;
    'Tis well enough.[9]
      [*Enter 1st* WAITING-WOMAN.]
              Look, see, these petulant[1] things,
    How they have done this!

VOLPONE.   [*aside*] I do feel the fever
    Entering in at mine ears; O, for a charm
    To fright it hence!

LADY POLITIC.   Come nearer: is this curl   10
    In his right place? Or this? Why is this higher
    Than all the rest? You have not washed your eyes yet!
    Or do they not stand even in your head?
    Where is your fellow? Call her.   [*Exit 1st* WOMAN.]

NANO.   [*aside*] Now, St. Mark
    Deliver us! Anon, she'll beat her women   15
    Because her nose is red.
      [*Re-enter 1st with 2nd* WOMAN.]

LADY POLITIC.   I pray you, view
    This tire,[2] forsooth: are all things apt, or no?

1 WOMAN. One hair a little, here, sticks out, forsooth.

LADY POLITIC. Does't so, forsooth! And where was your dear
    sight,

---

8. I.e., his loathing for Lady Politic may destroy his appetite for Celia.
9. The theme of talkative women was ancient and traditional; Jonson got a lot of Lady Politic's chatter from a Syrian sophist of the fourth century C.E., Libanius, who wrote a talkative book about talkative women.
1. Pert, rude.
2. Headdress, arrangement of hair.

When it did so, forsooth![3] What now! Bird-eyed?   20
And you, too? Pray you, both approach and mend it.
Now, by that light, I muse you're not ashamed!
I, that have preached these things so oft unto you,
Read you the principles, argued all the grounds,
Disputed every fitness, every grace,   25
Called you to counsel of so frequent dressings—
NANO. [aside] More carefully than of your fame or honor.
LADY POLITIC. Made you acquainted, what an ample dowry
   The knowledge of these things would be unto you,
   Able, alone, to get you noble husbands   30
   At your return; and you thus to neglect it!
   Besides, you seeing what a curious[4] nation
   The Italians are, what will they say of me?
   The English lady cannot dress herself.—
   Here's a fine imputation to our country!   35
   Well, go your ways, and stay in the next room.
   This fucus[5] was too coarse too; it's no matter.
   Good sir, you'll give them entertainment?
                          [*Exeunt* NANO *and* WAITING-WOMEN.]
VOLPONE. The storm comes toward me.
LADY POLITIC.   [*Goes to the couch*] How does my Volpone?
VOLPONE. Troubled with noise; I cannot sleep; I dreamt   40
   That a strange fury entered, now, my house,
   And, with the dreadful tempest of her breath,
   Did cleave my roof asunder.
LADY POLITIC.   Believe me, and I
   Had the most fearful dream, could I remember't—
VOLPONE. [aside] Out on my fate! I have given her the occasion   45
   How to torment me: she will tell me hers.
LADY POLITIC. Methought, the golden mediocrity,[6]
   Polite, and delicate—
VOLPONE   O, if you do love me,
   No more; I sweat, and suffer, at the mention
   Of any dream: feel how I tremble yet.   50
LADY POLITIC. Alas, good soul! The passion of the heart.[7]
   Seed-pearl were good now, boiled with syrup of apples,
   Tincture of gold, and coral, citron-pills,
   Your elecampane root, myrobalanes[8]—

---

3. She strikes at both women and jeers at their flinching. "Bird-eyed": sharp of sight.
4. Fastidious, particular.
5. Makeup. The last sentence is spoken to Nano.
6. She intends the "Golden Mean," where according to Horace virtue was to be found.
7. Heartburn.
8. An Oriental drug used for diarrhea. "Elecampane": a stimulant.

VOLPONE. [*aside*] Ay me, I have ta'en a grass-hopper by the
   wing!   55
LADY POLITIC. Burnt silk, and amber; you have muscadel
   Good in the house—
VOLPONE.   You will not drink, and part?
LADY POLITIC. No, fear not that, I doubt we shall not get
   Some English saffron, half a dram would serve;
   Your sixteen cloves, a little musk, dried mints,   60
   Bugloss,[9] and barley-meal—
VOLPONE.   [*aside*] She's in again!
   Before I feigned diseases, now I have one.
LADY POLITIC. And these applied with a right scarlet cloth.
VOLPONE. [*aside*] Another flood of words! A very torrent!
LADY POLITIC. Shall I, sir, make you a poultice?
VOLPONE.   No, no, no;   65
   I'm very well, you need prescribe no more.
LADY POLITIC. I have a little studied physic; but now,
   I'm all for music, save in the forenoons,
   An hour or two for painting. I would have
   A lady, indeed, to have all letters and arts,   70
   Be able to discourse, to write, to paint,
   But principal, as Plato holds, your music
   (And so does wise Pythagoras, I take it)
   Is your true rapture; when there is consent[1]
   In face, in voice, and clothes: and is, indeed,   75
   Our sex's chiefest ornament.
VOLPONE.   The poet
   As old in time as Plato, and as knowing,
   Says that your highest female grace is silence.[2]
LADY POLITIC. Which of your poets? Petrarch, or Tasso, or
   Dante?
   Guarini? Ariosto? Aretine?   80
   Cieco di Hadria?[3] I have read them all.
VOLPONE. [*aside*] Is everything a cause to my destruction?
LADY POLITIC. I think I have two or three of them about me.
VOLPONE. [*aside*] The sun, the sea, will sooner both stand still
   Than her eternal tongue! Nothing can 'scape it.   85

9. A common herb used as a mild stimulant.
1. Harmony, concord.
2. The poet as old as Plato is Sophocles (496–406 B.C.E.) (*Ajax*, line 293).
3. The poets Lady Politic named lived in much more modern times than Plato: Dante Alighieri
   (1265–1321) was author of the *Divine Comedy*; Petrarch was famous for his sonnets about
   Laura; Torquato Tasso (1544–1595) wrote the epic *Jerusalem Delivered*. Giovanni Battista
   Guarini (1538–1612) was the author of the pastoral *Il Pastor Fido* (1590), and Ludovico
   Ariosto (1474–1535) wrote *Orlando Furioso* (1532). Pietro Aretino (1492–1556) was well
   known for pornographic poems. Much less well known than these poets was Cieco di Hadria
   (1541–1585), "the blind man of Adria."

LADY POLITIC. Here's *Pastor Fido*—[4]
VOLPONE   [*aside*] Profess obstinate silence;
  That's now my safest.
LADY POLITIC.   All our English writers,
  I mean such as are happy in th' Italian,
  Will deign to steal out of this author, mainly;
  Almost as much as from Montagnié:[5]   90
  He has so modern and facile a vein,
  Fitting the time, and catching the court-ear!
  Your Petrarch is more passionate, yet he,
  In days of sonneting, trusted them with much:[6]
  Dante is hard, and few can understand him.   95
  But, for a desperate wit, there's Aretine;[7]
  Only, his pictures are a little obscene—
  You mark me not?
VOLPONE.   Alas, my mind's perturbed.
LADY POLITIC. Why, in such cases, we must cure ourselves,
  Make use of our philosophy—
VOLPONE.   Oh me!   100
LADY POLITIC. And as we find our passions do rebel,
  Encounter them with reason, or divert them,
  By giving scope unto some other humor
  Of lesser danger; as in politic bodies,
  There's nothing more doth overwhelm the judgment,   105
  And cloud the understanding, than too much
  Settling and fixing, and, as 'twere, subsiding
  Upon one object. For the incorporating
  Of these same outward things, into that part,
  Which we call mental, leaves some certain fæces[8]   110
  That stop the organs, and, as Plato says,
  Assassinate our knowledge.
VOLPONE.   [*aside*] Now the spirit
  Of patience help me!
LADY POLITIC.   Come, in faith, I must
  Visit you more a days, and make you well;
  Laugh and be lusty.
VOLPONE.   [*aside*] My good angel save me!   115
LADY POLITIC. There was but one sole man in all the world,

---

4. See preceding note.
5. The name of French essayist Montaigne (1533–1592) tended to be given three syllables by
   English tongues; his *Essays*, first published in 1580, were translated into English by Jonson's
   friend John Florio (1603).
6. Left to subsequent ages a substantial literary heritage.
7. Aretino's pornographic poems, illustrated by Guilio Romano and engraved by M. Raimondi,
   were internationally notorious.
8. Traces. Lady Politic is interested in orthodox, but very verbose, psychology.

With whom I e'er could sympathize; and he
Would lie you, often, three, four hours together
To hear me speak; and be sometime so rapt,
As he would answer me quite from the purpose,   120
Like you, and you are like him, just. I'll discourse,
An't be but only, sir, to bring you asleep,
How we did spend our time and loves together,
For some six years.
VOLPONE.   Oh, oh, oh, oh, oh, oh!
LADY POLITIC. For we were *coaetanei*,[9] and brought up—   125
VOLPONE. Some power, some fate, some fortune rescue me!

ACT III   SCENE 5

[*Enter* MOSCA.]
MOSCA. God save you, madam!
LADY POLITIC.   Good sir.
VOLPONE.   Mosca! Welcome,
Welcome to my redemption!
MOSCA.   Why, sir?
VOLPONE.   Oh,
Rid me of this my torture, quickly, there;
My madam, with the everlasting voice:
The bells, in time of pestilence, ne'er made   5
Like noise, or were in that perpetual motion!
The cock-pit comes not near it.[1] All my house,
But now, steamed like a bath with her thick breath.
A lawyer could not have been heard; nor scarce
Another woman, such a hail of words   10
She has let fall. For hell's sake, rid her hence.
MOSCA. Has she presented?
VOLPONE.   O, I do not care;
I'll take her absence, upon any price,
With any loss.
MOSCA.   Madam—
LADY POLITIC.   I have brought your patron
A toy, a cap here, of mine own work.
MOSCA.   'Tis well.   15
I had forgot to tell you, I saw your knight,
Where you would little think it—
LADY POLITIC.   Where?
MOSCA.   Marry,

9. Of an age (Italian).
1. When the plague struck, church bells were constantly tolling; at cockfights spectators constantly shouted bets and encouragement to the birds.

Where yet, if you make haste, you may apprehend him,
Rowing upon the water in a gondola,
With the most cunning courtesan of Venice.   20
LADY POLITIC. Is't true?
MOSCA.   Pursue them, and believe your eyes:
   Leave me to make your gift. [*Exit* LADY POLITIC *hastily.*]—I
      knew 'twould take:
   For, lightly,[2] they that use themselves most license,
   Are still most jealous.
VOLPONE.   Mosca, hearty thanks,
   For thy quick fiction, and delivery of me.   25
   Now to my hopes, what sayest thou?
      [*Re-enter* LADY POLITIC.]
LADY POLITIC.   But do you hear, sir?—
VOLPONE. Again! I fear a paroxysm.
LADY POLITIC.   Which way
   Rowed they together?
MOSCA.   Toward the Rialto.
LADY POLITIC. I pray you lend me your dwarf.
MOSCA.   I pray you take him—
                              [*Exit* LADY POLITIC.]
   Your hopes, sir, are like happy blossoms, fair,   30
   And promise timely fruit, if you will stay
   But the maturing; keep you at your couch,
   Corbaccio will arrive straight, with the will;
   When he is gone, I'll tell you more.   [*Exit.*]
VOLPONE.   My blood,
   My spirits are returned; I am alive: 35
   And, like your wanton gamester at primero,[3]
   Whose thought had whispered to him, not go less,
   Methinks I lie, and draw—for an encounter.
      [*The bed-curtains close upon* VOLPONE.]

ACT III   SCENE 6. *THE PASSAGE LEADING TO* VOLPONE'S *CHAMBER*

   [*Enter* MOSCA *and* BONARIO.]
MOSCA. Sir, here concealed, [*shows him a closet*] you may hear
      all. But, pray you,
   Have patience, sir. [*Knocking within.*]—The same's your father
      knocks:
   I am compelled to leave you.   [*Exit.*]
BONARIO.   Do so. Yet

2. Commonly (an old sense of the word).
3. An early form of the Spanish card game later known as ombre (the game played in Pope's
   Rape of the Lock). The phrases "go less," "draw," and "encounter" are all used in primero.

Cannot my thought imagine this a truth. [*Goes into the closet.*]

ACT III   SCENE 7. *ANOTHER PART OF THE SAME*

[*Enter* MOSCA *and* CORVINO, CELIA *following.*]

MOSCA. Death on me! You are come too soon; what meant you?
　　Did not I say I would send?
CORVINO.　　　　　　　　　　Yes, but I feared
　　You might forget it, and then they prevent us.
MOSCA. [*aside*] Prevent! Did e'er man haste so, for his horns?
　　A courtier would not ply it so, for a place.　　　　　　　5
　　—Well, now there is no helping it, stay here;
　　I'll presently return.　　　　[*Crosses stage to* BONARIO.]
CORVINO.　　　　　Where are you, Celia?
　　You know not wherefore I have brought you hither?
CELIA. Not well, except you told me.
CORVINO.　　　　　　　　Now, I will: [*He leads her
　　apart, and whispers to her.*]
　　Hark hither.
MOSCA. [*to* BONARIO] Sir your father hath sent word,　　　10
　　It will be half an hour ere he come;
　　And therefore, if you please to walk the while
　　Into that gallery—at the upper end,
　　There are some books to entertain the time;
　　And I'll take care no man shall come unto you, sir.　　15
BONARIO. Yes, I will stay there. [*aside*]—I do doubt this fellow.
　　　　　　　　　　　　　　　[*Exit* BONARIO.]
MOSCA. [*looking after him*] There; he is far enough; he can hear
　　nothing:
　　And, for his father, I can keep him off.　　　　[*Exit.*]
CORVINO. [*to* CELIA] Nay, now, there is no starting back, and
　　therefore,
　　Resolve upon it: I have so decreed.　　　　　　　　20
　　It must be done. Nor would I move't afore,
　　Because I would avoid all shifts and tricks,
　　That might deny me.
CELIA.　　　　　　Sir, let me beseech you,
　　Affect not these strange trials;[4] if you doubt
　　My chastity, why, lock me up forever;　　　　　　　25
　　Make me the heir of darkness. Let me live,
　　Where I may please your fears, if not your trust.
CORVINO. Believe it, I have no such humor, I.

---

4. Don't tempt me so.

All that I speak I mean; yet I'm not mad;
Not horn-mad, see you? Go to, show yourself   30
Obedient, and a wife.
CELIA.   O heaven!
CORVINO.   I say it,
Do so.
CELIA.   Was this the train?[5]
CORVINO.   I've told you reasons;
What the physicians have set down; how much
It may concern me; what my engagements are;
My means; and the necessity of those means,   35
For my recovery:[6] wherefore, if you be
Loyal, and mine, be won, respect my venture.[7]
CELIA. Before your honor?
CORVINO.   Honor! Tut, a breath;
There's no such thing in nature. A mere term
Invented to awe fools. What is my gold   40
The worse for touching, clothes for being looked on?
Why, this's no more. An old decrepit wretch,
That has no sense, no sinew; takes his meat
With others' fingers; only knows to gape,
When you do scald his gums;[8] a voice; a shadow;   45
And what can this man hurt you?
CELIA.   [aside] Lord! What spirit
Is this hath entered him?
CORVINO.   And for your fame,
That's such a jig;[9] as if I would go tell it,
Cry it on the Piazza! Who shall know it,
But he that cannot speak it, and this fellow,[1]   50
Whose lips are in my pocket? Save yourself
(If you'll proclaim't, you may), I know no other
Should come to know it.
CELIA.   Are heaven and saints then nothing?
Will they be blind or stupid?
CORVINO.   How!
CELIA.   Good sir,
Be jealous still, emulate them; and think   55
What hate they burn with toward every sin.
CORVINO. I grant you, if I thought it were a sin,

5. "Is this what you had in mind all the time?"
6. Corvino is evidently in financial straits.
7. In the sense of a commercial venture.
8. The old man has to be fed by others and doesn't even know enough to open his own mouth for food.
9. Farce, joke.
1. "He that cannot speak it": Volpone; "this fellow": Mosca.

I would not urge you. Should I offer this
To some young Frenchman, or hot Tuscan blood
That had read Aretine,[2] conned all his prints,   60
Knew every quirk within lust's labyrinth,
And were professed critic in lechery;
And I would look upon him, and applaud him,
This were a sin: but here, 'tis contrary,
A pious work, mere charity, for physic,   65
And honest polity, to assure mine own.[3]
CELIA. O heaven! Canst thou suffer such a change?
VOLPONE. Thou art mine honor, Mosca, and my pride,
    My joy, my tickling, my delight! Go bring them.
MOSCA. [advancing] Please you draw near, sir.
CORVINO.   Come on, what—   70
    You will not be rebellious? By that light—
MOSCA.   Sir,
    Signor Corvino, here, is come to see you—
VOLPONE.   Oh!
MOSCA. And hearing of the consultation had,
    So lately, for your health, is come to offer,
    Or rather, sir, to prostitute—
CORVINO.   Thanks, sweet Mosca.   75
MOSCA. Freely, unasked, or unentreated—
CORVINO.   Well.
MOSCA. As the true fervent instance of his love,
    His own most fair and proper wife, the beauty
    Only of price in Venice—
CORVINO.   'Tis well urged.
MOSCA. To be your comfortress, and to preserve you.   80
VOLPONE. Alas, I'm past, already! Pray you, thank him
    For his good care and promptness; but for that,
    'Tis a vain labor e'en to fight 'gainst heaven;
    Applying fire to stone—uh, uh, uh, uh! [Coughing.]
    Making a dead leaf grow again. I take   85
    His wishes gently, though; and you may tell him,
    What I have done for him: marry, my state is hopeless.
    Will him to pray for me; and to use his fortune
    With reverence, when he comes to't.
MOSCA.   Do you hear, sir?
    Go to him with your wife.
CORVINO.   Heart of my father!   90

2. See p. 51, note 3.
3. "Pious work" means it's good for your soul, "mere charity" says it's kindness to Volpone, "for
    physic" says it's for the benefit of his health, "honest policy" means it's prudent self-interest,
    and "to assure mine own" gets down to the basic motivation—greed.

Wilt thou persist thus? Come, I pray thee, come.
Thou seest 'tis nothing. Celia! By this hand,
I shall grow violent. Come, do't, I say.
CELIA. Sir, kill me, rather. I will take down poison,
Eat burning coals, do anything.
CORVINO.   Be damned!   95
Heart, I will drag thee hence, home, by the hair;
Cry thee a strumpet through the streets; rip up
Thy mouth unto thine ears; and slit thy nose,
Like a raw rochet[4]—Do not tempt me; come,
Yield, I am loath—Death! I will buy some slave   100
Whom I will kill, and bind thee to him, alive;
And at my window hang you forth, devising
Some monstrous crime which I, in capital letters,
Will eat into thy flesh with aquafortis,
And burning corsives,[5] on this stubborn breast.   105
Now, by the blood thou hast incensed, I'll do it!
CELIA. Sir, what you please you may, I am your martyr.
CORVINO. Be not thus obstinate, I have not deserved it:
Think who it is entreats you. 'Prithee, sweet;
Good faith, thou shalt have jewels, gowns, attires,   110
What thou wilt think, and ask. Do but go kiss him.
Or touch him, but. For my sake. At my suit.
This once. No? Not! I shall remember this.
Will you disgrace me thus? Do you thirst my undoing?
MOSCA. Nay, gentle lady, be advised.
CORVINO.   No, no,   115
She has watched her time. God's precious, this is scurvy,[6]
'Tis very scurvy; and you are—
MOSCA.   Nay, good sir.
CORVINO. An arrant locust, by heaven, a locust![7]
Crocodile, that hast thy tears prepared,
Expecting, how thou'lt bid them flow—
MOSCA.   Nay, pray you, sir!   120
She will consider.
CELIA.   Would my life would serve
To satisfy.
CORVINO.   S'death if she would but speak to him,
And save my reputation, it were somewhat;
But spitefully to effect my utter ruin!
MOSCA. Ay, now you have put your fortune in her hands.   125

4. A fish.
5. Acids and corrosives.
6. I.e., by God's precious blood, this is villainous.
7. A destructive plague. The lore of the crocodile says it sheds deceitful tears.

Why, i'faith, it is her modesty; I must quit[8] her.
If you were absent, she would be more coming;
I know it, and dare undertake for her.
What woman can before her husband? Pray you,
Let us depart, and leave her here.   130
CORVINO.   Sweet Celia,
Thou mayst redeem all, yet; I'll say no more:
If not, esteem yourself as lost. Nay, stay there.
                    [*Shuts the door, and exits with* MOSCA.]
CELIA. O God, and his good angels! Whither, whither,
Is shame fled human breasts? That with such ease
Men dare put off your honors, and their own?   135
Is that, which ever was a cause of life,
Now placed beneath the basest circumstance,
And modesty an exile made, for money?
VOLPONE. Ay, in Corvino, and such earth-fed minds, [*leaping
    from his couch*]
That never tasted the true heaven of love.   140
Assure thee, Celia, he that would sell thee,
Only for hope of gain, and that uncertain,
He would have sold his part of Paradise
For ready money, had he met a cope-man.[9]
Why art thou 'mazed to see me thus revived?   145
Rather applaud thy beauty's miracle;
'Tis thy great work: that hath, not now alone,
But sundry times raised me, in several shapes,
And, but this morning, like a mountebank,
To see thee at thy window. Ay, before   150
I would have left my practice for thy love,
In varying figures I would have contended
With the blue Proteus, or the hornèd flood.[1]
Now art thou welcome.
CELIA.   Sir!
VOLPONE.   Nay, fly me not.
Nor let thy false imagination   155
That I was bed-rid, make thee think I am so:
Thou shalt not find it. I am now as fresh,
As hot, as high, and in as jovial plight,
As when, in that so celebrated scene,

8. Acquit; "coming": forthcoming.
9. Buyer.
1. Proteus was a sea god who could take any shape at will; Virgil calls him "blue Proteus."
Achelous was a river god who fought with Hercules for possession of Deianeira; he fought
first as a river, then as a snake, and finally as a bull (hence "the horned flood"), but he was
beaten in all three shapes (Ovid, *Metamorphoses* 9).

At recitation of our comedy,   160
For entertainment of the great Valois,[2]
I acted young Antinous; and attracted
The eyes and ears of all the ladies present,
To admire each graceful gesture, note, and footing.

Song[3]

Come, my Celia, let us prove,   165
While we can, the sports of love,
Time will not be ours for ever,
He, at length, our good will sever;
Spend not then his gifts in vain:
Suns that set may rise again;   170
But if once we lose this light,
'Tis with us perpetual night.
Why should we defer our joys?
Fame and rumor are but toys.
Cannot we delude the eyes   175
Of a few poor household spies?
Or his easier ears beguile,
Thus removèd by our wile?—
'Tis no sin love's fruits to steal;
But the sweet thefts to reveal,   180
To be taken, to be seen,
These have crimes accounted been.

CELIA. Some serene[4] blast me, or dire lightning strike
    This my offending face!
VOLPONE.   Why droops my Celia?
Thou hast, in place of a base husband, found   185
A worthy lover: use thy fortune well,
With secrecy and pleasure. See, behold,
What thou art queen of; not in expectation,
As I feed others: but possessed and crowned.
See here a rope of pearl; and each, more orient   190
Than that the brave Egyptian queen caroused.[5]
Dissolve and drink them. See, a carbuncle[6]

---

2. Henry of Valois, Duke of Anjou and newly created King Henry III of France, visited Venice
   in 1574 and was entertained with splendid festivities. Antinous was the suitor of Penelope in
   the *Odyssey*; a less probable reference is to the young male favorite of Emperor Hadrian, in
   Roman antiquity.
3. The opening lines are adapted from Catullus, "Ode 5," boldest and bawdiest of Latin lyricists;
   the whole song emphasizes the theme of "carpe diem" (seize the day), which is a common
   erotic incitement.
4. Mist from heaven, malignant influence.
5. According to a common story, Cleopatra dissolved a precious pearl in wine and drank it
   during a banquet with Antony.
6. Ruby.

May put out both the eyes of our St. Mark;
A diamond, would have bought Lollia Paulina,
When she came in like star-light, hid with jewels,   195
That were the spoils of provinces;[7] take these,
And wear, and lose them: yet remains an earring
To purchase them again, and this whole state.
A gem but worth a private patrimony,
Is nothing: we will eat such at a meal.   200
The heads of parrots, tongues of nightingales,
The brains of peacocks, and of ostriches,
Shall be our food: and, could we get the phoenix,[8]
Though nature lost her kind, she were our dish.

CELIA. Good sir, these things might move a mind affected   205
    With such delights; but I, whose innocence
    Is all I can think wealthy, or worth th'enjoying,
    And which, once lost, I have nought to lose beyond it,
    Cannot be taken with these sensual baits:
    If you have conscience—
VOLPONE.   'Tis the beggar's virtue;   210
    If thou hast wisdom, hear me, Celia.
    Thy baths shall be the juice of gilly-flowers,[9]
    Spirit of roses, and of violets,
    The milk of unicorns, and panthers' breath
    Gathered in bags, and mixed with Cretan wines.[1]   215
    Our drink shall be preparèd gold and amber;
    Which we will take, until my roof whirl round
    With the vertigo: and my dwarf shall dance,
    My eunuch sing, my fool make up the antic,
    Whilst we, in changèd shapes, act Ovid's tales,[2]   220
    Thou, like Europa now, and I like Jove,
    Then I like Mars, and thou like Erycine:
    So, of the rest, till we have quite run through,
    And wearied all the fables of the gods.
    Then will I have thee in more modern forms,   225
    Attirèd like some sprightly dame of France,
    Brave Tuscan lady, or proud Spanish beauty;
    Sometimes, unto the Persian Sophy's wife,[3]
    Or the Grand Signor's mistress; and, for change,

---

7. Lollia Paulina, wife of a Roman governor, is said by Pliny (*Natural History* 9.117) to have
   worn in her hair jewels enough to represent the loot of several provinces.
8. Only one phoenix is said to be alive at any one time; eating it would eradicate the species.
9. Clove-scented flowers used to flavor drinks and as a light perfume.
1. The most expensive known to Jonson's age; the "panther's breath" was supposed to lure victims
   with its breath and then destroy them.
2. Enact all the fables in Ovid's *Metamorphoses*. "Erycine" is one of the names of Venus.
3. The "Sophy" is the shah of Persia, the "Grand Signor" the sultan of Turkey.

To one of our most artful courtesans,   230
Or some quick Negro, or cold Russian;
And I will meet thee in as many shapes:
Where we may so transfuse our wandering souls
Out at our lips, and score up sums of pleasures, [*sings*]

> That the curious shall not know   235
> How to tell them as they flow;
> And the envious, when they find
> What their number is, be pined.[4]

CELIA. If you have ears that will be pierced; or eyes
That can be opened; a heart may be touched;   240
Or any part that yet sounds man about you;
If you have touch of holy saints, or heaven,
Do me the grace to let me 'scape. If not,
Be bountiful and kill me. You do know,
I am a creature, hither ill betrayed,   245
By one, whose shame I would forget it were.
If you will deign me neither of these graces,
Yet feed your wrath, sir, rather than your lust
(It is a vice comes nearer manliness),
And punish that unhappy crime of nature,   250
Which you miscall my beauty; flay my face,
Or poison it with ointments, for seducing
Your blood to this rebellion. Rub these hands,
With what may cause an eating leprosy,
E'en to my bones and marrow: any thing,   255
That may disfavor[5] me, save in my honor—
And I will kneel to you, pray for you, pay down
A thousand hourly vows, sir, for your health;
Report, and think you virtuous—
VOLPONE.   Think me cold,
Frozen and impotent, and so report me?   260
That I had Nestor's hernia,[6] thou wouldst think.
I do degenerate, and abuse my nation,
To play with opportunity thus long;
I should have done the act, and then have parleyed.
Yield, or I'll force thee.   [*Seizes her.*]
CELIA.   O! Just God!
VOLPONE.   In vain—   265

---

4. Grieved, depressed. The verses, once again, are adapted from Catullus, "Ode 5."
5. Disfigure.
6. Senile impotence; the phrase is from the Roman satirist Juvenal's (60–ca. 136 C.E.) sixth
satire.

BONARIO. [*rushing in*] Forbear, foul ravisher! Libidinous swine!
    Free the forced lady, or thou diest, impostor!
    But that I'm loath to snatch thy punishment
    Out of the hand of justice, thou shouldst yet
    Be made the timely sacrifice of vengeance   270
    Before this altar, and this dross, thy idol.
    Lady, let's quit the place, it is the den
    Of villainy; fear nought, you have a guard:
    And he, ere long, shall meet his just reward. [*Exeunt* BONARIO
    and CELIA.]
VOLPONE. Fall on me, roof, and bury me in ruin!   275
    Become my grave, that wert my shelter! O!
    I am unmasked, unspirited, undone,
    Betrayed to beggary, to infamy—

ACT III   SCENE 8

[*Enter* MOSCA, *wounded, and bleeding.*]
MOSCA. Where shall I run, most wretched shame of men,
    To beat out my unlucky brains?
VOLPONE.   Here, here.
    What! Dost thou bleed?
MOSCA.   O that his well-driven sword
    Had been so courteous to have cleft me down
    Unto the navel, ere I lived to see   5
    My life, my hopes, my spirits, my patron, all
    Thus desperately engagèd, by my error!
VOLPONE. Woe on thy fortune!
MOSCA.   And my follies, sir.
VOLPONE. Thou hast made me miserable.
MOSCA.   And myself, sir.
    Who would have thought he would have hearkened so?   10
VOLPONE. What shall we do?
MOSCA.   I know not; if my heart
    Could expiate the mischance, I'd pluck it out.
    Will you be pleased to hang me? Or cut my throat?
    And I'll requite you, sir. Let's die like Romans,
    Since we have lived like Grecians.[7] [*Knocking within.*]
VOLPONE.   Hark! Who's there?   15
    I hear some footing; officers, the Saffi,[8]
    Come to apprehend us! I do feel the brand

---

7. Greeks, especially Corinthians, were famous for living in luxury, Romans for committing
    suicide with dignity when life no longer appeared worthy of them.
8. Police officers, investigators.

Hissing already at my forehead; now
Mine ears are boring.[9]
MOSCA.   To your couch, sir, you
Make that place good, however. [VOLPONE *lies down, as
before.*]—Guilty men   20
Suspect what they deserve still. Signor Corbaccio!

ACT III   SCENE 9

[*Enter* CORBACCIO.]
CORBACCIO. Why, how now, Mosca?
MOSCA.   O, undone, amazed, sir.
Your son, I know not by what accident,
Acquainted with your purpose to my patron,
Touching your will, and making him your heir,
Entered our house with violence, his sword drawn,   5
Sought for you, called you wretch, unnatural,
Vowed he would kill you.
CORBACCIO.   Me!
MOSCA.   Yes, and my patron.
CORBACCIO. This act shall disinherit him indeed:
Here is the will.
MOSCA.   Tis well, sir.
CORBACCIO.   Right and well;
Be you as careful now for me.
        [*Enter* VOLTORE *behind.*]
MOSCA.   My life, sir,   10
Is not more tendered; I am only yours.
CORBACCIO. How does he? Will he die shortly, think'st thou?
MOSCA.   I fear
He'll outlast May.
CORBACCIO.   Today?
MOSCA.   No, last out May, sir.
CORBACCIO. Couldst thou not give him a dram?
MOSCA.   O, by no means, sir.
CORBACCIO. Nay, I'll not bid you.
VOLTORE.   [*coming forward*] This is a knave, I see.   15
MOSCA. [*seeing* VOLTORE, *aside*] How! Signor Voltore! Did he
hear me?
VOLTORE.   Parasite!
MOSCA. Who's that? O, sir, most timely welcome—
VOLTORE.   Scarce,
To the discovery of your tricks, I fear.

9. Branding on the face and boring holes in the ears were common criminal punishments.

You are his, *only?* And mine also, are you not?
MOSCA. Who? I, sir!
VOLTORE.   You, sir. What device is this   20
About a will?
MOSCA.   A plot for you, sir.
VOLTORE.   Come,
Put not your foists[1] upon me; I shall scent them.
MOSCA. Did you not hear it?
VOLTORE.   Yes, I hear Corbaccio
Hath made your patron there his heir.
MOSCA.   'Tis true,
By my device, drawn to it by my plot,   25
With hope—
VOLTORE.   Your patron should reciprocate?
And you have promised?
MOSCA.   For your good, I did, sir.
Nay more, I told his son, brought, hid him here,
Where he might hear his father pass the deed;
Being persuaded to it by this thought, sir,   30
That the unnaturalness, first, of the act,
And then his father's oft disclaiming in him,
(Which I did mean t'help on), would sure enrage him
To do some violence upon his parent,
On which the law should take sufficient hold,   35
And you be stated[2] in a double hope:
Truth be my comfort, and my conscience,
My only aim was to dig you a fortune
Out of these two old rotten sepulchres—
VOLTORE. I cry thee mercy, Mosca.
MOSCA.   Worth your patience,   40
And your great merit, sir. And see the change!
VOLTORE. Why, what success?[3]
MOSCA.   Most hapless! You must help, sir.
Whilst we expected the old raven, in comes
Corvino's wife, sent hither by her husband—
VOLTORE. What, with a present?
MOSCA.   No, sir, on visitation   45
(I'll tell you how anon); and staying long,
The youth he grows impatient, rushes forth,
Seizeth the lady, wounds me, makes her swear
(Or he would murder her, that was his vow)

---

1. Tricks, but also bad smells.
2. Installed.
3. Result, outcome.

To affirm my patron to have done her rape: 50
Which how unlike it is, you see! And hence,
With that pretext he's gone to accuse his father,
Defame my patron, defeat you—
VOLTORE.   Where is her husband?
Let him be sent for straight.
MOSCA.   Sir, I'll go fetch him.
VOLTORE. Bring him to the Scrutineo.[4]
MOSCA.   Sir, I will.   55
VOLTORE. This must be stopped.
MOSCA.   O, you do nobly, sir.
Alas, 'twas labored all, sir, for your good;
Nor was there want of counsel in the plot:
But fortune can, at any time, o'erthrow
The projects of a hundred learned clerks,[5] sir.   60
CORBACCIO. [listening] What's that?
VOLTORE.   Will't please you, sir, to go
along?   [Exit CORBACCIO followed by VOLTORE.]
MOSCA. Patron, go in, and pray for our success.
VOLPONE. [rising from his couch] Need makes devotion: heaven
your labor bless!   [Exeunt.]

Act IV

ACT IV   SCENE 1. A STREET

[Enter SIR POLITIC WOULD-BE and PEREGRINE.]
SIR POLITIC. I told you, sir, it was a plot; you see
What observation is! You mentioned[6] me
For some instructions: I will tell you, sir,
(Since we are met here in this height[7] of Venice),
Some few particulars I have set down,   5
Only for this meridian, fit to be known
Of your crude traveler; and they are these.
I will not touch, sir, at your phrase, or clothes,
For they are old.
PEREGRINE.   Sir, I have better.
SIR POLITIC.   Pardon,
I meant, as they are themes.
PEREGRINE.   O, sir, proceed: 10
I'll slander you no more of wit, good sir.

---

4. The court of law. Jonson's court, like courts on the Continent generally, has power to look
   into abuses and investigate possible violations of the law, before any particular suit is filed.
5. Scholars.
6. Asked.
7. Part of the world.

SIR POLITIC. First, for your garb,[8] it must be grave and serious,
    Very reserved and locked; not tell a secret
    On any terms, not to your father; scarce
    A fable, but with caution; make sure choice   15
    Both of your company, and discourse; beware
    You never speak a truth—
PEREGRINE.   How!
SIR POLITIC.   Not to strangers,
    For those be they you must converse with most;
    Others I would not know, sir, but at distance,
    So as I still might be a saver in them:[9]   20
    You shall have tricks, else, passed upon you hourly.
    And then, for your religion, profess none,
    But wonder at the diversity of all;
    And, for your part, protest, were there no other
    But simply the laws o' th' land, you could content you.   25
    Nick Machiavel, and Monsieur Bodin, both
    Were of this mind.[1] Then must you learn the use
    And handling of your silver fork at meals.[2]
    The metal of your glass (these are main matters
    With your Italian), and to know the hour   30
    When you must eat your melons, and your figs.
PEREGRINE. Is that a point of state too?
SIR POLITIC.   Here it is;
    For your Venetian, if he see a man
    Preposterous[3] in the least, he has him straight;
    He has; he strips him. I'll acquaint you, sir.   35
    I now have lived here, 'tis some fourteen months;
    Within the first week of my landing here,
    All took me for a citizen of Venice,
    I knew the forms so well—
PEREGRINE.   [*aside*] And nothing else.
SIR POLITIC. I had read Contarine,[4] took me a house,   40
    Dealt with my Jews to furnish it with movables—

---

8. Behavior, as well as clothes.
9. The implication is clear: Don't lend anybody money.
1. The abbreviation "Nick Machiavel" implies casual familiarity; the sentiment attributed to
   Niccolò Machiavelli (1469–1527), Italian political philosopher, shows complete ignorance of
   him. Sir Politic Would-be is more nearly right in his estimate of Jean Bodin (1530–1596),
   the French political philosopher, who did advocate religious toleration.
2. Handling a fork was a new experience for Englishmen who traveled abroad in Jonson's time;
   back home, fingers were still the preferred instruments. "The metal of your glass": literally,
   the composition of your glass.
3. In its literal Latin sense, getting things back to front; inverted, monstrous.
4. Cardinal Gasparo Contarini (1483–1542) wrote *The Commonwealth and Government of Ven-*
   ice, translated into English in 1599, which Sir Politic would be quick to know. "My Jews":
   in the indefinite sense—the usual Jewish merchants that everybody goes to for furniture to set
   up a Venetian apartment.

Well, if I could but find one man, one man
To mine own heart, whom I durst trust, I would—
PEREGRINE. What, what, sir?
SIR POLITIC.   Make him rich; make him a fortune;
He should not think again. I would command it.   45
PEREGRINE. As how?
SIR POLITIC.   With certain projects[5] that I have
Which I may not discover.
PEREGRINE.   [aside] If I had
But one to wager with, I would lay odds now,
He tells me instantly.
SIR POLITIC.   One is (and that
I care not greatly who knows) to serve the state   50
Of Venice with red herrings for three years,
And at a certain rate, from Rotterdam[6]
Where I have correspondence. There's a letter,
Sent me from one o' the States,[7] and to that purpose;
He cannot write his name, but that's his mark.   55
PEREGRINE. He is a chandler?[8]
SIR POLITIC.   No, a cheese monger.
There are some others too with whom I treat
About the same negotiation;
And I will undertake it: for, 'tis thus.
I'll do't with ease, I've cast it all. Your hoy[9]   60
Carries but three men in her, and a boy;
And she shall make me three returns a year.
So, if there come but one of three, I save;
If two, I can defalk:[1]—but this is now,
If my main project fail.
PEREGRINE.   Then you have others?   65
SIR POLITIC. I should be loath to draw the subtle air
Of such a place, without my thousand aims.
I'll not dissemble, sir; where'er I come,
I love to be considerative; and 'tis true,
I have at my free hours thought upon   70
Some certain goods unto the state of Venice,
Which I do call my cautions; and, sir, which

---

5. Schemes for social improvement or making money (or preferably both) were favorite targets of seventeenth-century satire. "Discover": disclose.
6. The Venetians have plenty of fresh fish in the Adriatic, and would not like salt herring in any case.
7. I.e., from one of the States-General in Holland.
8. A candle merchant. Peregrine is perhaps joking about the greasiness of the paper.
9. A small North Sea fishing vessel; such a boat would have great trouble making a trip to Venice, let alone carrying a worthwhile cargo.
1. Reduce the amount, cut back, maybe even go into bankruptcy.

I mean, in hope of pension, to propound
To the Great Council, then unto the Forty,
So to the Ten.[2] My means are made already—   75
PEREGRINE. By whom?
SIR POLITIC.   Sir, one that, though his place be obscure,
Yet he can sway, and they will hear him. He's
A *commandatore.*
PEREGRINE.   What! A common sergeant?
SIR POLITIC. Sir, such as they are, put it in their mouths,
What they should say, sometimes, as well as greater.   80
I think I have my notes to show you—[*Searching his pockets.*]
PEREGRINE.   Good, sir.
SIR POLITIC. But you shall swear unto me, on your gentry[3]
Not to anticipate—
PEREGRINE.   I, sir!
SIR POLITIC.   Nor reveal
A circumstance—My paper is not with me.
PEREGRINE. O, but you can remember, sir.
SIR POLITIC.   My first is   85
Concerning tinder-boxes.[4] You must know,
No family is here without its box.
Now, sir, it being so portable a thing,
Put case, that you or I were ill affected
Unto the state, sir; with it in our pockets,   90
Might not I go into the Arsenal,[5]
Or you? Come out again? And none the wiser?
PEREGRINE. Except yourself, sir.
SIR POLITIC.   Go to, then. I therefore
Advertise to the state, how fit it were,
That none but such as were known patriots,   95
Sound lovers of their country, should be suffered
To enjoy them in their houses; and even those
Sealed at some office, and at such a bigness
As might not lurk in pockets.
PEREGRINE.   Admirable!
SIR POLITIC. My next is, how to inquire, and be resolved   100
By present demonstration, whether a ship,
Newly arrived from Syria, or from
Any suspected part of all the Levant,[6]

2. Representative legislative bodies, increasingly more selective and powerful, of the Venetian
government. "My means": my approaches to these eminent bodies.
3. As you are a gentleman.
4. Matchboxes or cigarette lighters.
5. Venice being largely a maritime power, the Arsenal where ships were built and repaired was
(and still is) an important part of the city.
6. The Middle East.

Be guilty of the plague; and where they use
To lie out forty, fifty days, sometimes,   105
About the Lazaretto,[7] for their trial,
I'll save that charge and loss unto the merchant,
And in an hour clear the doubt.
PEREGRINE.   Indeed, sir!
SIR POLITIC. Or—I will lose my labor.
PEREGRINE.   My faith, that's much.
SIR POLITIC. Nay, sir conceive me. 'Twill cost me in onions,   110
Some thirty livres[8]—
PEREGRINE.   Which is one pound sterling.
SIR POLITIC. Besides my water-works; for this I do, sir.
First, I bring in your ship 'twixt two brick-walls;
But those the state shall venture. On the one
I strain[9] me a fair tarpaulin, and in that   115
I stick my onions, cut in halves; the other
Is full of loop-holes, out at which I thrust
The noses of my bellows; and those bellows
I keep, with water-works[1] in perpetual motion,
Which is the easiest matter of a hundred.   120
Now, sir, your onion, which doth naturally
Attract the infection, and your bellows blowing
The air upon him, will show instantly,
By his changed color, if there be contagion,
Or else remain as fair as at the first.   125
—Now 'tis known, 'tis nothing.
PEREGRINE.   You are right, sir.
SIR POLITIC. I would I had my note.
PEREGRINE.   Faith, so would I:
But you have done well for once, sir.
SIR POLITIC.   Were I false,
Or would be made so, I could show you reasons
How I could sell this state now to the Turk,[2]   130
Spite of their galleys, or their—[*Examining his papers.*]
PEREGRINE.   Pray you, Sir Pol.
SIR POLITIC. I have them not about me.
PEREGRINE.   That I feared.

---

7. Place of quarantine. Bubonic plague, carried by lice living on shipboard rats, was a constant peril in Venice, where trade with the Middle East was particularly busy. Ships had to wait several months in port before debarking crew, passengers, or cargo.
8. A French coin of small value. Onions were reputed to be a defense against the plague; cut open, they supposedly absorbed the plague germs from the air.
9. Stretch.
1. Sir Politic's waterworks are apparently a waterwheel arranged to operate a bellows. Of course, there is no spot in the flat country around Venice where streams flow swiftly enough to turn a wheel.
2. Here Sir Politic is verging on real subversion, and Peregrine quickly shuts him off.

They are there, sir?

SIR POLITIC.   No, this is my diary,
   Wherein I note my actions of the day.

PEREGRINE. Pray you let's see, sir. What is here? *Notandum*,[3]   135

                                             [*Reads.*]

   A *rat had gnawn my spur-leathers; notwithstanding,*
   I put on new, and did go forth; but first
   I threw three beans over the threshold. Item,
   I went and bought two tooth-picks, whereof one
   I burst immediately, in a discourse   140
   With a Dutch merchant, 'bout ragion del stato.[4]
   From him I went and paid a mocenigo
   For piecing my silk stockings; by the way
   I cheapened sprats;[5] *and at St. Mark's I urined.*
   Faith, these are politic notes!

SIR POLITIC.   Sir, I do slip   145
   No action of my life, thus, but I quote it.

PEREGRINE. Believe me, it is wise!

SIR POLITIC.   Nay, sir, read forth.

ACT IV   SCENE 2

   [*Enter, at a distance,* LADY POLITIC WOULD-BE, NANO, *and*
   two WAITING-WOMEN.]

LADY POLITIC. Where should this loose knight be, trow? Sure
   he's housed.[6]

NANO. Why, then he's fast.

LADY POLITIC.   Ay, he plays both with me.[7]
   I pray you stay. This heat will do more harm
   To my complexion, than his heart is worth.
   (I do not care to hinder, but to take him.)   5
   How it[8] comes off! [*Rubbing her cheeks.*]

1 WOMAN.   My master's yonder.

LADY POLITIC.   Where?

2 WOMAN. With a young gentleman.

LADY POLITIC.   That same's the party,
   In man's apparel! Pray you, sir, jog my knight;
   I will be tender to his reputation,

3. Take special note.
4. Literally, "reason of state," but also the title of a famous book by Giovanni Botero (1544–
   1617), presenting a diluted version of Machiavelli's thought; "mocenigo": Venetian coin, as
   at 2.2.200.
5. Bargained over some trifling fish; "piecing": mending.
6. Gone into somebody's house. "He's fast" implies that he's securely fastened and in fast (promiscuous) company.
7. Both fast and loose.
8. I.e., her complexion.

However he demerit.

SIR POLITIC. [*seeing her*] My lady!

PEREGRINE.   Where?   10

SIR POLITIC. 'Tis she indeed, sir; you shall know her. She is,
Were she not mine, a lady of that merit,
For fashion and behavior; and for beauty
I durst compare—

PEREGRINE.   It seems you are not jealous,
That dare commend her.

SIR POLITIC.   Nay, and for discourse—   15

PEREGRINE. Being your wife, she cannot miss that.

SIR POLITIC.   [*introducing Peregrine*] Madam,
Here is a gentleman, pray you, use him fairly;
He seems a youth, but he is—

LADY POLITIC.   None.

SIR POLITIC.   Yes, one
Has put his face as soon into the world—

LADY POLITIC. You mean, as early? But today?

SIR POLITIC.   How's this?   20

LADY POLITIC. Why, in this habit, sir; you apprehend me.
Well, Master Would-be, this doth not become you;
I had thought the odor, sir, of your good name
Had been more precious to you; that you would not
Have done this dire massacre on your honor;   25
One of your gravity, and rank besides!
But knights, I see, care little for the oath
They make to ladies, chiefly, their own ladies.

SIR POLITIC. Now, by my spurs, the symbol of my knighthood[9]—

PEREGRINE. [*aside*] Lord, how his brain is humbled for an oath!   30

SIR POLITIC. I reach you not.

LADY POLITIC.   Right, sir, your polity
May bear it through thus. [*To* PEREGRINE.]—Sir, a word with
    you.
I would be loath to contest publicly
With any gentlewoman, or to seem
Froward, or violent, as *The Courtier* says;[1]   35
It comes too near rusticity in a lady,
Which I would shun by all means; and however
I may deserve from Master Would-be, yet
T'have one fair gentlewoman thus be made
The unkind instrument to wrong another,   40

---

9. Because King James created knights indiscriminately at his accession, knighthood was a broad
   joke in early seventeenth-century England.
1. Title of a famous book of courtesy by the Italian statesman Baldassare Castiglione (1478–
   1529), published in 1528 and translated into English by Thomas Hoby in 1561.

And one she knows not, ay, and to persever;
In my poor judgment, is not warranted
From being a solecism[2] in our sex,
If not in manners.

PEREGRINE.   How is this!

SIR POLITIC.   Sweet madam,
Come nearer to your aim.

LADY POLITIC.   Marry, and will, sir.   45
Since you provoke me with your impudence,
And laughter of your light land-siren here,
Your Sporus,[3] your hermaphrodite—

PEREGRINE.   What's here?
Poetic fury, and historic[4] storms!

SIR POLITIC. The gentleman, believe it, is of worth,   50
And of our nation.

LADY POLITIC.   Ay, your Whitefriars[5] nation!
Come, I blush for you, Master Would-be, ay;
And am ashamed you should have no more forehead,[6]
Than thus to be the patron, or St. George,
To a lewd harlot, a base fricatrice,[7]   55
A female devil, in a male outside.

SIR POLITIC.   Nay,
An you be such a one, I must bid adieu
To your delights. The case appears too liquid.   [*Exit.*]

LADY POLITIC. Ay, you may carry't clear, with your state-face![8]
But for your carnival concupiscence,   60
Who here is fled for liberty of conscience,
From furious persecution of the marshal,
Her will I dis'ple.[9]

PEREGRINE.   This is fine, i'faith,
And do you use this often? Is this part
Of your wit's exercise, 'gainst you have occasion?   65
Madam——

LADY POLITIC. Go to, sir.

PEREGRINE.   Do you hear me, lady?
Why, if your knight have set you to beg shirts,
Or to invite me home, you might have done it

---

2. Lapse in behavior.
3. Sporus was a favorite homosexual lover of Nero, who dressed him in drag and married him.
4. With reference to the historical allusion (Sporus), but "hysteric" is not far away.
5. Disreputable quarter of London, inhabited by whores.
6. Sense of shame.
7. Prostitute.
8. A solemn expression.
9. Discipline; specifically, whip. In England at least (although not in Venice) the marshal was directly charged with catching and punishing prostitutes.

A nearer way, by far.[1]

LADY POLITIC.   This cannot work you
 Out of my snare.

PEREGRINE.   Why, am I in it, then?   70
 Indeed your husband told me you were fair,
 And so you are; only your nose inclines,
 That side that's next the sun, to the queen-apple.[2]

LADY POLITIC. This cannot be endured, by any patience.

ACT IV SCENE 3

    [Enter MOSCA.]

MOSCA. What is the matter, madam?

LADY POLITIC.   If the Senate
 Right not my quest in this,[3] I will protest them
 To all the world, no aristocracy.

MOSCA. What is the injury, lady?

LADY POLITIC.   Why, the callet[4]
 You told me of, here I have ta'en disguised.   5

MOSCA. Who? This! What means your ladyship? The creature
 I mentioned to you is apprehended now,
 Before the Senate; you shall see her—

LADY POLITIC.   Where?

MOSCA. I'll bring you to her. This young gentleman,
 I saw him land this morning at the port.   10

LADY POLITIC. Is't possible! How has my judgment wandered?
 Sir, I must, blushing, say to you, I have erred;
 And plead your pardon.

PEREGRINE.   What, more changes yet!

LADY POLITIC. I hope you have not the malice to remember
 A gentlewoman's passion. If you stay   15
 In Venice here, please you to use me, sir—

MOSCA. Will you go, madam?

LADY POLITIC.   'Pray you, sir, use me; in faith,
 The more you see me, the more I shall conceive
 You have forgot our quarrel.

    [Exeunt LADY WOULD-BE, MOSCA, NANO, and WAITING-
    WOMEN.]

PEREGRINE.   This is rare!
 Sir Politic Would-be? No; Sir Politic Bawd! 20

---

1. Peregrine implies that the whole situation is a setup, that Sir Politic is pimping for his wife.
2. Lady Politic has a fiery red nose.
3. Doesn't do me justice.
4. Slut.

To bring me thus acquainted with his wife!
Well, wise Sir Pol, since you have practiced thus
Upon my freshman-ship,[5] I'll try your salt-head,
What proof it is against a counterplot.   [*Exit.*]

ACT IV   SCENE 4. *THE SCRUTINEO*

[*Enter* VOLTORE, CORBACCIO, CORVINO, *and* MOSCA.]
VOLTORE. Well, now you know the carriage of the business,
    Your constancy is all that is required
    Unto the safety of it.
MOSCA.   Is the lie[6]
    Safely conveyed amongst us? Is that sure?
    Knows every man his burden?[7]
CORVINO.   Yes.
MOSCA.   Then shrink not.   5
CORVINO. [*aside to* MOSCA] But knows the advocate the truth?
MOSCA.   O, sir,
    By no means; I devised a formal tale
    That salved your reputation. But be valiant, sir.
CORVINO. I fear no one but him, that this his pleading
    Should make him stand for a co-heir—
MOSCA.   Co-halter!   10
    Hang him; we will but use his tongue, his noise,
    As we do Croaker's[8] here.
CORVINO.   Ay, what shall he do?
MOSCA. When we have done, you mean?
CORVINO.   Yes.
MOSCA.   Why, we'll think:
    Sell him for mummia;[9] he's half dust already.
    [*To* VOLTORE.] Do you not smile to see this buffalo,[1]   15
    How he doth sport it with his head? [*aside*]—I should,
    If all were well and past. [*To* CORBACCIO.] Sir, only you
    Are he that shall enjoy the crop of all,
    And these know not for whom they toil.
CORBACCIO.   Ay, peace.
MOSCA. [*turning to* CORVINO] But you shall eat it. [*Aside.*]
    Much![2] [*to* VOLTORE] Worshipful sir,   20

5. Innocence, as of a freshman, but in opposition to Sir Politic's "salt-head": salacity, lewdness.
6. Untruth, but also the shape of things, as in the lay of the land.
7. "Part," as in part-singing. Mosca must be sure everyone has his story straight.
8. Corbaccio's.
9. Allegedly the powdered remains of the pharaohs, popularly sold as medicine.
1. An allusion to the cuckold's horns worn by Corvino.
2. I.e., "fat chance!"

Mercury sit upon your thundering tongue,
Or the French Hercules,[3] and make your language
As conquering as his club, to beat along,
As with a tempest, flat, our adversaries;
But much more yours, sir.

VOLTORE.   Here they come, have done.   25
MOSCA. I have another witness, if you need, sir,
I can produce.
VOLTORE.   Who is it?
MOSCA.   Sir, I have her.

ACT IV   SCENE 5

[*Enter* AVOCATORI *and take their seats*; BONARIO, CELIA, NO-
TARIO, COMMANDATORI, SAFFI, *and other* OFFICERS OF
JUSTICE.]

1 AVOCATORE. The like of this the Senate never heard of.
2 AVOCATORE. 'Twill come most strange to them when we report
   it.
4 AVOCATORE. The gentlewoman[4] has been ever held
   Of unreprovèd name.
3 AVOCATORE.   So has the youth.[5]
4 AVOCATORE. The more unnatural part that of his father.   5
2 AVOCATORE. More of the husband.[6]
1 AVOCATORE.   I not know to give
   His act a name, it is so monstrous!
4 AVOCATORE. But the impostor,[7] he's a thing created
   To exceed example!
1 AVOCATORE.   And all after-times!
2 AVOCATORE. I never heard a true voluptuary   10
   Described, but him.
3 AVOCATORE.   Appear yet those were cited?
NOTARIO. All but the old magnifico, Volpone.
1 AVOCATORE. Why is not he here?
MOSCA.   Please your fatherhoods,
   Here is his advocate: himself's so weak,
   So feeble—
4 AVOCATORE. What are you?
BONARIO.   His parasite,   15
   His knave, his pander: I beseech the court,

---

3. Both Mercury, Roman god of thieves, and the French Hercules were patrons of eloquence;
   the latter is specifically discussed by the classical burlesque-writer, Lucian.
4. Celia.
5. Bonario.
6. Corvino.
7. Volpone.

He may be forced to come, that your grave eyes
   May bear strong witness of his strange impostures.
VOLTORE. Upon my faith and credit with your virtues,
   He is not able to endure the air.   20
2 AVOCATORE. Bring him, however.
3 AVOCATORE.   We will see him.
4 AVOCATORE.   Fetch him.
VOLTORE. Your fatherhoods' fit pleasures be obeyed;
                                  [*Exeunt* OFFICERS.]
   But sure, the sight will rather move your pities
   Than indignation. May it please the court,
   In the meantime, he may be heard in me.   25
   I know this place most void of prejudice,
   And therefore crave it, since we have no reason
   To fear our truth should hurt our cause.
3 AVOCATORE.   Speak free.
VOLTORE. Then know, most honored fathers, I must now
   Discover to your strangely abusèd ears,   30
   The most prodigious and most frontless[8] piece
   Of solid impudence and treachery,
   That ever vicious nature yet brought forth
   To shame the state of Venice. This lewd woman,
   That wants[9] no artificial looks or tears   35
   To help the visor she has now put on,
   Hath long been known a close adulteress
   To that lascivious youth there; not suspected,
   I say, but known, and taken in the act
   With him; and by this man, the easy husband,   40
   Pardoned; whose timeless[1] bounty makes him now
   Stand here, the most unhappy, innocent person,
   That ever man's own goodness made accused.
   For these not knowing how to owe a gift
   Of that dear grace, but with their shame; being placed   45
   So above all powers of their gratitude,
   Began to hate the benefit; and, in place
   Of thanks, devise to extirp[2] the memory
   Of such an act. Wherein, I pray your fatherhoods
   To observe the malice, yea, the rage of creatures   50
   Discovered in their evils; and what heart
   Such take, even from their crimes. But that anon
   Will more appear. This gentleman, the father,

8. Shameless.
9. Lacks; "visor": artificial features, outward appearance.
1. Ill-timed.
2. Wipe out, erase.

Hearing of this foul fact, with many others,
Which daily struck at his too tender ears,   55
And grieved in nothing more than that he could not
Preserve himself a parent (his son's ills
Growing to that strange flood), at last decreed
To disinherit him.
1 AVOCATORE.   These be strange turns!
2 AVOCATORE. The young man's fame was ever fair and honest.   60
VOLTORE. So much more full of danger is his vice,
That can beguile so under shade of virtue.
But, as I said, my honored sires, his father
Having this settled purpose, by what means
To him betrayed, we know not, and this day   65
Appointed for the deed; that parricide,
I cannot style him better, by confederacy[3]
Preparing this his paramour to be there,
Entered Volpone's house (who was the man,
Your fatherhoods must understand, designed   70
For the inheritance), there sought his father;
But with what purpose sought he him, my lords?
I tremble to pronounce it, that a son
Unto a father, and to such a father,
Should have so foul, felonious intent!   75
It was to murder him; when, being prevented
By his more happy absence, what then did he?
Not check his wicked thoughts; no, now new deeds
(Mischief doth ever end where it begins);
An act of horror, fathers! He dragged forth   80
The agèd gentleman that had there lain bed-rid
Three years and more, out of his innocent couch,
Naked upon the floor, there left him; wounded
His servant in the face; and, with this strumpet,
The stale[4] to his forged practice, who was glad   85
To be so active (I shall here desire
Your fatherhoods to note but my collections,[5]
As most remarkable), thought at once to stop
His father's ends, discredit his free choice
In the old gentleman, redeem themselves,   90
By laying infamy upon this man,[6]
To whom, with blushing, they should owe their lives.
1 AVOCATORE. What proofs have you of this?

3. Conspiracy.
4. Pretext.
5. Deductions.
6. I.e., Corvino.

BONARIO.   Most honored fathers,
   I humbly crave there be no credit given
   To this man's mercenary tongue.
2 AVOCATORE.   Forbear.   95
BONARIO. His soul moves in his fee.
3 AVOCATORE.   O, sir.
BONARIO.   This fellow,
   For six sols more,[7] would plead against his maker.
1 AVOCATORE. You do forget yourself.
VOLTORE.   Nay, nay, grave fathers,
   Let him have scope; can any man imagine
   That he will spare his accuser, that would not   100
   Have spared his parent?
1 AVOCATORE.   Well, produce your proofs.
CELIA. I would I could forget I were a creature!
VOLTORE. Signor Corbaccio! [CORBACCIO comes forward.]
4 AVOCATORE.   What is he?
VOLTORE.   The father.
2 AVOCATORE. Has he had an oath?
NOTARIO.   Yes.
CORBACCIO.   What must I do now?
NOTARIO. Your testimony's craved.
CORBACCIO.   Speak to the knave?   105
   I'll have my mouth first stopped with earth; my heart
   Abhors his knowledge.[8] I disclaim in him.
1 AVOCATORE. But for what cause?
CORBACCIO.   The mere portent of nature!
   He is an utter stranger to my loins.
BONARIO. Have they made you to this?
CORBACCIO.   I will not hear thee,   110
   Monster of men, swine, goat, wolf, parricide!
   Speak not, thou viper.[9]
BONARIO.   Sir, I will sit down,
   And rather wish my innocence should suffer,
   Than I resist the authority of a father.
VOLTORE. Signor Corvino! [CORVINO comes forward.]
2 AVOCATORE.   This is strange.
1 AVOCATORE.   Who's this?   115
NOTARIO. The husband.
4 AVOCATORE.   Is he sworn?

---

7. Three pence.
8. Shudders to recognize him.
9. The parricide, as a creature wholly unnatural, was punished among the Romans by being
   whipped; sewed up in a sack with a dog, a cock, a viper, and an ape; and thrown into the
   sea.

NOTARIO.   He is.

3 AVOCATORE.   Speak, then.

CORVINO. This woman, please your fatherhoods, is a whore
    Of most hot exercise, more than a partridge[1]
    Upon record—

1 AVOCATORE.   No more.

CORVINO.   Neighs like a jennet.[2]

NOTARIO. Preserve the honor of the court.

CORVINO.   I shall,   120
    And modesty of your most reverend ears.
    And yet I hope that I may say, these eyes
    Have seen her glued unto that piece of cedar,
    That fine well-timbered gallant; and that here[3]
    The letters may be read, through the horn,   125
    That make the story perfect.

MOSCA.   Excellent, sir!

CORVINO. [aside to MOSCA] There is no shame in this now, is
    there?

MOSCA.   None.

CORVINO. Or if I said, I hoped that she were onward
    To her damnation, if there be a hell
    Greater than whore and woman; a good catholic[4]   130
    May make the doubt.

3 AVOCATORE.   His grief hath made him frantic.

1 AVOCATORE. Remove him hence.   [CELIA swoons.]

2 AVOCATORE.   Look to the woman.

CORVINO.   Rare!
    Prettily feigned, again!

4 AVOCATORE.   Stand from about her.

1 AVOCATORE. Give her the air.

3 AVOCATORE.   [to MOSCA] What can you say?

MOSCA.   My wound,
    May it please your wisdoms, speaks for me, received   135
    In aid of my good patron, when he missed
    His sought-for father[5] when that well-taught dame
    Had her cue given her, to cry out a rape.

BONARIO. O most laid impudence! Fathers—

3 AVOCATORE.   Sir, be silent;
    You had your hearing free, so must they theirs.   140

2 AVOCATORE. I do begin to doubt the imposture here.

---

1. The partridge vied with the sparrow as the most lustful of birds.
2. Mare.
3. Corvino holds two fingers over his head to make the horned sign of the cuckold.
4. The 1607 quarto reads "Christian" instead of "catholic."
5. Corbaccio.

4 AVOCATORE. This woman has too many moods.

VOLTORE.   Grave fathers,
  She is a creature of a most professed
  And prostituted lewdness.

CORVINO.   Most impetuous,
  Unsatisfied, grave fathers!

VOLTORE.   May her feignings   145
  Not take your wisdoms: but this day she baited
  A stranger, a grave knight, with her loose eyes,
  And more lascivious kisses. This man saw them
  Together on the water, in a gondola.

MOSCA. Here is the lady herself, that saw them too,   150
  Without; who then had in the open streets
  Pursued them, but for saving her knight's honor.

1 AVOCATORE. Produce that lady.

2 AVOCATORE.   Let her come.   [*Exit* MOSCA.]

4 AVOCATORE.   These things,
  They strike with wonder.

3 AVOCATORE.   I am turned a stone.

ACT IV   SCENE 6

     [*Enter* MOSCA *with* LADY WOULD-BE.]

MOSCA. Be resolute, madam.

LADY POLITIC.   Ay, this same is she. [*Pointing to*
  CELIA.]
  Out, thou chameleon[6] harlot! Now thine eyes
  Vie tears with the hyena. Dar'st thou look
  Upon my wrongèd face?—I cry your pardons,
  I fear I have forgettingly transgressed   5
  Against the dignity of the court—

2 AVOCATORE.   No, madam.

LADY POLITIC. And been exorbitant[7]—

2 AVOCATORE.   You have not, lady.

4 AVOCATORE. These proofs are strong.

LADY POLITIC.   Surely, I had no purpose
  To scandalize your honors, or my sex's.

3 AVOCATORE. We do believe it.

LADY POLITIC.   Surely, you may believe it.   10

2 AVOCATORE. Madam, we do.

LADY POLITIC.   Indeed you may; my breeding
  Is not so coarse——

4 AVOCATORE.   We know it.

---

6. An animal that changes colors. The hyena, an eater of carrion, is emblematic of treachery.
7. Excessive.

LADY POLITIC.   To offend
  With pertinacy——
3 AVOCATORE.   Lady—
LADY POLITIC.   Such a presence!
  No, surely.
1 AVOCATORE. We well think it.
LADY POLITIC.   You may think it.
1 AVOCATORE. Let her o'ercome. [*To* BONARIO.] What witnesses
      have you,   15
  To make good your report?
BONARIO.   Our consciences.
CELIA. And heaven, that never fails the innocent.
4 AVOCATORE. These are no testimonies.
BONARIO.   Not in your courts,
  Where multitude and clamor overcomes.
1 AVOCATORE. Nay, then you do wax insolent.   20
        [*Re-enter* OFFICERS, *bearing* VOLPONE *on a couch.*]
VOLTORE.   Here, here,
  The testimony comes, that will convince,
  And put to utter dumbness their bold tongues!
  See here, grave fathers, here's the ravisher,
  The rider on men's wives, the great impostor,
  The grand voluptuary! Do you not think   25
  These limbs should affect venery?[8] Or these eyes
  Covet a concubine? Pray you mark these hands;
  Are they not fit to stroke a lady's breasts?
  Perhaps he doth dissemble!
BONARIO.   So he does.
VOLTORE. Would you have him tortured?
BONARIO.   I would have him proved.   30
VOLTORE. Best try him then with goads, or burning irons;
  Put him to the strappado.[9] I have heard
  The rack hath cured the gout; 'faith, give it him,
  And help him of a malady; be courteous.
  I'll undertake, before these honored fathers,   35
  He shall have yet as many left diseases,
  As she has known adulterers, or thou strumpets.
  O, my most equal hearers, if these deeds,
  Acts of this bold and most exorbitant strain,
  May pass with sufferance, what one citizen   40
  But owes the forfeit of his life, yea, fame,

---

8. Be disposed to lust.
9. A common torture of the time: a man's hands were tied behind his back, and he was hoisted
  by his wrists on a gallows, to the usual effect of dislocating his shoulders.

To him that dares traduce him? Which of you
Are safe, my honored fathers? I would ask,
With leave of your grave fatherhoods, if their plot
Have any face or color like to truth?   45
Or if, unto the dullest nostril here,
It smell not rank, and most abhorrèd slander?
I crave your care of this good gentleman,
Whose life is much endangered by their fable;
And as for them, I will conclude with this,   50
That vicious persons, when they're hot, and fleshed
In impious acts, their constancy abounds:
Damned deeds are done with greatest confidence.
1 AVOCATORE. Take them to custody, and sever them. [CELIA *and*
    BONARIO *are taken out.*]
2 AVOCATORE. 'Tis pity two such prodigies should live.   55
1 AVOCATORE. Let the old gentleman be returned with care:
        [*Exeunt* OFFICERS *with* VOLPONE.]
    I'm sorry our credulity hath wronged him.
4 AVOCATORE. These are two creatures!
3 AVOCATORE.   I've an earthquake in me.[1]
2 AVOCATORE. Their shame, even in their cradles, fled their
    faces.
4 AVOCATORE. [*to* VOLTORE] You have done a worthy service to
    the state, sir,   60
    In their discovery.
1 AVOCATORE.   You shall hear, ere night,
What punishment the court decrees upon them.
VOLTORE. We thank your fatherhoods. [*Exeunt* AVOCATORI, NO-
    TARIO, and OFFICERS.] [*To* MOSCA.]—How like you it?
MOSCA.   Rare.
    I'd have your tongue, sir, tipped with gold for this;
    I'd have you be the heir to the whole city;   65
    The earth I'd have want men, ere you want living:
    They're bound to erect your statue in St. Mark's.
    Signor Corvino, I would have you go
    And show yourself, that you have conquered.
CORVINO.   Yes.
MOSCA. It was much better that you should profess   70
    Yourself a cuckold thus, than that the other
    Should have been proved.
CORVINO.   Nay, I considered that;
    Now it is her fault.
MOSCA.   Then it had been yours.

1. I'm overwhelmed.

CORVINO. True; I do doubt this advocate still.
MOSCA.   I'faith,
  You need not, I dare ease you of that care.   75
CORVINO. I trust thee, Mosca.   [*Exit.*]
MOSCA.   As your own soul, sir.
CORBACCIO.   Mosca!
MOSCA. Now for your business, sir.
CORBACCIO.   How! Have you business?
MOSCA. Yes, yours sir.
CORBACCIO.   O, none else?
MOSCA.   None else, not I.
CORBACCIO. Be careful then.
MOSCA.   Rest you with both your eyes, sir.
CORBACCIO. Dispatch it.[2]
MOSCA.   Instantly.
CORBACCIO.   And look that all,   80
  Whatever, be put in, jewels, plate, moneys,
  Household stuff, bedding, curtains.
MOSCA.   Curtain-rings, sir:
  Only the advocate's fee must be deducted.
CORBACCIO. I'll pay him now; you'll be too prodigal.
MOSCA. Sir, I must tender it.
CORBACCIO.   Two sequins is well.   85
MOSCA. No, six, sir.
CORBACCIO.   'Tis too much.
MOSCA.   He talked a great while;
  You must consider that, sir.
CORBACCIO.   Well, there's three—
MOSCA. I'll give it him.
CORBACCIO.   Do so, and there's for thee.   [*Exit.*]
MOSCA. Bountiful bones! What horrid strange offense
  Did he commit 'gainst nature, in his youth,   90
  Worthy this age? [*To* VOLTORE.]—You see, sir, how I work
  Unto your ends; take you no notice.
VOLTORE.   No,
  I'll leave you.   [*Exit.*]
MOSCA.   All is yours, the devil and all,
  Good advocate!—Madam, I'll bring you home.
LADY POLITIC. No, I'll go see your patron.
MOSCA.   That you shall not.   95
  I'll tell you why. My purpose is to urge
  My patron to reform his will;[3] and for

---

2. I.e., get the will made, with me in it.
3. Rewrite his testament, though also with the connotation of improving his disposition.

The zeal you have shown today, whereas before
You were but third or fourth, you shall be now
Put in the first; which would appear as begged,   100
If you were present. Therefore—
LADY POLITIC.   You shall sway me. [*Exeunt.*]

Act V

ACT V   SCENE 1. *A ROOM IN* VOLPONE*'S HOUSE*

[*Enter* VOLPONE.]
VOLPONE. Well, I am here, and all this brunt[4] is past.
  I ne'er was in dislike with my disguise
  Till this fled moment:[5] here 'twas good, in private,
  But in your public—*cavè*[6] whilst I breathe.
  'Fore God, my left leg 'gan to have the cramp,   5
  And I appre'nded[7] straight some power had struck me
  With a dead palsy. Well, I must be merry,
  And shake it off. A many of these fears
  Would put me into some villainous disease,
  Should they come thick upon me: I'll prevent 'em.   10
  Give me a bowl of lusty wine, to fright
  This humour from my heart. [*Drinks.*]—Hum, hum, hum!
  'Tis almost gone already, I shall conquer.
  Any device, now, of rare ingenious knavery,
  That would possess me with a violent laughter,   15
  Would make me up again. [*Drinks again.*]—So, so, so, so!
  This heat is life; 'tis blood by this time! Mosca!

ACT V   SCENE 2

[*Enter* MOSCA.]
MOSCA. How now, sir? Does the day look clear again?
  Are we recovered? And wrought out of error,
  Into our way, to see our path before us?
  Is our trade free once more?
VOLPONE.   Exquisite Mosca!
MOSCA. Was it not carried learnedly?
VOLPONE.   And stoutly.   5
  Good wits are greatest in extremities.
MOSCA. It were a folly beyond thought, to trust
  Any grand act unto a cowardly spirit.

4. Trouble.
5. Moment just past.
6. Beware, watch out (Latin).
7. Apprehended immediately.

You are not taken with it[8] enough, methinks.
VOLPONE. O, more than if I had enjoyed the wench;   10
    The pleasure of all womankind's not like it.
MOSCA. Why now you speak, sir. We must here be fixed;
    Here we must rest. This is our masterpiece;
    We cannot think to go beyond this.
VOLPONE.   True,
    Thou'st played thy prize, my precious Mosca.
MOSCA.   Nay, sir,   15
    To gull the court—
VOLPONE.   And quite divert the torrent
    Upon the innocent.
MOSCA.   Yes, and to make
    So rare a music out of discords—
VOLPONE.   Right.
    That yet to me's the strangest! How thou'st borne it
    That these, being so divided 'mongst themselves,   20
    Should not scent somewhat, or in me or thee,
    Or doubt their own side.
MOSCA.   True, they will not see't.
    Too much light blinds them, I think.[9] Each of them
    Is so possessed and stuffed with his own hopes,
    That anything unto the contrary,   25
    Never so true, or never so apparent,
    Never so palpable, they will resist it—
VOLPONE. Like a temptation of the devil.
MOSCA.   Right, sir.
    Merchants may talk of trade, and your great signors
    Of land that yields well; but if Italy   30
    Have any glebe[1] more fruitful than these fellows,
    I am deceived. Did not your advocate rare?[2]
VOLPONE. O—*My most honored fathers, my grave fathers,*
    Under correction of your fatherhoods,
    What face of truth is here? If these strange deeds   35
    May pass, most honored fathers—I had much ado
    To forbear laughing.
MOSCA.   It seemed to me you sweat, sir.
VOLPONE. In troth, I did a little.
MOSCA.   But confess, sir,
    Were you not daunted?
VOLPONE.   In good faith, I was

8. Pleased, satisfied with it.
9. An ancient adage.
1. Soil.
2. Did not your advocate (perform) rare(ly)?

A little in a mist, but not dejected;   40
Never, but still myself.
MOSCA.   I think it, sir.
  Now, so truth help me, I must needs say this, sir,
  And out of conscience for your advocate,
  He has taken pains, in faith, sir, and deserved,
  In my poor judgment, I speak it under favor,   45
  Not to contrary you, sir, very richly—
  Well—to be cozened.
VOLPONE.   Troth, and I think so too,
  By that I heard him, in the latter end.
MOSCA. O, but before, sir: had you heard him first
  Draw it to certain heads, then aggravate,   50
  Then use his vehement figures³—I looked still
  When he would shift a shirt;⁴ and, doing this
  Out of pure love, no hope of gain—
VOLPONE.   'Tis right.
  I cannot answer him Mosca, as I would,
  Not yet; but for thy sake, at thy entreaty,   55
  I will begin e'en now to vex them all,
  This very instant.
MOSCA.   Good, sir.
VOLPONE.   Call the dwarf
  And eunuch forth.
MOSCA.   Castrone, Nano!
          [*Enter* CASTRONE *and* NANO.]
NANO.   Here.
VOLPONE. Shall we have a jig now?
MOSCA.   What you please, sir.
VOLPONE.   Go,
  Straight give out about the streets, you two,   60
  That I am dead; do it with constancy,
  Sadly, do you hear? Impute it to the grief
  Of this late slander.   [*Exeunt* CASTRONE *and* NANO.]
MOSCA.   What do you mean, sir?
VOLPONE.   O,
  I shall have instantly my vulture, crow,
  Raven, come flying hither on the news,   65
  To peck for carrion, my she-wolf, and all,
  Greedy, and full of expectation—
MOSCA. And then to have it ravished from their mouths!
VOLPONE. 'Tis true. I will have thee put on a gown,

---

3. Terms of legal oratory.
4. I.e., he sweated so much over his speech, it seemed he might have to change his linen.

And take upon thee, as thou wert mine heir;   70
  Show them a will. Open that chest, and reach
  Forth one of those that has the blanks; I'll straight
  Put in thy name.
MOSCA.   It will be rare, sir. [*Gives him a paper.*]
VOLPONE.   Ay,
  When they e'en gape, and find themselves deluded—
MOSCA. Yes.
VOLPONE.   And thou use them scurvily! Dispatch,   75
  Get on thy gown.
MOSCA.   But what, sir, if they ask
  After the body?
VOLPONE.   Say it was corrupted.
MOSCA. I'll say it stunk, sir; and was fain to have it
  Coffined up instantly, and sent away.
VOLPONE. Anything, what thou wilt. Hold, here's my will.   80
  Get thee a cap, a count-book,[5] pen and ink,
  Papers afore thee; sit as thou wert taking
  An inventory of parcels. I'll get up
  Behind the curtain, on a stool, and hearken;
  Sometime peep over, see how they do look,   85
  With what degrees their blood doth leave their faces.
  O, 'twill afford me a rare meal of laughter!
MOSCA. [*putting on a cap, and setting out the table, & c.*] Your
    advocate will turn stark dull upon it.
VOLPONE. It will take off his oratory's edge.
MOSCA. But your clarissimo, old round-back,[6] he   90
  Will crump you like a hog-louse, with the touch.
VOLPONE. And what Corvino?
MOSCA.   O, sir, look for him,
  Tomorrow morning, with a rope and dagger
  To visit all the streets;[7] he must run mad.
  My lady too, that came into the court   95
  To bear false witness for your worship—
VOLPONE.   Yes,
  And kissed me 'fore the fathers, when my face
  Flowed all with oils.
MOSCA.   And sweat, sir. Why, your gold
  Is such another medicine, it dries up
  All those offensive savors; it transforms   100

---

5. Ledger.
6. Corbaccio is a *clarissimo*, a distinguished man in Venice. "Crump you": curl up on you;
  there is a species of wood louse or hog louse (the names are interchangeable) that curls up
  in a ball when touched.
7. I.e., looking for a place to commit suicide.

The most deformed, and restores them lovely,
As 'twere the strange poetical girdle.[8] Jove
Could not invent t' himself a shroud more subtle
To pass Acrisius' guards.[9] It is the thing
Makes all the world her grace, her youth, her beauty.   105
VOLPONE. I think she loves me.
MOSCA.   Who? The lady, sir?
    She's jealous of you.
VOLPONE.   Dost thou say so?   [*Knocking within.*]
MOSCA.   Hark,
    There's some already.
VOLPONE.   Look.
MOSCA.   It is the vulture;
    He has the quickest scent.
VOLPONE.   I'll to my place,
    Thou to thy posture.   [*Goes behind the curtain.*]
MOSCA.   I am set.
VOLPONE.   But, Mosca,   110
    Play the artificer now, torture them rarely.

ACT V   SCENE 3

        [*Enter* VOLTORE.]
VOLTORE. How now, my Mosca?
MOSCA.   [*writing*] *Turkey carpets, nine*[1]—
VOLTORE. Taking an inventory? That is well.
MOSCA. *Two suits of bedding, tissue—*
VOLTORE.   Where's the will?
    Let me read that the while.
        [*Enter* SERVANTS *with* CORBACCIO *in a chair.*]
CORBACCIO.   So, set me down,
    And get you home.   [*Exeunt servants.*]
VOLTORE.   Is he come now to trouble us?   5
MOSCA. *Of cloth of gold, two more—*
CORBACCIO.   Is it done, Mosca?
MOSCA. *Of several velvets, eight—*
VOLTORE.   I like his care.
CORBACCIO. Dost thou not hear?
        [*Enter* CORVINO.]
CORVINO.   Ha! Is the hour come, Mosca?
VOLPONE. [*peeping over the curtain*] Ay, now they muster.

8. The girdle of Venus (*cestus*) made any wearer irresistibly beautiful.
9. In Roman mythology, Acrisius was the father of Danae; he locked her up in a tower till Jove
   managed to get to her in the form of a shower of gold.
1. Turkey carpets (not necessarily from Turkey) were particularly thick and luxurious; cloth
   described as tissue often had threads of gold or silver interwoven.

CORVINO.   What does the advocate here,
   Or this Corbaccio?
CORBACCIO.   What do these here?
          [*Enter* LADY POLITIC WOULD-BE.]
LADY POLITIC.   Mosca!   10
   Is his thread spun?
MOSCA.   *Eight chests of linen—*
VOLPONE.   O,
   My fine dame Would-be, too!
CORVINO.   Mosca, the will,
   That I may show it these, and rid them hence.
MOSCA. *Six chests of diaper,*[2] *four of damask.*—There. [*Gives*
   them the will carelessly, over his shoulder.]
CORBACCIO. Is that the will?
MOSCA.   *Down-beds, and bolsters—*
VOLPONE.   Rare!   15
   Be busy still. Now they begin to flutter:
   They never think of me. Look, see, see, see!
   How their swift eyes run over the long deed,
   Unto the name, and to the legacies,
   What is bequeathed them there—
MOSCA.   *Ten suits of hangings—*[3]   20
VOLPONE. Ay, in their garters, Mosca. Now their hopes
   Are at the gasp.
VOLTORE.   Mosca the heir!
CORBACCIO.   What's that?
VOLPONE. My advocate is dumb; look to my merchant,
   He has heard of some strange storm, a ship is lost,
   He faints; my lady will swoon. Old glazen-eyes,[4]   25
   He hath not reached his despair yet.
CORBACCIO.   All these
   Are out of hope; I am, sure, the man. [*Takes the will.*]
CORVINO.   But, Mosca—
MOSCA. *Two cabinets—*
CORVINO.   Is this in earnest?
MOSCA.   *One*
   Of ebony—
CORVINO.   Or do you but delude me?
MOSCA. *The other, mother of pearl*—I am very busy.   30
   Good faith, it is a fortune thrown upon me—

2. Fine linen cloth; "damask" (from Damascus): a rich fabric woven with many figures.
3. Sets of tapestries on the walls. But Volpone is punning on the traditional mock, "Hang yourself
   in your own garters."
4. Corbaccio.

Item, one salt[5] *of agate*—not my seeking.

LADY POLITIC. Do you hear, sir?

MOSCA.   A *perfumed box*—'Pray you forbear,
You see I'm troubled—*made of an onyx*—

LADY POLITIC.   How!

MOSCA. To-morrow or next day, I shall be at leisure   35
To talk with you all.

CORVINO.   Is this my large hope's issue?

LADY POLITIC. Sir, I must have a fairer answer.

MOSCA.   Madam!
Marry, and shall: pray you, fairly[6] quit my house.
Nay, raise no tempest with your looks; but hark you:
Remember what your ladyship offered me   40
To put you in an heir;[7] go to, think on it:
And what you said e'en your best madams did
For maintenance;[8] and why not you? Enough.
Go home, and use the poor Sir Pol, your knight, well,
For fear I tell some riddles; go, be melancholic.   45

                              [*Exit* LADY POLITIC.]

VOLPONE. O, my fine devil!

CORVINO.   Mosca, 'pray you a word.

MOSCA. Lord! Will not you take your dispatch hence yet?
Methinks, of all, you should have been the example.
Why should you stay here? With what thought, what promise?
Hear you; do not you know, I know you an ass,   50
And that you would most fain have been a wittol,[9]
If fortune would have let you? That you are
A declared cuckold, on good terms? This pearl,
You'll say, was yours? Right. This diamond?
I'll not deny't, but thank you. Much here else?   55
It may be so. Why, think that these good works
May help to hide your bad. I'll not betray you;
Although you be but extraordinary,[1]
And have it only in title, it sufficeth;
Go home, be melancholic too, or mad.   [*Exit* CORVINO.]   60

VOLPONE. Rare Mosca! How his villainy becomes him!

VOLTORE. Certain he doth delude all these for me.

CORBACCIO. Mosca the heir!

---

5. Salt-cellar.
6. Once and for all.
7. Lady Would-be has apparently offered sexual favors to Mosca.
8. Money.
9. A pimp for your own wife.
1. I.e., not a full-fledged pimp or cuckold, just one who did his best to be such.

VOLPONE.   O, his four eyes have found it.[2]
CORBACCIO. I am cozened, cheated, by a parasite slave;
    Harlot,[3] thou hast gulled me.
MOSCA.   Yes, sir. Stop your mouth,   65
    Or I shall draw the only tooth is left.
    Are not you he, that filthy covetous wretch,
    With the three legs[4] that here, in hope of prey,
    Have, any time this three years, snuffed about
    With your most groveling nose, and would have hired   70
    Me to the poisoning of my patron, sir?
    Are not you he that have today in court
    Professed the disinheriting of your son?
    Perjured yourself? Go home, and die, and stink;
    If you but croak a syllable, all comes out: 75
    Away, and call your porters!   [*Exit* CORBACCIO.]
                         Go, go, stink.
VOLPONE. Excellent varlet!
VOLTORE.   Now, my faithful Mosca,
    I find thy constancy—
MOSCA.   Sir?
VOLTORE.   Sincere.
MOSCA.   [*writing*] A *table*
    Of *porphyry*—I mar'l you'll be thus troublesome.
VOLTORE. Nay, leave off now, they are gone.
MOSCA.   Why, who are you?   80
    What! Who did send for you? O, cry you mercy,
    Reverend sir! Good faith, I am grieved for you,
    That any chance of mine should thus defeat
    Your (I must needs say) most deserving travails:
    But I protest, sir, it was cast upon me,   85
    And I could almost wish to be without it,
    But that the will o' the dead must be observed.
    Marry, my joy is that you need it not;
    You have a gift, sir (thank your education),
    Will never let you want, while there are men,   90
    And malice, to breed causes. Would I had
    But half the like, for all my fortune, sir!
    If I have any suits (as I do hope,
    Things being so easy and direct, I shall not)
    I will make bold with your obstreperous[5] aid—   95

2. Corbaccio wears spectacles.
3. A term frequently used of men, in the sense of "scoundrel."
4. I.e., two plus a cane or crutch.
5. Noisy.

Conceive me—for your fee, sir. In meantime,
You that have so much law, I know have the conscience
Not to be covetous of what is mine.
Good sir, I thank you for my plate; 'twill help
To set up a young man.[6] Good faith, you look   100
As you were costive;[7] best go home and purge, sir.
                                        [Exit VOLTORE.]
VOLPONE. [comes from behind the curtain] Bid him eat lettuce
    well.[8] My witty mischief,
    Let me embrace thee. O that I could now
    Transform thee to a Venus!—Mosca, go,
    Straight take my habit of clarissimo,[9]   105
    And walk the streets; be seen, torment them more.
    We must pursue, as well as plot. Who would
    Have lost this feast?
MOSCA.   I doubt it will lose them.
VOLPONE. O, my recovery shall recover all.
    That I could now but think on some disguise   110
    To meet them in, and ask them questions;
    How I would vex them still at every turn!
MOSCA. Sir, I can fit you.
VOLPONE.   Canst thou?
MOSCA.   Yes, I know
    One o' the commandatori, sir, so like you;
    Him will I straight make drunk, and bring you his habit.[1]   115
VOLPONE. A rare disguise, and answering thy brain!
    O, I will be a sharp disease unto them.
MOSCA. Sir, you must look for curses—
VOLPONE.   Till they burst;
The fox fares ever best when he is cursed.   [Exeunt.]

ACT V   SCENE 4. A HALL IN SIR POLITIC'S HOUSE

[Enter PEREGRINE disguised, and three MERCHANTS.]
PEREGRINE. Am I enough disguised?
1 MERCHANT.   I warrant you.
PEREGRINE. All my ambition is to fright him only.
2 MERCHANT. If you could ship him away, 'twere excellent.

---

6. I.e., himself.
7. Constipated; "purge": take a laxative.
8. In classical days, lettuce was thought to have mild purgative powers.
9. Mosca, in putting on the distinctive dress of a nobleman (clarissimo), is running a big risk—
   laws about wearing the costume of one's rank were strict and severe.
1. Volpone now assumes a common sergeant's uniform, and over it a loose black robe, with a
   red cap and two brass buttons.

3 MERCHANT. To Zant, or to Aleppo?[2]
PEREGRINE.   Yes, and have his
  Adventures put i' the Book of Voyages,   5
  And his gulled story[3] registered for truth.
  Well, gentlemen, when I am in a while,
  And that you think us warm in our discourse,
  Know your approaches.
1 MERCHANT.   Trust it to our care. [*Exeunt* MERCHANTS.]
        [*Enter* WAITING WOMAN.]
PEREGRINE. Save you, fair lady! Is Sir Pol within?   10
WOMAN. I do not know, sir.
PEREGRINE.   Pray you say unto him,
  Here is a merchant, upon earnest business,
  Desires to speak with him.
WOMAN.   I will see, sir.   [*Exit*]
PEREGRINE.   Pray you.—
  I see the family is all female here.
        [*Re-enter* WAITING WOMAN.]
WOMAN. He says, sir, he has weighty affairs of state,   15
  That now require him whole; some other time
  You may possess him.
PEREGRINE.   Pray you say again.
  If those require him whole, these will exact him,[4]
  Whereof I bring him tidings. [*Exit* WOMAN.]—What might be
  His grave affair of state now? How to make   20
  Bolognian sausages[5] here in Venice, sparing
  One o' the ingredients?
        [*Re-enter* WAITING WOMAN.]
WOMAN.   Sir, he says, he knows
  By your word *tidings*, that you are no statesman,[6]
  And therefore wills you stay.
PEREGRINE.   Sweet, pray you return him;
  I have not read so many proclamations,   25
  And studied them for words, as he has done—
  But—here he deigns to come.   [*Exit* WOMAN.]
        [*Enter* SIR POLITIC.]
SIR POLITIC.   Sir, I must crave
  Your courteous pardon. There hath chanced today

---

2. Zant, an Ionian island famous for its currants and controlled by the Venetians (modern name, Zakynthos); from there, Sir Politic could be shipped to Aleppo, Smyrna, or any other remote city of the Middle East.
3. The story of his gulling.
4. Cause him to pay attention.
5. Sausages of Bologna were so famous that *boloney* is still a word in general use.
6. "Tidings" were what normal people received; a secret-service operative would get "intelligence."

Unkind disaster 'twixt my lady and me;
And I was penning my apology,   30
To give her satisfaction, as you came now.
PEREGRINE. Sir, I am grieved I bring you worse disaster:
The gentleman you met at the port today,
That told you he was newly arrived—
SIR POLITIC.   Ay, was
A fugitive punk?[7]
PEREGRINE.   No, sir, a spy set on you;   35
And he has made relation to the senate,
That you professed to him to have a plot
To sell the state of Venice to the Turk.[8]
SIR POLITIC. O me!
PEREGRINE.   For which, warrants are signed by this time,
To apprehend you, and to search your study   40
For papers—
SIR POLITIC.   Alas, sir, I have none but notes
Drawn out of play-books[9]—
PEREGRINE.   All the better, sir.
SIR POLITIC. And some essays. What shall I do?
PEREGRINE.   Sir, best
Convey yourself into a sugar-chest:
Or, if you could lie round, a frail[1] were rare,   45
And I could send you aboard.
SIR POLITIC.   Sir, I but talked so,
For discourse sake merely.   [Knocking within.]
PEREGRINE.   Hark! They are there.
SIR POLITIC. I am a wretch, a wretch!
PEREGRINE.   What will you do, sir?
Have you ne'er a currant-butt[2] to leap into?
They'll put you to the rack; you must be sudden.   50
SIR POLITIC. Sir, I have an engine—[3]
3 MERCHANT.   [within] Sir Politic Would-be!
2 MERCHANT. [within] Where is he?
SIR POLITIC.   That I have thought upon
    before time.
PEREGRINE. What is it?
SIR POLITIC.   I shall ne'er endure the torture.

7. A whore in flight from the marshal. (For all his vaulted subtlety, Sir Politic still believes his
   wife's deluded charge, that Peregrine was a woman in disguise.)
8. See above, 4.1.130.
9. Sir Politic's exotic information turns out to be very common. Playbooks in particular had then
   about the reputation of comic books now.
1. Flimsy fruit-basket.
2. Cask for holding currants.
3. Contrivance (i.e., the tortoise shell, below).

Marry, it is, sir, of a tortoise-shell,
Fitted for these extremities: pray you, sir, help me.   55
Here I've a place, sir, to put back my legs,
Please you to lay it on, sir, [*lies down while* PEREGRINE *places
   the shell upon him*]—With this cap,
And my black gloves, I'll lie, sir, like a tortoise,
Till they are gone.
PEREGRINE.   And call you this an engine?
SIR POLITIC. Mine own device—Good sir, bid my wife's women   60
   To burn my papers.   [*Exit* PEREGRINE.]
        [*The* MERCHANTS *rush in.*]
1 MERCHANT.   Where is he hid?
3 MERCHANT.   We must,
   And will sure find him.
2 MERCHANT.   Which is his study?
        [*Re-enter* PEREGRINE.]
1 MERCHANT.   What
   Are you, sir?
PEREGRINE.   I am a merchant, that came here
   To look upon this tortoise.
3 MERCHANT.   How!
1 MERCHANT.   St. Mark!
   What beast is this?
PEREGRINE.   It is a fish.
2 MERCHANT.   Come out here!   65
PEREGRINE. Nay, you may strike him, sir, and tread upon him:
   He'll bear a cart.
1 MERCHANT.   What, to run over him?
PEREGRINE.   Yes.
3 MERCHANT. Let's jump upon him.
2 MERCHANT.   Can he not go?
PEREGRINE.   He creeps, sir.
1 MERCHANT. Let's see him creep. [*Pokes* him.]
PEREGRINE.   No, good sir, you will hurt him.
2 MERCHANT. Heart, I will see him creep, or prick his guts.   70
3 MERCHANT. Come out here!
PEREGRINE.   Pray you, sir! [*aside to* SIR POLITIC]
                                  —Creep a little.
1 MERCHANT.   Forth.
2 MERCHANT. Yet farther.
PEREGRINE.   Good sir! [*aside to* SIR POLITIC] Creep!
2 MERCHANT.   We'll see his legs.
        [*They pull off the shell and discover him.*]
3 MERCHANT. Gods' so', he has garters!
1 MERCHANT.   Ay, and gloves!

2 MERCHANT.   Is this
  Your fearful tortoise?
PEREGRINE. [*discovering himself*] Now, Sir Pol, we are even;
  For your next project I shall be prepared.   75
  I am sorry for the funeral of your notes, sir.
1 MERCHANT. 'Twere a rare motion[4] to be seen in Fleet Street.
2 MERCHANT. Ay, in the Term.
1 MERCHANT.   Or Smithfield, in the fair.
3 MERCHANT. Methinks 'tis but a melancholic sight.
PEREGRINE. Farewell, most politic tortoise!
                            [*Exeunt* PEREGRINE *and* MERCHANTS.]
        [*Re-enter* WAITING-WOMAN.]
SIR POLITIC.   Where's my lady?   80
  Knows she of this?
WOMAN.   I know not, sir.
SIR POLITIC.   Inquire.
  O, I shall be the fable of all feasts,
  The freight of the *gazetti*,[5] ship-boys' tale;
  And, which is worst, even talk for ordinaries.
WOMAN. My lady's come most melancholic home,   85
  And says, sir, she will straight to sea, for physic.[6]
SIR POLITIC. And I, to shun this place and clime forever,
  Creeping with house on back, and think it well
  To shrink my poor head in my politic shell.   [*Exeunt.*]

        ACT V   SCENE 5. *A ROOM IN* VOLPONE'S HOUSE

  [*Enter* MOSCA *in the habit of a* clarissimo, *and* VOLPONE *in
  that of a* commandatore.]
VOLPONE. Am I then like him?
MOSCA.   O, sir, you are he.
  No man can sever[7] you.
VOLPONE.   Good.
MOSCA.   But what am I?
VOLPONE. 'Fore heaven, a brave *clarissimo*; thou becom'st it!
  Pity thou wert not born one.
MOSCA.   If I hold
  My made one, 'twill be well.
VOLPONE.   I'll go and see   5

---

4. Puppet show. "Fleet Street": then as now a busy street in central London. "Smithfield": where
   Bartholomew Fair was held. All fairs were especially busy in "Term," the time when the law
   courts were in session. These Venetian *mercatori* are remarkably conversant with London
   manners.
5. Subject of the newsletters; "talk for the ordinaries": tavern gossip.
6. For her health.
7. Distinguish.

What news first at the court.   [*Exit.*]
MOSCA.   Do so. My fox
   Is out of his hole, and ere he shall re-enter,
   I'll make him languish in his borrowed case,[8]
   Except he come to composition with me.—
   Androgyno, Castrone, Nano!
         [*Enter* ANDROGYNO, CASTRONE, *and* NANO.]
ALL.   Here.   10
MOSCA. Go, recreate yourselves abroad; go, sport.—   [*Exeunt.*]
   So, now I have the keys, and am possessed.
   Since he will needs be dead afore his time,
   I'll bury him, or gain by him. I am his heir,
   And so will keep me, till he share at least.   15
   To cozen him of all, were but a cheat
   Well placed; no man would construe it a sin:
   Let his sport pay for't. This is called the fox-trap.   [*Exit.*]

               ACT V   SCENE 6. *A STREET*

         [*Enter* CORBACCIO *and* CORVINO.]
CORBACCIO. They say the court is set.
CORVINO.   We must maintain
   Our first tale good, for both our reputations.
CORBACCIO. Why? Mine's no tale; my son would there have
   killed me.
CORVINO. That's true, I had forgot. [*aside*]—Mine is, I'm sure.
   But for your will, sir.
CORBACCIO.   Ay, I'll come upon him   5
   For that hereafter, now his patron's dead.
         [*Enter* VOLPONE *in disguise.*]
VOLPONE. Signor Corvino! And Corbaccio! Sir,
   Much joy unto you.
CORVINO.   Of what?
VOLPONE.   The sudden good
   Dropped down upon you—
CORBACCIO.   Where?
VOLPONE.   And none knows how,
   From old Volpone, sir,
CORBACCIO.   Out, arrant knave!   10
VOLPONE. Let not your too much wealth, sir, make you furious.
CORBACCIO. Away, thou varlet.
VOLPONE.   Why, sir?
CORBACCIO.   Dost thou mock me?

---

8. His false costume.

VOLPONE. You mock the world, sir; did you not change[9] wills?
CORBACCIO. Out, harlot!
VOLPONE.   O! Belike you are the man,
　Signor Corvino? Faith, you carry it well;   15
　You grow not mad withal; I love your spirit.
　You are not over-leavened[1] with your fortune.
　You should have some would swell now, like a wine-vat.
　With such an autumn—Did he give you all, sir?
CORVINO. Avoid, you rascal!
VOLPONE.   Troth, your wife has shown   20
　Herself a very woman,[2] but you are well,
　You need not care, you have a good estate
　To bear it out, sir; better by this chance.
　Except Corbaccio have a share.
CORBACCIO.   Hence, varlet.
VOLPONE. You will not be a 'known, sir; why, 'tis wise.   25
　Thus do all gamesters, at all games, dissemble,
　No man will seem to win. [*Exeunt* CORVINO *and* CORBACCIO.]
　　　　　　　　　　—Here comes my vulture,
　Heaving his beak up in the air, and snuffing.

ACT V   SCENE 7

　[*Enter* VOLTORE.]
VOLTORE. Outstripped thus, by a parasite! A slave,
　Would run on errands, and make legs[3] for crumbs!
　Well, what I'll do—
VOLPONE.   The court stays for your worship.
　I e'en rejoice, sir, at your worship's happiness,
　And that it fell into so learnèd hands,   5
　That understand the fingering—
VOLTORE.   What do you mean?
VOLPONE. I mean to be a suitor to your worship
　For the small tenement, out of reparations[4]—
　That at the end of your long row of houses,
　By the Piscaria;[5] it was, in Volpone's time,   10
　Your predecessor, ere he grew diseased,
　A handsome, pretty, customed[6] bawdy-house
　As any was in Venice, none dispraised;

9. Exchange.
1. Too puffed up (like a loaf of bread).
2. I.e., promiscuous.
3. Bow and scrape.
4. Repair.
5. The fish market on the Grand Canal.
6. Well-patronized; "none dispraised": without prejudice to any of the other splendid bawdy
　houses in Venice.

But fell with him. His body and that house
Decayed together.
VOLTORE. Come, sir, leave your prating. 15
VOLPONE. Why, if your worship give me but your hand
　　That I may have the refusal, I have done.
　　'Tis a mere toy to you, sir; candle-rents,[7]
　　As your learned worship knows—
VOLTORE. What do I know?
VOLPONE. Marry, no end of your wealth, sir; God decrease it! 20
VOLTORE. Mistaking knave! What, mock'st thou my misfortune?
VOLPONE. His blessing on your heart, sir; would 'twere more!—
　　　　　　　　　　　　　　　　　[Exit VOLTORE.]
　　—Now to my first again, at the next corner. [Exit.]

ACT V　SCENE 8. *ANOTHER PART OF THE STREET*

　　[*Enter* CORBACCIO *and* CORVINO;—MOSCA *passes over the
　　stage, before them.*]
CORBACCIO. See, in our habit![8] See the impudent varlet!
CORVINO. That I could shoot mine eyes at him, like gun-stones!
　　[*Enter* VOLPONE.]
VOLPONE. But is this true, sir, of the parasite?
CORBACCIO. Again, to afflict us! Monster!
VOLPONE. In good faith, sir,
　　I'm heartily grieved, a beard of your grave length 5
　　Should be so over-reached. I never brooked[9]
　　That parasite's hair; methought his nose should cozen.
　　There still was somewhat in his look did ·promise
　　The bane of a clarissimo.[1]
CORBACCIO. Knave—
VOLPONE. Methinks
　　Yet you, that are so traded in the world, 10
　　A witty merchant, the fine bird, Corvino,
　　That have such moral emblems on your name,
　　Should not have sung your shame, and dropped your cheese,
　　To let the fox laugh at your emptiness.[2]
CORVINO. Sirrah, you think the privilege of the place, 15
　　And your red saucy cap that seems to me
　　Nailed to your jolt-head[3] with those two sequins,
　　Can warrant your abuses. Come you hither;

7. Mere drippings and leftovers, enough to buy candles with.
8. In the clothes we aristocrats are accustomed to wear.
9. Could stand.
1. I.e., trouble for an aristocrat.
2. The recurrent refrain from Aesop's fable.
3. Blockhead.

You shall perceive, sir, I dare beat you; approach.

VOLPONE. No haste, sir, I do know your valor well,   20
Since you durst publish what you are, sir.[4]

CORVINO.   Tarry,
I'd speak with you.

VOLPONE.   Sir, sir, another time—

CORVINO. Nay, now.

VOLPONE.   O lord, sir! I were a wise man,
Would stand the fury of a distracted cuckold. [*As he is
running off, re-enter* MOSCA.]

CORBACCIO. What, come again!

VOLPONE.   Upon 'em, Mosca; save me.   25

CORBACCIO. The air's infected where he breathes.

CORVINO.   Let's fly him.
                    [*Exeunt* CORVINO *and* CORBACCIO.]

VOLPONE. Excellent basilisk![5] Turn upon the vulture.

ACT V   SCENE 9

[*Enter* VOLTORE.]

VOLTORE. Well, flesh-fly, it is summer with you now;
Your winter will come on.

MOSCA.   Good advocate,
Prithee not rail, nor threaten out of place thus;
Thou'lt make a solecism, as madam says.[6]
Get you a biggen[7] more; your brain breaks loose.   [*Exit.*]   5

VOLTORE. Well, sir.

VOLPONE.   Would you have me beat the insolent slave,
Throw dirt upon his first good clothes?

VOLTORE.   This same
Is doubtless some familiar.

VOLPONE.   Sir, the court,
In troth, stays for you. I am mad, a mule
That never read Justinian,[8] should get up,   10
And ride an advocate. Had you no quirk
To avoid gullage,[9] sir, by such a creature?
I hope you do but jest; he has not done it;
This's but confederacy[1] to blind the rest.

---

4. A cuckold.
5. A mythical beast capable of killing with a glance.
6. The "solecism" of Lady Politic is above, 4.2.43.
7. A little skullcap worn by lawyers.
8. Lawyers often rode mules to court; here Volpone tells Voltore that he is allowing the mule (i.e., Mosca), who never read Justinian (a Roman emperor who codified the legal code), to ride him.
9. Being deceived.
1. I.e., a conspiracy between you and Mosca.

You are the heir?

VOLTORE.   A strange, officious,   15
   Troublesome knave! Thou dost torment me.

VOLPONE.   I know—
   It cannot be, sir, that you should be cozened;
   'Tis not within the wit of man to do it;
   You are so wise, so prudent; and 'tis fit
   That wealth and wisdom still should go together.   [*Exeunt.*]   20

ACT V   SCENE 10. *THE SCRUTINEO*

   [*Enter* AVOCATORE, NOTARIO, BONARIO, CELIA, CORBACCIO,
      CORVINO, COMMANDATORI, SAFFI, *&c.*]

1 AVOCATORE. Are all the parties here?

NOTARIO.   All but the advocate.

2 AVOCATORE. And here he comes.
      [*Enter* VOLTORE *and* VOLPONE.]

1 AVOCATORE.   Then bring them forth to sentence.

VOLTORE. O, my most honored fathers, let your mercy
   Once win upon your justice, to forgive—
   I am distracted——

VOLPONE.   [*aside*] What will he do now?

VOLTORE.   O,   5
   I know not which to address myself to first;
   Whether your fatherhoods, or these innocents—

CORVINO. [*aside*] Will he betray himself?

VOLPONE.   Whom equally
   I have abused, out of most covetous ends—

CORVINO. The man is mad!

CORBACCIO.   What's that?

CORVINO.   He is possessed.   10

VOLTORE. For which, now struck in conscience, here I prostrate
   Myself at your offended feet, for pardon.

1, 2 AVOCATORI. Arise.

CELIA.   O heaven, how just thou art!

VOLPONE.   [*aside*] I am caught
   In mine own noose—

CORVINO. [*to Corbaccio*] Be constant, sir; nought now
   Can help, but impudence.

1 AVOCATORE.   Speak forward.

COMMENDATORE.   Silence!   15

VOLTORE. It is not passion in me, reverend fathers,
   But only conscience, conscience, my good sires,
   That makes me now tell truth. That parasite,

That knave, hath been the instrument of all.

1 AVOCATORE. Where is that knave? Fetch him.

VOLPONE.   I go.   [*Exit.*]

CORVINO.   Grave fathers,   20
    This man's distracted; he confessed it now;
    For, hoping to be old Volpone's heir,
    Who now is dead—

3 AVOCATORE.   How!

2 AVOCATORE.   Is Volpone dead?

CORVINO. Dead since, grave fathers.

BONARIO.   O sure vengeance!

1 AVOCATORE.   Stay,
    Then he was no deceiver.

VOLTORE.   O no, none;   25
    The parasite, grave fathers.

CORVINO.   He does speak
    Out of mere envy, 'cause the servant's made
    The thing he gaped for. Please your fatherhoods,
    This is the truth, though I'll not justify
    The other,[2] but he may be some-deal faulty.   30

VOLTORE. Ay, to your hopes, as well as mine, Corvino.
    But I'll use modesty. Pleaseth your wisdoms,
    To view these certain notes, and but confer them;
    As I hope favor, they shall speak clear truth.

CORVINO. The devil has entered him!

BONARIO.   Or bides in you.   35

4 AVOCATORE. We have done ill, by a public officer
    To send for him, if he be heir.

2 AVOCATORE.   For whom?

4 AVOCATORE. Him that they call the parasite.

3 AVOCATORE.   'Tis true,
    He is a man of great estate, now left.[3]

4 AVOCATORE. Go you, and learn his name, and say, the court   40
    Entreats his presence here, but to the clearing
    Of some few doubts.   [*Exit* NOTARIO.]

2 AVOCATORE.   This same's a labyrinth!

1 AVOCATORE. Stand you unto your first report?

CORVINO.   My state,
    My life, my fame—

BONARIO.   Where is it?

CORVINO.   Are at the stake.

---

2. I.e., Mosca.

3. As an aristocrat (which he is automatically if he has a lot of money), Mosca is not to be summoned by a common official.

1 AVOCATORE. Is yours so too?

CORBACCIO.   The advocate's a knave,   45
  And has a forkèd tongue—

2 AVOCATORE.   Speak to the point.

CORBACCIO. So is the parasite too.

1 AVOCATORE.   This is confusion.

VOLTORE. I do beseech your fatherhoods, read but those—
  [*Giving them papers.*]

CORVINO. And credit nothing the false spirit hath writ;
  It cannot be, but he's possessed,[4] grave fathers.   50

ACT V   SCENE 11. *A STREET*

  [*Enter* VOLPONE.]

VOLPONE. To make a snare for mine own neck! And run
  My head into it, wilfully! With laughter!
  When I had newly 'scaped, was free, and clear!
  Out of mere wantonness! O, the dull devil
  Was in this brain of mine when I devised it,   5
  And Mosca gave it second; he must now
  Help to sear up[5] this vein, or we bleed dead.
    [*Enter* NANO, ANDROGYNO, *and* CASTRONE.]
  How now! Who let you loose? Whither go you now?
  What? To buy gingerbread, or to drown kitlings?

NANO. Sir, Master Mosca called us out of doors,   10
  And bid us all go play, and took the keys.

ANDROGYNO.   Yes.

VOLPONE. Did Master Mosca take the keys? Why, so!
  I'm farther in. These are my fine conceits!
  I must be merry, with a mischief to me!
  What a vile wretch was I, that could not bear   15
  My fortune soberly! I must have my crotchets,
  And my conundrums![6] Well, go you, and seek him.
  His meaning may be truer than my fear.
  Bid him, he straight come to me to the court;
  Thither will I, and, if't be possible,   20
  Unscrew my advocate, upon new hopes.
  When I provoked him, then I lost myself.   [*Exeunt.*]

---

4. I.e., demonically possessed by a devil inside him.
5. Cauterize.
6. "Crotchets" and "conundrums" are both whims or fancies.

ACT V   SCENE 12. *THE SCRUTINEO*

[AVOCATORI, BONARIO, CELIA, CORBACCIO, CORVINO, COM-
     MANDATORI, SAFFI, &c. *as before.*]

1 AVOCATORE. [*showing the papers*] These things can ne'er be
     reconciled. He here
  Professeth that the gentleman was wronged,
  And that the gentlewoman was brought thither,
  Forced by her husband, and there left.
VOLTORE.   Most true.
CELIA. How ready is heaven to those that pray!
1 AVOCATORE.   But that   5
  Volpone would have ravished her, he holds
  Utterly false, knowing his impotence.
CORVINO. Grave fathers, he's possessed; again, I say,
  Possessed; nay, if there be possession and
  Obsession, he has both.[7]
3 AVOCATORE.   Here comes our officer.   10
     [*Enter* VOLPONE, *still in disguise.*]
VOLPONE. The parasite will straight be here, grave fathers.
4 AVOCATORE. You might invent some other name, sir varlet.
3 AVOCATORE. Did not the notary meet him?
VOLPONE.   Not that I know.
4 AVOCATORE. His coming will clear all.
2 AVOCATORE.   Yet, it is misty.
VOLTORE. May't please your fatherhoods.
VOLPONE.   [*Whispers to* VOLTORE.] Sir, the parasite   15
  Willed me to tell you, that his master lives;
  That you are still the man; your hopes the same;
  And this was only a jest—
VOLTORE.   How?
VOLPONE.   Sir, to try
  If you were firm, and how you stood affected.
VOLTORE. Art sure he lives?
VOLPONE.   Do I live, sir?
VOLTORE.   O me!   20
  I was too violent.
VOLPONE.   Sir, you may redeem it.
  They said you were possessed; fall down, and seem so.
  I'll help to make it good. [VOLTORE *falls.*]—God bless the
     man!
  [*aside*] Stop your wind hard, and swell.—See, see, see, see!

7. Possession is a devil attacking the mind from within, obsession is the same temptation from
without.

He vomits crooked pins![8] His eyes are set,   25
   Like a dead hare's hung in a poulter's[9] shop!
   His mouth's running away! Do you see, signor?
   Now it is in his belly.
CORVINO.   Ay, the devil!
VOLPONE. Now in his throat.
CORVINO.   Ay, I perceive it plain.
VOLPONE. 'Twill out, 'twill out! Stand clear! See where it flies,   30
   In shape of a blue toad with a bat's wings!
   Do not you see it, sir?
CORBACCIO.   What? I think I do.
CORVINO. 'Tis too manifest.
VOLPONE.   Look! He comes to himself!
VOLTORE. Where am I?
VOLPONE.   Take good heart, the worst is past, sir.
   You are dispossessed.
1 AVOCATORE.   What accident is this?   35
2 AVOCATORE. Sudden and full of wonder!
3 AVOCATORE.   If he were
   Possessed, as it appears, all this is nothing. [*He waves the
      notes.*]
CORVINO. He has been often subject to these fits.
1 AVOCATORE. Show him that writing.—Do you know it, sir?
VOLPONE. [*whispers to* VOLTORE] Deny it, sir, forswear it; know it
   not.   40
VOLTORE. Yes, I do know it well, it is my hand;
   But all that it contains is false.
BONARIO.   O practice![1]
2 AVOCATORE. What maze is this?
1 AVOCATORE.   Is he not guilty then,
   Whom you there name the parasite?
VOLTORE.   Grave fathers,
   No more than his good patron, old Volpone.   45
AVOCATORE. Why, he is dead.
VOLTORE.   O no, my honored fathers,
   He lives—
1 AVOCATORE. How! Lives?
VOLTORE.   Lives.
2 AVOCATORE.   This is subtler yet!
3 AVOCATORE. You said he was dead.
VOLTORE.   Never.

---

8. The symptoms that Volpone "sees," and persuades others to see, were standard. The "blue
   toad with bat's wings" below (line 31) is the demon himself.
9. A dealer in fowl and small game.
1. Deceit.

4 AVOCATORE.   [*to* CORVINO] You said so!

CORVINO.   I heard so.

4 AVOCATORE. Here comes the gentleman; make him way.[2]
    [*Enter* MOSCA *as a* clarissimo.]

3 AVOCATORE.   A stool.

4 AVOCATORE. [*aside*] A proper man; and, were Volpone dead,   50
  A fit match for my daughter.

3 AVOCATORE.   Give him way.

VOLPONE. [*aside to* MOSCA] Mosca, I was almost lost; the
    advocate
  Had betrayed all; but now it is recovered;
  All's on the hinge again—say, I am living.

MOSCA. What busy knave is this! Most reverend fathers,   55
  I sooner had attended your grave pleasures,
  But that my order for the funeral
  Of my dear patron did require me—

VOLPONE.   [*aside*] Mosca!

MOSCA. Whom I intend to bury like a gentleman.

VOLPONE. [*aside*] Ay, quick[3] and cozen me of all.

2 AVOCATORE.   Still stranger!   60
  More intricate!

1 AVOCATORE.   And come about again!

4 AVOCATORE. [*aside*] It is a match, my daughter is bestowed.

MOSCA. [*aside to* VOLPONE] Will you give me half?

VOLPONE.   First, I'll be hanged.

MOSCA.   I know
  Your voice is good, cry not so loud.

1 AVOCATORE.   Demand
  The advocate.—Sir, did you not affirm   65
  Volpone was alive?

VOLPONE.   Yes, and he is;
  This gentleman[4] told me so. [*aside to* MOSCA] Thou shalt have
    half.

MOSCA. Whose drunkard is this same? Speak, some that know
    him:
  I never saw his face. [*aside to* VOLPONE] I cannot now
  Afford it you so cheap.

VOLPONE.   No!

1 AVOCATORE.   What say you?   70

VOLTORE. The officer told me.

VOLPONE.   I did, grave fathers,

---

2. Jonson's audience would be scandalized at the instant transformation of a parasite into a
  gentleman, partly because they had seen it happen frequently in their own land.
3. Alive.
4. Mosca.

And will maintain he lives, with mine own life,
And that this creature [*points to* MOSCA] told me. [*aside*] I was
    born
With all good stars my enemies.
MOSCA.   Most grave fathers,
    If such an insolence as this must pass   75
    Upon me, I am silent: 'twas not this
    For which you sent, I hope.
2 AVOCATORE.   Take him away.
VOLPONE. [*aside*] Mosca!
3 AVOCATORE.   Let him be whipped.
VOLPONE.   Wilt thou betray me?
    Cozen me?
3 AVOCATORE. And taught to bear himself
    Toward a person of his rank.
                                    Away. [*The* OFFICERS *seize* VOLPONE.]   80
MOSCA. I humbly thank your fatherhoods.
VOLPONE.   [*aside*] Soft, soft. Whipped!
    And lose all that I have! If I confess,
    It cannot be much more.
4 AVOCATORE.   Sir, are you married?[5]
VOLPONE. They'll be allied anon; I must be resolute.
    The fox shall here uncase.[6] [*Throws off his disguise.*]
MOSCA.   Patron!
VOLPONE.   Nay, now   85
    My ruins shall not come alone; your match
    I'll hinder sure: my substance shall not glue you
    Nor screw you into a family.
MOSCA.   Why, patron!
VOLPONE. I am Volpone, and this [*pointing to* MOSCA] is my
        knave;
    This, [*to* VOLTORE] his own knave; this, [*to* CORBACCIO]
        avarice's fool;   90
    This, [*to* CORVINO] a chimera[7] of wittol, fool, and knave.
    And, reverend fathers, since we all can hope
    Nought but a sentence, let's not now despair it.
    You hear me brief.
CORVINO.   May it please your fatherhoods—
COMMANDATORE.   Silence!
1 AVOCATORE. The knot is now undone by miracle.   95
2 AVOCATORE. Nothing can be more clear.

---

5. The question is addressed to Mosca.
6. Remove his mask.
7. The chimera was an unnatural imaginary creature compounded of lion, goat, and serpent;
   "wittol": one who willingly gives in to his wife's adultery.

3 AVOCATORE.   Or can more prove
   These innocent.
1 AVOCATORE.   Give them their liberty.
BONARIO. Heaven could not long let such gross crimes be hid.
2 AVOCATORE. If this be held the highway to get riches,
   May I be poor!
3 AVOCATORE.   This is not gain, but torment.   100
1 AVOCATORE. These possess wealth, as sick men possess fevers.
   Which trulier may be said to possess them.[8]
2 AVOCATORE.   Disrobe that parasite.
CORVINO, MOSCA.   Most honored fathers!
1 AVOCATORE. Can you plead aught to stay the course of justice?
   If you can, speak.
CORVINO, VOLTORE. We beg favor.
CELIA.   And mercy.   105
1 AVOCATORE. You hurt your innocence, suing for the guilty.
   Stand forth; and first, the parasite. You appear
   T'have been the chiefest minister, if not plotter,
   In all these lewd impostures; and now, lastly,
   Have with your impudence abused the court,   110
   And habit of a gentleman of Venice,
   Being a fellow of no birth or blood:
   For which our sentence is, first, thou be whipped;
   Then live perpetual prisoner in our galleys.
VOLPONE. I thank you for him.
MOSCA.   Bane[9] to thy wolfish nature!   115
1 AVOCATORE. Deliver him to the Saffi.   [MOSCA *is led out.*]
     —Thou, Volpone,
   By blood and rank a gentleman, canst not fall
   Under like censure; but our judgment on thee
   Is, that thy substance all be straight confiscate
   To the hospital of the Incurabili.[1]   120
   And, since the most was gotten by imposture,
   By feigning lame, gout, palsy, and such diseases,
   Thou art to lie in prison, cramped with irons,
   Till thou be'st sick and lame indeed. Remove him. [*He is
    taken away.*]
VOLPONE. This is called mortifying of a fox.   125
1 AVOCATORE. Thou, Voltore, to take away the scandal
   Thou hast given all worthy men of thy profession,
   Art banished from their fellowship, and our state.

---

8. The aphorism is Seneca's (Epistle 119, par. 12).
9. Poison. Wolfsbane is a poisonous plant. "Saffi": guards.
1. There was a Hospital of the Incurables in Venice.

Corbaccio!—bring him near—we here possess
Thy son of all thy state[2] and confine thee   130
To the monastery of San Spirito;
Where, since thou knew'st not how to live well here,
Thou shalt be learned[3] to die well.
CORBACCIO.   Ha! What said he?
COMMANDATORE. You shall know anon, sir.
1 AVOCATORE.   Thou, Corvino, shalt
Be straight embarked from thine own house, and rowed   135
Round about Venice, through the Grand Canal,
Wearing a cap with fair long ass's ears
Instead of horns; and so to mount, a paper
Pinned on thy breast, to the Berlina[4]——
CORVINO.   Yes,
And have mine eyes beat out with stinking fish,   140
Bruised fruit, and rotten eggs—'Tis well. I'm glad
I shall not see my shame yet.
1 AVOCATORE.   And to expiate
Thy wrongs done to thy wife, thou art to send her
Home to her father, with her dowry trebled:
And these are all your judgments—
ALL.   Honored fathers.   145
1 AVOCATORE. Which may not be revoked. Now you begin,
When crimes are done, and past, and to be punished,
To think what your crimes are: away with them!
Let all that see these vices thus rewarded,
Take heart, and love to study 'em! Mischiefs feed   150
Like beasts, till they be fat, and then they bleed.   [Exeunt.]
     [VOLPONE comes forward.]
The seasoning of a play is the applause.
Now, though the fox be punished by the laws,
He yet doth hope, there is no suffering due,
For any fact which he hath done 'gainst you;   155
If there be, censure him; here he doubtful stands:
If not, fare jovially, and clap your hands.   [Exit.]

THE END.

1606

---

2. I.e., convey to your son your entire estate.
3. Taught.
4. Pillory.

Epicoene

or

The Silent Woman

The Persons of the Play[1]

MOROSE, *a gentleman that loves no noise.*

SIR DAUPHINE EUGENIE, *his nephew.*

CLERIMONT, *a gentleman, his friend.*

TRUEWIT, *another friend.*

EPICOENE, *a young gentleman supposed the Silent Woman.*

SIR JOHN DAW, *a Knight, her servant.*

SIR AMOROUS LA FOOLE, *a Knight.*

THOMAS OTTER, *a land and sea captain.*

CUTBEARD, *a barber.*

MUTE, *one of* MOROSE'S *servants.*

PARSON.

LADY HAUGHTY
LADY CENTAUR } *Ladies Collegiates.*
MISTRESS MAVIS

MISTRESS OTTER, *the Captain's wife*
MISTRESS TRUSTY, *the* LADY HAUGHTY'S *woman* } *Pretenders.*

PAGES, SERVANTS, &c.

---

1. As is customary in Jonson's plays, the names of his dramatic persons indicate their character. Some that are not especially obvious are: Morose: his name carries the modern meaning of "sullen" but also suggests the older sense of being overly attached to a habit (from the Latin *mos/moris*, custom); Sir Dauphine Eugenie: the dauphin was the successor to the king of France, although Sir Dauphine's name is given in the feminine form—here he is only heir to Morose's estate; Clerimont: brightness, clarity; Truewit: "wit" means here not just amusing or clever but denotes one of intellectual ability and talent as well; Epicoene: pertaining to both the male and female sexes; Sir John Daw: his name is reminiscent of the jackdaw, a bird known for its chattering and petty thefts; Thomas Otter and Mistress Otter: the otter is an amphibious creature who lives on both land and sea, and the Otter marriage is similarly difficult to classify; Lady Centaur: the centaur was a mythological animal who was half horse, half human; Ladies Collegiates: a self-governed academy of women dedicated to a knowledge of literature and society; Mavis: ill-face; Pretenders: pretenders to the "learning" that the Ladies Collegiate claim to embody.

THE SCENE: *LONDON*

Prologue

Truth says, of old, the art of making plays
　　Was to content the people; and their praise
　　Was to the poet money, wine, and bays.[2]
But in this age a sect of writers are,
　　That only for particular likings care,   5
　　And will taste nothing that is popular.
With such we mingle neither brains nor breasts;[3]
　　Our wishes, like to those make public feasts,
　　Are not to please the cook's taste, but the guests.
Yet if those cunning palates hither come,   10
　　They shall find guests' entreaty, and good room;
　　And though all relish not, sure there will be some,
That when they leave their seats shall make them say,
　　Who wrote that piece, could so have wrote a play;
　　But that he knew this was the better way.   15
For, to present all custard or all tart,
　　And have no other meats to bear a part,
　　Or to want[4] bread and salt, were but coarse art.
The poet prays you, then, with better thought
　　To sit; and when his cates[5] are all in brought,   20
　　Though there be none far-fet,[6] there will dear-bought
Be, fit for ladies: some for lords, knights, squires;
　　Some for your waiting-wench, and city-wires;[7]
　　Some for your men and daughters of Whitefriars.
Nor is it only while you keep your seat   25
　　Here, that his feast will last; but you shall eat
　　A week at ord'naries[8] on his broken meat;
　　　　　If his muse be true,
　　　　　Who commends her to you.

---

2. Laurels, the poet's crown.
3. Hearts.
4. Lack.
5. Dishes.
6. Farfetched, exotic.
7. Fancy ladies (from the wires holding up their ruffs). Whitefriars was the London district, named from a long-abolished monastery, where *Epicoene* was first performed.
8. Public taverns; "broken meats": leftovers.

Another

The ends of all, who for the scene do write,
Are, or should be, to profit and delight.
And still't hath been the praise of all best times,
So persons were not touched, to tax the crimes.
Then in this play, which we present tonight,   5
And make the object of your ear and sight,
On forfeit of your selves, think nothing true;
Lest so you make the maker to judge you.
For he knows poet never credit gained
By writing truths, but things like truths, well feigned.   10
If any yet will, with particular sleight
Of application, wrest what he doth write,
And that he meant or him or her, will say;
They make a libel, which he made a play.

Act I

ACT 1   SCENE 1. CLERIMONT'S HOUSE

[*Enter* CLERIMONT, *making himself ready, followed by his*
PAGE.]

CLERIMONT. Have you got the song yet perfect I gave you, boy?

PAGE. Yes, sir.

CLERIMONT. Let me hear it.

PAGE. You shall, sir; but, i' faith, let nobody else.

CLERIMONT. Why, I pray?   5

PAGE. It will get you the dangerous name of a poet in town, sir,
besides me a perfect deal of ill will at the mansion you wot[1] of,
whose lady is the argument of it; where now I am the welcom'st
thing under a man that comes there.

CLERIMONT. I think; and above a man, too, if the truth were   10
racked[2] out of you.

PAGE. No, faith, I'll confess before, sir. The gentlewomen play with

9. *Epicoene* got into trouble, and may even have been suppressed on its first run, because of an allusion in Act 5, scene 1, to the prince of Moldavia: he was a fraud who visited England in 1607, talked King James out of some money, and after his departure gave out that he was going to marry the king's cousin, Lady Arabella Stuart. Since Lady Arabella was, according to the lineage-experts, next in line for the throne of England, both Elizabeth and James had long ago determined that she should not marry. Whether Jonson really alluded to the lady in Act 5 of *Epicoene*, Arabella thought he did; though out of the royal favor, she was strong enough to have steps taken against Jonson, in response to which he evidently wrote this prologue.
1. Know.
2. The rack was a common instrument of torture for dragging confessions out of criminals.

me, and throw me o' the bed, and carry me in to my Lady; and she
kisses me with her oiled face, and puts a peruke[3] o' my head, and
asks me an[4] I will wear her gown; and I say no. And then she   15
hits me a blow o' the ear, and calls me innocent, and lets me go.

CLERIMONT. No marvel if the door be kept shut against your master, when the entrance is so easy to you——Well, sir, you shall
go there no more, lest I be fain to seek your voice in my lady's
rushes a fortnight hence.[5] Sing, sir.   [PAGE *sings*.]   20
    [*Enter* TRUEWIT.]

TRUEWIT. Why, here's the man that can melt away his time, and
never feels it! What between his mistress abroad and his ingle[6]
at home, high fare, soft lodging, fine clothes, and his fiddle, he
thinks the hours have no wings, or the day no post-horse.[7] Well,
Sir Gallant, were you struck with the plague this minute, or   25
condemned to any capital punishment tomorrow, you would
begin then to think, and value every article o' your time, esteem
it at the true rate, and give all for't.

CLERIMONT. Why, what should a man do?

TRUEWIT. Why, nothing; or that which, when 'tis done, is as idle.   30
Hearken after the next horse-race or hunting-match, lay wagers,
praise Puppy, or Peppercorn, Whitefoot, Franklin; swear upon
Whitemane's party;[8] speak aloud, that my lords may hear you; visit
my ladies at night, and be able to give them the character of every
bowler or better on the green.[9] These be the things where in   35
your fashionable men exercise themselves, and I for company.

CLERIMONT. Nay, if I have thy authority, I'll not leave yet. Come,
the other are considerations when we come to have gray heads
and weak hams, moist eyes and shrunk members. We'll think
on 'em then; then we'll pray and fast.   40

TRUEWIT. Ay, and destine only that time of age to goodness, which
our want of ability will not let us employ in evil?

CLERIMONT. Why, then 'tis time enough.

TRUEWIT. Yes; as if a man should sleep all the term,[1] and think to
effect his business the last day. O, Clerimont, this time, because   45
it is an incorporeal thing, and not subject to sense, we mock ourselves the fineliest out of it, with vanity and misery indeed; not seek-

---

3. Wig, hairpiece.
4. If.
5. Boy sopranos lose their elegant voices as they mature; Clerimont is afraid precocious experience will leave his boy's voice on the "rushes," spread on the floor of the lady's bedroom.
6. Bosom friend, sometimes with the overtone of a boy kept for homosexual purposes.
7. The post-horse—one used by messengers—should remind Clerimont that time is passing.
8. Racehorses.
9. Bowling and betting on bowling were popular pastimes for Jacobean idlers.
1. Law-terms ran for several months while the judges held sittings; even by nonlawyers, the terms
   were commonly used as measures of time.

ing an end of wretchedness, but only changing the matter still.

CLERIMONT. Nay, thou'lt not leave now——

TRUEWIT. See but our common disease! With what justice can we   50
complain that great men will not look upon us, nor be at leisure
to give our affairs such dispatch as we expect, when we will never
do it to our selves; nor hear, nor regard our selves?

CLERIMONT. Foh! Thou hast read Plutarch's 'Morals,' now,[2] or
some such tedious fellow, and it shows so vilely with thee, 'fore   55
God, 'twill spoil thy wit utterly! Talk me of pins and feathers and
ladies and rushes and such things, and leave this Stoicity alone
till thou mak'st sermons.[3]

TRUEWIT. Well, sir, if it will not take, I have learned to lose as
little of my kindness as I can. I'll do good to no man against his   60
will, certainly. When were you at the college?

CLERIMONT. What college?

TRUEWIT. As if you knew not!

CLERIMONT. No, faith, I came but from court yesterday.

TRUEWIT. Why, is it not arrived there yet, the news? A new foun-   65
dation, sir, here in the town, of ladies that call themselves the
Collegiates, an order between courtiers and country madams,
that live from their husbands and give entertainment to all the
wits and braveries of the time, as they call them; cry down, or
up, what they like or dislike in a brain or a fashion, with most   70
masculine, or rather, hermaphroditical authority;[4] and every day
gain to their college some new probationer.

CLERIMONT. Who is the president?

TRUEWIT. The grave and youthful matron, the Lady Haughty.

CLERIMONT. A pox of her autumnal face, her pieced beauty!   75
There's no man can be admitted till she be ready nowadays, till
she has painted, and perfumed, and washed, and scoured, but
the boy here; and him she wipes her oiled lips upon, like a
sponge. I have made a song—I pray thee hear it—o' the subject.
    [PAGE *sings.*]

> Still to be neat, still to be dressed   80
> As you were going to a feast,
> Still to be powdered, still perfumed;
> Lady, it is to be presumed,
> Though art's hid cause are not found,
> All is not sweet, all is not sound.   85

2. The moral essays of Greek biographer Plutarch (46–ca. 119), the so-called *Moralia*, are his
miscellaneous writings.
3. "Stoicity" is used in the loose sense of "solemn moralizing."
4. Authority of both sexes. Societies of literary ladies were novelties in the seventeenth century,
and they seemed to be encroachments on male privilege.

> Give me a look, give me a face,
> That makes simplicity a grace;
> Robes loosely flowing, hair as free—
> Such sweet neglect more taketh me,
> Than all the adulteries of art.   90
> They strike mine eyes, but not my heart.

TRUEWIT. And I am clearly on the other side; I love a good dressing before any beauty o' the world. O, a woman is then like a delicate garden, nor is there one kind of it. She may vary every hour, take often counsel of her glass, and choose the best. If she 95 have good ears, show 'em; good hair, lay it out; good legs, wear short clothes; a good hand, discover it often; practice any art to mend breath, cleanse teeth, repair eyebrows; paint, and profess it.

CLERIMONT. How! Publicly?

TRUEWIT. The doing of it, not the manner; that must be private. 100 Many things that seem foul in the doing, do please done. A lady should, indeed, study her face, when we think she sleeps; nor, when the doors are shut, should men be inquiring; all is sacred within, then. Is it for us to see their perukes put on, their false teeth, their complexion, their eyebrows, their nails? You see 105 gilders will not work, but enclosed.⁵ They must not discover how little serves, with the help of art, to adorn a great deal. How long did the canvas hang afore Aldgate?⁶ Were the people suffered to see the City's Love and Charity, while they were rude stone, before they were painted and burnished? No. No more should 110 servants approach their mistresses, but when they are complete and finished.

CLERIMONT. Well said, my Truewit.

TRUEWIT. And a wise lady will keep a guard always upon the place, that she may do things securely. I once followed a rude fellow 115 into a chamber, where the poor madam, for haste, and troubled, snatched at her peruke to cover her baldness, and put it on the wrong way.

CLERIMONT. O prodigy!

TRUEWIT. And the unconscionable knave held her in compliment 120 an hour with that reversed face, when I still looked when she should talk from the t'other side.

CLERIMONT. Why, thou shouldst have relieved her.

TRUEWIT. No, faith, I let her alone, as we'll let this argument, if you please, and pass to another. When saw you Dauphine 125 Eugenie?

---

5. Men who work with gold leaf require closed rooms to keep the airy stuff from blowing around.
6. Aldgate, a gate in the city walls, was evidently hidden behind a canvas while being reworked; Love and Charity were two painted statues on the new structure.

CLERIMONT. Not these three days. Shall we go to him this morning? He is very melancholy, I hear.

TRUEWIT. Sick of the uncle, is he? I met that stiff piece of formality, his uncle, yesterday, with a huge turban of nightcaps on his head, buckled over his ears.   130

CLERIMONT. O, that's his custom when he walks abroad. He can endure no noise, man.

TRUEWIT. So I have heard. But is the disease so ridiculous in him as it is made? They say he has been upon divers treaties with the fishwives and orange-women, and articles propounded between them. Marry, the chimney-sweepers will not be drawn in.[7]   135

CLERIMONT. No, nor the broom-men; they stand out stiffly. He cannot endure a costermonger;[8] he swoons if he hear one.

TRUEWIT. Methinks a smith should be ominous.   140

CLERIMONT. Or any hammer-man. A brazier[9] is not suffered to dwell in the parish, nor an armorer. He would have hanged a pewterer's prentice once upon a Shrove Tuesday's riot,[1] for being of that trade, when the rest were quit.

TRUEWIT. A trumpet should fright him terribly, or the hautboys![2]   145

CLERIMONT. Out of his senses. The waits[3] of the City have a pension of him, not to come near that ward.[4] This youth practiced on him one night, like the bellman,[5] and never left till he had brought him down to the door with a long-sword, and there left him flourishing with the air.   150

PAGE. Why, sir, he hath chosen a street to lie in, so narrow at both ends that it will receive no coaches, nor carts, nor any of these common noises. And therefore we that love him devise to bring him in such as we may, now and then, for his exercise, to breathe him. He would grow resty[6] else, in his ease; his virtue would rust without action. I entreated a bear-ward[7] one day to come down with the dogs of some four parishes that way, and I thank him, he did; and cried his games under Master Morose's window, till he was sent crying away with his head made a most   155

---

7. All the jokes have to do with Morose's efforts to prevent street-cries in his area of town, or to muffle noisy workshops.
8. Pushcart salesman.
9. Worker in brass.
1. Shrove Tuesday (the day before Ash Wednesday), known in other cultures as Mardi Gras, was a day of licentiousness, especially for the tradesmen's helpers and shop-assistants called as a group "prentices."
2. Oboes.
3. Bands of itinerant musicians.
4. District.
5. Bellmen wandered the streets by night, ringing their bells to indicate the hours and shouting any spectacular news aloud.
6. Restless.
7. The keeper of the bears at the garden where they were baited often roamed the streets, advertising future shows.

bleeding spectacle to the multitude. And another time, a fencer   160
marching to his prize had his drum most tragically run through,
for taking that street in his way, at my request.

TRUEWIT. A good wag! How does he for the bells?

CLERIMONT. O, in the Queen's time,[8] he was wont to go out of
town every Saturday at ten o'clock, or on holiday eves. But now,   165
by reason of the sickness,[9] the perpetuity of ringing has made
him devise a room with double walls and treble ceilings, the
windows close shut and caulked, and there he lives by candlelight. He turned away a man last week, for having a pair of new
shoes that creaked. And this fellow waits on him now in tennis-   170
court socks, or slippers soled with wool; and they talk each to
other in a trunk.[1] See, who comes here!

ACT I   SCENE 2

[*Enter* SIR DAUPHINE EUGENIE.]

DAUPHINE. How now! What ail you, sirs? Dumb?

TRUEWIT. Struck into stone, almost, I am here, with tales o' thine
uncle. There was never such a prodigy heard of.

DAUPHINE. I would you would once lose this subject, my masters,
for my sake. They are such as you are, that have brought me into   5
that predicament I am, with him.

TRUEWIT. How is that?

DAUPHINE. Marry, that he will disinherit me, no more. He thinks
I and my company are authors of all the ridiculous acts and
monuments[2] are told of him.   10

TRUEWIT. 'Slid, I would be the author of more to vex him; that
purpose deserves it; it gives thee law of plaguing him. I'll tell
thee what I would do. I would make a false almanac, get it
printed, and then have him drawn out on a coronation day to
the Tower Wharf, and kill him with the noise of the ordnance.[3]   15
Disinherit thee! He cannot, man. Art not thou next of blood,
and his sister's son?

DAUPHINE. Ay, but he will thrust me out of it, he vows, and marry.

TRUEWIT. How! That's a more portent. Can he endure no noise,
and will venture on a wife?   20

CLERIMONT. Yes. Why, thou art a stranger, it seems, to his best

---

8. Queen Elizabeth, who was strict about church attendance, had the bells rung on Sunday
   mornings; James was less insistent on the point.
9. Frequent funerals during plague-time made for much tolling of bells.
1. Speaking tube.
2. John Foxe (1516–1587) wrote the history of the Protestant martyrs under the title of *Acts and
   Monuments*: the title became proverbial.
3. On ceremonial occasions the cannons in London Tower were fired off.

trick yet. He has employed a fellow this half-year all over England to hearken him out a dumb woman, be she of any form
or any quality, so she be able to bear children; her silence is
dowry enough, he says.   25

TRUEWIT. But I trust to God he has found none.

CLERIMONT. No, but he has heard of one that's lodged in the next
street to him, who is exceedingly soft-spoken, thrifty of her
speech, that spends but six words a day. And her he's about now,
and shall have her.   30

TRUEWIT. Is't possible! Who is his agent in the business?

CLERIMONT. Marry, a barber, one Cutbeard; an honest fellow, one
that tells Dauphine all here.

TRUEWIT. Why, you oppress me with wonder: a woman and a barber, and love no noise!   35

CLERIMONT. Yes, faith. The fellow trims him silently, and has not
the knack with his shears or his fingers;[4] and that continence in
a barber he thinks so eminent a virtue, as it has made him chief
of his counsel.

TRUEWIT. Is the barber to be seen, or the wench?   40

CLERIMONT. Yes, that they are.

TRUEWIT. I pray thee, Dauphine, let's go thither.

DAUPHINE. I have some business now; I cannot, i' faith.

TRUEWIT. You shall have no business shall make you neglect this,
sir. We'll make her talk, believe it; or, if she will not, we can   45
give out at least so much as shall interrupt the treaty. We will
break it. Thou art bound in conscience, when he suspects thee
without cause, to torment him.

DAUPHINE. Not I, by any means. I'll give no suffrage to't. He shall
never have that plea against me, that I opposed the least fancy   50
of his. Let it lie upon my stars to be guilty, I'll be innocent.

TRUEWIT. Yes, and be poor, and beg; do, innocent; when some
groom of his has got an heir, or this barber, if he himself cannot.
Innocent! I pray thee, Ned, where lies she? Let him be innocent
still.   55

CLERIMONT. Why, right over against the barber's, in the house
where Sir John Daw lies.

TRUEWIT. You do not mean to confound me!

CLERIMONT. Why?

TRUEWIT. Does he that would marry her know so much?   60

CLERIMONT. I cannot tell.

TRUEWIT. 'Twere enough of imputation to her, with him.[5]

---

4. I.e., the art of snipping with scissors or cracking the knuckles.
5. I.e., if Morose knew she was acquainted with Daw, that would be enough for him.

CLERIMONT. Why?

TRUEWIT. The only talking Sir in the town! Jack Daw! An he teach
her not to speak—God b'w'you.[6] I have some business too.   65

CLERIMONT. Will you not go thither, then?

TRUEWIT. Not with the danger to meet Daw, for mine ears.

CLERIMONT. Why? I thought you two had been upon very good
terms.

TRUEWIT. Yes, of keeping distance.   70

CLERIMONT. They say he is a very good scholar.

TRUEWIT. Ay, and he says it first. A pox on him, a fellow that
pretends only to learning, buys titles, and nothing else of books
in him!

CLERIMONT. The world reports him to be very learned.   75

TRUEWIT. I am sorry the world should so conspire to belie him.

CLERIMONT. Good faith, I have heard very good things come from
him.

TRUEWIT. You may. There's none so desperately ignorant to deny
that; would they were his own! God b'w'you, gentlemen.   80

[*Exit hastily.*]

CLERIMONT. This is very abrupt!

ACT I   SCENE 3

DAUPHINE. Come, you are a strange, open man, to tell everything
thus.

CLERIMONT. Why, believe it, Dauphine, Truewit's a very honest
fellow.

DAUPHINE. I think no other; but this frank nature of his is not for   5
secrets.

CLERIMONT. Nay then, you are mistaken, Dauphine. I know where
he has been well trusted, and discharged the trust very truly and
heartily.

DAUPHINE. I contend not, Ned; but with the fewer a business is   10
carried, it is ever the safer. Now we are alone, if you'll go thither,
I am for you.

CLERIMONT. When were you there?

DAUPHINE. Last night; and such a Decameron[7] of sport fallen out!
Boccace never thought of the like. Daw does nothing but court   15
her, and the wrong way. He would lie with her, and praises her
modesty; desires that she would talk and be free, and commends
her silence in verses, which he reads, and swears are the best that

---

6. The phrase "God be with you" was in the process, during the early seventeenth century, of
being shortened to "Goodbye."
7. A hundred comical and often bawdy tales by Italian author Giovanni Boccaccio (1313–1375).

ever man made. Then rails at his fortunes, stamps, and mutines,[8]
why he is not made a councillor, and called to affairs of state.   20

CLERIMONT. I pray thee, let's go. I would fain partake this.—
    Some water, boy.   [Exit PAGE.]

DAUPHINE. We are invited to dinner together, he and I, by one
    that came thither to him, Sir La Foole.

CLERIMONT. O, that's a precious mannikin!   25

DAUPHINE. Do you know him?

CLERIMONT. Ay, and he will know you too, if e'er he saw you but
    once, though you should meet him at church in the midst of
    prayers. He is one of the braveries,[9] though he be none o' the
    wits. He will salute a judge upon the bench, and a bishop in   30
    the pulpit, a lawyer when he is pleading at the bar, and a lady
    when she is dancing in a masque, and put her out. He does give
    plays and suppers, and invites his guests to them aloud, out of
    his window, as they ride by in coaches. He has a lodging in the
    Strand for the purpose; or to watch when ladies are gone to the   35
    china-houses, or the Exchange,[1] that he may meet them by
    chance, and give them presents, some two or three hundred
    pounds worth of toys, to be laughed at. He is never without a
    spare banquet, or sweetmeats in his chamber, for their women
    to alight at, and come up to, for a bait.   40

DAUPHINE. Excellent! He was a fine youth last night, but now
    he is much finer! What is his Christian name? I have forgot.
    [Re-enter PAGE.]

CLERIMONT. Sir Amorous La Foole.

PAGE. The gentleman is here below that owns that name.

CLERIMONT. Heart, he's come to invite me to dinner, I hold my   45
    life.

DAUPHINE. Like enough. Pray thee, let's have him up.

CLERIMONT. Boy, marshal[2] him.

PAGE. With a truncheon, sir?

CLERIMONT. Away, I beseech you. [Exit PAGE.] I'll make him tell   50
    us his pedigree now, and what meat he has to dinner, and who
    are his guests, and the whole course of his fortunes, with a
    breath.

---

8. Complains.
9. Fine dressers, fops. "Putting a lady out" is embarrassing her by revealing her identity when
   she's wearing a mask to conceal it.
1. The New Exchange, where millinery was sold, and the china shops, where one might buy
   tableware, were fashionable shopping areas. They were also often places of assignation.
2. I.e., show him up. The Page plays on the word by asking for a regular marshal's staff, a
   truncheon.

ACT I   SCENE 4

[*Enter* SIR AMOROUS LA FOOLE.]

LA FOOLE. Save, dear Sir Dauphine! Honored Master Clerimont!

CLERIMONT. Sir Amorous! You have very much honested my lodging with your presence.

LA FOOLE. Good faith, it is a fine lodging! Almost as delicate a
lodging as mine.   5

CLERIMONT. Not so, sir.

LA FOOLE. Excuse me, sir, if it were in the Strand, I assure you. I
am come, Master Clerimont, to entreat you to wait upon two
or three ladies to dinner today.

CLERIMONT. How, sir! Wait upon them? Did you ever see me carry   10
dishes!

LA FOOLE. No, sir, dispense with me; I meant, to bear them
company.

CLERIMONT. O, that I will, sir. The doubtfulness of your phrase,
believe it, sir, would breed you a quarrel once an hour with the 15
terrible boys,[3] if you should but keep them fellowship a day.

LA FOOLE. It should be extremely against my will, sir, if I contested
with any man.

CLERIMONT. I believe it, sir. Where hold you your feast?

LA FOOLE. At Tom Otter's, sir.   20

DAUPHINE. Tom Otter! What's he?

LA FOOLE. Captain Otter, sir; he is a kind of gamester, but he has
had command both by sea and by land.

DAUPHINE. O, then he is *animal amphibium?*[4]

LA FOOLE. Ay, sir. His wife was the rich china-woman that the   25
courtiers visited so often, that gave the rare entertainment. She
commands all at home.

CLERIMONT. Then she is Captain Otter.

LA FOOLE. You say very well, sir. She is my kinswoman, a La Foole
by the mother side, and will invite any great ladies for my sake. 30

DAUPHINE. Not of the La Fooles of Essex?

LA FOOLE. No, sir, the La Fooles of London.

CLERIMONT. [*aside*]—Now he's in.

LA FOOLE. They all come out of our house, the La Fooles of the
north, the La Fooles of the west, the La Fooles of the east and   35
south—we are as ancient a family as any is in Europe—but I
myself am descended lineally of the French La Fooles—and we
do bear for our coat yellow, or Or, checkered Azure, and Gules,

---

3. Roughnecks-about-town.
4. Amphibious animals, like the frog, are equally at home on land or water. The imputation
   about his wife is that she is not only bossy but promiscuous.

and some three or four colors more,[5] which is a very noted coat, and has sometimes been solemnly worn by divers nobility of our house—but let that go, antiquity is not respected now—I had a brace of fat does sent me, gentlemen, and half a dozen of pheasants, a dozen or two of godwits,[6] and some other fowl, which I would have eaten while they are good, and in good company— there will be a great lady or two, my Lady Haughty, my Lady Centaur, Mistress Doll Mavis—And they come o' purpose to see the silent gentlewoman, Mistress Epicoene, that honest Sir John Daw has promised to bring thither—and then, Mistress Trusty, my lady's woman, will be there, too, and this honorable knight, Sir Dauphine, with yourself, Master Clerimont—And we'll be very merry, and have fiddlers, and dance—I have been a mad wag in my time, and have spent some crowns since I was a page in court, to my Lord Lofty, and after, my Lady's gentleman-usher, who got me knighted in Ireland, since it pleased my elder brother to die—I had as fair a gold jerkin[7] on that day as any was worn in the island voyage, or at Cadiz,[8] none dispraised; and I came over in it hither, showed myself to my friends in court, and after went down to my tenants in the country, and surveyed my lands, let new leases, took their money, spent it in the eye o' the land here, upon ladies—and now I can take up[9] at my pleasure.

DAUPHINE. Can you take up ladies, sir?

CLERIMONT. O, let him breathe, he has not recovered.

DAUPHINE. Would I were your half in that commodity!

LA FOOLE. No, sir, excuse me; I meant money, which can take up anything. I have another guest or two to invite, and say as much to, gentlemen. I'll take my leave abruptly, in hope you will not fail——Your servant.   [Exit.]

DAUPHINE. We will not fail you, Sir Precious La Foole; but she shall, that your ladies come to see, if I have credit afore Sir Daw.

CLERIMONT. Did you ever hear such a windfucker[1] as this?

DAUPHINE. Or such a rook as the other, that will betray his mistress to be seen! Come, 'tis time we prevented it.

CLERIMONT. Go.   [Exeunt.]

---

5. The La Foole coat of arms is suspiciously like motley, a fool's many-colored garment.
6. Long-billed wading bird.
7. Man's close-fitting jacket.
8. Semi-piratical expeditions were sent out by the English, in 1596 against the Spanish seaport of Cadiz and in 1597 against "the islands"—the Azores. The adventurers, all eager for court positions and confident of booty, wore their finest clothes.
9. Borrow, but also preempt, take for one's own. The "eye of the land" is London.
1. The windhover, or falcon, which hunts by hovering in the air.

Act II

ACT II   SCENE 1. MOROSE'S HOUSE

[*Enter* MOROSE *with a tube in his hand, followed by* MUTE.]

MOROSE. Cannot I yet find out a more compendious method, than
by this trunk, to save my servants the labor of speech, and mine
ears the discord of sounds? Let me see: all discourses but mine
own afflict me; they seem harsh, impertinent, and irksome. Is it
not possible that thou shouldst answer me by signs, and I ap-   5
prehend thee, fellow? Speak not, though I question you. You
have taken the ring off from the street door, as I bade you?
Answer me not by speech, but by silence, unless it be otherwise.
[MUTE *makes a leg.*]² Very good. And you have fastened on a
thick quilt, or flock-bed, on the outside of the door, that if they   10
knock with their daggers, or with brickbats, they can make no
noise? But with your leg, your answer, unless it be otherwise. [*A
leg.*] Very good.—This is not only fit modesty in a servant, but
good state and discretion in a master.—And you have been with
Cutbeard the barber, to have him come to me? [*A leg.*] Good.   15
And he will come presently? Answer me not but with your leg,
unless it be otherwise; if it be otherwise, shake your head, or
shrug. [*A leg.*] So.—Your Italian and Spaniard are wise in these,
and it is a frugal and comely gravity!—How long will it be ere
Cutbeard come? Stay, if an hour, hold up your whole hand; if   20
half an hour, two fingers; if a quarter, one. [*A finger, bent.*]
Good, half a quarter? 'Tis well. And have you given him a key,
to come in without knocking? [*A leg.*] Good. And is the lock
oiled, and the hinges, today? [*A leg.*] Good. And the quilting of
the stairs nowhere worn out and bare? [*A leg.*] Very good. I see,   25
by much doctrine and impulsion,³ it may be effected. Stand
by.—The Turk, in this divine discipline, is admirable, exceeding
all the potentates of the earth; still waited on by mutes, and all
his commands so executed; yea, even in the war, as I have heard,
and in his marches, most of his charges and directions given by   30
signs, and with silence—an exquisite art! And I am heartily
ashamed, and angry oftentimes, that the princes of Christendom
should suffer a barbarian to transcend them in so high a point
of felicity. I will practice it hereafter. [*One winds⁴ a horn without.*] How now? O! O! What villain, what prodigy of mankind is   35
that? Look. [*Exit* MUTE. *Horn again.*] O, cut his throat, cut his
throat! What murderer, hell-hound, devil can this be?

---

2. I.e., a perfunctory bow or scrape.
3. External influence; instigation.
4. Blows.

[*Re-enter* MUTE.]

MUTE. It is a post[5] from the court——

MOROSE. Out, rogue! And must thou blow thy horn, too?

MUTE. Alas, it is a post from the court, sir, that says he must speak   40
with you, pain of death——

MOROSE. Pain of thy life, be silent!

ACT II   SCENE 2

[*Enter* TRUEWIT *with a post-horn and a halter in his hand.*]

TRUEWIT. By your leave, sir—I am a stranger here—is your name
Master Morose? Is your name Master Morose? Fishes![6] Pythagoreans all! This is strange. What say you, sir! Nothing! Has Harpocrates[7] been here with his club among you? Well, sir, I will
believe you to be the man at this time; I will venture upon you,   5
sir. Your friends at court commend them to you, sir——

MOROSE. O men! O manners! Was there ever such an impudence?

TRUEWIT. And are extremely solicitous for you, sir.

MOROSE. Whose knave are you?

TRUEWIT. Mine own knave, and your compeer,[8] sir.   10

MOROSE. Fetch me my sword——

TRUEWIT. You shall taste the one half of my dagger, if you do,
groom; and you the other, if you stir, sir. Be patient, I charge
you, in the King's name, and hear me without insurrection.
They say you are to marry; to marry! Do you mark, sir?[9]   15

MOROSE. How then, rude companion!

TRUEWIT. Marry, your friends do wonder, sir, the Thames being
so near, wherein you may drown so handsomely; or London
Bridge, at a low fall, with a fine leap, to hurry you down the
stream; or such a delicate steeple i' the town, as Bow, to vault   20
from; or a braver height, as Paul's;[1] or, if you affected to do it
nearer home, and a shorter way, an excellent garret-window into
the street; or a beam in the said garret, with this halter—[*shows
him the halter*] which they have sent, and desire that you would
sooner commit your grave head to this knot, than to the wedlock   25
noose; or take a little sublimate,[2] and go out of the world like a
rat, or a fly—as one said—with a straw i' your arse; any way rather
than to follow this goblin, matrimony. Alas, sir, do you ever think

5. Messenger.
6. "Mute as fishes!" is understood. "Pythagoreans all!" implies that they have taken a vow of
silence, like members of the ancient Greek philosophical sect.
7. Harpocrates was the Greek and Roman god of silence.
8. Equal.
9. Most of Truewit's long and virulent diatribe against women and marriage is adapted from
Juvenal's sixth satire against women.
1. St. Mary le Bow in Cheapside or St. Paul's Cathedral would provide heights to leap from.
2. Mercury chloride, a violent poison.

to find a chaste wife in these times? Now? When there are so
many masques, plays, Puritan preachings, mad folks, and other   30
strange sights to be seen daily, private and public? If you had
lived in King Ethelred's time, sir, or Edward the Confessor's,[3]
you might perhaps have found in some cold country hamlet,
then, a dull, frosty wench, would have been contented with one
man. Now, they will as soon be pleased with one leg or one eye.   35
I'll tell you, sir, the monstrous hazards you shall run with a wife.

MOROSE. Good sir, have I ever cozened[4] any friends of yours of
their land? Bought their possessions? Taken forfeit of their mortgage? Begged a reversion[5] from 'em? Bastarded their issue? What
have I done that may deserve this?   40

TRUEWIT. Nothing, sir, that I know, but your itch of marriage.

MOROSE. Why, if I had made an assassinate upon your father, vitiated[6] your mother, ravished your sisters——

TRUEWIT. I would kill you, sir, I would kill you, if you had.

MOROSE. Why, you do more in this, sir. It were a vengeance cen-   45
tuple, for all facinorous[7] acts that could be named, to do that
you do——

TRUEWIT. Alas, sir, I am but a messenger. I but tell you what you
must hear. It seems your friends are careful after your soul's
health, sir, and would have you know the danger; but you may   50
do your pleasure for all them, I persuade not, sir. If, after you
are married, your wife do run away with a vaulter, or the Frenchman that walks upon ropes, or him that dances the jig, or a
fencer for his skill at his weapon; why, it is not their fault; they
have discharged their consciences, when you know what may   55
happen. Nay, suffer valiantly, sir, for I must tell you all the perils
that you are obnoxious[8] to. If she be fair, young, and vegetous,
no sweetmeats ever drew more flies; all the yellow doublets and
great roses[9] i' the town will be there. If foul and crooked, she'll
be with them, and buy those doublets and roses, sir. If rich, and   60
that you marry her dowry, not her, she'll reign in your house as
imperious as a widow. If noble, all her kindred will be your
tyrants. If fruitful, as proud as May and humorous[1] as April; she
must have her doctors, her midwives, her nurses, her longing
every hour, though it be for the dearest morsel of man. If   65
learned, there was never such a parrot; all your patrimony will

3. Kings of England, 978–1016 and 1042–1066.
4. Deceived.
5. A right of succession to their property (which would make a pauper of Truewit).
6. Corrupted; "assassinate": killed.
7. Wicked to the highest degree; "centuple": hundredfold.
8. Subject (to something harmful); "vegetous": full of vigor.
9. "Yellow doublets and great roses": fancy attire.
1. Changeable (in allusion to April showers).

be too little for the guests that must be invited to hear her speak
Latin and Greek; and you must lie with her in those languages
too, if you will please her. If precise, you must feast all the
silenced brethren,[2] once in three days; salute the sisters; enter-   70
tain the whole family, or wood[3] of 'em; and hear long-winded
exercises, singings, and catechizings, which you are not given
to, and yet must give for, to please the zealous matron your wife,
who, for the holy cause, will cozen you over and above. You
begin to sweat, sir? But this is not half, i' faith! You may do your   75
pleasure, notwithstanding as I said before; I come not to persuade you. [MUTE *is stealing away.*] Upon my faith, Master
Serving-man, if you do stir, I will beat you.

MOROSE. O, what is my sin? What is my sin?

TRUEWIT. Then, if you love your wife, or rather, dote on her, sir,   80
O how she'll torture you, and take pleasure i' your torments!
You shall lie with her but when she lists;[4] she will not hurt her
beauty, her complexion; or it must be for that jewel, or that
pearl, when she does. Every half-hour's pleasure must be bought
anew, and with the same pain and charge you wooed her at first.   85
Then you must keep what servants she please, what company
she will; that friend must not visit you without her licence; and
him she loves most, she will seem to hate eagerliest, to decline[5]
your jealousy; or feign to be jealous of you first, and for that
cause go live with her she-friend, or cousin at the College, that   90
can instruct her in all the mysteries of writing letters, corrupting
servants, taming spies; where she must have that rich gown for
such a great day, a new one for the next, a richer for the third;
be served in silver; have the chamber filled with a succession of
grooms, footmen, ushers, and other messengers, besides em-   95
broiderers, jewellers, tire-women, sempsters,[6] feather-men, per-
fumers; while she feels not how the land drops away, nor the
acres melt;[7] nor foresees the change, when the mercer[8] has your
woods for her velvets; never weighs what her pride costs, sir, so
she may kiss a page, or a smooth chin that has the despair of a   100
beard; be a stateswoman, know all the news, what was done at
Salisbury, what at the Bath,[9] what at court, what in progress; or

2. Puritan preachers, once in the Church of England, but now censored or ejected and so
dependent on the charity of sympathizers. "Precise": puritanical.
3. Tribe.
4. Chooses.
5. Lessen.
6. Seamster, tailor.
7. I.e., her expenses cause her husband's estate to drop away and disappear.
8. Dealer in fabrics.
9. Salisbury and Bath were fashionable places where the latest news or scandal was likely to be
heard; "progress": tours of the countryside made by the king and his court.

so she may censure poets and authors and styles, and compare
'em—Daniel with Spenser, Jonson with the t'other youth,[1] and so
forth; or be thought cunning in controversies or the very knots of   105
divinity, and have often in her mouth the state of the question;[2]
and then skip to the mathematics and demonstration; and answer, in religion to one, in state to another, in bawdry to a third.

MOROSE. O! O!

TRUEWIT. All this is very true, sir. And then her going in disguise   110
to that conjurer, and this cunning-woman,[3] where the first question is how soon you shall die? Next, if her present servant[4] love
her? Next that, if she shall have a new servant? And how many?
Which of her family would make the best bawd, male or female?
What precedence she shall have by her next match? And sets   115
down the answers, and believes 'em above the scriptures. Nay,
perhaps she'll study the art.

MOROSE. Gentle sir, have you done? Have you had your pleasure
o' me? I'll think of these things.

TRUEWIT. Yes, sir, and then comes reeking home of vapor and   120
sweat, with going afoot, and lies in, a month, of a new face, all
oil and birdlime; and rinses in asses' milk, and is cleansed with
a new fucus.[5] God b'w'you, sir. One thing more, which I had
almost forgot. This too, with whom you are to marry, may have
made a conveyance of her virginity aforehand, as your wise wid-   125
ows do of their states,[6] before they marry, in trust to some friend,
sir. Who can tell? Or if she have not done it yet, she may do,
upon the wedding day, or the night before, and antedate you
cuckold. The like has been heard of in nature. 'Tis no devised,
impossible thing, sir. God b'w'you. I'll be bold to leave this rope   130
with you, sir, for a remembrance.—Farewell, Mute!   [*Exit.*]

MOROSE. Come, have me to my chamber; but first shut the door.
[*The horn again.*] O, shut the door, shut the door! Is he come
again?

[*Enter* CUTBEARD.]

CUTBEARD. 'Tis, I, sir, your barber.   135

MOROSE. O Cutbeard, Cutbeard, Cutbeard! Here has been a cut-
throat with me. Help me in to my bed, and give me physic with
thy counsel.   [*Exeunt.*]

---

1. The standard comparison was Jonson and Shakespeare, but Jonson may not want to be too
   particular here.
2. "The state of the question" implies formal logical disputations.
3. Female witch doctor.
4. With the overtone of Italian *cavalier sirvente*, half lover, half domestic convenience.
5. Makeup.
6. Estates.

ACT II SCENE 3. SIR JOHN DAW'S *HOUSE*

[*Enter* DAW, CLERIMONT, DAUPHINE, *and* EPICOENE.]

DAW. Nay, an she will, let her refuse at her own charges; 'tis nothing to me, gentlemen. But she will not be invited to the like
feasts or guests every day.

CLERIMONT. O, by no means, she may not refuse——[*they dis-
suade her privately*] to stay at home, if you love your reputation.   5
'Slight, you are invited thither o' purpose to be seen, and
laughed at by the lady of the College and her shadows. This
trumpeter hath proclaimed you.

DAUPHINE. You shall not go. Let him be laughed at in your stead,
for not bringing you; and put him to his extemporal faculty of   10
fooling and talking loud to satisfy the company.

CLERIMONT. He will suspect us; talk aloud.—Pray, Mistress Epicoene, let's see your verses; we have Sir John Daw's leave. Do
not conceal your servant's merit, and your own glories.

EPICOENE. They'll prove my servant's glories, if you have his leave   15
so soon.

DAUPHINE. His vainglories, lady!

DAW. Show them, show them, mistress! I dare own them.

EPICOENE. Judge you what glories.

DAW. Nay, I'll read them myself, too; an author must recite his   20
own works. It is a madrigal[7] of modesty:

    Modest and fair, for fair and good are near
          Neighbors, howe'er.

DAUPHINE. Very good.

CLERIMONT. Ay, is't not?   25

DAW.   *No noble virtue ever was alone,*
          But two in one.

DAUPHINE. Excellent!

CLERIMONT. That again, I pray, Sir John.

DAUPHINE. It has something in't like rare wit and sense.   30

CLERIMONT. Peace.

DAW.   *No noble virtue ever was alone,*
          But two in one.
    Then, when I praise sweet modesty, I praise
          Bright beauty's rays;   35
    And having praised both beauty and modesty,
          I have praised thee.

DAUPHINE. Admirable!

CLERIMONT. How it chimes and cries tink in the close[8] divinely!

DAUPHINE. Ay, 'tis Seneca.   40

7. Short love poem.
8. Conclusion.

CLERIMONT. No, I think 'tis Plutarch.[9]

DAW. The *dor* on Plutarch and Seneca,[1] I hate it! They are mine own imaginations, by that light! I wonder those fellows have such credit with gentlemen.

CLERIMONT. They are very grave authors. 45

DAW. Grave asses! Mere essayists! A few loose sentences, and that's all. A man would talk so his whole age. I do utter as good things every hour, if they were collected and observed, as either of 'em.

DAUPHINE. Indeed, Sir John!

CLERIMONT. He must needs, living among the wits, and braveries 50 too.

DAUPHINE. Ay, and being president of 'em, as he is.

DAW. There's Aristotle, a mere commonplace fellow; Plato, a discourser; Thucydides and Livy, tedious and dry; Tacitus, an entire knot—sometimes worth the untying, very seldom.[2] 55

CLERIMONT. What do you think of the poets, Sir John?

DAW. Not worthy to be named for authors. Homer, an old, tedious, prolix ass, talks of curriers and chines of beef;[3] Virgil, of dunging of land, and bees; Horace, of I know not what.

CLERIMONT. —I think so. 60

DAW. And so Pindarus, Lycophron, Anacreon, Catullus, Seneca the tragedian, Lucan, Propertius, Tibullus, Martial, Juvenal, Ausonius, Statius, Politian, Valerius Flaccus,[4] and the rest——

CLERIMONT. —What a sack-full of their names he has got!

DAUPHINE. And how he pours 'em out! Politian with Valerius 65 Flacus!

CLERIMONT. Was not the character right of him?[5]

DAUPHINE. As could be made, i' faith.

DAW. And Persius, a crabbed coxcomb, not to be endured.[6]

DAUPHINE. Why, whom do you account for authors, Sir John Daw? 70

DAW. *Syntagma Juris Civilis, Corpus Juris Civilis, Corpus Juris Canonici,* the King of Spain's Bible[7]——

DAUPHINE. Is the King of Spain's Bible an author?

CLERIMONT. Yes, and *Syntagma.*

9. Seneca and Plutarch, grave and moral authors of antiquity, are the least appropriate authors under the circumstances.
1. I.e., To the devil with Plutarch and Seneca.
2. Sir John Daw's opinions of the great classical authors are the trite formulas of lazy and reluctant readers.
3. Curriers, that is, groomers of horses, and sides of beef.
4. Sir John Daw rattles off a miscellaneous list of Latin poets, concluding with Politian (Polizian), an Italian poet of the fifteenth century, and Valerius Flaccus, a Roman poet of the first century.
5. I.e., Didn't I tell you what sort of fellow he was?
6. Persius (34–62 C.E.) a sharp and witty satirist, is indeed rather hard reading.
7. I.e., The Collection of Civil Law, The Body of Civil Law, The Body of Canon Law, and even The King of Spain's Bible—Sir John thinks they are all personal names.

DAUPHINE. What was that *Syntagma*, sir?   75

DAW. A civil lawyer, a Spaniard.

DAUPHINE. Sure, *Corpus* was a Dutchman.

CLERIMONT. Ay, both the *Corpuses*, I knew 'em; they were very corpulent authors.

DAW. And then there's Vatablus, Pomponatius, Symancha;[8] the others are not to be received within the thought of a scholar.   80

DAUPHINE. [*aside*] 'Fore God, you have a simple learned servant, lady—in titles.

CLERIMONT. I wonder that he is not called to the helm, and made a councillor!

DAUPHINE. He is one extraordinary.   85

CLERIMONT. Nay, but in ordinary![9] To say truth, the state wants such.

DAUPHINE. Why, that will follow.

CLERIMONT. I muse a mistress can be so silent to the dotes[1] of such a servant.   90

DAW. 'Tis her virtue, sir. I have written somewhat of her silence, too.

DAUPHINE. In verse, Sir John?

CLERIMONT. What else?   95

DAUPHINE. Why, how can you justify your own being of a poet, that so slight all the old poets?

DAW. Why, every man that writes in verse is not a poet; you have of the wits that write verses, and yet are no poets. They are poets that live by it, the poor fellows that live by it.   100

DAUPHINE. Why, would not you live by your verses, Sir John?

CLERIMONT. No, 'twere pity he should. A knight live by his verses? He did not make them to that end, I hope.

DAUPHINE. And yet the noble Sidney lives by his,[2] and the noble family not ashamed.   105

CLERIMONT. Ay, he professed himself; but Sir John Daw has more caution. He'll not hinder his own rising i' the state so much! Do you think he will? Your verses, good Sir John, and no poems.

DAW.   *Silence in woman is like speech in man,*
        Deny 't who can.   110

DAUPHINE. Not I, believe it; your reason, sir.

DAW.   *Nor is't a tale,*
        That female vice should be a virtue male,

---

8. Renaissance scholars: Vatable, Pomponazzi, Simancus.
9. I.e., to be a councillor on the regular staff, as opposed to being a councillor "extraordinary."
1. Endowments.
2. Sir Philip Sidney (1554–1586), living in fame through his poetry, though dead for 23 years at the time of the play's writing.

Or masculine vice a female virtue be.
You shall it see   115
Proved with increase;
I know to speak, and she to hold her peace.
Do you conceive me, gentlemen?

DAUPHINE. No, faith; how mean you *with increase,* Sir John?

DAW. Why, *with increase* is when I court her for the common   120
cause of mankind, and she says nothing, but *consentire videtur,*
and in time is *gravida.*[3]

DAUPHINE. Then this is a ballad of procreation?

CLERIMONT. A madrigal of procreation, you mistake.

EPICOENE. Pray give me my verses again, servant.   125

DAW. If you'll ask them aloud, you shall.

CLERIMONT. See, here's Truewit again!

ACT II   SCENE 4

[*Enter* TRUEWIT *with his horn.*]

CLERIMONT. Where hast thou been, in the name of madness, thus
accoutred with thy horn?

TRUEWIT. Where the sound of it might have pierced your senses
with gladness, had you been in ear-reach of it. Dauphine, fall
down and worship me; I have forbid the banns,[4] lad. I have been   5
with thy virtuous uncle, and have broke the match.

DAUPHINE. You have not, I hope.

TRUEWIT. Yes, faith, an thou shouldst hope otherwise, I should
repent me. This horn got me entrance; kiss it. I had no other
way to get in, but by feigning to be a post;[5] but when I got in   10
once, I proved none, but rather the contrary, turned him into a
post, or a stone, or what is stiffer, with thundering into him the
incommodities of a wife, and the miseries of marriage. If ever
Gorgon[6] were seen in the shape of a woman, he hath seen her
in my description. I have put him off o' that scent forever. Why   15
do you not applaud and adore me, sirs? Why stand you mute?
Are you stupid? You are not worthy of the benefit.

DAUPHINE. Did not I tell you? Mischief!

CLERIMONT. I would you had placed this benefit somewhere else.

TRUEWIT. Why so?   20

CLERIMONT. 'Slight, you have done the most inconsiderate, rash,
weak thing, that ever man did to his friend.

---

3. I.e., she says nothing but seems to consent and in time is pregnant.
4. Banns are public announcements of a proposed marriage.
5. Messenger.
6. The Gorgons were frightful females of Greek mythology, the most famous being Medusa,
whose very glance turned men to stone.

DAUPHINE. Friend! If the most malicious enemy I have, had studied to inflict an injury upon me, it could not be a greater.

TRUEWIT. Wherein, for God's sake? Gentlemen, come to yourselves again.   25

DAUPHINE. But I presaged[7] thus much afore to you.

CLERIMONT. Would my lips had been soldered when I spake on't! 'Slight, what moved you to be thus impertinent?

TRUEWIT. My masters, do not put on this strange face to pay my   30
courtesy; off with this visor.[8] Have good turns done you, and thank 'em this way!

DAUPHINE. 'Fore heaven, you have undone me. That which I have plotted for, and been maturing now these four months, you have blasted in a minute. Now I am lost I may speak. This gentle-   35
woman was lodged here by me o' purpose, and, to be put upon my uncle, hath professed this obstinate silence for my sake, being my entire friend, and one that for the requital of such a fortune as to marry him, would have made me very ample conditions; where now all my hopes are utterly miscarried by this   40
unlucky accident.

CLERIMONT. Thus 'tis when a man will be ignorantly officious, do services and not know his why. I wonder what courteous itch possessed you! You never did absurder part i' your life, nor a great trespass to friendship, to humanity.   45

DAUPHINE. Faith, you may forgive it best; 'twas your cause principally.

CLERIMONT. I know it, would it had not!

[*Enter* CUTBEARD.]

DAUPHINE. How now, Cutbeard! What news?

CUTBEAD. The best, the happiest that ever was, sir. There has been   50
a mad gentleman with your uncle this morning—I think this be the gentleman—that has almost talked him out of his wits, with threatening him from marriage——

DAUPHINE. On, I pray thee.

CUTBEARD. And your uncle, sir, he thinks 'twas done by your pro-   55
curement. Therefore he will see the party you wot of presently; and if he like her, he says, and that she be so inclining to dumb as I have told him, he swears he will marry her today, instantly, and not defer it a minute longer.

DAUPHINE. Excellent! Beyond our expectation!   60

TRUEWIT. Beyond your expectation! By this light, I knew it would be thus.

7. Predicted.
8. False face.

DAUPHINE. Nay, sweet Truewit, forgive me.

TRUEWIT. No, I was *ignorantly officious, impertinent*; this was the *absurd, weak part.*   65

CLERIMONT. Wilt thou ascribe that to merit now, was mere fortune?

TRUEWIT. Fortune? Mere providence! Fortune had not a finger in't. I saw it must necessarily in nature fall out so; my genius is never false to me in these things. Show me how it could be   70 otherwise.

DAUPHINE. Nay, gentlemen, contend not; 'tis well now.

TRUEWIT. Alas, I let him go on with *inconsiderate*, and *rash*, and what he pleased.

CLERIMONT. Away, thou strange justifier of thyself, to be wiser than   75 thou wert, by the event!

TRUEWIT. Event! By this light, thou shalt never persuade me but I foresaw it as well as the stars themselves.

DAUPHINE. Nay, gentlemen, 'tis well now. Do you two entertain Sir John Daw with discourse, while I send her away with   80 instructions.

TRUEWIT. I'll be acquainted with her first, by your favor.

CLERIMONT. Master Truewit, lady, a friend of ours.

TRUEWIT. I am sorry I have not known you sooner, lady, to celebrate this rare virtue of your silence.   85

[*Exeunt* DAUPHINE, EPICOENE, *and* CUTBEARD.]

CLERIMONT. Faith, an you had come sooner, you should have seen and heard her well celebrated in Sir John Daw's madrigals.

TRUEWIT. [*advances to* DAW.] Jack Daw, God save you! When saw you La Foole?

DAW. Not since last night, Master Truewit.   90

TRUEWIT. That's a miracle! I thought you two had been inseparable.

DAW. He's gone to invite his guests.

TRUEWIT. God's so'! 'Tis true! What a false memory have I towards that man! I am one.[9] I met him e'en now upon that he calls his   95 delicate, fine black horse, rid into foam with posting from place to place and person to person, to give them the cue——

CLERIMONT. Lest they should forget?

TRUEWIT. Yes. There was never poor captain took more pains at a muster to show men, than he at this meal to show friends.   100

DAW. It is his quarter-feast, sir.[1]

CLERIMONT. What! Do you say so, Sir John?

---

9. I.e., I am one of the party, I am invited.
1. Held on quarter-day, when rents or allowances were paid.

TRUEWIT. Nay, Jack Daw will not be out at the best friends he has, to the talent of his wit. Where's his mistress, to hear and applaud him? Is she gone?   105

DAW. Is Mistress Epicoene gone?

CLERIMONT. Gone afore, with Sir Dauphine, I warrant, to the place.

TRUEWIT. Gone afore! That were a manifest injury, a disgrace and a half; to refuse him at such a festival time as this, being a   110 bravery, and a wit too!

CLERIMONT. Tut, he'll swallow it like cream. He's better read in *Jure Civili*[2] than to esteem anything a disgrace is offered him from a mistress.

DAW. Nay, let her e'en go; she shall sit alone and be dumb in her   115 chamber a week together, for John Daw, I warrant her! Does she refuse me?

CLERIMONT. No, sir, do not take it so to heart; she does not refuse you, but a little neglect you. Good faith, Truewit, you were to blame, to put it into his head that she does refuse him.   120

TRUEWIT. Sir, she does refuse him, palpably, however you mince it. An I were as he, I would swear to speak ne'er a word to her today, for't.

DAW. By this light, no more I will not!

TRUEWIT. Nor to anybody else, sir.   125

DAW. Nay, I will not say so, gentlemen.

CLERIMONT. [*aside*]—It had been an excellent happy condition for the company, if you could have drawn him to it.

DAW. I'll be very melancholy, i' faith.

CLERIMONT. As a dog, if I were as you, Sir John.   130

TRUEWIT. Or a snail, or a hog-louse. I would roll myself up for this day; in troth, they should not unwind me.[3]

DAW. By this picktooth, so I will.

CLERIMONT. [*aside*]—'Tis well done, he begins already to be angry with his teeth.   135

DAW. Will you go, gentlemen?

CLERIMONT. Nay, you must walk alone, if you be right melancholy, Sir John.

TRUEWIT. Yes, sir, we'll dog you; we'll follow you afar off.

[*Exit* DAW.]

CLERIMONT. Was there ever such a two yards of knighthood   140 measured out by Time to be sold to Laughter?

---

2. In civil law, with a special ironic allusion to the courtesies governing behavior toward a mistress.
3. A hog-louse, when touched, rolls itself up in a ball.

TRUEWIT. A mere talking mole, hang him! No mushroom was ever
so fresh. A fellow so utterly nothing, as he knows not what he
would be.

CLERIMONT. Let's follow him. But first let's go to Dauphine; he's   145
hovering about the house to hear what news.

TRUEWIT. Content.   [*Exeunt.*]

ACT II   SCENE 5. MOROSE'*S HOUSE*

[*Enter* MOROSE *and* MUTE, *followed by* CUTBEARD *with*
EPICOENE.]

MOROSE. Welcome, Cutbeard! Draw near with your fair charge,
and in her ear softly entreat her to unmask. [EPICOENE *takes off
her mask.*] So! Is the door shut? [MUTE *makes a leg.*] Enough!
Now, Cutbeard, with the same discipline I use to my family, I
will question you. As I conceive, Cutbeard, this gentlewoman is   5
she you have provided, and brought, in hope she will fit me in
the place and person of a wife? Answer me not but with your
leg, unless it be otherwise. [CUTBEARD *makes a leg.*] Very well
done, Cutbeard. I conceive besides, Cutbeard, you have been
pre-acquainted with her birth, education, and qualities, or else   10
you would not prefer her to my acceptance, in the weighty consequence of marriage. This I conceive, Cutbeard. Answer me
not but with your leg, unless it be otherwise. [*A leg.*] Very well
done, Cutbeard. Give aside now a little, and leave me to examine her condition and aptitude to my affection. [*Goes about*   15
her and views her.] She is exceeding fair, and of a special good
favor; a sweet composition, or harmony of limbs; her temper of
beauty has the true height of my blood. The knave hath exceedingly well fitted me without; I will now try her within.—
Come near, fair gentlewoman. Let not my behavior seem rude,   20
though unto you, being rare, it may haply appear strange. [EPI-
COENE *curtsies.*]—Nay, lady, you may speak, though Cutbeard
and my man might not; for of all sounds, only the sweet voice
of a fair lady has the just length of mine ears. I beseech you,
say, lady—out of the first fire of meeting eyes, they say, love is   25
stricken—do you feel any such emotion suddenly shot into you,
from any part you see in me? Ha, lady? [*Curtsy.*] Alas, lady, these
answers by silent curtsies from you, are too courtless and simple.
I have ever had my breeding in court, and she that shall be my
wife must be accomplished with courtly and audacious orna-   30
ments. Can you speak, lady?

EPICOENE. [*softly*] Judge you, forsooth.

MOROSE. What say you, lady? Speak out, I beseech you.

EPICOENE. Judge you, forsooth.

MOROSE. On my judgment, a divine softness! But can you natu- 35
  rally, lady, as I enjoin these by doctrine and industry, refer yourself to the search of my judgment, and—not taking pleasure in
  your tongue, which is a woman's chiefest pleasure—think it
  plausible to answer me by silent gestures, so long as my speeches
  jump right with what you conceive? [*Curtsy.*] Excellent! Divine! 40
  If it were possible she should hold out thus! Peace, Cutbeard,
  thou art made forever, as thou hast made me, if this felicity have
  lasting: but I will try her further. Dear lady, I am courtly, I tell
  you, and I must have mine ears banqueted with pleasant and
  witty conferences, pretty girds,[4] scoffs, and dalliance in her that 45
  I mean to choose for my bed-fere.[5] The ladies in court think it
  a most desperate impair to their quickness of wit, and good carriage, if they cannot give occasion for a man to court 'em; and
  when an amorous discourse is set on foot, minister as good matter to continue it as himself. And do you alone so much differ 50
  from all them, that what they, with so much circumstance, affect
  and toil for—to seem learned, to seem judicious, to seem sharp
  and conceited—you can bury in yourself with silence? And
  rather trust your graces to the fair conscience of virtue, than to
  the world's or your own proclamation? 55
EPICOENE. [*softly*] I should be sorry else.
MOROSE. What say you, lady? Good lady, speak out.
EPICOENE. I should be sorry else.
MOROSE. That sorrow doth fill me with gladness! O Morose, thou
  art happy above mankind! Pray that thou mayst contain thyself. 60
  I will only put her to it once more, and it shall be with the
  utmost touch and test of their sex.—But hear me, fair lady: I do
  also love to see her whom I shall choose for my heifer[6] to be
  the first and principal in all fashions, precede all the dames at
  court by a fortnight, have her council of tailors, lineners, lace- 65
  women, embroiderers, and sit with 'em sometimes twice a day
  upon French intelligences;[7] and then come forth varied like Nature, or oftener than she, and better by the help of Art, her
  emulous servant. This do I affect. And how will you be able,
  lady, with this frugality of speech, to give the manifold but nec- 70
  essary instructions for that bodice, these sleeves, those skirts, this
  cut, that stitch, this embroidery, that lace, this wire, those knots,
  that ruff, those roses, this girdle, that fan, the t'other scarf, these
  gloves, ha? What say you, lady?

---

4. Sharp or biting comments; "scoffs": taunts.
5. Bedmate.
6. In the seventeenth century, the word "heifer" could be used without contempt to describe a
  wife.
7. Talking about the latest news of French fashions.

EPICOENE. [*softly*] I'll leave it to you, sir.   75
MOROSE. How, lady? Pray you rise a note.
EPICOENE. I leave it to wisdom and you, sir.
MOROSE. Admirable creature! I will trouble you no more. I will
  not sin against so sweet a simplicity. Let me now be bold to
  print on those divine lips the seal of being mine. Cutbeard, I   80
  give thee the lease of thy house free: thank me not but with thy
  leg [CUTBEARD *shakes his head.*] I know what thou wouldst say:
  she's poor and her friends deceased. She has brought a wealthy
  dowry in her silence, Cutbeard; and in respect of her poverty,
  Cutbeard, I shall have her more loving and obedient, Cutbeard.   85
  Go thy ways, and get me a minister presently, with a soft, low
  voice, to marry us; and pray him he will not be impertinent, but
  brief as he can; away. Softly, Cutbeard. [*Exit* CUTBEARD.] Sirrah,
  conduct your mistress into the dining-room, your now mistress.
  [*Exit* MUTE, *followed by* EPICOENE.] O my felicity! How I shall   90
  be revenged on mine insolent kinsman, and his plots to fright
  me from marrying! This night I will get an heir, and thrust him
  out of my blood like a stranger. He would be knighted, forsooth,
  and thought by that means to reign over me; his title must do
  it. No, kinsman, I will now make you bring me the tenth lord's   95
  and the sixteenth lady's letter, kinsman; and it shall do you no
  good, kinsman. Your knighthood itself shall come on its knees,
  and it shall be rejected; it shall be sued for its fees to execution,
  and not be redeemed; it shall cheat at the twelvepenny ordinary,
  it knighthood,[8] for its diet all the term time, and tell tales for it   100
  in the vacation to the hostess; or it knighthood shall do worse,
  take sanctuary in Cole Harbor,[9] and fast. It shall fright all it
  friends with borrowing letters; and when one of the fourscore
  hath brought it knighthood ten shillings, it knighthood shall go
  to the Cranes, or the Bear at the Bridge-foot,[1] and be drunk in   105
  fear. It shall not have money to discharge one tavern reckoning,
  to invite the old creditors to forbear it knighthood, or the new,
  that should be, to trust it knighthood. It shall be the tenth name
  in the bond to take up the commodity of pipkins and stone-
  jugs,[2] and the part thereof shall not furnish it knighthood forth   110
  for the attempting of a baker's widow, a brown baker's widow.
  It shall give it knighthood's name for a stallion to all gamesome

---

8. The form "it" was very new in 1609, and Morose uses the archaic form sarcastically, almost
   as a form of baby talk.
9. Cole (or Cold) Harbor was a sorry tenement where debtors often took sanctuary from their
   creditors and bailiffs.
1. Seedy taverns in the suburbs of town. Even there, Dauphine would be drunk only because
   of his fear of bailiffs and debt collectors.
2. Morose is straining to think of the most miserable dodges to which Dauphine can be reduced
   to raise a few pennies; this one involves a shabby trick on a greedy pawnbroker.

citizens' wives, and be refused, when the master of a dancing-
school, or—how do you call him?—the worst reveler in the town,
is taken.[3] It shall want clothes, and by reason of that, wit to fool   115
lawyers. It shall not have hope to repair itself by Constantinople,
Ireland, or Virginia;[4] but the best and last fortune to it knighthood shall be to make Doll Tearsheet[5] or Kate Common a lady;
and so, it knighthood may eat.   [Exit.]

ACT II   SCENE 6. *A LANE NEAR* MOROSE'S *HOUSE*

[*Enter* TRUEWIT, DAUPHINE, *and* CLERIMONT.]

TRUEWIT. Are you sure he is not gone by?

DAUPHINE. No, I stayed in the shop ever since.

CLERIMONT. But he may take the other end of the lane.

DAUPHINE. No, I told him I would be here at this end; I appointed
him hither.   5

TRUEWIT. What a barbarian it is to stay then!

DAUPHINE. Yonder he comes.

CLERIMONT. And his charge left behind him, which is a very good
sign, Dauphine.

[*Enter* CUTBEARD.]

DAUPHINE. How now, Cutbeard! Succeeds it or no?   10

CUTBEARD. Past imagination, sir, *omnia secunda*;[6] you could not
have prayed to have had it so well. *Saltat senex*;[7] as it is in the
proverb; he does triumph in his felicity, admires the party! He
has given me the lease of my house, too! And I am now going
for a silent minister to marry 'em, and away.   15

TRUEWIT. 'Slight! Get one o' the silenced ministers; a zealous
brother would torment him purely.[8]

CUTBEARD. *Cum privilegio*, sir.

DAUPHINE. O, by no means; let's do nothing to hinder it now.
When 'tis done and finished, I am for you, for any device of   20
vexation.

CUTBEARD. And that shall be within this half hour, upon my dex-
terity, gentlemen. Contrive what you can in the meantime, *bonis
avibus*.[9]   [Exit.]

CLERIMONT. How the slave doth Latin it!   25

---

3. Dauphine, after trying to seduce a citizen's wife by using his knighthood as a lure, will be
   rejected in favor of a dancing master. There is something in the phrasing ("how do you call
   him?") that suggests Jonson had in mind a particular man named Howe.
4. Traditional places for repairing broken fortunes.
5. Since Shakespeare's *Merry Wives of Windsor*, the traditional name of a prostitute.
6. All things favorable.
7. I.e., the old man leaps for joy.
8. Puritan preachers were notoriously long talkers; they talked "with privilege" because, as clergy,
   they could not be interrupted.
9. Literally, with good birds—i.e., under favorable auspices.

TRUEWIT. It would be made a jest to posterity, sirs, this day's mirth, if ye will.

CLERIMONT. Beshrew his heart that will not, I pronounce.

DAUPHINE. And for my part. What is't?

TRUEWIT. To translate all La Foole's company and his feast hither   30
today, to celebrate this bridal.

DAUPHINE. Ay, marry, but how will't be done?

TRUEWIT. I'll undertake the directing of all the lady-guests thither, and then the meat must follow.

CLERIMONT. For God's sake, let's effect it! It will be an excellent   35
comedy of affliction, so many several noises.

DAUPHINE. But are they not at the other place already, think you?

TRUEWIT. I'll warrant you for the College Honors;[1] one o' their faces has not the priming color laid on yet, nor the other her smock[2] sleeked.   40

CLERIMONT. O, but they'll rise earlier than ordinary, to a feast.

TRUEWIT. Best go see, and assure ourselves.

CLERIMONT. Who knows the house?

TRUEWIT. I'll lead you. Were you never there yet?

DAUPHINE. Not I.   45

CLERIMONT. Nor I.

TRUEWIT. Where have you lived then? Not know Tom Otter!

CLERIMONT. No. For God's sake, what is he?

TRUEWIT. An excellent animal, equal with your Daw or La Foole, if not transcendent, and does Latin it as much as your barber.   50
He is his wife's subject; he calls her princess, and at such times as these follows her up and down the house like a page, with his hat off, partly for heat, partly for reverence. At this instant he is marshalling of his Bull Bear, and Horse.

DAUPHINE. What be those, in the name of Sphinx?[3]   55

TRUEWIT. Why, sir, he has been a great man at the bear-garden[4] in his time, and from that subtle sport has ta'en the witty denomination of his chief carousing[5] cups. One he calls his Bull, another his Bear, another his Horse. And then he has his lesser glasses, that he calls his Deer and his Ape; and several degrees   60
of them too; and never is well, nor thinks any entertainment perfect, till these be brought out and set o' the cupboard.

CLERIMONT. For God's love! We should miss this if we should not go.

TRUEWIT. Nay, he has a thousand things as good, that will speak   65

---

1. I.e., the literary ladies.
2. Petticoat.
3. The Sphinx is a Greek mythological figure renowned for asking difficult questions.
4. The bearpit, where bulls and bears were baited.
5. Drinking. The covers of the cups might have represented animals.

him all day. He will rail on his wife, with certain commonplaces, behind her back; and to her face——

DAUPHINE. No more of him. Let's go see him, I petition you.

[*Exeunt.*]

Act III

ACT III   SCENE 1. MISTRESS OTTER'S *HOUSE*

[*Enter* CAPTAIN OTTER *with his cups, and* MISTRESS OTTER.]

OTTER. Nay, good Princess, hear me, *pauca verba.*[6]

MISTRESS OTTER. By that light, I'll have you chained up, with your bull-dogs and bear-dogs, if you be not civil the sooner. I'll send you to kennel, i' faith. You were best bait me with your Bull, Bear, and Horse! Never a time that the courtiers or Collegiates come to the house, but you make it a Shrove Tuesday![7] I would have you get your Whitsuntide velvet cap, and your staff in your hand, to entertain them. Yes, in troth, do.   5

OTTER. No so, Princess, neither, but under correction, sweet Princess, give me leave—these things I am known to the courtiers by. It is reported to them for my humor, and they receive it so, and do expect it. Tom Otter's Bull, Bear, and Horse is known all over England, *in rerum natura.*[8]   10

MISTRESS OTTER. 'Fore me, I will na-ture 'em over to Paris Garden,[9] and na-ture you thither too, if you pronounce them again. Is a bear a fit beast, or a bull, to mix in society with great ladies? Think in your discretion, in any good policy.   15

OTTER. The horse then, good Princess.

MISTRESS OTTER. Well, I am contented, for the horse; they love to be well horsed, I know.[1] I love it myself.   20

OTTER. And it is a delicate fine horse this. *Poetarum Pegasus.*[2] Under correction, Princess, Jupiter did turn himself into a—taurus, or bull, under correction, good Princess.

[*Enter* TRUEWIT, CLERIMONT, *and* DAUPHINE *behind.*]

MISTRESS OTTER. By my integrity, I'll send you over to the Bankside, I'll commit you to the Master of the Garden,[3] if I hear but a syllable more. Must my house or my roof be polluted with the   25

---

6. A few words.
7. Mardi Gras, the day before Lent begins, and hence a day of festivity; it was a particularly riotous one for roughnecks at the bear gardens. "Whitsuntide" begins fifty days after Easter and was also a festive time; velvet caps were worn during such seasons.
8. "In the nature of things," with an allusion to the Roman poet Lucretius's (ca. 99–55 B.C.E.) work of that name.
9. The bearbaiting pit; it also served as a part-time theater.
1. Well provided with horses, but also with an obscene meaning.
2. Pegasus is the poet's winged horse of inspiration.
3. The Master of the Garden was the keeper of the bears.

scent of bears and bulls, when it is perfumed for great ladies? Is this according to the instrument, when I married you? That I would be princess, and reign in mine own house; and you would be my subject, and obey me? What did you bring me, should make you thus peremptory? Do I allow you your half-crown a day, to spend where you will, among your gamesters, to vex and torment me at such times as these? Who gives you your maintenance, I pray you? Who allows you your horse-meat and man's-meat? Your three suits of apparel a year? Your four pair of stockings, one silk, three worsted? Your clean linen, your bands[4] and cuffs, when I can get you to wear 'em? 'Tis mar'l[5] you have 'em on now. Who graces you with courtiers or great personages, to speak to you out of their coaches and come home to your house? Were you ever so much as looked upon by a lord or a lady before I married you, but on the Easter or Whitsun-holidays? And then out at the Banqueting House window, when Ned Whiting or George Stone[6] were at the stake.

TRUEWIT. [aside]—For God's sake, let's go stave her off him.

MISTRESS OTTER. Answer me to that. And did not I take you up from thence, in an old, greasy buff doublet, with points,[7] and green velvet sleeves out at the elbows? You forget this.

TRUEWIT. [aside]—She'll worry[8] him, if we help not in time.
[They come forward.]

MISTRESS OTTER. O, here are some of the gallants! Go to, behave yourself distinctly, and with good morality; or, I protest, I'll take away your exhibition.[9]

ACT III   SCENE 2

TRUEWIT. By your leave, fair Mistress Otter, I'll be bold to enter these gentlemen in your acquaintance.

MISTRESS OTTER. It shall not be obnoxious or diffcil, sir.

TRUEWIT. How does my noble Captain? Is the Bull, Bear, and Horse in rerum natura still?

OTTER. Sir, sic visum superis.[1]

MISTRESS OTTER. I would you would but intimate[2] 'em, do. Go your ways in, and get toasts and butter made for the woodcocks.[3] That's a fit province for you.   [Drives him out.]

---

4. Strips of linen worn at the wrists.
5. Marvel.
6. Bears were named after their owners; George Stone was particularly famous.
7. Laces, cords.
8. Hunting term: a hound's biting or striking its quarry to injure or kill it.
9. Daily allowance.
1. As it pleases the gods.
2. Perhaps "imitate."
3. Birds easily caught, and therefore, figuratively, fools.

CLERIMONT. Alas, what a tyranny is this poor fellow married to.   10
TRUEWIT. O, but the sport will be anon, when we get him loose.
DAUPHINE. Dares he ever speak?
TRUEWIT. No Anabaptist[4] ever railed with the like licence. But
    mark her language in the meantime, I beseech you.
MISTRESS OTTER. Gentlemen, you are very aptly come. My cousin,   15
    Sir Amorous, will be here briefly.
TRUEWIT. In good time, lady. Was not Sir John Daw here, to ask
    for him, and the company?
MISTRESS OTTER. I cannot assure you, Master Truewit. Here was
    a very melancholy knight in a ruff, that demanded my subject[5]   20
    for somebody, a gentleman, I think.
CLERIMONT. Ay, that was he, lady.
MISTRESS OTTER. But he departed straight, I can resolve you.
DAUPHINE. What an excellent, choice phrase this lady expresses in!
TRUEWIT. O, sir, she is the only authentical courtier, that is not   25
    naturally bred one, in the City!
MISTRESS OTTER. You have taken that report upon trust, gentle-
    men.
TRUEWIT. No, I assure you, the court governs it so, lady, in your
    behalf.   30
MISTRESS OTTER. I am the servant of the court and courtiers, sir.
TRUEWIT. They are rather your idolaters.
MISTRESS OTTER. Not so, sir.
        [*Enter* CUTBEARD.]
DAUPHINE. How now, Cutbeard! Any cross?[6]
CUTBEARD. O no, sir, *omnia bene*. 'Twas never better o'the hinges;   35
    all's sure. I have so pleased him with a curate, that he's gone
    to't almost with the delight he hopes for soon.
DAUPHINE. What is he, for a vicar?[7]
CUTBEARD. One that has catched a cold sir, and can scarce be
    heard six inches off; as if he spoke out of a bulrush that were   40
    not picked, or his throat were full of pith;[8] a fine, quick fellow,
    and an excellent barber of prayers. I came to tell you, sir, that
    you might '*omnem movere lapidem*,'[9] as they say, be ready with
    your vexation.
DAUPHINE. Gramercy, honest Cutbeard! Be thereabouts with thy   45
    key to let us in.

---

4. Traditionally a violent, ranting, radical Protestant sect.
5. I.e., her husband.
6. Accident; "omnia bene": all's well.
7. "What sort of vicar is he?" "Curate" and "vicar" are both names that may be applied to a
   clergyman of the Church of England.
8. Phlegm. A "barber of prayers" clips the prayers short.
9. Leave no stone unturned.

CUTBEARD. I will not fail you, sir. *Ad manum.*[1]   [*Exit.*]

TRUEWIT. Well, I'll go watch my coaches.

CLERIMONT. Do; and we'll send Daw to you, if you meet him not.

MISTRESS OTTER. Is Master Truewit gone?   50

DAUPHINE. Yes, lady, there is some unfortunate business fallen out.

MISTRESS OTTER. So I judged by the physiognomy of the fellow
that came in; and I had a dream last night, too, of the new
pageant[2] and my Lady Mayoress, which is always very ominous
to me. I told it my Lady Haughty t'other day, when her honor   55
came hither to see some China stuffs, and she expounded it out
of Artemidorus[3] and I have found it since very true. It has done
me many affronts.

CLERIMONT. Your dream, lady?

MISTRESS OTTER. Yes, sir, anything I do but dream of the City.[4] It   60
stained me a damask tablecloth, cost me eighteen pound at one
time, and burnt me a black satin gown, as I stood by the fire at
my Lady Centaur's chamber in the College, another time. A
third time, at the Lord's masque, it dropped all my wire and my
ruff[5] with wax candle, that I could not go up to the banquet. A   65
fourth time, as I was taking coach to go to Ware, to meet a
friend, it dashed me a new suit all over—a crimson satin doublet
and black velvet skirts—with a brewer's horse, that I was fain to
go in and shift me,[6] and kept my chamber a leash of days for
the anguish of it.   70

DAUPHINE. These were dire mischances, lady.

CLERIMONT. I would not dwell in the City an 'twere so fatal to
me.

MISTRESS OTTER. Yes, sir, but I do take advice of my doctor to
dream of it as little as I can.   75

DAUPHINE. You do well, Mistress Otter.

[*Enter* SIR JOHN DAW, *and is taken aside by* CLERIMONT.]

MISTRESS OTTER. Will it please you to enter the house farther,
gentlemen?

DAUPHINE. And your favor, lady. But we stay to speak with a knight,
Sir John Daw, who is here come. We shall follow you, lady.   80

MISTRESS OTTER. At your own time, sir. It is my cousin, Sir Amorous, his feast——

DAUPHINE. I know it, lady.

1. Right at hand.
2. The city government of London had a great many pageants and parades.
3. Artemidorus (late second century C.E.) wrote a treatise in Greek on the interpretation of
dreams.
4. London City, as contrasted with court. The next word, "It," refers to Mistress Otter's dream.
5. The large lace ruffs of fine ladies were stiffened with wires.
6. Change my clothes; "leash": set of three, originally used of hounds or hares.

MISTRESS OTTER. And mine together. But it is for his honor, and
  therefore I take no name of it, more than of the place.   85
DAUPHINE. You are a bounteous kinswoman.
MISTRESS OTTER. Your servant, sir.   [*Exit.*]

ACT III   SCENE 3

CLERIMONT. [*coming forward with* DAW] Why, do not you know it,
  Sir John Daw?
DAW. No, I am a rook if I do.
CLERIMONT. I'll tell you then: she's married by this time. And
  whereas you were put i' the head, that she was gone with Sir   5
  Dauphine, I assure you Sir Dauphine has been the noblest,
  honestest friend to you, that ever gentleman of your quality
  could boast of. He has discovered[7] the whole plot, and made
  your mistress so acknowledging, and indeed so ashamed of her
  injury to you, that she desires you to forgive her, and but grace   10
  her wedding with your presence today—She is to be married to
  a very good fortune, she says, his uncle, old Morose; and she
  willed me in private to tell you that she shall be able to do you
  more favors, and with more security, now, than before.
DAW. Did she say so, i' faith?   15
CLERIMONT. Why, what do you think of me, Sir John? Ask Sir
  Dauphine!
DAW. Nay, I believe you. Good Sir Dauphine, did she desire me
  to forgive her?
DAUPHINE. I assure you, Sir John, she did.   20
DAW. Nay, then, I do with all my heart, and I'll be jovial.
CLERIMONT. Yes, for look you, sir, this was the injury to you. La
  Foole intended this feast to honor her bridal day, and made you
  the property[8] to invite the College ladies, and promise to bring
  her; and then at the time she should have appeared—as his   25
  friend—to have given you the dor.[9] Whereas now Sir Dauphine
  has brought her to a feeling of it, with this kind of satisfaction,
  that you shall bring all the ladies to the place where she is, and
  be very jovial. And there she will have a dinner, which shall be
  in your name; and so disappoint La Foole, to make you good   30
  again, and, as it were, a saver in the main.
DAW. As I am a knight, I honor her, and forgive her heartily.
CLERIMONT. About it then presently. Truewit is gone before to
  confront the coaches, and to acquaint you with so much, if he

7. Exposed.
8. Pretext.
9. Disgraced you.

meet you. Join with him, and 'tis well. See, here comes your   35
antagonist; but take you no notice, but be very jovial.

[*Enter* SIR AMOROUS LA FOOLE.]

LA FOOLE. Are the ladies come, Sir John Daw, and your mistress?
[*Exit* DAW.]—Sir Dauphine! You are exceeding welcome, and
honest Master Clerimont. Where's my cousin? Did you see no
Collegiates, gentlemen?   40

DAUPHINE. Collegiates! Do you not hear, Sir Amorous, how you
are abused?

LA FOOLE. How, sir!

CLERIMONT. Will you speak so kindly to Sir John Daw, that has
done you such an affront?   45

LA FOOLE. Wherein, gentlemen? Let me be a suitor to you to
know, I beseech you!

CLERIMONT. Why, sir, his mistress is married today to Sir Dauphine's uncle, your cousin's neighbor, and he has diverted all
the ladies, and all your company thither, to frustrate your pro- 50
vision, and stick a disgrace upon you. He was here now to have
enticed us away from you too, but we told him his own,[1] I think.

LA FOOLE. Has Sir John Daw wronged me so inhumanely?

DAUPHINE. He has done it, Sir Amorous, most maliciously and
treacherously; but if you'll be ruled by us, you shall quit him, i' 55
faith.

LA FOOLE. Good gentlemen, I'll make one, believe it. How, I pray?

DAUPHINE. Marry, sir, get me your pheasants, and your godwits,
and your best meat, and dish it in silver dishes of your cousin's
presently; and say nothing, but clap me a clean towel about you, 60
like a sewer;[2] and bareheaded, march afore it with a good
confidence—'tis but over the way, hard by—and we'll second
you, where you shall set it off the board;[3] and bid 'em welcome
to 't, which shall show 'tis yours, and disgrace his preparation
utterly. And for your cousin, whereas she should be troubled 65
here at home with care of making and giving welcome, she shall
transfer all that labor thither, and be a principal guest herself;
sit ranked with the College Honors, and be honored, and have
her health drunk as often, as bare,[4] and as loud as the best
of 'em.   70

LA FOOLE. I'll go tell her presently. It shall be done, that's resolved.   [*Exit.*]

CLERIMONT. I thought he would not hear it out but 'twould take
him.

1. Told him off.
2. Steward.
3. Put it on the table.
4. Bareheaded, in token of respect.

DAUPHINE. Well, there be guests and meat now; how shall we do   75
for music?

CLERIMONT. The smell of the venison, going through the street,
will invite one noise[5] of fiddlers or other.

DAUPHINE. I would it would call the trumpeters thither!

CLERIMONT. Faith, there is hope; they have intelligence of all   80
feasts. There's good correspondence betwixt them and the London cooks. 'Tis twenty to one but we have 'em.

DAUPHINE. 'Twill be a most solemn day for my uncle, and an
excellent fit of mirth for us.

CLERIMONT. Ay, if we can hold up the emulation betwixt Foole   85
and Daw, and never bring them to expostulate.[6]

DAUPHINE. Tut, flatter 'em both, as Truewit says, and you may take
their understandings in a pursenet.[7] They'll believe themselves
to be just such men as we make 'em, neither more nor less.
They have nothing, not the use of their senses, but by tradition.   90

[Re-enter LA FOOLE, like a sewer.]

CLERIMONT. See! Sir Amorous has his towel on already. Have you
persuaded your cousin?

LA FOOLE. Yes, 'tis very feasible. She'll do anything, she says, rather
than the La Fooles shall be disgraced.

DAUPHINE. She is a noble kinswoman. It will be such a pestling[8]   95
device, Sir Amorous, it will pound all your enemy's practices to
powder, and blow him up with his own mine, his own train![9]

LA FOOLE. Nay, we'll give fire, I warrant you.

CLERIMONT. But you must carry it privately, without any noise, and
take no notice by any means——   100

[Re-enter CAPTAIN OTTER.]

OTTER. Gentlemen, my Princess says you shall have all her silver
dishes, festinate;[1] and she's gone to alter her tire[2] a little, and go
with you——

CLERIMONT. And yourself too, Captain Otter?

DAUPHINE. By any means, sir.   105

OTTER. Yes, sir, I do mean it; but I would entreat my cousin Sir
Amorous, and you, gentlemen, to be suitors to my Princess, that
I may carry my Bull and my Bear, as well as my Horse.

CLERIMONT. That you shall do, Captain Otter.

LA FOOLE. My cousin will never consent, gentlemen.   110

---

5. I.e., a pickup group of itinerant street musicians.
6. To explain things to one another; "emulation": competition.
7. A small sack closed by a string, fit to hold both their brains; "tradition": literally, "what they are handed."
8. A trick that works like a mortar and pestle.
9. I.e., a track of gunpowder leading to the enemy's bomb; ignite it and you blow him up.
1. Soon.
2. Attire, specifically hairdo.

DAUPHINE. She must consent, Sir Amorous, to reason.

LA FOOLE. Why, she says they are no decorum among ladies.

OTTER. But they are *decora*,³ and that's better, sir.

CLERIMONT. Ay, she must hear argument. Did not Pasiphae, who
was a queen, love a bull?⁴ And was not Callisto, the mother of   115
Arcas, turned into a bear, and made a star, Mistress Ursula, i'
the heavens?

OTTER. O God! That I could ha' said as much! I will have these
stories painted in the bear-garden, *ex Ovidii Metamorphosi.*⁵

DAUPHINE. Where is your Princess, Captain? Pray be our leader.   120

OTTER. That I shall, sir.

CLERIMONT. Make haste, good Sir Amorous.   [*Exeunt.*]

ACT III   SCENE 4. MOROSE'S *HOUSE*

[*Enter* MOROSE, EPICOENE, PARSON, *and* CUTBEARD.]

MOROSE. Sir, there's an angel⁶ for yourself, and a brace of angels
for your cold. Muse not at this manage of my bounty. It is fit
we should thank fortune, double to nature, for any benefit she
confers upon us; besides, it is your imperfection, but my solace.

PARSON. [*speaks as having a cold.*] I thank your worship; so is it   5
mine now.

MOROSE. What says he, Cutbeard?

CUTBEARD. He says, presto, sir, whensoever your worship needs
him, he can be ready with the like. He got this cold with sitting
up late, and singing catches⁷ with cloth-workers.   10

MOROSE. No more. I thank him.

PARSON. God keep your worship, and give you much joy with your
fair spouse! [*Coughs.*] Uh, uh!

MOROSE. O, O! Stay, Cutbeard! Let him give me five shillings of
my money back. As it is bounty to reward benefits, so it is equity   15
to mulct injuries. I will have it. What says he?

CLERIMONT. He cannot change it, sir.

MOROSE. It must be changed.

CUTBEARD. [*aside.*]—Cough again.

MOROSE. What says he?   20

CUTBEARD. He will cough out the rest, sir.

PARSON. [*Coughs.*] Uh, uh, uh!

---

3. *Decora* are fine things, though they may not be decorous (i.e., suitable to the occasion).
4. In Greek mythology, Pasiphae, queen of Crete, loved a bull, and so gave birth to the Minotaur;
Callisto was turned into a bear and is now Ursa Major, a constellation in the heavens.
5. Out of the Roman poet Ovid's (43 B.C.E.–17 C.E.) *Metamorphoses.*
6. A gold coin bearing the image of St. Michael and worth a handsome sum of money.
7. Songs in several parts. Huguenot weavers, refugees from Catholic persecution in France, were
celebrated for singing at their work.

MOROSE. Away, away with him! Stop his mouth! Away! I forgive
it——.   [*Exit* CUTBEARD *thrusting out the* PARSON.]

EPICOENE. Fie, Master Morose, that you will use this violence to   25
a man of the church!

MOROSE. How!

EPICOENE. It does not become your gravity or breeding, as you
pretend in court, to have offered this outrage on a waterman,[8]
or any more boisterous creature, much less on a man of his civil   30
coat.

MOROSE. You can speak then!

EPICOENE. Yes, sir.

MOROSE. Speak out, I mean.

EPICOENE. Ay, sir. Why, did you think you had married a statue,   35
or a motion[9] only? One of the French puppets, with the eyes
turned with a wire? Or some innocent out of the hospital, that
would stand with her hands thus, and a plaice-mouth,[1] and look
upon you?

MOROSE. O immodesty! A manifest woman! What, Cutbeard!   40

EPICOENE. Nay, never quarrel with Cutbeard, sir; it is too late now.
I confess it doth bate[2] somewhat of the modesty I had, when I
writ simply maid; but I hope I shall make it a stock still competent to the estate and dignity of your wife.

MOROSE. She can talk!   45

EPICOENE. Yes indeed, sir.
          [*Enter* MUTE.]

MOROSE. What, sirrah! None of my knaves there? Where is this
impostor Cutbeard?

EPICOENE. Speak to him, fellow, speak to him! I'll have none of
this coacted,[3] unnatural dumbness in my house, in a family   50
where I govern.   [*Exit* MUTE.]

MOROSE. She is my regent already! I have married a Penthesilea,
a Semiramis![4] Sold my liberty to a distaff!

ACT III   SCENE 5

          [*Enter* TRUEWIT.]

TRUEWIT. Where's Master Morose?

MOROSE. Is he come again? Lord have mercy upon me!

---

8. A hired boatman on the Thames.
9. Puppet.
1. Puckered-up, wry mouth, like that of a flatfish.
2. Abate, diminish.
3. Forced.
4. Penthesilea and Semiramis were warrior queens of Greek mythology. A "distaff," used in
spinning, is not only a stick, but one that whirs and clatters.

TRUEWIT. I wish you all joy, Mistress Epicoene, with your grave
and honorable match.

EPICOENE. I return you the thanks, Master Truewit, so friendly a   5
wish deserves.

MOROSE. She has acquaintance, too!

TRUEWIT. God save you, sir, and give you all contentment in your
fair choice here! Before, I was the bird of night to you, the
owl;[5] but now I am the messenger of peace, a dove, and bring   10
you the glad wishes of my friends to the celebration of this good
hour.

MOROSE. What hour, sir?

TRUEWIT. Your marriage hour, sir. I commend your resolution,
that—notwithstanding all the dangers I laid afore you, in the   15
voice of a night-crow—would yet go on, and be yourself. It shows
you are a man constant to your own ends, and upright to your
purposes, that would not be put off with left-handed cries.[6]

MOROSE. How should you arrive at the knowledge of so much?

TRUEWIT. Why did you ever hope, sir, committing the secrecy of   20
it to a barber, that less than the whole town should know it?
You might as well have told it the conduit,[7] or the bakehouse,
or the infantry that follow the court, and with more security.
Could your gravity forget so old and noted a remnant as *'lippis
et tonsoribus notum'*?[8] Well, sir, forgive it yourself now, the fault,   25
and be communicable with your friends. Here will be three or
four fashionable ladies from the College to visit you presently,
and their train of minions and followers.

MOROSE. Bar my doors! Bar my doors! Where are all my eaters,[9]
my mouths, now?——   30

    [*Enter* SERVANTS.]

Bar up my doors, you varlets!

EPICOENE. He is a varlet that stirs to such an office. Let 'em stand
open. I would see him that dares move his eyes toward it. Shall
I have a *barricado*[1] made against my friends, to be barred of any
pleasure they can bring in to me with honorable visitation?   35

        [*Exeunt* SERVANTS.]

MOROSE. O Amazonian[2] impudence!

TRUEWIT. Nay, faith, in this, sir, she speaks but reason; and, me
thinks, is more continent than you. Would you go to bed so

---

5. Traditional bird of ill omen.
6. The left or sinister hand is always associated with bad luck.
7. All these phrases are more or less metaphorical ways of referring to the rabble, the common
herd.
8. The phrase, from a satire by Horace, means "known to everyone, to the blear-eyed and the
barbers" (Latin).
9. Servants, i.e., those who have all this time eaten my bread.
1. Barrier.
2. As of Amazons, fierce female warriors of Greek mythology.

presently, sir, afore noon? A man of your head and hair should
owe more to that reverend ceremony, and not mount the mar-   40
riage bed like a town-bull, or a mountain-goat; but stay the due
season, and ascend it then with religion and fear. Those delights
are to be steeped in the humor and silence of the night; and
give the day to other open pleasures, and jollities of feast, of
music, of revels, of discourse. We'll have all, sir, that may make   45
your Hymen[3] high and happy.

MOROSE. O my torment, my torment!

TRUEWIT. Nay, if you endure the first half hour, sir, so tediously,
and with this irksomeness, what comfort or hope can this fair
gentlewoman make to herself hereafter, in the consideration of   50
so many years as are to come——

MOROSE. Of my affliction. Good sir, depart, and let her do it alone.

TRUEWIT. I have done, sir.

MOROSE. That cursed barber!

TRUEWIT. Yes, faith, a cursed wretch indeed, sir.   55

MOROSE. I have married his cittern,[4] that's common to all men.
Some plague above the plague——

TRUEWIT. All Egypt's ten plagues.[5]

MOROSE. Revenge me on him!

TRUEWIT. 'Tis very well, sir. If you laid on a curse or two more,   60
I'll assure you he'll bear 'em. As that he may get the pox with
seeking to cure it, sir. Or that, while he is curling another man's
hair, his own may drop off. Or, for burning some male bawd's
lock, he may have his brain beat out with the curling-iron.

MOROSE. No, let the wretch live wretched. May he get the itch,   65
and his shop so lousy, as no man dare come at him, nor he
come at no man!

TRUEWIT. Ay, and if ye would swallow all his balls[6] for pills, let
not them purge him.

MOROSE. Let his warming-pan be ever cold!   70

TRUEWIT. A perpetual frost underneath it, sir.

MOROSE. Let him never hope to see fire again!

TRUEWIT. But in hell, sir.

MOROSE. His chairs be always empty, his scissors rust, and his
combs mold in their cases!   75

TRUEWIT. Very dreadful that! And may he lose the invention, sir,
of carving lanterns in paper.[7]

---

3. God of marriage, hence by extension the ceremony itself.
4. A guitar, often kept in barbershops for customers to fool with while they waited—hence, a
common floozie.
5. In the Bible, the Lord visited ten plagues on Egypt, so that the children of Israel might go
free.
6. Of soap, commonly used in that form by barbers; "lousy": full of lice.
7. Barber signs, for the twilight hours.

MOROSE. Let there be no bawd carted that year, to employ a basin of his;[8] but let him be glad to eat his sponge for bread!

TRUEWIT. And drink lotion[9] to it, and much good do him!　　　80

MOROSE. Or, for want of bread——

TRUEWIT. Eat ear-wax, sir! I'll help you. Or draw his own teeth, and add them to the lute-string!

MOROSE. No, beat the old ones to powder, and make bread of them!　　　85

TRUEWIT. Yes, make meal of the millstones.

MOROSE. May all the botches and burns that he has cured on others, break out upon him!

TRUEWIT. And he now forget the cure of them in himself, sir; or, if he do remember it, let him have scraped all his linen into　　90 lint for't, and have not a rag left him to set up with!

MOROSE. Let him never set up[1] again, but have the gout in his hands forever! Now, no more sir.

TRUEWIT. O, that last was too high set; you might go less with him, i' faith, and be revenged enough: as, that he be never able to　　95 new-paint his pole——

MOROSE. Good sir, no more. I forgot myself.

TRUEWIT. Or, want credit to take up with a comb-maker——

MOROSE. No more, sir.

TRUEWIT. Or, having broken his glass in a former despair, fall now　　100 into a much greater, of ever getting another——

MOROSE. I beseech you, no more.

TRUEWIT. Or, that he never be trusted with trimming of any but chimney-sweepers——

MOROSE. Sir——　　　105

TRUEWIT. Or, may he cut a collier's[2] throat with his razor, by chance-medley, and yet hang for't.

MOROSE. I will forgive him rather than hear any more. I beseech you, sir.

ACT III　SCENE 6

[*Enter* DAW, *with* LADY HAUGHTY, LADY CENTAUR, MISTRESS MAVIS, *and* TRUSTY.]

DAW. This way, madam.

MOROSE. O, the sea breaks in upon me! Another flood! An inundation! I shall be o'erwhelmed with noise. It beats already at my shores. I feel an earthquake in myself for't.

8. Bawds, i.e., pimps, being whipped through the streets in a cart were preceded by a man banging on a basin to invite public attention.
9. Stale urine used by barbers on hair.
1. Set up shop.
2. Literally, a coal miner, figuratively, a rascal, a worthless person; "chance-medley": accident.

DAW. Give you joy, mistress.   5

MOROSE. Has she servants too!

DAW. I have brought some ladies here to see and know you. My
    Lady Haughty—[EPICOENE *kisses them severally, as he presents
    them*]—this my Lady Centaur—Mistress Doll Mavis—Mistress
    Trusty, my Lady Haughty's woman. Where's your husband?   10
    Let's see him. Can he endure no noise? Let me come to him.

MOROSE. What nomenclator³ is this?

TRUEWIT. Sir John Daw, sir, your wife's servant, this.

MOROSE. A Daw, and her servant! O, 'tis decreed, 'tis decreed of
    me, an she have such servants.   15

TRUEWIT. Nay, sir, you must kiss the ladies; you must not go away
    now. They come toward you to seek you out.

HAUGHTY. I' faith, Master Morose, would you steal a marriage thus,
    in the midst of so many friends, and not acquaint us? Well, I'll
    kiss you, notwithstanding the justice of my quarrel. You shall   20
    give me leave, mistress, to use a becoming familiarity with your
    husband.

EPICOENE. Your ladyship does me an honor in it, to let me know
    he is so worthy your favor; as you have done both him and me
    grace to visit so unprepared a pair to entertain you.   25

MOROSE. Compliment! Compliment!

EPICOENE. But I must lay the burden of that upon my servant here.

HAUGHTY. It shall not need, Mistress Morose; we will all bear,
    rather than one shall be oppressed.

MOROSE. I know it; and you will teach her the faculty, if she be   30
    to learn it.   [*Walks aside.*]

HAUGHTY. Is this the Silent Woman?

CENTAUR. Nay, she has found her tongue since she was married,
    Master Truewit says.

HAUGHTY. O, Master Truewit, save you! What kind of creature is   35
    your bride here? She speaks, methinks!

TRUEWIT. Yes, madam, believe it, she is a gentlewoman of very
    absolute behavior, and of a good race.

HAUGHTY. And Jack Daw told us she could not speak!

TRUEWIT. So it was carried in plot, madam, to put her upon this   40
    old fellow, by Sir Dauphine, his nephew, and one or two more
    of us. But she is a woman of an excellent assurance, and an
    extraordinary happy wit and tongue. You shall see her make rare
    sport with Daw ere night.

HAUGHTY. And he brought us to laugh at her!   45

TRUEWIT. That falls out often, madam, that he that thinks himself

---

3. Someone who announces the names of guests.

the master-wit, is the master-fool. I assure your ladyship, ye cannot laugh at her.

HAUGHTY. No, we'll have her to the College. An she have wit, she
shall be one of us! Shall she not, Centaur? We'll make her a   50
Collegiate.

CENTAUR. Yes, faith, madam, and Mavis and she will set up a side.[4]

TRUEWIT. Believe it, madam and Mistress Mavis, she will sustain
her part.

MAVIS. I'll tell you that when I have talked with her, and tried her.   55

HAUGHTY. Use her very civilly, Mavis.

MAVIS. So I will, madam.   [Whispers to her.]

MOROSE. [aside]—Blessed minute! that they would whisper thus
ever!

TRUEWIT. In the meantime, madam, would but your ladyship help   60
to vex him a little. You know his disease; talk to him about the
wedding ceremonies, or call for your gloves, or——

HAUGHTY. Let me alone. Centaur, help me. Master Bridegroom,
where are you?

MOROSE. [aside]—O, it was too miraculously good to last!   65

HAUGHTY. We see no ensigns[5] of a wedding here, no character of
a bridal. Where be our scarfs and our gloves? I pray you, give
'em us. Let us know your bride's colors, and yours, at least.[6]

CENTAUR. Alas, madam, he has provided none.

MOROSE. Had I known your ladyship's painter,[7] I would.   70

HAUGHTY. He has given it you, Centaur, i' faith. But do you hear,
Master Morose? A jest will not absolve you in this manner. You
that have sucked the milk of the court, and from thence have
been brought up to the very strong meats and wine of it; been
a courtier from the biggen to the nightcap,[8] as we may say; and   75
you to offend in such a high point of ceremony as this, and let
your nuptials want all marks of solemnity! How much plate have
you lost today—if you had but regarded your profit—what gifts,
what friends, through your mere rusticity!

MOROSE. Madam——   80

HAUGHTY. Pardon me, sir, I must insinuate[9] your errors to you. No
gloves? No garters? No scarfs? No epithalamium?[1] No masque?

---

4. I.e., make a pair in a game of cards.
5. I.e., special emblems.
6. The bride and her bridesmaids and the groom and his followers wore distinctive colors.
7. Painting (wearing makeup) was not well thought of in those days; Morose indicates that if he
   had known Lady Centaur's makeup man, he would have had her daubed, say, green and
   orange.
8. I.e., from the cradle to the grave.
9. Introduce subtly.
1. Marriage poem; masques were also performed for very fancy weddings.

DAW. Yes, madam, I'll make an *epithalamium*, I promised my mistress. I have begun it already. Will your ladyship hear it?

HAUGHTY. Ay, good Jack Daw.   85

MOROSE. Will it please your ladyship command a chamber, and be private with your friend? You shall have your choice of rooms to retire to after. My whole house is yours. I know it hath been your ladyship's errand into the City at other times,[2] however now you have been unhappily diverted upon me; but I shall be loath   90
to break any honorable custom of your ladyship's. And therefore, good madam——

EPICOENE. Come, you are a rude bridegroom, to entertain ladies of honor in this fashion.

CENTAUR. He is a rude groom[3] indeed.   95

TRUEWIT. By that light, you deserve to be grafted, and have your horns[4] reach from one side of the island to the other—[*aside to Morose*] Do not mistake me, sir, I but speak this to give the ladies some heart again, not for any malice to you.

MOROSE. Is this your bravo,[5] ladies?   100

TRUEWIT. As God help me, if you utter such another word, I'll take Mistress Bride in, and begin to you in a very sad cup,[6] do you see? Go to, know your friends and such as love you.

ACT III   SCENE 7

[*Enter* CLERIMONT *followed by a number of musicians.*]

CLERIMONT. By your leave, ladies. Do you want any music? I have brought you variety of noises—Play, sirs, all of you.

[Music of all sorts.]

MOROSE. O, a plot, a plot, a plot, a plot upon me! This day I shall be their anvil to work on; they will grate me asunder. 'Tis worse than the noise of a saw.   5

CLERIMONT. No, they are hair, rosin, and guts. I can give you the receipt.[7]

TRUEWIT. Peace, boys!

CLERIMONT. Play, I say!

TRUEWIT. Peace, rascals! You see who's your friend now, sir? Take   10
courage, put on a martyr's resolution. Mock down all their attemptings with patience. 'Tis but a day, and I would suffer heroically. Should an ass exceed me in fortitude? No. You betray

---

2. I.e., she has gone into the city from the court to be alone in a bedroom with a courtier.
3. Not just a rude bridegroom but rude by the standards of stableboys (grooms).
4. The cuckold's traditional horns.
5. A hired bully, who may protect prostitutes—implying that they are whores.
6. I.e., get your marriage off to a very bad start.
7. Recipe.

your infirmity with your hanging dull ears, and make them insult. Bear up bravely, and constantly. [LA FOOLE *passes over,*   15
serving the meat, followed by servants carrying dishes, and MIS-
TRESS OTTER.]—Look you here sir, what honor is done you unexpected, by your nephew; a wedding dinner come, and a
knight-sewer before it, for the more reputation; and fine Mistress
Otter, your neighbor, in the rump or tail of it.   20
MOROSE. Is that Gorgon, that Medusa[8] come? Hide me, hide me!
TRUEWIT. I warrant you, sir, she will not transform you. Look upon
her with a good courage. Pray you entertain her, and conduct
your guests in. No?—Mistress Bride, will you entreat in the la-
dies? Your bridegroom is so shamefaced here——   25
EPICOENE. Will it please your ladyship, madam?
HAUGHTY. With the benefit of your company, mistress.
EPICOENE. Servant, pray you perform your duties.
DAW. And glad to be commanded, mistress.
CENTAUR. How like you her wit, Mavis?   30
MAVIS. Very prettily, absolutely well.
MISTRESS OTTER. 'Tis my place.
MAVIS. You shall pardon me, Mistress Otter.
MISTRESS OTTER. Why, I am a Collegiate.
MAVIS. But not in ordinary.[9]   35
MISTRESS OTTER. But I am.
MAVIS. We'll dispute that within.   [*Exeunt* LADIES.]
CLERIMONT. Would this had lasted a little longer!
TRUEWIT. And that they had sent for the heralds!
        [*Enter* CAPTAIN OTTER.]
    Captain Otter! What news?   40
OTTER. I have brought my Bull, Bear, and Horse, in private, and
yonder are the trumpeters without, and the drum, gentlemen.[1]
                    [*The drum and trumpets sound.*]
MOROSE. O, O, O!
OTTER. And we will have a rouse[2] in each of 'em, anon, for bold
Britons, i' faith!   [*They sound again.*]   45
MOROSE. O, O, O!   [*Exit.*]
ALL. Follow, follow, follow![3]   [*Exeunt all.*]

---

8. Medusa the Gorgon had frightful features that turned men to stone.
9. The ladies have their dignities and precedences: "in ordinary" implies "with all the titles and
   formalities."
1. At serious drinking bouts a flourish of trumpets and a drumroll saluted each emptying of the
   glasses.
2. Toast.
3. "Follow, follow, follow" is the Elizabethan playwright's way of indicating a confused gabble
   of many people.

Act IV

ACT IV   SCENE 1. MOROSE'S HOUSE

[*Enter* TRUEWIT *and* CLERIMONT]

TRUEWIT. Was there ever poor bridegroom so tormented? Or man, indeed?

CLERIMONT. I have not read of the like in the chronicles of the land.

TRUEWIT. Sure, he cannot but go to a place of rest, after all this   5
purgatory.[4]

CLERIMONT. He may presume it, I think.

TRUEWIT. The spitting, the coughing, the laughter, the sneezing, the farting, dancing, noise of the music, and her masculine and loud commanding, and urging the whole family, makes him   10
think he has married a fury.[5]

CLERIMONT. And she carries it up bravely.

TRUEWIT. Ay, she takes any occasion to speak; that's the height on't.

CLERIMONT. And how soberly Dauphine labors to satisfy him, that   15
it was none of his plot!

TRUEWIT. And has almost brought him to the faith, in the article. Here he comes.

[*Enter* SIR DAUPHINE.]

Where is he now? What's become of him, Dauphine?

DAUPHINE. O, hold me up a little, I shall go away in the jest[6] else.   20
He has got on his whole nest of nightcaps, and locked himself up in the top of the house, as high as ever he can climb from the noise. I peeped in at a cranny, and saw him sitting over a crossbeam of the roof, like him on the saddler's horse in Fleet Street,[7] upright; and he will sleep there.   25

CLERIMONT. But where are your Collegiates?

DAUPHINE. Withdrawn with the bride in private.

TRUEWIT. O, they are instructing her in the College grammar. If she have grace with them, she knows all their secrets instantly.

CLERIMONT. Methinks the Lady Haughty looks well today, for all   30
my dispraise of her in the morning. I think I shall come about to thee again, Truewit.

TRUEWIT. Believe it, I told you right. Women ought to repair the losses time and years have made in their features, with dressings.

---

4. In Catholic theology, the place of purification after death; used here with the overtone that Morose has been purged of his fear of noise and may go to his "place of rest," or Heaven.
5. In Greek mythology the Furies were three frightful females appointed to punish human crimes; Epicoene looks like one of them.
6. Die laughing.
7. A bootmaker in Fleet Street evidently had a sign consisting of a wooden horse and rider.

And an intelligent woman, if she know by herself the least defect 35
will be most curious to hide it; and it becomes her. If she be
short, let her sit much, lest, when she stands, she be thought to
sit. If she have an ill foot, let her wear her gown the longer, and
her shoe the thinner. If a fat hand and scald nails, let her carve
the less,[8] and act in gloves. If a sour breath, let her never dis- 40
course fasting,[9] and always talk at her distance. If she have black
and rugged teeth, let her offer the less at laughter, especially if
she laugh wide and open.

CLERIMONT. O, you shall have some women, when they laugh you
would think they brayed, it is so rude and—— 45

TRUEWIT. Ay, and others that will stalk in their gait like an ostrich,
and take huge strides. I cannot endure such a sight. I love measure in the feet, and number in the voice.[1] They are gentlenesses
that oftentimes draw no less than the face.

DAUPHINE. How camest thou to study these creatures so exactly? I 50
would thou wouldst make me a proficient.

TRUEWIT. Yes, but you must leave to live i' your chamber, then, a
month together upon Amadis de Gaul, or Don Quixote as you
are wont;[2] and come abroad where the matter is frequent, to
court, to tiltings,[3] public shows, and feasts, to plays, and church 55
sometimes. Thither they come to show their new tires too, to
see and to be seen. In these places a man shall find whom to
love, whom to play with, whom to touch once, whom to hold
ever. The variety arrests his judgment. A wench to please a man
comes not down dropping from the ceiling, as he lies on his 60
back droning a tobacco-pipe. He must go where she is.

DAUPHINE. Yes, and be never the nearer.

TRUEWIT. Out, heretic! That diffidence makes thee worthy it
should be so.

CLERIMONT. He says true to you, Dauphine. 65

DAUPHINE. Why?

TRUEWIT. A man should not doubt to overcome any woman.
Think he can vanquish them, and he shall; for though they
deny, their desire is to be tempted. Penelope herself cannot
hold out long. Ostend, you saw, was taken at last.[4] You must 70
persevere and hold to your purpose. They would solicit us, but

---

8. I.e., if she has rough, scabby hands, she shouldn't carve at table, when everyone will be
watching them.
9. Talk on an empty stomach (when her breath would be bad).
1. Small feet and a soft voice.
2. Romantic and impractical reading.
3. Mock jousts.
4. In Homer's *Odyssey*, Penelope, Odysseus's wife, held out against the solicitation of her many
suitors for 20 years; Ostend, a port in Belgium, was under siege by the Spaniards from 1601
to 1604.

that they are afraid. Howsoever, they wish in their hearts we
should solicit them. Praise them, flatter them, you shall never
want eloquence or trust; even the chastest delight to feel themselves that way rubbed. With praises you must mix kisses too; if   75
they take them, they'll take more. Though they strive, they
would be overcome.

CLERIMONT. O, but a man must beware of force.

TRUEWIT. It is to them an acceptable violence, and has oft-times
the place of the greatest courtesy. She that might have been   80
forced, an you let her go free without touching, though then
she seem to thank you, will ever hate you after; and, glad in the
face, is assuredly sad at the heart.

CLERIMONT. But all women are not to be taken all ways.

TRUEWIT. 'Tis true. No more than all birds, or all fishes. If you   85
appear learned to an ignorant wench, or jocund to a sad, or
witty to a foolish, why, she presently begins to mistrust herself.
You must approach them in their own height, their own line;
for the contrary makes many that fear to commit themselves to
noble and worthy fellows, run into the embraces of a rascal. If   90
she love wit, give verses, though you borrow them of a friend,
or buy them, to have good. If valor, talk of your sword, and be
frequent in the mention of quarrels, though you be staunch in
fighting.[5] If activity, be seen on your barbary[6] often, or leaping
over stools, for the credit of your back. If she love good clothes   95
or dressing, have your learned counsel about you every morning,
your French tailor, barber, linener, etc. Let your powder, your
glass, and your comb be your dearest acquaintance. Take more
care for the ornament of your head, than the safety; and wish
the commonwealth rather troubled, than a hair about you. That   100
will take her. Then, if she be covetous and craving, do you
promise anything, and perform sparingly; so shall you keep her
in appetite still. Seem as you would give, but be like a barren
field that yields little, or unlucky dice to foolish and hoping
gamesters. Let your gifts be slight and dainty, rather than pre-   105
cious. Let cunning be above cost. Give cherries at time of year,[7]
or apricots, and say they were sent you out of the country,
though you bought them in Cheapside. Admire her tires; like
her in all fashions; compare her in every habit to some deity;
invent excellent dreams to flatter her, and riddles; or, if she be 110
a great one, perform always the second parts to her: like what
she likes, praise whom she praises, and fail not to make the

---

5. The passage would be clearer if it said, as it evidently means, staunch *against* fighting.
6. Arabian horse.
7. I.e., at the odd time of year, out of season.

household and servants yours, yea, the whole family, and salute
them by their names—'tis but light cost, if you can purchase
them so—and make her physician your pensioner; and her chief   115
woman.[8] Nor will it be out of your gain to make love to her too,
so she follow, not usher her lady's pleasure. All blabbing is taken
away, when she comes to be a part of the crime.

DAUPHINE. On what courtly lap hast thou late slept, to come forth
so sudden and absolute a courtling?   120

TRUEWIT. Good faith, I should rather question you, that are so
hearkening after these mysteries. I began to suspect your diligence, Dauphine. Speak, art thou in love in earnest?

DAUPHINE. Yes, by my troth, am I! 'Twere ill dissembling before
thee.   125

TRUEWIT. With which of 'em, I pray thee?

DAUPHINE. With all the Collegiates.

CLERIMONT. Out on thee! We'll keep you at home, believe it, in
the stable, an you be such a stallion.

TRUEWIT. No, I like him well. Men should love wisely, and all   130
women: some one for the face, and let her please the eye; another for the skin, and let her please the touch; a third for the
voice, and let her please the ear; and where the objects mix, let
the senses so, too. Thou wouldst think it strange if I should make
them all in love with thee afore night!   135

DAUPHINE. I would say thou hadst the best philter[9] in the world,
and couldst do more than Madam Medea, or Doctor Forman.

TRUEWIT. If I do not, let me play the mountebank[1] for my meat,
while I live, and the bawd for my drink.

DAUPHINE. So be it, I say.   140

ACT IV   SCENE 2

[*Enter* OTTER, *with his three cups,* DAW, *and* LA FOOLE.]

OTTER. O Lord, gentlemen, how my knights and I have missed
you here!

CLERIMONT. Why, Captain, what service, what service?

OTTER. To see me bring up my Bull, Bear, and Horse to fight.

DAW. Yes, faith, the Captain says we shall be his dogs to bait them.   5

DAUPHINE. A good employment.

TRUEWIT. Come on, let's see a course, then.

LA FOOLE. I am afraid my cousin will be offended, if she come.

OTTER. Be afraid of nothing. Gentlemen, I have placed the drum

---

8. Bribe her doctor and maid—the former just with money, the latter with sex in addition;
"usher": precede.
9. Love potion. Medea was the witch-sorceress of Greek mythology; Doctor Simon Forman was
an astrologer, physician, and druggist of Jonson's day.
1. Quack.

and the trumpets, and one to give them the sign when you are   10
ready. Here's my Bull for myself, and my Bear for Sir John Daw,
and my Horse for Sir Amorous. Now set your foot to mine, and
yours to his and—[2]

LA FOOLE. Pray God my cousin come not.

OTTER. Saint George and Saint Andrew, fear no cousins—Come,   15
sound, sound!—*Et rauco strepuerunt cornua cantu.*[3] [*Drum
and trumpets. They drink.*]

TRUEWIT. Well said, Captain, i' faith! Well fought at the Bull.

CLERIMONT. Well held at the Bear.

TRUEWIT. Low, low, Captain!

DAUPHINE. O, the Horse has kicked off his dog already.   20

LA FOOLE. I cannot drink it, as I am a knight.

TRUEWIT. God's so! Off with his spurs, somebody!

LA FOOLE. It goes against my conscience. My cousin will be angry
with it.

DAW. I have done mine.   25

TRUEWIT. You fought high and fair, Sir John.

CLERIMONT. At the head.

DAUPHINE. Like an excellent bear-dog.

CLERIMONT. —You take no notice of the business,[4] I hope?

DAW. Not a word, sir, you see we are jovial.   30

OTTER. Sir Amorous, you must not equivocate.[5] It must be pulled
down, for all my cousin.

CLERIMONT. —'Sfoot, if you take not your drink, they'll think you
are discontented with something. You'll betray all, if you take
the least notice.   35

LA FOOLE. Not I, I'll both drink and talk then.

OTTER. You must pull the horse on his knees, Sir Amorous; fear
no cousins. *Jacta est alea.*[6]

TRUEWIT. —O, now he's in his vein, and bold. The least hint given
him of his wife now will make him rail desperately.   40

CLERIMONT. Speak to him of her.

TRUEWIT. Do you, and I'll fetch her to the hearing of it.   [*Exit.*]

DAUPHINE. Captain he-Otter, your she-Otter is coming, your wife.

OTTER. Wife! buzz! Titivilitium![7] There's no such thing in nature.
I confess, gentleman, I have a cook, a laundress, a house drudge,   45
that serves my necessary turns, and goes under that title; but he's
an ass that will be so uxorious to tie his affections to one circle.

---

2. Otter is suggesting that they toast their cups.
3. "And the trumpets gave off a roaring sound."
4. I.e., the supposed quarrel with La Foole.
5. Stall—in drinking contests, no excuses were accepted till a man lay insensible.
6. "The die is cast"—as Caesar said when he crossed the Rubicon to seize imperial power.
7. A thing of no value.

Come, the name dulls appetite. Here, replenish again; another
bout. [*Fills the cups again.*] Wives are nasty, sluttish animals.

DAUPHINE. O, Captain.   50

OTTER. As ever the earth bare, *tribus verbis.*[8] Where's Master
   Truewit?

DAW. He's slipped aside, sir.

CLERIMONT. But you must drink and be jovial.

DAW. Yes, give it me.   55

LA FOOLE. And me too.

DAW. Let's be jovial.

LA FOOLE. As jovial as you will.

OTTER. Agreed. Now you shall have the Bear, cousin, and Sir John
   Daw the Horse, and I'll have the Bull still.—Sound, Tritons[9] of   60
   the Thames!—*Nunc est bibendum, nunc pede libero*——[1]

MOROSE. [*Speaks from above, as the drum beats and the trumpets
   sound.*] Villains, murderers, sons of the earth, and traitors, what
   do you there?

CLERIMONT. O, now the trumpets have waked him, we shall have
   his company.   65

OTTER. A wife is a scurvy clogdogdo,[2] an unlucky thing, a very
   fore-said bear-whelp, without any good fashion or breeding, *mala
   bestia.*[3]

[*Re-enter* TRUEWIT *behind with* MISTRESS OTTER.]

DAUPHINE. Why did you marry one then, Captain?

OTTER. A pox! I married with six thousand pound, I. I was in love   70
   with that. I have not kissed my Fury these forty weeks.

CLERIMONT. The more to blame you, Captain.

TRUEWIT. [*aside*]—Nay, Mistress Otter, hear him a little first.

OTTER. She has a breath worse than my grandmother's, *profecto!*[4]

MISTRESS OTTER. [*aside*]—O treacherous liar! Kiss me, sweet Mas-   75
   ter Truewit, and prove him a slandering knave.

TRUEWIT. I'll rather believe you, lady.

OTTER. And she has a peruke that's like a pound of hemp, made
   up in shoe-threads.

MISTRESS OTTER. [*aside*]—O viper, mandrake!   80

OTTER. A most vile face! And yet she spends me forty pound a
   year in mercury and hogs'-bones.[5] All her teeth were made in

---

8. In three words.
9. Sea gods who carry shell trumpets.
1. From the Roman poet Horace (65–8 B.C.E.), Odes 1.37.1: "Now's the time to drink, now we
   dance lightly."
2. A perplexing word—perhaps used in the old sense of fastening a clog to an animal, especially
   a dog, to impede movement.
3. Ugly beast.
4. For a fact.
5. The disgusting ingredients of cosmetics were a favorite theme of satirists.

the Blackfriars, both her eyebrows in the Strand, and her hair
in Silver Street. Every part o' the town owns a piece of her.

MISTRESS OTTER. [*Comes forward.*]—I cannot hold.   85

OTTER. She takes herself asunder still when she goes to bed, into
some twenty boxes; and about next day noon is put together
again, like a great German clock; and so come forth, and rings
a tedious 'larum to the whole house, and then is quiet again for
an hour, but for her quarters.—Have you done me right, gen-   90
tlemen?

MISTRESS OTTER. [*Falls upon him and beats him.*] No, sir, I'll do
you right with my quarters, with my quarters!

OTTER. O, hold, good Princess.

TRUEWIT. Sound, sound!   [*Drum and trumpets.*]   95

CLERIMONT. A battle, a battle!

MISTRESS OTTER. You notorious stinkardly bear-ward,[6] does my
breath smell?

OTTER. Under correction, dear Princess—Look to my Bear and my
Horse, gentlemen.   100

MISTRESS OTTER. Do I want teeth and eyebrows, thou bulldog?

TRUEWIT. Sound, sound still!   [*Trumpets again.*]

OTTER. No, I protest, under correction——

MISTRESS OTTER. Ay, now you are under correction, you protest;
but you did not protest before correction, sir. Thou Judas, to   105
offer to betray thy Princess! I'll make thee an example——
                                                      [*Beats him.*]

[MOROSE *descends with a long-sword.*]

MOROSE. I will have no such examples in my house, Lady Otter.

MISTRESS OTTER. Ah——

                     [*Exeunt* MISTRESS OTTER, DAW *and* LA FOOLE.]

MOROSE. Mistress Mary Ambree,[7] your examples are dangerous.—
Rogues, hellhounds, Stentors![8] Out of my doors, you sons of   110
noise and tumult, begot on an ill May-day, or when the galley-
foist is afloat to Westminster.[9] [*Drives out the musicians.*] A trumpeter could not be conceived but then!

DAUPHINE. What ails you, sir?

MOROSE. They have rent my roof, walls, and all my windows asun-   115
der with their brazen throats.   [*Exit.*]

TRUEWIT. Best follow him, Dauphine.

---

6. Bear-warden, keeper of the bears.
7. A legendary English Amazon supposed to have helped defend Ghent against the Spaniards
   in 1584.
8. Stentor was the herald of the gods in Greek mythology—the memory of his thunderous voice
   is preserved in the word "stentorian."
9. Distracted Morose thinks that May-day and the day of the Lord Mayor's entry into office
   (when the official galley, loaded with musicians, firecrackers, and ceremonial artillery, carried
   him to Westminster) were the only days on which trumpeters could have been begotten.

DAUPHINE. So I will.   [*Exit.*]

CLERIMONT. Where's Daw and La Foole?

OTTER. They are both run away, sir. Good gentlemen, help to   120
pacify my Princess, and speak to the great ladies for me. Now
must I go lie with the bears this fortnight, and keep out o' the
way, till my peace be made, for this scandal she has taken. Did
you not see my bull-head, gentlemen?

CLERIMONT. Is't not on, Captain?[1]   125

TRUEWIT. No; but he may make a new one, by that is on.

OTTER. O, here 'tis. An you come over, gentlemen, and ask for
Tom Otter, we'll go down to Ratcliffe, and have a course, i'
faith, for all these disasters. There's *bona spes*[2] left.

TRUEWIT. Away, Captain, get off while you are well. [*Exit* OTTER.]   130

CLERIMONT. I am glad we are rid of him.

TRUEWIT. You had never been, unless we had put his wife upon
him. His humor is as tedious at last as it was ridiculous at first.

ACT IV   SCENE 3. MOROSE'*S HOUSE*

[*Enter* LADY HAUGHTY, MISTRESS OTTER, LADY MAVIS, DAW,
LA FOOLE, LADY CENTAUR, *and* EPICOENE.]

HAUGHTY. We wondered why you shrieked so, Mistress Otter.

MISTRESS OTTER. O God, madam, he came down with a huge,
long, naked weapon in both his hands, and looked so dreadfully!
Sure, he's beside himself.

MAVIS. Why, what made you there, Mistress Otter?   5

MISTRESS OTTER. Alas, Mistress Mavis, I was chastising my subject,
and thought nothing of him.

DAW. Faith, mistress, you must do so, too. Learn to chastise. Mistress Otter corrects her husband so, he dares not speak but under
correction.   10

LA FOOLE. And with his hat off to her. 'Twould do you good to
see.

HAUGHTY. In sadness, 'tis good and mature counsel. Practise it,
Morose. I'll call you Morose still now, as I call Centaur and
Mavis; we four will be all one.   15

CENTAUR. And you'll come to the College, and live with us?

HAUGHTY. Make him give milk and honey.

MAVIS. Look how you manage him at first, you shall have him ever
after.

CENTAUR. Let him allow you your coach and four horses, your   20

---

1. The joke is that Otter, a cuckold, wears the legendary horns.
2. Good hope. Ratcliff, in the outer suburbs, had a lot of low taverns and so was a good place
for a "course," a drinking spree.

woman, your chambermaid, your page, your gentleman-usher, your French cook, and four grooms.

HAUGHTY. And go with us to Bedlam, to the chinahouses, and to the Exchange.[3]

CENTAUR. It will open the gate to your fame.   25

HAUGHTY. Here's Centaur has immortalized herself with taming of her wild male.

MAVIS. Ay, she has done the miracle of the kingdom.

[*Enter* CLERIMONT *and* TRUEWIT.]

EPICOENE. But, ladies, do you count it lawful to have such plurality of servants, and do 'em all graces?   30

HAUGHTY. Why not? Why should women deny their favors to men? Are they the poorer, or the worse?

DAW. Is the Thames the less for the dyers' water,[4] mistress?

LA FOOLE. Or a torch for lighting many torches?

TRUEWIT. Well said, La Foole.—What a new one he has got!   35

CENTAUR. They are empty losses women fear in this kind.

HAUGHTY. Besides, ladies should be mindful of the approach of age, and let no time want his due use. The best of our days pass first.

MAVIS. We are rivers that cannot be called back, madam. She that   40
now excludes her lovers may live to lie a forsaken beldam[5] in a frozen bed.

CENTAUR. 'Tis true, Mavis; and who will wait on us to coach then? Or write, or tell us the news then? Make anagrams of our names, and invite us to the Cockpit,[6] and kiss our hands all the playtime,   45
and draw their weapons for our honors?

HAUGHTY. Not one.

DAW. Nay, my mistress is not altogether unintelligent of these things. Here be in presence have tasted of her favors.

CLERIMONT. [*aside*]—What a neighing hobby-horse is this!   50

EPICOENE. But not with intent to boast 'em again, servant.—And have you those excellent receipts, madam, to keep yourselves from bearing of children?

HAUGHTY. O yes, Morose. How should we maintain our youth and beauty else? Many births of a woman make her old, as many   55
crops make the earth barren.

---

3. Fine ladies commonly amused themselves with trips to Bedlam (a madhouse), to the china shops where they shopped for porcelain and picked up lovers, and to the Royal Exchange where they bargained over lace and worthless trifles.
4. Dyers of cloth use a lot of water, most of which they return (somewhat the worse for wear) to the source from which they got it. The reference is very local, but the basic idea, like many others in this scene, comes from Ovid's *Art of Love*, Book 3.
5. Crone.
6. I.e., the theater, but just as likely the pit where cockfights were held.

ACT IV   SCENE 4

[*Enter* MOROSE *and* DAUPHINE.]

MOROSE. O my cursed angel, that instructed me to this fate!

DAUPHINE. Why, sir?

MOROSE. That I should be seduced by so foolish a devil as a barber will make!

DAUPHINE. I would I had been worthy, sir, to have partaken your   5
counsel; you should never have trusted it to such a minister.

MOROSE. Would I could redeem it with the loss of an eye, nephew, a hand, or any other member.

DAUPHINE. Marry, God forbid, sir, that you should geld yourself to anger your wife.   10

MOROSE. So it would rid me of her! And that I did supererogatory[7] penance in a belfry, at Westminister Hall, i' the Cockpit, at the fall of a stag, the Tower Wharf,—what place is there else?— London Bridge, Paris Garden, Billingsgate when the noises are at their height and loudest.[8] Nay, I would sit out a play, that   15 were nothing but fights at sea, drum, trumpet, and target!

DAUPHINE. I hope there shall be no such need, sir. Take patience, good uncle. This is but a day, and 'tis well worn, too, now.

MOROSE. O, 'twill be so forever, nephew, I foresee it, forever. Strife and tumult are the dowry that comes with a wife.   20

TRUEWIT. I told you so, sir, and you would not believe me.

MOROSE. Alas, do not rub those wounds, Master Truewit, to blood again. 'Twas my negligence. Add not affliction to affliction. I have perceived the effect of it too late in Madam Otter.

EPICOENE. How do you, sir?   25

MOROSE. Did you ever hear a more unnecessary question? As if she did not see! Why, I do as you see, Empress, Empress.

EPICOENE. You are not well, sir; you look very ill; something has distempered you.

MOROSE. O horrible, monstrous impertinencies! Would not one of   30 these have served, do you think, sir? Would not one of these have served?

TRUEWIT. Yes, sir, but these are but notes of female kindness, sir, certain tokens that she has a voice, sir.

MOROSE. O, is't so! Come, an't be no otherwise——What say you?   35

EPICOENE. How do you feel yourself, sir?

MOROSE. Again that!

---

7. More than is necessary.
8. All of these are places of excessive noise—Westminster Hall, full of loud lawyers; the Cockpit, full of noisy spectators; the stag, surrounded by howling dogs and blaring horns; the Tower Wharf, covered with cannons; Paris Garden, where bull-baitings were held; Billingsgate, where fishwives called out their wares.

TRUEWIT. Nay, look you, sir, you would be friends with your wife upon unconscionable terms—her silence.

EPICOENE. They say you are run mad, sir.   40

MOROSE. Not for love, I assure you, of you, do you see?

EPICOENE. O Lord, gentlemen, lay hold on him, for God's sake! What shall I do! Who's his physician—can you tell?—that knows that state of his body best, that I might send for him? Good sir, speak; I'll send for one of my doctors else.   45

MOROSE. What, to poison me, that I might die intestate,[9] and leave you possessed of all?

EPICOENE. Lord, how idly he talks, and how his eyes sparkle! He looks green about the temples! Do you see what blue spots he has?   50

CLERIMONT. Ay, it's melancholy.

EPICOENE. Gentlemen, for Heaven's sake, counsel me. Ladies!— Servant, you have read Pliny and Paracelsus;[1] ne'er a word now to comfort a poor gentlewoman? Ay me, what fortune had I to marry a distracted man!   55

DAW. I'll tell you, mistress——

TRUEWIT. [aside to CLERIMONT]—How rarely she holds it up!

MOROSE. What mean you, gentlemen?

EPICOENE. What will you tell me, servant?

DAW. The disease in Greek is called μανία, in Latin insania, furor,   60
vel ecstasis melancholica, that is, egressio, and a man ex melan-
cholico evadit fanaticus.[2]

MOROSE. Shall I have a lecture read upon me alive.

DAW. But he may be but phreneticus yet, mistress; and phrenesis is only delirium, or so.[3]   65

EPICOENE. Ay, that is for the disease, servant; but what is this to the cure? We are sure enough of the disease.

MOROSE. Let me go.

TRUEWIT. Why, we'll entreat her to hold her peace, sir.

MOROSE. O no, labor not to stop her. She is like a conduit-pipe,   70
that will gush out with more force when she opens again.

HAUGHTY. I'll tell you, Morose, you must talk divinity to him altogether, or moral philosophy.

LA FOOLE. Ay, and there's an excellent book of moral philosophy,
madam, of Reynard the Fox and all the beasts, called 'Doni's   75

9. Without a will.
1. These are natural historians, one of Roman times, one of the Renaissance.
2. I.e., " 'madness, fury, or melancholy ecstasy,' that is, 'being beside yourself,' and a man 'from being melancholy turns to a fanatic.' "
3. I.e., he may be only "frenetic," and "frenzy" is nothing more than "delirium," but not absolute insanity.

Philosophy.'[4]

CENTAUR. There is indeed, Sir Amorous La Foole.

MOROSE. O misery!

LA FOOLE. I have read it, my Lady Centaur, all over, to my cousin
here.   80

MISTRESS OTTER. Ay, and 'tis a very good book as any is, of the
moderns.

DAW. Tut, he must have Seneca read to him, and Plutarch, and
the ancients.[5] The moderns are not for this disease.

CLERIMONT. Why, you discommended them too, today, Sir John.   85

DAW. Ay, in some cases; but in these they are best; and Aristotle's
'Ethics.'

MAVIS. Say you so, Sir John? I think you are deceived; you took it
upon trust.

HAUGHTY. Where's Trusty, my woman? I'll end this difference. I   90
pray thee, Otter, call her. Her father and mother were both mad,
when they put her to me.

MOROSE. I think so.—Nay, gentlemen, I am tame. This is but an
exercise, I know, a marriage ceremony, which I must endure.

HAUGHTY. And one of 'em, I know not which, was cured with 'The   95
Sick Man's Salve,' and the other with 'Green's Groatsworth of
Wit.'[6]

TRUEWIT. A very cheap cure, madam.

HAUGHTY. Ay, it's very feasible.

                 [Enter TRUSTY.]

MISTRESS OTTER. My lady called for you, Mistress Trusty. You   100
must decide a controversy.

HAUGHTY. O, Trusty, which was it you said, your father or your
mother, that was cured with 'The Sick Man's Salve'?

TRUSTY. My mother, madam, with the 'Salve.'

TRUEWIT. Then it was the sick woman's salve.   105

TRUSTY. And my father with the 'Groatsworth of Wit.' But there
was other means used: we had a preacher that would preach
folk asleep still; and so they were prescribed to go to church, by
an old woman that was their physician, thrice a week—

EPICOENE. To sleep?   110

TRUSTY. Yes, forsooth, and every night they read themselves asleep
on those books.

4. The latter book is a collection of ragbag lore, translated into Italian by Doni, and into English
   (1601) by Sir Thomas North. The story of Reynard the Fox is quite different, a good deal
   older, and much cleverer. It is one of the sources for Jonson's *Volpone*.
5. Seneca and Plutarch, grave moral authors, are prescribed by Sir John Daw as psychotherapy.
6. Cheap moral pamphlets of the day: *Sick Man's Salve* by Thomas Becon was published in
   1561 and many times reprinted; Robert Greene's *Groatsworth of Wit*, his deathbed autobi-
   ography, was published in 1592.

EPICOENE. Good faith, it stands with great reason. I would I knew
where to procure those books.

MOROSE. O!   115

LA FOOLE. I can help you with one of 'em, Mistress Morose, the
'Groatsworth of Wit.'

EPICOENE. But I shall disfurnish you, Sir Amorous; can you spare
it?

LA FOOLE. O yes, for a week or so; I'll read it myself to him.   120

EPICOENE. No, I must do that, sir; that must be my office.

MOROSE. O, O!

EPICOENE. Sure, he would do well enough if he could sleep.

MOROSE. No, I should do well enough if you could sleep. Have I
no friend that will make her drunk? Or give her a little lauda-   125
num, or opium?

TRUEWIT. Why, sir, she talks ten times worse in her sleep.

MOROSE. How!

CLERIMONT. Do you not know that, sir? Never ceases all night.

TRUEWIT. And snores like a porpoise.   130

MOROSE. O, redeem me, fate; redeem me, fate! For how many
causes may a man be divorced, nephew?

DAUPHINE. I know not truly, sir.

TRUEWIT. Some divine must resolve you[7] in that, sir, or canon
lawyer.   135

MOROSE. I will not rest, I will not think of any other hope or
comfort, till I know.   [Exit with DAUPHINE.]

CLERIMONT. Alas, poor man!

TRUEWIT. You'll make him mad indeed, ladies, if you pursue this.

HAUGHTY. No, we'll let him breathe now, a quarter of an hour   140
or so.

CLERIMONT. By my faith, a large truce!

HAUGHTY. Is that his keeper that is gone with him?

DAW. It is his nephew, madam.

LA FOOLE. Sir Dauphine Eugenie.   145

CENTAUR. He looks like a very pitiful knight——

DAW. As can be. This marriage has put him out of all.

LA FOOLE. He has not a penny in his purse, madam——

DAW. He is ready to cry all this day.

LA FOOLE. A very shark; he set me i' the nick t'other night at   150
primero.[8]

TRUEWIT. [aside]—How these swabbers[9] talk!

7. Settle all your doubts.
8. He won money from me by cheating at primero, a card game.
9. Loutish persons.

CLERIMONT. Ay, Otter's wine has swelled their humors above a spring-tide.

HAUGHTY. Good Morose, let's go in again. I like your couches 155 exceeding well; we'll go lie and talk there.

[*Exeunt* LADY CENTAUR, MISTRESS MAVIS, TRUSTY, LA FOOLE, *and* DAW.]

EPICOENE. [*following them*] I wait on you, madam.

TRUEWIT. [*stopping her*] 'Slight, I will have 'em silent as signs, and their post[1] too, ere I have done. Do you hear, Lady Bride? I pray thee now, as thou art a noble wench, continue this discourse of 160 Dauphine within; but praise him exceedingly. Magnify him with all the height of affection thou canst—I have some purpose in't—and but beat off these two rooks, Jack Daw and his fellow, with any discontentment, hither, and I'll honor thee forever.

EPICOENE. I was about it here. It angered me to the soul, to hear 165 'em begin to talk so malapert.[2]

TRUEWIT. Pray thee perform it, and thou winn'st me an idolater to thee everlasting.

EPICOENE. Will you go in and hear me do 't?

TRUEWIT. No, I'll stay here. Drive 'em out of your company, 'tis 170 all I ask; which cannot be any way better done than by extolling Dauphine, whom they have so slighted.

EPICOENE. I warrant you; you shall expect one of 'em presently.

[*Exit.*]

CLERIMONT. What a cast of kastrils[3] are these, to hawk after ladies thus! 175

TRUEWIT. Ay, and strike at such an eagle as Dauphine.

CLERIMONT. He will be mad when we tell him. Here he comes.

ACT IV   SCENE 5

[*Re-enter* DAUPHINE.]

CLERIMONT. O, sir, you are welcome.

TRUEWIT. Where's thine uncle?

DAUPHINE. Run out of doors in his nightcaps to talk with a casuist about his divorce. It works admirably.

TRUEWIT. Thou wouldst have said so, an thou hadst been here! 5 The ladies have laughed at thee most comically, since thou went'st, Dauphine.

CLERIMONT. And asked if thou went thine uncle's keeper.

TRUEWIT. And the brace of baboons answered yes; and said thou

---

1. Their messenger (Daw), with a pun on the notion of someone being deaf or mute as a post.
2. Impudently.
3. Pair of scavengers. Kastrils or kestrels were small hawks, not as noble as falcons.

were a pitiful, poor fellow, and didst live upon posts,[4] and hadst   10
nothing but three suits of apparel, and some few benevolences
that the lords gave thee to fool to 'em and swagger.

DAUPHINE. Let me not live, I'll beat 'em! I'll bind them both to
grand Madam's bed-posts, and have them baited with monkeys.

TRUEWIT. Thou shalt not need; they shall be beaten to thy hand,   15
Dauphine. I have an execution to serve upon them, I warrant
thee shall serve; trust my plot.

DAUPHINE. Ay, you have many plots. So you had one to make all
the wenches in love with me!

TRUEWIT. Why, if I do it not yet afore night, as near as 'tis, and   20
that they do not every one invite thee, and be ready to scratch[5]
for thee, take the mortgage of my wit.

CLERIMONT. 'Fore God, I'll be his witness, thou shalt have it,
Dauphine!—Thou shalt be his fool forever, if thou dost not.

TRUEWIT. Agreed. Perhaps 'twill be the better estate. Do you ob-   25
serve this gallery, or rather lobby, indeed? Here are a couple of
studies, at each end one: here will I act such a tragi-comedy
between the Guelphs and the Ghibellines,[6] Daw and La
Foole—Which of 'em comes out first, will I seize on. You two
shall be the chorus behind the arras,[7] and whip out between the   30
acts and speak. If I do not make them keep the peace for this
remnant of the day, if not of the year, I have failed once——I
hear Daw coming. Hide [*they withdraw*], and do not laugh, for
God's sake!
    [*Re-enter* DAW.]

DAW. Which is the way into the garden, trow?[8]   35

TRUEWIT. O, Jack Daw! I am glad I have met with you. In good
faith, I must have this matter go no further between you. I must
have it taken up.

DAW. What matter, sir? Between whom?

TRUEWIT. Come, you disguise it: Sir Amorous and you. If you love   40
me, Jack, you shall make use of your philosophy now, for this
once, and deliver me your sword. This is not the wedding the
Centaurs were at,[9] though there be a she-one here. [*Takes his
sword.*] The bride has entreated me I will see no blood shed at
her bridal; you saw her whisper me erewhile.   45

DAW. As I hope to finish Tacitus,[1] I intend no murder.

---

4. Made a living by running errands.
5. Claw each other's faces.
6. Traditional opponents in Italian politics.
7. The commentators behind the curtain.
8. Can you tell me?
9. In the Greek mythological story, the Centaurs and Lapiths got into a battle royal at the
   marriage of Hippodamia with Peirithous.
1. The Roman historian Tacitus (ca. 55–after 115 C.E.) is notoriously a hard study.

TRUEWIT. Do you not wait for Sir Amorous?

DAW. Not I, by my knighthood.

TRUEWIT. And your scholarship too?

DAW. And my scholarship too.   50

TRUEWIT. Go to, then I return you your sword, and ask you mercy;
but put it not up, for you will be assaulted. I understood that
you had apprehended it, and walked here to brave him; and that
you had held your life contemptible, in regard of your honor.

DAW. No, no; no such thing, I assure you. He and I parted now   55
as good friends as could be.

TRUEWIT. Trust not you to that visor.[2] I saw him since dinner with
another face. I have known many men in my time vexed with
losses, with deaths, and with abuses, but so offended a wight[3] as
Sir Amorous did I never see or read of. For taking away his   60
guests, sir, today, that's the cause; and he declares it behind your
back with such threatenings and contempts——He said to Dauphine you were the arrant'st ass——

DAW. Ay, he may say his pleasure.

TRUEWIT. And swears you are so protested a coward, that he knows   65
you will never do him any manly or single right, and therefore
he will take his course.

DAW. I'll give him any satisfaction, sir—but fighting.

TRUEWIT. Ay, sir, but who knows what satisfaction he'll take? Blood
he thirsts for, and blood he will have; and whereabouts on you   70
he will have it, who knows but himself?

DAW. I pray you, Master Truewit, be you a mediator.

TRUEWIT. Well, sir, conceal yourself then in this study till I return.
[Puts him into the study.] Nay, you must be content to be locked
in; for, for mine own reputation, I would not have you seen to   75
receive a public disgrace, while I have the matter in managing.
God's so, here he comes. Keep your breath close, that he do
not hear you sigh.—In good faith, Sir Amorous, he is not this
way. I pray you be merciful, do not murder him; he is a Christian, as good as you. You are armed as if you sought a revenge   80
on all his race. Good Dauphine, get him away from this place.
I never knew a man's choler[4] so high, but he would speak to his
friends, he would hear reason.—Jack Daw, Jack Daw! Asleep?

DAW. [within] Is he gone, Master Truewit?

TRUEWIT. Ay, did you hear him?   85

DAW. O God, yes!

2. Mask.
3. Person.
4. Anger, rage.

TRUEWIT. —What a quick ear fear has!

DAW. [*Comes out of the closet.*]—But is he so armed as you say?

TRUEWIT. Armed! Did you ever see a fellow set out to take possession?[5]

DAW. Ay, sir.

TRUEWIT. That may give you some light to conceive of him, but
'tis nothing to the principal. Some false brother in the house
has furnished him strangely; or, if it were out of the house, it
was Tom Otter.

DAW. Indeed, he's a captain, and his wife is his kinswoman.

TRUEWIT. He has got somebody's old two-hand sword, to mow you
off at the knees; and that sword hath spawned such a dagger!
But then he is so hung with pikes, halberds, petronels, calivers,[6]
and muskets, that he looks like a Justice of Peace's hall. A man
of two thousand a year is not cessed[7] at so many weapons as he
has on. There was never fencer challenged at so many several
foils.[8] You would think he meant to murder all Saint 'Pulchre's
parish.[9] If he could but victual himself for half a year in his
breeches, he is sufficiently armed to overrun a country.

DAW. Good Lord! What means he, sir? I pray you, Master Truewit,
be you a mediator.

TRUEWIT. Well, I'll try if he will be appeased with a leg or an arm;
if not, you must die once.

DAW. I would be loath to lose my right arm, for writing madrigals.

TRUEWIT. Why, if he will be satisfied with a thumb or a little
finger, all's one to me. You must think, I'll do my best. [*Shuts
him up again.*]

DAW. Good sir, do.

[CLERIMONT *and* DAUPHINE *come forward.*]

CLERIMONT. What hast thou done?

TRUEWIT. He will let me do nothing, man, he does all afore me;
he offers his left arm.

CLERIMONT. His left wing, for a jackdaw.

DAUPHINE. Take it, by all means.

TRUEWIT. How! Maim a man forever, for a jest? What a conscience hast thou!

90

95

100

105

110

115

120

---

5. I.e., of a new property, when real fighting with the old owner was not out of the question.
6. These are weapons used by armies but not in dueling. Pikes had a long shaft ending in a
sharp point; halberds also had long handles, which ended, however, in a combination of
spearhead and battleaxe; petronels and calivers are varieties of pistol. All these weapons, supplied by the citizenry, would be lodged with the Justice of the Peace for use in time of
emergency.
7. Taxed—rich men had to contribute more weapons than poor ones.
8. With so many different weapons.
9. The parish of Saint Sepulchre in London City.

DAUPHINE. 'Tis no loss to him; he has no employment for his arms but to eat spoon-meat. Beside, as good maim his body as his reputation.

TRUEWIT. He is a scholar and a wit, and yet he does not think so. But he loses no reputation with us, for we all resolved him an 125 ass before. To your places again.

CLERIMONT. I pray thee, let me be in it at the other a little.

TRUEWIT. Look, you'll spoil all; these be ever your tricks.

CLERIMONT. No, but I could hit off some things that thou wilt miss, and thou wilt say are good ones.   130

TRUEWIT. I warrant you. I pray, forbear, I'll leave it off else.

DAUPHINE. Come away, Clerimont.

> [DAUPHINE *and* CLERIMONT *withdraw.*]

> [*Enter* LA FOOLE.]

TRUEWIT. Sir Amorous!

LA FOOLE. Master Truewit.

TRUEWIT. Whither were you going?   135

LA FOOLE. Down into the court to make water.

TRUEWIT. By no means, sir, you shall rather tempt your breeches.

LA FOOLE. Why, sir?

TRUEWIT. Enter here, if you love your life. [*Opens the door of the other study.*]

LA FOOLE. Why? Why?   140

TRUEWIT. Question till your throat be cut, do! Dally till the enraged soul find you.

LA FOOLE. Who's that?

TRUEWIT. Daw it is! Will you in?

LA FOOLE. Ay, ay. I'll in. What's the matter?   145

TRUEWIT. Nay, if he had been cool enough to tell us that, there had been some hope to atone[1] you; but he seems so implacably enraged!

LA FOOLE. 'Slight, let him rage! I'll hide myself.

TRUEWIT. Do, good sir. But what have you done to him within, 150 that should provoke him thus? You have broke some jest upon him afore the ladies.

LA FOOLE. Not I, never in my life broke jest upon any man. The bride was praising Sir Dauphine, and he went away in snuff,[2] and I followed him—unless he took offense at me in his drink 155 ere-while, that I would not pledge all the Horse full.

TRUEWIT. By my faith, and that may be; you remember well. But he walks the round up and down, through every room o' the house, with a towel in his hand, crying, 'Where's La Foole? Who

---

1. Reconcile, make you at one.
2. In a rage.

saw La Foole?' And when Dauphine and I demanded the cause,   160
we can force no answer from him but, 'O revenge, how sweet
art thou! I will strangle him in this towel!' Which leads us to
conjecture that the main cause of his fury is for bringing your
meat today with a towel about you, to his discredit.

LA FOOLE. Like enough. Why, an he be angry for that, I'll stay   165
here till his anger be blown over.

TRUEWIT. A good, becoming resolution, sir, if you can put it on o'
the sudden.

LA FOOLE. Yes, I can put it on. Or, I'll away into the country
presently.   170

TRUEWIT. How will you get out of the house, sir? He knows you
are in the house, and he'll watch you this se'nnight,[3] but he'll
have you. He'll outwait a sergeant[4] for you.

LA FOOLE. Why, then I'll stay here.

TRUEWIT. You must think how to victual yourself in time, then.   175

LA FOOLE. Why, sweet Master Truewit, will you entreat my cousin
Otter to send me a cold venison pasty, a bottle or two of wine,
and a chamber-pot?

TRUEWIT. A stool were better, sir, of Sir Ajax's invention.[5]

LA FOOLE. Ay, that will be better indeed; and a pallet to lie on.   180

TRUEWIT. O, I would not advise you to sleep, by any means.

LA FOOLE. Would you not, sir? Why, then I will not.

TRUEWIT. Yet there's another fear——

LA FOOLE. Is there! What is't?

TRUEWIT. No, he cannot break open this door with his foot, sure.   185

LA FOOLE. I'll set my back against it, sir. I have a good back.

TRUEWIT. But then if he should batter.

LA FOOLE. Batter! If he dare, I'll have an action of battery against
him.

TRUEWIT. Cast you the worst. He has sent for powder already, and   190
what he will do with it no man knows—perhaps blow up the
corner of the house where he suspects you are. Here he comes;
in quickly. [*Thrusts in* LA FOOLE, *and shuts the door*.]—I protest,
Sir John Daw, he is not this way. What will you do? Before God,
you shall hang no petard[6] here! I'll die rather. Will you not take   195
my word? I never knew one but would be satisfied—Sir Amorous, there's no standing out. He has made a petard of an old
brass pot, to force your door. Think upon some satisfaction, or
terms, to offer him.

3. Seven nights.
4. Sergeants—who arrest debtors—are traditionally tenacious men.
5. According to Sir John Harington's farce *The Metamorphosis of Ajax* (1596), the Homeric hero
Ajax was transformed into a jakes—a toilet.
6. Bomb, mortar shell.

LA FOOLE. [*within*] Sir, I'll give him any satisfaction. I dare give   200
  any terms.

TRUEWIT. You'll leave it to me then?

LA FOOLE. Ay, sir. I'll stand to any conditions.

TRUEWIT. [*Calls forth* CLERIMONT *and* DAUPHINE.] How now!
  What think you, sirs? Were't not a difficult thing to determine   205
  which of these two feared most?

CLERIMONT. Yes, but this fears the bravest; the other a whiniling[7],
  dastard jackdaw! But La Foole, a brave, heroic coward! And is
  afraid in a great look and a stout accent. I like him rarely.

TRUEWIT. Had it not been pity these two should have been   210
  concealed?

CLERIMONT. Shall I make a motion?

TRUEWIT. Briefly, for I must strike while 'tis hot.

CLERIMONT. Shall I go fetch the ladies to the catastrophe?

TRUEWIT. Umh? Ay, by my troth.   215

DAUPHINE. By no mortal means. Let them continue in the state of
  ignorance, and err still; think 'em wits and fine fellows, as they
  have done. 'Twere sin to reform them.

TRUEWIT. Well, I will have them fetched, now I think on't, for a
  private purpose of mine. Do, Clerimont, fetch them, and dis-   220
  course to them all that's passed, and bring them into the gallery
  here.

DAUPHINE. This is thy extreme vanity, now! Thou think'st thou
  wert undone if every jest thou mak'st were not published.

TRUEWIT. Thou shalt see how unjust thou art presently—Cleri-   225
  mont, say it was Dauphine's plot. [*Exit* CLERIMONT.] Trust me
  not if the whole drift be not for thy good. There's a carpet in
  the next room; put it on, with this scarf over thy face, and a
  cushion on thy head, and be ready when I call Amorous. Away.
  [*Exit* DAUPHINE.] John Daw! [*Goes to* DAW's *closet, and brings*   230
  him out.]

DAW. What good news, sir?

TRUEWIT. Faith, I have followed, and argued with him hard for
  you. I told him you were a knight and a scholar, and that you
  knew fortitude did consist *magis patiendo quam faciendo, magis
  ferendo quam feriendo.*[8]   235

DAW. It doth so indeed, sir.

TRUEWIT. And that you would suffer, I told him. So at first he
  demanded, by my troth, in my conceit[9] too much.

DAW. What was it, sir?

---

7. Whining.
8. "More in suffering than in inflicting pain, more in bearing than in striking blows."
9. In my judgment.

TRUEWIT. Your upper lip and six of your foreteeth.   240

DAW. 'Twas unreasonable.

TRUEWIT. Nay, I told him plainly, you could not spare them all.
So after long argument—*pro et con*, as you know—I brought him
down to your two butter-teeth,[1] and them he would have.

DAW. O, did you so? Why, he shall have them.   245

TRUEWIT. But he shall not, sir, by your leave. The conclusion is
this, sir: because you shall be very good friends hereafter, and
this never to be remembered or upbraided; besides, that he may
not boast he has done any such thing to you in his own person;
he is to come here in disguise, give you five kicks in private, sir,   250
take your sword from you, and lock you up in that study during
pleasure; which will be but a little while, we'll get it released
presently.

DAW. Five kicks? He shall have six, sir, to be friends.

TRUEWIT. Believe me, you shall not overshoot yourself, to send   255
him that word by me.

DAW. Deliver it, sir, he shall have it with all my heart, to be friends.

TRUEWIT. Friends! Nay, an he should not be so, and heartily too,
upon these terms, he shall have me to enemy while I live.
Come, sir, bear it bravely.   260

DAW. O God, sir, 'tis nothing.

TRUEWIT. True. What's six kicks to a man that reads Seneca?[2]

DAW. I have had a hundred, sir.

TRUEWIT. Sir Amorous! No speaking one to another, or rehearsing
old matters. [DAUPHINE *comes forth disguised, and kicks* DAW.]   265

DAW. One, two, three, four, five. I protest, Sir Amorous, you shall
have six.

TRUEWIT. Nay, I told you you should not talk. Come, give him
six, and he will needs. [DAUPHINE *kicks him again.*] Your sword.
[*He takes it.*] Now return to your safe custody. You shall pres-   270
ently meet afore the ladies, and be the dearest friends one to
another. [*Puts* DAW *in the study.*]—Give me the scarf now, thou
shalt beat the other barefaced. Stand by. [DAUPHINE *retires, and*
TRUEWIT *goes to the other closet and releases* LA FOOLE.]—Sir
Amorous!   275

LA FOOLE. What's here? A sword!

TRUEWIT. I cannot help it, without I should take the quarrel upon
myself. Here he has sent you his sword——

LA FOOLE. I'll receive none on't.

TRUEWIT. And he wills you to fasten it against a wall, and break   280

---

1. Front teeth; *pro et con*: for and against.
2. Roman philosopher Seneca (ca. 4 B.C.E.–65 C.E.) counsels his readers to endure misfortune
(but not disgrace and humiliation) patiently.

your head in some few several places against the hilts.

LA FOOLE. I will not; tell him roundly. I cannot endure to shed
my own blood.

TRUEWIT. Will you not?

LA FOOLE. No. I'll beat it against a fair flat wall, if that will satisfy   285
him. If not, he shall beat it himself, for Amorous.

TRUEWIT. Why, this is strange starting off, when a man undertakes
for you! I offered him another condition; will you stand to that?

LA FOOLE. Ay, what is't?

TRUEWIT. That you will be beaten in private.   290

LA FOOLE. Yes, I am content, at the blunt.[3]

     [*Enter above* LADY HAUGHTY, LADY CENTAUR, MISTRESS MA-
     VIS, MISTRESS OTTER, EPICOENE, *and* TRUSTY.]

TRUEWIT. Then you must submit yourself to be hoodwinked in
this scarf and be led to him, where he will take your sword from
you, and make you bear a blow over the mouth *gules*, and tweaks
by the nose, *sans nombre*.[4]   295

LA FOOLE. I am content. But why must I be blinded?

TRUEWIT. That's for your good, sir; because if he should grow insolent upon this, and publish it hereafter to your disgrace—
which I hope he will not do—you might swear safely and protest
he never beat you to your knowledge.   300

LA FOOLE. O, I conceive.

TRUEWIT. I do not doubt but you'll be perfect good friends upon't,
and not dare to utter an ill thought, one of another, in future.

LA FOOLE. Not I, as God help me, of him.

TRUEWIT. Nor he of you, sir. If he should [*Blindfolds him.*]—   305
Come, sir. All hid, Sir John!

     [DAUPHINE *enters to tweak him by the nose.*]

LA FOOLE. Oh, Sir John, Sir John! Oh, o-o-o-o-o-oh—

TRUEWIT. Good Sir John, leave tweaking, you'll blow his nose
off.—'Tis Sir John's pleasure you should retire into the study.
[*Puts him back again.*] Why, now you are friends. All bitterness   310
between you, I hope, is buried; you shall come forth, by and by,
Damon and Pythias upon't, and embrace with all the rankness[5]
of friendship that can be.—I trust we shall have 'em tamer in
their language hereafter. Dauphine, I worship thee. God's will,
the ladies have surprised us!   315

---

3. If it comes to that.

4. Numberless; *gules*, the heraldic term for scarlet, implies that the blow must draw blood.

5. Abundance. Damon and Pythias were students of the Greek philosopher Pythagoras (sixth
century B.C.E.), who were condemned to die by Dionysius of Syracuse for their beliefs. Each,
however, wanted to die for the other, and the tyrant, impressed by their devotion to one
another, pardoned both.

ACT IV   SCENE 6

[*Enter* CLERIMONT, *with* LADY HAUGHTY, LADY CENTAUR,
MISTRESS MAVIS, MISTRESS OTTER, EPICOENE, *and* TRUSTY.]

HAUGHTY. Centaur, how our judgments were imposed on by these
   adulterate[6] knights!

CENTAUR. Nay, madam, Mavis was more deceived then we; 'twas
   her commendation uttered them in the College.

MAVIS. I commended but their wits, madam, and their braveries.[7]   5
   I never looked toward their valors.

HAUGHTY. Sir Dauphine is valiant, and a wit too, it seems.

MAVIS. And a bravery too.

HAUGHTY. Was this his project?

MISTRESS OTTER. So Master Clerimont intimates, madam.   10

HAUGHTY. Good Morose, when you come to the College, will you
   bring him with you? He seems a very perfect gentleman.

EPICOENE. He is so, madam, believe it.

CENTAUR. But when will you come, Morose?

EPICOENE. Three or four days hence, madam, when I have got me   15
   a coach and horses.

HAUGHTY. No, tomorrow, good Morose; Centaur shall send you
   her coach.

MAVIS. Yes, faith, do, and bring Sir Dauphine with you.

HAUGHTY. She has promised that, Mavis.   20

MAVIS. He is a very worthy gentleman in his exteriors, madam.

HAUGHTY. Ay, he shows he is judicial in his clothes.

CENTAUR. And yet not so superlatively neat as some, madam, that
   have their faces set in a brake.[8]

HAUGHTY. Ay, and have every hair in form.   25

MAVIS. That wear purer linen than ourselves, and profess more
   neatness than the French hermaphrodite.

EPICOENE. Ay, ladies, they, what they tell one of us, have told a
   thousand; and are the only thieves of our fame, that think to
   take us with that perfume, or with that lace, and laugh at us   30
   unconscionably when they have done.

HAUGHTY. But Sir Dauphine's carelessness becomes him.

CENTAUR. I could love a man for such a nose!

MAVIS. Or such a leg!

CENTAUR. He has an exceeding good eye, madam!   35

MAVIS. And a very good lock![9]

6. Degenerate.
7. Finery.
8. A rigid form (originally from a rig used to confine a horse's feet while it was being shod).
9. Lock of hair.

CENTAUR. Good Morose, bring him to my chamber first.

MISTRESS OTTER. Please your honors to meet at my house, madam.

TRUEWIT. —See how they eye thee, man! They are taken, I warrant
thee.   40

[LADY HAUGHTY *comes forward.*]

HAUGHTY. You have unbraced our brace of knights here, Master
Truewit.

TRUEWIT. Not I, madam, it was Sir Dauphine's engine;[1] who, if
he have disfurnished your ladyship of any guard or service by
it,[2] is able to make the place good again in himself.   45

HAUGHTY. There's no suspicion of that, sir.

CENTAUR. God's so, Mavis, Haughty is kissing.

MAVIS. Let us go, too, and take part.

[*They come forward.*]

HAUGHTY. But I am glad of the fortune—beside the discovery of
two such empty caskets—to gain the knowledge of so rich a mine   50
of virtue as Sir Dauphine.

CENTAUR. We would be all glad to style him of our friendship, and
see him at the College.

MAVIS. He cannot mix with a sweeter society, I'll prophesy, and I
hope he himself will think so.   55

DAUPHINE. I should be rude to imagine otherwise, lady.

TRUEWIT. [*aside*]—Did not I tell thee, Dauphine? Why, all their
actions are governed by crude opinion, without reason or cause.
They know not why they do anything; but as they are informed,
believe, judge, praise, condemn, love, hate, and in emulation   60
one of another, do all these things alike. Only they have a natural inclination sways them generally to the worst, when they
are left to themselves. But pursue it, now thou hast them.

HAUGHTY. Shall we go in again, Morose?

EPICOENE. Yes, madam.   65

CENTAUR. We'll entreat Sir Dauphine's company.

TRUEWIT. Stay, good madam, the interview of the two friends, Py-
lades and Orestes.[3] I'll fetch them out to you straight.

HAUGHTY. Will you, Master Truewit?

DAUPHINE. Ay, but noble ladies, do not confess in your counte-   70
nance, or outward bearing to them, any discovery of their follies,
that we may see how they will bear up again, with what assurance and erection.

HAUGHTY. We will not, Sir Dauphine.

CENTAUR, MAVIS. Upon our honors, Sir Dauphine.   75

1. Idea, device.
2. If he has deprived you of any servants or protectors.
3. Another pair of proverbial classical friends.

TRUEWIT. [*Goes to the first closet.*] Sir Amorous! Sir Amorous! The
ladies are here.

LA FOOLE. Are they?

TRUEWIT. Yes, but slip out by and by, as their backs are turned,
and meet Sir John here, as by chance, when I call you [*Goes to*   80
the other closet.]—Jack Daw!

DAW. [*within*] What say you, sir?

TRUEWIT. Whip out behind me suddenly; and no anger in your
looks to your adversary. Now, now!

　　　[LA FOOLE *and* DAW *slip out of their closets and greet each
　　　other.*]

LA FOOLE. Noble Sir John Daw! Where have you been?   85

DAW. To seek you, Sir Amorous.

LA FOOLE. Me! I honor you.

DAW. I prevent you, sir.

CLERIMONT. They have forgot their rapiers!

TRUEWIT. O, they meet in peace, man.   90

DAUPHINE. Where's your sword, Sir John?

CLERIMONT. And yours, Sir Amorous?

DAW. Mine? My boy had it forth to mend the handle, c'en now.

LA FOOLE. And my gold handle was broke, too, and my boy had
it forth.   95

DAUPHINE. Indeed, sir!—How their excuses meet!

CLERIMONT. What a consent there is, in the handles!

TRUEWIT. Nay, there is so in the points too, I warrant you.

　　　[*Enter* MOROSE *with the two swords, drawn, in his hands.*]

MISTRESS OTTER. O me! Madam, he comes again, the madman!
Away!　　　　　　　　　[*Exeunt* LADIES, DAW, *and* LA FOOLE.]   100

ACT IV　　SCENE 7

MOROSE. What make these naked weapons here, gentlemen?

TRUEWIT. O sir! Here hath like to been murder since you went—
a couple of knights fallen out about the bride's favors! We were
fain to take away their weapons; your house had been begged[4]
by this time else.   5

MOROSE. For what?

CLERIMONT. For manslaughter, sir, as being accessory.

MOROSE. And for her favors?

TRUEWIT. Ay, sir, heretofore, not present. Clerimont, carry them
their swords now. They háve done all the hurt they will do.   10

　　　　　　　　　[*Exit* CLERIMONT *with the swords.*]

DAUPHINE. Have you spoke with the lawyer sir?

---

4. Forfeit to the crown for breach of the peace; the crown would then bestow it on a third party
who asked (begged) for it.

MOROSE. O no! There is such a noise in the court that they have
frighted me home with more violence than I went! Such speaking and counterspeaking, with their several voices of citations,
appelations, allegations, certificates, attachments, interrogatories,   15
references, convictions, and afflictions indeed, among the doctors and proctors, that the noise here is silence to't, a kind of
calm midnight!

TRUEWIT. Why, sir, if you would be resolved indeed, I can bring
you hither a very sufficient lawyer, and a learned divine, that   20
shall inquire into every least scruple for you.

MOROSE. Can you, Master Truewit?

TRUEWIT. Yes, and are very sober, grave persons, that will dispatch
it in a chamber, with a whisper or two.

MOROSE. Good sir, shall I hope this benefit from you, and trust   25
myself into your hands?

TRUEWIT. Alas, sir! Your nephew and I have been ashamed and
oft-times mad,[5] since you went, to think how you are abused.
Go in, good sir, and lock yourself up till we call you; we'll tell
you more anon, sir.   30

MOROSE. Do your pleasure with me, gentlemen. I believe in you,
and that deserves no delusion—   [*Exit.*]

TRUEWIT. You shall find none, sir,—but heaped, heaped plenty of
vexation.

DAUPHINE. What wilt thou do now, Wit?   35

TRUEWIT. Recover me hither Otter and the barber, if you can, by
any means, presently.

DAUPHINE. Why? To what purpose?

TRUEWIT. O, I'll make the deepest divine and gravest lawyer out
of them two, for him——   40

DAUPHINE. Thou canst not, man; these are waking dreams.

TRUEWIT. Do not fear me. Clap but a civil gown with a welt on
the one, and a canonical cloak with sleeves on the other, and
give them a few terms in their mouths; if there come not forth
as able a doctor and complete a parson, for this turn, as may be   45
wished, trust not my election. And I hope, without wronging the
dignity of either profession, since they are but persons put on,
and for mirth's sake, to torment him.[6] The barber smatters Latin,
I remember.

DAUPHINE. Yes, and Otter, too.   50

TRUEWIT. Well then, if I make them not wrangle out this case to
his no comfort, let me be thought a jackdaw, or La Foole, or

---

5. Angry, frustrated.
6. Jonson's carefulness about the parody of lawyers and clergymen that follows suggests that there
   had been some complaint about it; his previous parody of lawyers in his play *The Poetaster*
   (1601) had caused trouble.

anything worse. Go you to your ladies, but first send for them.

DAUPHINE. I will.   [*Exeunt*]

Act V

ACT V   SCENE 1. MOROSE'*S HOUSE*

[*Enter* LA FOOLE, CLERIMONT, *and* DAW.]

LA FOOLE. Where had you our swords, Master Clerimont?

CLERIMONT. Why, Dauphine took them from the madman.

LA FOOLE. And he took them from our boys, I warrant you!

CLERIMONT. Very like, sir.

LA FOOLE. Thank you, good Master Clerimont. Sir John Daw and   5
I are both beholden to you.

CLERIMONT. Would I knew how to make you so, gentlemen.

DAW. Sir Amorous and I are your servants, sir.

[*Enter* MISTRESS MAVIS.]

MAVIS. Gentlemen, have any of you a pen and ink? I would fain
write out a riddle in Italian, for Sir Dauphine to translate.   10

CLERIMONT. Not I, in troth, lady, I am no scrivener.[7]

DAW. I can furnish you, I think, lady.   [*Exeunt* DAW *and* MAVIS.]

CLERIMONT. He has it in the haft of a knife, I believe.

LA FOOLE. No, he has his box of instruments.

CLERIMONT. Like a surgeon!   15

LA FOOLE. For the mathematics—his square, his compasses, his
brass pens, and black-lead, to draw maps of every place and
person where he comes.

CLERIMONT. How, maps of persons!

LA FOOLE. Yes, sir, of Nomentack, when he was here, and of the   20
Prince of Moldavia, and of his mistress, Mistress Epicoene.[8]

[*Re-enter* DAW.]

CLERIMONT. Away! He hath not found out her latitude, I hope.

LA FOOLE. You are a pleasant gentleman, sir.

CLERIMONT. Faith, now we are in private, let's wanton it a little,
and talk waggishly.—Sir John, I am telling Sir Amorous here,   25
that you two govern the ladies; where'er you come, you carry the
feminine gender afore you.

DAW. They shall rather carry us afore them, if they will, sir.

CLERIMONT. Nay, I believe that they do withal—But that you are the
prime men in their affections, and direct all their actions——   30

---

7. Draftsmen of legal documents who might well carry pen and ink with them.
8. Nomentack was an Indian chief from the colony in Virginia who visited London in 1605–
   09. The Prince of Moldavia was a con man who passed through England in 1607. In the
   text, "his" mistress clearly refers to Sir John Daw's mistress, but Lady Arabella Stuart thought
   it referred to the Prince of Moldavia's mistress (i.e., herself), and the more so because she
   had been involved in an epicene escapade, which involved her dressing up as a boy.

DAW. Not I; Sir Amorous is.

LA FOOLE. I protest, Sir John is.

DAW. As I hope to rise in the state, Sir Amorous, you have the person.

LA FOOLE. Sir John, you have the person, and the discourse too.   35

DAW. Not I, sir. I have no discourse—and then you have activity beside.

LA FOOLE. I protest, Sir John, you come as high from Tripoli[9] as I do, every whit; and lift as many joint-stools, and leap over them, if you would use it—   40

CLERIMONT. Well, agree on't together, knights, for between you, you divide the kingdom or commonwealth of ladies' affections. I see it, and can perceive a little how they observe you, and fear you indeed. You could tell strange stories, my masters, if you would, I know.   45

DAW. Faith, we have seen somewhat, sir.

LA FOOLE. That we have—velvet petticoats, and wrought smocks, or so.

DAW. Ay, and——

CLERIMONT. Nay, out with it, Sir John! Do not envy your friend the pleasure of hearing, when you have had the delight of tasting.   50

DAW. Why—a—do you speak, Sir Amorous.

LA FOOLE. No, do you, Sir John Daw.

DAW. I' faith, you shall.   55

LA FOOLE. I' faith, you shall.

DAW. Why, we have been——

LA FOOLE. In the great bed at Ware[1] together in our time. On, Sir John.

DAW. Nay, do you, Sir Amorous.   60

CLERIMONT. And these ladies with you, knights?

LA FOOLE. No, excuse us, sir.

DAW. We must not wound reputation.

LA FOOLE. No matter—they were these, or others. Our bath cost us fifteen pound when we came home.   65

CLERIMONT. Do you hear, Sir John? You shall tell me but one thing truly, as you love me.

DAW. If I can, I will, sir.

CLERIMONT. You lay in the same house with the bride here?

DAW. Yes, and conversed with her hourly, sir.   70

9. I.e., are able to skip and frisk as well. The phrase is simply a play on the word "trip"; it has nothing to do with North Africa.
1. The great Bed of Ware was a public curiosity—it measured nearly eleven feet in each direction and naturally became a byword for erotic overachievement.

CLERIMONT. And what humor is she of? Is she coming and open, free?

DAW. O, exceeding open, sir. I was her servant, and Sir Amorous was to be.

CLERIMONT. Come, you have both had favors from her: I know, 75 and have heard so much.

DAW. O no, sir.

LA FOOLE. You shall excuse us, sir; we must not wound reputation.

CLERIMONT. Tut, she is married now, and you cannot hurt her with any report, and therefore speak plainly: how many times, 80 i' faith? Which of you led first? Ha?

LA FOOLE. Sir John had her maidenhead, indeed.

DAW. O, it pleases him to say so, sir, but Sir Amorous knows what's what as well.

CLERIMONT. Dost thou, i' faith, Amorous? 85

LA FOOLE. In a manner, sir.

DAW. Why, I commend you, lads. Little knows Don Bridegroom of this; nor shall he, for me.

DAW. Hang him, mad ox!

CLERIMONT. Speak softly, here comes his nephew, with the Lady 90 Haughty. He'll get the ladies from you, sirs, if you look not to him in time.

LA FOOLE. Why, if he do, we'll fetch them home again, I warrant you.   [*Exit with* DAW. CLERIMONT *walks aside.*]

ACT V   SCENE 2

[*Enter* DAUPHINE *and* LADY HAUGHTY.]

HAUGHTY. I assure you, Sir Dauphine, it is the price and estimation of your virtue only, that hath embarked me to this adventure, and I could not but make out to tell you so. Nor can I repent me of the act, since it is always an argument of some virtue in ourselves, that we love and affect it so in others. 5

DAUPHINE. Your ladyship sets too high a price on my weakness.

HAUGHTY. Sir, I can distinguish gems from pebbles——

DAUPHINE. [*aside*]—Are you so skilful in stones?

HAUGHTY. And howsoever I may suffer in such a judgment as yours, by admitting equality of rank or society with Centaur or 10 Mavis—

DAUPHINE. You do not, madam; I perceive they are your mere foils.

HAUGHTY. Then are you a friend to truth, sir. It makes me love you the more. It is not the outward but the inward man that I 15 affect. They are not apprehensive of an eminent perfection, but love flat, and dully.

CENTAUR. [*Calls from offstage.*] Where are you, my Lady Haughty?

HAUGHTY. I come presently, Centaur.—My chamber, sir, my page
shall show you; and Trusty, my woman, shall be ever awake for   20
you. You need not fear to communicate anything with her, for
she is a Fidelia.[2] I pray you wear this jewel for my sake, Sir
Dauphine.

    [*Enter* LADY CENTAUR.]

Where's Mavis, Centaur?

CENTAUR. Within, madam, a-writing. I'll follow you presently.   25
[*Exit* HAUGHTY.] I'll but speak a word with Sir Dauphine.

DAUPHINE. With me, madam?

CENTAUR. Good Sir Dauphine, do not trust Haughty, nor make
any credit to her, whatever you do besides. Sir Dauphine, I give
you this caution: she is a perfect courtier, and loves nobody but   30
for her uses; and for her uses, she loves all. Besides, her physicians give her out to be none o' the clearest; whether she pay
them or no, Heaven knows! And she's above fifty, too, and par-
gets![3] See her in a forenoon. Here comes Mavis, a worse face
than she! You would not like this by candlelight.   35

    [*Re-enter* MISTRESS MAVIS.]

If you'll come to my chamber one of these mornings early, or
late in an evening, I'll tell you more.—Where's Haughty, Mavis?

MAVIS. Within, Centaur.

CENTAUR. What have you there?

MAVIS. An Italian riddle for Sir Dauphine. You shall not see it, i'   40
faith, Centaur. [*Exit* CENTAUR.] Good Sir Dauphine, solve it for
me. I'll call for it anon.   [*Exit.*]

CLERIMONT. [*coming forward*] How now, Dauphine! How dost
thou quit thyself of these females?

DAUPHINE. 'Slight, they haunt me like fairies, and give me jewels   45
here; I cannot be rid of them.

CLERIMONT. O, you must not tell though.

DAUPHINE. Mass, I forgot that! I was never so assaulted. One loves
for virtue, and bribes me with this [*shows the jewel*]. Another
loves me with caution, and so would possess me. A third brings   50
me a riddle here; and all are jealous, and rail each at other.

CLERIMONT. A riddle! Pray let me see't.   [*Reads the paper.*]

    Sir Dauphine: I chose this way of intimation for privacy.
The ladies here, I know, have both hope and purpose to make
a Collegiate and servant of you. If I might be so honored as to   55
appear at any end of so noble a work, I would enter into a

---

2. Trustworthy.
3. Uses a lot of makeup.

fame of taking physic tomorrow,[4] *and continue it four or five*
days, or longer, for your visitation.

                                                                Mavis.

By my faith, a subtle one! Call you this a riddle? What's their   60
plain-dealing, trow?
DAUPHINE. We lack Truewit, to tell us that.
CLERIMONT. We lack him for somewhat else, too: his knights *re-*
formados[5] are wound up as high and insolent as ever they were.
DAUPHINE. You jest.   65
CLERIMONT. No drunkards, either with wine or vanity, ever confessed such stories of themselves. I would not give a fly's leg in
balance against all the women's reputations here, if they could
be but thought to speak truth; and for the bride, they have made
their affidavit against her directly——   70
DAUPHINE. What, that they have lain with her?
CLERIMONT. Yes, and tell times and circumstances, with the cause
why, and the place where. I had almost brought them to affirm
that they had done it today.
DAUPHINE. Not both of them?   75
CLERIMONT. Yes, faith, with a sooth[6] or two more I had effected
it. They would have set it down under their hands.
DAUPHINE. Why, they will be our sport, I see, still, whether we will
or no.

ACT V   SCENE 3

[*Enter* TRUEWIT.]
TRUEWIT. O are you here? Come, Dauphine, go call your uncle
presently. I have fitted my divine and my canonist, dyed their
beards and all. The knaves do not know themselves, they are so
exalted and altered. Preferment changes any man. Thou shalt
keep one door and I another, and then Clerimont in the midst,   5
that he may have no means of escape from their cavilling,[7] when
they grow hot once. And then the women—as I have given the
bride her instructions—to break in upon him in the *l'envoy*.[8] O,
'twill be full and twanging! Away, fetch him! [*Exit* DAUPHINE]
   [*Enter* OTTER, *disguised as a divine, and* CUTBEARD *as a*
   canon lawyer.][9]

---

4. I'll give out that I'm sick and confined to my bed.
5. In the military sense of an officer left without a command because of reorganization but
   retaining his rank and seniority.
6. Flattery, blandishment.
7. Making frivolous objections.
8. Conclusion; "twanging": noisy and exciting.
9. Otter is a clergyman, Cutbeard a lawyer specializing in ecclesiastical cases.

Come, Master Doctor, and Master Parson, look to your parts   10
now, and discharge them bravely. You are well set forth, perform
it as well. If you chance to be out, do not confess it with standing
still or humming or gaping one at another; but go on, and talk
aloud, and eagerly; use vehement action, and only remember
your terms, and you are safe. Let the matter go where it will;   15
you have many will do so. But at first be very solemn and grave,
like your garments, though you loose yourselves after, and skip
out like a brace of jugglers on a table. Here he comes! Set your
faces, and look superciliously, while I present you.

    [*Re-enter* DAUPHINE *with* MOROSE.]

MOROSE. Are these the two learned men?   20
TRUEWIT. Yes, sir, please you salute them.
MOROSE. Salute them! I had rather do anything than wear out time
    so unfruitfully, sir. I wonder how these common forms, as God
    save you, and *You are welcome*, are come to be a habit in our
    lives; or *I am glad to see you*—when I cannot see what the profit   25
    can be of these words, so long as it is no whit better with him
    whose affairs are sad and grievous, that he hears this salutation.
TRUEWIT. 'Tis true, sir; we'll go to the matter then.—Gentlemen,
    Master Doctor and Master Parson, I have acquainted you suf-
    ficiently with the business for which you are come hither, and   30
    you are not now to inform yourselves in the state of the question,
    I know. This is the gentleman who expects your resolution, and
    therefore, when you please, begin.
OTTER. Please you, Master Doctor.
CUTBEARD. Please you, good Master Parson.   35
OTTER. I would hear the canon law speak first.
CUTBEARD. It must give place to positive divinity, sir.[1]
MOROSE. Nay, good gentlemen, do not throw me into circum-
    stances. Let your comforts arrive quickly at me, those that are.
    Be swift in affording me my peace, if so I shall hope any. I love   40
    not your disputations or your court tumults. And that it be not
    strange to you, I will tell you: my father, in my education, was
    wont to advise me that I should always collect and contain my
    mind, not suffering it to flow loosely; that I should look to what
    things were necessary to the carriage of my life, and what not,   45
    embracing the one and eschewing the other; in short, that I
    should endear myself to rest and avoid turmoil; which now is
    grown to be another nature to me. So that I come not to your
    public pleadings, or your places of noise; not that I neglect those
    things that make for the dignity of the commonwealth; but for   50

---

1. "Positive divinity," based on the scripture, is Otter's province; canon law (Cutbeard's) is the
    entire body of regulations governing the church.

the mere avoiding of clamors, and impertinences of orators that know not how to be silent. And for the cause of noise am I now a suitor to you. You do not know in what a misery I have been exercised this day, what a torrent of evil! My very house turns round with the tumult! I dwell in a windmill! The perpetual   55
motion is here and not at Eltham.[2]

TRUEWIT. Well, good Master Doctor, will you break the ice? Master Parson will wade after.

CUTBEARD. Sir, though unworthy, and the weaker, I will presume.

OTTER. 'Tis no presumption, *Domine* Doctor.[3]   60

MOROSE. Yet again!

CUTBEARD. Your question is, for how many causes a man may have *divortium legitimum*, a lawful divorce? First you must understand the nature of the word 'divorce,' *a divertendo*[4]——

MOROSE. No excursions upon words, good Doctor, to the question   65
briefly.

CUTBEARD. I answer then, the canon law affords divorce but in few cases; and the principal is in the common case, the adulterous case. But there are *duodecim impedimenta*, twelve impediments as we call 'em, all which do not *dirimere contractum*, but *irritum*   70
reddere matrimonium as we say in the canon law, not take away the bond but cause a nullity therein.

MOROSE. I understood you before, good sir, avoid your impertinency of translation.

OTTER. He cannot open this too much, sir, by your favor.   75

MOROSE. Yet more!

TRUEWIT. O, you must give the learned men leave, sir.—To your impediments, Master Doctor.

CUTBEARD. The first is *impedimentum erroris*.[5]

OTTER. Of which there are several species.   80

CUTBEARD. Ay, as *error personae*.[6]

OTTER. If you contract yourself to one person thinking her another.

CUTBEARD. Then, *error fortunae*.[7]

OTTER. If she be a beggar, and you thought her rich.

CUTBEARD. Then, *error qualitatis*.[8]   85

---

2. A Dutch inventor named Drebbel exhibited what he called a perpetual-motion machine at Eltham.
3. *Domine*: Master. Much of the comedy of the following scene derives from the learned disputants' increasing intoxication with Latin. Many of their Latin phrases are either followed or preceded by a translation in the text, and so they will not be annotated.
4. *A divertendo*: from the word "divide" or separate. But *diverto* has a secondary sense, which is to digress.
5. The impediment of error.
6. An error of the person.
7. An error as to fortune.
8. An error of quality.

OTTER. If she prove stubborn or headstrong, that you thought obedient.

MOROSE. How! Is that, sir, a lawful impediment? One at once, I pray you, gentlemen.

OTTER. Ay, *ante copulam*, but not *post copulam*,[9] sir.   90

CUTBEARD. Master Parson says right. *Nec post nuptiarum benedictionem*. It doth indeed but *irrita reddere sponsalia*, annul the contract; after marriage it is of no obstancy.[1]

TRUEWIT. Alas, sir, what a hope are we fallen from by this time!

CUTBEARD. The next is *conditio*: if you thought her free-born and   95
she prove a bondwoman there is impediment of estate and condition.

OTTER. Ay, but Master Doctor, those servitudes are *sublatae*[2] now, among us Christians.

CUTBEARD. By your favor, Master Parson——   100

OTTER. You shall give me leave, Master Doctor.

MOROSE. Nay, gentlemen, quarrel not in that question; it concerns not my case. Pass to the third.

CUTBEARD. Well, then, the third is *votum*: if either party have made a vow of chastity. But that practice, as Master Parson said   105
of the other, is taken away among us, thanks be to discipline. The fourth is *cognatio*; if the persons be of kin within the degrees.

OTTER. Ay; do you know what the degrees are, sir?

MOROSE. No, nor I care not, sir. They offer me no comfort in the   110
question, I am sure.

CUTBEARD. But there is a branch of this impediment may, which is *cognatio spiritualis*. If you were her godfather, sir, then the marriage is incestuous.

OTTER. That comment is absurd and superstitious, Master Doctor.   115
I cannot endure it. Are we not all brothers and sisters, and as much akin in that as god-fathers and god-daughters?

MOROSE. O me! To end the controversy, I never was a godfather, I never was a godfather in my life, sir. Pass to the next.

CUTBEARD. The fifth is *crimen adulterii*,[3] the known case. The   120
sixth, *cultus disparitas*, difference of religion; have you ever examined her, what religion she is of?

MOROSE. No, I would rather she were of none, than be put to the trouble of it.

9. Before marriage but not after marriage.
1. "It's grounds for breaking an engagement but not the marriage itself." "Obstancy" (a made-up word from the Latin): obstacle.
2. Laid aside, obsolete.
3. The crime of adultery.

OTTER. You may have it done for you, sir.   125

MOROSE. By no means, good sir; on to the rest. Shall you ever come to an end, think you?

TRUEWIT. Yes, he has done half, sir.—On to the rest.—Be patient, and expect, sir.

CUTBEARD. The seventh is *vis*: if it were upon compulsion or force.   130

MOROSE. O no, it was too voluntary, mine, too voluntary.

CUTBEARD. The eighth is *ordo*: if ever she have taken holy orders.

OTTER. That's superstitious too.

MOROSE. No matter, Master Parson; would she would go into a nunnery yet!   135

CUTBEARD. The ninth is *ligamen*: if you were bound, sir, to any other before.

MOROSE. I thrust myself too soon into these fetters.

CUTBEARD. The tenth is *publica honestas*: which is *inchoata quaedam affinitas*.[4]   140

OTTER. Ay, or *affinitas orta ex sponsalibus*; and is but *leve impedimentum*.[5]

MOROSE. I feel no air of comfort blowing to me in all this.

CUTBEARD. The eleventh is *affinitas ex fornicatione*.[6]

OTTER. Which is no less *vera affinitas* than the other, Master   145
Doctor.

CUTBEARD. True, *quae oritur ex legitimo matrimonio*.[7]

OTTER. You say right, venerable Doctor; and, *nascitur ex eo, quod per conjugium duae personae efficiuntur una caro*——[8]

TRUEWIT. Hey-day, now they begin!   150

CUTBEARD. I conceive you, Master Parson. *Ita per fornicationem aeque est verus pater, qui sic generat*——[9]

OTTER. *Et vere filius qui sic generatur*——[1]

MOROSE. What's all this to me?

CLERIMONT. —Now it grows warm.   155

CUTBEARD. The twelfth and last is, *si forte coire nequibis*.[2]

OTTER. Ay, that is *impedimentum gravissimum*. It doth utterly annul and annihilate, that. If you have *manifestam frigiditatem*, you are well, sir.[3]

TRUEWIT. Why, there is comfort come at length, sir. Confess your-   160

---

4. Public probity, which is a certain indefinite affinity (between the parties).
5. Ay, or an affinity rising out of the marriage itself; but it's only a minor impediment.
6. Affinity by way of fornication—just as valid an impediment as any other.
7. Affinity through adultery is just as valid as that which rises from legitimate marriage.
8. And derives from the fact that in marriage two persons are made one flesh.
9. And so he is a true father who begets a child in fornication.
1. And he is truly a son who is thus begotten.
2. If for some reason you cannot consummate the marriage.
3. That is a very heavy impediment; if you can show manifest frigidity, you've made your case.

self but a man unable, and she will sue to be divorced first.

OTTER. Ay, or if there be *morbus perpetuus et insanabilis*,[4] as paralysis, elephantiasis, or so——

DAUPHINE. O, but *frigiditas* is the fairer way, gentlemen.

OTTER. You say troth, sir, and as it is in the canon, Master Doctor——   165

CUTBEARD. I conceive you, sir.

CLERIMONT. [*aside*]—Before he speaks!

OTTER. That a boy, or child under years, is not fit for marriage, because he cannot *reddere debitum*.[5] So your *omnipotentes*——   170

TRUEWIT. [*aside to* OTTER]—Your *impotentes*, you whoreson lobster!

OTTER. Your *impotentes*, I should say, are *minime apti ad contrahenda matrimonium*.[6]

TRUEWIT. —*Matrimonium?* We shall have most unmatrimonial   175
Latin with you. *Matrimonia*, and be hanged!

DAUPHINE. —You put them out, man.

CUTBEARD. But then there will arise a doubt, Master Parson, in our case, *post matrimonium*: that *frigiditate praeditus*—do you conceive me, sir?   180

OTTER. Very well, sir.

CUTBEARD. Who cannot *uti uxore pro uxore*, may *habere eam pro sorore*.[7]

OTTER. Absurd, absurd, absurd, and merely apostatical!

CUTBEARD. You shall pardon me, Master Parson, I can prove it.   185

OTTER. You can prove a will, Master Doctor, you can prove nothing else. Does not the verse of your own canon say:
Haec socianda vetant connubia, facta retractant?[8]

CUTBEARD. I grant you; but how do they *retractare*, Master Parson?

MOROSE. O, this was it I feared.   190

OTTER. *In aeternum*,[9] sir.

CUTBEARD. That's false in divinity, by your favor.

OTTER. 'Tis false in humanity to say so. Is he not *prorsus inutilis ad thorum?* Can he *praestare fidem datam?*[1] I would fain know.

CUTBEARD. Yes; how if he do *convalere?*   195

---

4. A chronic and incurable illness; "elephantiasis": a condition in which a part of the body, usually a limb, is grossly enlarged.
5. Perform his matrimonial duties. Otter's slip confuses "omnipotents" with "impotents."
6. Your impotents are by no means fit to undertake matrimony. But again he botches the Latin.
7. Cutbeard proposes that since Morose was impotent when he entered into the marriage, and cannot be to his wife what a husband should be, he can live with her as if she were his sister ("pro sorore"); apostatical: heretical.
8. These associations can't be marriages, the conditions aren't met.
9. Permanent; for eternity.
1. Is he not wholly useless in the marriage bed? Can he fulfill the promise he made? Then Cutbeard questions whether he might not afterward recover (*convalere*).

OTTER. He cannot *convalere*, it is impossible.

TRUEWIT. Nay, good sir, attend the learned men; they'll think you neglect them else.

CUTBEARD. Or if he do *simulare* himself *frigidum, odio uxoris*,[2] or so?   200

OTTER. I say he is *adulter manifestus*, then.

DAUPHINE. —They dispute it very learnedly, i' faith.

OTTER. And *prostitutor uxoris*,[3] and this is positive.

MOROSE. Good sir, let me escape.

TRUEWIT. You will not do me that wrong, sir?   205

OTTER. And, therefore, if he be *manifeste frigidus*, sir——

CUTBEARD. Ay, if he be *manifeste frigidus*, I grant you——

OTTER. Why, that was my conclusion.

CUTBEARD. And mine too.

TRUEWIT. Nay, hear the conclusion, sir.   210

OTTER. Then, *frigiditatis causa*——

CUTBEARD. Yes, *causa frigiditatis*——

MOROSE. O mine ears!

OTTER. She may have *libellum divortii*[4] against you.

CUTBEARD. Ay, *divortii libellum* she will sure have.   215

MOROSE. Good echoes, forbear.

OTTER. If you confess it——

CUTBEARD. Which I would do, sir——

MOROSE. I will do anything.

OTTER. And clear myself, *in foro conscientiae*[5]——   220

CUTBEARD. Because you want indeed——

MOROSE. Yet more?

OTTER. *Exercendi potestate.*[6]

ACT V   SCENE 4

[*Enter* EPICOENE, *followed by* LADY HAUGHTY, LADY CEN-
TAUR, MISTRESS MAVIS, MISTRESS OTTER, DAW, *and* LA
FOOLE.]

EPICOENE. I will not endure it any longer. Ladies, I beseech you, help me. This is such a wrong as never was offered to poor bride before. Upon her marriage day to have her husband conspire against her, and a couple of mercenary companions to be brought in for form's sake, to persuade a separation! If you had   5
blood or virtue in you, gentlemen, you would not suffer such

2. Or else he might be feigning frigidity, out of hatred for his spouse.
3. In that case, says Otter, he is a manifest adulterer and one who prostitutes his own wife.
4. Bill of divorce.
5. In the forum of conscience.
6. The power of performance.

earwigs[7] about a husband, or scorpions to creep between man
and wife——

MOROSE. O, the variety and changes of my torment!

HAUGHTY. Let them be cudgeled out of doors by our grooms.   10

CENTAUR. I'll lend you my footman.

MAVIS. We'll have our men blanket them in the hall.[8]

MISTRESS OTTER. As there was one at our house, madam, for peeping in at the door.

DAW. Content, i' faith.   15

TRUEWIT. Stay, ladies and gentlemen; you'll hear before you proceed?

MAVIS. I'd have the bridegroom blanketed, too.

CENTAUR. Begin with him first.

HAUGHTY. Yes, by my troth.   20

MOROSE. O mankind generation![9]

DAUPHINE. Ladies, for my sake forbear.

HAUGHTY. Yes, for Sir Dauphine's sake.

CENTAUR. He shall command us.

LA FOOLE. He is as fine a gentleman of his inches, madam, as any   25
is about the town, and wears as good colors when he list.[1]

TRUEWIT. Be brief, sir, and confess your infirmity. She'll be afire
to be quit of you, if she but hear that named once. You shall
not entreat her to stay; she'll fly you like one that had the marks[2]
upon him.   30

MOROSE. Ladies, I must crave all your pardons——

TRUEWIT. Silence, ladies.

MOROSE. For a wrong I have done to your whole sex, in marrying
this fair and virtuous gentlewoman——

CLERIMONT. Hear him, good ladies.   35

MOROSE. Being guilty of an infirmity which, before I conferred
with these learned men, I thought I might have concealed——

TRUEWIT. But now being better informed in his conscience by
them, he is to declare it, and give satisfaction by asking your
public forgiveness.   40

MOROSE. I am no man, ladies.

ALL. How!

MOROSE. Utterly unabled in nature, by reason of frigidity, to perform the duties or any of the least office of a husband.

MAVIS. Now out upon him, prodigious creature!   45

CENTAUR. Bridegroom uncarnate!

---

7. An insect formerly believed to crawl into the human ear.
8. Toss them in a blanket.
9. I.e., O generation of vipers! "Mankind" is an old term of disapproval.
1. Choose; "colors": the heraldic insignia of a knight.
2. I.e., of the plague.

HAUGHTY. And would you offer it to a young gentlewoman?

MISTRESS OTTER. A lady of her longings?

EPICOENE. Tut, a device, a device, this! It smells rankly, ladies. A
mere comment of his own.   50

TRUEWIT. Why, if you suspect that, ladies, you may have him
searched.

DAW. As the custom is, by a jury of physicians.

LA FOOLE. Yes, faith, 'twill be brave.

MOROSE. O me, must I undergo that?   55

MISTRESS OTTER. No, let women search him, madam. We can do
it ourselves.

MOROSE. Out on me, worse!

EPICOENE. No, ladies, you shall not need; I'll take him with all
his faults.   60

MOROSE. Worst of all!

CLERIMONT. Why then, 'tis no divorce, Doctor, if she consent not.

CUTBEARD. No, if the man be *frigidus*, it is *parte uxoris*, that we
grant *libellum divortii* in the law.[3]

OTTER. Ay, it is the same in theology.   65

MOROSE. Worse, worse than worst!

TRUEWIT. Nay, sir, be not utterly disheartened; we have yet a small
relic of hope left, as near as our comfort is blown out.—Clerimont, produce your brace of knights.—What was that, Master
Parson, you told me, in *errore qualitatis*,[4] e'en now? [*aside*]—   70
Dauphine, whisper the bride, that she carry it as if she were
guilty and ashamed.

OTTER. Marry, sir, *in errore qualitatis*,—which Master Doctor did
forbear to urge—if she be found *corrupta*, that is, vitiated
or broken up, that was *pro virgine desponsa*, espoused for a   75
maid——

MOROSE. What then, sir?

OTTER. It doth *dirimere contractum*, and *irritum reddere*, too.[5]

TRUEWIT. If this be true, we are happy again, sir, once more. Here
are an honorable brace of knights that shall affirm so much.   80

DAW. Pardon us, good Master Clerimont.

LA FOOLE. You shall excuse us, Master Clerimont.

CLERIMONT. Nay, you must make it good now, knights, there is no
remedy. I'll eat no words for you, nor no men; you know you
spoke it to me.   85

DAW. Is this gentlemanlike, sir?

TRUEWIT. [*aside to* DAW] Jack Daw, he's worse than Sir Amorous,

---

3. No, if the man is frigid, it's only on the wife's complaint that we grant a bill of divorce.
4. About an error of quality.
5. If she was married as a virgin, but wasn't really, it breaks the bond and renders it void too.

fiercer a great deal. [*aside to* LA FOOLE]—Sir Amorous, beware,
there be ten Daws in this Clerimont.

LA FOOLE. I'll confess it, sir.   90

DAW. Will you, Sir Amorous? Will you wound reputation?

LA FOOLE. I am resolved.

TRUEWIT. So should you be too, Jack Daw. What should keep you
off? She's but a woman, and in disgrace. He'll be glad on't.

DAW. Will he? I thought he would have been angry.   95

CLERIMONT. You will despatch, knights, it must be done, i' faith.

TRUEWIT. Why, an it must, it shall, sir, they say. They'll ne'er go
back. [*aside to them*]—Do not tempt his patience.

DAW. It is true indeed, sir.

LA FOOLE. Yes, I assure you, sir.   100

MOROSE. What is true, gentlemen? What do you assure me?

DAW. That we have known your bride, sir——

LA FOOLE. In good fashion. She was our mistress, or so——

CLERIMONT. You must be plain, knights, as you were to me.

OTTER. Ay, the question is, if you have *carnaliter*,[6] or no?   105

LA FOOLE. *Carnaliter!* What else, sir?

OTTER. It is enough; a plain nullity.

EPICOENE. I am undone, I am undone!

MOROSE. O, let me worship and adore you, gentlemen!

EPICOENE. I am undone!   110

MOROSE. Yes, to my hand, I thank these knights. Master Parson,
let me thank you otherwise.

CENTAUR. And have they confessed?

MAVIS. Now, out upon them, informers!

TRUEWIT. You see what creatures you may bestow your favors on,   115
madams.

HAUGHTY. I would except against them as beaten knights, wench,
and not good witnesses in law.[7]

MISTRESS OTTER. Poor gentlewoman, how she takes it!

HAUGHTY. Be comforted, Morose, I love you the better for 't.   120

CENTAUR. So do I, I protest.

CUTBEARD. But, gentlemen, you have not known her since *matrimonium*?

DAW. Not today, Master Doctor.

LA FOOLE. No, sir, not today.   125

CUTBEARD. Why, then I say, for any act before, the *matrimonium*
is good and perfect; unless the worshipful bridegroom did precisely, before witnesses, demand if she were *virgo ante nuptias*.[8]

---

6. If you've had carnal knowledge of her.
7. If they have been cowardly, they have forfeited their honor and are not to be believed under
oath.
8. A virgin before her marriage.

EPICOENE. No, that he did not, I assure you, Master Doctor.

CUTBEARD. If he cannot prove that, it is *ratum conjugium*, not-   130
withstanding the premises; and they do no way *impedire*.[9] And
this is my sentence, this I pronounce.

OTTER. I am of Master Doctor's resolution, too, sir, if you made
not that demand *ante nuptias*.[1]

MOROSE. O my heart! Wilt thou break? Wilt thou break? This is   135
worst of all worst worsts that Hell could have devised! Marry a
whore, and so much noise!

DAUPHINE. Come, I see now plain confederacy in this doctor and
this parson, to abuse a gentleman. You study his affliction. I pray
begone, companions.—And, gentlemen, I begin to suspect you   140
for having parts with 'em.—Sir, will it please you, hear me?

MOROSE. O do not talk to me; take not from me the pleasure of
dying in silence, nephew.

DAUPHINE. Sir, I must speak to you. I have been long your poor,
despised kinsman, and many a hard thought has strengthened   145
you against me; but now it shall appear if either I love you or
your peace, and prefer them to all the world beside. I will not
be long or grievous to you, sir. If I free you of this unhappy
match absolutely and instantly, after all this trouble, and almost
in your despair, now——   150

MOROSE. It cannot be.

DAUPHINE. Sir, that you be never troubled with a murmur of it
more, what shall I hope for, or deserve of you?

MOROSE. O, what thou wilt, nephew! Thou shalt deserve me, and
have me.   155

DAUPHINE. Shall I have your favor perfect to me, and love
hereafter?

MOROSE. That, and anything beside. Make thine own conditions.
My whole estate is thine. Manage it; I will become thy ward.

DAUPHINE. Nay, sir, I will not be so unreasonable.   160

EPICOENE. Will Sir Dauphine be mine enemy, too?

DAUPHINE. You know I have been long a suitor to you, uncle, that
out of your estate, which is fifteen hundred a year, you would
allow me but five hundred during life, and assure the rest upon
me after; to which I have often, by myself and friends, tendered   165
you a writing to sign, which you would never consent or incline
to. If you please but to effect it now——

MOROSE. Thou shalt have it, nephew. I will do it, and more.

DAUPHINE. If I quit you not, presently and forever, of this cumber,[2]

9. I.e., it is a valid marriage, and her affairs before marriage in no way flaw it.
1. Before marriage.
2. Trouble.

you shall have power instantly, afore all these, to revoke your 170
act, and I will become whose slave you will give me to, forever.

MOROSE. Where is the writing? I will seal to it, that, or to a blank,
and write thine own conditions.

EPICOENE. O me, most unfortunate, wretched gentlewoman!

HAUGHTY. Will Sir Dauphine do this? 175

EPICOENE. Good sir, have some compassion on me.

MOROSE. O, my nephew knows you, belike; away, crocodile![3]

CENTAUR. He does it not, sure, without good ground.

DAUPHINE. Here, sir. [*Gives him the parchments.*]

MOROSE. Come, nephew, give me the pen. I will subscribe to any- 180
thing, and seal to what thou wilt, for my deliverance. Thou art
my restorer. Here I deliver it thee as my deed. If there be a word
in it lacking, or writ with false orthography,[4] I protest before God
I will not take the advantage. [*Returns the paper.*]

DAUPHINE. Then here is your release, sir: [*Takes off* EPICOENE'S 185
peruke.] You have married a boy, a gentleman's son that I have
brought up this half year at my great charges, and for this composition which I have now made with you. What say you, Master
Doctor? This is *justum impedimentum*, I hope, *error personae?*[5]

OTTER. Yes sir, *in primo gradu.*[6] 190

CUTBEARD. *In primo gradu.*

DAUPHINE. I thank you, good Doctor Cutbeard, and Parson Otter.
[*Pulls off their beards and disguise.*] You are beholden to them,
sir, that have taken this pains for you; and my friend, Master
Truewit, who enabled them, for the business. Now you may go 195
in and rest; be as private as you will, sir. [*Exit* MOROSE.] I'll not
trouble you till you trouble me with your funeral, which I care
not how soon it come.—Cutbeard, I'll make your lease good.
Thank me not, but with your leg, Cutbeard. And Tom Otter,
your Princess shall be reconciled to you.—How now, gentlemen, 200
do you look at me?

CLERIMONT. A boy!

DAUPHINE. Yes, Mistress Epicoene.

TRUEWIT. Well, Dauphine, you have lurched[7] your friends of the
better half of the garland, by concealing this part of the plot; 205
but much good do it thee, thou deserv'st it, lad! And, Clerimont,
for thy unexpected bringing in these two to confession, wear my
part of it freely. Nay, Sir Daw and Sir La Foole, you see the

---

3. Crocodile tears are proverbially hypocritical.
4. Spelling.
5. This is a valid impediment, I hope, a mistaken identity?
6. Of the highest degree.
7. Cheated. The "garland" is the victor's crown, imaginary in this case, for having done the best job of plotting.

gentlewoman that has done you the favors! We are all thankful
to you, and so should the womankind here, specially for lying   210
on her,[8] though not with her! You meant so, I am sure. But that
we have stuck it upon you today, in your own imagined persons,
and so lately, this Amazon, the champion of the sex, should beat
you now thriftily,[9] for the common slanders which ladies receive
from such cuckoos as you are. You are they that, when no merit   215
or fortune can make you hope to enjoy their bodies, will yet lie
with their reputations, and make their fame suffer. Away, you
common moths of these and all ladies' honors. Go travel, to
make legs and faces, and come home with some new matter
to be laughed at. You deserve to live in an air as corrupted as   220
that where with you feed rumor. [*Exeunt* DAW *and* LA FOOLE.]
Madams, you are mute upon this new metamorphosis! But here
stands she that has vindicated your fames. Take heed of such
insectae hereafter.[1] And let it not trouble you that you have discovered any mysteries to this young gentleman. He is almost of   225
years, and will make a good visitant[2] within this twelvemonth.
In the meantime, we'll all undertake for his secrecy, that can
speak so well of his silence.—[*Coming forward.*] *Spectators, if
you like this comedy, rise cheerfully, and now Morose is gone in,
clap your hands. It may be that noise will cure him, at least please*   230
him.

THE END.

1609

---

8. Rather, "lying about her."
9. Handsomely, thoroughly. The meaning of the sentence is, "if we hadn't already had our
   revenge, we would let Epicoene, the boy, beat you up."
1. Because she has metamorphosed so radically, Epicoene is an "insect."
2. Secret lover.

The Alchemist

The Persons of the Play[1]

SUBTLE, *the alchemist.*
FACE, *the housekeeper.*
DOL COMMON, *their colleague.*
DAPPER, *a clerk.*
DRUGGER, *a tobacco-man.*
LOVEWIT, *master of the house.*
EPICURE MAMMON, *a knight.*
SURLY, *a gamester.*
TRIBULATION, *a pastor of Amsterdam.*
ANANIAS, *a deacon there.*
KASTRIL, *the angry boy.*
DAME PLIANT, *his sister, a widow.*

NEIGHBORS, OFFICERS, MUTES.

THE SCENE: *LONDON.*

The Argument

> *The sickness hot, a master quit for fear*
> *His house in town, and left one servant there.*
> *Ease him corrupted, and gave means to know*
> *A cheater and his punk, who, now brought low,*
> *Leaving their narrow practice, were become*　　　　　　5

---

1. As usual in Jonson's plays, people's names indicate their character. Subtle: reminiscent of the serpent in Genesis, who is "more subtle than any beast of the field" (Gen. 3.1); Face: his name as Lovewit's steward is "Jeremy," but this is the name he uses to perform his swindles, and it suggests the multiplicity of his identities—i.e., he has many "faces"—and also his unreliable nature ("two-faced"); Dol Common: a generic name for a prostitute; Dapper: a small person who is neat, even fastidious, in appearance; Drugger: a druggist; Lovewit: one who loves intelligence and ingenuity; Epicure Mammon: An epicurean was one devoted to the pursuit of sensual pleasure, and Mammon was the name given to riches in the New Testament; Surly: haughty, arrogant; Tribulation: suggests the persecutions that the Puritans endured, here used of course comically; Ananias: a name taken from Acts 5.1–10 in the New Testament of a man who tried to withhold money belonging to the Christian community; Kastril: a small hawk; Dame Pliant: yielding, accomodating; Mutes: i.e., characters with no lines to speak.

Cozeners[2] *at large; and only wanting some*
House to set up, with him they here contract,
Each for a share, and all begin to act.
Much company they draw, and much abuse,
In casting figures,[3] telling fortunes, news,   10
Selling of flies,[4] flat bawdry, with the stone:
Till it and they and all in fume[5] are gone.

Prologue

Fortune, that favors fools, these two short hours
  We wish away, both for your sakes and ours,[6]
Judging spectators; and desire, in place,
  To th' author justice, to ourselves but grace.
Our scene is London, 'cause we would make known   5
  No country's mirth is better than our own:
No clime breeds better matter for your whore,
  Bawd, squire, impostor, many persons more,
Whose manners, now called humors,[7] feed the stage;
  And which have still been subject for the rage   10
Or spleen of comic writers. Though this pen
  Did never aim to grieve, but better men;
Howe'er the age he lives in doth endure
  The vices that she breeds, above their cure.
But when the wholesome remedies are sweet,   15
  And in their working gain and profit meet,
He hopes to find no spirit so much diseased,
  But will with such fair correctives be pleased:
For here he doth not fear who can apply.
  If there be any that will sit so nigh   20
Unto the stream, to look what it doth run,
  They shall find things, they'd think or wish were done;
They are so natural follies, but so shown,
  As even the doers may see, and yet not own.[8]

---

2. Con-men.
3. Telling fortunes.
4. Selling familiar spirits, supernatural helpers; "stone": the philosopher's stone, reputed capable
   of curing all diseases and converting base metals to gold.
5. Smoke.
6. In dismissing fortune for the period of the play, Jonson is appealing to more judicious and
   rational powers—justice for the author, grace for the actors.
7. Humors are the idiosyncrasies of individual temperaments, caused, according to the old medical theories, by an imbalance among the four basic humors of the body, choler, phlegm,
   blood, and black bile; "rage" (line 10) includes the idea of inspiration; "spleen" (line 11):
   the seat of passionate laughter or mirth.
8. Even those who share in the follics mocked onstage will be able to see (recognize) and yet
   not own (admit to) them.

Act I

ACT 1   SCENE 1. *A ROOM IN* LOVEWIT'*S HOUSE*

[*Enter* FACE, *in a captain's uniform, with his sword drawn,
and* SUBTLE *with a vial, quarrelling, and followed by* DOL
COMMON.]

FACE. Believe't, I will.

SUBTLE.   Thy worst. I fart at thee.

DOL. Have you your wits? Why, gentlemen! For love—

FACE. Sirrah, I'll strip you——[1]

SUBTLE.   What to do? Lick figs[2]

Out at my—

FACE.   Rogue, rogue! Out of all your sleights.[3]

DOL. Nay, look ye! Sovereign, General, are you madmen?   5

SUBTLE. O, let the wild sheep loose. I'll gum your silks
With good strong water, an' you come.[4]

DOL.   Will you have
The neighbors hear you? Will you betray all?
Hark! I hear somebody.

FACE.   Sirrah——

SUBTLE.   I shall mar
All that the tailor has made, if you approach.[5]   10

FACE. You most notorious whelp,[6] you insolent slave,
Dare you do this?

SUBTLE.   Yes, faith; yes, faith.

FACE.   Why, who
Am I, my mongrel? Who am I?

SUBTLE.   I'll tell you,
Since you know not yourself.

FACE.   Speak lower, rogue.

SUBTLE. Yes, you were once (time's not long past) the good,   15
Honest, plain, livery-three-pound-thrum,[7] that kept
Your master's worship's house here in the Friars,
For the vacations—

FACE.   Will you be so loud?

SUBTLE. Since, by my means, translated[8] Suburb-Captain.

1. I.e., strip you of your astrologer's robes.
2. Piles, hemorrhoids.
3. Tricks.
4. Subtle has corrosive acid in his vial.
5. I.e., Face as a man is entirely the product of his tailor.
6. Puppy.
7. A drudge, working for his livery (his butler's uniform) plus three pounds a year. The Friars
   are the Blackfriars, an area where Jonson lived and where the play may well have had its first
   performance. The name came from the fact that the Dominican monks once had a monastery
   there; by the seventeenth century, it was a humdrum district of middle-class houses.
8. Transformed into.

FACE. By your means, Doctor Dog?

SUBTLE.   Within man's memory,   20
   All this I speak of.

FACE.   Why, I pray you, have I
   Been countenanced by you? Or you by me?
   Do but collect, sir, where I met you first.

SUBTLE. I do not hear well.

FACE.   Not of this, I think it.
   But I shall put you in mind, sir;—at Pie-corner,[9]   25
   Taking your meal of steam in, from cooks' stalls,
   Where, like the father of hunger, you did walk
   Piteously costive, with your pinched-horn-nose,
   And your complexion of the Roman wash,[1]
   Stuck full of black and melancholic worms,   30
   Like powder corns shot at the artillery-yard.

SUBTLE. I wish you could advance[2] your voice a little.

FACE. When you went pinned up in the several rags
   You had raked and picked from dunghills, before day;
   Your feet in moldy slippers, for your kibes,[3]   35
   A felt of rug, and a thin threaden cloak,
   That scarce would cover your no-buttocks——

SUBTLE.   So, sir!

FACE. When all your alchemy, and your algebra,
   Your minerals, vegetals,[4] and animals,
   Your conjuring, cozening, and your dozen of trades,   40
   Could not relieve your corpse with so much linen
   Would make you tinder, but to see a fire.[5]
   I gave you countenance, credit for your coals,
   Your stills, your glasses, your materials,
   Built you a furnace, drew you customers,   45
   Advanced all your black arts; lent you, beside,
   A house to practice in——

SUBTLE.   Your master's house!

FACE. Where you have studied the more thriving skill
   Of bawdry since.

SUBTLE.   Yes, in your master's house.

---

9. I.e., a corner where meat pies could be bought on the street for immediate consumption. The idea of dining on steam goes back to the French humanist Rabelais's (ca. 1494–ca. 1553) work *Gargantua*, 3.37.
1. Everything about Subtle's earlier estate bespoke the starved and melancholic scholar, from his constipation ("piteously costive"), to his nose like a slender horn, to his sallow complexion ("of the Roman wash"), to his blackheads ("black and melancholic worms"); "powder corns": grains of gunpowder.
2. Raise.
3. Sores on the heel; "felt of rug": a shaggy hat.
4. All things that grow.
5. "Linen": underclothes; pieces of linen were used to light fires.

You and the rats here kept possession.   50
Make it not strange.[6] I know you were one could keep
The buttery-hatch still locked, and save the chippings,[7]
Sell the dole beer to aqua-vitæ men,
The which, together with your Christmas vails,[8]
At post-and-pair, your letting out of counters,   55
Made you a pretty stock, some twenty marks,[9]
And gave you credit to converse with cobwebs,
Here, since your mistress' death hath broke up house.
FACE. You might talk softlier, rascal.
SUBTLE.   No, you scarab,[1]
I'll thunder you in pieces. I will teach you   60
How to beware to tempt a fury again,
That carries tempest in his hand and voice.
FACE. The place has made you valiant.
SUBTLE.   No, your clothes.
Thou vermin, have I ta'en thee out of dung,
So poor, so wretched, when no living thing   65
Would keep thee company, but a spider, or worse?
Raised thee from brooms, and dust, and watering-pots,
Sublimed thee, and exalted thee, and fixed thee
In the third region, called our state of grace?[2]
Wrought thee to spirit, to quintessence, with pains   70
Would twice have won me the philosopher's work?
Put thee in words and fashion, made thee fit
For more than ordinary fellowships?
Giv'n thee thy oaths, thy quarreling dimensions,[3]
Thy rules to cheat at horse-race, cock-pit, cards,   75
Dice, or whatever gallant tincture else?
Made thee a second in mine own great art?
And have I this for thanks! Do you rebel,
Do you fly out in the projection?[4]
Would you be gone now?
DOL.   Gentlemen, what mean you?   80

6. Don't make a mystery out of it.
7. I.e., Face kept the pantry door locked, and clung to the leftovers he should have given away.
   He even sold stale beer to "aqua-vitae men," so called because they accumulated alcoholic
   dregs of all sorts, redistilled them, and sold the product as new liquor.
8. Tips. "Post and pair" was an old card game that required counters; the man who provided
   them got a tiny cut of the pot.
9. As a result of all these devices, Face had 20 marks—worth as much as $150 today.
1. Dung-beetle.
2. "Sublimed," "exalted," and "state of grace" are all alchemical terms; the "philosopher's work"
   is, of course, the philosopher's stone. Subtle has transformed Face, as the stone transforms
   base metals to gold.
3. I.e., rules and regulations, not only for quarreling (provoking a duel), but for cloaking all
   kinds of sharp practice with a "gallant tincture," a coloring of gallantry.
4. Explode, just in the last stages of the process of making gold.

Will you mar all?
SUBTLE.   Slave, thou hadst had no name——
DOL. Will you undo yourselves with civil war?
SUBTLE. Never been known, past *equi clibanum*,[5]
  The heat of horse-dung, under ground, in cellars,
  Or an ale-house darker than deaf John's; been lost   85
  To all mankind, but laundresses and tapsters,
  Had not I been.
DOL.   Do you know who hears you, Sovereign?
FACE. Sirrah—
DOL.   Nay, general, I thought you were civil.
FACE. I shall turn desperate, if you grow thus loud.
SUBTLE. And hang thyself, I care not.
FACE.   Hang thee, collier,   90
  And all thy pots, and pans, in picture,[6] I will,
  Since thou hast moved me——
DOL.   O, this will o'erthrow all.
FACE. Write thee up bawd in Paul's;[7] have all thy tricks
  Of cozening with a hollow coal,[8] dust, scrapings;
  Searching for things lost, with a sieve and shears,   95
  Erecting figures in your rows of houses,
  And taking in of shadows with a glass,[9]
  Told in red letters; and a face cut for thee,
  Worse than Gamaliel Ratsey's.[1]
DOL.   Are you sound?
  Have you your senses, masters?
FACE.   I will have   100
  A book, but barely reckoning thy impostures,
  Shall prove a true philosopher's stone to printers.[2]
SUBTLE. Away, you trencher-rascal![3]
FACE.   Out, you dog-leech!
  The vomit of all prisons——
DOL.   Will you be
  Your own destructions, gentlemen?

5. Horse manure, used in the early stages of alchemy to provide moist and moderate heat.
6. Expose him publicly as an impostor by an illustrated advertisement he will post in St. Paul's (note 7); "collier": cheat, by allusion to the dirtiness and sharp practice of charcoal dealers.
7. St. Paul's was the place for public notices, respectable and scandalous.
8. The "hollow coal" trick involved pouring a bit of molten gold into a hollow piece of charcoal and then burning off the charcoal: this would be proof of the transmutation of metals. Searching for lost things is a traditional activity of magicians; "erecting figures in rows of houses" is constructing a horoscope.
9. Looking in a crystal ball; "told in red letters": Face's advertisement will have special printing; "face cut for thee": engraved picture.
1. Gamaliel Ratsey was a highwayman, hanged in 1605, who wore a hideous mask while robbing people.
2. I.e., the printers will get rich off the book.
3. Parasite.

FACE.   Still spewed out   105
  For lying too heavy on the basket.[4]
SUBTLE.   Cheater!
FACE.   Bawd!
SUBTLE. Cow-herd!
FACE.   Conjurer!
SUBTLE.   Cut-purse!
FACE.   Witch!
DOL.   O me!
  We are ruined! Lost! Have you no more regard
  To your reputations? Where's your judgment? 'Slight,
  Have yet some care of me, of your republic—[5]   110
FACE. Away, this brach! I'll bring thee, rogue, within
  The statute of sorcery, *tricesimo tertio*
  Of Harry the eighth;[6] Ay, and perhaps thy neck
  Within a noose, for laundering gold and barbing it.[7]
DOL. [*snatches* FACE'S *sword*] You'll bring your head within a
    cockscomb, will you?   115
  And you, sir, with your menstrue[8] [*dashes* SUBTLE'S *vial out of
    his hand*]—gather it up.—
  'Sdeath, you abominable pair of stinkards,
  Leave off your barking, and grow one again,
  Or, by the light that shines, I'll cut your throats.
  I'll not be made a prey unto the marshal,[9]   120
  For ne'er a snarling dog-bolt of you both.
  Have you together cozened[1] all this while,
  And all the world, and shall it now be said
  You've made most courteous shift to cozen yourselves?
  [*to* FACE] You will accuse him! You will bring him in   125
  Within the statute! Who shall take your word?
  A whoreson, upstart, apocryphal captain,
  Whom not a Puritan in Blackfriars will trust
  So much as for a feather. [*to* SUBTLE] And you, too,
  Will give the cause, forsooth! You will insult,   130
  And claim a primacy in the divisions!
  You must be chief! As if you only had

4. For cheating in the distribution of food within the prison.
5. "Republic" means "public thing" in Latin, and saying that she is what Face and Subtle hold
   in common. Dol is "brach": bitch.
6. The statute Face cites (against alchemy and multiplying metal) was passed in the thirty-third
   year of the reign of Henry VIII, 1541.
7. "Laundering gold" was washing coins in acid, which ate away their weight; "barbing it" was
   clipping the edges. Both were hanging offenses.
8. Stinking concoction; cockscomb: a fool's cap.
9. As a prostitute, Dol was always in danger from the marshal; "dog-bolt": worthless pup.
1. Cheated.

The powder to project with, and the work
Were not begun out of equality?
The venture tripartite? All things in common?   135
Without priority? 'Sdeath! You perpetual curs,
Fall to your couples again, and cozen kindly,
And heartily, and lovingly, as you should,
And lose not the beginning of a term,[2]
Or, by this hand, I shall grow factious[3] too,   140
And take my part, and quit you.
FACE.   'Tis his fault;
  He ever murmurs, and objects his pains,
  And says the weight of all lies upon him.
SUBTLE. Why, so it does.
DOL.   How does it? Do not we
  Sustain our parts?
SUBTLE.   Yes, but they are not equal.   145
DOL. Why, if your part exceed today, I hope
  Ours may, tomorrow, match it.
SUBTLE.   Ay, they may.
DOL. May, murmuring mastiff? Ay, and do. Death on me!
  Help me to throttle him. [*seizes* SUBTLE, *by the throat.*]
SUBTLE.   Dorothy! Mistress Dorothy!
  'Ods precious,[4] I'll do any thing. What do you mean?   150
DOL. Because o' your fermentation and cibation?[5]
SUBTLE. Not I, by heaven——
DOL.   Your Sol and Luna[6]——[*to* FACE] Help me.
SUBTLE. Would I were hanged then! I'll conform myself.
DOL. Will you, sir? Do so then, and quickly: swear.
SUBTLE. What should I swear?
DOL.   To leave your faction, sir,   155
  And labor kindly in the common work.
SUBTLE. Let me not breathe if I meant aught beside.
  I only used those speeches as a spur
  To him.
DOL.   I hope we need no spurs, sir. Do we?
FACE. 'Slid, prove today, who shall shark best.
SUBTLE.   Agreed.   160
DOL. Yes, and work close and friendly.
SUBTLE.   'Slight, the knot

---

2. The first days of a court term, implying the prime time for business.
3. Make my own faction.
4. By God's precious body and blood.
5. Moistening, in the fancy language of alchemy.
6. Alchemical terms for gold and silver.

Shall grow the stronger for this breach, with me. [*They shake
    hands.*]
DOL. Why, so, my good baboons! Shall we go make
    A sort of sober, scurvy, precise neighbors,[7]
    That scarce have smiled twice since the king came in,   165
    A feast of laughter at our follies? Rascals,
    Would run themselves from breath, to see me ride,[8]
    Or you t' have but a hole to thrust your heads in,
    For which you should pay ear-rent? No, agree.
    And may Don Provost ride a feasting long,[9]   170
    In his old velvet jerkin[1] and stained scarfs,
    My noble Sovereign, and worthy General,
    Ere we contribute a new crewel[2] garter
    To his most worsted worship.
SUBTLE.   Royal Dol!
    Spoken like Claridiana,[3] and thyself.   175
FACE. For which at supper thou shalt sit in triumph,
    And not be styled Dol Common, but Dol Proper,
    Dol Singular: the longest cut at night,[4]
    Shall draw thee for his Dol Particular.   [*Bell rings without.*]
SUBTLE. Who's that? One rings. To the window, Dol. [*Exit* DOL.]
    Pray heaven,   180
    The master do not trouble us this quarter.[5]
FACE. O, fear not him. While there dies one a week
    O' the plague, he's safe from thinking toward London.
    Beside, he's busy at his hop-yards now;
    I had a letter from him. If he do,   185
    He'll send such word, for airing of the house,
    As you shall have sufficient time to quit it.
    Though we break up a fortnight, 'tis no matter.
        [*Re-enter* DOL.]
SUBTLE. Who is it, Dol?
DOL.   A fine young quodling.[6]

---

7. "Precise" defines the neighbors as Puritans, earnest to observe the law of God (as they understood it) precisely; "since the king came in": 1603, i.e., seven years before.
8. Dol would ride in a cart, stripped and whipped, to the workhouse. Face and Subtle, as pimps,
   would be pilloried and have their ears cut off—all this to the great delight of the neighbors.
9. Don Provost, though a specific officer of the law, stands here for the whole legal apparatus,
   especially the public executioner, who got as part of his fee the best clothes of those he
   whipped or executed.
1. Close-fitting leather jacket.
2. "Crewel": worsted, but with a pun on "cruel" and another on "worsted" in the sense of
   cheated or defeated.
3. The heroine of an epic Spanish romance, *The Mirror of Knighthood*. The terms applied to
   Dol—"proper," "singular," and "particular"—are parodies of terms used in heraldry.
4. I.e., they'll draw straws to decide who sleeps with her.
5. Periods when the law courts were in session.
6. Sprout.

FACE.   O,
   My lawyer's clerk, I lighted on last night,   190
   In Holborn, at the Dagger.⁷ He would have
   (I told you of him) a familiar,⁸
   To rifle with at horses, and win cups.
DOL. O, let him in.
SUBTLE.   Stay. Who shall do't?
FACE.   Get you
   Your robes on. I will meet him, as going out.   195
DOL. And what shall I do?
FACE.   Not be seen; away!   [*Exit* DOL.]
   Seem you very reserved.
SUBTLE.   Enough.   [*Exit.*]
FACE.   [*aloud and retiring*] God be wi' you, sir,
   I pray you let him know that I was here;
   His name is Dapper. I would gladly have stayed, but—

ACT I   SCENE 2

DAPPER. [*within*] Captain, I am here.
FACE.   Who's that?—He's come, I
   think, doctor.
        [*Enter* DAPPER.]
   Good faith, sir, I was going away.
DAPPER.   In truth,
   I'm very sorry captain.
FACE.   But I thought
   Sure I should meet you.
DAPPER.   Ay, I'm very glad.
   I had a scurvy writ or two to make,   5
   And I had lent my watch last night to one
   That dines today at the sheriff's, and so was robbed
   Of my pass-time.⁹
        [*Re-enter* SUBTLE *in his velvet cap and gown.*]
                 Is this the cunning-man?¹
FACE. This is his worship.
DAPPER.   Is he a doctor?
FACE.   Yes.
DAPPER. And have you broke with him,² captain?
FACE.   Aye.

7. A particularly low tavern of the district.
8. Short for "familiar spirit," a magic spiritual helper; "rifle": gamble (a variant form of "raffle").
9. Watches were expensive and conferred social prestige on the owner.
1. A country term for "magician."
2. Explained the matter to him.

DAPPER.   And how?   10
FACE. Faith, he does make the matter, sir, so dainty,
  I know not what to say.
DAPPER.   Not so, good captain.
FACE. Would I were fairly rid of it, believe me.
DAPPER. Nay, now you grieve me, sir. Why should you wish so?
  I dare assure you, I'll not be ungrateful.   15
FACE. I cannot think you will, sir. But the law
  Is such a thing——and then he says, Read's matter[3]
  Falling so lately.
DAPPER.   Read! he was an ass,
  And dealt, sir, with a fool.
FACE.   It was a clerk, sir.
DAPPER. A clerk!
FACE.   Nay, hear me, sir, you know the law   20
  Better, I think——
DAPPER.   I should, sir, and the danger.
  You know, I showed the statute to you.[4]
FACE. You did so.
DAPPER.   And will I tell then? By this hand of flesh,
  Would it might never write good court-hand[5] more,
  If I discover. What do you think of me,   25
  That I am a *chiaus*?[6]
FACE.   What's that?
DAPPER.   The Turk, was here.
  As one would say, do you think I am a Turk?
FACE. I'll tell the doctor so.
DAPPER.   Do, good sweet captain.
FACE. Come, noble doctor, pray thee let's prevail;
  This is the gentleman, and he is no *chiaus*.   30
SUBTLE. Captain, I have returned you all my answer.
  I would do much, sir, for your love——But this
  I neither may, nor can.
FACE.   Tut, do not say so.
  You deal now with a noble fellow, doctor,
  One that will thank you richly; and he is no *chiaus*:   35
  Let that, sir, move you.
SUBTLE.   Pray you, forbear—

---

3. In 1608 Simon Read was charged with necromancy—he had called up some spirits to ask
   them who had stolen a sum of money from his client. King James pardoned him.
4. This is the source of Face's remarkable erudition above (1.1.112–13); it is part of Jonson's
   point that con-men learn their trade from their victims.
5. The particular script used by clerks in the courts of law.
6. A messenger (Turkish—pronounced "chouse"). In 1607 a messenger named Mustafa arrived
   in England claiming to be from Turkey; he collected a lot of money from gullible folk and
   made off with it, leaving behind a new word for "cheat."

FACE.   He has

Four angels here.[7]

SUBTLE.   You do me wrong, good sir.

FACE. Doctor, wherein? To tempt you with these spirits?

SUBTLE. To tempt my art and love, sir, to my peril.

'Fore heaven, I scarce can think you are my friend,   40

That so would draw me to apparent danger.

FACE. I draw you! A horse draw you, and a halter,

You, and your flies together—[8]

DAPPER.   Nay, good Captain.

FACE. That know no difference of men.

SUBTLE.   Good words, sir.

FACE. Good deeds, sir Doctor Dogs'-Meat. 'Slight, I bring you   45

No cheating Clim-o' the-Cloughs, or Claribels,[9]

That look as big as five-and-fifty, and flush;[1]

And spit out secrets like hot custard—

DAPPER.   Captain?

FACE. Nor any melancholic under-scribe,

Shall tell the vicar; but a special gentle,   50

That is the heir to forty marks a year,

Consorts with the small poets of the time,

Is the sole hope of his old grandmother;

That knows the law, and writes you six fair hands,

Is a fine clerk, and has his ciphering perfect,   55

Will take his oath o' the Greek Testament,

If need be, in his pocket; and can court

His mistress out of Ovid.[2]

DAPPER.   Nay, dear captain—

FACE. Did you not tell me so?

DAPPER.   Yes; but I'd have you

Use master Doctor with some more respect.   60

FACE. Hang him, proud stag, with his broad velvet head![3]

But for your sake, I'd choke, ere I would change

An article of breath with such a puckfist—[4]

Come, let's be gone.   [Going.]

---

7. Coins bearing an image of Michael the archangel. The total bribe is about two pounds.

8. As in the Argument, familiar spirits, sometimes taking the form of flies, but just as often assuming other shapes.

9. Clim o' the Clough was one of Robin Hood's playmates, Claribel a lewd and wicked knight in Edmund Spenser's *The Faeire Queen* (1590–96)—unsavory characters, in other words.

1. In the old card game of primero, this would be as good a hand as a royal straight flush in poker.

2. I.e., will have the smartest and sexiest possible things to say to her. The Roman poet Ovid (43 B.C.E.–18 C.E.) wrote the *Metamorphoses*.

3. Doctors wore velvet caps, and Face also alludes to the "velvet" on a stag's (and cuckold's) antlers.

4. Literally, tightwad, but Face is accusing Subtle of being a "stingy receiver."

SUBTLE.   Pray you let me speak with you.

DAPPER. His worship calls you, Captain.

FACE.   I am sorry   65
  I e'er embarked myself in such a business.

DAPPER. Nay, good sir; he did call you.

FACE.   Will he take then?

SUBTLE. First, hear me—

FACE.   Not a syllable, 'less you take.

SUBTLE. Pray you, sir—

FACE.   Upon no terms, but an *assumpsit*.[5]

SUBTLE. Your humor must be law. [*He takes the four angels.*]

FACE.   Why now, sir, talk.   70
  Now I dare hear you with mine honor. Speak.
  So may this gentleman too.

SUBTLE.   Why, sir—[*Pretending to whisper*
  to FACE.]

FACE.   No whispering.

SUBTLE. 'Fore heaven, you do not apprehend the loss
  You do yourself in this.

FACE.   Wherein? For what?

SUBTLE. Marry, to be so importunate for one,   75
  That, when he has it, will undo you all.
  He'll win up all the money in the town.

FACE. How!

SUBTLE.   Yes, and blow up gamester after gamester,
  As they do crackers[6] in a puppet-play.
  If I do give him a familiar,   80
  Give you him all you play for; never set him;[7]
  For he will have it.

FACE.   You are mistaken, Doctor.
  Why, he does ask one but for cups and horses,
  A rifling fly;[8] none of your great familiars.

DAPPER. Yes, Captain, I would have it for all games.   85

SUBTLE. I told you so.

FACE. [*taking* DAPPER *aside*] 'Slight, that's a new business!
  I understood you, a tame bird, to fly
  Twice in a term, or so, on Friday nights,
  When you had left the office, for a nag
  Of forty or fifty shillings.

DAPPER.   Ay, 'tis true, sir;   90

---

5. Literally, a taking. Subtle must take Dapper's money (reluctant as he is to do so) to avoid a quarrel with Face.
6. Firecrackers.
7. Never bet against him.
8. A spirit for use in now-and-then gambling situations.

But I do think now I shall leave the law,
And therefore——
FACE.   Why, this changes quite the case.
Do you think that I dare move him?
DAPPER.   If you please, sir;
All's one to him, I see.
FACE.   What! For that money?
I cannot with my conscience; nor should you   95
Make the request, methinks.
DAPPER.   No, sir, I mean
To add consideration.[9]
FACE.   Why then, sir,
I'll try. [*Goes to* SUBTLE.] Say that it were for all games,
    Doctor?
SUBTLE. I say then, not a mouth shall eat for him
At any ordinary, but on the score;[1]   100
That is a gaming mouth, conceive me.
FACE.   Indeed!
SUBTLE. He'll draw you all the treasure of the realm,
If it be set him.
FACE.   Speak you this from art?
SUBTLE. Ay, sir, and reason too, the ground of art.
He is of the only best complexion,   105
The Queen of Fairy loves.
FACE.   What! Is he?
SUBTLE.   Peace,
He'll overhear you. Sir, should she but see him—
FACE. What?
SUBTLE.   Do not you tell him.
FACE.   Will he win at cards too?
SUBTLE. The spirits of dead Holland, living Isaac,[2]
You'd swear, were in him; such a vigorous luck   110
As cannot be resisted. 'Slight, he'll put
Six of your gallants to a cloak,[3] indeed.
FACE. A strange success, that some man shall be born to!
SUBTLE. He hears you, man——
DAPPER.   Sir, I'll not be ungrateful.
FACE. Faith, I have confidence in his good nature: 115
You hear, he says he will not be ungrateful.

---

9. Money.
1. I.e., no gamester will have a bit of cash left to buy food at a tavern ("ordinary"); they'll all
   have to eat on credit.
2. John and Isaac Holland were Dutch alchemists; Subtle implies that they are masters of good
   luck.
3. I.e., he'll strip six gallants to their cloaks.

SUBTLE. Why, as you please; my venture follows yours.
FACE. Troth, do it, Doctor; think him trusty, and make him.
 He may make us both happy in an hour;
 Win some five thousand pound, and send us two on't. 120
DAPPER. Believe it, and I will, sir.
FACE.   And you shall, sir.
 You have heard all?   [*Takes him aside.*]
DAPPER.   No, what was't? Nothing, I, sir.
FACE. Nothing?
DAPPER.   A little, sir.
FACE.   Well, a rare star
 Reigned at your birth.
DAPPER.   At mine, sir! No.
FACE.   The doctor
 Swears that you are—
SUBTLE.   Nay, captain, you'll tell all now. 125
FACE. Allied to the Queen of Fairy.
DAPPER.   Who? That I am?
 Believe it, no such matter—
FACE.   Yes, and that
 You were born with a caul on your head.[4]
DAPPER.   Who says so?
FACE.   Come,
 You know it well enough, though you dissemble it.
DAPPER. I'fac, I do not: you are mistaken.
FACE.   How! 130
 Swear by your fac,[5] and in a thing so known
 Unto the Doctor? How shall we, sir, trust you
 In the other matter? Can we ever think,
 When you have won five or six thousand pound,
 You'll send us shares in't, by this rate?
DAPPER.   By Jove, sir, 135
 I'll win ten thousand pound, and send you half.
 I'fac's no oath.
SUBTLE. No, no, he did but jest.
FACE. Go to. Go thank the doctor: he's your friend,
 To take it so.
DAPPER. I thank his worship.
FACE.   So?
 Another angel.

---

4. A membrane on the head of a newborn child, considered a mark of good luck.
5. "In faith," but diluted to the point at which it's not much more of an oath than "Gosh" or "Golly."

DAPPER.   Must I?

FACE.   Must you! 'Slight,   140
What else is thanks? Will you be trivial?—Doctor,
                    [DAPPER *gives him the money.*]
When must he come for his familiar?

DAPPER. Shall I not have it with me?

SUBTLE.   O, good sir!
There must a world of ceremonies pass;
You must be bathed and fumigated first;   145
Besides, the Queen of Fairy does not rise
Till it be noon.

FACE.   Not if she danced tonight.

SUBTLE. And she must bless it.

FACE.   Did you never see
Her royal grace yet?

DAPPER.   Whom?

FACE.   Your aunt of Fairy?

SUBTLE. Not since she kissed him in the cradle, Captain;   150
I can resolve you that.

FACE.   Well, see her Grace,
Whate'er it cost you, for a thing that I know.
It will be somewhat hard to compass; but
However, see her. You are made, believe it,
If you can see her. Her Grace is a lone woman,   155
And very rich; and if she take a fancy,
She will do strange things. See her, at any hand.
'Slid, she may hap to leave you all she has:
It is the doctor's fear.

DAPPER.   How will't be done, then?

FACE. Let me alone, take you no thought. Do you   160
But say to me, "Captain, I'll see her Grace."

DAPPER. Captain, I'll see her Grace.

FACE.   Enough. [*Knocking within.*]

SUBTLE.   Who's there?
Anon! [*aside to* FACE]—Conduct him forth by the back way.—
Sir, against one o'clock prepare yourself;
Till when you must be fasting; only take   165
Three drops of vinegar in at your nose,
Two at your mouth, and one at either ear;
Then bathe your fingers' ends and wash your eyes,
To sharpen your five senses, and *cry hum*
Thrice, and then *buz* as often; and then come. [*Exit.*] 170

FACE. Can you remember this?

DAPPER.   I warrant you.

FACE. Well then, away. It is but your bestowing
　　Some twenty nobles 'mong her Grace's servants,[6]
　　And put on a clean shirt. You do not know
　　What grace her Grace may do you in clean linen.　　　　　175
　　　　　　　　　　　　　　[*Exeunt* FACE *and* DAPPER.]

ACT 1   SCENE 3

SUBTLE. [*within*] Come in! [*He calls out through the door.*]
　　—Good wives, I pray you forbear me now;[7]
　　Troth, I can do you no good till afternoon—
　　　　　　[*Re-enters, followed by* DRUGGER.]
　　What is your name, say you, Abel Drugger?
DRUGGER.　　　　　　　　　　　　　　　Yes, sir.
SUBTLE. A seller of tobacco?
DRUGGER.　　　　　　　　Yes, sir.
SUBTLE.　　　　　　　　　　Umph!
　　Free of the grocers?[8]
DRUGGER.　　　　　　　Ay, an't please you.
SUBTLE.　　　　　　　　　　　　Well——　　　　　　　　　5
　　Your business, Abel?
DRUGGER.　　　　　　　　This, an't please your worship;
　　I am a young beginner, and am building
　　Of a new shop, an't like your worship, just
　　At corner of a street: here is the plot[9] on't.
　　And I would know by art, sir, of your worship,　　　　10
　　Which way I should make my door, by necromancy,[1]
　　And where my shelves; and which should be for boxes,
　　And which for pots. I would be glad to thrive, sir;
　　And I was wished to your worship by a gentleman,
　　One Captain Face, that says you know men's planets,　　15
　　And their good angels, and their bad.
SUBTLE.　　　　　　　　　　　　　I do,
　　　　[*Enter* FACE.]
　　If I do see them—
FACE.　　　　　　　What! My honest Abel?
　　Thou art well met here.
DRUGGER.　　　　　　　　Troth, sir, I was speaking,
　　Just as your worship came here, of your worship.
　　I pray you speak for me to master Doctor.　　　　　　20
FACE. He shall do anything. Doctor, do you hear?

6. For a man of Dapper's class, this is a stiff sum, perhaps one to two hundred dollars today.
7. Subtle is putting off tradeswomen to whom he owes money.
8. Are you a full member of the grocer's company? (i.e., have you served your apprenticeship?).
9. Plan, layout.
1. Communication with the dead.

This is my friend Abel, an honest fellow;
He lets me have good tobacco, and he does not
Sophisticate[2] it with sack-lees or oil,
Nor washes it in muscadel and grains,   25
Nor buries it in gravel, under ground,
Wrapped up in greasy leather, or pissed clouts:[3]
But keeps it in fine lily pots, that, opened,
Smell like conserve of roses, or French beans.
He has his maple block, his silver tongs,   30
Winchester pipes, and fire of juniper;
A neat, spruce, honest fellow, and no goldsmith.[4]
SUBTLE. He is a fortunate fellow, that I am sure on.
FACE. Already, sir, have you found it? Lo thee, Abel!
SUBTLE. And in right way toward riches—
FACE.   Sir!
SUBTLE.   This summer   35
He will be of the clothing of his company,[5]
And next spring called to the scarlet; spend what he can.
FACE. What, and so little beard?
SUBTLE.   Sir, you must think,
He may have a receipt to make hair come.
But he'll be wise, preserve his youth, and fine for't;[6]   40
His fortune looks for him another way.
FACE. 'Slid, Doctor, how canst thou know this so soon?
I am amused[7] at that!
SUBTLE.   By a rule, Captain,
In metoposcopy,[8] which I do work by;
A certain star in the forehead, which you see not.   45
Your chestnut or your olive-colored face
Does never fail; and your long ear doth promise.
I knew't, by certain spots, too, in his teeth,
And on the nail of his mercurial finger.
FACE. Which finger's that?
SUBTLE.   His little finger.[9] Look.   50

---

2. Adulterate.
3. Rags.
4. As usual, Jonson's technical details are precise: the maple block was used to shred the tobacco, the silver tongs to hold a coal of glowing juniper to get the pipe lit, and Winchester pipes were thought to be the best. The highest commendation is that Abel is no goldsmith, i.e., not a usurer, as grocers tended to be.
5. I.e., an officer of the grocers' company, for whom the next step up would be appointment as sheriff ("called to the scarlet"); all this despite his extreme youth ("so little beard").
6. He'll be smart enough not to accept the office, with its responsibilities; he'll do better to pay a fine for refusing it.
7. Bemused, puzzled.
8. Telling of fortunes by looking in someone's face.
9. This astrological gibberish, which Drugger takes very seriously, may be understood to say that he is in particular danger from thieves—as he obviously is.

You were born upon a Wednesday?

DRUGGER.   Yes, indeed, sir.

SUBTLE. The thumb, in chiromancy,[1] we give Venus;
The fore-finger, to Jove; the midst, to Saturn;
The ring, to Sol; the least, to Mercury,
Who was the lord, sir, of his horoscope,   55
His house life being Libra; which fore-showed
He should be a merchant, and should trade with balance.

FACE. Why, this is strange! Is it not, honest Nab?

SUBTLE. There is a ship now, coming from Ormuz,[2]
That shall yield him such a commodity   60
Of drugs [*pointing to the plan*]——This is the west, and this
the south?

DRUGGER. Yes, sir.

SUBTLE.   And those are your two sides?

DRUGGER.   Ay, sir.

SUBTLE. Make me your door, then, south; your broad side, west;
And on the east side of your shop, aloft,
Write Mathlai, Tarmiel, and Baraborat;[3]   65
Upon the north part, Rael, Velel, Thiel.
They are the names of those mercurial spirits
That do fright flies from boxes.

DRUGGER.   Yes, sir.

SUBTLE.   And
Beneath your threshold, bury me a lodestone
To draw in gallants that wear spurs; the rest,   70
They'll seem to follow.

FACE.   That's a secret, Nab!

SUBTLE. And, on your stall, a puppet, with a vice[4]
And a court-fucus, to call city-dames.
You shall deal much with minerals.

DRUGGER.   Sir, I have
At home, already——

SUBTLE.   Ay, I know you have arsenic,   75
Vitriol,[5] sal-tartar, argaile, alkali,
Cinoper: I know all.—This fellow, Captain,
Will come, in time, to be a great distiller,
And give a say[6]—I will not say directly,

---

1. Divination by the hand.
2. An island in the Persian gulf, source of many drugs.
3. Gibberish names for occult spirits that will protect Drugger's stock on the shelves.
4. Device, for making the puppet move; "court-focus": the kind of makeup used at court, not
   bound to sell well to city ladies who never go there.
5. Sulphuric acid; "sal-tartar": carbonate of potash; "argaile": cream of tartar; "alkali": soda ash;
   "cinoper": cinnabar, red mercuric sulphide.
6. Essay, attempt.

But very fair—at the philosopher's stone.   80
FACE. Why, how now, Abel! Is this true?
DRUGGER.   [*aside to* FACE.] Good Captain,
  What must I give?
FACE.   Nay, I'll not counsel thee.
  Thou hear'st what wealth he says, spend what thou canst,
  Thou'rt like to come to.
DRUGGER.   I would gi' him a crown.
FACE. A crown! And toward such a fortune? Heart,   85
  Thou shalt rather gi' him thy shop. No gold about thee?
DRUGGER. Yes, I have a portague[7] I have kept this half year.
FACE. Out on thee, Nab! 'Slight, there was such an offer—
  Shalt keep't no longer, I'll give't him for thee.—Doctor,
  Nab prays your worship to drink this, and swears   90
  He will appear more grateful, as your skill
  Does raise him in the world.
DRUGGER.   I would entreat
  Another favor of his worship.
FACE.   What is't, Nab?
DRUGGER. But to look over, sir, my almanac,
  And cross out my ill-days, that I may neither   95
  Bargain, nor trust upon them.
FACE.   That he shall, Nab;
  Leave it, it shall be done, 'gainst afternoon.
SUBTLE. And a direction for his shelves.
FACE.   Now, Nab,
  Art thou well pleased, Nab?
DRUGGER.   Thank, sir, both your worships.
FACE.   Away.
                            [*Exit* DRUGGER.]
  Why, now, you smoky persecutor of nature!   100
  Now do you see, that something's to be done,
  Beside your beech-coal, and your corsive waters,
  Your crosslets, crucibles, and cucurbites?[8]
  You must have stuff, brought home to you, to work on.
  And yet you think, I am at no expense   105
  In searching out these veins, then following them,
  Then trying them out. 'Fore God, my intelligence
  Costs me more money, than my share oft comes to,
  In these rare works.
SUBTLE.   You are pleasant, sir.—How now?

---

7. Portuguese gold piece worth nearly four pounds.
8. Acids, furnaces, and cupping-glasses, used in alchemical demonstrations.

ACT I   SCENE 4

[*Re-enter* DOL.]
What says my dainty Dolkin?
DOL.   Yonder fishwife
Will not away. And there's your giantess,
The bawd of Lambeth.[9]
SUBTLE.   Heart, I cannot speak with them.
DOL. Not afore night, I have told them in a voice,
Through the trunk,[1] like one of your familiars.   5
But I have spied Sir Epicure Mammon——
SUBTLE.   Where?
DOL. Coming along, at far end of the lane,
Slow of his feet, but earnest of his tongue
To one that's with him.
SUBTLE.   Face, go you, and shift.[2]   [*Exit* FACE.]
Dol, you must presently make ready, too.   10
DOL. Why, what's the matter?
SUBTLE.   O, I did look for him
With the sun's rising: marvel he could sleep!
This is the day I am to perfect for him
The *magisterium*,[3] our great work, the stone;
And yield it, made, into his hands, of which   15
He has, this month, talked as he were possessed.
And now he's dealing pieces on't away.
Methinks I see him entering ordinaries,[4]
Dispensing for the pox,[5] and plaguy houses,
Reaching[6] his dose, walking Moorfields for lepers,   20
And offering citizens' wives pomander-bracelets,
As his preservative, made of the elixir;
Searching the spittle,[7] to make old bawds young,
And the highways, for beggars, to make rich;
I see no end of his labors. He will make   25
Nature ashamed of her long sleep, when art,
Who's but a stepdame, shall do more than she,
In her best love to mankind, ever could.
If his dream last, he'll turn the age to gold.   [*Exeunt.*]

9. A disreputable area.
1. Speaking-tube.
2. Change your clothes.
3. Masterwork.
4. Inns.
5. Venereal diseases.
6. Offering; Moorfields, in the suburbs, was a hangout for beggars, cripples, the feeble-minded, and the hopelessly diseased; "pomander-bracelets": medicine-bracelets.
7. Hospital. Sir Epicure will cure all the epidemic diseases of the time when he has the stone.

Act II

ACT II   SCENE 1. *AN OUTER ROOM IN* LOVEWIT'*S HOUSE*

[*Enter* SIR EPICURE MAMMON *and* SURLY.]

MAMMON. Come on, sir. Now, you set your foot on shore
In *Novo Orbe*;[8] here's the rich Peru;
And there within, sir, are the golden mines,
Great Solomon's Ophir![9] He was sailing to't
Three years, but we have reached it in ten months.   5
This is the day, wherein, to all my friends,
I will pronounce the happy word, "Be rich";[1]
This day you shall be *spectatissimi*.[2]
You shall no more deal with the hollow die
Or the frail card. No more be at charge of keeping   10
The livery-punk[3] for the young heir, that must
Seal, at all hours, in his shirt. No more,
If he deny, have him beaten to't, as he is
That brings him the commodity. No more
Shall thirst of satin, or the covetous hunger   15
Of velvet entrails for a rude-spun cloak,
To be displayed at Madam Augusta's,[4] make
The sons of Sword and Hazard fall before
The golden calf, and on their knees, whole nights,
Commit idolatry with wine and trumpets,   20
Or go a feasting after drum and ensign.
No more of this. You shall start up young viceroys
And have your punks[5] and punketees, my Surly.
And unto thee I speak it first, "Be rich."
Where is my Subtle, there? Within, ho!
FACE.   [*within*] Sir,   25
He'll come to you by and by.
MAMMON.   That is his fire-drake,[6]

---

8. The New World, with its legends of El Dorado, the mythical man of gold, whom Pizarro
   found to be real and actual in the Inca of Peru.
9. Solomon was understood from a biblical text (1 Kings 10.22) to have found great wealth in
   the Arabian city of Ophir, to which he sent a fleet every three years.
1. Mammon is parodying the divine word of creation, e.g., "Let there be light" (Gen. 1.3).
2. Most distinguished.
3. Professed pimp. The general sense is that the man with the philosopher's stone no longer has
   to resort to dishonest and degrading ways of making a living—such as by rounding up girls
   for young heirs.
4. Clearly a brothel, where the wretched servant has resorted to recruit girls for his master. The
   "sons of Sword and Hazard" are highwaymen and (like Surly) gamesters—these represent
   alternative ways for the desperate fellow to make money. And if all else fails, he can "go a-
   feasting after drum and ensign"—enlist in the army.
5. Pimps; "punketees": bawds (evidently an invented word).
6. A fire-dragon, supposed to live in the element of fire; all Mammon's fanciful names for Face
   imply his role as a stimulator of fire.

His Lungs, his Zephyrus, he that puffs his coals,
Till he firk[7] nature up, in her own center.
You are not faithful,[8] sir. This night, I'll change
All that is metal in my house to gold;   30
And early in the morning will I send
To all the plumbers and the pewterers
And buy their tin and lead up; and to Lothbury[9]
For all the copper.
SURLY.   What, and turn that too?
MAMMON. Yes, and I'll purchase Devonshire and Cornwall   35
    And make them perfect Indies![1] You admire now?
SURLY. No, faith.
MAMMON.   But when you see th' effects of the great
        medicine,
Of which one part projected on a hundred
Of Mercury, or Venus, or the Moon,[2]
Shall turn it to as many of the Sun;   40
Nay, to a thousand, so *ad infinitum*—
You will believe me.
SURLY.   ·   Yes, when I see't, I will.
But if my eyes do cozen me so, and I
Giving them no occasion, sure I'll have
A whore shall piss them out next day.
MAMMON.   Ha! Why?   45
Do you think I fable with you? I assure you,
He that has once the flower of the sun,
The perfect ruby, which we call elixir,[3]
Not only can do that, but, by its virtue,
Can confer honor, love, respect, long life;   50
Give safety, valor, yea, and victory
To whom he will. In eight and twenty days,
I'll make an old man of fourscore a child.
SURLY. No doubt; he's that already.
MAMMON.   Nay, I mean
Restore his years, renew him like an eagle   55
To the fifth age;[4] make him get sons and daughters,

7. Stir.
8. A true believer.
9. The street of the coppersmiths in London.
1. I.e., the Americas. Tin and copper mines were found in Devon and Cornwall; Mammon will
   convert them to storehouses of gold.
2. Alchemically speaking, quicksilver, copper, or silver. The sun is, of course, gold itself.
3. The fluid that changes base metals to gold and cures all diseases instantly.
4. I.e., to the Fifth (the years between 41 and 56) of the Seven Ages of Man. Mars ("Marses,"
   line 61) was the planet that predominated the Fifth Age in the Ptolemaic astrological scheme.

    Young giants; as our philosophers have done,
The ancient patriarchs, afore the flood,
But taking once a week, on a knife's point,
The quantity of a grain of mustard of it;[5]   60
Become stout Marses and beget young Cupids.
SURLY. The decayed vestals[6] of Pict-hatch would thank you,
  That keep the fire alive, there.
MAMMON.   'Tis the secret
  Of nature naturized[7] 'gainst all infections,
  Cures all diseases coming of all causes;   65
  A month's grief in a day, a year's in twelve;
  And, of what age soever, in a month,
  Past all the doses of your drugging doctors.
  I'll undertake, withal, to fright the plague
  Out of the kingdom in three months.
SURLY.   And I'll   70
  Be bound the players shall sing your praises, then,[8]
  Without their poets.
MAMMON.   Sir, I'll do't. Meantime,
  I'll give away so much unto my man
  Shall serve the whole city, with preservative,[9]
  Weekly; each house his dose, and at the rate—   75
SURLY. As he that built the water-work, does with water?[1]
MAMMON. You are incredulous.
SURLY.   Faith, I have a humor.
  I would not willingly be guiled.[2] Your stone
  Cannot transmute me.
MAMMON.   Pertinax, my Surly,
  Will you believe antiquity? Records?   80
  I'll show you a book where Moses and his sister
  And Solomon have written of the art;
  Ay, and a treatise penned by Adam[3]—
SURLY.   How!
MAMMON. Of the philosopher's stone, and in High Dutch.
SURLY. Did Adam write, sir, in High Dutch?

---

5. Mammon attributed the longevity and the potency of the biblical patriarchs (e.g., Noah and Abraham) to their use of the elixir.
6. Virgins, sardonically. "Pict-hatch": district near Blackfriars famous for prostitutes.
7. Referring to the distinction in medieval philosophy between *natura naturata* ("nature naturized"), which is finished, created nature, and *natura naturans*, the active, divine creative force behind nature. Here the stone is the created product, the alchemist the creating force.
8. When the plague ran rampant, theaters closed and actors were unemployed.
9. Stuff that's good for what ails you.
1. About 1595 the first public waterworks were established in London, supplying Thames water to households for a fee.
2. Tricked.
3. Moses, Miriam, Solomon, and Adam were only a few of the early worthies whom the alchemists claimed as members of their craft.

MAMMON.   He did;   85
  Which proves it was the primitive tongue.
SURLY.   What paper?
MAMMON. On cedar board.
SURLY.   O that, indeed, they say,
  Will last 'gainst worms.
MAMMON.   'Tis like your Irish wood
  'Gainst cobwebs. I have a piece of Jason's fleece, too,
  Which was no other than a book of alchemy,   90
  Writ in large sheepskin, a good fat ram-vellum.
  Such was Pythagoras' thigh, Pandora's tub,
  And all that fable of Medea's charms,
  The manner of our work;[4] the bulls, our furnace,
  Still breathing fire; our argent-vive, the dragon: 95
  The dragon's teeth, mercury sublimate,
  That keeps the whiteness, hardness, and the biting;
  And they are gathered into Jason's helm,
  The alembic,[5] and then sowed in Mars his field,
  And thence sublimed so often, till they're fixed.   100
  Both this, the Hesperian garden,[6] Cadmus' story,
  Jove's shower, the boon of Midas, Argus' eyes,
  Boccace his Demogorgon, thousands more,
  All abstract riddles of our stone.[7]—How now?

ACT II   SCENE 2

  [*Enter* FACE *as the servant Lungs.*]
  Do we succeed? Is our day come? And holds it?
FACE. The evening will set red upon you, sir;
  You have color for it, crimson: the red ferment
  Has done his office; three hours hence prepare you
  To see projection.[8]
MAMMON.   Pertinax, my Surly,   5

---

4. Pythagoras (ca. 580–500 B.C.E.) was reputed to have a golden thigh, and the box the gods
   gave Pandora was also thought golden. In addition, Mammon interprets as an emblem of the
   stone the story of Jason and Medea. Jason had to plough a field with a pair of brazen-footed,
   fire-breathing bulls (the furnace), sow the furrows with dragon's teeth (mercury sublimate),
   kill the armed men who sprang from those teeth, and then overcome a sleepless dragon
   ("argent-vive," quicksilver) guarding the golden fleece. Medea, a prototype of the witch,
   helped him pass these various tests.
5. Jason's helmet is the retort in which ingredients were heated and distilled.
6. A mythical garden where golden apples grew, guarded by a dragon.
7. Like the tale of Jason and the golden fleece, the stories of Cadmus and the sowing of dragon's
   teeth, of Jove wooing Danae in a shower of gold, of Argus the watchman with a hundred
   eyes, and of Boccaccio's Demogorgon (who was the original god of all gods) are all versions
   of a single basic story: the transmutation of metals.
8. The twelfth and final work of the alchemist: the creation of gold.

Again I say to thee, aloud, "Be rich."
This day thou shalt have ingots; and, tomorrow,
Give lords th' affront.—Is it, my Zephyrus,[9] right?
Blushes the bolt's-head?

FACE.   Like a wench with child, sir,
That were but now discovered to her master.   10

MAMMON. Excellent witty Lungs!—My only care is
Where to get stuff enough now to project on;
This town will not half serve me.

FACE.   No, sir? Buy
The covering off o' churches.

MAMMON.   That's true.

FACE.   Yes.
Let them stand bare, as do their auditory;   15
Or cap them new with shingles.

MAMMON.   No, good thatch:[1]
Thatch will lie light upon the rafters, Lungs.
Lungs, I will manumit[2] thee from the furnace;
I will restore thee thy complexion, Puff,
Lost in the embers; and repair this brain,   20
Hurt with the fume o' the metals.

FACE.   I have blown, sir,
Hard for your worship; thrown by many a coal,
When 'twas not beech;[3] weighed those I put in, just,
To keep your heat still even; these bleared eyes
Have waked to read your several colors, sir,   25
Of the pale citron, the green lion, the crow,
The peacock's tail, the plumed swan.[4]

MAMMON.   And, lastly,
Thou hast descried the flower, the *sanguis agni*?[5]

FACE. Yes, sir.

MAMMON.   Where's master?

FACE.   At his prayers, sir, he;
Good man, he's doing his devotions   30
For the success.

MAMMON.   Lungs, I will set a period

---

9. The west wind; "bolt's head": a long-necked vessel, the top of which turns red ("blushes") at
the height of the process.
1. Having taken the lead off church roofs, and toyed with Face's fancy of leaving them bareheaded like the audiences inside them, Mammon replaces them (in his fantasy) with cheap
thatch.
2. Liberate.
3. Only beech, a particularly dense and expensive wood, yielded the right coal for alchemy.
4. The various colors through which the basic materials pass on their way to becoming the
philosopher's stone.
5. Blood of the lamb, the final blood-red color of projection.

To all thy labors; thou shalt be the master
Of my seraglio.[6]

FACE.   Good, sir.

MAMMON.   But do you hear?
I'll geld you, Lungs.

FACE.   Yes, sir.

MAMMON.   For I do mean
To have a list of wives and concubines,   35
Equal with Solomon, who had the stone
Alike with me; and I will make me a back
With the elixir, that shall be as tough
As Hercules, to encounter fifty a night.—
Thou art sure thou saw'st it blood?

FACE.   Both blood and spirit, sir.   40

MAMMON. I will have all my beds blown up, not stuffed:
Down is too hard. And then, mine oval room
Filled with such pictures as Tiberius took
From Elephantis,[7] and dull Aretine
But coldly imitated. Then, my glasses   45
Cut in more subtle angles, to disperse
And multiply the figures, as I walk
Naked between my succubae.[8] My mists
I'll have of perfume, vapored 'bout the room,
To lose ourselves in; and my baths, like pits   50
To fall into; from whence we will come forth,
And roll us dry in gossamer and roses.—
Is it arrived at ruby?——Where I spy
A wealthy citizen, or a rich lawyer,
Have a sublimed pure wife, unto that fellow   55
I'll send a thousand pound to be my cuckold.

FACE. And I shall carry it?

MAMMON.   No, I'll have no bawds,
But fathers and mothers: they will do it best,[9]
Best of all others. And my flatterers
Shall be the pure and gravest of divines,   60
That I can get for money. My mere fools,
Eloquent burgesses,[1] and then my poets

---

6. Harem.
7. The Roman biographer Suetonius's life of the emperor Tiberius (ruled 14–37 C.E.) describes the obscene decorations of the villa on Capri where the emperor held his orgies. Elephantis was a Greek erotic writer of antiquity and Pietro Aretino an Italian pornographer of more recent vintage.
8. Whores with demonic overtones.
9. The detail comes from the Tenth Satire by Roman poet Juvenal (ca. 60–136 C.E.), but the streak of perversity is Mammon's own.
1. He'll have so much money that he'll hire respectable bourgeois ("burgesses") to play the fool before him.

The same that writ so subtly of the fart,[2]
Whom I will entertain still for that subject.
The few that would give out themselves to be   65
Court and town-stallions, and each-where belie
Ladies who are known most innocent, for them,
Those will I beg, to make me eunuchs of:
And they shall fan me with ten ostrich tails
Apiece, made in a plume to gather wind.   70
We will be brave,[3] Puff, now we have the medicine.
My meat shall all come in, in Indian shells,
Dishes of agate set in gold, and studded
With emeralds, sapphires, hyacinths,[4] and rubies.
The tongues of carps, dormice, and camels heels,   75
Boiled in the spirit of Sol,[5] and dissolved pearl,
Apicius' diet, 'gainst the epilepsy:
And I will eat these broths with spoons of amber,
Headed with diamond and carbuncle.
My foot-boy shall eat pheasants, calvered salmons,   80
Knots, godwits, lampreys:[6] I myself will have
The beards of barbels served instead of salads;
Oiled mushrooms; and the swelling unctuous paps
Of a fat pregnant sow newly cut off,
Dressed with an exquisite and poignant sauce;[7]   85
For which, I'll say unto my cook, "There's gold,
Go forth, and be a knight."
FACE.   Sir, I'll go look
A little, how it heightens.

                                        [*Exit.*]

MAMMON.   Do.—My shirts
I'll have of taffeta-sarsnet,[8] soft and light
As cobwebs; and for all my other raiment   90
It shall be such as might provoke the Persian
Were he to teach the world riot[9] anew.
My gloves of fishes and bird skins perfumed
With gums of paradise and eastern air—

2. An episode of a fart let in the House of Commons created a minor stir in the session of 1607;
   a number of poets, including Jonson himself, took occasion to display their wit.
3. Splendid.
4. Rare blue stones; "dormice": plural of "dormouse," a rodent that was edible.
5. I.e., liquid gold. Roman gourmets recommended these and many of the other delicacies
   described below as preventives of epilepsy. Apicius, the best-known of them, had a better
   remedy: after eating himself out of a huge fortune, he hanged himself.
6. "Calvered" salmon are simply sliced. "Knots" and "godwits" are game birds, "lampreys" eels.
   "Barbels" are fish like catfish, with soft, fleshy chin-whiskers.
7. Many of the gastronomic details are from the *Life of Heliogabalus* (Roman emperor 218–222
   C.E.) by the late Roman historian Lampridius.
8. A particularly soft and luxurious fabric.
9. Luxury. The Persians were famous for rich living.

SURLY. And do you think to have the stone with this?

MAMMON. No, I do think t'have all this with the stone.

SURLY. Why, I have heard he must be *homo frugi*,[1]
  A pious, holy, and religious man,
  One free from mortal sin, a very virgin.

MAMMON. That makes it, sir; he is so. But I buy it;   100
  My venture brings it me. He, honest wretch,
  A notable, superstitious, good soul,
  Has worn his knees bare, and his slippers bald,
  With prayer and fasting for it: and, sir, let him
  Do it alone, for me, still. Here he comes.   105
  Not a profane word afore him; 'tis poison.

ACT II   SCENE 3

MAMMON. Good morrow, father.
      [*Enter* SUBTLE.]

SUBTLE.   Gentle son, good morrow
  And to your friend there. What is he, is with you?

MAMMON. An heretic, that I did bring along
  In hope, sir, to convert him.

SUBTLE.   Son, I doubt[2]
  You are covetous, that thus you meet your time   5
  In the just point—prevent your day at morning.[3]
  This argues something, worthy of a fear
  Of importune and carnal appetite.
  Take heed you do not cause the blessing leave you
  With your ungoverned haste. I should be sorry   10
  To see my labors, now even at perfection,
  Got by long watching and large patience,
  Not prosper where my love and zeal hath placed them.
  Which (heaven I call to witness with your self,
  To whom I have poured my thoughts) in all my ends,   15
  Have looked no way but unto public good,
  To pious uses, and dear charity,
  Now grown a prodigy[4] with men. Wherein
  If you, my son, should now prevaricate,[5]
  And, to your own particular lusts employ   20
  So great and catholic[6] a bliss, be sure

.1. A man of temperate habits. It was, of course, accepted by alchemists that a man who discovered the secret of nature's perfection must himself be perfect.
2. Suspect.
3. Anticipate the arrival of day by coming early.
4. Rarity.
5. Not the modern "lie" but rather the Latin sense of "walk crookedly."
6. Universal.

A curse will follow, yea, and overtake
Your subtle and most secret ways.
MAMMON.   I know, sir;
You shall not need to fear me. I but come
To have you confute this gentleman.
SURLY.   Who is,   25
Indeed, sir, somewhat costive[7] of belief
Toward your stone; would not be gulled.
SUBTLE.   Well, son,
All that I can convince him in, is this,
The work is done, bright Sol is in his robe.
We have a medicine of the triple soul,   30
The glorified spirit. Thanks be to heaven,
And make us worthy of it!—Ulen Spiegel![8]
FACE. [within] Anon, sir.
SUBTLE.   Look well to the register.[9]
And let your heat still lessen by degrees,
To the aludels.[1]
FACE.   [within] Yes, sir.
SUBTLE.   Did you look   35
O' the bolt's-head yet?
FACE.   [within] Which? On D, sir?
SUBTLE.   Aye;
What's the complexion?
FACE.   [within] Whitish.
SUBTLE.   Infuse vinegar,
To draw his volatile substance and his tincture:
And let the water in glass E be filtered,
And put into the gripe's egg.[2] Lute him well;   40
And leave him closed in balneo.
FACE.   [within] I will, sir.
SURLY. What a brave language here is! Next to canting.[3]
SUBTLE. I have another work, you never saw, son,
That three days since passed the philosopher's wheel,
In the lent heat of Athanor;[4] and's become   45
Sulphur of Nature.
MAMMON.   But 'tis for me?

---

7. Reluctant to grant consent.
8. Till Eulenspiegel, literally, "Owl-glass," was a German joker of the Renaissance, a trickster
   and con-man with whom Face and Subtle recognize kinship.
9. Damper of the furnace.
1. Pots without bottoms, fitted together to form a condenser.
2. A specially shaped vessel, like a vulture's egg. Face is to pack this vessel in clay to make it
   airtight and leave it "in balneo," in the bath of hot water.
3. Thieves' slang, but also a special jargon developed by extreme Puritans.
4. The gentle heat of a slow furnace. "Sulphur of Nature" is just pure sulphur.

SUBTLE.   What need you?
  You have enough in that is perfect.
MAMMON.   O but——
SUBTLE. Why, this is covetise!
MAMMON.   No, I assure you,
  I shall employ it all in pious uses,
  Founding of colleges and grammar schools,   50
  Marrying young virgins, building hospitals,
  And now and then a church.
        [*Re-enter* FACE]
SUBTLE.   How now?
FACE.   Sir, please you,
  Shall I not change the filter?
SUBTLE.   Marry, yes;
  And bring me the complexion of glass B.   [*Exit* FACE.]
MAMMON. Have you another?
SUBTLE.   Yes, son; were I assured   55
  Your piety were firm, we would not want
  The means to glorify it; but I hope the best.
  I mean to tinct C in sand-heat tomorrow,
  And give him imbition.[5]
MAMMON.   Of white oil?
SUBTLE. No, sir, of red. F is come over the helm too,   60
  I thank my maker, in Saint Mary's bath,[6]
  And shows *lac virginis*. Blessed be heaven!
  I sent you of his faeces there calcined:
  Out of that calx,[7] I have won the salt of mercury.
MAMMON. By pouring on your rectified water?   65
SUBTLE. Yes, and reverberating[8] in Athanor.
        [*Re-enter* FACE.]
  How now! What color says it?
FACE.   The ground black, sir.
MAMMON. That's your crow's head?[9]
SURLY.   Your cockscomb's, is it not?
SUBTLE. No, 'tis not perfect. Would it were the crow.
  That work wants something.
SURLY.   [*aside*] O, I looked for this.   70
  The hay's a pitching.[1]
SUBTLE.   Are you sure you loosed them

---

5. Moistening.
6. Essentially, a double boiler; "lac virginis": literally, milk of the virgin, dissolved mercury.
7. "Faeces": literally, excrement, actually sediment; "calx": powder.
8. Heating in a furnace in which the heat is reflected off the top of the furnace.
9. Jet-black; Surly's correction implies mammon is a fool, a coxcomb.
1. The trap is being set—a "hay" was a snare to catch a rabbit.

In their own menstrue?[2]

FACE.   Yes, sir, and then married them,
And put them in a bolt's-head nipped to digestion,
According as you bade me, when I set
The liquor of Mars to circulation   75
In the same heat.

SUBTLE.   The process then was right.

FACE. Yes, by the token, sir; the retort brake,
And what was saved was put into the pelican,
And signed with Hermes' seal.[3]

SUBTLE.   I think 'twas so.
We should have a new amalgama.[4]

SURLY.   [aside] O, this ferret   80
Is rank as any pole cat.

SUBTLE.   But I care not:
Let him e'en die; we have enough beside,
In embrion.[5] H has his white shirt on?

FACE.   Yes sir,
He's ripe for inceration,[6] he stands warm
In his ash-fire. I would not you should let   85
Any die now, if I might counsel, sir,
For luck's sake to the rest: it is not good.

MAMMON. He says right.

SURLY.   [aside] Ay, are you bolted?[7]

FACE.   Nay, I know't, sir,
I have seen the ill fortune. What is some three ounces
Of fresh materials?

MAMMON.   Is't no more?

FACE.   No more, sir,   90
Of gold, t'amalgam with some six of mercury.

MAMMON. Away, here's money. What will serve?

FACE.   Ask him, sir.

MAMMON. How much?

SUBTLE.   Give him nine pound; you may give him ten.

SURLY. Yes, twenty, and be cozened, do.

MAMMON.   There 'tis.
          [Gives FACE the money.]

---

2. Solvents.
3. The "pelican" was a retort whose outlet led back into itself. "Hermes' seal" was a way of
closing off a tube (hermetically, so to speak) by twisting it shut.
4. Combination.
5. Embryo. The "white shirt" signified a stage in distillation when all the ingredients appeared
white.
6. The stage of waxiness.
7. Driven into the net. Surly sees the whole process of trapping Mammon as a rabbit hunt, in
which the net is laid (pitched) and the rabbit driven into it.

SUBTLE. This needs not; but that you will have it so,   95
    To see conclusions of all; for two
    Of our inferior works are at fixation,
    A third is in ascension.[8] Go your ways.
    Have you set the oil of luna in kemia?[9]
FACE. Yes, sir.
SUBTLE.   And the philosopher's vinegar?[1]
FACE.   Ay.   [*Exit.*]   100
SURLY. We shall have a salad!
MAMMON.   When do you make projection?
SUBTLE. Son, be not hasty, I exalt our med'cine,
    By hanging him *in balneo vaporoso*,[2]
    And giving him solution; congeal him;
    And then dissolve him; then again congeal him.   105
    For look, how oft I iterate the work,
    So many times I add unto his virtue.
    As, if at first one ounce converts a hundred,
    After his second loose, he'll turn a thousand;
    His third solution, ten; his fourth, a hundred.   110
    After his fifth, a thousand thousand ounces
    Of any imperfect metal, into pure
    Silver or gold, in all examinations
    As good as any of the natural mine.
    Get you your stuff here against afternoon,   115
    Your brass, your pewter, and your andirons.
MAMMON. Not those of iron?
SUBTLE.   Yes, you may bring them too:
    We'll change all metals.
SURLY.   I believe you in that.
MAMMON. Then I may send my spits?
SUBTLE.   Yes, and your racks.
SURLY. And dripping-pans, and pot-hangers, and hooks,   120
    Shall he not?
SUBTLE.   If he please.
SURLY.   —To be an ass.
SUBTLE. How, sir!
MAMMON.   This gentleman you must bear withal.
    I told you he had no faith.

---

8. The two "inferior works" are Dapper and Drugger, both set aside for the moment in "fixation";
   Mammon is in "ascension"—he's getting crazier and crazier in his ambitious lust.
9. "Oil of luna" contains an allusion to the moon and to the silver of which it is an emblem;
   "kemia" is the process of alchemy itself: Mammon is being transmuted.
1. Some sort of corrosive.
2. In a steam bath.

SURLY.   And little hope, sir;
 But much less charity, should I gull myself.
SUBTLE. Why, what have you observed, sir, in our art   125
 Seems so impossible?
SURLY.   But your whole work, no more.
 That you should hatch gold in a furnace, sir,
 As they do eggs in Egypt![3]
SUBTLE.   Sir, do you
 Believe that eggs are hatched so?
SURLY.   If I should?
SUBTLE. Why, I think that the greater miracle.   130
 No egg but differs from a chicken more
 Than metals in themselves.
SURLY.   That cannot be.
 The egg's ordained by nature to that end,
 And is a chicken *in potentia*.[4]
SUBTLE. The same we say of lead and other metals,   135
 Which would be gold, if they had time.
MAMMON.   And that
 Our art doth further.
SUBTLE.   Ay, for 'twere absurd
 To think that nature in the earth bred gold
 Perfect in the instant. Something went before.
 There must be remote matter.
SURLY.   Ay, what is that?   140
SUBTLE. Marry, we say—
MAMMON.   Ay, now it heats; stand, father,
 Pound him to dust.
SUBTLE.   It is, of the one part,
 A humid exhalation, which we call
 Materia liquida, or the unctuous water;[5]
 On the other part, a certain crass and viscous   145
 Portion of earth; both which, concorporate,
 Do make the elementary matter of gold;
 Which is not yet *propria materia*,[6]
 But common to all metals and all stones.
 For, where it is forsaken of that moisture,   150
 And hath more dryness, it becomes a stone;

---

3. In incubators, supposed to be an Egyptian invention.
4. Potentially.
5. I.e., oily water. The lecture on alchemy that Subtle delivers here had been put forward in all seriousness by the alchemists themselves. Its premise is that all inferior metals would be gold if they could; the work of the alchemist is simply to help them fulfill their basic disposition.
6. Proper material.

Where it retains more of the humid fatness,
It turns to sulphur, or to quicksilver,
Who are the parents of all other metals.
Nor can this remote matter suddenly   155
Progress so from extreme unto extreme,
As to grow gold and leap o'er all the means.
Nature doth first beget the imperfect, then
Proceeds she to the perfect. Of that airy
And oily water, mercury is engendered;   160
Sulphur of the fat and earthy part; the one,
Which is the last, supplying the place of male,
The other of the female, in all metals.
Some do believe hermaphrodeity,[7]
That both do act and suffer.[8] But these two   165
Make the rest ductile, malleable, extensive.
And even in gold they are; for we do find
Seeds of them, by our fire, and gold in them,
And can produce the species of each metal
More perfect thence, than nature doth in earth.[9]   170
Beside, who doth not see in daily practice
Art can beget bees, hornets, beetles, wasps,
Out of the carcasses and dung of creatures?[1]
Yea, scorpions of an herb, being rightly placed?
And these are living creatures, far more perfect   175
And excellent than metals.
MAMMON.   Well said, father!
    Nay, if he take you in hand, sir, with an argument,
    He'll bray you in a mortar.[2]
SURLY.   Pray you, sir, stay.
    Rather than I'll be brayed, sir, I'll believe
    That alchemy is a pretty kind of game,   180
    Somewhat like tricks o' the cards, to cheat a man
    With charming.
SUBTLE.   Sir?
SURLY.   What else are all your terms,
    Whereon no one of your writers 'grees with other?

---

7. A great deal of alchemical terminology extended a sexual principle into chemical processes;
   thus, gold was the product of a fortunate marriage between sulphur and mercury.
8. Acting and suffering define the active and passive energies of a relationship.
9. Outdoing mere nature, the philosopher's art could produce—or so the alchemists believed—
   a kind of supergold, capable of creating new gold.
1. Aristotle had taught the reality of spontaneous generation, i.e., living creatures developing
   from inorganic material; if that can happen, why not transmutation of metals?
2. Crush you to powder.

Of your *elixir*, your *lac virginis*,[3]
Your *stone*, your *med'cine*, and your *chrysosperme*,   185
Your *sal*, your *sulphur*, and your *mercury*,
Your *oil of height*, your *tree of life*, your *blood*,
Your *marchesite*, your *tutie*, your *magnesia*,
Your *toad*, your *crow*, your *dragon*, and your *panther*;
Your *sun*, your *moon*, your *firmanent*, your *adrop*,   190
Your *lato, azoch, zernich, chibrit, heautarit*,
And then your *red man*, and your *white woman*,
With all your broths, your menstrues, and materials,
Of piss and egg-shells, women's terms, man's blood,
Hair o' the head, burnt clouts, chalk, merds, and clay,   195
Powder of bones, scalings of iron, glass,
And worlds of other strange *ingredients*,
Would burst a man to name?
SUBTLE.   And all these named,
Intending but one thing; which art our writers
Used to obscure their art.
MAMMON.   Sir, so I told him   200
Because the simple idiot should not learn it,
And make it vulgar.
SUBTLE.   Was not all the knowledge
Of the Egyptians writ in mystic symbols?[4]
Speak not the Scriptures oft in parables?
Are not the choicest fables of the poets,   205
That were the fountains and first springs of wisdom,
Wrapped in perplexed allegories?
MAMMON.   I urged that,
And cleared to him, that Sisyphus was damned
To roll the ceaseless stone, only because
He would have made ours common.[5] [DOL *appears at the
door.*]   —Who is this?   210

3. The phrases of the following vehement catalog are all legitimate alchemical expressions. Note
   that the list starts with technical terms and gradually works down to ingredients that are not
   only common but disgusting. "Lac virginis": virgin's milk (another name for mercury); "chrysosperme": seed of gold; "oil of height": oil was thought to be one of the five supposed
   principles of matter; "tree of life": the philosopher's stone, but with allusion to the tree in the
   Garden of Eden; "marchesite": white iron pyrites; "tutie": impure zinc oxide; "magnesia":
   thick, salty water; "toad [black] . . . crow [blue-black] . . . dragon [mercury] . . . panther
   [spotted]" all indicate colors that appear during alchemical transformation; "adrop": an alchemical term for "lead"; "lato": a metal similar to brass; "azoch": mercury; "zernich": tri-
   sulphide of arsenic; "chibrit": sulphur; "heautarit": mercury; "red man . . . white woman":
   sulphur and mercury; "women's terms": menstrual discharge; "clouts": rags or, perhaps, clods
   of earth; "merds": excrement.
4. Hieroglyphics—which, in spite of many pretenses, nobody could read before the nineteenth
   century.
5. In Greek mythology, Sisyphus was condemned to roll a stone in the underworld because he
   betrayed the secrets of the gods: Mammon says that secret was the philosopher's stone.

SUBTLE. God's precious!—What do you mean? Go in, good lady,
    Let me entreat you. [DOL *retires.*] Where's this varlet?
       [*Re-enter* FACE.]

FACE.   Sir.

SUBTLE. You very knave! Do you use me thus?

FACE.   Wherein, sir?

SUBTLE. Go in and see, you traitor. Go!   [*Exit* FACE.]

MAMMON.   Who is it, sir?

SUBTLE. Nothing, sir, nothing.

MAMMON.   What's the matter, good sir?   215
    I have not seen you thus distempered. Who is it?

SUBTLE. All arts have still had, sir, their adversaries;
    But ours the most ignorant. [*Re-enter* FACE.] What now?

FACE. 'Twas not my fault, sir; she would speak with you.

SUBTLE. Would she, sir! Follow me.   [*Exit.*]

MAMMON.   [*stopping him*] Stay, Lungs.

FACE.   I dare not, sir.   220

MAMMON. Stay, man; what is she?

FACE.   A lord's sister, sir.

MAMMON. How! Pray thee, stay.

FACE.   She's mad, sir, and sent hither—
    He'll be mad too.

MAMMON.   I warrant thee. Why sent hither?

FACE. Sir, to be cured.

SUBTLE.   [*within*] Why, rascal!

FACE.   Lo you!—Here, sir!   [*Exit.*]

MAMMON. 'Fore God, a Bradamante,[6] a brave piece.   225

SURLY. Heart, this is a bawdy-house! I'll be burnt else.

MAMMON. O, by this light, no. Do not wrong him. He's
    Too scrupulous that way; it is his vice.
    No, he's a rare physician, do him right,
    An excellent Paracelsian,[7] and has done   230
    Strange cures with mineral physic. He deals all
    With spirits, he; he will not hear a word
    Of Galen,[8] or his tedious recipes.
    How now, Lungs!

FACE.   Softly, sir; speak softly. I meant
    To have told your worship all. This[9] must not hear.   235

MAMMON. No, he will not be gulled; let him alone.

---

6. Bradamante, a heroine of Italian poet Ludovico Ariosto's *Orlando Furioso* (1532) and, like
   Dol, as bold at war as love.
7. A follower of Theophrastus Bombastus von Hohenheim (Paracelsus), the sixteenth-century
   Swiss physician and alchemist.
8. Galen, late Roman doctor and chief authority cited by conventional physicians, whom
   Paracelsus and his followers despised.
9. With a gesture at Surly.

FACE. You're very right, sir; she is a most rare scholar,
   And is gone mad with studying Broughton's works.[1]
   If you but name a word touching the Hebrew,
   She falls into her fit, and will discourse   240
   So learnedly of genealogies,
   As you would run mad too, to hear her, sir.
MAMMON. How might one do t' have conference with her,
   Lungs?
FACE. O divers[2] have run mad upon the conference.
   I do not know, sir. I am sent in haste.   245
   To fetch a vial.
SURLY.   Be not gulled, sir Mammon.
MAMMON. Wherein? Pray ye, be patient.
SURLY.   Yes, as you are,
   And trust confederate knaves and bawds and whores.
MAMMON. You are too foul, believe it.—Come here, Ulen,
   One word.
FACE.   I dare not, in good faith.   [*Going.*]
MAMMON.   Stay, knave.   250
FACE. He is extreme angry that you saw her, sir.
MAMMON. Drink that. [*Gives him money.*] What is she when
   she's out of her fit?
FACE. O, the most affablest creature, sir! So merry!
   So pleasant! She'll mount you up, like quick-silver,
   Over the helm;[3] and circulate like oil,   255
   A very vegetal: discourse of state,[4]
   Of mathematics, bawdry, anything——
MAMMON. Is she no way accessible? No means,
   No trick to give a man a taste of her——wit——
   Or so?
SUBTLE. [*within*] Ulen!
FACE.   I'll come to you again, sir.   [*Exit.*]   260
MAMMON. Surly, I did not think one of your breeding
   Would traduce personages of worth.
SURLY.   Sir Epicure,
   Your friend to use; yet still, loath to be gulled.
   I do not like your philosophical bawds.
   Their stone is lechery enough to pay for   265
   Without this bait.
MAMMON.   'Heart, you abuse yourself.

---

1. Hugh Broughton (1549–1612) was a scholar of Hebrew whom Jonson often satirized.
2. Various people.
3. Face's commendations of Dol are phrased in alchemical terms but can be understood to apply to a whore.
4. Talk of politics; "vegetal": a stimulant.

I know the lady, and her friends, and means,
The original of this disaster. Her brother
Has told me all.
SURLY.   And yet you ne'er saw her
    Till now!
MAMMON.   O yes, but I forgot. I have, believe it,   270
    One of the treacherousest memories, I do think,
    Of all mankind.
SURLY.   What call you her brother?
MAMMON.   My lord——
    He will not have his name known, now I think on't.
SURLY. A very treacherous memory!
MAMMON.   On my faith——
SURLY. Tut, if you have it not about you, pass it,   275
    Till we meet next.
MAMMON.   Nay, by this hand, 'tis true.
    He's one I honor, and my noble friend;
    And I respect his house.
SURLY.   Heart! can it be
    That a grave sir, a rich, that has no need,
    A wise sir, too, at other times, should thus   280
    With his own oaths and arguments make hard means
    To gull himself? An this be your elixir,
    Your *lapis mineralis*,⁵ and your lunary,
    Give me your honest trick yet at primero,
    Or gleek; and take your *lutum sapientis*,   285
    Your *menstruum simplex*! I'll have gold before you,
    And with less danger of the quicksilver,
    Or the hot sulphur.⁶
        [*Enter* FACE, *still as Lungs.*]
FACE. [*to* SURLY] Here's one from Captain Face, sir,
    Desires you meet him in the Temple-church,
    Some half hour hence, and upon earnest business.   290
    Sir, [*whispers to* MAMMON] if you please to quit us now, and
        come
    Again within two hours, you shall have
    My master busy examining o'the works;
    And I will steal you in, unto the party,
    That you may see her converse. [*Aloud to* SURLY.]
                                Sir, shall I say,   295

5. Mineral stone. Surly is saying that if this is alchemy, he'd rather lose his money at cards, at
   "primero or gleek" (lines 284–85).
6. "Lutum sapientis": wise man's glue; "menstrum simplex": plain solvent. Both phrases refer to
   Dol. Surly's road to wealth involves less danger from quicksilver or sulphur, both used to cure
   venereal diseases.

You'll meet the captain's worship?

SURLY.   Sir, I will.   [*Walks aside.*]
But, by attorney,[7] and to a second purpose.
Now, I am sure it is a bawdy-house;
I'll swear it, were the marshal here to thank me;
The naming this commander doth confirm it.   300
Don Face! Why he's the most authentic dealer
In these commodities, the superintendent
To all the quainter traffickers[8] in town!
He is the visitor, and does appoint
Who lies with whom, and at what hour; what price;   305
Which gown, and in what smock; what fall, what tire.[9]
Him will I prove by a third person, to find
The subtleties of this dark labyrinth;
Which if I do discover, dear sir Mammon,
You'll give your poor friend leave, though no philosopher,   310
To laugh; for you that are, 'tis thought, shall weep.[1]

FACE. Sir, he does pray, you'll not forget.

SURLY.   I will not, sir.
Sir Epicure, I shall leave you.

MAMMON.   I follow you, straight.

FACE. But do so, good sir, to avoid suspicion.
This gentleman has a parlous head.[2]

MAMMON.   But wilt thou, Ulen,   315
Be constant to thy promise?

FACE.   As my life, sir.

MAMMON. And wilt thou insinuate what I am, and praise me,
And say, I am a noble fellow?

FACE.   O, what else, sir?
And that you'll make her royal with the stone,
An empress; and your self, king of Bantam.[3]   320

MAMMON. Wilt thou do this?

FACE.   Will I, sir!

MAMMON.   Lungs, my Lungs!
I love thee.

FACE.   Send your stuff, sir, that my master
May busy himself about projection.

MAMMON. Thou has witched me, rogue; take, go. [*Gives him
    money.*]

---

7. Through a representative, at second hand.
8. Traders in sex.
9. I.e., what ruff or collar the woman wears, how she dresses her hair.
1. Surly plays on the old contrast between Democritus the laughing philosopher and Heraclitus
   the weeping philosopher.
2. Dangerously clever mind.
3. A rich East Indian kingdom.

FACE.   Your jack,[4] and
     all, sir.
MAMMON. Thou art a villain—I will send my jack,   325
     And the weights too. Slave, I could bite thine ear.[5]
     Away, thou dost not care for me.
FACE.   Not I, sir!
MAMMON. Come, I was born to make thee, my good weasel,
     Set thee on a bench, and have thee twirl a chain
     With the best lord's vermin of 'em all.[6]
FACE.   Away, sir.   330
MAMMON. A count, nay, a count palatine[7]——
FACE.   Good, sir, go.
MAMMON. Shall not advance thee better; no nor faster.   [*Exit.*]

ACT II   SCENE 4

[*Enter* SUBTLE *and* DOL.]
SUBTLE. Has he bit? Has he bit?
FACE.   And swallowed too, my Subtle.
     I have given him line, and now he plays, i' faith.
SUBTLE. And shall we twitch him?
FACE.   Through both the gills.
     A wench is a rare bait, with which a man
     No sooner's taken, but he straight firks mad.[8]   5
SUBTLE. Dol, my lord What's'hum's sister, you must now
     Bear your self *statelich.*[9]
DOL.   O let me alone.
     I'll not forget my race, I warrant you.
     I'll keep my distance, laugh and talk aloud,
     Have all the tricks of a proud scurvy lady,   10
     And be as rude as her woman.
FACE.   Well said, sanguine![1]
SUBTLE. But will he send his andirons?
FACE.   His jack, too,
     And's iron shoeing-horn; I have spoke to him. Well,
     I must not lose my wary gamester yonder.
SUBTLE. O monsieur Caution, that will not be gulled.
FACE.   Ay,   15

4. An iron machine for turning a spit holding meat over the fire. It worked by means of weights
   on chains, wound up and allowed to unwind.
5. I.e., in exultant, erotic affection.
6. Lords are entitled to wear ermine trimming on their robes, playfully referred to as "vermin."
7. One who has authority in a territory or county rather than the king.
8. Runs mad, with the added overtone of sexual activity.
9. German for "stately," to suggest strangeness as well as dignity.
1. One of the four humors, derived from the blood (Latin: "sanguis"), signifying a courageous
   and amorous disposition.

If I can strike a fine hook into him, now!
The Temple-church, there I have cast mine angle.[2]
Well, pray for me. I'll about it. [*Knocking without.*]
SUBTLE.   What, more gudgeons![3]
Dol, scout, scout! [DOL *goes to the window.*]
                      Stay, Face, you must go to the door.
'Pray God it be my anabaptist.[4] Who is't, Dol?   20
DOL. I know him not; he looks like a gold-end-man.[5]
SUBTLE. God's so! 'Tis he, he said he would send——what call
    you him?
The sanctified elder,[6] that should deal
For Mammon's jack and andirons. Let him in.
Stay, help me off, first, with my gown. [*Exit* FACE *with the
    gown.*] Away   25
Madam, to your withdrawing chamber. [*Exit* DOL.] Now,
In a new tune, new gesture, but old language.
This fellow is sent from one negotiates with me
About the stone too; for the holy brethren
Of Amsterdam, the exiled saints,[7] that hope   30
To raise their discipline by it. I must use him
In some strange fashion, now, to make him admire me.

ACT II   SCENE 5

    [*Enter* ANANIAS.]
SUBTLE. [*calling loudly*] Where is my drudge?
    [*Enter* FACE.]
FACE.   Sir!
SUBTLE.   Take away the
    recipient,
And rectify your menstrue from the phlegma.
Then pour it on the Sol, in the cucurbite,
And let them macerate together.[8]
FACE.   Yes, sir.
And save the ground?
SUBTLE.   No: *terra damnata*[9]   5
Must not have entrance in the work. Who are you?

2. Fishing line.
3. A proverbially simpleminded breed of small fish.
4. A member of an extreme group of Puritans.
5. A buyer of odds and ends of gold and silver.
6. Pastor of a Puritan sect.
7. Amsterdam had a colony of English Puritans in exile who still maintained relations with the
   old country. Within a few years, some of them would depart for the New World, to become
   the Pilgrim Fathers.
8. This jargon means something like, "Take a pot and develop a solvent from the mixture. Pour
   it on the gold in a retort and let them soak together."
9. Corrupt materials.

ANANIAS. A faithful brother, if it please you.
SUBTLE.   What's that?
   A Lullianist? A Ripley?[1] *Filius artis?*
   Can you sublime and dulcify? Calcine?
   Know you the *sapor pontic? Sapor stiptic?*[2]   10
   Or what is *homogene,* or *heterogene?*
ANANIAS. I understand no heathen language, truly.
SUBTLE. Heathen, you Knipper-doling![3] Is *Ars sacra,*
   Or *chrysopoeia,* or *spagyrica,*
   Or the pamphysic, or panarchic knowledge,[4]   15
   A heathen language?
ANANIAS.   Heathen Greek, I take it.
SUBTLE. How! Heathen Greek?
ANANIAS.   All's heathen but the Hebrew.[5]
SUBTLE. Sirrah, my varlet, stand you forth and speak to him,
   Like a philosopher; answer, in the language.
   Name the vexations, and the martyrizations   20
   Of metals in the work.
FACE.   Sir, putrefaction,[6]
   Solution, ablution, sublimation,
   Cohobation, calcination, ceration, and
   Fixation.
SUBTLE.   This is heathen Greek to you, now?
   And when comes vivification?
FACE.   After mortification.   25
SUBTLE. What's cohobation?
FACE.   'Tis the pouring on
   Your aqua regis,[7] and then drawing him off,

---

1. Subtle wants to know what "faith" Ananias holds to—that of Raymond Lull, the thirteenth-
   century Catalonian mystic, or of George Ripley, the fifteenth-century English monk. Both
   were alchemists of renown. "Filius artis": son of the art, a general term for any alchemical
   devotee.
2. There were nine "sapors" or tastes in alchemy; "pontic" is very sour, "styptic" less so.
3. Bernt Knipperdoling was a leading figure in the bloody attempt of the Anabaptists to establish
   the kingdom of God in Münster, Germany, in 1534; "ars sacra": sacred art.
4. "Chrysopoeia" is gold-making, "spagyrica" is a fancy word for alchemy; "pamphysic" and
   "panarchic" are words made up by Subtle, meaning knowledge of "all nature" and "all
   power."
5. Because it was regarded as the language spoken by Adam in Paradise. Puritans were much
   more skeptical of Greek and of all classical learning.
6. The meaning of the terms in this dialogue are as follows: "putrefaction": chemical disintegration, decomposition; "solution": changing a solid or a gas to a liquid state by using a
   solvent; "ablution": washing off impurities; "sublimation": changing a solid to a gas by heat;
   "cohobation": repeated distillation; "calcination": reduction to powder by heat; "ceration":
   process of softening a hard substance; "fixation": conversion of a volatile substance (e.g.,
   mercury) into a solid substance; "vivification": restoration of a metal to its original state;
   "mortification": to chemically alter the form of a metal.
7. From Latin, "royal water": a mixture of nitric and hydrochloric acid that can dissolve gold.

To the trine circle of the seven spheres.[8]

SUBTLE. What's the proper passion of metals?

FACE.   Malleation.

SUBTLE. What's your *ultimum supplicium auri?*[9]

FACE.   Antimonium.   30

SUBTLE. This is heathen Greek to you? And what's your
    mercury?

FACE. A very fugitive, he will be gone, sir.

SUBTLE. How know you him?

FACE.   By his viscosity,
    His oleosity, and his suscitability.[1]

SUBTLE. How do you sublime[2] him?

FACE.   With the calce of egg-shells,   35
    White marble, talc.

SUBTLE.   Your *magisterium,*[3] now,
    What's that?

FACE.   Shifting, sir, your elements,
    Dry into cold, cold into moist, moist into hot,
    Hot into dry.

SUBTLE.   This is heathen Greek to you still?
    Your *lapis philosophicus?*[4]

FACE.   'Tis a stone,   40
    And not a stone; a spirit, a soul, and a body;
    Which if you do dissolve, it is dissolved;
    If you coagulate, it is coagulated;
    If you make it to fly, it flieth.

SUBTLE.   Enough.   [*Exit* FACE.]
    This is heathen Greek to you? What are you, sir?   45

ANANIAS. Please you, a servant of the exiled brethren,
    That deal with widows and with orphans' goods;
    And make a just account unto the saints,
    A deacon.

SUBTLE.   O, you are sent from master Wholesome,
    Your teacher?

ANANIAS.   From Tribulation Wholesome,   50
    Our very zealous pastor.

SUBTLE.   Good! I have

---

8. Alchemical jargon is being enriched by jargon from astrology: "trine" is the favorable astrological aspect of two heavenly bodies 120° apart, which would be a good time for the alchemist
   to project; the "seven spheres" are the first five planets plus the sun and moon.
9. Antimony is the "final punishment of gold," because it hardens and fixes the gold; "malleation" is the hammering of the metal to make it expand.
1. Activity; "viscosity": semifluidity; "oleosity": oiliness.
2. Sublimate, purify; "calce": what remains after burning a mineral or metal.
3. Masterwork.
4. Philosopher's stone.

Some orphans' goods to come here.
ANANIAS. Of what kind, sir?
SUBTLE. Pewter and brass, andirons and kitchen-ware,
Metals, that we must use our medicine on,
Wherein the brethren may have a pennyworth 55
For ready money.
ANANIAS. Were the orphans' parents
Sincere professors?[5]
SUBTLE. Why do you ask?
ANANIAS. Because
We then are to deal justly and give in truth
Their utmost value.
SUBTLE. 'Slid, you'd cozen else,
And if their parents were not of the faithful? 60
I will not trust you, now I think on it,
'Till I have talked with your pastor. Have you brought money
To buy more coals?
ANANIAS. No, surely.
SUBTLE. No! How so?
ANANIAS. The brethren bid me say unto you, sir,
Surely they will not venture any more 65
Till they may see projection.
SUBTLE. How!
ANANIAS. You have had,
For the instruments, as bricks and loam and glasses,
Already thirty pound; and for materials,
They say, some ninety more; and they have heard since,
That one at Heidelberg made it of an egg, 70
And a small paper of pin-dust.
SUBTLE. What's your name?
ANANIAS. My name is Ananias.
SUBTLE. Out, the varlet
That cozened the apostles! Hence, away!
Flee, mischief! Had your holy consistory[6]
No name to send me, of another sound, 75
Than wicked Ananias?[7] Send your elders
Hither, to make atonement for you, quickly,
And give me satisfaction; or out goes
The fire; and down th'alembics, and the furnace,
Piger Henricus,[8] or what not. Thou wretch! 80

5. Good protestants of our cause.
6. Church council.
7. The biblical Ananias tried to cheat the Apostles; his failure and its consequences are described in the Acts of the Apostles, chapter 5.
8. Literally, "Lazy Henry," a many-chambered furnace heated by a single fire.

Both sericon and bufo[9] shall be lost,
Tell them. All hope of rooting out the bishops,
Or the antichristian hierarchy, shall perish
If they stay threescore minutes. The aqueity,
Terreity, and sulphureity[1]   85
Shall run together again, and all be annulled,
Thou wicked Ananias! [*Exit* ANANIAS.] This will fetch 'em,
And make them haste towards their gulling more.
A man must deal like a rough nurse, and fright
Those that are froward, to an appetite.   90

ACT II   SCENE 6

[FACE *in his captain's uniform*, SUBTLE, DRUGGER.]
FACE. He is busy with his spirits, but we'll upon him.
SUBTLE. How now! What mates, what Bayards[2] have we here?
FACE. I told you, he would be furious. Sir, here's Nab,
  Has brought you another piece of gold to look on;
      [*aside to* DRUGGER.]
  —We must appease him. Give it me.—and prays you,   5
  You would devise—what is it, Nab?
DRUGGER.   A sign, sir.
FACE. Ay, a good lucky one, a thriving sign, doctor.
SUBTLE. I was devising now.
FACE.   [*aside to* SUBTLE.] 'Slight, do not say so,
  He will repent he gave you any more—
  What say you to his constellation, doctor,   10
  The Balance?[3]
SUBTLE.   No, that way is stale, and common.
  A townsman born in Taurus, gives the bull,
  Or the bull's head; in Aries, the ram.
  A poor device! No, I will have his name
  Formed in some mystic character, whose radii,   15
  Striking the senses of the passers by,
  Shall, by a virtual influence, breed affections,
  That may result upon the party owns it:
  As thus——
FACE.   Nab!
SUBTLE.   He shall have *a bell*, that's *Abel*;
  And by it standing one whose name is *Dee*,   20
  In a *rug* gown, there's D, and *Rug*, that's *drug*;

---

9. The red and black stages of the experiment.
1. Water, earth, and sulphur, all the ingredients of the mixture.
2. The chevalier Bayard was a daredevil soldier of the early sixteenth century: hence any bold
   and reckless fellow.
3. The Scales, a zodiacal sign naturally suited to a merchant.

And right anenst him a dog snarling *Er;*[4]
There's *Drugger,* Abel Drugger. That's his sign.
And here's now mystery and hieroglyphic![5]
FACE. Abel, thou art made.
DRUGGER.   Sir, I do thank his worship.   25
FACE. Six o' thy legs[6] more will not do it, Nab.
He has brought you a pipe of tobacco, doctor.
DRUGGER.   Yes, sir.
I have another thing I would impart——
FACE. Out with it, Nab.
DRUGGER.   Sir, there is lodged, hard by me,
A rich young widow——
FACE.   Good! a bona roba?[7]   30
DRUGGER. But nineteen, at the most.
FACE.   Very good, Abel.
DRUGGER. Marry, she's not in fashion yet; she wears
A hood, but it stands a cop.[8]
FACE.   No matter, Abel.
DRUGGER. And I do now and then give her a fucus[9]——
FACE. What! Dost thou deal,[1] Nab?
SUBTLE.   I did tell you, captain.   35
DRUGGER. And physic too, sometimes, sir; for which she trusts
    me
With all her mind. She's come up here of purpose
To learn the fashion.
FACE.   Good (his match too!)—On, Nab.
DRUGGER. And she does strangely long to know her fortune.
FACE. God's lid, Nab, send her to the doctor, hither.   40
DRUGGER. Yes, I have spoke to her of his worship already;
But she's afraid it will be blown abroad,[2]
And hurt her marriage.
FACE.   Hurt it! 'Tis the way
To heal it, if 'twere hurt; to make it more
Followed and sought. Nab, thou shalt tell her this: 45
She'll be more known, more talked of; and your widows

---

4. Doctor John Dee was a well-known alchemist in Jonson's London. A rug gown is one made of rough wool; "Er" is a rather strained representation of "Grrr"; "anenst": opposite.
5. The ancient Egyptians were thought to be the true founders of alchemy, which they expressed in hieroglyphics.
6. Scrapes and bows.
7. Literally, "well dressed," but also implying "available" and even suggesting whoredom.
8. Hoods were out of fashion; the lady's came to a point, which amounted to making the best of a bad job.
9. The materials of makeup—cosmetics being unusual at the time, especially among young women.
1. Do you do business with her—with a sexual innuendo.
2. Gossiped about.

Are ne'er of any price till they be famous;
Their honor is their multitude of suitors.
Send her, it may be *thy* good fortune. What?
Thou dost not know.
DRUGGER.   No, sir, she'll never marry   50
Under a knight; her brother has made a vow.
FACE. What! And dost thou despair, my little Nab,
Knowing what the doctor has set down for thee,
And seeing so many of the city dubbed?[3]
One glass o' thy water, with a madam I know,   55
Will have it done, Nab.[4] What's her brother, a knight?
DRUGGER. No, sir, a gentleman newly warm in his land, sir,
Scarce cold in his one-and-twenty, that does govern
His sister here; and is a man himself
Of some three thousand a year, and is come up   60
To learn to quarrel, and to live by his wits,
And will go down again, and die in the country.
FACE. How! To quarrel?
DRUGGER.   Yes, sir, to carry quarrels,
As gallants do, and manage them by line.[5]
FACE. 'Slid, Nab, the doctor is the only man   65
In Christendom for him. He has made a table,
With mathematical demonstrations,
Touching the art of quarrels; he will give him
An instrument to quarrel by. Go, bring them both,
Him and his sister. And, for thee, with her   70
The doctor haply may persuade. Go to;
'Shalt give his worship a new damask suit
Upon the premises.[6]
SUBTLE.   O, good captain!
FACE.   He shall;
He is the honestest fellow, doctor.—Stay not,
No offers; bring the damask, and the parties.   75
DRUGGER. I'll try my power, sir.
FACE.   And thy will too, Nab.
SUBTLE. 'Tis good tobacco, this! What is't an ounce?
FACE. He'll send you a pound, doctor.
SUBTLE.   O, no.
FACE.   He will do't.
It is the goodest soul! Abel, about it.
Thou shalt know more anon. Away, be gone.   [*Exit* ABEL.]   80

3. Made a knight.
4. Given a specimen of Drugger's urine, a witch can enchant the lady into loving him.
5. According to the rules.
6. Prospects.

A miserable rogue, and lives with cheese,
And has the worms. That was the cause, indeed,
Why he came now. He dealt with me in private
To get a med'cine for them.
SUBTLE.   And shall, sir. This works.
FACE. A wife, a wife for one of us, my dear Subtle!   85
We'll e'en draw lots, and he that fails, shall have
The more in goods, the other has in tail.[7]
SUBTLE. Rather the less; for she may be so light
She may want grains.[8]
FACE.   Ay, or be such a burden,
A man would scarce endure her for the whole.   90
SUBTLE. Faith, best let's see her first and then determine.
FACE. Content. But Dol must have no breath on't.
SUBTLE.   Mum.
Away you, to your Surly yonder, catch him.
FACE. Pray God I have not stayed too long.
SUBTLE.   I fear it.   [Exeunt.]

Act III

ACT III   SCENE 1. *THE LANE BEFORE* LOVEWIT'S *HOUSE*

[*Enter* TRIBULATION WHOLESOME *and* ANANIAS.]
TRIBULATION. These chastisements are common to the saints,
And such rebukes we of the separation[9]
Must bear with willing shoulders, as the trials
Sent forth to tempt our frailties.
ANANIAS.   In pure zeal,
I do not like the man; he is a heathen,   5
And speaks the language of Canaan, truly.[1]
TRIBULATION. I think him a profane person indeed.
ANANIAS.   He bears
The visible mark of the beast[2] in his forehead.
And for his stone, it is a work of darkness,
And with philosophy blinds the eyes of man.   10
TRIBULATION. Good brother, we must bend unto all means
That may give furtherance to the holy cause.

---

7. With a sexual meaning, but also with a glance at the legal expression "entail," in the sense
   of a commitment of future property.
8. Need extra ballast to make legal weight.
9. I.e., separated from the Church of England, which extreme Puritans considered too corrupt
   to be reformed.
1. Likening themselves to the Jews as specially chosen people, the Puritans often referred to
   their opponents by the name of the enemies of ancient Israel—Philistines, Canaanites, etc.
2. According to the Book of Revelation (16.2, 19.20), the "beast" with his distinguishing mark
   would persecute Christians near the end of the world.

ANANIAS. Which his cannot; the sanctified cause
  Should have a sanctified course.
TRIBULATION   Not always necessary.
  The children of perdition are oft-times   15
  Made instruments even of the greatest works.[3]
  Beside, we should give somewhat to man's nature,
  The place he lives in, still about the fire,
  And fume of metals, that intoxicate
  The brain of man, and make him prone to passion.   20
  Where have you greater atheists than your cooks?
  Or more profane, or choleric, than your glass-men?[4]
  More antichristian than your bell-founders?
  What makes the devil so devilish, I would ask you,
  Satan our common enemy, but his being   25
  Perpetually about the fire, and boiling
  Brimstone and arsenic? We must give, I say,
  Unto the motives, and the stirrers up
  Of humors in the blood. It may be so,
  When as the work is done, the stone is made,   30
  This heat of his may turn into a zeal,
  And stand up for the beauteous discipline
  Against the menstruous cloth and rag of Rome.[5]
  We must await his calling, and the coming
  Of the good spirit. You did fault, t' upbraid him   35
  With the brethren's blessing of Heidelberg, weighing
  What need we have to hasten on the work,
  For the restoring of the silenced saints,[6]
  Which ne'er will be, but by the philosopher's stone.
  And so a learned elder, one of Scotland,   40
  Assured me; *aurum potabile*[7] being
  The only medicine, for the civil magistrate
  T' incline him to a feeling of the cause,
  And must be daily used in the disease.
ANANIAS. I have not edified more, truly, by man,   45
  Not since the beautiful light first shone on me;
  And I am sad my zeal hath so offended.
TRIBULATION. Let us call on him then.

---

3. "The children of this world are in their generation wiser than the children of light" (Luke 16.8).
4. Glass-blowers, subject to unusual temptations because of their fiery calling.
5. The "beauteous discipline" is that established by John Calvin (1509–1564), French theologian and reformer, in his *Institutes*, and exemplified in the city of Geneva; the rags and tatters of Rome (i.e., Roman Catholicism) were a standard feature of Puritan rhetoric.
6. Those Puritan reformers who had been dismissed from their posts in the Church of England (silenced) for preaching against its ruling bishops.
7. Drinkable gold.

ANANIAS.   The motion's[8] good,
And of the spirit; I will knock first. [*Knocks*.] Peace be within!
  [*The door is opened, and they enter.*]

ACT III   SCENE 2. *A ROOM IN* LOVEWIT'*S HOUSE*

  [SUBTLE *opens the door to* TRIBULATION *and* ANANIAS.]
SUBTLE. O, are you come? 'Twas time. Your threescore minutes
  Were at the last thread, you see; and down had gone
  Furnus acediae, turris circulatorius,[9]
  Limbec, bolt's-head, retort, and pelican
  Had all been cinders. Wicked Ananias!   5
  Art thou returned? Nay then, it goes down yet.
TRIBULATION. Sir, be appeased; he is come to humble
  Himself in spirit, and to ask your patience,
  If too much zeal hath carried him aside
  From the due path.
SUBTLE.   Why, this doth qualify!   10
TRIBULATION. The brethren had no purpose, verily,
  To give you the least grievance: but are ready
  To lend their willing hands to any project
  The spirit and you direct.
SUBTLE.   This qualifies more!
TRIBULATION. And for the orphans' goods, let them be valued,   15
  Or what is needful else to the holy work,
  It shall be numbered; here, by me, the saints
  Throw down their purse before you.
SUBTLE.   This qualifies most!
  Why, thus it should be, now you understand.
  Have I discoursed so unto you of our stone,   20
  And of the good that it shall bring your cause?
  Showed you (beside the main of hiring forces
  Abroad, drawing the Hollanders, your friends,
  From the Indies, to serve you, with all their fleet)[1]
  That even the medicinal use shall make you a faction,   25
  And party in the realm? As, put the case,
  That some great man in state, he have the gout,
  Why, you but send three drops of your elixir,
  You help him straight: there you have made a friend.
  Another has the palsy or the dropsy,   30

---

8. Impulse, idea.
9. "Furnus acediae," or the furnace of sloth, is like "Piger Henricus," or Lazy Henry, above, a
  furnace with several chambers but only one fire. "Turris circulatorius," or circulating tower,
  is a kind of elaborate still.
1. Subtle accuses the Puritans of treachery, in hoping to hire the Dutch to mount an attack on
  England.

He takes of your incombustible stuff,[2]
He's young again: there you have made a friend.
A lady that is past the feat of body,
Though not of mind, and hath her face decayed
Beyond all cure of paintings, you restore,   35
With the oil of talc: there you have made a friend,
And all her friends. A lord that is a leper,
A knight that has the bone-ache,[3] or a squire
That hath both these, you make them smooth and sound,
With a bare fricace[4] of your medicine: still   40
You increase your friends.
TRIBULATION.   Ay, it is very pregnant.
SUBTLE. And then the turning of this lawyer's pewter
    To plate at Christmas—
ANANIAS.   Christ-tide, I pray you.[5]
SUBTLE. Yet, Ananias!
ANANIAS.   I have done.
SUBTLE.   Or changing
    His parcel gilt[6] to massy gold. You cannot   45
    But raise you friends. Withal, to be of power
    To pay an army in the field, to buy
    The king of France out of his realms, or Spain
    Out of his Indies. What can you not do
    Against lords spiritual or temporal,   50
    That shall oppone you?
TRIBULATION.   Verily, 'tis true.
    We may be temporal lords ourselves, I take it.
SUBTLE. You may be anything, and leave off to make
    Long-winded exercises; or suck up
    Your *ha*! And *hum*! in a tune. I not deny,   55
    But such as are not graced in a state,
    May, for their ends, be adverse in religion,
    And get a tune to call the flock together.
    For, to say sooth, a tune does much with women,
    And other phlegmatic people; it is your bell.[7]   60
ANANIAS. Bells are profane; a tune may be religious.
SUBTLE. No warning with you? Then farewell my patience.

---

2. I.e., so perfectly tempered it would neither decay nor burn.
3. Syphilis.
4. Rubdown.
5. Because "Christmas" included the hateful word "mass," the Puritans preferred to call it
   "Christ-tide" or, more elaborately, "the day of Christ's nativity."
6. Silverware covered with gold plate or simply gilded.
7. Puritans were famous for singing psalms; Subtle equates this with bell-ringing, but Ananias
   will have none of it, thinking bells to be rags of popery and superstition; "phlegmatic": dull,
   sluggish.

'Slight, it shall down; I will not be thus tortured.

TRIBULATION. I pray you, sir.

SUBTLE.   All shall perish. I have spoke it.

TRIBULATION. Let me find grace, sir, in your eyes; the man   65
    He stands corrected; neither did his zeal,
    But as yourself, allow a tune somewhere.[8]
    Which now, being toward the stone, we shall not need.

SUBTLE. No, nor your holy vizard, to win widows
    To give you legacies; or make zealous wives   70
    To rob their husbands for the common cause;
    Nor take the start of bonds broke but one day,
    And say, they were forfeited by providence.[9]
    Nor shall you need o'ernight to eat huge meals,
    To celebrate your next day's fast the better,   75
    The whilst the brethren and the sisters humbled,
    Abate the stiffness of the flesh. Nor cast
    Before your hungry hearers scrupulous bones;
    As whether a Christian may hawk or hunt,
    Or whether matrons of the holy assembly   80
    May lay their hair out, or wear doublets,[1]
    Or have that idol starch about their linen.

ANANIAS. It is indeed an idol.

TRIBULATION.   Mind him not, sir.
    I do command thee, spirit of zeal, but trouble,
    To peace within him! Pray you, sir, go on.   85

SUBTLE. Nor shall you need to libel 'gainst the prelates,
    And shorten so your ears against the hearing
    Of the next wire-drawn grace.[2] Nor of necessity
    Rail against plays, to please the alderman
    Whose daily custard you devour. Nor lie   90
    With zealous rage till you are hoarse. Not one
    Of these so singular arts. Nor call your selves
    By names of Tribulation, Persecution,
    Restraint, Long-patience, and such like, affected
    By the whole family or wood[3] of you,   95
    Only for glory, and to catch the ear

---

8. Tribulation tries to smooth things over by saying everyone considers "tunes" (psalms) to be lawful.
9. Puritans, being generally of the middle class and subject to the frailties of petty merchants, were often reproached with the difference between their scruples in religion and their sharp commercial practices.
1. Dress considered appropriate to men; "lay their hair out": wear in a fashionable style.
2. Libeling the prelates (bishops) sometimes led Puritans to the pillory, where their ears might well be clipped—Subtle says, at least that will make it easier for them to sit through the next long, drawn-out sermon.
3. Clutch, gang, tribe.

Of the disciple.

TRIBULATION.   Truly, sir, they are
Ways that the godly brethren have invented,
For propagation of the glorious cause,
As very notable means, and whereby also   100
Themselves grow soon, and profitably, famous.

SUBTLE. O, but the stone, all's idle to it! Nothing!
The art of angels, nature's miracle,
The divine secret that doth fly in clouds
From east to west; and whose tradition   105
Is not from men, but spirits.

ANANIAS.   I hate traditions;[4]
I do not trust them——

TRIBULATION.   Peace!

ANANIAS.   They are popish all.
I will not peace. I will not——

TRIBULATION.   Ananias!

ANANIAS. Please the profane, to grieve the godly; I may not.

SUBTLE. Well, Ananias, thou shall overcome.   110

TRIBULATION. It is an ignorant zeal that haunts him, sir:
But truly, else, a very faithful brother,
A botcher,[5] and a man, by revelation,
That hath a competent knowledge of the truth.

SUBTLE. Has he a competent sum there in the bag   115
To buy the goods within? I am made guardian,
And must, for charity, and conscience sake,
Now see the most be made for my poor orphans;
Though I desire the brethren too good gainers.
There they are within. When you have viewed and bought
    'em,   120
And ta'en the inventory of what they are,
They are ready for projection; there's no more
To do. Cast on the medicine, so much silver
As there is tin there, so much gold as brass,
I'll give't you in by weight.

TRIBULATION.   But how long time,   125
Sir, must the saints expect yet?[6]

SUBTLE.   Let me see,
How's the moon now? Eight, nine, ten days hence,

---

4. Mere human traditions (of councils, church fathers, or other church authorities) were of no force against the pure, undiluted word of God in the Scriptures.
5. A low-grade tailor who patches clothes.
6. The "saints" were always expecting the second coming, so their language adapts naturally to the dream of the philosopher's stone.

He will be silver potate;[7] then three days
Before he citronise; some fifteen days,
The magisterium will be perfected.   130
ANANIAS. About the second day of the third week,
　In the ninth month?[8]
SUBTLE.   Yes, my good Ananias.
TRIBULATION. What will the orphans' goods arise[9] to, think you?
SUBTLE. Some hundred marks, as much as filled three cars,
　Unladed now: you'll make six million of them.   135
　But I must have more coals laid in.
TRIBULATION.   How!
SUBTLE.   Another load,
　And then we've finished. We must now increase
　Our fire to *ignis ardens*, we are past
　Fimus equinus, balnei, cineris,[1]
　And all those lenter heats. If the holy purse   140
　Should with this draught fall low, and that the saints
　Do need a present sum, I have a trick
　To melt the pewter, you shall buy now, instantly,
　And with a tincture make you as good Dutch dollars
　As any are in Holland.[2]
TRIBULATION.   Can you so?   145
SUBTLE. Aye, and shall 'bide the third examination.
ANANIAS. It will be joyful tidings to the brethren.
SUBTLE. But you must carry it secret.
TRIBULATION.   Ay, but stay,
　This act of coining, is it lawful?
ANANIAS.   Lawful!
　We know no magistrate; or, if we did,   150
　This is foreign coin.
SUBTLE.   It is no coining, sir.
　It is but casting.
TRIBULATION.   Ha! You distinguish well.
　Casting of money may be lawful.
ANANIAS.   'Tis, sir.
TRIBULATION. Truly, I take it so.

---

7. The moon must turn first to liquid silver, then yellow like a lemon ("citronise") before turning
　rosy red when projection is completed. Making the philosopher's stone takes just about as
　long as it does to make a normal human baby, and analogies are constantly implied between
　the two processes.
8. November 16; the old-style English calendar, which began the year in March was then in
　use; the Puritans avoided the normal English names of the months as "pagan."
9. Amount.
1. In the graduated series of heats, they have passed "Fimus equinus" (horse manure), "balnei"
　(the double boiler), and "cineris" (ashes), all "lenter," or more moderate, heats; now is the
　time for "ignis ardens," or glowing fire.
2. Pewter, which is tin and lead, can be made to look like silver coins.

SUBTLE.   There is no scruple,
Sir, to be made of it; believe Ananias.   155
This case of conscience he is studied in.
TRIBULATION. I'll make a question of it to the brethren.
ANANIAS. The brethren shall approve it lawful, doubt not.
Where shall it be done?   [*Knocking without.*]
SUBTLE.   For that we'll talk anon.
There's some to speak with me. Go in, I pray you,   160
And view the parcels. That's the inventory.
I'll come to you straight.   [*Exeunt* TRIBULATION *and* ANANIAS.]
                    Who is it? [*He gestures, as if conjur-*
ing.]—Face! Appear!

ACT III   SCENE 3

    [*Enter* FACE *in his uniform.*]
How now! Good prize?
FACE.   Good pox! Yond' costive[3] cheater
Never came on.
SUBTLE.   How then?
FACE.   I have walked the round[4]
Till now, and no such thing.
SUBTLE.   And have you quit him?
FACE. Quit him! An hell would quit him too, he were happy.
'Slight! Would you have me stalk like a mill-jade,   5
All day, for one that will not yield us grains?
I know him of old.
SUBTLE.   O, but to have gulled him
Had been a mastery.
FACE.   Let him go, black boy![5]
And turn thee, that some fresh news may possess thee.
A noble count, a don of Spain (my dear   10
Delicious compeer, and my party-bawd),
Who is come hither private for his conscience,
And brought munition with him, six great slops,[6]
Bigger than three Dutch hoys, beside round trunks.
Furnished with pistolets,[7] and pieces of eight,   15
Will straight be here, my rogue, to have thy bath[8]
(That is the color), and to make his battery

---

3. I.e., Surly.
4. The Temple Church was round in shape.
5. Subtle wears a black academic robe and is dark from attending his smoky furnaces.
6. Loose-fitting trousers, bigger than "Dutch hoys" (i.e., fishing boats), in addition to "round trunks," i.e., the kind of leggings that puff out around the waist.
7. Spanish gold coins; "pieces of eight": Spanish dollars.
8. A specially luxurious bath, furnished in high-class whorehouses as a preliminary ceremony; "color": pretext.

Upon our Dol, our castle, our cinque-port,[9]
Our Dover pier, our what thou wilt. Where is she?
She must prepare perfumes, delicate linen,   20
The bath in chief, a banquet, and her wit,
For she must milk his epididymis.[1]
Where is the doxy?
SUBTLE.   I'll send her to thee,
And but dispatch my brace of little John Leydens,[2]
And come again myself.   25
FACE.   Are they within then?
SUBTLE. Numbering the sum.
FACE.   How much?
SUBTLE.   A hundred marks, boy.
                                                  [*Exit.*]
FACE. Why, this is a lucky day. Ten pounds of Mammon!
Three of my clerk! A portague of my grocer!
This of the brethren! Beside reversions,[3]
And states to come in the widow, and my count!   30
My share today will not be bought for forty—
     [*Enter* DOL.]
DOL.   What?
FACE. Pounds, dainty Dorothy! Art thou so near?
DOL. Yes; say, Lord General, how fares our camp?
FACE. As with the few that had entrenched themselves
Safe, by their discipline, against a world, Dol;   35
And laughed within those trenches, and grew fat
With thinking on the booties, Dol, brought in
Daily by their small parties. This dear hour,
A doughty don is taken with my Dol;
And thou mayst make his ransom what thou wilt,   40
My Dousabel;[4] he shall be brought here fettered
With thy fair looks, before he sees thee; and thrown
In a down-bed, as dark as any dungeon;
Where thou shalt keep him waking with thy drum;
Thy drum, my Dol, thy drum; till he be tame   45
As the poor blackbirds were in the great frost,[5]
Or bees are with a basin; and so hive him

---

9. The five channel ports, through which England could most easily be entered from the Continent. Dover pier was where most travelers from abroad first disembarked.
1. Seminal vesicles.
2. I.e., Anabaptist or Puritan leaders—after John Bockelhausen, who came from Leyden in Holland, and led the fanatical Puritan insurrection at Münster in 1534.
3. Future benefits; "portague": Portuguese gold piece; see 1.3.87.
4. From *douce et belle* (French), "sweet and lovely."
5. During the winter of 1607–08 the Thames froze over, and the blackbirds obviously suffered.
   One could attract swarming bees by banging on a basin.

In the swan-skin coverlid, and cambric sheets,
Till he work honey and wax, my little God's-gift.[6]
DOL. What is he, General?
FACE.   An *adalantado*,[7]   50
A grandee, girl. Was not my Dapper here yet?
DOL. No.
FACE.   Nor my Drugger?
DOL.   Neither.
FACE.   A pox on 'em,
They are so long a furnishing! Such stinkards
Would not be seen upon these festival days.
    [*Enter* SUBTLE]
How now! Have you done?
SUBTLE.   Done. They are gone. The sum   55
Is here in bank, my Face. I would we knew
Another chapman[8] now would buy 'em outright.
FACE. 'Slid, Nab shall do't against he have the widow,
To furnish household.
SUBTLE.   Excellent, well thought on;
Pray God he come.
FACE.   I pray he keep away   60
Till our new business be o'erpassed.
SUBTLE.   But, Face,
How cam'st thou by this secret don?
FACE.   A spirit
Brought me th' intelligence in a paper here,
As I was conjuring yonder in my circle
For Surly; I have my flies abroad.[9] Your bath   65
Is famous, Subtle, by my means. Sweet Dol,
You must go tune your virginal,[1] no losing
O' the least time. And, do you hear? Good action.
Firk, like a flounder; kiss, like a scallop, close;
And tickle him with thy mother-tongue. His great   70
Verdugoship[2] has not a jot of language;
So much the easier to be cozen'd, my Dolly.
He will come here in a hired coach, obscure,
And our own coachman, whom I have sent as guide,
No creature else. [*Knocking without.*] Who's that?   [*Exit* DOL.]
SUBTLE.   It is not he?   75

6. Dorothy means "God's gift" in Greek.
7. Mayor or governor (Spanish); "grandee": dignitary.
8. Merchant.
9. What happened was simply that he was handed a written note as he walked around looking
   for Surly.
1. Put your harpsichord in tune (with obvious double-entendre).
2. From the Spanish word for hangman.

FACE. O no, not yet this hour.
    [*Re-enter* DOL.]
SUBTLE.   Who is't?
DOL.   Dapper,
   Your clerk.
FACE.   God's will then, Queen of Fairy,
   On with your tire;[3] [*Exit* DOL.] and, Doctor, with your robes.
   Let's dispatch him for God's sake.
SUBTLE.   'Twill be long.
FACE. I warrant you, take but the cues I give you,   80
   It shall be brief enough. [*Goes to the window.*]
               'Slight, here are more!
   Abel, and I think the angry boy, the heir,
   That fain would quarrel.
SUBTLE.   And the widow?
FACE.   No,
   Not that I see. Away!   [*Exit* SUBTLE.]

             ACT III   SCENE 4

   [*Enter* DAPPER.]
              O sir, you are welcome.
   The doctor is within a moving for you;
   I have had the most ado to win him to it!
   He swears you'll be the darling of the dice.
   He never heard her highness dote till now.   5
   Your aunt has given you the most gracious words
   That can be thought on.
DAPPER.   Shall I see her grace?
FACE. See her, and kiss her too.
   [*Enter* ABEL, *followed by* KASTRIL.]
              What, honest Nab!
   Hast brought the damask?
DRUGGER.   No, sir; here's tobacco.
FACE. 'Tis well done, Nab; thou'lt bring the damask too?   10
DRUGGER. Yes. Here's the gentleman, Captain, master Kastril,
   I have brought to see the Doctor.
FACE.   Where's the widow?
DRUGGER. Sir, as he likes, his sister, he says, shall come.
FACE. O, is it so? 'Good time. Is your name Kastril, sir?
KASTRIL. Ay, and the best of the Kastrils, I'd be sorry else,   15
   By fifteen hundred a year.[4] Where is this Doctor?
   My mad tobacco-boy, here, tells me of one

---

3. Attire, costume.
4. If he weren't an elder son, he wouldn't have an estate of this value.

That can do things: has he any skill?
FACE.   Wherein, sir?
KASTRIL. To carry a business, manage a quarrel fairly,
    Upon fit terms.
FACE.   It seems, sir, you're but young   20
    About the town, that can make that a question.
KASTRIL. Sir, not so young, but I have heard some speech
    Of the angry boys,[5] and seen 'em take tobacco;
    And in his shop; and I can take it too.
    And I would fain be one of 'em, and go down   25
    And practice in the country.
FACE.   Sir, for the duello,
    The doctor, I assure you, shall inform you
    To the least shadow of a hair; and show you
    An instrument he has of his own making,
    Wherewith no sooner shall you make report   30
    Of any quarrel, but he will take the height on't
    Most instantly, and tell in what degree
    Of safety it lies in, or mortality.[6]
    And how it may be borne, whether in a right line,
    Or a half circle; or may else be cast   35
    Into an angle blunt, if not acute:
    All this he will demonstrate.[7] And then, rules
    To give and take the lie by.
KASTRIL.   How! To take it?
FACE. Yes, in oblique he'll show you, or in circle;
    But never in diameter.[8] The whole town   40
    Study his theorems, and dispute them ordinarily
    At the eating academies.[9]
KASTRIL.   But does he teach
    Living by the wits too?
FACE.   Anything whatever.
    You cannot think that subtlety but he reads it.
    He made me a Captain. I was a stark pimp,   45
    Just of your standing, 'fore I met with him,
    It is not two months since. I'll tell you his method.
    First, he will enter you at some ordinary.[1]

5. Town swaggerers and bullies; taking tobacco, as a new art, required some skill and practice.
6. Subtle's "instrument" is some kind of chart on which one can look up any particular quarrel
    and discover how serious it is ("the height on't"), how safely it may be embarked on, and
    what the danger of getting killed in it is ("mortality").
7. The art of quarreling is the art, not of encountering an opponent directly, but of coming at
    him at an angle, social or political.
8. I.e., the lie direct. Subtle will teach him to accuse his opponent indirectly, in an "oblique"
    or devious ("in circle") way.
9. Common taverns or public houses.
1. Public eating-house, tavern.

KASTRIL. No, I'll not come there; you shall pardon me.
FACE.   For why, sir?
KASTRIL. There's gaming there, and tricks.
FACE.   Why, would you be   50
   A gallant, and not game?
KASTRIL.   Ay, 'twill spend[2] a man.
FACE. Spend you! It will repair you when you are spent.
   How do they live by their wits there, that have vented
   Six times your fortunes?
KASTRIL.   What, three thousand a year!
FACE. Ay, forty thousand.
KASTRIL.   Are there such?
FACE.   Ay, sir,   55
   And gallants yet. Here's a young gentleman
   Is born to nothing, [*points to* DAPPER] forty marks a year,
   Which I count nothing. He is to be initiated,
   And have a fly[3] of the doctor. He will win you,
   By unresistible luck, within this fortnight,   60
   Enough to buy a barony. They will set him
   Upmost, at the groom porter's, all the Christmas,[4]
   And for the whole year through, at every place
   Where there is play, present him with the chair;
   The best attendance, the best drink; sometimes   65
   Two glasses of canary, and pay nothing;
   The purest linen, and the sharpest knife,
   The partridge next his trencher; and somewhere
   The dainty bed in private with the dainty.
   You shall have your ordinaries bid for him,   70
   As playhouses for a poet; and the master
   Pray him aloud to name what dish he affects,
   Which must be buttered shrimps; and those that drink
   To no mouth else, will drink to his, as being
   The goodly president mouth of all the board.[5]   75
KASTRIL. Do you not gull one?
FACE.   'Ods my life! Do you think it?
   You shall have a cast commander (can but get
   In credit with a glover, or a spurrier,
   For some two pair of either's ware aforehand),
   Will, by most swift posts, dealing with him,   80

2. Bankrupt.
3. A familiar spirit.
4. The groom porter was in charge of gambling at the court; Christmas, and the period of
   Twelfth Night associated with it, was the gambling season. To be "set upmost" on these
   occasions was to head up the gambling table.
5. I.e., those who will drink a toast to nobody else will be glad to toast him.

Arrive at competent means to keep himself,[6]
His punk and naked boy, in excellent fashion,
And be admired for't.
KASTRIL.   Will the doctor teach this?
FACE. He will do more, sir; when your land is gone,
    (As men of spirit hate to keep earth long)   85
    In a vacation, when small money is stirring,
    And ordinaries suspended till the term,
    He'll show a perspective,[7] where on one side
    You shall behold the faces and the persons
    Of all sufficient young heirs in town,   90
    Whose bonds are current for commodity;
    On th' other side, the merchants' forms, and others,
    That without help of any second broker,
    Who would expect a share, will trust such parcels:
    In the third square, the very street and sign   95
    Where the commodity dwells, and does but wait
    To be delivered, be it pepper, soap,
    Hops, or tobacco, oatmeal, woad,[8] or cheeses.
    All which you may so handle, to enjoy
    To your own use, and never stand obliged.   100
KASTRIL. I' faith! Is he such a fellow?
FACE.   Why, Nab here knows him.
    And then for making matches for rich widows,
    Young gentlewomen, heirs, the fortunat'st man!
    He's sent to, far and near, all over England
    To have his counsel and to know their fortunes.   105
KASTRIL. God's will, my suster[9] shall see him.
FACE.   I'll tell you, sir,
    What he did tell me of Nab. It's a strange thing!—
    (By the way, you must eat no cheese, Nab, it breeds
        melancholy,
    And that same melancholy breeds worms; but pass it)—
    He told me, honest Nab here was ne'er at tavern   110
    But once in's life!
DRUGGER.   Truth, and no more I was not.
FACE. And then he was so sick—

---

6. I.e., a dismissed soldier, who can get credit only for a pair of gloves or spurs, will quickly
    make a fortune under his guidance.
7. Image, chart.
8. A dyestuff. The racket is to discover some desperate heir-to-be who, in his anxiety to borrow
    money, has been forced to accept some part of the loan in damaged commodities; having no
    particular use for them, he leaves them in a warehouse, where a sly operator can easily
    appropriate them.
9. Kastril comes from the country, probably the West Country, and tends to pronounce the *ih*
    sound as *uh*—*suster* for *sister*, *kuss* for *kiss*.

DRUGGER.   Could he tell you that too?
FACE. How should I know it?
DRUGGER.   In troth we had been a shooting,
    And had a piece of fat ram-mutton to supper,
    That lay so heavy o' my stomach—
FACE.   And he has no head   115
    To bear any wine; for what with the noise of the fiddlers,
    And care of his shop, for he dares keep no servants—
DRUGGER. My head did so ache—
FACE.   As he was fain to be brought
        home,
    The Doctor told me; and then a good old woman—
DRUGGER. Yes, faith, she dwells in Sea-coal-lane,—did cure me,   120
    With sodden ale, and pellitory of the wall;[1]
    Cost me but twopence. I had another sickness
    Was worse than that.
FACE.   Ay, that was with the grief
    Thou took'st for being cessed at eighteenpence,
    For the water-work.[2]
DRUGGER.   In truth, and it was like   125
    T' have cost me almost my life.
FACE.   Thy hair went off?
DRUGGER. Yes, sir; 'twas done for spite.
FACE.   Nay, so says the Doctor.
KASTRIL. Pray thee, tobacco-boy, go fetch my suster;
    I'll see this learned boy before I go;
    And so shall she.
FACE.   Sir, he is busy now: 130
    But if you have a sister to fetch hither,
    Perhaps your own pains may command her sooner;
    And he by that time will be free.
KASTRIL.   I go.   [*Exit* KASTRIL.]
FACE. Drugger, she's thine: the damask!—   [*Exit* ABEL.]
                    [*aside*] Subtle and I
    Must wrestle for her.—Come on, master Dapper,   135
    You see how I turn clients here away,
    To give your cause despatch. Have you performed
    The ceremonies were enjoined you?
DAPPER.   Yes, of the vinegar,
    And the clean shirt.
FACE.   'Tis well; that shirt may do you

---

1. Boiled ale and a purgative made of local weeds.
2. The new waterwork was a recent economic fact of life, and having to pay for water was a painful experience for Englishmen. "Cessed": assessed.

More worship than you think. Your aunt's afire,   140
But that she will not show it, t' have a sight of you.
Have you provided for her Grace's servants?
DAPPER. Yes, here are six score Edward shillings.[3]
FACE.   Good!
DAPPER. And an old Harry's sovereign.
FACE.   Very good!
DAPPER. And three James shillings, and an Elizabeth groat,   145
Just twenty nobles.
FACE.   O, you are too just.
I would you had had the other noble in Maries.
DAPPER. I have some Philip and Maries.[4]
FACE.   Ay, those same
Are best of all. Where are they? Hark, the Doctor.

ACT III   SCENE 5

> [Enter SUBTLE, *disguised like a priest of Fairy, with an old
> petticoat.*]

SUBTLE. [*in a feigned voice*] Is yet her grace's cousin come?
FACE.   He is
come.
SUBTLE. And is he fasting?
FACE.   Yes.
SUBTLE.   And hath cried *hum*?
FACE. Thrice, you must answer.
DAPPER.   Thrice.
SUBTLE.   And as oft *buz*?
FACE. If you have, say.
DAPPER.   I have.
SUBTLE.   Then, to her coz,
Hoping that he hath vinegared his senses,   5
As he was bid, the Fairy Queen dispenses,
By me, this robe, the petticoat of Fortune;
Which that he straight put on, she doth importune. [*They put
it on him.*]
And though to fortune near be her petticoat,
Yet nearer is her smock, the Queen doth note: 10
And therefore, ev'n of that a piece she hath sent,
Which, being a child, to wrap him in was rent;
And prays him for a scarf he now will wear it,

---

3. I.e., minted during the reign of Edward VI. English coins varied in value according to the
reign during which they were minted, because the amounts of precious metals in them also
varied; "old Harry's sovereign": from the reign of Henry VIII (1509–47); "groat": small English
coin worth a few pence.
4. From the reign of King Philip of Spain and Queen Mary Tudor (1553–58).

With as much love as then her Grace did tear it,
About his eyes, [*they blind him with a rag*] to show he is
    fortunate.   15
And, trusting unto her to make his state,
He'll throw away all worldly pelf about him;
Which that he will perform, she doth not doubt him.
FACE. She need not doubt him, sir. Alas, he has nothing,
    But what he will part withal as willingly,   20
    Upon her Grace's word—throw away your purse—
    As she would ask it:—handkerchiefs and all—[*He throws away,*
    as they bid him.]
    She cannot bid that thing, but he'll obey.
    If you have a ring about you, cast it off,
    Or a silver seal at your wrist; her grace will send   25
    Her fairies here to search you, therefore deal
    Directly with her Highness. If they find
    That you conceal a mite, you are undone.
DAPPER. Truly, there's all.
FACE.   All what?
DAPPER.   My money; truly.
FACE. Keep nothing that is transitory about you.   30
    [*aside to* SUBTLE] Bid Dol play music.—Look, the elves are
    come [DOL *plays on the cittern*[5] *within.*]
    To pinch you, if you tell not truth. Advise you. [*They pinch*
    him.]
DAPPER. O! I have a paper with a spur-ryal[6] in't.
FACE.   *Ti, ti.*
    They knew't, they say,
SUBTLE.   *Ti, ti, ti, ti.* He has more yet.
FACE. *Ti, ti-ti-ti.* [*aside to* SUBTLE] In the other pocket?
SUBTLE.   *Titi, titi,*
    titi, titi.   35
    They must pinch him or he will never confess, they say. [*They*
    pinch him again.]
DAPPER. O, O!
FACE. Nay, pray you hold: he is her Grace's nephew,
    Ti, ti, ti? What care you? Good faith, you shall care.
    Deal plainly, sir, and shame the fairies. Show
    You are an innocent.
DAPPER.   By this good light, I have nothing.   40
SUBTLE. *Ti, ti, ti, ti, to, ta.* He does equivocate,[7] she says:

5. Guitar.
6. A gold coin bearing on its face a blazing sun that resembled the rowels of a spur.
7. Use a word ambiguously in order to mislead.

Ti, ti do ti, ti ti do, ti da; and swears by the light when he is
   blinded.
DAPPER. By this good dark, I have nothing but a half-crown
   Of gold about my wrist, that my love gave me;
   And a leaden heart I wore since she forsook me.[8]   45
FACE. I thought 'twas something. And would you incur
   Your aunt's displeasure for these trifles? Come,
   I had rather you had thrown away twenty half-crowns.
                                             [*Takes it off.*]
   You may wear your leaden heart still.
                                        How now!
         [*Enter* DOL *hastily.*]
SUBTLE. What news, Dol?
DOL.   Yonder's your knight, sir Mammon.   50
FACE. God's lid, we never thought of him till now.
   Where is he?
DOL.   Here hard by. He is at the door.
SUBTLE. And you are not ready, now! Dol, get his suit.[9]
                                             [*Exit* DOL.]
   He must not be sent back.
FACE.   O by no means.
   What shall we do with this same puffin[1] here,   55
   Now he's on the spit?
SUBTLE.   Why, lay him back awhile,
   With some device.
         [*Re-enter* DOL *with* FACE'S *clothes.*]
   —*Ti, ti, ti, ti, ti.* Would her Grace speak with me?
   I come.—Help, Dol!   [*Knocking without.*]
FACE. [*speaks through the key-hole*] Who's there? Sir Epicure,
   My master's in the way. Please you to walk
   Three or four turns, but till his back be turned,   60
   And I am for you.—Quickly, Dol!
SUBTLE.   Her Grace
   Commends her kindly to you, master Dapper.
DAPPER. I long to see her Grace.
SUBTLE.   She now is set
   At dinner in her bed, and she has sent you
   From her own private trencher,[2] a dead mouse,   65
   And a piece of gingerbread, to be merry withal,
   And stay your stomach, lest you faint with fasting.

---

8. These little love-devices were characteristic of humble middle-class citizens such as Dapper.
9. Face's costume as Lungs, the alchemist's drudge.
1. I.e., Dapper. A "puffin" is a seabird noted for its brightly colored bill; by saying Dapper is
   "on the spit," Face means he is ready to be roasted.
2. Plate.

Yet if you could hold out till she saw you, she says,
It would be better for you.
FACE.   Sir, he shall
Hold out, an 'twere this two hours, for her Highness;   70
I can assure you that. We will not lose
All we have done.——
SUBTLE.   He must not see, nor speak
To anybody, till then.
FACE.   For that we'll put, sir,
A stay³ in's mouth.
SUBTLE.   Of what?
FACE.   Of gingerbread.
Make you it fit. He that hath pleased her Grace   75
Thus far, shall not now crinkle⁴ for a little.—
Gape sir, and let him fit you. [*They thrust a gag of
    gingerbread in his mouth.*]
SUBTLE.   Where shall we now
Bestow him?
DOL.   In the privy.
SUBTLE.   Come along, sir,
I now must show you Fortune's privy lodgings.
FACE. Are they perfumed, and his bath ready?
SUBTLE.   All.   80
Only the fumigation's somewhat strong.
FACE. [*speaking through the key-hole*] Sir Epicure, I am yours,
    sir, by and by.   [*Exeunt with* DAPPER.]

Act IV

ACT IV   SCENE 1. *A ROOM IN* LOVEWIT'S *HOUSE*

[*Enter* FACE *dressed as* LUNGS, *and* MAMMON.]
FACE. O, sir you are come in the only finest time—
MAMMON. Where's master?
FACE.   Now preparing for projection, sir.
Your stuff will be all changed shortly.
MAMMON.   Into gold?
FACE. To gold and silver, sir.
MAMMON.   Silver I care not for.
FACE. Yes, sir, a little to give beggars.
MAMMON.   Where's the lady?   5
FACE. At hand here. I have told her such brave things of you,
    Touching your bounty, and your noble spirit—

3. Impediment, gag.
4. Give up, fall short.

MAMMON.   Hast thou?

FACE. As she is almost in her fit to see you.
But, good sir, no divinity in your conference,[5]
For fear of putting her in rage—

MAMMON.   I warrant thee.   10

FACE. Six men will not hold her down; and then,
If the old man should hear or see you—

MAMMON.   Fear not.

FACE. The very house, sir, would run mad. You know it,
How scrupulous he is, and violent,
'Gainst the least act of sin. Physic, or mathematics,   15
Poetry, state, or bawdry, as I told you,
She will endure, and never startle; but
No word of controversy.

MAMMON.   I am schooled, good Ulen.

FACE. And you must praise her house, remember that,
And her nobility.

MAMMON.   Let me alone: 20
No herald, no, nor antiquary, Lungs,
Shall do it better. Go.

FACE.   [aside] Why, this is yet
A kind of modern happiness,[6] to have
Dol Common for a great lady.   [Exit FACE.]

MAMMON.   [alone, to himself] Now, Epicure,
Heighten thyself, talk to her all in gold;   25
Rain her as many showers as Jove did drops
Unto his Danäe;[7] show the god a miser,
Compared with Mammon. What the stone will do't.
She shall feel gold, taste gold, hear gold, sleep gold;
Nay, we will concumbere[8] gold: I will be puissant,   30
And mighty in my talk to her.
          [Enter FACE with DOL, richly dressed.]
                          Here she comes.

FACE. [aside] To him, Dol, suckle him.—This is the noble
    knight, I told your ladyship—

MAMMON.   Madam, with your pardon,
I kiss your vesture.

DOL.   Sir, I were uncivil
If I would suffer that; my lip to you, sir. [Kisses him.]   35

MAMMON. I hope my lord your brother be in health, lady.

---

5. Don't talk religion to her.
6. Modern happiness is the vulgar sort, the only kind available nowadays.
7. The Roman god Jove wooed and won Danäe in the form of a shower of gold.
8. Copulate; "puissant": overpowering.

DOL. My lord, my brother is, though I no lady, sir.

FACE. [*aside*] Well said, my Guinea bird.[9]

MAMMON.   Right noble madam—

FACE. [*aside*] O, we shall have most fierce idolatry.

MAMMON. 'Tis your prerogative.

DOL.   Rather your courtesy.   40

MAMMON. Were there nought else t'enlarge your virtues to me,
   These answers speak your breeding, and your blood.

DOL. Blood we boast none, sir, a poor baron's daughter.

MAMMON. Poor! And gat you? Profane not. Had your father
   Slept all the happy remnant of his life   45
   After that act, lain but there still, and panted,
   He had done enough to make himself, his issue,
   And his posterity noble.

DOL.   Sir, although
   We may be said to want the gilt and trappings,
   The dress of honor, yet we strive to keep   50
   The seeds and the materials.

MAMMON.   I do see
   The old ingredient, virtue, was not lost,
   Nor the drug money used to make your compound.
   There is a strange nobility in your eye,
   This lip, that chin! Methinks you do resemble   55
   One of the Austriac princes.[1]

FACE.   [*aside*] Very like!
   Her father was an Irish costermonger.[2]

MAMMON. The house of Valois, just, had such a nose,
   And such a forehead, yet, the Medici
   Of Florence boast.[3]   60

DOL.   Troth, and I have been likened
   To all these princes.

FACE.   [*aside*] I'll be sworn, I heard it.

MAMMON. I know not how! It is not any one,
   But e'en the very choice of all their features.

FACE. [*aside*] I'll in, and laugh.   [*Exit.*]

MAMMON.   A certain touch, or air,
   That sparkles a divinity beyond   65
   An earthly beauty!

DOL.   O, you play the courtier.

MAMMON. Good lady, give me leave—

---

9. Slang for prostitute.
1. The Hapsburgs, princes of Austria, tended to a heavy jaw and hanging lower lip.
2. Pushcart salesman.
3. The Valois were the royal house of France; the Medici of Florence were never particularly
   handsome, but Mammon is determined to flatter.

DOL.   In faith, I may not,
  To mock me, sir.
MAMMON.   To burn in this sweet flame;
  The phoenix[4] never knew a nobler death.
DOL. Nay, now you court the courtier, and destroy   70
  What you would build; this art, sir, in your words,
  Calls your whole faith in question.
MAMMON.   By my soul——
DOL. Nay, oaths are made of the same air, sir.
MAMMON.   Nature
  Never bestowed upon mortality
  A more unblamed, a more harmonious feature;   75
  She played the stepdame in all faces else.
  Sweet madam, let me be particular[5]—
DOL. Particular, sir? I pray you know your distance.
MAMMON. In no ill sense, sweet lady; but to ask
  How your fair graces pass the hours. I see   80
  You are lodged here, in the house of a rare man,
  An excellent artist; but what's that to you?
DOL. Yes, sir; I study here the mathematics,
  And distillation.
MAMMON.   O, I cry your pardon.
  He's a divine instructor! Can extract   85
  The souls of all things by his art; call all
  The virtues; and the miracles of the sun,
  Into a temperate furnace: teach dull nature
  What her own forces are. A man the Emperor
  Has courted above Kelly;[6] sent his medals   90
  And chains to invite him.
DOL.   Ay, and for his physic, sir—
MAMMON. Above the art of Aesculapius,
  That drew the envy of the thunderer![7]
  I know all this, and more.
DOL.   Troth, I am taken, sir,
  Whole with these studies, that contemplate nature.   95
MAMMON. It is a noble humor; but this form
  Was not intended to so dark a use.
  Had you been crooked, foul, of some coarse mould,
  A cloister had done well; but such a feature

4. The mythical bird that builds itself a special pyre on which to enact its own death.
5. Mammon means "precise," "detailed"; Dol thinks, or affects to think, he is making a pass.
6. Edward Kelly (1555–1595) worked with Doctor John Dee (1527–1608) very much as Face
  works with Subtle. The Holy Roman Emperor Rudolph II invited Kelly to his court, where
  he promised to make gold; after failing, he was jailed, and he died while trying to escape.
7. In Greek mythology, Aesculapius the physician was so successful in his cures that Zeus ("the
  thunderer") destroyed him lest he render men immortal.

That might stand up the glory of a kingdom,   100
To live recluse! is a mere solecism,[8]
Though in a nunnery. It must not be.
I muse my lord your brother will permit it:
You should spend half my land first, were I he.
Does not this diamond better on my finger,   105
Than in the quarry?
DOL.   Yes.
MAMMON.   Why, you are like it.
You were created, lady, for the light.
Here, you shall wear it; take it, the first pledge
Of what I speak, to bind you to believe me.
DOL. In chains of adamant?[9]
MAMMON.   Yes, the strongest bands.   110
And take a secret too—here, by your side,
Doth stand this hour the happiest man in Europe.
DOL. You are contented, sir?
MAMMON.   Nay, in true being,
The envy of princes and the fear of states.
DOL. Say you so, sir Epicure?
MAMMON.   Yes, and thou shalt prove it, 115
Daughter of honor. I have cast mine eye
Upon thy form, and I will rear this beauty
Above all styles.
DOL.   You mean no treason, sir?
MAMMON. No, I will take away that jealousy.[1]
I am the lord of the philosopher's stone,   120
And thou the lady.
DOL.   How, sir! Have you that?
MAMMON. I am the master of the mastery.[2]
This day the good old wretch here o' the house
Has made it for us; now he's at projection.
Think therefore thy first wish now, let me hear it;   125
And it shall rain into thy lap, no shower,
But floods of gold, whole cataracts, a deluge,
To get a nation on thee.[3]
DOL.   You are pleased, sir,
To work on the ambition of our sex.
MAMMON. I am pleased the glory of her sex should know   130

8. Anomaly, absurdity.
9. Literally, diamond; practically, a very hard metal.
1. Suspicion.
2. "I own the masterwork," i.e., the stone.
3. Beget a whole population.

This nook, here, of the Friars[4] is no climate
For her to live obscurely in, to learn
Physic and surgery, for the constable's wife
Of some odd hundred in Essex;[5] but come forth,
And taste the air of palaces; eat, drink   135
The toils of empirics,[6] and their boasted practice,
Tincture of pearl, and coral, gold and amber;
Be seen at feasts and triumphs; have it asked,
What miracle she is? Set all the eyes
Of court afire, like a burning glass,   140
And work 'em into cinders, when the jewels
Of twenty states adorn thee, and the light
Strikes out the stars! That, when thy name is mentioned,
Queens may look pale; and we but showing our love,
Nero's Poppæa may be lost in story![7]   145
Thus will we have it.

DOL.   I could well consent, sir.
But, in a monarchy, how will this be?
The prince will soon take notice, and both seize
You and your stone, it being a wealth unfit
For any private subject.

MAMMON.   If he knew it.   150

DOL. Yourself do boast it, sir.

MAMMON.   To thee, my life.

DOL. O, but beware, sir! You may come to end
The remnant of your days in a loathed prison
By speaking of it.

MAMMON.   'Tis no idle fear.
We'll therefore go withal,[8] my girl, and live   155
In a free state, where we will eat our mullets,[9]
Soused in high-country wines, sup pheasants' eggs,
And have our cockles boiled in silver shells;
Our shrimps to swim again, as when they lived,
In a rare butter made of dolphins' milk,   160
Whose cream does look like opals; and with these
Delicate meats set ourselves high for pleasure,
And take us down again, and then renew

---

4. Blackfriars.
5. I.e., the wife of a modest rural official in a country town.
6. The alchemical followers of Paracelsus were called "empirics" because they disregarded the
rules of the ancient medical authority Galen and followed what they saw as "experience."
7. Poppaea was the second wife of Nero—she will be lost in history when the newer and greater
love of Mammon and Dol is made manifest.
8. At once.
9. A fish that was a Roman delicacy; "cockles": shellfish.

Our youth and strength with drinking the elixir,
And so enjoy a perpetuity   165
Of life and lust! And thou shalt have thy wardrobe
Richer than nature's, still to change thyself,
And vary oftener, for thy pride, than she,
Or art, her wise and almost-equal servant.
      [*Re-enter* FACE.]
FACE. Sir, you are too loud. I hear you, every word,   170
  Into the laboratory. Some fitter place;
  The garden, or great chamber above. How like you her?
MAMMON. Excellent, Lungs! There's for thee. [*Gives him money.*]
FACE.   But do you hear?
  Good sir, beware, no mention of the rabbins.[1]
MAMMON. We think not on 'em.   [*Exeunt* MAMMON *and* DOL.]
FACE.   O, it is well, sir.—Subtle!   175

ACT IV   SCENE 2

      [*Enter* SUBTLE.]
  Dost thou not laugh?
SUBTLE.   Yes; are they gone?
FACE.   All's clear.
SUBTLE. The widow is come.
FACE.   And your quarreling disciple?
SUBTLE. Ay.
FACE.   I must to my Captainship again then.
SUBTLE. Stay, bring them in first.
FACE.   So I meant. What is she?
  A bonnibel?[2]
SUBTLE.   I know not.
FACE.   We'll draw lots;   5
  You'll stand to that?[3]
SUBTLE.   What else?
FACE.   O, for a suit
  To fall now like a curtain, flap![4]
SUBTLE.   To the door, man.
FACE. You'll have the first kiss, 'cause I am not ready.
                                    [*Exit* FACE.]
SUBTLE. Yes, and perhaps hit you through both the nostrils.[5]

1. Rabbis, Hebrew commentators on the Old Testament and other Jewish law.
2. From *bonne et belle* (French), "beauty."
3. Agree to that.
4. Face needs his captain's uniform and is getting tired of the frequent quick-changes required of his many plots.
5. Perhaps from the old poacher's sport of spear fishing: "get the best of you before you're ready." Cf. above, "twitch him through both gills" (2.4.3).

FACE. [*within*] Who would you speak with?
KASTRIL.   [*within*] Where's the Captain?
FACE.   [*within*] Gone, sir,   10
  About some business.
KASTRIL.   [*within*] Gone!
FACE.   [*within*] He'll return straight.
  But master Doctor, his lieutenant, is here.
      [*Enter* KASTRIL, *followed by* DAME PLIANT.]
SUBTLE. Come near, my worshipful boy, my *terræ fili*,[6]
  That is, my boy of land; make thy approaches.
  Welcome; I know thy lusts, and thy desires,   15
  And I will serve and satisfy them. Begin,
  Charge me from thence, or thence, or in this line;
  Here is my center; ground thy quarrel.
KASTRIL.   You lie.
SUBTLE. How, child of wrath and anger! The loud lie?
  For what, my sudden boy?
KASTRIL.   Nay, that look you to,   20
  I am afore-hand.[7]
SUBTLE.   O, this's no true grammar,
  And as ill logic! You must render causes, child,
  Your first and second intentions, know your canons[8]
  And your divisions, moods, degrees, and differences,
  Your predicaments, substance, and accident,   25
  Series extern and intern, with their causes,
  Efficient, material, formal, final,
  And have your elements perfect—
KASTRIL.   What is this
  The angry tongue he talks in?
SUBTLE.   That false precept,
  Of being afore-hand, has deceived a number,   30
  And made them enter quarrels, oftentimes,
  Before they were aware; and afterward,
  Against their wills.
KASTRIL.   How must I do then, sir?
SUBTLE. I cry this lady mercy: she should first
  Have been saluted. [*Kisses her.*] I do call you lady,   35
  Because you are to be one, ere 't be long,
  My soft and buxom widow.

6. Subtle translates this Latin phrase in the next line; Kastril is a landowner, but the phrase also
    refers to a kind of spirit in alchemy.
7. To be "aforehand" in a quarrel was to gain certain advantages in the duel that was bound to
    follow.
8. "First and second intentions," "canons," "divisions, moods, degrees," and so forth are all
    Aristotelian categories—terms of art for dressing nature in learned jargon, which in this case
    are applied to dueling.

KASTRIL.   Is she, i'faith?

SUBTLE. Yes, or my art is an egregious liar.

KASTRIL. How know you?

SUBTLE.   By inspection on her forehead,
   And subtlety of her lip, which must be tasted   40
   Often to make a judgment. [*Kisses her again.*]—'Slight, she
      melts
   Like a myrobolane.[9]—Here is yet a line,
   In *rivo frontis*, tells me he is no knight.

DAME PLIANT. What is he then, sir?

SUBTLE.   Let me see your hand.
   O, your *linea fortunæ* makes it plain;   45
   And stella here in *monte Veneris*.
   But, most of all, *junctura annularis*.[1]
   He is a soldier, or a man of art, lady,
   But shall have some great honor shortly.

DAME PLIANT.   Brother,
   He's a rare man, believe me!

      [*Enter* FACE, *in his Captain's uniform.*]

KASTRIL.   Hold your peace.   50
   Here comes the t' other rare man.—'Save you, Captain.

FACE. Good master Kastril. Is this your sister?

KASTRIL.   Ay, sir.
   Please you to kuss her, and be proud to know her.

FACE. I shall be proud to know you, lady. [*Kisses her.*]

DAME PLIANT.   Brother,
   He calls me lady too.

KASTRIL.   Ay, peace; I heard it.   55

                    [KASTRIL *takes her aside.*]

FACE. The Count is come.

SUBTLE.   Where is he?

FACE.   At the door.

SUBTLE. Why, you must entertain him.

FACE.   What will you do
   With these the while?

SUBTLE.   Why, have them up, and show them
   Some fustian[2] book, or the dark glass.

FACE.   'Fore God,
   She is a delicate dabchick![3] I must have her.   [*Exit* FACE.]   60

9. Candied plum from the East that melted in the mouth; "rivo frontis": a line on the forehead,
     supposed to be significant in fortune-telling.
1. The "linea fortunae," or line of fortune, is one of the main lines in the palm of the hand;
     the "stella," or star, on the mount of Venus at the base of the thumb and loose joints on the
     ring finger ("junctura annularis") are evidence of sexual appetite.
2. Pompous and phony; "the dark glass": the crystal ball.
3. Small bird.

SUBTLE. Must you? Ay, if your fortune will, you must.
   Come, sir, the Captain will come to us presently.
   I'll have you to my chamber of demonstrations,
   Where I will show you both the grammar and logic
   And rhetoric of quarreling; my whole method   65
   Drawn out in tables;[4] and my instrument,
   That hath the several scales upon't, shall make you
   Able to quarrel at a straw's breadth by moonlight.[5]
   And, lady, I'll have you look in a glass,
   Some half an hour, but to clear your eyesight,   70
   Against you see your fortune; which is greater,
   Than I may judge upon the sudden, trust me.
                [*Exit, followed by* KASTRIL *and* DAME PLIANT.]

ACT IV   SCENE 3

     [*Enter* FACE, *as Captain.*]
FACE. Where are you, Doctor?
SUBTLE.   [*within*] I'll come to you presently.
FACE. I will have this same widow, now I've seen her,
   On any composition.[6]
     [*Enter* SUBTLE.]
SUBTLE.   What do you say?
FACE. Have you disposed of them?
SUBTLE.   I've sent them up.
FACE. Subtle, in troth, I needs must have this widow.   5
SUBTLE. Is that the matter?
FACE.   Nay, but hear me.
SUBTLE.   Go to,
   If you rebel once, Dol shall know it all.
   Therefore be quiet, and obey your chance.
FACE. Nay, thou art so violent now—Do but conceive,
   Thou art old, and canst not serve—
SUBTLE.   Who cannot? I?   10
   'Slight, I will serve her with thee, for a—
FACE.   Nay,
   But understand: I'll give you composition.[7]
SUBTLE. I will not treat with thee; what! Sell my fortune?
   'Tis better than my birthright. Do not murmur.
   Win her, and carry her. If you grumble, Dol   15
   Knows it directly.

---

4. Diagrams.
5. I.e., able to pick a quarrel over something ordinary persons can't even see.
6. On any terms whatever.
7. Make a deal with you.

FACE.   Well, sir, I am silent.
Will you go help to fetch in Don in state?
SUBTLE. I follow you, sir. [*Exit* FACE.] We must keep Face in
   awe,
Or he will over-look[8] us like a tyrant.
   [*Enter* FACE, *introducing* SURLY *disguised as a Spaniard.*]
Brain of a tailor! Who comes here? Don John[9]   20
SURLY. *Señores, beso las manos à vuestras mercedes.*[1]
SUBTLE. Would you had stooped a little, and kissed our *anos*!
FACE. Peace, Subtle.
SUBTLE.   Stab me; I shall never hold, man.[2]
He looks in that deep ruff like a head in a platter,
Served in by a short cloak upon two trestles.[3]   25
FACE. Or, what do you say to a collar of brawn,[4] cut down
Beneath the souse, and wriggled with a knife?
SUBTLE. 'Slud, he does look too fat to be a Spaniard.
FACE. Perhaps some Fleming or some Hollander got him
In d'Alva's time; Count Egmont's bastard.[5]
SUBTLE.   Don,   30
Your scurvy, yellow Madrid face is welcome.
SURLY. *Gratia.*
SUBTLE.   He speaks out of a fortification.
Pray God he have no squibs in those deep sets.[6]
SURLY. *Por dios, señores, muy linda casa!*[7]
SUBTLE. What says he?
FACE.   Praises the house, I think;   35
I know no more but's action.
SUBTLE.   Yes, the *casa*,
My precious Diego, will prove fair enough
To cozen you in. Do you mark? You shall
Be cozened, Diego.
FACE.   Cozened, do you see,
My worthy Donzel, cozened.
SURLY.   *Entiendo.*[8]   40
SUBTLE. Do you intend it? So do we, dear Don.

---

8. Domineer.
9. Don John was a common name for a Spaniard. Surly wears an ornate costume, both as a
   disguise and because Spaniards were understood to be elaborate dressers.
1. Gentlemen, I kiss the hands of your honors.
2. I shall never keep a straight face.
3. His legs.
4. Pig's head and neck; "souse": ears.
5. Dutchmen and Flemings, over whom the Spanish had ruled for years, were supposed to be
   fat. The Duke of Alva was governor-general of the Netherlands for Spain from 1567 to 1573;
   Count Egmont was a Dutch patriot executed in 1568.
6. The folds of his ruff; "squibs": firecrackers, i.e., unpleasant surprises.
7. By heaven, gentlemen, a very fine house.
8. I understand.

Have you brought pistolets, or portagues,
My solemn Don?—Dost thou feel any?
FACE.   [*feels his pockets*] Full.
SUBTLE. You shall be emptied, Don, pumped and drawn
    Dry, as they say.
FACE.   Milked, in troth, sweet Don.   45
SUBTLE. See all the monsters; the great lion of all, Don.[9]
SURLY. *Con licencia, se puede ver à esta señora?*[1]
SUBTLE. What talks he now?
FACE.   Of the señora.
SUBTLE.   O, Don,
    That is the lioness, which you shall see
    Also, my Don.
FACE.   'Slid, Subtle, how shall we do?   50
SUBTLE. For what?
FACE.   Why, Dol's employed, you know.
SUBTLE.   That's true.
    'Fore heaven, I know not; he must stay, that's all.
FACE. Stay! That he must not by no means.
SUBTLE.   No, why?
FACE. Unless you'll mar all. 'Slight, he will suspect it,
    And then he will not pay, not half so well.   55
    This is a traveled punk-master,[2] and does know
    All the delays; a notable hot rascal,
    And looks already rampant.[3]
SUBTLE.   'Sdeath, and Mammon
    Must not be troubled.
FACE.   Mammon! In no case.
SUBTLE. What shall we do then?
FACE.   Think: you must be sudden.   60
SURLY. *Entiendo que la señora es tan hermosa, que codicio tan*
    verla, como la bien aventuranza de mi vida.[4]
FACE. *Mi vida!* 'Slid, Subtle, he puts me in mind o' the widow.
    What dost thou say to draw her to it? Ha!
    And tell her 'tis her fortune? All our venture   65
    Now lies upon't. It is but one man more,
    Which of us chance to have her; and beside,
    There is no maidenhead to be feared or lost.
    What dost thou think on't, Subtle?

---

9. Subtle pretends to be master of an amusement park; the Don will see all the sideshows.
1. "Please, can this lady be seen?"
2. An experienced whoremaster.
3. Up on his hind legs and ready to go.
4. "I understand the lady is so lovely that seeing her will be the greatest piece of good luck in my life."

SUBTLE. Who, I? Why—

FACE. The credit of our house too is engaged. 70

SUBTLE. You made me an offer for my share ere-while.
What wilt thou give me, i' faith?

FACE. O, by that light
I'll not buy now. You know your doom[5] to me.
"E'en take your lot, obey your chance, sir; win her,
And wear her out, for me."

SUBTLE. 'Slight, I'll not work her then. 75

FACE. It is the common cause; therefore bethink you.
Dol else must know it, as you said.

SUBTLE. I care not.

SURLY. *Señores, porqué se tarda tanto?*[6]

SUBTLE. Faith, I am not fit, I am old.

FACE. That's now no reason, sir.

SURLY. *Puede ser de hazer burla de mi amor?*[7] 80

FACE. You hear the Don too? By this air, I call,
And loose the hinges.[8] Dol!

SUBTLE. A plague of hell——

FACE. Will you then do?

SUBTLE. You're a terrible rogue!
I'll think of this: will you, sir, call the widow?

FACE. Yes, and I'll take her too with all her faults, 85
Now I do think on't better.

SUBTLE. With all my heart, sir;
Am I discharged o' the lot?

FACE. As you please.

SUBTLE. Hands. [*They shake
hands.*]

FACE. Remember now, that upon any change,
You never claim her.

SUBTLE. Much good joy, and health to you, sir.
Marry a whore! Fate, let me wed a witch first. 90

SURLY. *Por estas honradas barbas*[9]——

SUBTLE. He swears by his beard.
Despatch, and call the brother too. [*Exit* FACE.]

SURLY. *Tengo duda, señores,
Que no me hagan alguna traición.*[1]

SUBTLE. How, issue on? Yes, *presto, señor.* Please you

---

5. Expression. Face quotes Subtle back at himself.
6. "Gentlemen, what is all the delay?"
7. "Perhaps you're making sport of my love?"
8. Dissolve our association.
9. By this honorable beard.
1. I'm afraid, gentlemen, that you may be playing some trick on me.

Enthratha the *chambratha*, worthy Don: 95
Where if you please the fates, in your *bathada*,
You shall be soaked, and stroked, and tubbed, and rubbed,
And scrubbed, and fubbed,[2] dear Don, before you go.
You shall in faith, my scurvy baboon Don,
Be curried,[3] clawed and flawed, and tawed, indeed.   100
I will the heartlier go about it now,
And make the widow a punk so much the sooner,
To be revenged on this impetuous Face.
The quickly doing of it, is the grace.
                              [*Exeunt* SUBTLE *and* SURLY.]

ACT IV   SCENE 4. *ANOTHER ROOM IN* LOVEWIT'S *HOUSE*

[*Enter* FACE, KASTRIL, *and* DAME PLIANT.]

FACE. Come, lady; I knew the Doctor would not leave,
    Till he had found the very nick[4] of her fortune.
KASTRIL. To be a countess, say you?
FACE.   A Spanish countess, sir.
DAME PLIANT. Why, is that better than an English countess?
FACE. Better! 'Slight, make you that a question, lady?   5
KASTRIL. Nay, she is a fool, Captain, you must pardon her.
FACE. Ask from your courtier, to your inns-of-court-man,
    To your mere milliner;[5] they will tell you all,
    Your Spanish jennet is the best horse; your Spanish
    Stoop[6] is the best garb; your Spanish beard   10
    Is the best cut; your Spanish ruffs are the best
    Wear; your Spanish payanne the best dance;
    Your Spanish titillation[7] in a glove
    The best perfume; and for your Spanish pike,
    And Spanish blade, let your poor Captain speak.   15
    Here comes the Doctor.
            [*Enter* SUBTLE, *with a paper.*]
SUBTLE.   My most honored lady,
    (For so I am now to style you, having found
    By this my scheme, you are to undergo
    An honorable fortune, very shortly)
    What will you say now, if some—
FACE.   I have told her all, sir;   20
    And her right worshipful brother here, that she shall be

2. Tricked.
3. Soaking, scraping, beating, especially leather; "flawed": flayed; "tawed": tanned.
4. Exact character.
5. Seller of women's hats.
6. Bow; "garb": fashion.
7. Scent.

A countess; do not delay them, sir. A Spanish countess!
SUBTLE. Still, my scarce-worshipful Captain, you can keep
   No secret! Well, since he has told you, madam,
   Do you forgive him, and I do.
KASTRIL.   She shall do that, sir;   25
   I'll look to't, 'tis my charge.
SUBTLE.   Well then, nought rests
   But that she fit her love now to her fortune.
DAME PLIANT. Truly I shall never brook[8] a Spaniard.
SUBTLE.   No?
DAME PLIANT. Never since eighty-eight[9] could I abide them,
   And that was some three year afore I was born, in truth.   30
SUBTLE. Come, you must love him, or be miserable;
   Choose which you will.
FACE.   By this good rush,[1] persuade her;
   She will cry strawberries else within this twelve-month.[2]
SUBTLE. Nay, shads and mackerel, which is worse.
FACE.   Indeed, sir!
KASTRIL. God's lid, you shall love him, or I'll kick you.
DAME PLIANT.   Why,   35
   I'll do as you will have me, brother.
KASTRIL.   Do,
   Or by this hand I'll maul you.
FACE.   Nay, good sir,
   Be not so fierce.
SUBTLE.   No, my enragèd child;
   She will be ruled. What, when she comes to taste
   The pleasures of a countess! To be courted—   40
FACE. And kissed, and ruffled!
SUBTLE.   Ay, behind the hangings.
FACE. And then come forth in pomp!
SUBTLE.   And know her state!
FACE. Of keeping all the idolaters of the chamber
   Barer to her, than at their prayers![3]
SUBTLE.   Is served
   Upon the knee!
FACE.   And has her pages, ushers,   45
   Footmen, and coaches—
SUBTLE.   Her six mares—

---

8. Endure.
9. 1588, the year of the Spanish Armada.
1. He picks up a rush from the floor.
2. I.e., peddle strawberries in the street as an itinerant huckster—only one stage above selling
   fish from a fish-stall.
3. I.e., the courtiers will remove their caps to her more reverently than at their prayers.

FACE.   Nay, eight!
SUBTLE. To hurry her through London, to the Exchange,[4]
   Bedlam, the china-houses—
FACE.   Yes, and have
   The citizens gape at her, and praise her tires,
   And my lord's goose-turd[5] bands, that ride with her!   50
KASTRIL. Most brave! By this hand, you are not my suster,
   If you refuse.
DAME PLIANT. I will not refuse, brother.
      [*Enter* SURLY.]
SURLY. *Qué es esto, señores, que non se venga?*
   Esta tardanza me mata![6]
FACE.   It is the Count come;
   The Doctor knew he would be here, by his art.   55
SUBTLE. *En gallanta madama, Don! Gallantissima!*
SURLY. *Por todos los dioses, la más acabada*
   Hermosura, que he visto en mi vida![7]
FACE. Is't not a gallant language that they speak?
KASTRIL. An admirable language! Is't not French?   60
FACE. No, Spanish, sir.
KASTRIL.   It goes like law-French,[8]
   And that, they say, is the courtliest language.
FACE.   List, sir.
SURLY. *El sol ha perdido su lumbre, con el*
   Resplandor que trae esta dama! Válgame dios![9]
FACE. He admires your sister.
KASTRIL.   Must not she make curtsey?   65
SUBTLE. God's will, she must go to him, man, and kiss him!
   It is the Spanish fashion, for the women
   To make first court.
FACE.   'Tis true he tells you, sir;
   His art knows all.
SURLY.   *Porqué no se acude?*[1]
KASTRIL. He speaks to her, I think.
FACE.   That he does, sir.   70
SURLY. *Por el amor de Dios, que es esto que se tarda?*[2]

---

4. The Exchange in the Strand was where fashionable ladies went shopping; Bedlam (the mad-house) was where they went for amusement.
5. Ribbons of a fashionable shade of greenish-yellow—also the traditional colors of a fool.
6. "How is it she doesn't come, gentlemen? The delay is killing me!"
7. "A fine lady, Don! Very fine!" "By all the gods, the most gorgeous creature I've ever seen in my life!"
8. The variety of Norman French long spoken in English law courts, of which we still have remnants in words such as "oyez," "torts," and "mortgage." "Courtliest" is a pun.
9. "The sun has lost its glitter before the splendor of this lady. Lord bless me."
1. "Why doesn't she come to me?"
2. "For the love of God, why is she holding back?"

KASTRIL. Nay, see: she will not understand him! Gull!
　Noddy!

DAME PLIANT. What say you, brother?

KASTRIL. 　　　　　　　　　　　Ass, my suster,
　Go kiss him, as the cunning man would have you;
　I'll thrust a pin in your buttocks else.

FACE. 　　　　　　　　　　　O no, sir. 　　　　　　75

SURLY. *Señora mía, mi persona muy indigna está*
　A llegar a tanta hermosura.[3]

FACE. Does he not use her bravely?

KASTRIL. 　　　　　　　　　　Bravely, i' faith!

FACE. Nay, he will use her better.

KASTRIL. 　　　　　　　　Do you think so?

SURLY. *Señora, si sera servida, entremos.*[4] [*Exit with* DAME PLIANT.] 　80

KASTRIL. Where does he carry her?

FACE. 　　　　　　　　　　Into the garden, sir;
　Take you no thought: I must interpret for her.

SUBTLE. [*Aside to* FACE, *who goes out*] Give Dol the word.—
　　Come, my fierce child, advance,
　We'll to our quarreling lesson again.

KASTRIL. 　　　　　　　　　　Agreed.
　I love a Spanish boy with all my heart. 　　　　　　85

SUBTLE. Nay, and by this means, sir, you shall be brother
　To a great count.

KASTRIL. 　　　　Ay, I knew that at first.
　This match will advance the house of the Kastrils.

SUBTLE. 'Pray God your sister prove but pliant!

KASTRIL. 　　　　　　　　　　　Why,
　Her name is so, by her other husband.

SUBTLE. 　　　　　　　　　　How! 　　　　　　90

KASTRIL. The widow Pliant. Knew you not that?

SUBTLE. 　　　　　　　　　　No, faith, sir;
　Yet, by erection of her figure,[5] I guessed it.
　Come, let's go practice.

KASTRIL. 　　　　　　Yes, but do you think, doctor,
　I e'er shall quarrel well?

SUBTLE. 　　　　　　I warrant you. 　　　　[*Exeunt.*]

---

3. "My lady, my person is altogether unworthy of approaching such loveliness."
4. "Lady, if you will, let us retire."
5. By casting her horoscope, but there's an obvious pun.

ACT IV   SCENE 5

[*Enter* DOL *in her fit of raving, followed by* MAMMON.]
DOL. *For after Alexander's death*[6]—
MAMMON.   Good lady—
DOL. *That Perdiccas and Antigonus were slain,*
    The two that stood, Seleuc', and Ptolomey—
MAMMON. Madam.
DOL.   *Made up the two legs, and the fourth beast,*
    That was Gog-north, and Egypt-south; which after   5
    Was called Gog-iron-leg, and South-iron-leg—
MAMMON.   Lady—
DOL. *And then Gog-hornèd. So was Egypt, too;*
    Then Egypt-clay-leg, and Gog-clay-leg—
MAMMON.   Sweet madam.
DOL. *And last Gog-dust, and Egypt-dust, which fall*
    In the last link of the fourth chain. And these   10
    Be stars in story, which none see, or look at—
MAMMON. What shall I do?
DOL.   *For, as he says, except*
    We call the rabbins and the heathen Greeks—
MAMMON. Dear lady.
DOL.   *To come from Salem, and from Athens,*
    And teach the people of Great Britain—
        [*Enter* FACE *hastily, dressed as Lungs.*]
FACE.   What's the matter, sir?   15
DOL. *To speak the tongue of Eber, and Javan*—
MAMMON.   O,
    She's in her fit.
DOL.   *We shall know nothing*—
FACE.   Death, sir,
    We are undone!
DOL.   *Where then a learned linguist*
    Shall see the ancient used communion
    Of vowels and consonants—
FACE.   My master will hear!   20
DOL. *A wisdom, which Pythagoras held most high*—
MAMMON. Sweet honorable lady!
DOL.   *To comprise*
    All sounds of voices, in few marks of letters—
FACE. Nay, you must never hope to lay[7] her now.

---

6. Dol's ravings come mostly from Hugh Broughton's book *The Consent of Scripture* (1590),
which tried to establish a conclusive, comprehensive chronology of the Bible. It is neither
necessary nor possible to understand completely the gibberish she recites. The biblical imagery
of her ravings comes from Daniel, ch. 2. See p. 474 of this volume.
7. Quiet.

[*They all speak together.*]

DOL. *And so we may arrive by Talmud*
    skill,
  And profane Greek, to raise the build-
    ing up
  Of Helen's house,[8] *against the*
    Ishmaelite,
  King of Thogarma, and his
    habergions[9]
  Brimstony, blue, and fiery; and the
    force
  Of king Abaddon, and the beast of
    Cittim;
  Which rabbi David Kimchi, Onkelos,
  And Ibn Ezra do interpret Rome.

FACE. How did you put her into't?

MAMMON.   Alas, I talked
  Of a fifth monarchy I would erect,[1]
  With the philosopher's stone, by
    chance, and she
  Falls on the other four straight.

FACE.   Out of Broughton!
  I told you so. 'Slid, stop her mouth.

MAMMON.   Is't best?

FACE. She'll never leave else. If the old
  man hear her,
  We are but faeces, ashes.

SUBTLE.   [*within*] What's to do there?

FACE. O, we are lost! Now she hears
  him, she is quiet.

[*Enter* SUBTLE; *they run different ways.*]

MAMMON. Where shall I hide me!

SUBTLE.   How! What sight is here?
  Close deeds of darkness, and that shun the light!
  Bring him again. Who is he? What, my son!   35
  O, I have lived too long.

MAMMON.   Nay, good dear father,
  There was no unchaste purpose.

SUBTLE.   Not! And flee me,
  When I come in?

MAMMON.   That was my error.

SUBTLE.   Error?
  Guilt, guilt, my son. Give it the right name. No marvel,
  If I found check in our great work within,   40
  When such affairs as these were managing!

MAMMON. Why, have you so?

SUBTLE.   It has stood still this half hour:
  And all the rest of our less works gone back.
  Where is the instrument of wickedness,
  My lewd false drudge?

MAMMON.   Nay, good sir, blame not him;   45
  Believe me, 'twas against his will or knowledge.
  I saw her by chance.

SUBTLE.   Will you commit more sin,
  To excuse a varlet?

---

8. I.e., the house of the Hellenes.
9. Coats of mail, but senseless in this context.
1. The fifth monarchy, predicted in the book of Revelation, was a concept dear to the Puritans; it was the period of Christ's second coming, hence of divine perfection. Mammon anticipates its emergence through application of the philosopher's stone.

MAMMON.   By my hope, 'tis true, sir.

SUBTLE. Nay, then I wonder less, if you, for whom
  The blessing was prepared, would so tempt heaven,   50
  And lose your fortunes.

MAMMON.   Why, sir?

SUBTLE.   This'll retard
  The work a month at least.

MAMMON.   Why, if it do,
  What remedy? But think it not, good father;
  Our purposes were honest.

SUBTLE.   As they were,
  So the reward will prove. [A *loud explosion within.*] How now!
    Ay me!   55
  God, and all saints[2] be good to us. [*Enter* FACE.] What's that?

FACE. O sir, we are defeated! All the works
  Are flown *in fumo,*[3] every glass is burst.
  Furnace and all rent down! As if a bolt
  Of thunder had been driven through the house.   60
  Retorts, receivers, pelicans, bolt-heads,
  All struck in shivers!   [SUBTLE *falls down as in a swoon.*]
                    Help, good sir! Alas,
  Coldness and death invades him. Nay, Sir Mammon,
  Do the fair offices of a man! You stand,
  As you were readier to depart than he.   [*Knocking within.*] 65
  Who's there? My lord her brother is come.

MAMMON.   Ha, Lungs!

FACE. His coach is at the door. Avoid his sight,
  For he's as furious as his sister's mad.

MAMMON. Alas!

FACE.   My brain is quite undone with the fume, sir,
  I ne'er must hope to be mine own man again.   70

MAMMON. Is all lost, Lungs? Will nothing be preserved
  Of all our cost?

FACE.   Faith, very little, sir;
  A peck of coals or so, which is cold comfort, sir.

MAMMON. O my voluptuous mind! I am justly punished.

FACE. And so am I, sir.

MAMMON.   Cast from all my hopes—   75

FACE. Nay, certainties, sir.

MAMMON.   By mine own base affections.

SUBTLE. [*seeming to come to himself*] O, the cursed fruits of vice
    and lust!

2. The date of the play's action, November 1, was All Saint's Day in the church calendar.
3. In smoke.

MAMMON.   Good father,
  It was my sin. Forgive it.
SUBTLE.   Hangs my roof
  Over us still, and will not fall? O justice
  Upon us, for this wicked man!
FACE.   Nay, look, sir,   80
  You grieve him now with staying in his sight.
  Good sir, the nobleman will come too, and take you,
  And that may breed a tragedy.
MAMMON.   I'll go.
FACE. Ay, and repent at home, sir. It may be,
  For some good penance you may have it yet;   85
  A hundred pound to the box at Bedlam[4]
MAMMON.   Yes.
FACE. For the restoring such as—have their wits.
MAMMON.   I'll do't.
FACE. I'll send one to you to receive it.
MAMMON.   Do.
  Is no projection left?
FACE.   All flown, or stinks, sir.
MAMMON. Will nought be saved that's good for medicine,
    think'st thou?   90
FACE. I cannot tell, sir. There will be, perhaps,
  Something about the scraping of the shards,
  Will cure the itch [aside]—though not your itch of mind,
    sir.—
  It shall be saved for you, and sent home. Good sir,
  This way for fear the lord should meet you.   [Exit MAMMON.]
SUBTLE.   [raising his head] Face!   95
FACE. Ay.
SUBTLE.   Is he gone?
FACE.   Yes, and as heavily
  As all the gold he hoped for were in's blood.
  Let us be light, though.
SUBTLE.   [leaping up] Ay, as balls, and bound
  And hit our heads against the roof for joy.
  There's so much of our care now cast away.   100
FACE. Now to our Don.
SUBTLE.   Yes, your young widow by this time
  Is made a countess, Face; she's been in travail[5]
  Of a young heir for you.

---

4. Giving money for support of lunatics was a common gesture of repentance, very appropriate
  here.
5. At work on.

FACE.   Good, sir.
SUBTLE.   Off with your case,[6]
And greet her kindly, as a bridegroom should,
After these common hazards.
FACE.   Very well, sir.   105
Will you go fetch Don Diego off the while?
SUBTLE. And fetch him over too, if you'll be pleased, sir;
Would Dol were in her place to pick his pockets now!
FACE. Why, you can do't as well, if you would set to't.
I pray you prove your virtue.[7]
SUBTLE.   For your sake, sir.   [*Exeunt.*]   110

ACT IV   SCENE 6

[*Enter* SURLY *and* DAME PLIANT.]
SURLY. Lady, you see into what hands you are fallen;
'Mongst what a nest of villains! And how near
Your honor was t'have catched a certain clap,
Through your credulity, had I but been
So punctually forward, as place, time,   5
And other circumstances would have made a man;
For you're a handsome woman. Would you were wise too!
I am a gentleman come here disguised,
Only to find the knaveries of this citadel;
And where I might have wronged your honor, and have not,   10
I claim some interest in your love. You are,
They say, a widow, rich; and I'm a bachelor,
Worth nought. Your fortunes may make me a man,
As mine have preserved you a woman. Think upon it,
And whether I have deserved you or no.
DAME PLIANT.   I will, sir.   15
SURLY. And for these household-rogues, let me alone
To treat with them.
        [*Enter* SUBTLE.]
SUBTLE.   How doth my noble Diego,
And my dear madam countess? Hath the count
Been courteous, lady? Liberal, and open?
Donzel, methinks you look melancholic,   20
After your *coitum*, and scurvy! Truly,
I do not like the dulness of your eye;
It hath a heavy cast, 'tis upsee Dutch,[8]

6. His costume as Lungs.
7. Talents.
8. Dull, stupefied, like a man who has drunk too much strong beer.

And says you are a lumpish whoremaster.
Be lighter, I will make your pockets so.					25
		[*Attempts to pick them.*]
SURLY. [*Throws open his cloak.*] Will you, Don bawd and pick-
	purse? [*Strikes him down.*] How now! Reel you?
Stand up, sir, you shall find, since I'm so heavy,
I'll give you equal weight.
SUBTLE.					Help! Murder!
SURLY.					No, sir,
There's no such thing intended: a good cart,
And a clean whip[9] shall ease you of that fear.					30
I am the Spanish don *that should be cozened*,
Do *you see, cozened*? Where's your Captain Face,
That parcel broker,[1] and whole-bawd, all rascal?
		[*Enter* FACE *in his uniform.*]
FACE. How, Surly!
SURLY.			O, make your approach, good Captain.
I have found from whence your copper rings and spoons					35
Come, now, wherewith you cheat abroad in taverns.
'Twas here you learned t'anoint your boot with brimstone,
Then rub men's gold on't for a kind of touch,
And say 'twas naught, when you had changed the color,
That you might have't for nothing.[2] And this doctor,					40
Your sooty, smoky-bearded compeer, he
Will close you so much gold, in a bolt's-head,
And, on a turn, convey in the stead another
With sublimed mercury, that shall burst in the heat,
And fly out all *in fumo!*[3] Then weeps Mammon;					45
Then swoons his worship. [FACE *slips out.*] Or, he is the
	Faustus[4]
That casteth figures and can conjure, cures
Plague, piles, and pox, by the ephemerides,[5]
And holds intelligence with all the bawds
And midwives of three shires: while you send in—					50
Captain!—What! Is he gone?—damsels with child,
Wives that are barren, or the waiting-maid

---

9. Cart and whip were the usual fate of bawds.
1. Part-time pimp.
2. The swindle seems to involve persuading men that the real gold they have is worthless, and
	then buying it cheaply.
3. This trick is to take real gold from a victim, pretend to use it in an experiment, and, when
	the experiment fails, keep the original gold.
4. I.e., magician.
5. The astrological calendar; "holds intelligence": keeps in touch with.

With the green sickness.[6] [*Seizes Subtle as he is slipping off.*]
                                —Nay, sir, you must tarry,
Though he be scaped; and answer by the ears, sir.

ACT IV   SCENE 7

[*Enter* FACE *with* KASTRIL.]
FACE. Why, now's the time, if ever you will quarrel
  Well, as they say, and be a true-born child.[7]
  The doctor and your sister both are abused.
KASTRIL. Where is he? Which is he? He is a slave,
  Whate'er he is, and the son of a whore. Are you   5
  The man, sir, I would know?
SURLY.   I should be loath, sir,
  To confess so much.
KASTRIL.   Then you lie in your throat.[8]
SURLY.   How!
FACE. [*to* KASTRIL] A very arrant rogue, sir, and a cheater,
  Employed here by another conjurer
  That does not love the Doctor, and would cross him,   10
  If he knew how.
SURLY.   Sir, you are abused.
KASTRIL.   You lie;
  And 'tis no matter.
FACE.   Well said, sir! He is
  The impudent'st rascal—
SURLY.   You are indeed. Will you hear me,
    sir?
FACE. By no means: bid him be gone.
KASTRIL.   Be gone, sir, quickly.
SURLY. This's strange! Lady, do you inform your brother.   15
FACE. There is not such a foist[9] in all the town.
  The Doctor had him presently;[1] and finds yet,
  The Spanish count will come here. [*aside*]—Bear up, Subtle.
SUBTLE. Yes, sir, he must appear within this hour.
FACE. And yet this rogue would come in a disguise,   20
  By the temptation of another spirit,
  To trouble our art, though he could not hurt it!
KASTRIL.   Ay,

6. Chlorosis: anemia found in young women, due to an iron deficiency, causing a characteristic
  greenish color on the skin.
7. I.e., knight-errant.
8. All Kastril knows of is the direct assault.
9. Cheating rogue.
1. Caught on to him at once.

.   I know. [DAME PLIANT *whispers to her brother.*]—Away, you talk
     like a foolish mauther.[2]
SURLY. Sir, all is truth she says.
FACE.   Do not believe him, sir.
     He is the lyingest swabber! Come your ways, sir.   25
SURLY. You are valiant, out of company![3]
KASTRIL.   Yes, how then, sir?
     [*Enter* DRUGGER *with a piece of damask.*]
FACE. Nay, here's an honest fellow, too, that knows him,
     And all his tricks. [*aside to* DRUGGER]—Make good what I say,
        Abel,
     This cheater would have cozened thee o' the widow.—
     He owes this honest Drugger here seven pound   30
     He has had on him two-penny' orths of tobacco.
DRUGGER. Yes, sir. And he's damned himself three terms to pay
        me.[4]
FACE. And what does he owe for *lotium?*
DRUGGER.   Thirty shillings, sir;
     And for six syringes.
SURLY.   Hydra of villainy![5]
FACE. Nay, sir, you must quarrel him out o'the house.
KASTRIL.   I will.   35
     —Sir, if you get not out o' doors, you lie;
     And you are a pimp.
SURLY.   Why, this is madness, sir,
     Not valor in you; I must laugh at this.
KASTRIL. It is my humor: you are a pimp and a trig,[6]
     And an *Amadis de Gaul,* or a *Don Quixote.*   40
DRUGGER. Or a knight o' the curious coxcomb, do you see?
     [*Enter* ANANIAS.]
ANANIAS. Peace to the household.
KASTRIL.   I'll keep peace for no man.
ANANIAS. Casting of dollars is concluded lawful.
KASTRIL. Is he the constable?
SUBTLE.   Peace, Ananias.
FACE.   No, sir.
KASTRIL. Then you are an otter, and a shad, a whit,   45

---

2. Stupid girl.
3. I.e., you're brave now that you have someone to back you up.
4. I.e., has sworn for the last three terms (of court) to pay me back; "lotium": stale urine, used
   as a hair tonic.
5. The Hydra was a many-headed dragon of mythology; the more heads Hercules cut off, the
   more grew back again.
6. Coxcomb—i.e., a fop, simpleton; *Amadis de Gault* eponymous hero of a Spanish romance
   translated into English about 1590; *Don Quixote*: the famous knight who tries to revive chiv-
   alry in Cervantes's tale, the first part of which was published in 1605. Jonson professed an
   aversion to this sort of romantic literature.

   A very tim.[7]

SURLY.   You'll hear me, sir?

KASTRIL.   I will not.

ANANIAS. What is the motive?

SUBTLE.   Zeal in the young gentleman,
   Against his Spanish slops.[8]

ANANIAS.   They are profane,
   Lewd, superstitious, and idolatrous breeches.

SURLY. New rascals!

KASTRIL.   Will you be gone, sir?

ANANIAS.   Avoid,[9] Satan!   50
   Thou art not of the light! That ruff of pride
   About thy neck, betrays thee; and is the same
   With that which the unclean birds, in seventy seven,[1]
   Were seen to prank it with on divers coasts.
   Thou look'st like antichrist, in that lewd hat.   55

SURLY. I must give way.

KASTRIL.   Be gone, sir.

SURLY.   But I'll take
   A course with you—

ANANIAS.   Depart, proud Spanish fiend!

SURLY. Captain and Doctor—

ANANIAS.   Child of perdition!

KASTRIL.   Hence, sir!
                       [*Exit* SURLY.]

   Did I not quarrel bravely?

FACE.   Yes, indeed, sir.

KASTRIL. Nay, an I give my mind to't, I shall do't.   60

FACE. O, you must follow, sir, and threaten him tame.
   He'll turn again else.

KASTRIL.   I'll re-turn him then.   [*Exit* KASTRIL.]
             [SUBTLE *takes* ANANIAS *aside.*]

FACE. Drugger, this rogue prevented[2] us, for thee;
   We had determined that thou shouldst have come
   In a Spanish suit, and have carried her so; and he,   65
   A brokerly[3] slave, goes, puts it on himself.
   Hast brought the damask?

---

7. Otter: an animal of uncertain classification—neither fish nor fowl; "shad": a herring—used also, as here, as a term of abuse; "whit": smallest amount (Capt. Whit in Jonson's play *Bartholomew Fair* is a bawd); "tim" is of unknown origin.
8. Breeches.
9. Begone.
1. Perhaps a reference to Spanish troops that in 1567, under the duke of Alva, invaded Holland to put down a Protestant rising there.
2. Forestalled.
3. Meddling.

DRUGGER.   Yes, sir.
FACE.   Thou must borrow
  A Spanish suit. Hast thou no credit with the players?
DRUGGER. Yes, sir; did you never see me play the Fool?[4]
FACE. I know not, Nab. [*aside*]—Thou shalt, if I can help it.—   70
  Hieronimo's[5] old cloak, ruff, and hat will serve;
  I'll tell thee more when thou bring'st 'em.   [*Exit* DRUGGER.]
ANANIAS.   Sir, I know
  The Spaniard hates the brethren,[6] and hath spies
  Upon their actions: and that this was one
  I make no scruple.[7] But the holy synod   75
  Have been in prayer and meditation for it;
  And 'tis revealed no less to them than me,
  That casting of money is most lawful.
SUBTLE.   True,
  But here I cannot do it; if the house
  Should chance to be suspected, all would out,   80
  And we be locked up in the Tower[8] forever,
  To make gold there for the state, never come out,[9]
  And then are you defeated.
ANANIAS.   I will tell
  This to the elders and the weaker brethren
  That the whole company of the separation   85
  May join in humble prayer again.
SUBTLE.   And fasting.
ANANIAS. Yea, for some fitter place. The peace of mind
  Rest with these walls!   [*Exit* ANANIAS.]
SUBTLE.   Thanks, courteous Ananias.
FACE. What did he come for?
SUBTLE.   About casting dollars,
  Presently out of hand.[1] And so I told him,   90
  A Spanish minister came here to spy,
  Against the faithful—
FACE.   I conceive. Come, Subtle,
  Thou art so down upon the least disaster!
  How wouldst thou have done, if I had not helped thee out?

---

4. There may be an in-company joke here, if the part of Drugger was played in the first production by the man who generally took fools' roles for the King's Men.
5. Hieronimo was a figure in Thomas Kyd's play *The Spanish Tragedy*, published anonymously
   in 1592.
6. I.e., the Puritan brethren.
7. Have no doubt.
8. The Tower of London, reserved for traitors and criminals of distinction—not the common jail
   in which vulgar con-men would actually be held.
9. If they were ever arrested, the government would use their magical powers for its own
   advantage.
1. On the spot, right away.

SUBTLE. I thank thee, Face, for the angry boy, i' faith.   95
FACE. Who would have looked it should have been that rascal
  Surly? He had dyed his beard and all. Well, sir,
  Here's damask come to make you a suit.
SUBTLE.   Where's Drugger?
FACE. He is gone to borrow me a Spanish habit;
  I'll be the count, now.
SUBTLE.   But where's the widow?   100
FACE. Within, with my lord's sister; madam Dol
  Is entertaining her.
SUBTLE.   By your favor, Face,
  Now she is honest, I will stand again.
FACE. You will not offer it?
SUBTLE.   Why?
FACE.   Stand to your word,
  Or—here comes Dol!—she knows—
SUBTLE.   You're tyrannous still.   105
     [*Enter* DOL *hastily.*]
FACE. Strict for my right. How now, Dol! Hast told her,
  The Spanish count will come?
DOL.   Yes; but another is come,
  You little looked for!
FACE.   Who's that?
DOL.   Your master;
  The master of the house.
SUBTLE.   How, Dol!
FACE.   She lies,
  This is some trick. Come, leave your quiblins,[2] Dorothy.   110
DOL. Look out, and see.   [FACE *goes to the window.*]
SUBTLE.   Art thou in earnest?
DOL.   'Slight,
  Forty o' the neighbors are about him, talking.
FACE. 'Tis he by this good day.
DOL.   'Twill prove ill day
  For some on us.
FACE.   We are undone and taken.
DOL. Lost, I'm afraid.
SUBTLE.   You said he would not come,   115
  While there died one a week within the liberties.[3]
FACE. No: 'twas within the walls.
SUBTLE.   Was't so? Cry you mercy;

---

2. Jokes.
3. The suburbs, outside the city itself, and so at "liberty" from its regulations. "Within the walls":
  within the city proper.

I thought the liberties. What shall we do now, Face?
FACE. Be silent. Not a word, if he call or knock.
I'll into mine old shape again and meet him,   120
Of Jeremy, the butler. In the mean time,
Do you two pack up all the goods and purchase[4]
That we can carry in the two trunks. I'll keep him
Off for today, if I cannot longer; and then
At night, I'll ship you both away to Ratcliff,[5]   125
Where we will meet tomorrow, and there we'll share.
Let Mammon's brass and pewter keep the cellar;
We'll have another time for that. But, Dol,
'Prithee go heat a little water quickly;
Subtle must shave me. All my Captain's beard   130
Must off, to make me appear smooth Jeremy.
You'll do it?
SUBTLE.   Yes, I'll shave you, as well as I can.
FACE. And not cut my throat, but trim me?
SUBTLE.   You shall see, sir.
                                          [*Exeunt.*]

Act V

ACT V   SCENE 1. *THE LANE BEFORE* LOVEWIT'*S DOOR*

[*Enter* LOVEWIT, *with several of the* NEIGHBORS.]
LOVEWIT. Has there been such resort,[6] say you?
1 NEIGHBOR.   Daily, sir.
2 NEIGHBOR. And nightly, too.
3 NEIGHBOR.   Ay, some as brave as lords.
4 NEIGHBOR. Ladies and gentlewomen.
5 NEIGHBOR.   Citizens' wives.
1 NEIGHBOR. And knights.
6 NEIGHBOR.   In coaches.
2 NEIGHBOR.   Yes, and oyster-women.
1 NEIGHBOR. Beside other gallants.
3 NEIGHBOR.   Sailors' wives.
4 NEIGHBOR.   Tobacco men.   5
5 NEIGHBOR. Another Pimlico![7]
LOVEWIT.   What should my knave advance,
To draw this company? He hung out no banners
Of a strange calf with five legs to be seen?

---

4. Booty, loot.
5. Down the Thames, to the East.
6. Throng of visitors.
7. A popular carnival held at Hogsden, now Hoxton, outside London.

Or a huge lobster with six claws?
6 NEIGHBOR.   No, sir.
3 NEIGHBOR. We had gone in then, sir.
LOVEWIT.   He has no gift   10
  Of teaching in the nose that e'er I knew of.[8]
  You saw no bills set up that promised cure
  Of agues, or the tooth-ache?
2 NEIGHBOR.   No such thing, sir.
LOVEWIT. Nor heard a drum struck for baboons or puppets?
5 NEIGHBOR. Neither, sir.
LOVEWIT.   What device should he bring forth now?   15
  I love a teeming wit as I love my nourishment.
  Pray God he have not kept such open house,
  That he hath sold my hangings and my bedding!
  I left him nothing else. If he have eat them,
  A plague o' the moth,[9] say I! Sure he has got   20
  Some bawdy pictures to call all this ging;[1]
  The friar and the nun; or the new motion
  Of the knight's courser covering the parson's mare,
  The boy of six year old with the great thing.
  Or't may be, he has the fleas that run at tilt[2]   25
  Upon a table, or some dog to dance.
  When saw you him?
1 NEIGHBOR.   Who, sir, Jeremy?
2 NEIGHBOR.   Jeremy butler?
  We saw him not this month.
LOVEWIT.   How!
4 NEIGHBOR.   Not these five weeks, sir.
1 NEIGHBOR. These six weeks at the least.
LOVEWIT.   You amaze me, neighbors!
5 NEIGHBOR. Sure, if your worship know not where he is,   30
  He's slipped away.
NEIGHBOR.   Pray god, he be not made away!
LOVEWIT. Ha! It's no time to question, then. [Knocks at the door.]
6 NEIGHBOR.   About
  Some three weeks since, I heard a doleful cry,
  As I sat up a-mending my wife's stockings.
LOVEWIT. 'Tis strange that none will answer! Didst thou hear   35
  A cry, sayst thou?
6 NEIGHBOR.   Yes, sir, like unto a man

---

8. Teaching how to cant, or preach through the nose, was not a real activity, but Jonson lists it
  as another stroke against the Puritans.
9. The locution was proverbial; it implies irritation but not deep distress.
1. Gang; "motion": show.
2. In a flea circus, creatures trained to imitate a knightly joust.

That had been strangled an hour, and could not speak.
2 NEIGHBOR. I heard it too, just this day three weeks, at two
o'clock
Next morning.
LOVEWIT.   These be miracles, or you make 'em so!
A man an hour strangled, and could not speak,   40
And both you heard him cry?
3 NEIGHBOR.   Yes, downward, sir.
LOVEWIT. Thou art a wise fellow. Give me thy hand, I pray thee.
What trade art thou on?
3 NEIGHBOR.   A smith, an't please your worship.
LOVEWIT. A smith! Then lend me thy help to get this door open.
3 NEIGHBOR. That I will presently, sir, but fetch my tools— [Exit]   45
1 NEIGHBOR. Sir, best to knock again, afore you break it.
LOVEWIT. [Knocks again.] I will.

ACT V   SCENE 2

[Enter FACE, in his butler's livery.]
FACE.   What mean you, sir?
1. 2. 4. NEIGHBORS.   O, here's
Jeremy!
FACE. Good sir, come from³ the door.
LOVEWIT.   Why, what's the matter?
FACE. Yet farther, you are too near yet.
LOVEWIT.   In the name of wonder,
What means the fellow?
FACE.   The house, sir, has been visited.
LOVEWIT. What, with the plague? Stand thou then farther.
FACE.   No, sir,   5
I had it not.
LOVEWIT.   Who had it then? I left
None else but thee in the house.
FACE.   Yes, sir, my fellow,
The cat that kept the buttery, had it on her
A week before I spied it; but I got her
Conveyed away in the night: and so I shut   10
The house up for a month—
LOVEWIT.   How!
FACE.   Purposing then, sir,
T'have burnt rose-vinegar, treacle, and tar,
And have made it sweet, that you should ne'er have known it;
Because I knew the news would but afflict you, sir.

3. Step away from.

LOVEWIT. Breathe less, and farther off! Why this is stranger!   15
  The neighbors tell me all here that the doors
  Have still been open—
FACE.   How, sir!
LOVEWIT.   Gallants, men and women,
  And of all sorts, tag-rag, been seen to flock here
  In threaves,[4] these ten weeks, as to a second Hogsden,
  In days of Pimlico and Eye-bright.
FACE.   Sir,   20
  Their wisdoms will not say so.
LOVEWIT.   Today they speak
  Of coaches and gallants; one in a French-hood
  Went in, they tell me; and another was seen
  In a velvet gown at the window! Divers more
  Pass in and out!
FACE.   They did pass through the doors then,   25
  Or walls, I assure their eyesights, and their spectacles;
  For here, sir, are the keys, and here have been,
  In this my pocket, now above twenty days!
  And for before, I kept the fort alone there.
  But that 'tis yet not deep in the afternoon,   30
  I should believe my neighbors had seen double
  Through the black pot,[5] and made these apparitions!
  For, on my faith to your worship, for these three weeks
  And upwards, the door has not been opened.
LOVEWIT.   Strange!
1 NEIGHBOR. Good faith, I think I saw a coach.
2 NEIGHBOR.   And I too,   35
  I'd have been sworn.
LOVEWIT.   Do you but think it now?
  And but one coach?
4 NEIGHBOR.   We cannot tell, sir; Jeremy
  Is a very honest fellow.
FACE.   Did you see me at all?
1 NEIGHBOR. No; that we are sure on.
2 NEIGHBOR.   I'll be sworn o' that.
LOVEWIT. Fine rogues to have your testimonies built on!   40
    [*Enter third* NEIGHBOR, *with his tools.*]
3 NEIGHBOR. Is Jeremy come!
1 NEIGHBOR.   O, yes; you may leave your tools;
  We were deceived, he says.

---

4. Throngs. Pimlico and Eye-bright were places where cakes and ale could be consumed by
  holiday crowds.
5. I.e., of liquor.

2 NEIGHBOR.   He has had the keys;
And the door has been shut these three weeks.
3 NEIGHBOR.   Like enough.
LOVEWIT. Peace, and get hence, you changelings.
        [*Enter* SURLY *and* MAMMON.]
FACE. [*aside*]   Surly come!
And Mammon made acquainted! They'll tell all.   45
How shall I beat them off? What shall I do?
Nothing's more wretched than a guilty conscience.

                    ACT V   SCENE 3

SURLY. No, sir, he was a great physician. This,
    It was no bawdy-house, but a mere chancel![6]
    You knew the lord and his sister.
MAMMON.   Nay, good Surly—
SURLY. *The happy word, "Be rich"*—
MAMMON.   Play not the tyrant—
SURLY. *Should be today pronounced to all your friends.*   5
    And where be your andirons now? And your brass pots,
    That should have been golden flagons and great wedges?
MAMMON. Let me but breathe. What, they have shut their doors,
    Methinks!
SURLY.   Ay, now 'tis holiday with them.
MAMMON.   Rogues, [*He and*
        SURLY *knock.*]
    Cozeners, impostors, bawds!
FACE.   What mean you, sir?   10
MAMMON. To enter if we can.
FACE.   Another man's house!
    Here is the owner, sir. Turn you to him,
    And speak your business.
MAMMON.   Are you, sir, the owner?
LOVEWIT. Yes, sir.
MAMMON.   And are those knaves within your cheaters?
LOVEWIT. What knaves? What cheaters?
MAMMON.   Subtle and his Lungs.   15
FACE. The gentleman is distracted, sir! No lungs,
    Nor lights[7] have been seen here these three weeks, sir,
    Within these doors, upon my word.
SURLY.   Your word,

---

6. I.e., the house was not a brothel but pure as a church (Surly reminds Mammon of his own
    words).
7. Lungs of animals sold for food (Face is pretending to misunderstand the sense of "Lungs,"
    his role as Subtle's assistant, in line 15).

Groom arrogant?

FACE.   Yes, sir, I am the housekeeper,
And know the keys have not been out of my hands.   20

SURLY. This's a new Face.

FACE.   You do mistake the house, sir:
What sign was't at?

SURLY.   You rascal! This is one
Of the confederacy. Come, let's get officers,
And force the door.

LOVEWIT.   Pray you stay, gentlemen.

SURLY. No, sir, we'll come with warrant.

MAMMON.   Ay, and then   25
We shall have your doors open. [*Exeunt* MAMMON *and* SURLY.]

LOVEWIT.   What means this?

FACE. I cannot tell, sir.

1 NEIGHBOR.   These are two of the gallants
That we do think we saw.

FACE.   Two of the fools!
You talk as idly as they. Good faith, sir,
I think the moon has crazed 'em all. [*aside*]—O me,   30
          [*Enter* KASTRIL.]
The angry boy come too! He'll make a noise,
And ne'er away till he have betrayed us all.

KASTRIL. [*knocking*] What, rogues, bawds, slaves, you'll open the
          door, anon!
Punk, cockatrice,[8] my suster! By this light
I'll fetch the marshal to you. You are a whore   35
To keep your castle—

FACE.   Who would you speak with, sir?

KASTRIL. The bawdy Doctor, and the cozening Captain,
And puss my suster.[9]

LOVEWIT.   This is something, sure!

FACE. Upon my trust, the doors were never open, sir.

KASTRIL. I have heard all their tricks told me twice over,   40
By the fat knight and the lean gentleman.[1]

LOVEWIT. Here comes another.
          [*Enter* ANANIAS *and* TRIBULATION.]

FACE.   Ananias too?
And his pastor!

TRIBULATION. [*beating at the door*] The doors are shut against us.

ANANIAS. Come forth, you seed of sulphur, sons of fire![2]

---

8. Slang for a prostitute. A whore in a house was often spoken of as keeping a castle.
9. "Puss" is as likely to refer to a rabbit as a cat.
1. I.e., Mammon and Surly.
2. Much of Ananias's language is from the book of Revelation.

Your stench it is broke forth; abomination   45
Is in the house.
KASTRIL.   Ay, my suster's there.
ANANIAS.   The place,
It is become a cage of unclean birds.[3]
KASTRIL. Yes, I will fetch the scavenger,[4] and the constable.
TRIBULATION. You shall do well.
ANANIAS.   We'll join to weed them out.
KASTRIL. You will not come then, punk device,[5] my sister.   50
ANANIAS. Call her not sister; she's a harlot verily.
KASTRIL. I'll raise the street.
LOVEWIT.   Good gentleman, a word.
ANANIAS. Satan avoid, and hinder not our zeal!
                    [*Exeunt* ANANIAS TRIBULATION, *and* KASTRIL.]
LOVEWIT. The world's turned Bedlam.[6]
FACE.   These are all broke loose
Out of St. Katherine's, where they use to keep   55
The better sort of mad-folks.
1 NEIGHBOR.   All these persons
We saw go in and out here.
2 NEIGHBOR.   Yes, indeed, sir.
3 NEIGHBOR. These were the parties.
FACE.   Peace, you drunkards! Sir,
I wonder at it! Please you to give me leave
To touch the door, I'll try an the lock be changed.   60
LOVEWIT. It 'mazes me!
FACE. [*Goes to the door.*] Good faith, sir, I believe
There's no such thing. 'Tis all *deceptio visus.*[7] —
[*aside*] Would I could get him away.
DAPPER.   [*within*] Master Captain! Master Doctor!
LOVEWIT. Who's that?
FACE.   [*aside*] Our clerk within, that I forgot!—I know
not, sir.
DAPPER. [*within*] For God's sake, when will her Grace be at
leisure?
FACE.   Ha!   65
Illusions, some spirit o' the air! [*aside*]—His gag is melted,
And now he sets out the throat.
DAPPER.   [*within*] I am almost stifled—

3. Cf. 4.7.53 and also Revelation 18.2 ("Babylon the great is fallen, is fallen, and is become . . .
a cage of every unclean and hateful bird").
4. Street sweeper.
5. She is a prostitute proclaimed by her device, i.e., her heraldic emblem, with a play on the
old French phrase for perfection, *point devise.*
6. Run mad. St. Katherine's (line 55) was another, older, madhouse.
7. Optical illusion.

FACE. [*aside*] Would you were altogether.

LOVEWIT.   'Tis in the house.
   Ha! list.

FACE.   Believe it, sir, in the air.

LOVEWIT.   Peace, you—

DAPPER. [*within*] Mine aunt's grace does not use me well.

SUBTLE.   [*within*] You fool,   70
   Peace, you'll mar all.

FACE. [*speaks through the key-hole, while* LOVEWIT *advances to
      the door unobserved*] Or you will else, you rogue.

LOVEWIT. O, is it so? Then you converse with spirits!—
   Come, sir. No more of your tricks, good Jeremy,
   The truth, the shortest way.

FACE.   Dismiss this rabble, sir.—
   [*aside.*] What shall I do? I am catched.

LOVEWIT.   Good neighbors,   75
   I thank you all. You may depart. [*Exeunt* NEIGHBORS.]—Come
      sir,
   You know that I am an indulgent master;
   And therefore, conceal nothing. What's your medicine,
   To draw so many several sorts of wild fowl?[8]

FACE. Sir, you were wont to affect mirth and wit: 80
   (But here's no place to talk on't in the street)
   Give me but leave to make the best of my fortune,
   And only pardon me the abuse of your house;
   It's all I beg. I'll help you to a widow,
   In recompense, that you shall give me thanks for,   85
   Will make you seven years younger, and a rich one.
   'Tis but your putting on a Spanish cloak.
   I have her within. You need not fear the house;
   It was not visited.[9]

LOVEWIT.   But by me, who came
   Sooner than you expected.

FACE.   It is true, sir.   90
   'Pray you forgive me.

LOVEWIT.   Well; let's see your widow.   [*Exeunt.*]

ACT V   SCENE 4. *A ROOM IN* LOVEWIT'S *HOUSE*

   [*Enter* SUBTLE, *leading in* DAPPER, *with his eyes bound as
   before.*]

SUBTLE. How! Have you eaten your gag?

DAPPER.   Yes, faith, it crumbled

8. Geese and ducks to be snared.
9. Touched by the plague.

Away in my mouth.

SUBTLE.   You have spoiled all then.

DAPPER.   No,

I hope my aunt of Fairy will forgive me.

SUBTLE. Your aunt's a gracious lady; but in troth
You were to blame.

DAPPER.   The fume did overcome me,   5

And I did do't to stay my stomach. 'Pray you
So satisfy her Grace.[1]

    [*Enter* FACE *in his uniform*].

Here comes the Captain.

FACE. How now! Is his mouth down?[2]

SUBTLE.   Ay, he has spoken!

FACE. [*aside*] A pox, I heard him, and you too.—[*loudly*]
    He's undone then.—[*He pushes* DAPPER *away and whispers
    to* SUBTLE.]

I have been fain to say, the house is haunted   10
With spirits, to keep churl[3] hack.

SUBTLE.   And hast thou done it?

FACE. Sure, for this night.

SUBTLE.   Why, then triumph and sing
Of Face so famous, the precious king
Of present wits.

FACE.   Did you not hear the coil[4]
About the door?

SUBTLE.   Yes, and I dwindled with it.   15

FACE. Show him his aunt, and let him be dispatched;
I'll send her to you.   [*Exit* FACE.]

SUBTLE.   Well, sir, your aunt her Grace
Will give you audience presently, on my suit,[5]
And the Captain's word that you did not eat your gag
In any contempt of her highness. [*Unbinds his eyes.*]

DAPPER.   Not I, in troth, sir.   20

    [*Enter* DOL *like the queen of Fairy.*]

SUBTLE. Here she is come. Down o' your knees and wriggle.
She has a stately presence. [DAPPER *kneels and shuffles towards
    her.*] Good! Yet nearer,
And bid, God save you!

DAPPER.   Madam!

SUBTLE.   And your aunt.

---

1. Explain it all to her Grace.
2. Has he opened his mouth?
3. I.e., Lovewit, the man from the country.
4. Racket.
5. At my request.

DAPPER. And my most gracious aunt, God save your Grace.

DOL. Nephew, we thought to have been angry with you;   25
   But that sweet face of yours hath turned the tide.
   And made it flow with joy, that ebbed of love.
   Arise, and touch our velvet gown.

SUBTLE.   The skirts,
   And kiss 'em. So!

DOL.   Let me now stroke that head.
   Much, nephew, shalt thou win, much shalt thou spend;   30
   Much shalt thou give away, much shalt thou lend.

SUBTLE. [*aside*] Ay, much indeed—Why do you not thank her
   Grace?

DAPPER. I cannot speak for joy.

SUBTLE.   See, the kind wretch!
   Your Grace's kinsman right.[6]

DOL.   Give me the bird.
   Here is your fly in a purse, about your neck, cousin;   35
   Wear it and feed it about this day se'en-night,[7]
   On your right wrist—

SUBTLE.   Open a vein with a pin,
   And let it suck but once a week; till then,
   You must not look on't.

DOL.   No. And, kinsman,
   Bear yourself worthy of the blood you come on.   40

SUBTLE. Her Grace would have you eat no more *Woolsack* pies,[8]
   Nor *Dagger* frumety.

DOL.   Nor break his fast
   In *Heaven* and *Hell*.[9]

SUBTLE.   She's with you everywhere!
   Nor play with costermongers, at mum-chance, tray-trip,[1]
   God-make-you-rich (whenas your aunt has done it); but keep   45
   The gallant'st company, and the best games—

DAPPER.   Yes, sir.

SUBTLE. Gleek and primero;[2] and what you get, be true to us.

DAPPER. By this hand, I will.

SUBTLE.   You may bring's a thousand pound
   Before tomorrow night, if but three thousand
   Be stirring, an you will.

---

6. True kinsman; "kind": tender-hearted.
7. A week from today.
8. Subtle advises against the kind of pies sold at the Woolsack, a London tavern, and "frumety," a kind of spiced pudding sold at the Dagger, another tavern.
9. Heaven and Hell were a pair of low taverns in Westminster; there was a third nearby, known as Purgatory.
1. "Mum-chance," "tray-trip," and "God-make-you-rich" were simple games of chance.
2. See 2.3.284–85.

DAPPER.   I swear I will then.   50
SUBTLE. Your fly will learn you all games.
FACE.   [*within*] Have you done there?
SUBTLE. Your Grace will command him no more duties?
DOL.   No;
    But come, and see me often. I may chance
    To leave him three or four hundred chests of treasure,
    And some twelve thousand acres of Fairyland,   55
    If he game well and comely with good gamesters.
SUBTLE. There's a kind aunt! Kiss her departing part.—
    But you must sell your forty mark a year, now.
DAPPER. Ay, sir, I mean.
SUBTLE.   Or, give't away; pox on't!
DAPPER. I'll give't mine aunt; I'll go and fetch the writings. [*Exit.*]   60
SUBTLE. 'Tis well, away.
        [*Enter* FACE.]
FACE.   Where's Subtle?
SUBTLE.   Here; what news?
FACE. Drugger is at the door, go take his suit,
    And bid him fetch a parson, presently;
    Say, he shall marry the widow. Thou shalt spend
    A hundred pound by the service![3] [*Exit* SUBTLE.] Now, Queen
        Dol,   65
    Have you packed up all?
DOL.   Yes.
FACE.   And how do you like
    The lady Pliant?
DOL.   A good dull innocent.
        [*Enter* SUBTLE.]
SUBTLE. Here's your Hieronimo's cloak and hat.
FACE.   Give me them.
SUBTLE. And the ruff too?
FACE.   Yes; I'll come to you presently.   [*Exit.*]
SUBTLE. Now he is gone about his project, Dol,   70
    I told you of, for the widow.
DOL.   'Tis direct
    Against our articles.[4]
SUBTLE.   Well, we will fit him, wench.
    Hast thou gulled her of her jewels or her bracelets?
DOL. No; but I'll do't.
SUBTLE.   Soon at night, my Dolly,
    When we are shipped, and all our goods aboard,   75

3. You'll gain a hundred pounds by doing this.
4. Articles of incorporation by which Face, Dol, and Subtle formed their original league.

Eastward for Ratcliff; we will turn our course
To Brainford,[5] westward, if thou sayst the word,
And take our leaves of this o'erweening rascal,
    This peremptory Face.
DOL.   Content, I'm weary of him.
SUBTLE. Thou'st cause, when the slave will run a wiving, Dol,   80
    Against the instrument that was drawn between us.
DOL. I'll pluck his bird as bare as I can.
SUBTLE.   Yes, tell her
    She must by any means address some present
    To the cunning man, make him amends for wronging
    His art with her suspicion; send a ring,   85
    Or chain of pearl; she will be tortured else
    Extremely in her sleep, say, and have strange things
    Come to her. Wilt thou?
DOL.   Yes.
SUBTLE.   My fine flitter-mouse,[6]
    My bird o' the night! We'll tickle it at the Pigeons,[7]
    When we have all, and may unlock the trunks   90
    And say, this's mine, and thine; and thine, and mine. [*They
        kiss.*]
            [*Enter* FACE.]
FACE. What now! a-billing?
SUBTLE.   Yes, a little exalted
    In the good passage of our stock-affairs.
FACE. Drugger has brought his parson; take him in, Subtle,
    And send Nab back again to wash his face.   95
SUBTLE. I will: and shave himself?   [*Exit.*]
FACE.   If you can get him.
DOL. You are hot upon it, Face, whate'er it is!
FACE. A trick that Dol shall spend ten pound a month by.
        [*Enter* SUBTLE.]
    Is he gone?
SUBTLE.   The chaplain waits you in the hall, sir.
FACE. I'll go bestow him.[8]   [*Exit* FACE.]
DOL.   He'll now marry her, instantly.   100
SUBTLE. He cannot yet, he is not ready. Dear Dol,
    Cozen her of all thou canst. To deceive him
    Is no deceit, but justice, that would break
    Such an inextricable tie as ours was.

---

5. Instead of going down the Thames to Ratcliff, and hence presumably outward-bound, Dol and Subtle will go upriver to Brainford (Brentford), heading to the West Country.
6. Bat—as a prostitute, Dol is a night-bird.
7. The Three Pigeons Inn at Brentford, famous into the first years of the twentieth century.
8. Get him ready.

DOL. Let me alone to fit him.[9]
   [*Enter* FACE.]
FACE.   Come, my ventures,[1]   105
  You have packed up all? Where be the trunks? Bring forth.
SUBTLE. Here.
FACE.   Let us see them. Where's the money?
SUBTLE.   Here,
  In this.
FACE.   Mammon's ten pound; eight score before.
  The brethren's money, this. Drugger's and Dapper's.
  What paper's that?
DOL.   The jewel of the waiting maid's,   110
  That stole it from her lady, to know certain—
FACE. If she should have precedence of her mistress?
DOL.   Yes.
FACE. What box is that?
SUBTLE.   The fishwives' rings, I think;
  And the alewives' single money.[2] Is't not, Dol?
DOL. Yes; and the whistle that the sailor's wife   115
  Brought you to know an her husband were with Ward.[3]
FACE. We'll wet it tomorrow; and our silver beakers
  And tavern cups. Where be the French petticoats,
  And girdles and hangers?
SUBTLE.   Here, in the trunk,
  And the bolts of lawn.
FACE.   Is Drugger's damask there,   120
  And the tobacco?
SUBTLE.   Yes.
FACE.   Give me the keys.
DOL. Why you the keys?
SUBTLE.   No matter, Dol; because
  We shall not open them before he comes.   [*She gives them.*]
FACE. 'Tis true, you shall not open them, indeed;
  Nor have them forth, do you see? Not forth, Dol.
DOL.   No!   125
FACE. No, my smock-rampant.[4] The right is, my master
  Knows all, has pardoned me, and he will keep 'em;
  Doctor, 'tis true—you look—for all your figures;[5]

---

9. I.e., I'll manage to give him what he deserves.
1. Partners.
2. Loose change.
3. A notorious pirate. The whistle was evidently a silver boatswain's whistle, and Face puns off
  it: i.e., we'll wet our whistles tomorrow.
4. In mock-heraldic language, Dol's smock or slip is the emblem of her trade, and she is rampant,
  i.e., rearing up to attack Face.
5. I.e., Doctor—there's no need to stare—it's true in spite of all your calculations.

I sent for him, indeed. Wherefore, good partners,
Both he and she, be satisfied; for here   130
Determines the *indenture tripartite*[6]
'Twixt Subtle, Dol, and Face. All I can do
Is to help you over the wall, o' the backside,
Or lend you a sheet to save your velvet gown, Dol.
Here will be officers presently; bethink you   135
Of some course suddenly to 'scape the dock:[7]
For thither you'll come else. [*Loud knocking.*] Hark you,
    thunder.

SUBTLE. You are a precious fiend!

OFFICERS.   [*without*] Open the door.

FACE. Dol, I am sorry for thee, i' faith; but hearest thou?
It shall go hard but I will place thee somewhere: 140
Thou shalt have my letter to mistress Amo—[8]

DOL.   Hang you!

FACE. Or madam Cæsarean.

DOL.   Pox upon you, rogue,
Would I had but time to beat thee!

FACE.   Subtle,
Let's know where you set up next; I will send you
A customer now and then, for old acquaintance.   145
What new course have you?

SUBTLE.   Rogue, I'll hang myself;
That I may walk a greater devil than thou,
And haunt thee in the flock-bed and the buttery.[9]   [*Exeunt.*]

ACT V   SCENE 5. *AN OUTER ROOM IN* LOVEWIT'S *HOUSE*

[*Enter* LOVEWIT *in Spanish dress, with the* PARSON. *Loud
knocking at the door.*]

LOVEWIT. What do you mean, my masters?

MAMMON.   [*without*] Open your door,
Cheaters, bawds, conjurers.

OFFICERS.   [*without*] Or we'll break it open.

LOVEWIT. What warrant have you?

OFFICERS.   [*without*] Warrant enough, sir, doubt not,
If you'll not open it.

LOVEWIT.   Is there an officer, there?

OFFICERS. [*without*] Yes, two or three for failing.[1]

6. Here ends ("determines") the three-way agreement.
7. The prisoner's dock, perhaps also the executioner's dock.
8. Mistress Amo(retta) or Madam Caesarean are obviously brothel-keepers.
9. I.e., when you are sleeping and when you are eating in the "buttery," or kitchen.
1. I.e., for good measure.

LOVEWIT.   Have but patience,   5
　And I will open it straight
　　　[*Enter* FACE, *as butler.*]
FACE.   Sir, have you done?
　Is it a marriage? Perfect?
LOVEWIT.   Yes, my brain.
FACE. Off with your ruff and cloak, then; be yourself, sir.
SUBTLE. [*without*] Down with the door.
KASTRIL.   [*without*] 'Slight, ding it open.[2]
LOVEWIT.   [*opening the door*] Hold,
　Hold, gentlemen, what means this violence?   10
　　　[MAMMON, SURLY, KASTRIL, ANANIAS, TRIBULATION, *and* OF-
　　　FICERS *rush in.*]
MAMMON. Where is this collier?[3]
SURLY.   And my Captain Face?
MAMMON. These day owls.
SURLY.   That are birding in men's purses.
MAMMON. Madam suppository.
KASTRIL.   Doxy,[4] my suster.
ANANIAS.   Locusts
　Of the foul pit.
TRIBULATION.   Profane as Bel and the dragon.[5]
ANANIAS. Worse than the grasshoppers, or the lice of Egypt.   15
LOVEWIT. Good gentlemen, hear me. Are you officers,
　And cannot stay this violence?
1 OFFICER.   Keep the peace.
LOVEWIT. Gentlemen, what is the matter? Whom do you seek?
MAMMON. The chemical cozener.
SURLY.   And the Captain pander.
KASTRIL. The nun[6] my suster.
MAMMON.   Madam Rabbi.
ANANIAS.   Scorpions,   20
　And caterpillars.
LOVEWIT.   Fewer at once, I pray you.
2 OFFICER. One after another, gentlemen, I charge you,
　By virtue of my staff.[7]
ANANIAS.   They are the vessels
　Of pride, lust, and the cart.

---

2. Break it down.
3. Cheat.
4. Slut. "Madam suppository" is, of course, Dol, a "supposed" lady.
5. One of the apocryphal books of the Bible bears this title. Daniel wars upon a pagan deity (Baal) and a dragon. The grasshoppers and lice of Egypt were plagues visited on that land before the Exodus.
6. Cant term for a prostitute in a house.
7. The officers carry long rods as emblems of their authority.

LOVEWIT.   Good zeal, lie still
  A little while.
TRIBULATION.   Peace, deacon Ananias.   25
LOVEWIT. The house is mine here, and the doors are open;
  If there be any such persons as you seek for,
  Use your authority, search on o' God's name.
  I am but newly come to town, and finding
  This tumult 'bout my door, to tell you true,   30
  It somewhat 'mazed me; till my man, here, fearing
  My more displeasure, told me he had done
  Somewhat an insolent part, let out my house
  (Belike presuming on my known aversion
  From any air o' the town while there was sickness)   35
  To a Doctor and a Captain; who, what they are
  Or where they be, he knows not.
MAMMON.   Are they gone?
LOVEWIT. You may go in and search, sir. [MAMMON, ANANIAS *and*
    TRIBULATION *go in.*] Here, I find
  The empty walls worse than I left them, smoked,
  A few cracked pots and glasses, and a furnace;   40
  The ceiling fill'd with poesies of the candle,[8]
  And madam with a dildo writ o' the walls:
  Only one gentlewoman I met here,
  That is within, that said she was a widow—
KASTRIL. Ay, that's my suster; I'll go thump her. Where is she?   45
                                    [*Goes in.*]
LOVEWIT. And should have married a Spanish count, but he,
  When he come to't, neglected her so grossly
  That I, a widower, am gone through with her.
SURLY. How! Have I lost her then?
LOVEWIT.   Were you the don, sir?
  Good faith, now, she does blame you extremely, and says   50
  You swore, and told her you had ta'en the pains
  To dye your beard, and umber o'er your face,
  Borrowed a suit, and ruff, all for her love;
  And then did nothing. What an oversight
  And want of putting forward, sir, was this!   55
  Well fare an old harquebusier,[9] yet,
  Could prime his powder, and give fire, and hit,
  All in a twinkling!
    [*Enter* MAMMON.]

---

8. I.e., poems traced on the walls in candle smoke; "madam with a dildo" is obviously an obscene
  picture.
9. Musketeer.

MAMMON.   The whole nest are fled!
LOVEWIT. What sort of birds were they?
MAMMON.   A kind of choughs,[1]
    Or thievish daws, sir, that have picked my purse   60
    Of eight score and ten pounds within these five weeks,
    Beside my first materials; and my goods,
    That lie in the cellar, which I am glad they have left,
    I may have home yet.
LOVEWIT.   Think you so, sir?
MAMMON.   Ay.
LOVEWIT. By order of law, sir, but not otherwise.   65
MAMMON. Not mine own stuff?
LOVEWIT.   Sir, I can take no knowledge
    That they are yours, but by public means.
    If you can bring certificate that you were gulled of 'em,
    Or any formal writ out of a court
    That you did cozen yourself, I will not hold them.   70
MAMMON. I'll rather lose 'em.
LOVEWIT.   That you shall not, sir,
    By me, in troth. Upon these terms, they're yours.
    What should they have been, sir, turned into gold, all?
MAMMON.   No.
    I cannot tell. It may be they should. What then?
LOVEWIT. What a great loss in hope have you sustained!   75
MAMMON. Not I, the commonwealth has.
FACE.   Ay, he would have built
    The city new; and made a ditch about it
    Of silver, should have run with cream from Hogsden;
    That, every Sunday, in Moorfields,[2] the younkers,
    And tits and tom-boys should have fed on, gratis.   80
MAMMON. I will go mount a turnip-cart, and preach
    The end of the world, within these two months. Surly,
    What! In a dream?
SURLY.   Must I needs cheat myself,
    With that same foolish vice of honesty!
    Come, let us go and hearken out the rogues.   85
    That Face I'll mark for mine, if e'er I meet him.
FACE. If I can hear of him, sir, I'll bring you word,
    Unto your lodging; for in troth, they were strangers
    To me, I thought 'em honest as myself, sir.
                          [*Exeunt* MAMMON *and* SURLY.]
        [*Enter* ANANIAS *and* TRIBULATION.]

---

1. Thievish magpies.
2. See 1.4.20; "younkers": young men; "tits and tom-boys": young girls.

TRIBULATION. 'Tis well, the saints shall not lose all yet. Go,   90
  And get some carts—
LOVEWIT.   For what, my zealous friends?
ANANIAS. To bear away the portion of the righteous
  Out of this den of thieves.
LOVEWIT.   What is that portion?
ANANIAS. The goods sometime the orphans', that the brethren
  Bought with their silver pence.
LOVEWIT.   What, those in the cellar,   95
  The knight Sir Mammon claims?
ANANIAS.   I do defy
  The wicked Mammon, so do all the brethren,
  Thou profane man! I ask thee with what conscience
  Thou canst advance that idol against us,
  That have the seal?[3] Were not the shillings numbered,   100
  That made the pounds? Were not the pounds told out,
  Upon the second day of the fourth week,
  In the eighth month, upon the table dormant,[4]
  The year of the last patience of the saints,
  Six hundred and ten?[5]
LOVEWIT.   Mine earnest vehement botcher,   105
  And deacon also, I cannot dispute with you:
  But if you get you not away the sooner,
  I shall confute you with a cudgel.
ANANIAS.   Sir!
TRIBULATION. Be patient, Ananias.
ANANIAS.   I am strong,
  And will stand up, well girt, against an host,   110
  That threaten Gad in exile.[6]
LOVEWIT.   I shall send you
  To Amsterdam, to your cellar.
ANANIAS.   I will pray there
  Against thy house. May dogs defile thy walls,
  And wasps and hornets breed beneath thy roof,
  This seat of falsehood, and this cave of cozenage!   115
                        [*Exeunt* ANANIAS *and* TRIBULATION.]
          [*Enter* DRUGGER.]
LOVEWIT. Another, too?

---

3. Referring to Revelation 9.4, in which locusts are permitted to hurt "those men which have
   not the seal of god in their foreheads."
4. Fixed table.
5. I.e., October 23, 1610—the year, in this counting, beginning in March; "last patience": a
   reference to the millennium, described in Revelation, chapter 20, the thousand-year period
   before the second coming of Christ.
6. The persecuted saints, with an allusion to Genesis 49.19, in which Gad is one of the sons of
   Jacob.

DRUGGER.   Not I, sir, I am no brother.
LOVEWIT. [*beats him*] Away, you Harry Nicholas![7] Do you talk?
                                      [*Exit* DRUGGER.]
FACE. No, this was Abel Drugger. Good sir, [*to the* PARSON] go,
  And satisfy him; tell him all is done:
  He stayed too long a washing of his face.   120
  The Doctor, he shall hear of him at Westchester;[8]
  And of the Captain, tell him, at Yarmouth, or
  Some good port-town else, lying for a wind.   [*Exit* PARSON.]
  If you get off the angry child, now, sir—
    [*Enter* KASTRIL *dragging in his sister.*]
KASTRIL. Come on, you ewe, you have matched most sweetly,
    have you not?   125
  Did not I say, I would never have you tupped[9]
  But by a dubbed boy, to make you a lady-tom?
  'Slight, you are a mammet![1] O, I could touse you, now.
  Death, mun' you marry with a pox?
LOVEWIT.   You lie, boy;
  As sound as you; and I'm aforehand with you.
KASTRIL.   Anon!   130
LOVEWIT. Come, will you quarrel? I will feize[2] you, sirrah;
  Why do you not buckle to your tools?
KASTRIL.   God's light,
  This is a fine old boy as e'er I saw!
LOVEWIT. What, do you change your copy[3] now? Proceed,
  Here stands my dove; stoop[4] at her, if you dare.   135
KASTRIL. 'Slight, I must love him! I cannot choose, i' faith,
  An I should be hanged for't! Suster, I protest,
  I honor thee for this match.
LOVEWIT.   O, do you so, sir?
KASTRIL. Yes, an thou canst take tobacco and drink, old boy,
  I'll give her five hundred pound more to her marriage,   140
  Than her own state.[5]
LOVEWIT.   Fill a pipe full, Jeremy.
FACE. Yes; but go in and take it, sir.
LOVEWIT.   We will.
  I will be ruled by thee in anything, Jeremy.

---

7. Lovewit mistakes Drugger for another Puritan and calls him "Harry Nicholas" in allusion to
   the Dutch founder of a radical protestant sect, the Family of Love.
8. Face's message sends Drugger off on a couple of wild-goose chases.
9. Mated (the term is commonly applied to sheep); "a dubbed boy": a knight; "lady-tom": the
   wife of a knight.
1. Doll, puppet, idiot; "touse": beat.
2. Beat, fight.
3. Style.
4. As a hawk stoops (dives) to clutch its prey.
5. I.e., five hundred pounds in dowry, beyond what she already has from her first marriage.

KASTRIL. 'Slight, thou art not hide-bound, thou art a jovy boy.[6]
   Come, let us in, I pray thee, and take our whiffs.   145
LOVEWIT. Whiff in with your sister, brother boy.

             [*Exeunt* KASTRIL *and* DAME PLIANT.]
                               That master
  That had received such happiness by a servant,
  In such a widow, and with so much wealth,
  Were very ungrateful, if he would not be
  A little indulgent to that servant's wit,   150
  And help his fortune, though with some small strain
  Of his own candor. [*advancing*]—*Therefore, gentlemen,*
  And kind spectators, if I have outstripped
  An old man's gravity, or strict canon, think
  What a young wife and a good brain may do;   155
  Stretch age's truth sometimes, and crack it too.
  Speak for thyself, knave.
FACE.   *So I will, sir.*
  [*Advancing to the front of the stage.*] *Gentlemen,*
  My part a little fell in this last scene,
  Yet 'twas decorum.[7] *And though I am clean*
  Got off from Subtle, Surly, Mammon, Dol,   160
  Hot Ananias, Dapper, Drugger, all
  With whom I traded; yet I put myself
  On you, that are my country,[8] *and this pelf,*
  Which I have got, if you do quit me, rests
  To feast you often, and invite new guests.   165

               THE END.

                            1610

---

6. Jovial good fellow.
7. I.e., the rule that a character must not violate the nature assigned him or her at the start of
   the play. He was a bold rogue as Face, a sly rogue as Jeremy, but always a rogue.
8. I.e., appeal to a jury of my peers; "pelf": wealth, "quit": acquit.

The Queen's Masques
The first, of BLACKNESS

Personated at the court at Whitehall on the Twelfth-night, 1605.

The honor and splendor of these spectacles was such in the performance as, could those hours have lasted, this of mine now had been a
most unprofitable work. But, when it is the fate even of the greatest
and most absolute births to need and borrow a life of posterity, little
had been done to the study of magnificence in these, if presently with 5
the rage of the people, who, as a part of greatness, are privileged by
custom[1] to deface their carcasses, the spirits had also perished. In duty,
therefore, to that Majesty who gave them their authority and grace and,
no less than the most royal of predecessors, deserves eminent celebration for these solemnities, I add this later hand to redeem them as well 10
from ignorance as envy, two common evils, the one of censure, the
other of oblivion.

Pliny, Solinus, Ptolemy, and of late Leo the African[2] remember unto
us a river in Ethiopia, famous by the name of Niger, of which the
people were called *Nigritae*, now Negroes, and are the blackest nation 15
of the world. This river taketh spring out of a certain lake eastward,[3]
and after a long race, falleth into the western ocean. Hence, because
it was her majesty's will to have them blackamoors[4] at first, the invention was derived by me, and presented thus.

First, for the scene, was drawn a Landtschap,[5] consisting of small 20
woods, and here and there a void place filled with huntings; which

---

1. The "custom" Jonson mentions is the "rage" of the audience's taking home the decoration
   and pagentry of the masque's scenery (i.e., its "carcass") after the performance. He intends to
   preserve the "spirit" of the masque by writing out his text.
2. Pliny (c. 23/4–79 C.E.) was a Roman writer on natural history; Solinus, about 200 C.E., wrote
   summary of Pliny's *Natural History*; Ptolemy (c. 100–c. 178 C.E.) was an Egyptian-born
   astronomer and geographer who wrote the authoritative (until the age of Renaissance explo-
   ration) *Outline of Geography*; Leo the African was sixteenth-century Moslem authority on the
   geography of North Africa, who ultimately became a Christian with the name of Giovanni
   Leone.
3. Lake Chad, in north central Africa.
4. Black Africans.
5. Landscape.

falling,[6] *an artificial sea was seen to shoot forth, as if it flowed to the
land, raised with waves which seemed to move and in some places the billow to break, as imitating that orderly disorder which is common in nature.
In front of this sea were placed six Tritons*[7] *in moving and sprightly*   25
*actions, their upper parts human, save that their hairs were blue, as
partaking of the sea color, their desinent*[8] *parts fish, mounted above their
heads, and all varied in disposition. From their backs were borne out
certain light pieces of taffeta, as if carried by the wind, and their music
made out of wreathed shells. Behind these, a pair of sea-maids, for song,*   30
*were as conspicuously seated; between which two great sea-horses (as big
as the life) put forth themselves, the one mounting aloft and writhing his
head from the other, which seemed to sink forwards, so intended for
variation—and that the figure behind might come off better. Upon their
backs Oceanus and Niger were advanced.*   35

   Oceanus,[9] *presented in a human form, the color of his flesh blue, and
shadowed with a robe of sea-green; his head gray, and horned, as he is
described by the ancients; his beard of the like mixed color. He was
garlanded with algae, or sea-grass, and in his hand a trident.*

   Niger, in form and color of an Ethiop, his hair and rare beard curled,   40
*shadowed with a blue and bright mantle; his front, neck, and wrists
adorned with pearl; and crowned with an artificial wreath of cane and
paper-rush.*[1]

   *These induced the masquers, which were twelve nymphs, Negroes, and
the daughters of Niger, attended by so many of the Oceaniae,*[2] *which*   45
were their light-bearers.

   *The masquers were placed in a great concave shell like mother of pearl,
curiously made to move on those waters and rise with the billow; the top
thereof was stuck with a chevron*[3] *of lights which, indented to the proportion of the shell, struck a glorious beam upon them as they were*   50
*seated, one above another, so that they were all seen, but in an extrav-
agant order.*

   *On sides of the shell did swim six huge sea-monsters, varied in their
shapes and dispositions, bearing on their backs the twelve torch-bearers;
who were planted there in several greces,*[4] *so as the backs of some were*   55
*seen, some in purfle, or side; others in face; and all having their lights
burning out of whelks or murex shells.*[5]

---

6. The landscape curtain fell to the floor to reveal the scene next described.
7. Sea gods.
8. Lower.
9. In Greek mythology, one of the Titns, son of Uranus (Heaven) and Gala (Earth); Oceanus
was thought to be a wide river that encircled the whole earth.
1. Papyrus.
2. Sea nymphs, daughters of Oceanus and Tethys; "induced"; introduced.
3. I.e., in an inverted "V" shape.
4. Steps; "purfle": profile.
5. Marine shellfish.

The attire of the masquers was alike in all, without difference; the
colors, azure and silver, their hair thick and curled upright in tresses like
pyramids, but returned on the top with a scroll and antique dressing of   60
feathers and jewels interlaced with ropes of pearl. And for the front, ear,
neck, and wrists, the ornament was of the most choice and orient pearl,
best setting off from the black.

For the light-bearers, sea-green, waved about the skirts with gold and
silver, their hair loose and flowing, garlanded with sea-grass, and that   65
stuck with branches of coral.

These thus presented, the scene behind seemed a vast sea and united
with this that flowed forth from the termination or horizon of which,
being the level of the state,[6] which was placed in the upper end of the
hall, was drawn, by the lines of perspective, the whole work shooting   70
downwards from the eye; which decorum[7] made it more conspicuous, and
caught the eye afar off with a wandering beauty. To which was added
an obscure and cloudy night-piece that made the whole set off. So much
for the bodily part,[8] which was of Master Inigo Jones[9] his design and act.

By this, one of the tritons, with the two sea-maids, began to sing to   75
the others' loud music, their voices being a tenor and two trebles.

SONG

Sound, sound aloud
The welcome of the orient flood
Into the west;
Fair Niger,[1] son to great Oceanus,   80
Now honored thus,
With all his beauteous race,
Who, though but black in face,
Yet are they bright
And full of life and light,   85
To prove that beauty best,
Which not the color, but the feature
Assures unto the creature.

OCEANUS

Be silent, now the ceremony's done,
And Niger, say, how comes it, lovely son,   90
That thou, the Ethiop's river, so far east,

6. King's chair.
7. Suitableness, appropriateness.
8. Scenery and decoration.
9. Scenic designer and Jonson's collaborator on the masque.
1. "All rivers are said to be the sons of the Ocean: for, as the Ancients thought, out of the
   vapours, exhaled by the heat of the sun, rivers and fountains were begotten" [Jonson's note].

Art seen to fall into th'extremest west
Of me, the king of floods, Oceanus,
And in mine empire's heart, salute me thus?
My ceaseless current now amazèd stands!   95
To see thy labor, through so many lands,
Mix thy fresh billow with my brackish stream,
And in thy sweetness stretch thy diadem
To these far distant and unequaled skies,
This squarèd circle of celestial bodies.   100

NIGER

Divine Oceanus, 'tis not strange at all,
That since the immortal souls of creatures mortal
Mix with their bodies, yet reserve forever
A power of separation, I should sever
My fresh streams from thy brackish, like things fixed,   105
Though with thy powerful saltness thus far mixed.
Virtue, though chained to earth, will still live free,
And hell itself must yield to Industry.[2]

OCEANUS

But what's the end of thy Herculean labors,
Extended to these calm and blessèd shores?   110

NIGER

To do a kind and careful father's part
In satisfying every pensive heart
Of these my daughters, my most lovèd birth,
Who though they were the first formed dames of earth,[3]
And in whose sparkling and refulgent eyes   115
The glorious sun did still delight to rise,
Though he—the best judge and most formal cause
Of all dames' beauties—in their firm hues draws
Signs of his fervent'st love, and thereby shows
That in their black the perfect'st beauty grows,[4]   120
Since the fixed color of their curlèd hair,
Which is the highest grace of dames most fair,
No cares no age can change or there display

---

2. From Roman poet Horace (65–8 B.C.E.), *Odes*, 1.3.36, "Herculean effort broke through Hell,"
   referred to in the next line.
3. "It is A conjecture of the old ethics that they which dwell under the South were the first
   begotten of the earth" [Jonson's note].
4. Thus opposing the common Elizbethan idea that black is not beautiful. The speaker in the
   biblical Song of Solomon declares, "I am black, but comely" (1.5).

The fearful tincture of abhorrèd gray,
Since Death herself (herself being pale and blue)   125
Can never alter their most faithful hue;
All which are arguments to prove how far
Their beauties conquer, in great beauty's war,
And more, how near divinity they be
That stand from passion or decay so free.   130
Yet since the fabulous voices of some few
Poor brainsick men, styled poets, here with you,
Have, with such envy of their graces, sung
The painted beauties, other empires sprung;
Letting their loose and wingèd fictions fly   135
To infect all climates, yea our purity;
As of one Phaethon,[5] that fired the world,
And that before his heedless flames were hurled
About the globe, the Ethiops were as fair
As other dames; now black, with black despair;   140
And in respect of their complexions changed,
Are eachwhere since for luckless creatures ranged.
Which, when my daughters heard, as women are
Most jealous of their beauties, fear and care
Possessed them whole; yea, and believing them,[6]   145
They wept such ceaseless tears into my stream,
That it hath thus far overflowed his shore
To seek them patience; who have since e'ermore
As the sun riseth charged his burning throne
With volleys of revilings, 'cause he shone   150
On their scorch'd cheeks with such intemperate fires,
And other dames made queens of all desires.
To frustrate which strange error oft I sought,
Though most in vain, against a settled thought
As women's are, till they confirmed at length   155
By miracle what I with so much strength
Of argument resisted; else they feigned:
For in the lake where their first spring they gained,
As they sat cooling their soft limbs, one night
Appeared a face all circumfused with light;   160
(And sure they saw't, for Ethiops never dream)
Wherein they might decipher through the stream
These words:
That they a land must forthwith seek,

5. In Roman mythology, the son of the Sun God who, when allowed to drive the chariot of his
   father across the sky, could not control the horses and scorched the earth. Jupiter destroyed
   him with thunderbolt so that he would not completely destroy the earth.
6. "The poets" [Jonson's note].

Whose termination (of the Greek)   165
Sounds -*tania*; where bright Sol, that heat
Their bloods, doth never rise or set,
But in his journey passeth by
And leaves that climate of the sky,
To comfort of a greater light   170
Who forms all beauty with his sight.
In search of this have we three princedoms passed
That speak out -*tania* in their accents last;
Black Mauretania[7] first, and secondly
Swarth Lusitania; next we did descry   175
Rich Aquitania; and yet cannot find
The place unto these longing nymphs designed.
Instruct and aid me, great Oceanus,
What land is this that now appears to us?

OCEANUS

This land that lifts into the temperate air   180
His snowy cliff is Albion[8] the fair,
So called of Neptune's son who ruleth here;
For whose dear guard myself four thousand year
Since old Deucalion's[9] days have walked the round
About his empire, proud to see him crowned   185
Above my waves.

At this the moon was discovered in the upper part of the house, tri-
umphant in a silver throne made in figure of a pyramid. Her garments
white and silver, the dressing of her head antique and crowned with a
luminary or sphere of light, which striking on the clouds, and heightened 190
with silver, reflected as natural clouds do by the splendor of the moon.
The heaven about her was vaulted with blue silk and set with stars of
silver which had in them their several lights burning. The sudden sight
of which made Niger to interrupt Oceanus with this present passion.

NIGER

O see, our silver star!   195
Whose pure, auspicious light greets us thus far!
Great Aethiopia,[1] goddess of our shore,
Since with particular worship we adore
Thy general brightness, let particular grace

7. Parts of Morocco and Algeria; "Lusitania": Portugal; "Aquitania": southwestern France;
   "swarth": swarthy, of a dark hue.
8. The Greek and Roman name for Britain.
9. In ancient mythology the survivor (along with his wife) of the worldwide flood.
1. The moon goddess.

Shine on my zealous daughters; show the place   200
Which long their longings urged their eyes to see.
Beautify them, which long have deifièd thee.

AETHIOPIA

Niger, be glad; resume thy native cheer.
Thy daughters' labors have their period[2] here,
And so thy errors.[3] I was that bright face   205
Reflected by the lake in which thy race
Read mystic lines, which skill Pythagoras
First taught to men[4] by a reverberate glass.
This blessèd isle doth with that -tania end,
Which there they saw inscribed, and shall extend   210
Wished satisfaction to their best desires.
Britannia, which the triple world[5] admires,
This isle hath now recovered for her name;
Where reign those beauties that with so much fame
The sacred muses' sons have honorèd,   215
And from bright Hesperus[6] to Eos spread.
With that great name Britannia this blest isle
Hath won her ancient dignity and style,
A *world divided from the world*,[7] and tried
The abstract of it, in his general pride.[8]   220
For were the world with all his wealth a ring,
Britannia, whose new name[9] makes all tongues sing,
Might be a diamond worthy to enchase[1] it,
Ruled by a sun[2] that to this height doth grace it,
Whose beams shine day and night and are of force   225
To blanch an Ethiop and revive a cor's.
His light sciential[3] is, and, past mere nature,
Can salve the rude defects of every creature.
     Call forth thy honored daughters, then,
     And let them, 'fore the Britain men,   230

---

2. End.
3. Wanderings.
4. Pythagoras was said to be able to write on the moon through the reflection of letters written in blood on a mirror. "Reverberate": reflecting.
5. Heaven, earth, hell; "Britannia": Latin name for Britain.
6. Evening star; "Eos": goddess of the dawn.
7. A world unto itself.
8. "Britain's pride has been justified ('tried'), as it is the epitome, the ideal ('abstract'), of the rest of the world ('it')."
9. King James I of England, previously James VI of Scotland, proclaimed in October 1604 that his title would be King of Great Britain. The two kingdoms of England and Scotland, he declared, make "the whole a little world within itself."
1. Adorn.
2. I.e., King James I.
3. Knowledgeable; "cor's": corpse.

Indent[4] the land with those pure traces
They flow with, in their native graces.
Invite them boldly to the shore,
Their beauties shall be scorched no more,
This sun is temperate and refines
All things on which his radiance shines.

Here the Tritons sounded, and they danced on shore, every couple as they advanced, severally presenting their fans, in one of which were inscribed their mixed names, in the other a mute hieroglyphic[5] *expressing their mixed qualities. Which manner of symbol I rather chose than* imprese, *as well for strangeness as relishing of antiquity, and more applying to that original doctrine of sculpture which the Egyptians are said first to have brought from the Ethiopians.*

		The names	The symbols
The Queen	1.	*Euphoris*[6]	A golden tree laden with fruit.
Countess of Bedford		*Aglaia*	
Lady Herbert	2.	*Diaphane*	The figure icosahedron of crystal.
Countess of Derby		*Eucampse*	
Lady Rich	3.	*Ocyte*	A pair of naked feet in a river.
Countess of Suffolk		*Kathare*	
Lady Bevill	4.	*Notis*	The salamander simple.
Lady Effingham		*Psychrote*	
Lady Elizabeth Howard	5.	*Glycyte*	A cloud full of rain, dropping.

4. Make deep marks on; "traces": footprints.
5. Symbol standing for a word or idea; "imprese": an emblem or symbol accompnied by a motto.
6. Fertility; "Golden Tree": symbol of fertility (which is particularly appropriate for the queen). "Aglaia": one of the three graces, daughters of Zeus—her name means "splendor," beauty." "Diaphane": transparency; "icosahedron": twenty-sided figure of crystal symbolizing water. "Eucampse": flexibility. "Ocyte": swiftness; "naked feet in river": symbolizes purity. "Kathare": spotless. "Notis": moisture; "salmander": cold-blooded animal that can walk in a fire and extinguish it without harm. "Psychrote": coldness; "Glycyte": sweetness; "cloud full of rain": symbolizes education. "Malacia": delicacy. "Bryte": weight; "urn sphered with wine": perhaps the globe of the earth, crowned with wine, but an obscure symbol. "Periphere": revolving, circular.

Lady Susan de Vere	Malacia	
Lady Wroth	Baryte	An urn, sphered with wine.
	6.	
Lady Walsingham	Periphere	255

The names of the Oceaniae were
Doris, Petraea, Ocyrhoe, Cydippe, Glauce, Tyche, Beroe, Acaste, Clytia,
Ianthe, Lycoris, Plexaure

Their own single dance ended, as they were about to make choice of their
men, one from the sea was heard to call 'em with this charm, sung by a   260
tenor voice.

SONG

Come away, come away,
We grow jealous of your stay;
If you do not stop your car,
We shall have more cause to fear   265
Sirens of the land, than they
To doubt the sirens[7] of the sea.

Here they danced with their men several measures[8] and corantos. All
which ended, they were again accited[9] to sea with a song of two trebles,
whose cadences were iterated by a double echo from several parts of the   270
land.

SONG

Daughters of the subtle flood,
Do not let earth longer entertain you;
1st Echo. Let earth longer entertain you.
2nd Echo. Longer entertain you.   275

'Tis to them enough of good,
That you give this little hope to gain you.
1st Echo. Give this little hope to gain you.
2nd Echo. Little hope to gain you.

If they love,   280
You shall quickly see;
For when to flight you move,
They'll follow you, the more you flee.

7. Greek mythological female creatures whose song lured sailors to their destruction.
8. Stately dances; "corntos": courtly dances with glides and light hops.
9. Summoned; "trebles": sopranos.

1st Echo. Follow you, the more you flee.
2nd Echo. The more you flee.   285

   If not, impute it each to other's matter;
They are but earth,
    1st Echo. But earth,
      2nd Echo. Earth.
             And what you vowed was water.   290
   1st Echo. And what you vowed ws water.
    2nd Echo. You vowed was water.

AETHIOPIA

Enough, bright nymphs, the night grows old,
And we are grieved we cannot hold
You longer light. But comfort take: 295
Your father only to the lake
Shall make return; yourselves, with feasts,
Must here remain the Ocean's guests.
Nor shall this veil the sun hath cast
Above your blood more summers last.   300
For which you shall observe these rites:
Thirteen times thrice, on thirteen nights,
So often as I fill my sphere
With glorious light, throughout the year,
You shall (when all things else do sleep   305
Save your chaste thoughts) with reverence steep
Your bodies in that purer brine
And wholesome dew called rosmarine.[1]
Then with that soft and gentler foam,
Of which the Ocean yet yields some,   310
Whereof bright Venus, beauty's queen,
Is said to have begotten been,
You shall your gentler limbs o'er-lave,[2]
And for your palm perfection have;
So that this night, the year gone round,[3]   315
You do gin salute this ground,
And in the beams of yond' bright sun
Your faces dry, and all is done.

*At which, in a dance they returned to the sea, where they took their shell
and with this full song, went out.*   320

---

1. Se dew.
2. Wash.
3. The masque that was to follow this, *The Masque of Beauty,* was not produced until three
years later, in 1608.

SONG

Now Dian[4] with her burning face
　　Declines space;
　By which our waters know
　To ebb, that late did flow.
Back seas, back nymphs; but with a forward grace   325
　Keep, still, your reverence to the place;
And shout with joy of favor you have won
　In sight of Albion, Neptune's son.

So ended the first masque, which (beside the singular grace of music and
dances) had that success in the nobility of performance, as nothing needs　330
to the illustration but the memory by whom it was personated.

4. The moon.

Mercury Vindicated from the Alchemists at Court

By Gentlemen the King's Servants

After the loud music, the scene discovered; being a laboratory, or Alchemist's workhouse: Vulcan looking to the Registers,[1] while a Cyclops tending the fire to the cornets began to sing.

CYCLOPS

Soft, subtle fire, thou soul of Art,
   Now do thy part 5
On weaker Nature, that through age is lamed.
   Take but thy time, now she is old,
   And the Sun, her friend, grown cold,
She will no more in strife with thee be named.[2]
Look but how few confess her now, 10
   In cheek or brow!
From every head, almost, how she is frighted!
   The very age abhors her so,
   That it learns to speak and go
As if by Art alone it could be righted. 15

The song ended, Mercury[3] appeared, thrusting out his head and afterward his body at the tunnel of the middle furnace; which Vulcan espying, cried out to the Cyclops.

VULCAN

Stay, see! our Mercury is coming forth. Art and all the elements assist! Call forth our philosophers! He will be gone, he will evap- 20
orate! Dear Mercury! Help! He flies! He is 'scaped! Precious,

---

1. Vulcan, as Roman god of the forge, is dressed like a blacksmith and tending the "registers," or dampers, of the alchemical furnace. Cyclops is a one-eyed giant (the actor must have worn a mask, and perhaps high-heeled shoes); he sings to a trumpet.
2. The contrast between Nature and Art was a commonplace of the age, fueled by the thought that Nature was decaying.
3. Throughout the masque, Mercury is both the Roman deity and the metal quicksilver, a major ingredient in the process by which the alchemists proposed to make gold.

golden Mercury, be fixed; be not so volatile! Will none of the Sons of Art[4] appear?

In which time Mercury, having run once or twice around the room, takes breath and speaks.   25

MERCURY

Now the place and goodness of it protect me. One tender-hearted creature or other, save Mercury and free him. Ne'er an old gentlewoman in the house that has a wrinkle about her to hide me in? I could run into a serving-woman's pocket now, her glove, any little hole. Some merciful farthingale[5] among so many,   30 be bounteous and undertake me; I will stand close up anywhere to escape this polt-footed philosopher, old Smug here of Lemnos,[6] and his smoky family. Has he given me time to breathe? Oh, the variety of torment that I have endured in the reign of the Cyclops, beyond the exquisite wit of tyrants! The whole household of 'em   35 are become Alchemists (since their trade of armor-making failed them)[7] only to keep themselves in fire for this winter; for the mischief of a secret that they know, above the consuming of coals and drawing of usquebaugh.[8] Howsoever they may pretend under the specious names of Geber, Arnold, Lully, Bombast of Hohenheim[9]   40 to commit miracles in art and treason against nature. And, as if the title of philosopher, that creature of glory, were to be fetched out of a furnace, abuse the curious and credulous nation of metal-men through the world, and make Mercury their instrument. I am their crude and their sublimate; their precipitate and their unctu-   45 ous; their male and their female; sometimes their hermaphrodite; what they list to style me.[1] It is I that am corroded and exalted and sublimed and reduced and fetched over and filtered and washed and wiped; what between their salts and their sulphurs, their oils and their tartars, their brines and their vinegars, you might take   50 me out now a soused Mercury, now a salted Mercury, now a smoked and dried Mercury, now a powdered and pickled Mercury. Never herring, oyster, or cucumber passed so many vexations. My whole life with 'em hath been an exercise of torture; one, two,

---

4. "Philosophers" and "Sons of Art" were titles assumed by alchemists.
5. Hoopskirt.
6. I.e., Vulcan, "smug" because a complacent cuckold (as a result of Mars's intrigue with Venus), and "of Lemnos" because he fell on that Aegean island when Jove threw him out of Olympus. He is "polt-footed," or lame, because of his hard landing on that occasion.
7. Vulcan was a maker of armor for heroes such as Achilles and Aeneas.
8. Coal and "usquebaugh" (whiskey) are two ways to keep warm in winter.
9. Geber (Abu Abdullah Jubor ben Hayyam ben Abdullah al-Kufi), Arnoldus de Villa Nova, Raymond Lull or Lully, and Paracelsus (Phlippus Aureolus Theophrastus Bombastus ab Hohenheim) were well-known alchemists.
1. Mercury overflows with terms of alchemical art.

three, four, and five times an hour have they made me dance the   55
philosophical circle, like an ape through a hoop or a dog in a
wheel.[2] I am their turnspit indeed; they eat or smell no roast meat
but in my name. I am their bill of credit still, that passes for their
victuals and houseroom. It is through me they have got this corner
of the court to cozen in, where they shark for a hungry diet below   60
stairs, and cheat upon your under-officers, promising mountains
for their meat, and all upon Mercury's security.[3] A poor page of
the larder they have made obstinately believe he shall be physician
for the household next summer: they will give him a quantity of
the quintessence shall serve him to cure kibes or the mort-mal of   65
the shin, take away the pustules in the nose[4] and Mercury is engaged for it. A child of the scullery steals all their coals for 'em
too, and he is bid sleep secure, he shall find a corner of the philosopher's stone for it under his bolster one day, and have the
proverb inverted.[5] Against which one day I am to deliver the but-   70
tery in so many firkins of *Aurum potabile*, as it delivers out bombards of budge to them, between this and that.[6] For the pantry,
they are at a certainty with me, and keep a tally, an ingot, a loaf,
or a wedge of some five pound weight, which is a thing of nothing,
a trifle. And so the black guard are pleased with a toy, a lease of   75
life (for some 999),[7] especially those of the boiling house: they are
to have Medea's kettle[8] hung up, that they may souse into it when
they will, and come out renewed like so many striped snakes at
their pleasure. But these are petty engagements and (as I said)
below the stairs; marry, above here, perpetuity of beauty (do you   80
hear, Ladies), health, riches, honors, a matter of immortality is
nothing. They will calcine[9] you a grave matron (as it might be a
mother of the maids) and spring up a young virgin out of her ashes,
as fresh as a phoenix:[1] lay you an old courtier on the coals like a
sausage or a bloat-herring, and after they have broiled him enough,   85
blow a soul into him with a pair of bellows, till he start up into

2. Dogs running in wheels connected to spits were used to turn roasting meat.
3. The alchemists are accused of dealing with the cooks and butlers ("under-officers") of the
   court, promising them a share in the philosopher's stone in return for a free meal in the
   pantry. The philosopher's stone was, of course, supposed to turn any common metal to gold
   at a touch. "Cozen": cheat.
4. "Pustules of the nose" were from syphilis, cured (sometimes) by injections of mercury; "kibes":
   a chapped blister; "mort-mal": gangrene.
5. An old proverb says one may mistake a stone for a treasure—the scullery boy is promised by
   the alchemists that he will find a treasure in a stone.
6. Mercury delivers tubs of potable gold, those in the buttery hand out in return leather sacks
   ("bombards") of foodstuffs to the hungry alchemists.
7. Leases on land were written sometimes for life, sometimes for 999 years; the kitchen help
   ("black guard") have, so to speak, mortgaged themselves for life to the alchemists.
8. Medea, the archetypical witch of Greek mythology, had a kettle of herbs in which she im-
   mersed Aeson, Jason's father; it bestowed on him eternal youth.
9. Reduce to chalk.
1. A mythical bird that was supposed to rise afresh from its own ashes every thousand years.

his galliard,[2] that was made when Monsieur was here. They profess
familiarly to melt down all the old sinners of the suburbs once in
half a year into fresh gamesters again—get all the cracked maid-
enheads and cast 'em into new ingots; half the wenches of the   90
town are Alchemy. See, they begin to muster again, and draw their
forces out against me! The Genius[3] of the place defend me! You
that are both the Sol and Jupiter of this sphere, Mercury invokes
your majesty against the sooty tribe here; for in your favor only, I
grow recovered and warm.   95

At which time Vulcan entering with a troop of threadbare Alche-
mists, prepares them to the first Antimasque.

VULCAN

Begin your charm, sound music, circle him in and take him: if
he will not obey, bind him.

They all danced about Mercury with variety of changes, while he   100
defends himself with his caduceus,[4] *and after the dance spake.*

MERCURY

It is in vain, Vulcan, to pitch your net in the sight of the fowl,
thus; I am no sleepy Mars to be catched in your subtle toils.[5] I
know what your aims are, sir, to tear the wings from my head and
heels, and lute[6] me up in a glass with my own seals, while you   105
might wrest the caduceus out of my hand, to the adultery and spoil
of Nature, and make your accesses by it to her dishonor more easy.
Sir,[7] would you believe it should be come to that height of impudence in mankind that such a nest of fire-worms as these are
(because their patron Mulciber heretofore has made stools stir and   110
statues dance, a dog of brass to bark, and—which some will say
was his worst act—a woman to speak[8] should therefore with their
heats called *Balnei, Cineris,* or horse-dung[9] profess to outwork the

---

2. A sprightly dance. The duke of Anjou, known as "Monsieur," visited England as a potential
   suitor of Queen Elizabeth in 1579.
3. Mercury here comes forward and importunes King James directly for help. James is the "Sol"
   (Sun) of the cosmos within which Mercury is a planet, and "Jupiter" (father of the gods) in
   the family of which Mercury is a member; on both scores he is the "Genius"—guiding spirit
   or tutelary guardian—of the troubled speaker.
4. The serpent-entwined, winged wand traditionally carried by Mercury.
5. Mars, sleeping with Venus, was netted by Vulcan, her husband.
6. Fasten. Hermes's seals are traditional means of sealing a container, as we say, "hermetically."
7. Again the address is directly to King James.
8. Mulciber is a secondary name of Vulcan, the archartificer, who made moving chairs and
   dancing statues (*Iliad*, chap. 18), barking dogs (*Odyssey*, chap. 7), and a talking woman in
   the person of Pandora.
9. A traditional source of slow alchemical heat; "Balnei": of the bath; "Cineris": of ashes.

sun in virtue, and contend to the great act of generation, nay, almost creation? It is so, though. For in yonder vessels which you see in their laboratory they have enclosed materials to produce men, beyond the deeds of Deucalion or Prometheus (of which one, they say, had the philosopher's stone and threw it over his shoulder, the other the fire, and lost it).[1] And what men are they, they are so busy about, think you? Not common or ordinary creatures, but of rarity and excellence, such as the times wanted, and the age had a special deal of need of: such, as there was a necessity they should be artificial, for Nature could never have thought or dreamt of their composition. I can remember some of their titles to you and the ingredients. Do not look for Paracelsus' man among them,[2] that he promised you out of white bread and dele-wine,[3] for he never came to light. But of these, let me see: the first that occurs, a master of the duel, a carrier of the differences.[4] To him went spirit of ale, a good quantity, with the amalgam of sugar and nutmegs, oil of oaths, sulphur of quarrel, strong waters, valor precipitate, vapored o'er the helm with tobacco and the rosin of Mars, with a dram of the business,[5] for that's the word of tincture, the business. Let me alone with the business, I will carry the business. I do understand the business, I do find an affront in the business. Then another is a fencer in the mathematics or the town's cunning-man, a creature of art too, a supposed secretary to the stars;[6] but indeed a kind of lying intelligencer from those parts. His materials, if I be not deceived, were juice of almanacs, extraction of ephemerides,[7] scales of the *Globe*, filings of figures, dust of the twelve houses,[8] conserve of questions, salt of confederacy, a pound of adventure, a grain of skill, and a drop of truth. I saw vegetals[9] too, as well as minerals, put into one glass there, as adder's tongue, title-bane, nitre of clients, tartar of false conveyance, *Aurum palpabile*[1] with a huge deal of talk, to which they added a tincture of conscience, with the faeces of honesty;[2] but for what this was I

1. In classical mythology, Deucalion created men by throwing stones over his shoulder, and Prometheus by stealing fire out of heaven. These interpretations of classical fables are reminiscent of those in *The Alchemist* 2.1.
2. Paracelsus in his book *On the Nature of Things* gave a recipe for creating a man.
3. A kind of Rhine wine.
4. Among the special men created by alchemists is the master of quarreling (very reminiscent of Subtle in *The Alchemist*).
5. "Business" is mocked as a catch-all word; any quarrel is "the business."
6. The universal shyster-about-town, Mr. Know-it-All.
7. Records of trivial, momentary happenings. The Globe was the public theater, where gossip could be picked up, but the "scales" are a lost allusion.
8. The dust of the twelve (astrological) houses is trivial nonsense.
9. Plants; the adder's tongue is forked as well as poisonous; "title-bane" is a poison that destroys not only titles of honor but legal titles too—a lawyer's poisonous tongue.
1. Palpable, i.e., tangible gold.
2. The dregs of truth.

could not learn, only I have overheard one of the artists say, Out of the corruption of a lawyer was the best generation of a broker in suits:[3] whether this were he or no, I know not.

VULCAN

Thou art a scorner, Mercury, and out of the pride of thy protection here makest it thy study to revile Art, but it will turn to thine own contumely soon. Call forth the creatures of the first class,[4] and let them move to the harmony of our heat, till the slanderer have sealed up his own lips to his own torment.   150

MERCURY

Let 'em come, let 'em come, I would not wish a greater punishment to thy impudence.   155

There enters the second Antimasque *of imperfect creatures, with helms of limbecks[5] on their heads: whose dance ended,*

MERCURY *proceeded*

Art thou not ashamed, Vulcan, to offer in defense of thy fire and Art, against the excellence of the Sun and Nature, creatures more imperfect than the very flies and insects that are her trespasses and 'scapes? Vanish with thy insolence, thou and thy impostors, and all mention of you melt before the Majesty of this light[6] whose Mercury henceforth I profess to be, and never again the philosophers'. Vanish, I say, that all who have but their senses may see and judge the difference between thy ridiculous monsters and his absolute features.   160   165

At which the whole scene changed to a glorious bower, wherein Nature was placed, with Prometheus at her feet; and the twelve masquers standing about them. After they had been a while viewed, Prometheus descended, and Nature after him, singing.   170

NATURE

How young and fresh am I tonight
To see't kept day by so much light,
And twelve my sons stand in their Maker's sight.

---

3. "The corruption of *this* is the generation of *that*" was a favorite, semi-serious formula of Renaissance popular scientists. A "broker in suits" is a seller of second-hand clothes.
4. I.e., the phony men I and my alchemists are alleged to have created; "contumely": disgrace, ignominy.
5. I.e., with retorts on their heads.
6. Once more the reference is to King James.

Help, wise Prometheus, something must be done
To show they are the creatures of the Sun,   175
   That each to other
   Is a brother,
And Nature here no stepdame, but a mother.
CHORUS { Come forth, come forth, prove all the numbers then,[7]
       { That make perfection up, and may absolve you men. 180

NATURE

But show thy winding ways and arts,
Thy risings and thy timely starts
Of stealing fire from Ladies' eyes and hearts.[8]
   Those softer circles are the young man's heaven,
   And there more orbs and planets are than seven,   185
    To know whose motion
    Were a notion
As worthy of youth's study as devotion.
CHORUS { Come forth, come forth, prove all the time will gain,
       { For Nature bids the best, and never bade in vain. 190

The first dance;
After which this song:

PROMETHEUS, NATURE

PROMETHEUS How many, 'mongst these Ladies here
     Wish now they such a mother were!
NATURE   Not one, I fear,   195
    And read it in their laughters.
   There's more, I guess, would wish to be my daughters.
PROMETHEUS You think they would not be so old
     For so much glory.
NATURE   I think that thought so told   200
     Is no false piece of story.
   'Tis yet with them but beauty's noon,
   They would not grandames be too soon.
PROMETHEUS   Is that your sex's humor?[9]
 Tis then since Niobe was changed that they have left
    that tumor.[1]   205

7. Arrange all the numerical combinations that create perfection. The Chorus invites the
   masquers (not without some hyperbole) to form the dance that figures ideal man.
8. Prometheus as stealer of fire and inspirer of men is in his element with the ladies' eyes.
9. Taste, preference.
1. Vanity. In Greek mythology, Niobe was the mother of fourteen, or perhaps fifty, children, all
   of whom were killed by Apollo. Since then, women have not been eager to have many
   children.

CHORUS   Move, move again, in forms as heretofore.
NATURE   'Tis form allures.
              Then move, the Ladies here are store.[2]
PROMETHEUS Nature is motion's mother, as she's yours.
CHORUS The spring whence order flows, that all directs,   210
              And knits the causes with th'effects.

> *The main dance,*
> *Then dancing with the Ladies;*
> *Then their last dance,*
> *After which, Prometheus calls to them in song.*   215

PROMETHEUS

        What, have you done
          So soon?
    And can you from such beauty part?
        You'll do a wonder more than I,
        I woman with her ills did fly,   220
    But you their good and them deny.
CHORUS   Sure each hath left his heart
    In pawn to come again, or else he durst not start.

NATURE

    They are loath to go,
          I know,   225
    Or sure they are no sons of mine.
    There is no banquet, boys, like this,
    If you hope better, you will miss;
    Stay here, and take each one a kiss.[3]
CHORUS Which, if you can refine,   230
    The taste knows no such cates,[4] nor yet the palate wine.
        No cause of tarrying shun,
    They are not worth his light, go backward from the Sun.[5]

THE END.

1615   1616

---

2. Abundant.
3. At the end of the dance, each gentleman received a kiss from his lady.
4. Delicacies.
5. I.e., they are not worthy of the sun's light who go backward from it.

Pleasure Reconciled to Virtue

A Masque as It Was Presented at Court Before King James. 1618.

*The scene was the mountain Atlas, who had his top ending in the
figure of an old man, his head and beard all hoary and frost as if
his shoulders were covered with snow; the rest wood and rock. A
grove of ivy at his feet, out of which, to a wild music of cymbals,
flutes and tabors, is brought forth Comus,[1] the god of cheer, or the* 5
*belly, riding in triumph, his head crowned with roses and other
flowers, his hair curled; they that wait upon him crowned with ivy,
their javelins done about with it; one of them going with Hercules
his bowl bare before him, while the rest presented him with this*

HYMN

Room, room! Make room for the bouncing belly, 10
First father of sauce, and deviser of jelly;
Prime master of arts, and the giver of wit,
That found out the excellent engine, the spit,
The plow and the flail, the mill and the hopper,
The hutch and the bolter, the furnace and copper. 15
The oven, the bavin, the mawkin, the peel,
The hearth and the range, the dog and the wheel.[2]
He, he first invented the hogshead and tun,
The gimlet and vice too, and taught them to run.
And since, with the funnel, an Hippocras bag 20

1. Comus is the traditional classical and Renaissance figure of sensual indulgence; many of his
properties here (ivy, wild music, and the flowing bowl) suggest his kinship with Dionysus.
The bowl of Hercules, given to him by the Sun-god, was so big that the hero sailed across
the ocean in it. At the root of the masque is the ancient story that early in his life Hercules
had to choose between a life of easy pleasure and one of strenuous virtue. But now, under
King James, the two principles are at last going to be reconciled. Jonson's stage directions,
being partly descriptive (for the reader), partly instructive (for the performer), are rather casual
about observing consistency of tense.
2. "Hutch" (bin), "mill," and "hopper" were used in grinding grain; the "bolter" was a grain
sifter; "bavin," "mawkin," and "peel" are different sorts of apparatus used in a bakeshop. A
dog harnessed to a wheel served to keep a roasting-spit turning.

He's made of himself, that now he cries swag.[3]
Which shows, though the pleasure be but of four inches,
Yet he is a weasel, the gullet that pinches,
Of any delight, and not spares from the back
Whatever to make of the belly a sack.[4]   25
Hail, hail, plump paunch! O the founder of taste
For fresh meats, or powdered, or pickle, or paste;
Devourer of broiled, baked, roasted or sod,[5]
And emptier of cups, be they even or odd;
All which have now made thee so wide i' the waist   30
As scarce with no pudding thou art to be laced;
But eating and drinking until thou dost nod,
Thou break'st all thy girdles, and break'st forth a god.

To this, the BOWL-BEARER

Do you hear, my friends? To whom did you sing all this now?   35
Pardon me only that I ask you, for I do not look for an answer; I'll
answer myself. I know it is now such a time as the Saturnals[6] for
all the world, that every man stands under the eaves of his own
hat and sings what pleases him; that's the right and the liberty of
it. Now you sing of god Comus here, the Belly-god. I say it is well,   40
and I say it is not well. It is well as it is a ballad, and the belly
worthy of it, I must needs say, an 'twere forty yards of ballad
more—as much ballad as tripe. But when the belly is not edified
by it, it is not well; for where did you ever read or hear that the
belly had any ears? Come, never pump for an answer, for you are   45
defeated. Our fellow Hunger there, that was as ancient a retainer
to the belly as any of us, was turned away for being unseasonable
—not unreasonable, but unseasonable—and now is he (poor thin-
gut) fain to get his living with teaching of starlings, magpies, parrots
and jackdaws, those things he would have taught the belly. Beware   50
of dealing with the belly; the belly will not be talked to, especially
when he is full. Then there is no venturing upon Venter,[7] he will
blow you all up; he will thunder indeed, la: some in derision call
him the father of farts. But I say he was the first inventor of great
ordnance, and taught us to discharge them on festival days. Would   55

3. "Hogshead" and "tun" are large barrels; "gimlet" and "vice" are tools for tapping a keg. A
   "Hippocras bag" is a cloth filter for clearing wine, and to "cry swag" is to reveal a drooping,
   pendulous belly.
4. The gullet, though only four inches long, is a harsh master: it imposes the belly's great weight
   on the back.
5. Boiled.
6. The Roman Saturnalia, which came about the end of the year, were a time of license; Jonson
   compares them to the Twelfth Night festivities in the English court, at which this masque
   was produced.
7. Belly, in Latin.

we had a fit feast for him, i' faith, to show his activity: I would
have something now fetched in to please his five senses, the throat;
or the two senses, the eyes. Pardon me for my two senses; for I
that carry Hercules' bowl[8] in the service may see double by my
place, for I have drunk like a frog today. I would have a tun now   60
brought in to dance, and so many bottles about him. Ha! You look
as if you would make a problem of this. Do you see? Do you see?
a problem: why bottles? and why a tun? and why a tun? and why
bottles to dance? I say that men that drink hard and serve the belly
in any place of quality (as *The Jovial Tinkers*, or *The Lusty Kin-*   65
dred[9]) are living measures of drink, and can transform themselves,
and do every day, to bottles or tuns when they please; and when
they have done all they can, they are, as I say again (for I think I
said somewhat like it afore) but moving measures of drink; and
there is a piece in the cellar can hold more than all they. This   70
will I make good if it please our new god but to give a nod; for
the belly does all by signs, and I am for the belly, the truest clock
in the world to go by.

> *Here the first antimasque*[1] *danced by men in the shape of bottles,*
> *tuns, etc., after which,* HERCULES: 75

What rites are these? Breeds earth more monsters yet?
Antaeus[2] scarce is cold: what can beget
This store?—And stay such contraries[3] upon her?
Is earth so fruitful of her own dishonor?
Or 'cause his vice was inhumanity,   80
Hopes she by vicious hospitality
To work an expiation first?[4] And then
(Help, Virtue!) these are sponges and not men.
Bottles? Mere vessels? Half a tun of paunch?
How? And the other half thrust forth in haunch?   85
Whose feast? The belly's! Comus'! And my cup
Brought in to fill the drunken orgies up
And here abused! That was the crowned reward
Of thirsty heroes after labor hard!
Burdens and shames of nature, perish, die;   90

8. To carry Hercules' bowl would clearly imply drinking a lot.
9. These seem to be names of taverns.
1. The antimasque, or antic masque, was a group of dancers, grotesquely or comically dressed,
   who served to contrast with the main group of masquers.
2. An earth-born giant whom Hercules destroyed in the course of his labors. As his favored sport
   was wrestling, and he grew stronger every time he touched the ground, Hercules had to kill
   him by holding him up in the air till he died.
3. "How can earth support such opposites?" "Store": abundance.
4. Hercules thinks that Comus is another child of the earth—earth, he supposes, is trying to
   expiate her guilt by producing one monster after another. "Vicious hospitality": hospitality to
   vice.

For yet you never lived, but in the sty
Of vice have wallowed, and in that swine's strife
Been buried under the offense of life.
Go, reel and fall under the load you make,
Till your swoll'n bowels burst with what you take.   95
Can this be pleasure, to extinguish man?
Or so quite change him in his figure? Can
The belly love his pain, and be content
With no delight but what's a punishment?
These monsters plague themselves, and fitly, too.   100
For they do suffer what and all they do.
But here must be no shelter, nor no shroud
For such: sink grove, or vanish into cloud!

*After this the whole grove vanished, and the whole music was
discovered, sitting at the foot of the mountain, with Pleasure and*   105
*Virtue seated above them. The choir invited Hercules to rest with
this*

SONG

Great friend and servant of the good,
Let cool awhile thy heated blood,
And from thy mighty labor cease.   110
Lie down, lie down,
And give thy troubled spirits peace,
Whilst Virtue, for whose sake
Thou dost this godlike travail take,
May of the choicest herbage[5] make,   115
Here on this mountain bred,
A crown, a crown
For thy immortal head.

*Here Hercules lay down at their feet, and the second antimasque,
which was of pygmies, appeared.*   120

1ST PYGMY. Antaeus dead and Hercules yet live!
Where is this Hercules? What would I give
To meet him now? Meet him? Nay three such other,
If they had hand in murder of our brother![6]

---

5. Plants and branches; "travail": labor, trouble.
6. Pygmies and giants, minimals and maximals, are disproportioned offspring of mere earth,
therefore brothers to one another. The pygmies don't know how many Hercules-figures there
are, because so many tales were told about the hero that even Renaissance mythographers
were forced to think there must have been several persons of that name.

With three? With four, with ten, nay, with as many   125
As the name yields! Pray anger there be any
Whereon to feed my just revenge, and soon!
How shall I kill him? Hurl him 'gainst the moon,
And break him in small portions! Give to Greece
His brain, and every tract of earth a piece!   130
2ND PYGMY. He is yonder.
1ST PYGMY. Where?
3RD PYGMY. At the hill foot, asleep.
1ST PYGMY. Let one go steal his club.
2ND PYGMY. My charge; I'll creep.   135
4TH PYGMY. He's ours.
1ST PYGMY. Yes, peace.
3RD PYGMY. Triumph, we have him, boy.
4TH PYGMY. Sure, sure, he's sure.
1ST PYGMY. Come, let us dance for joy.   140

*At the end of their dance they thought to surprise him, when
suddenly, being awaked by the music, he roused himself, and they
all ran into holes.*

SONG

CHOIR. Wake, Hercules, awake: but heave up thy black eye,
    'Tis only asked from thee to look and these will die,   145
            Or fly.
      Already they are fled,
      Whom scorn had else left dead.

*At which Mercury descended from the hill with a garland of pop-
lar to crown him.*   150

MERCURY. Rest still, thou active friend of Virtue; these
    Should not disturb the peace of Hercules.
    Earth's worms and honor's dwarfs, at too great odds,
    Prove or provoke the issue of the gods.
    See here a crown the agèd hill hath sent thee,   155
    My grandsire Atlas, he that did present thee
    With the best sheep that in his fold were found,
    Or golden fruit in the Hesperian ground,
    For rescuing his fair daughters, then the prey
    Of a rude pirate, as thou cam'st this way;   160
    And taught thee all the learning of the sphere,
    And how, like him, thou might'st the heavens up-bear,

As that thy labor's virtuous recompense.[7]
He, though a mountain now, hath yet the sense
Of thanking thee for more, thou being still   165
Constant to goodness, guardian of the hill;
Antaeus, by thee suffocated here,
And the voluptuous Comus, god of cheer,
Beat from his grove, and that defaced. But now
The time's arrived that Atlas told thee of: how   170
By unaltered law, and working of the stars,
There should be a cessation of all jars[8]
'Twixt Virtue and her noted opposite,
Pleasure; that both should meet here in the sight
Of Hesperus, the glory of the west,[9]   175
The brightest star, that from his burning crest
Lights all on this side the Atlantic seas
As far as to thy pillars, Hercules.[1]
See where he shines, Justice and Wisdom placed
About his throne, and those with Honor graced,   180
Beauty and Love! It is not with his brother
Bearing the world, but ruling such another
Is his renown.[2] Pleasure, for his delight,
Is reconciled to Virtue, and this night
Virtue brings forth twelve princes have been bred   185
In this rough mountain and near Atlas' head,
The hill of knowledge; one and chief of whom
Of the bright race of Hesperus is come,
Who shall in time the same that he is be,
And now is only a less light than he.[3]   190
These now she trusts with Pleasure, and to these
She gives an entrance to the Hesperides,
Fair Beauty's garden; neither can she fear
They should grow soft or wax effeminate here,
Since in her sight and by her charge all's done,   195
Pleasure the servant, Virtue looking on.[4]

---

7. When Hercules was seeking the golden apples of the Hesperides, he took for a while Atlas's
   job of holding up the heavens, so that the giant could wade out in the ocean and get the
   apples. Atlas himself was originally an astronomer, and thus he knew "all the learning of the
   sphere."
8. Quarrels.
9. Jonson followed the mythographers in making Hesperus a brother of Atlas; as the evening star
   and guardian of the western isles, he is easily identified with King James.
1. The "pillars of Hercules" are the straits of Gilbraltar.
2. As Hesperus, King James does not hold up the sky, like his brother Atlas, but rules over a
   special world of his own, England.
3. Tradition has it that Prince Charles was one of the masquers; he was just eighteen at the
   time, and it was his first masque.
4. Having grown up inside Atlas itself, so that virtue comes naturally to them, the masquers can
   now be allowed to mingle freely with the daughters of Hesperus, in pursuit of pleasure.

*Here the whole choir of music called the twelve masquers forth
from the lap of the mountain, which then opened with this*

SONG

Ope, agèd Atlas, open then thy lap,
And from thy beamy bosom strike a light,   200
That men may read in thy mysterious map
    All lines
    And signs
Of royal education and the right,
    See how they come and show,   205
    That are but born to know,
        Descend,
        Descend,
Though pleasure lead,
    Fear not to follow: 210
They who are bred
    Within the hill
    Of skill
May safely tread
    What path they will: 215
No ground of good is hollow.

*In their descent from the hill Daedalus[5] came down before them,
of whom Hercules questioned Mercury.*

HERCULES. But Hermes, stay a little, let me pause:
  Who's this that leads?
MERCURY.   A guide that gives them laws   220
  To all their motions: Daedalus the wise.
HERCULES. And doth in sacred harmony comprise
  His precepts?
MERCURY.   Yes.
HERCULES.   They may securely prove[6]
  Then, any labyrinth, though it be of love.

Here, while they put themselves in form, Daedalus has his first   225

SONG

Come on, come on! And where you go,
So interweave the curious knot,

---

5. Daedalus, the mythical Greek maker of mazes, acts here as master of the intricate steps of
the dance that interweaves pleasure with virtue under the guidance of art.
6. Experience.

As ev'n th' observer scarce may know
   Which lines are Pleasure's and which not.

First, figure out the doubtful way   230
   At which awhile all youth should stay,[7]
Where she and Virtue did contend
   Which should have Hercules to friend.

Then, as all actions of mankind
   Are but a labyrinth or maze,   235
So let your dances be entwined,
   Yet not perplex men unto gaze;

But measured, and so numerous too,
   As men may read each act you do,
And when they see the graces meet,   240
   Admire the wisdom of your feet.

For dancing is an exercise
   Not only shows the mover's wit,
But maketh the beholder wise,
   As he hath power to rise to it.   245

The first dance.

After which Daedalus again.

SONG 2

O more, and more! This was so well
   As praise wants half his voice to tell;
      Again yourselves compose;   250
And now put all the aptness on
   Of figure, that proportion
      Or color can disclose.

That if those silent arts were lost,
   Design and picture, they might boast   255
      From you a newer ground;[8]
Instructed to the height'ning sense
   Of dignity and reverence
      In your true motions found:

---

7. The dancers are to "figure out" the doubtful moment of Hercules' choice in the sense of illustrating it; they are beyond the occasion of making it themselves, having already reconciled pleasure with virtue.
8. Put on the "aptness of figure," i.e., significance of expression, of which art (proportion or color) is capable; thus, if design and picture, the silent arts, were lost, they could be rebuilt out of the dance alone.

Begin, begin; for look, the fair   260
Do longing listen to what air
    You form your second touch;[9]
That they may vent their murmuring hymns
Just to the tune you move your limbs,
    And wish their own were such.   265

Make haste, make haste, for this
  The labyrinth of beauty is.

The second dance:

That ended, DAEDALUS:

SONG 3

It follows now you are to prove   270
  The subtlest maze of all, that's love,
    And if you stay too long,
    The fair will think you do 'em wrong,

Go choose among—but with a mind
  As gentle as the stroking wind   275
    Runs o'er the gentler flowers.
And so let all your actions smile
  As if they meant not to beguile
    The ladies, but the hours.

Grace, laughter and discourse may meet,   280
  And yet the beauty not go less:
For what is noble should be sweet,
  But not dissolved in wantonness.

  Will you that I give the law
    To all your sport, and sum it?   285
It should be such should envy draw,
    But ever overcome it.

Here they danced with the ladies, and the whole revels followed;[1]
which ended, Mercury called to Daedalus in this following speech,
which was after repeated in song by two trebles, two tenors, a bass, 290
and the whole chorus.

SONG 4

An eye of looking back were well,
  Or any murmur that would tell

9. Endeavor.
1. Group of onlookers and courtiers.

Your thoughts, how you were sent
　　　　And went,　　　　　　　　　　　　295
To walk with Pleasure, not to dwell.

These, these are hours by Virtue spared
　　Herself, she being her own reward,
　　　　But she will have you know
　　　　　　That though　　　　　　　　300
Her sports be soft, her life is hard.

You must return unto the hill,
　　　　And there advance
With labor, and inhabit still
　　　　　　That height and crown　　　　305
From whence you ever may look down
　　　　　　Upon triumphèd Chance.

She, she it is, in darkness shines.
　　'Tis she that still herself refines
　　　　　　By her own light, to every eye　　310
More seen, more known when Vice stands by.
　　And though a stranger here on earth,
　　In heaven she hath her right of birth.
　　　　　　There, there is Virtue's seat,
Strive to keep her your own;　　　　　　315
　　'Tis only she can make you great,
Though place here make you known.

*After which, they danced their last dance, and returned into the
scene, which closed and was a mountain again as before.*

　　　　And so it ended.　　　　　　　　320

This pleased the king so well, as he would see it again; when it
was presented with these additions.[2]

1618　　　　　　　　　　　　　　　1640

---

2. The "additions" were another short masque, *For the Honor of Wales.*

CONTEXTS

Jonson on His Work

Discourses on Poetry

Jonson's relation to his readers was always peculiarly direct and personal: far from rhapsodizing in a vacuum, he always conceived of himself as a man talking to other men. Part of the poet's duty, as he saw it (and a long tradition helped him see it this way) was to provide his readers with instruction about both life and art, and he was rarely devious or indirect in doing so. In his prologues, his plays, his poems, and his prose he often went out of his way to lay down a set of ethical and esthetic principles. These allocutions tell us a great deal about the character of the man, something too about the best way to approach his work; with both these ends in view, we have arranged a selection of representative passages.

From Every Man in His Humour (first version, 1598)[1]

LORENZO SENIOR. * * * Go to; you see
How abjectly your poetry is ranked   310
In general opinion.
LORENZO JUNIOR. Opinion! O God, let gross opinion
Sink and be damned as deep as Barathrum.[2]
If it may stand with your most wished content,
I can refell[3] opinion, and approve   315
The state of poesy, such as it is,
Blessèd, eternal, and most true divine.
Indeed, if you will look on poesy
As she appears in many, poor and lame,
Patched up in remnants and old worn rags,   320
Half starved for want of her peculiar food,
Sacred invention, then I must confirm

1. The play, first performed in 1598, exists in two versions, the quarto of 1601 and the heavily revised folio of 1616. In the first version, Lorenzo junior is having trouble with his father, Lorenzo senior, who wants his son to give up poetry and devote himself to something practical such as making money. His assertion that poetry is not highly valued by "the general opinion" provokes a long and earnest rebuttal by his son—through whose voice one can surely hear that of Jonson himself. The passage is found in Act 5, scene 3, lines 309 and following.
2. A pit in ancient Athens into which criminals condemned to death were thrown.
3. Refute; "approve": prove.

Both your conceit and censure of her merit.
But view her in her glorious ornaments,
Attired in the majesty of art,   325
Set high in spirit with the precious taste
Of sweet philosophy, and, which is most,
Crowned with the rich traditions of a soul
That hates to have her dignity profaned
With any relish of an earthly thought: 330
Oh, then how proud a presence doth she bear!
Then is she like herself, fit to be seen
Of none but grave and consecrated eyes;
Nor is it any blemish to her fame
That such lean, ignorant, and blasted wits,   335
Such brainless gulls,[4] should utter their stol'n wares
With such applauses in our vulgar[5] ears,
Or that their slubbered lines have current pass
From the fat judgments of the multitude,
But that this barren and infected age   340
Should set no difference 'twixt these empty spirits
And a true poet: than which reverend name
Nothing can more adorn humanity.

Prologue to Every Man in His Humour (second version, 1616)[1]

Though need make many Poets, and some such
As art and nature have not bettered[2] much,
Yet ours, for want, hath not so loved the stage
As he dare serve th'ill customs of the age,
Or purchase your delight at such a rate   5
As for it he himself must justly hate:
To make a child, now swaddled, to proceed
Man, and then shoot up, in one beard and weed[3]
Past threescore years; or with three rusty swords
And help of some few foot-and-half-foot words   10
Fight over York and Lancaster's long jars,
And in the tiring-house[4] bring wounds to scars.
He rather prays you will be pleased to see
One such today as other plays should be:

---

4. Simpletons.
5. Gross, undiscriminating—from *vulgus*, mob (Latin); "slubbered": careless, messy.
1. In this second version of the play, Lorenzo junior's defense of poetry has disappeared, along with Lorenzo junior (his name is now Edward Kno'well), but the Prologue introduces the play with a forthright account of what Jonson thinks a play should and should not be.
2. Improved over their original ignorance.
3. Suit of clothing.
4. Dressing and makeup room.

Where neither *Chorus* wafts you o'er the seas,[5]   15
Nor creaking throne comes down, the boys to please,
Nor nimble squib is seen, to make afeared
The gentlewomen,[6] nor rolled bullet heard,
To say, *It thunders*; nor tempestuous drum
Rumbles to tell you when the storm doth come: 20
But deeds and language, such as men do use,
And persons such as *Comedy* would choose
When she would show an image of the times,
And sport with human follies, not with crimes—
Except, we make 'em such by loving still   25
Our popular errors, when we know they're ill.
I mean such errors as you'll all confess
By laughing at them, they deserve no less:
Which when you heartily do, there's hope left then,
You that have so graced monsters may like men.   30

Prologue to Cynthia's Revels
(produced 1600, published 1601)[1]

If gracious silence, sweet attention,
Quick sight, and quicker apprehension
(The lights of judgment's throne) shine anywhere,
Our doubtful[2] author hopes this is their sphere,
And therefore opens he himself to those,   5
To other weaker beams his labors close,
As loth to prostitute their virgin strain
To every vulgar and adulterate brain.
In this alone his Muse her sweetness hath,
She shuns the print of any beaten path,   10
And proves[3] new ways to come to learned ears:
Pied ignorance[4] she neither loves nor fears.
Nor hunts she after popular applause,
Or foamy praise, that drops from common jaws.
The garland that she wears their hands must twine   15
Who can both censure, understand, define

---

5. Jonson is reflecting on Shakespeare's *Henry V*, when the Chorus invites the audience to imagine themselves aboard a fleet crossing the Channel to invade France; his preceding allusion is to stage fights such as that of Shrewsbury in *Henry IV, Part I*.
6. Squibs were firecrackers, sometimes set off onstage or amid the audience, as in Marlowe's *Doctor Faustus*; to imitate thunder, a cannonball was rolled down a wooden trough.
1. *Cynthia's Revels* is a satirical comedy in which satire all but overwhelms its comic partner. In declaring here that only the knowing few can judge him, Jonson comes close to arrogance; in placing "matter"—i.e., thought—far above "action," he comes close to disdaining the first commandment of the storyteller: "Dramatize!"
2. Uncertain (of the success of his play).
3. Attempts.
4. Fools wore a harlequin jacket, and ignorance was associated with motley ("pied").

What merit is: then cast those piercing rays
Round as a crown, instead of honored bays,[5]
About his poesy; which (he knows) affords
Words above action, matter above words.   20

From Poetaster (1601)[1]

CAESAR. Say then, loved Horace, thy true thought of Virgil.
HORACE. I judge him of a rectified spirit,   100
By many revolutions of discourse
(In his bright reason's influence) refined
From all the tartarous moods of common men;[2]
Bearing the nature and similitude
Of a right heavenly body; most severe   105
In fashion and collection of himself,
And then as clear and confident as Jove.
GALLUS. And yet so chaste and tender is his ear,
In suffering any syllable to pass
That he thinks may become the honored name   110
Of issue to his so examined self,[3]
That all the lasting fruits of his full merit
In his own poems, he doth so distaste
As if his mind's peace, which he strove to paint,
Could not with fleshly pencils have her right.   115
TIBULLUS. But, to approve his works of sovereign worth,
This observation (methinks) more than serves,
And is not vulgar;[4] That which he hath writ
Is with such judgment labored and distilled
Through all the needful uses of our lives,   120
That could a man remember but his lines,
He should not touch at any serious point,
But he might breathe his spirit out of him.
CAESAR. You mean, he might repeat part of his works,
As fit for any conference he can use?   125
TIBULLUS. True, royal Caesar. CAESAR. Worthily observed,
And a most worthy virtue in his works.
What thinks material[5] Horace of his learning?

---

5. Bays, or laurel, traditionally composed the poet's crown.
1. *Poetaster* (the word means "minipoet" or "pseudopoet") carried forward the set of literary
   quarrels that animated *Cynthia's Revels*. Its action centers on a plot to defame Horace, which
   is exposed and defeated; in the course of rendering judgment, Caesar asks Horace what he
   thinks of Virgil, and the answer turns into an extended description, if not quite a definition,
   of what Horace (i.e., Jonson) thinks a real poet should be. The passage is found in Act 5,
   scene 1, lines 99 and following.
2. The basic metaphor is that he is a heavenly body, a star, purified of the earthy deposits
   ("tartarous moods") of ordinary humans.
3. I.e., he is so careful of letting anything pass that might be attributed to him as its author, that
   he criticizes sharply his own writings.
4. Commonplace.
5. Substantial, solid.

HORACE. His learning labors not the school-like gloss
That most consists in echoing words and terms   130
And soonest wins a man an empty name,
Nor any long or far-fetched circumstance
Wrapped in the curious generalties of arts;
But a direct and analytic sum
Of all the worth and first effects of arts.   135
And for his poesy, 'tis so rammed with life
That it shall gather strength of life with being,
And live hereafter more admired than now.

From "Epistle Dedicatory" *to* Volpone[1]

For if men will impartially, and not asquint, look toward the offices
and function of a poet, they will easily conclude to themselves the
impossibility of any man's being the good poet without first being a
good man. He that is said to be able to inform[2] young men to all good
disciplines, inflame grown men to all great virtues, keep old men in
their best and supreme state or, as they decline to childhood, recover
them to their first strength; that comes forth the interpreter and arbiter
of nature, a teacher of things divine no less than human, a master in
manners; and can alone, or with a few, effect the business of mankind;
this, I take him, is no subject for pride and ignorance to exercise their
railing rhetoric upon.

⁎   ⁎   ⁎

⁎ ⁎ ⁎ [D]octrine ⁎ ⁎ ⁎ is the principal end of poesy, to inform men
in the best reason of living. And though my catastrophe[3] may, in the
strict rigor of comic law, meet with censure, as turning back to my
promise, I desire the learned and charitable critic to have so much faith
in me to think it was done of industry; for with what ease I could have
varied it nearer his scale, but that I fear to boast my own faculty, I could
here insert. But my special aim being to put the snaffle[4] in their mouths
that cry out we never punish vice in our interludes, etc., I took the
more liberty; though not without some lines of example drawn even in
the ancients themselves, the goings out of whose comedies are not
always joyful, but oft-times the bawds,[5] the servants, the rivals, yea, and
the masters are mulcted;[6] and fitly, it being the office of a comic poet

---

1. Johnson addresses his "Epistle" to "The most noble and most equal sisters, the two famous universities," Oxford and Cambridge, from whom Jonson received honorary degrees. An early production of the play took place at Oxford. The second of the two passages is Jonson's defense of the conclusion of his play, which has frequently drawn criticism for being too harsh.
2. Shape.
3. Denouement, conclusion; "turning back to my promise": i.e., his promise to keep distinct comedy and more serious drama.
4. Bridle-bit.
5. Prostitutes, panders.
6. Punished.

to imitate justice, and instruct to life, as well as purity of language, or stir up gentle affections.

JONSON'S SHOPTALK

A spacious, talkative, and opinionated man, Jonson frequently unburdened himself on a wide variety of miscellaneous topics. We have two compendia of these sayings. The first consists of a manuscript or group of manuscripts, found after his death by Jonson's literary executor, Sir Kenelm Digby, and by him bundled into the 1640 Folio edition of Jonson's Works. The material has at least three titles—*Timber, Explorata, Discoveries*—but the subtitle of the original edition best describes the contents. They are discoveries "made upon men and matter as they have flowed out of his daily readings or had their reflux to his peculiar notion of the times"—a sort of commonplace book, as it were, in which he made notes and observations as things struck him. They constitute, effectually, our first glimpse inside an English poet's workshop. We see here what he thought about his trade, what his stylistic aims were and how he trained himself to carry them out. Many of his ideas are not really his, but are transcribed out of the classical and continental authors whom he read avidly; but that doesn't lessen their interest, or his sincerity in professing them.

The second collection of Jonson's talk is more picturesque in its origins. In mid-summer of 1618 he took off on a walking trip to Scotland, having a mind to see the country and write a poetical account of his adventures on the way. Against all the odds, for he was a corpulent man in his middle years and since the military days of his youth given more to eating and drinking than to exercise, he completed the tour, and was feted royally by the literary society of Edinburgh. Among his hosts on the trip was the Anglo-Scottish poet William Drummond, at whose estate of Hawthornden Jonson lingered for a couple of weeks. Drummond wasn't altogether enchanted with his English guest, who seemed to drink a lot, boast of his own doings, and run down everybody else. But he jotted down the memoranda of his conversations with Jonson—or rather, of Jonson's monologues to him. These notes lay hidden for many years but were discovered in 1833 by David Laing and published. They furnish a vivid and intimate picture —unique in the early history of our literature—of Jonson talking off the top of his head and through a growing army of empty bottles.

From Discoveries

[The comic writer] * * * in moving the minds of men and stirring of affections * * * chiefly excels. What figure of a body was Lysippus[1]

---

1. Lysippus was a sculptor in bronze in the fourth century B.C.E. and Apelles was a great painter of the same period; Alexander the Great declared that no one but Lysippus should make his statue and no one but Apelles paint his picture; "graver": an engraver's tool.

ever able to form with his graver, or Apelles to paint with his pencil, as the comedy to life expresses so many and various affections of the mind? There shall the spectator see some insulting[2] with joy, others fretting with melancholy, raging with anger, mad with love, boiling with avarice, undone with riot, tortured with expectation, consumed with fear.

          ✻   ✻   ✻

For a man to write well, there are required three necessaries: to read the best authors, observe the best speakers, and much exercise of his own style. In style, to consider what ought to be written, and after what manner. He must first think and excogitate his matter, then choose his words and examine the weight of either. Then take care in placing and ranking both matter and words that the composition be comely; and to do this with diligence, and often. No matter how slow the style be at first, so it be labored and accurate; seek the best, and be not glad of the forward conceits or first words that offer themselves to us, but judge of what we invent and order what we approve. Repeat often what we have formerly written, which besides that it helps the consequence and makes the juncture better, it quickens the heat of imagination that often cools in the time of setting down, and gives it new strength as if it grew lustier by the going back. As we see in the contention of leaping, they jump farthest that fetch their race largest; or, as in throwing a dart or javelin, we force back our arms to make our loose[3] the stronger. Yet, if we have a fair gale of wind, I forbid not the steering out of our sail,[4] so the favor of the gale deceive us not. For all that we invent doth please us in the conception or birth, else we would never set it down. But the safest is to return to our judgment and handle over again those things the easiness of which might make them justly suspected.

So did the best writers in their beginnings; they imposed upon themselves care and industry. They did nothing rashly. They obtained first to write well, and then custom made it easy and a habit. By little and little their matter showed itself to them more plentifully; their words answered, their composition followed; and all, as in a well-ordered family, presented itself in the place. So that the sum of all is: Ready writing makes not good writing, but good writing brings on ready writing. Yet when we think we have got the faculty, it is even then good to resist it, as to give a horse a check sometimes with a bit, which doth not so much stop his course as stir his mettle. Again, whither a man's genius is best able to reach, thither it should more and more contend, lift, and dilate[5] itself, as men of low stature raise themselves on their toes, and so ofttimes get even, if not eminent. Besides, as it is fit for grown

2. Literally, "jumping" (from Latin).
3. Release.
4. Letting out the sheet, running before the wind.
5. Expand, puff up.

and able writers to stand of themselves and work with their own
strength, to trust and endeavor by their own faculties, so it is fit for the
beginner and learner to study others, and the best. For the mind and   45
memory are more sharply exercised in comprehending another man's
things than our own, and such as accustom themselves and are familiar
with the best authors shall ever and anon find somewhat of them in
themselves, and in the expression of their minds, even when they feel
it not, be able to utter something like theirs, which hath an authority   50
above their own. Nay, sometimes it is the reward of a man's study, the
praise of quoting another man fitly. And though a man be more prone
and able for one kind of writing than another, yet he must exercise all.
For as in an instrument, so in style, there must be a harmony and
consent of parts.   55
   * * * Talking and eloquence are not the same: to speak and to speak
well are two things. A fool may talk but a wise man speaks, and out of
the observation, knowledge, and use of things. Many writers perplex
their readers and hearers with mere nonsense. Their writings need sun-
shine. Pure and neat language I love, yet plain and customary. A bar-   60
barous phrase hath often made me out of love with a good sense, and
doubtful writing hath racked me beyond my patience. The reason why
a poet is said that he ought to have all knowledges is that he should
not be ignorant of the most, especially of those he will handle. And
indeed when the attaining of them is possible, it were a sluggish and   65
base thing to despair. For frequent imitation of anything becomes a
habit quickly. If a man should prosecute[6] as much as could be said of
every thing, his work would find no end.
   Speech is the only benefit man hath to express his excellency of mind
above other creatures. It is the instrument of society. Therefore Mer-   70
cury, who is the president[7] of language is called *Deorum hominumque*
interpres.[8] In all speech, words and sense are as the body and the soul.
The sense is as the life and soul of language, without which all words
are dead. Sense is wrought out of experience, the knowledge of human
life and actions, or of the liberal arts which the Greeks called *Encyclo-*   75
paideian.[9] Words are the people's, yet there is a choice of them to be
made. For *Verborum delectus, origo est eloquentiae.*[1] They are to be
chosen according to the persons we make speak, or the things we speak
of. Some are of the camp, some of the council-board, some of the shop,
some of the sheep-cote,[2] some of the pulpit, some of the bar, etc. And   80
herein is seen their elegance and propriety, when we use them fitly

6. Follow out, give expression to.
7. Presiding deity.
8. "The interpreter of Gods and men."
9. The Greek word means, literally, "instruction in a circle," the complete corpus of what a
person needs to know.
1. "Choice of words is the source of eloquence."
2. Sheep-fold.

and draw them forth to their just strength and nature by way of translation or metaphor.[3] But in this translation we must only serve necessity
. . . or commodity, which is a kind of necessity. * * * Metaphors far-
fetched hinder to be understood, and, affected, lose their grace. * * *   85
All attempts that are new in this kind are dangerous and somewhat hard
before they be softened with use. A man coins not a new word without
some peril and less fruit; for if it happen to be received, the praise is
but moderate; if refused, the scorn is assured. Yet we must adventure,
for things at first hard and rough are by use made tender and gentle.   90
It is an honest error that is committed, following great chiefs.

Custom is the most certain mistress of language, as the public stamp
makes the current money. But we must not be too frequent with the
mint, every day coining, nor fetch words from the extreme and utmost
ages, since the chief virtue of a style is perspicuity, and nothing so   95
vicious[4] in it as to need an interpreter. Words borrowed of antiquity do
lend a kind of majesty to style, and are not without their delight sometimes. For they have the authority of years, and out of their intermission
do win to themselves a kind of grace like newness. But the eldest of
the present and newness of the past language is best. For what was the   100
ancient language, which some men so dote upon, but the ancient custom? Yet when I name custom, I understand not the vulgar custom,
for that were a precept no less dangerous to language than life, if we
should speak or live after the manners of the vulgar. But that I call
custom of speech which is the consent of the learned; as custom of   105
life, which is the consent of the good. * * *

Our composition must be more accurate in the beginning and end,
than in the midst, and in the end more than in the beginning; for
through the midst the stream bears us. And this is attained by custom
more than care or diligence. We must express readily and fully, not   110
profusely. There is difference between a liberal and a prodigal hand.
As it is a great point of art, when our matter requires it, to enlarge and
veer out all sail, so to take it in and contract it is of no less praise when
the argument doth ask it. Either of them hath their fitness in the place.
A good man always profits by his endeavor, by his help—yea, when he   115
is absent, nay when he is dead by his example and memory. So good
authors in their style.

A strict and succinct style is that where you can take away nothing
without loss, and that loss to be manifest. The brief style is that which
expresseth much in little. The concise style, which expresseth not   120
enough, but leaves somewhat to be understood. The abrupt style, which
hath many breaches and doth not seem to end, but fall. The congruent

3. "Metaphor" is derived from Greek, "translation" from Latin, but the root sense of both is the
   same: to carry across.
4. Corrupt, debased.

and harmonious fitting of parts in a sentence hath almost the fastening
and force of knitting and connexion: as in stones well squared, which
will rise strong a great way without mortar. Periods[5] are beautiful when   125
they are not too long, for so they have their strength too, as in a pike
or javelin. As we must take the care that our words and sense be clear,
so if the obscurity happen through the hearer's or reader's want of understanding, I am not to answer for them, no more than for their not
listening or marking—I must neither find them ears nor mind. * * *   130
Whatsoever loseth the grace and clearness converts into a riddle; the
obscurity is marked, but not the value. That perisheth and is passed by,
like the pearl in the fable. Our style should be like a skein of silk to
be carried and found by the right thread, not raveled and perplexed;
then all is a knot, a heap.   135

* * *

The parts of a comedy are the same with a tragedy, and the end is
partly the same. For they both delight and teach; the comics are called
didaskaloi[6] of the Greeks, no less than the tragics.

Nor is the moving of laughter always the end of comedy, that is rather
a fowling[7] for the people's delight, or their fooling. For, as Aristotle says   140
rightly, the moving of laughter is a fault in comedy, a kind of turpitude
that depraves some part of man's nature without a disease.[8] As a wry
face without pain moves laughter, or a deformed vizard,[9] or a rude
clown dressed in a lady's habit and using her actions: we dislike and
scorn such representations, which made the ancient philosophers ever   145
think laughter unfitting in a wise man. And this induced Plato to esteem of Homer as a sacrilegious person, because he presented the gods
sometimes laughing.[1] As also it is divinely said of Aristotle, that to seem
ridiculous is a part of dishonesty and foolish.

So that what, either in the words or sense of an author, or in the   150
language or actions of men, is awry or depraved, doth strangely stir
mean affections and provoke for the most part to laughter. And therefore it was clear that all insolent and obscene speeches; jest upon the
best men; injuries to particular persons; perverse and sinister sayings
(and the rather unexpected) in the old comedy[2] did move laughter,   155
especially where it did imitate any dishonesty. And scurrility came forth
in the place of wit, which who understands the nature and genius of
laughter cannot but perfectly know.

---

5. Sentences.
6. Teachers.
7. Hunting.
8. Jonson has here misinterpreted badly a statement in the *Poetics*, 5.1.
9. Mask.
1. Referring to the *Republic*, 3.388–89, where Plato mentions the laughter of the gods (in the
   Iliad, 1.599) at the lame god of the forge, Hephaestus.
2. The "old" comedy is that of Aristophanes, satirical and personal; the "new" that of Menander,
   presenting primarily types, not individuals.

Of which Aristophanes[3] affords an ample harvest, having not only outgone Plautus or any other in that kind, but expressed all the moods and figures of what is ridiculous, oddly. In short, as vinegar is not accounted good until the wine be corrupted, so jests that are true and natural seldom raise laughter with the beast, the multitude. They love nothing that is right and proper; the farther it runs from reason or possibility, with them, the better it is.

What could have made them laugh like to see Socrates presented, that example of all good life, honesty, and virtue, to have him hoisted up with a pulley and there play the philosopher in a basket, measure how many foot a flea could skip geometrically by a just scale, and edify the people from the engine?[4] This was theatrical wit, right stage-jesting, and relishing a playhouse, invented for scorn and laughter; whereas, if it had savored of equity, truth, perspicuity, and candor, to have tasted a wise or a learned palate, spit it out presently. "This is bitter and profitable, this instructs and would inform us; what need we know anything, that are nobly born, more than a horse race or a hunting match, our day to break with citizens, and such innate mysteries."[5]

This is truly leaping from the stage to the tumbril again, reducing all wit to the original dung-cart.[6]

From Ben Jonson's Conversations with William Drummond of Hawthornden (1619)[1]

Of his own life, education, birth, actions.

His grandfather came from Carlisle and he thought from Annandale to it;[2] he served King Henry VIII and was a gentleman. His father lost all his estate under Queen Mary; having been cast in prison and forfeited, at last turned minister. So he was a minister's son; he himself was posthumous born a month after his father's decease, brought up

3. Aristophanes (448–385 B.C.E.) was the greatest of the Greek comic poets. Jonson's own work was often compared with that of Aristophanes on the score of its bitter personalities, so it is curious to see him raising this objection against his predecessor.
4. In *The Clouds*, Aristophanes introduces Socrates onstage in an aerial basket (the "engine"), thinking airy and useless thoughts.
5. Jonson imagines Greek audiences of complacent aristocrats, approving of Aristophanes because he doesn't teach them anything (they know it all anyway): the animus in his mind is clearly against contemporary English audiences. "Our day to break with the citizens" is the gentleman's day to renege on his debts to the tradesman.
6. Tradition says the first dramas were performed on wagons or carts, drawn up in village marketplaces; Jonson thinks savage personal satire reduces comedy to the crudity of its original.
1. The conversations with Drummond were held at his estate of Hawthornden in the course of Jonson's walking tour to Scotland, which he began in the summer of 1618. During that winter he visited Drummond (1585–1649), who was himself a poet and an historian of Scotland. The text is presented in modernized English.
2. At the mouth of Solway Firth leading into the Irish Sea, Carlisle is just a few miles from the Scottish border. There are no Jonsons or Johnsons recorded as living in the hamlet of Annandale, but there are many Johnstones; Jonson may have been of their stock.

poorly, put to school by a friend (his master Camden[3]); after taken from it, and put to another craft (I think was to be a wright or bricklayer) which he could not endure. Then went he to the Low Countries but returning soon he betook himself to his wonted studies. In his service in the Low Countries he had, in the face of both the camps, killed an enemy and taken *opima spolia*[4] from him; and since his coming to England, being appealed to the fields, he had killed his adversary, which had hurt him in the arm, and whose sword was ten inches longer than his; for the which he was imprisoned and almost at the gallows.[5] Then took he his religion by trust of a priest who visited him in prison; thereafter he was twelve years a Papist.

He was Master of Arts in both the universities by their favor, not his study.

He married a wife who was a shrew yet honest; five years he had not bedded with her but remained with my Lord Aubigny.[6]

In the time of his close imprisonment under Queen Elizabeth his judges could get nothing of him to all their demands but "aye" and "no." They placed two damned villains to catch advantage of him, with him, but he was advertised by his keeper; of the spies he has an epigram.

When the King came in England—at that time the pest was in London—he being in the country at Sir Robert Cotton's[7] house with old Camden, he saw in a vision his eldest son (then a child and at London) appear unto him with the mark of a bloody cross on his forehead as if it had been cutted with a sword; at which amazed he prayed unto God, and in the morning he came to Mr. Camden's chamber to tell him, who persuaded him it was but an apprehension of his fantasy at which he should not be disjected. In the meantime comes there letters from his wife of the death of that boy in the plague. He appeared to him, he said, of a manly shape and of that growth that he thinks he shall be at the resurrection.

He was delated[8] by Sir James Murray to the King for writing something against the Scots in a play, *Eastward Ho*, and voluntarily imprisoned himself with Chapman[9] and Marston, who had written it amongst

10

15

20

25

30

35

40

3. William Camden, famous antiquary, is reported to have taught Jonson himself and paid his way through Westminster School.
4. The armor of an enemy whom one has killed in hand-to-hand combat.
5. This is the duel with a fellow actor, Gabriel Spenser, on September 22, 1598. Jonson escaped execution by claiming "benefit of clergy," that is, by proving his ability to translate a verse of the Latin Bible.
6. Esmé Stewart, Lord of Aubigny, a Scottish lord with estates in France, living in London.
7. Cotton was a great English antiquary and a fellow schoolmate of Jonson's under Camden's tutelage.
8. Accused.
9. George Chapman (best known for his translations of Homer) and John Marston, satirical playwright. *Eastward Ho* (1605) was a joint production of all three men.

them. The report was that they should then had their ears cut and noses. After their delivery he banqueted all his friends; there was Camden, Selden, and others. At the midst of the feast his old mother drank to him and show[ed] him a paper which she had (if the sentence had taken execution) to have mixed in the prison among his drink, which was full of lusty strong poison, and, that she was no churl, she told she minded first to have drunk of it herself.

He had many quarrels with Marston, beat him, and took his pistol from him, wrote his *Poetaster*[1] on him. The beginning of them were that Marston represented him in the stage.

In his youth given to venery.[2] He thought the use of a maid nothing in comparison to the wantonness of a wife and would never have another mistress. He said two accidents strange befell him: one, that a man made his own wife to court him, whom he enjoyed two years ere he knew of it, and one day finding them by chance, was passingly delighted with it; one other, lay diverse times with a woman, who show[ed] him all that he wished except the last act, which she would never agree unto.

Sir W. Raleigh sent him governor with his son, anno 1613, to France.[3] This youth, being knavishly inclined, among other pastimes (as the setting of the favors of damsels on a codpiece),[4] caused him to be drunken and dead drunk, so that he knew not where he was; thereafter laid him on a car which he made to be drawn by pioneers[5] through the streets, at every corner showing his governor stretched out and telling them that was a more lively image of the crucifix than any they had; at which sport young Raleigh's mother delighted much (saying his father young was so inclined), though the father abhorred it.

He can set horoscopes, but trusts not in them. He, with the consent of a friend, cozened a lady, with whom he had made an appointment to meet an old astrologer in the suburbs, which she kept; and it was himself disguised in a long gown and a white beard at the light of [a] dim-burning candle up in a little cabinet reached unto by a ladder.

Every first day of the New Year he had £20 sent him from the Earl of Pembroke[6] to buy books.

---

1. *Poetaster* (1601), one of the most savagely satirical of Jonson's plays. Marston portrayed Jonson as the character Chrisogamus in his play *Histriomastix* (1599).
2. Lust.
3. Since 1603 Sir Walter Raleigh had been living with his family in the Tower of London, under suspicion of treason for conspiring against King James. In 1616 he was released to head an expedition to El Dorado in America; the expedition failing, he returned to England and was executed in 1618.
4. A damsel's "favor" is her handkerchief or garter; a codpiece is a conspicuous ornamented flap in the front of a man's breeches.
5. Soldiers with engineering training and equipment, i.e., shovels.
6. Jonson had praised this nobleman in the dedication to his *Epigrams* (1616); Pembroke was the nephew of Sir Philip Sidney.

After he was reconciled with the Church, and left off to be a recu- 75
sant,[7] at his first communion in token of true reconciliation, he drank
out all the full cup of wine.

Being at the end of my Lord Salisbury's table with Inigo Jones, and
demanded by my Lord why he was not glad: "My lord," said he, "you
promised I should dine with you, but I do not," for he had none of his 80
meat. He esteemed only that his meat which was of his own dish.

He has consumed a whole night in lying looking to his great toe,
about which he has seen Tartars and Turks, Romans and Carthaginians,
fight in his imagination.

Northampton was his mortal enemy for brawling, on a St. George's 85
Day, one of his attenders. He was called before the Council for his
Sejanus[8] and accused both of popery and treason by him.

Sundry times he has devoured his books; i.e., sold them all for necessity.

He has a mind to be a churchman, and so he might have favor to 90
make one sermon to the King; he careth not what thereafter should
befall him, for he would not flatter though he saw death.

At his hither coming Sir Francis Bacon said to him, he loved not to
see poesy go on other feet than poetical dactyls and spondees.

Drummond's Summary of Jonson's Character (January 19, 1619)

He is a great lover and praiser of himself, a contemner and scorner 95
of others, given rather to lose a friend than a jest, jealous of every word
and action of those about him (especially after drink, which is one of
the elements in which he lives), a dissembler of ill parts which reign
in him, a bragger of some good that he wants, thinks nothing well but
what either he himself, or some of his friends and countrymen has said 100
or done. He is passionately kind and angry, careless either to gain or
keep, vindicative, but if he be well answered, at himself.

For any religion, as being versed[9] in both. Interprets best sayings and
deeds often to the worst. Oppressed with fantasy, which has ever mas-
tered his reason, a general disease in many poets. His inventions are 105
smooth and easy, but above all he excels in a translation. When his
play of a Silent Woman was first acted, there was found verses after on
the stage against him, concluding that that play was well named The
Silent Woman: there was never one man to say plaudite[1] to it.

---

7. A "recusant" refuses to attend the services of the Church of England; in those days such
   refusal was taken to be proof that one belonged to the Church of Rome. Drinking the full
   cup at communion would be taken as a sign of full reconciliation to the English Church.
8. Saint George's Day is April 23; as he is patron saint of England, it is a festive day. Henry
   Howard, Earl of Northampton, was a tough and tricky antagonist; Sejanus, Jonson's first tragedy (1603), contains many passages suggestive of a resentful and even conspiratorial
   disposition.
9. Practiced. The two religions are Protestantism and Catholicism.
1. Bravo, well done (from the Latin).

Contemporary Readers
on Jonson

Jonson himself was a generous as well as a judicious appreciator of other men's work; his poems on Shakespeare, Donne, Beaumont, Selden, and Camden are ample evidence of his gift for warm yet dignified praise. In return he received from a choir of lesser poets tributes of complimentary verse which swelled to a chorus the year after his death with the appearance of a volume, *Jonsonius Virbius* (Jonson Reborn). Much of this verse is simply social or ceremonial in character, but from the best of it we may learn what qualities in Jonson and his work appealed most deeply to his own times.

SIDNEY GODOLPHIN

On Ben Jonson[1]

The Muses' fairest light in no dark time,
The wonder of a learnèd age; the line
Which none can pass; the most proportioned wit
To nature; the best judge of what was fit;
The deepest, plainest, highest, clearest pen;   5
The voice most answered by consenting[2] men,
The soul which answered best to all well said
By others, and which most requital made;
Tuned to the highest key of ancient Rome,
Returning all her music with his own;   10
In whom, with nature, study claimed a part,
And yet who to himself owed all his art:
    Here lies Ben Jonson. Every age will look
    With sorrow here, with wonder on his book.

1. Sidney Godolphin (1610–1643) was more a politician and diplomat than a man of letters; with his friend Lord Falkland he was of the group that admired and helped support Jonson in his last years, and he contributed this eloquent poem to the memorial volume.
2. The metaphor, which works throughout the poem, is of two stringed instruments, one of which vibrates in response to chords played on the other.

EDMUND WALLER

Upon Ben Jonson[1]

Mirror of poets! mirror of our age!
Which her whole face beholding on stage,
Pleased and displeased with her own faults, endures
A remedy like those whom music cures.[2]
Thou hast alone those various inclinations   5
Which Nature gives to ages, sexes, nations
So tracèd with thy all-resembling pen,
That whate'er custom has imposed on men,
Or ill-got habits (which distort them so
That scarce the brother can the brother know)   10
Is represented to the wondering eyes
Of all that see or read thy comedies.
Whoever in those glasses looks, may find
The spots returned, or graces, of his mind,
And by the help of so divine an art,   15
At leisure view and dress[3] his nobler part.
Narcissus, cozened by that flattering well
Which nothing could but of his beauty tell,
Had here, discov'ring the deformed estate
Of his fond mind, preserved himself with hate.[4]   20
But virtue too, as well as vice, is clad
In flesh and blood so well, that Plato had
Beheld what his high fancy once embraced,[5]
Virtue with colors, speech, and motion graced.
The sundry postures of thy copious Muse   25
Who would express, a thousand tongues must use,
Whose fate's no less peculiar than thy art;
For as thou couldst all characters impart,
So none could render thine, which still escapes,
Like Proteus,[6] in variety of shapes—   30

---

1. Edmund Waller (1606–1687) survived the civil wars to exercise a strong influence on the polished and graceful poetry fashionable during the Restoration. His contribution to *Jonsonius Virbius* emphasizes the universality of Jonson's vision and the therapeutic powers of his dramas.
2. Music was thought to cure madness by driving out one frenzy with another.
3. Not simply adorn, but in the stronger sense of correct, redress.
4. In Greek mythology, Narcissus fell in love with his own image and starved to death; had he recognized his vanity (as Jonson's plays could have taught him to do), he would have hated that vice, and so been preserved.
5. Looking at Jonson's plays, Plato would have seen the pure and ideal form of virtue clothed in flesh and blood.
6. Proteus, the old man of the sea, had the power to assume an infinite variety of shapes.

Who was nor this nor that, but all we find
And all we can imagine in mankind.

JASPER MAYNE

From To the Memory of Ben. Jonson[1]

He that writes well, writes quick, since the rule's true,   65
Nothing is slowly done, that's always new.
So when thy FOX had ten times acted been,
Each day was first, but that 'twas cheaper seen.[2]
And so thy ALCHEMIST, played o'er and o'er,
Was new o'th' Stage when 'twas not at the door.[3]   70
We like the Actors did repeat, the Pit
The first time saw, the next conceived thy Wit:
Which was cast in those forms, such rules, such Arts,
That but to some not half thy Acts were parts:
Since of some silken judgments we may say,   75
They filled a Box two hours, but saw no Play.[4]
So that th'unlearned lost their money, and
Scholars saved only, that could understand.
    Thy Scene was free from Monsters, no hard Plot
Called down a God t'untie th'unlikely knot.[5]   80
The Stage was still a Stage, two entrances
Were not two parts o'th' World, disjoined by Seas.
Thine were land-Tragedies, no prince was found
To swim a whole Scene out, then o'th' stage drowned;[6]
Pitched fields, as Red-Bull wars,[7] still felt thy doom,   85
Thou laidst no sieges to the Music-Room;[8]
Nor wouldst allow to thy best Comedies

1. Jasper Mayne or Maine (1604–1672) was a lively if not particularly gifted divine, poet, play-wright, translator, controversialist, and man of letters, who contributed to the Jonson memorial volume. Precisely because they're not very original, his comments express with clarity and force the literary standards of the time.
2. In the seventeenth century, as in the twentieth, tickets to the first performance cost more than those for the regular run of the play.
3. The play was ever fresh onstage though it had been presented a number of times. The "pit," where admission was cheapest, is understood to contain the dullest spectators.
4. The "silken" judgments are clearly those of the fine gentlemen, to whom Jonson himself was hostile.
5. Having a god float down from heaven to resolve a knotty plot is a cheap theatrical device, known as a *deus ex machina*, a god out of the machine.
6. Shipwrecks and drownings onstage (as in Shakespeare's *Pericles* and *The Tempest*) taxed the credulity of spectators in ways that Jonson did not accept.
7. The Red Bull was a theater famous for putting on loud, swashbuckling shows.
8. The phrase implies that there may have been a special room on some Elizabethan stages for musicians: sieges of cities might then be sketchily represented by a couple of actors in armor attacking the music room.

Humors that should above the people rise:
Yet was thy language and thy style so high,
Thy Sock to th' Ankle, Buskin reached to th' thigh;[9]　　90
And both so chaste, so 'bove Dramatic clean,
That we both safely saw and lived thy Scene.
No foul loose line did prostitute thy wit,
Thou wrot 'st thy Comedies, did not commit.[1]
We did the vice arraigned not tempting hear,　　　　95
And were made Judges, not bad parts,[2] by th'ear.
For thou ev'n sin didst in such words array,
That some who came bad parts went out good play.
Which ended not with th' Epilogue; the Age
Still acted, which grew innocent from th' stage.　　　100
'Tis true thou hadst some sharpness, but thy salt
Served but with pleasure to reform the fault.
Men were laughed into virtue, and none more
Hated Face acted than were such before.
So did thy sting not blood, but humors draw,　　　105
So much doth satire more correct than law.

※　　※　　※

THOMAS CAREW

To Ben Jonson upon Occasion of His Note of Defiance Annexed to His Play of *The New Inn*[1]

'Tis true, dear Ben, thy just chastising hand
Hath fixed upon the sotted age a brand
To their swoll'n pride and empty scribbling due;
It cannot judge nor write;—and yet, 'tis true
Thy comic muse from the exalted line　　　　　5
Touched by thy *Alchemist* doth since decline
From that her zenith, and foretells a red
And blushing evening when she goes to bed,
Yet such as shall out-shine the glimmering light
With which all stars shall gild the following night.　　10

9. The comic "sock" or slipper is a metaphor for the "low" style of comedy, as the high-heeled boot or "buskin" represents the exalted style of tragedy.
1. Mayne plays on the familiar prohibition, "Thou shalt not commit adultery."
2. "Bad parts" would be the equivalent of "a bad lot"; "good play" implies what we would call "a good sort," with a punning compliment on Jonson's dramatic workmanship.
1. Thomas Carew (1594–1640) was a brilliant, charming man who hung about the fringes of the Stuart court, chasing girls and writing verses. His poem to Jonson, whose play *The New Inn* (1629) had been a catastrophic failure, and who promptly wrote a poem denouncing the taste of the whole audience, neatly combines truth with tact.

Nor think it much (since all thy eaglets may
Endure the sunny trial)[2] if we say
This hath the stronger wing, or that doth shine
Tricked up in fairer plumes, since all are thine.
Who hath his flock of cackling geese compared   15
With thy tuned choir of swans? Or else who dared
To call thy births deformed? But if thou bind
By city-custom or by gavelkind[3]
In equal shares thy love on all thy race,
We may distinguish of their sex and place.   20
Though one hand from them, and though one brain strike
Souls into all, they are not all alike.
Why should the follies then of this dull age
Draw from thy pen such an immodest rage
As seems to blast thy (else-immortal) bays.[4]   25
When thine own tongue proclaims thy itch of praise?
Such thirst will argue drouth. No, let be hurled
Upon thy works by the detracting world
What malice can suggest; let the rout say,
The running sands that ere thou make a play   30
Count the slow minutes might a *Goodwin* frame[5]
To swallow when th' hast done thy shipwrecked name.
Let them the dear[6] expense of oil upbraid,
Sucked by thy watchful lamp, that hath betrayed
To theft the blood of martyred authors, spilt   35
Into thy ink, whilst thou growest pale with guilt.[7]
Repine not at the taper's thrifty waste
That sleeks thy terser poems, nor is haste
Praise but excuse; and if thou overcome
A knotty writer, bring the booty home;   40
Nor think it theft if the rich spoils so torn
From conquered authors be as trophies worn.
Let others glut on the extorted praise
Of vulgar breath, trust thou to after days:
Thy labored works shall live when Time devours   45
Th' abortive offspring of their hasty hours.

---

2. To make sure the young birds in his nest are genuine eaglets, the eagle is reputed to fly with them up toward the sun; any bird that isn't an authentic eagle is blinded by the rays.
3. City-custom (i.e., London city custom) and gavelkind (a system of land tenure once common in Kent) were two legal ways of dividing an estate equally among all the heirs—as opposed to the normal English rule of primogeniture (under which the eldest son received everything).
4. Bays, or laurel, make up the poet's crown.
5. Goodwin-sands was a sandbar, shifty and treacherous, on which many ships were lost. Jonson's slowness in composition was proverbial.
6. Extravagant.
7. The other great charge against Jonson was that he copied or translated too liberally from other authors.

Thou art not of their rank, the quarrel lies
Within thine own verge.[8] Then let this suffice:
The wiser world doth greater thee confess
Then all men else, than thyself only less.   50

8. I.e., within your own territory, against yourself. Duels cannot properly take place between two
   men of different rank, and as Jonson is out of everyone else's class, he can fight only himself.

BACKGROUNDS
AND SOURCES

Volpone

BEAST FABLE

Underlying all of the machinations of Volpone upon the foolish dupes seeking his wealth is the ancient fable of Aesop, who probably lived in the early sixth century B.C.E., that tells how a fox flattered a crow, sitting safely in a treetop with a piece of cheese, into trying to sing. When the bird opened its mouth, the cheese fell to the ground for the fox to devour. Below are a number of variations and expansions upon this fable. All would have been known to Jonson except the last, that of La Fontaine, which was published in 1668; it is included here because it was destined in subsequent literary history to become the most famous short version of the story.

MIDDLE ENGLISH BESTIARY

Natura Wulpis[†]

A wild creature there is
That is full of many tricks;
She is called "Fox."
Householders hate her
For her craftiness   5
And harmful deeds.
The cock and the capon
She drags often from their pen,
And the gander and the goose
By the neck and by the beak   10
She hauls to her hole.
Therefore man hates her;
They hate and howl,
Both men and fowl.

---

† Translated by Norma J. Engberg. The title means "nature of the fox." Medieval bestiaries, or collections of fabulous stories about animals, with morals attached at the end, had their origins in Aesop's *Fables* and other collections from earlier times, such as the Greek *Physiologus*. The Middle English Bestiary appeared in the northeast Midlands in the latter half of the thirteenth century and was written in verse. Its application to Volpone is clear.

367

Hear now a wonder   15
This creature does for hunger:
She goes afield to a furrow
And falls into it,
In ploughed earth or a gully
In order to deceive birds.   20
Nor does she stir from the spot
The better part of a day
But lies still as if dead,
Drawing no breath.
The raven is very ready   25
He thinks that she is rotting,
And other birds light down by her
In order to get food,
Boldly and without fear.
They think that she is dead.   30
They hop on the fox's skin
And she feels them.
Quickly she leaps up
And stops them at once;
She requites their pecking   35
With swift ill-feeling;
She rends and rips them
With her sharp teeth;
She gulps down her fill
And goes where she will.   40

Significacio prima[1]

Of use as a twofold example
We may find this creature,
To teach prudence and wisdom
Against the devil and evil men.

The devil lies secretly.   5
Pretending he will not mislead us,
That he will do us no harm,
He leads us into sin
And there he slays us.
He bids us do our belly's will,   10
To eat and drink to excess,
And during our diversion
He takes the fox's role.

He jabs at the fox's skin
Whosoever tells a lying tale.   15

1. "First moral."

And he rips at his carcass
Whosoever feeds himself with sin.
The devil requites such pecking
With shame and disgrace
And, for his sinful work,   20
Leads man to hell's murk.

Significacio secunda[2]

Thus the devil is like the fox
With evil tricks and stratagems.
And men also the fox's name
Are worthy to have in shame.
For whosoever says good to another   5
And thinks evil in his mind,
Fox he is and fiend indeed.
The Book does not lie about this.
So was Herod fox and beguiler
When Christ came on earth;   10
He said he would believe in him
And planned to kill him.[3]

WILLIAM CAXTON

How Corbant the Crow Made Complaint against the Fox for the Death of his Wife[†]

Just as soon as the rabbit had made an end to his complaint, Corbant the crow came flying into the place before the king, and cried, "Dear lord, hear me! I bring you here a piteous complaint.

"I went this morning with Sharpbeak, my wife, to play upon the heath and there, like a lifeless wretch in the dirt, lay Reynard the fox.

2. "Second moral."
3. King Herod asked the wise men who were searching for the place of Christ's birth to return to him when they had found him "that I may come and worship him also" (Matthew 2.8). After finding the child, the wise men were warned by God in a dream not to return to Herod: "Then Herod, when he saw that he was mocked of the wise men, was exceeding wroth, and sent forth, and slew all the children that were in Bethlehem . . . from two years old and under" (Matthew 2.16).
† This story is taken from the English version of the adventures of Reynard the Fox published in 1481 by the early English printer William Caxton, translated by Norma J. Engberg. The source of this book, the French *Le Roman de Renart,* was a group of twenty-seven octosyllabic poems composed by clerics between 1175 and 1250, and it parodies the *chanson de geste* (French epic poem), such as *The Song of Roland,* as well as the courtly romance. Recounting the adventures of the wily fox Renart, who unfailingly outwits his fellow animals, the poems written before 1205 offer lighthearted satire of feudal society, while the later poems take on a darker quality, with Renart personifying evil and hypocrisy.
   In this selection from Caxton, the fox pretends that he is dead in order to get his way. The moral is incorporated into the text in the crow's warning to the king.

His eyes stared and his tongue lolled out of his mouth like a hound that was dead. We tasted and felt his belly, but we found no life in it. Then my wife went to listen and laid her ear before his mouth to see if he drew breath. This was the cause of her troubles. For the treacherous, deadly fox awaited well his time, and when he saw her so near him, he caught her by the head and bit it off.

"Then I was in great sorrow and cried aloud, 'Alas! Alas! What is going on here?' He stood up hastily and reached for me so gluttonously that for fear of death I trembled and flew up into a nearby tree. Then I saw from afar how the wily deceiver chewed and swallowed her up so hungrily that he left neither flesh nor bone, no more than a few feathers. Indeed, he gobbled the small feathers with the flesh. He was so hungry he would have eaten two of her, if he could. Then he went his way.

"I flew down with great sorrow and gathered up these feathers in order to show them to you here. I would not again be in such peril and fear as I was then for a thousand marks of the finest Arabian gold.

"My lord the king, see here this piteous work! These are the feathers of Sharpbeak, my wife. My lord, if you will have honor, you must do justice for this and avenge yourself in such a way that a man may respect you and be indebted to you. For if you suffer thus your safe-conduct to be violated, you yourself shall not go peacefully upon the highways. Those lords that are unjust and withhold the law from thieves, murderers, and other transgressors are partners before God in all of those evildoers' misdeeds and trespasses. Everyone then will be a lord unto himself. Dear lord, look to this matter so as to preserve yourself!"

GEOFFREY CHAUCER

The Nun's Priest's Tale[†]

When that the month in which the world began,
That one called March, when God did first make man,
Was complete; and also had passed a few
Since March had gone, say thirty days and two,   3190
It befell that Chauntecleer in his pride
Seven wives with him, walking by his side,
Cast up his eyes toward the bright sun,
That in the sign of Taurus had run
Twenty and one degrees and somewhat more,   3195

[†] From *The Canterbury Tales* (largely planned and composed between 1387 and 1399), translated by Norma J. Engberg. This is the most famous English version of Aesop's fable of the fox and the crow, or, in this case, the fox and the chicken Chauntecleer.

He knew by kind, but by no other lore,
That it was Prime and crowed with blissful sound.
"The sun," he said, "Has climbed up heaven's round.
Forty and one degrees and more it is.
Madame Pertelote, my own worldly bliss,   3200
Hear these rapturous birds and how they sing.
And see the new-made flowers, how they spring;
Full is my heart of revel and relief!"
But all too soon on him fell sudden grief,
For every joy the final end is woe,   3205
God knows that worldly joys are soon to go;
And if a rhetorician could explain
He in a chronicle might write it plain—
A simple fact with notability.
Now every wise man, let him hark to me;   3210
This story is as true, I undertake,
As is the book of Launcelot de Lake,[1]
Whom women hold in highest reverence.
Now will I turn again to my sentence.
    A black-tipped fox of sly iniquity,   3215
That in the grove had lived three years, you see,
With great imagination had foretold,
And that same night broke through the hedge so bold
Into the yard where Chauntecleer the fair
Was with his wives accustomed to repair;   3220
And in a cabbage bed so still he lay
Until was passed the ninth hour of day,
Waiting his chance on Chauntecleer to fall,
As gladly do these homicides withal
That wicked lie in wait to murder men.   3225
O false murderer, lurking in your den!
O new Iscariot,[2] new Ganelon,
False deceiver, O second Greek Sinon,
That left all Trojans utterly forlorn!
O Chautecleer, accursed be that morn   3230
When you into that yard flew from the beams!
You certainly were warned by your dreams
Of peril this day held—which you should flee;
But that which God foreknows must ever be.

                        *   *   *

    Fair in the sand, to bathe her suitably,
Lies Pertelote, and all her sisters by

---

1. A famous knight of Arthur's roundtable. In some versions of the story, his love affair with
   Queen Guinevere leads to the destruction of Arthur's kingdom; "sentence": subject.
2. The betrayer in the New Testament Gospels who sells information about Jesus to the chief
   priests for thirty pieces of silver; "Ganelon": the stepfather of Roland in *The Song of Roland*
   who betrays Roland and the rear guard to the Saracen enemy as Charlemagne and his troops
   triumphantly march back to France; "Sinon": the Greek soldier left behind by the Greek
   army to be discovered by the Trojans so that his testimony would persuade them to bring the
   wooden horse, containing Greek troops, into the city.

Facing the sun; and Chauntecleer so free
Sings merrier than mermaids in the sea   3270
* * *
And so befell it, as he cast his eye
Among cabbages on a butterfly,
He caught sight of this fox, lying so low.   3275
Nothing would have less pleased him than to crow
But he cried "Cok! Cok!" at once and did start
As a man who was frightened in his heart.
For naturally a beast desires to flee
From his contrary, if he it can see,   3280
Though he had not before seen it with eye.
　　This Chauntecleer, when he him did espy,
Wanted to flee, except the fox anon
Said, "Gentle sir, alas, would you have gone?
Are you afraid of me who am your friend?   3285
Now, certainly were I worse than a fiend
If I to you did harm or villainy!
I am not come your gathering to espy,
But actually the cause of my coming
Was only in order to hear you sing.   3290
You certainly have as merry a voice
As any angel ever of God's choice;
You express in music feelings deeper
Than Boethius,[3] or other singer.
My lord your father—may God his soul bless!—   3295
And also your mother, true gentilesse,
Have in my house been guests to my great ease;
And likewise, am I eager you to please.
But, if men speak of singing, I would say—
So must I use well my two eyes today—   3300
Save you, I never heard a man so sing
As did your father in early morning.
Certainly from his heart outpoured his song,
And to make his voice ever the more strong
He put so much effort out that both eyes   3305
Had to be shut, so loudly he did cry,
And he would stand on tiptoes therewithal
And stretch his neck forth very long and small.
Furthermore, he was of such discretion
That there was no man in any region   3310
* * *
That surpassed him in song or subtlety.
Now sing out, sir, for holy charity;   3320
Let's see; can you your father counterfeit?
　　Then Chauntecleer his wings began to beat,

---

3. Author of *De Musica*, a famous Latin textbook on the mathematical aspect of music.

Just as a man that treason could not see,
So was he ravished with this flattery.

      *   *   *

This Chauntecleer stood high upon his toes,
Stretching his neck, and holding his eyes closed,
And at that time began to crow loudly.
Then up jumped Don Russell, the fox, quickly
And, grabbing Chauntecleer around the neck,   3335
He bore him to the woods thrown on his back,
For all this while, no man there had him viewed.
O destiny, that may not be eschewed!
Alas, that Chauntecleer flew from the beams!
Alas, that his wife had no care for dreams!   3340
Thus a Friday's ill luck did he measure.
O Venus,[4] that are goddess of pleasure,
Since he your servant was, this Chauntecleer,
And he did service with all his power,
More for delight than kind to multiply,   3345
Why suffer him on your own day to die?

      *   *   *

Certainly, no cries and lamentation
Were made by ladies, even when Ilion[5]
Was won, and Pyrrhus, brandishing his sword,
Rushed in to seize King Priam, their old lord,
And slay him—as recounts the Roman bard—   3360
To equal those made by the hens in yard.

      *   *   *

O woeful hens, it was fitting that you wept
Just as when fire throughout the city crept   3370
And for Rome's senators did cry their wives
Because all of their husbands lost their lives—
Without compunction, Nero[6] had them slain.
Now will I turn back to my tale again.
This hapless widow and her daughters two   3375
Heard these hens' lamenting and making woe;
Hastening to the door they looked around
And spied the fox, who toward the grove had run
And bore upon his back the cock caught fast.
Aloud, they cried, "Out, Help! Help!" and "Alas!   3380
Ah ha! The Fox!" and after him they ran;
Also, carrying staves, many a man.
Coll our dog ran, and Talbot and Gerland

4. Roman name for the goddess of love and beauty to whom Fridays were sacred, but in the
   Middle Ages Fridays were associated with bad luck.
5. Another name for Troy, a city in Asia Minor besieged for ten years by the Greeks, who finally
   captured it by trickery. The death of Troy's king, Priam, at the hand of Achilles' son, Pyrrhus,
   is recounted in Book II of *The Aeneid* (29–19 B.C.E.) by Virgil ("the Roman bard").
6. An insane emperor of Rome who set fire to his own city in 64 C.E. but blamed the senators
   for the fire.

And Malkyn, with a distaff in her hand;
Too ran the cow and calf, and too the hogs   3385
So frightened by the barking of the dogs
The shouting men, and women from the first—
All ran as if they thought their hearts would burst.
They yelled as friends do in darkest hell,
The ducks shrieked as if being killed, as well.   3390
The geese for fear flew high above the trees;
Out of the hive burst forth a swarm of bees.
So hideous was the racket—Bless me!—
Certainly, Jack Straw[7] and his company
Never made cacophony half so shrill   3395
When they sought out any Fleming to kill,
As this fine day was made upon the fox.
Trumpets made of brass they brought and of box,
Of horn, of bone, in which they blew and puffed
And, joining all together, shrieked and huffed.   3400
It seemed as if the high heaven should fall.
    Now, good men, I pray you to harken all:
Observe Dame Fortune turning suddenly
The hope and pride too of their enemy!
This cock, that lay upon the fox's back,   3405
In all his fear unto the fox he spoke,
And said, "Sir, if indeed I were as you,
Yet—so God help me—should I shout out, too,
'Turn back again, you proud churls each and all!
A very pestilence upon you fall!   3410
Now am I come into the woods beside;
Do as you can, the cock shall here abide
I will him eat, in faith, and that anon!' "
    The fox answered, "In faith, it shall be done."
And as he spoke those words, all suddenly   3415
This cock broke from his mouth quite nimbly
And high up in a tree he flew anon.
When the fox realized that the cock was gone,
"Alas!" said he, "O Chauntecleer, alas!
I have to you," he said, "Done some tresspass,   3420
Inasmuch as I have made you afraid
When I you grabbed and brought out of the yard.
But sir, I harbored no wicked intent.
Come down, and I shall tell you what I meant;
I shall speak truth—so God me help—to you!"   3425
    "Nay, then," he said, "I curse both of us two.
And first I curse myself, both blood and bone,
If you beguile me oftener than once.
You shall no more by means of flattery

---

7. Leader of an uprising as part of the Peasants' Revolt of 1381. His mob wandered London
   seeking to kill "Flemings" (Flemish wool merchants and weavers) because they were
   foreigners.

Persuade me both to sing and shut my eye;   3430
For he that winks when he should rather watch
—God grant that he makes of his life a botch!"
    "Nay," said the fox, "But God give him mischance,
Who is so lacking in self-governance,
That he chatters when closed mouths are the goal."   3435
    Low, such it is to be out-of-control
And negligent, and trust in flattery.
    But you that this tale hold to be folly,
As of a fox, or of a cock and hen,
Take up the moral lesson, my good men.   3440
For Saint Paul says[8] that all that is in books
Is meant to show us how great learning looks.
Take up the fruit and let the chaff lie still.
Now, good God, if it may be by thy will,
As my lord says, so make us all good men,   3445
And bring us to his highest bliss! Amen.

LA FONTAINE

The Crow and the Fox[†]

Mister Crow, perched in a tree,
Held in his beak a cheese:
Mister Fox, enticed by its aroma,
Addressed him more or less in this way:
"Hey! Good day, Monsieur de Corbeau,   5
How pretty you are! How beautiful you seem to me!
Without lying, if your voice
Equals your plumage
You are the phoenix of this wood's inhabitants."
At these words the Crow is entranced;   10
And, in order to show off his beautiful voice,
He opens a wide beak, lets fall his quarry.
The Fox seizes upon it and says: "My dear Monsieur,
Learn that every flatterer
Lives at the expense of the one who listens to him.   15
This lesson is well worth a cheese, no doubt."
The Crow, ashamed and embarrassed,
Swore, but a little too late, that he would not be fooled again.

---

8. Romans 15.4.
† Translated by Margaret Harp. La Fontaine's *Fables* were written for King Louis XIV of
  France's son as a type of moral instruction. Based on Aesop's *Fables*, they are narrative poems
  that reflect sarcastically on seventeenth-century French society as well as the passions and
  weaknesses of humanity in general. The originality of La Fontaine's *Fables* lies in their poetic
  rhythm, linguistic richness, and dramatic concision.

LEGACY HUNTING

There are a number of classical sources that gave Jonson ideas for his portrayal of greedy heirs, such as parts of the *Satyricon* by the Roman writer Petronius (d. 65 C.E.) and *Dialogues of the Dead* by the Greek writer Lucian (d. ca. 200 C.E.). The most vivid of all such pictures, though, is by Horace, in one of his satires.

HORACE

Satire 2.5†

ULYSSES. Respond to this question, Tiresias,[1] in addition to
    what has already been said. By which arts and practices
    may I rebuild my stunted fortunes? You laugh?
TIRESIAS.   Is it not enough
    now for the crafty man to return to Ithaca and see
    paternal lands and household gods?
ULYSSES.   O One-reputed-truthful,   5
    you can see, as a prophet, that I come home, naked and poor
    and find neither wine room nor flocks untouched by the
        suitors.
    High birth and virtue are cheaper than seaweed—without
        wealth.
TIRESIAS. When, to put it plainly, you shudder at poverty, accept
    by what reasoning you can become rich.

                                If a thrush[2]   10
or other special thing be given you, let it fly away
to where a large fortune glitters under an agèd lord.
If your tilled soil bears sweet fruits and other produce, let the
    rich man,
as being more venerable than a Lar,[3] enjoy them first.
Although he be a perjured person, of low origin,   15
stained with fraternal blood or a fugitive, still you may not

---

† Translated, with notes, by Norma J. Engberg. The Roman poet Horace lived from 65 to
  8 B.C.E.
1. A blind Greek prophet. Horace imagines some additions to the dialogue that Ulysses has with
  him in the underworld in Book 11 of *The Odyssey*. Ulysses is returning to his home of Ithaca
  after many years. When he does get home Ulysses finds that his wealth has been squandered
  by the dozens of local suitors who had taken advantage of his long absence to court his wife,
  Penelope.
2. This bird, considered a great delicacy in Imperial Rome, is to be given as a gift to the old
  man from whom Ulysses wishes favors.
3. These are deified ancestors (plural *Lares*) who watched over the households of their
  descendants.

refuse to walk as his attendant on his left side, if he asks.

ULYSSES. Are you telling me to shield the flank of a filthy Dama?[4]
Not thus did I at Troy, contending always with my betters.

TIRESIAS. Therefore a pauper you will be.

ULYSSES.   I shall order my tough
    soul   20
to endure this, for at times I have borne greater. Tell further,
prophet, whence I may scrape together riches and heaps of
    copper.

TIRESIAS. I have been and am speaking truly. Being clever, you
    can
everywhere lay hold of old men's last wills, and if an artful
one or two flee the lurker by means of a chewed-off fishhook,   25
neither give up hope nor, having been made sport of, let go
    your craft.
Or perhaps a matter large or less will at some time be
disputed in the forum; whichever of the two lives richly
and without sons—though he be a reprobate who audaciously
summons the better man to court—defend that one and
    despise   30
the man of good name and cause, if son or fruitful wife be at
    his home.
Say "Quintus" or "Publius" (sensitive ears delight in first
    names)
"Your manly excellence has made me your friend. I know the
    court
of justice on both sides and I am able to defend cases;
anyone will sooner pluck out my eyes than rob you, rendered   35
thus contemptible, of a hollow nut. My care is this,
that you neither lose the case nor be made a joke of." Order
him home to take care of his skin. Be made his advocate
yourself; stand firm and be hard whether "the red dog star
cleaves the speechless statues" or Furius with a fat paunch   40
"sputters over the wintry Alps with whitish-gray snow."[5]
"Do you not see?" someone says, touching with his elbow the
    person
near him, "How enduring he is, how allied to friends, how
    keen?"
More tuna will swim near and your stock of caught fish will
    grow.

Beyond this, if someone of great wealth nourishes a sickly son 45

---

4. A common name for a slave.
5. Lines from the (bad) poetry of Furius Bibaculus, contemporary to Horace, are being quoted
and made fun of here.

as heir, let not clear deference to an unmarried man
expose you, but be obliging and in a friendly manner
creep to him, in hopes both that he will write you in as
    second heir
and, if any mishap drive the boy to Orcus,[6] that you may fill
the empty place; very rarely is this dice game lost.   50

Whenever someone entrusts his last will to you to read,
remember to refuse by a motion of the head and push
the tablets from you so your sideways glance catches what the
    first wax
ordains on its second line; read quickly whether you are alone
or a coheir. A clerk new molded from a police magistrate   55
will delude the open-mouthed raven,[7] and the legacy hunter
Nasica will give opportunity for laughter to Coranus.[8]
ULYSSES. Are you mad? Or making sport of me with nonsensical
    forecasts?
TIRESIAS. Oh, son of Laertes, whatever I say either will be
or not.[9] Truly, great Apollo grants divination to me.   60
ULYSSES. Still divulge, if it is allowed, the meaning of your fable.
TIRESIAS. In days to come, when a young man,[1] frightful to the
    Parthians,
a scion of high-born Aeneas, will be great on land and sea,
the tall daughter of Nasica (seeking to avoid paying
the whole debt) will be married to durable Coranus.   65
Then the son-in-law will do this: give the tablets to his
father-in-law and beg him to read them; after numerous
refusals, he will accept and read silently, only to find
that nothing has been bequeathed to him and his own—
    except to wail.

In addition, I command these things: if by chance a freedman   70
or cunning matron gains control over a doting old man,
associate with them. Praise them so that behind your back
    they praise
you. This is useful. But to take the summit itself by storm
will bind your intended victim far better. Will the foolish
    thing

---

6. The name of the god of the land of the dead, here used to mean the underworld itself.
7. A reference to the fable of the raven and the fox.
8. Gossips of Horace's day enjoyed the tale of the debtor who, by giving his daughter in marriage, hoped not only to avoid paying what he owed, but also to inherit part of her father-in-law's assets.
9. Tiresias here burlesques his own prophetic utterances.
1. Octavius, born 63 B.C.E., who became the first Roman emperor, taking the name Augustus; the Parthians were longtime enemies of the Romans from Asia Minor; Aeneas, ancestor of the Romans, brought a band of Trojans to Italy after the Trojan War.

write bad poems? Praise them! Will he be a fornicator? Don't
   make   75
him ask. Volunteer Penelope good-naturedly.
ULYSSES.   Do you think
   that someone so temperate and virtuous, whom the suitors
   have not been able to drive from the right course, can be
   seduced?
TIRESIAS. But those young men came, tight-fisted about
   bestowing
great gifts and anxious not so much for love as for victuals.   80
Thus your Penelope is discrete; that one, if she once tasted
a little profit—sharing it with you—from one old man would
be like a dog that never can be kept off a greasy hide.
Let me tell you what happened when I yet lived. A depraved
   old Theban—
according to her will—was thus to be borne to the grave: 85
the heir had to carry the anointed corpse on his bare
   shoulders,
to test if she, having died, would slip away from him, I
   suppose,
because he had too greatly harassed her in life.

                                 Be cautious
in your approach; neither give up the effort or overdo it.
Being talkative will displease the surly and morose; yet   90
you may not be silent beyond a certain point. Be like Davus,[2]
a comic actor, and stand with head bowed down, much
   overawed.
Proceed with obsequiousness: urge him, if the wind gets gusty,
to cover his dear head; extract him from a disorderly crowd
with interposed shoulders; prick up your ear when he is
   talkative.   95
Is he burdensome in his love of praise? Press on until
"Enough certainly!" will have been said with hands raised up
to heaven; puff up the swelling windbag with pompous
   discourse.

When he will have relieved you from the weight of your long
   servitude,
stay wide awake to hear "Let Ulysses be heir to a fourth part."   100
Accordingly say, "Is Dama, my comrade, now no more?
Whence shall come someone so brave and so faithful to me?"

2. A reference to New Comedy, such as the works of Roman playwright Terence (193?–159
   B.C.E.).

from time to time scatter a few tears and if you are able,
    weep;
it is possible to hide the delight your face projects. Build up
his tomb—if it's left up to you—without being stingy about   105
expenses. Let the neighbors praise the funeral's execution.
If an older coheir has a weak cough, tell him if he wants
to purchase a farm or home out of your share, that you will
    ask
only a small sum.

       Queen Proserpina[3] beckons! Live and fare well!

3. The queen of the underworld.

The Alchemist

Alchemists believed that base metals, such as lead, could be changed into gold by certain primitive chemical processes. A number of serious writers in the Middle Ages and Renaissance found alchemy to be a fruitful source of poetic metaphors and allusions, but it was clearly a "science" that could be abused by its practitioners. Below is a famous account of such a charlatan in one of Erasmus's *Colloquies*, as well as a description from Stanton Linden's study of literature and alchemy of the context in which alchemy thrived.

ERASMUS

The Alchemy Swindle[†]

PHILECOUS.[1] What new thing is Lalus laughing to himself about, from time to time making the sign of the cross? I shall disturb the felicity of the man. I hope you are well, Lalus, my good friend; you seem to me completely happy.

LALUS. Nevertheless, I shall be happier if I may share with you what delights me.   5

PHILECOUS. Therefore, make me happy as soon as possible.

LALUS. Are you acquainted with Balbinus?[2]

PHILECOUS. I know him to be an old man, erudite and considered fortunate in life.   10

LALUS. Thus it is as you say, but there is no mortal man who is in every way perfect. This man, among his many excellent qualities, has this one mole on his body: he is seized with madness for the art that is named alchemy.

---

† Translated by Norma J. Engberg. Erasmus (1466?–1536) was one of the most famous men of the Renaissance and was noted, among other things, for being an early advocate of Greek studies and for the copiousness and variety of his writings. His *Colloquia*, from which this dialogue is taken, are a vividly imagined group of conversations on topics of the day. "The Alchemy Swindle" was first published in 1524 and, along with Chaucer's "The Canon's Yeoman's Tale" and Jonson's *The Alchemist*, is the most famous picture of this combination of early "chemist" and confidence man.

1. The name means one "who loves to listen"; "Lalus" means "talkative."
2. A name of a man in one of Horace's satires (1.3.40) who does not see the imperfections of his mistress.

PHILECOUS. Truly, you describe no mere mole on the body, but a   15
remarkable sickness.

LALUS. Whichever it is—a blemish or a sickness—Balbinus has
been cheated many times, yet he permitted himself to be ex-
traordinarily deceived a little while ago.

PHILECOUS. In what respect?   20

LALUS. A certain priest came to him and greeted him respectfully.
Presently he made a beginning to his speech, thus: "Most
learned Balbinus, you will be astonished perhaps that I, an unknown person, might dare to disturb you thus, whom I know
always to be busy with most pious studies." Balbinus nodded—   25
a customary behavior for that man—for he is wonderfully sparing
of words.

PHILECOUS. You are providing proof of his sagacity.

LALUS. Nevertheless, the other man, being more experienced, continues thus, "Yet you will forgive my rudeness once you will   30
have understood the reason why I might have approached you."
"Speak," says Balbinus, "but in as few words as possible." "I shall
explain," says he, "as briefly as I can: You know, most learned
man, I do not know whether to consider myself lucky or unlucky. And indeed, if I consider carefully my fate from one point   35
of view, I seem to myself admirably fortunate; if from the other,
no one is more unfortunate than I." When Balbinus urges him
to tie up the loose ends quickly, he says, "I shall finish, most
learned Balbinus. It will be easier for me to explain this to a
man, to whom this entire business is so completely known, in-   40
deed better known than to anyone else."

PHILECOUS. To me, you are picturing a rhetorician, not an
alchemist.

LALUS. Presently you will hear the alchemist. "This good fortune,"
he says, "befell me from boyhood, that I might learn the art   45
most to be desired of all things—alchemy, which I declare the
marrow of all philosophy." Balbinus sat up straighter at the word,
"alchemy"; sighing, he ordered the other to proceed. Then that
man says, "O wretched me! I who might not have fallen into
the way which I have." As soon as Balbinus asked of what "way"   50
he spoke, he said, "You know, most gracious sir (for what escapes
your notice, Balbinus, a man most learned in all things?) that
the means of this art is twofold; the one method is called *Longation*, 'Lengthening,' the other method is called *Curtation*,
'Shortening.' But it has befallen me by a certain ill-fate to learn   55
about Longation." With Balbinus then inquiring into what the
distinction between the ways might be, he says, "Shameless me,
who speak of these things before you—you to whom all these
things are so much better known than to anyone else. And thus

I have hastened here, in supplication that you, having compas- 60
sion on us, may deign to impart to us that most fortunate method
of Curtation. Indeed, the more practiced you are in this method,
the less difficulty you will have imparting it to us. Do not hide
this great divine favor from a brother who could die from sorrow.
In such wise, may Jesus Christ enrich you always with greater 65
gifts."

When this man would not make an end to his entreaties,
Balbinus has been driven to admit himself entirely ignorant as
to what Longation and Curtation might be: he orders his visitor
to explain the meaning of those terms himself. "Since you order, 70
thus I do. They, who consume their whole lives in this divine
art, change the species of things by two methods, the one which
is shorter but more perilous, the other which is longer but safer.
I consider myself unfortunate because up to this point I have
toiled hard in that second method, although it does not please 75
my soul; and I have not been able to find anyone who would
reveal the first method, for the love of which I perish. At length,
God sent it into my mind that I should approach you, a man
no less pious than well informed. Knowledge excels in you so
that you are easily able to give what I beg; piety will move you 80
so that you may wish to assist a brother whose welfare is in your
hand."

That I not make this tedious, when that cunning fellow had
removed any suspicion of deceit from himself by conversation
of this sort, and might even have inspired confidence in his 85
understanding of the second method, Balbinus could not get it
out of his mind. At length, overcoming his usual reticence, Balbinus says, "Away with that Curtation, whose name I have certainly never heard, and therefore for me to comprehend it is
very unlikely. Tell me in good faith, do you understand the 90
process of Longation precisely?" "Pah!" says that one, "To a hair,
but the length of time it takes is displeasing." When Balbinus
asked how long a period of time would be required, "Too
much," he says, "nearly a whole year, but in the meantime, it
is very safe." "Don't be distressed," says Balbinus, "even if the 95
business were to take as long as two years, provided that you
believe in your art."

So that I may conclude this matter in a few words it was
agreed between them that they might attempt the business in
the house of Balbinus on the following basis. The priest would 100
supply the labor; Balbinus, the expense; and the profit would be
divided equally, although the modest deceiver of his own accord
kept offering the entire gain which might come forth to Balbinus. Both parties swear silence, as they do who are being initi-

ated into secret rites. Now, on the spot, money is counted out, with which the alchemist might buy pots, glasses, charcoal and other things needed to set up a laboratory. Thereupon, our alchemist agreeably melts away the money on prostitutes, dice games and drinking parties. 105

PHILECOUS. This is to change the nature of things, assuredly. 110

LALUS. With Balbinus urging that he start immediately, he says, "But do you not understand that he who has begun well, has half the job done? It is a great thing to prepare the materials rightly." At last, the furnace has begun to be furnished. Again this action required new gold, as an enticement to the gold about to come. Just as a fish is not caught without bait, so gold does not come forth to alchemists, unless a portion of gold is added by mixing. In the meantime, Balbinus was caught up in his computations. For he kept calculating if an ounce might provide fifteen, what amount of gain might be expected from two thousand ounces, for he had resolved to expend so much. When the alchemist had melted away this money also, and now put on the appearance of great effort about the bellows and the charcoal—for one month and then another—Balbinus kept questioning whether the matter might be advancing. At first he was silent, but at last he answered the man's urgent query, "It is advancing, just as remarkable things—which are always difficult of access—are wont to do." He cited an error in purchasing charcoal as a pretext: for he had bought oak where there was a need for fir or hazel. There one hundred gold coins vanished, not stingily having been returned to the dice game. With new money having been given, the charcoal is changed; and now the matter has been taken in hand with greater eagerness than formerly: just as soldiers in war, if anything happens otherwise than they might wish, repair things with their courage. 115 120 125 130 135

When the laboratory might have been boiling hot now several months and a golden product might therefore be expected, but not even a crumb of gold was in the utensils (for now alchemy has melted all that away also), another excuse has been discovered. Truly, the glasses, in which the application had been made, had not been tempered as is proper. As mercury may not be drawn from just any wood, so gold is not brought about in just any glasses. Anyway, the more that had been laid out, the less it pleased the man to stop the undertaking. 140

PHILECOUS. Thus are gamblers wont to be—as if it were not more advantageous to waste a limited amount, rather than the whole. 145

LALUS. Thus it is. The alchemist kept swearing that he himself had never before been so deceived, that now, with the error having been detected, the rest is about to be more secure, that he him-

self is about to make up for the losses in their business with high   150
interest. With the glasses having been changed, the laboratory
has been begun anew for the third time. The alchemist kept
admonishing him that things would turn out more fortunately,
if he might send some gold as a gift to the Virgin Mother, who
is worshipped, as you know, at Paralia.[3] Because the art is sacred,   155
the thing is not to be managed prosperously without the favor
of the saints. This advice has exceedingly pleased Balbinus, a
pious man who might let no day pass on which he did not attend
Divine Service. The alchemist took on himself the pilgrimage,
doubtless into the nearest town, and there also he melted away   160
the money in debauchery. Having come back home, he an-
nounced that he himself was of the highest hope, that the business was about to succeed to their wishes, and what is more,
that the divine had seemed to nod to his prayers.

When the furnace might have been sweated already for a long   165
time, but not even a grain of gold might be produced anywhere,
he had to answer Balbinus's complaints. He said that no such
thing had happened to him at any time in his life, having proven
his art so many times, and that he was not able to guess the
cause. The question was given lengthy consideration; at last it   170
occurred to Balbinus to wonder whether he might have neglected on any day to hear the Mass or to say the Rosary, as they
call it. For no thing might succeed with these having been omit-
ted. Thereupon the impostor says, "Wretched me! Such
omissions have been allowed through my forgetfulness once and   175
again. Not long ago, rising up from a long banquet, I forgot to
say the Salutation to the Virgin." Balbinus says, "Then, it is not
astonishing, that our business does not succeed." Therefore, the
alchemist takes upon himself, for two Masses having been omit-
ted, to hear twelve; and for one Salutation, to requite ten.   180

When immediately thereafter money failed the prodigal alchemist and reasons for asking it were not at hand, at length he
invented this cunning trick. He has come back home quite
senseless with terror, and with a mournful voice he says, "I am
undone; I am completely undone, Balbinus! It is all over with   185
me!" Balbinus was astonished and kept desiring to know the
cause of so great a disaster. "Courtiers have smelled out," he
says, "what we have set in motion, and I look for no other thing
than that I may be led off to prison." At these words, Balbinus
becomes very pale in earnest. "For you know that if anyone   190
practices alchemy without the permission of the prince—as we

---

3. An uncertain reference. Perhaps it refers to the great English shrine to the Virgin Mary at
Walsingham.

have been doing—his life is imperiled." That one continues. "I
do not fear death," he says, "would that death might befall me;
I fear something inhuman." When Balbinus asks what that
might be, he says, "I may be dragged off to a tower somewhere.   195
I may be compelled to work there through my whole life for
those who don't please me. Is not any possible death bound to
be better than such a life?" Because Balbinus was adept in rhetorical theory, he moved all sides of the question if by any way
the danger could be avoided. "Can't you deny the accusation?"   200
he says. "By no means," asserts that one. "The matter has been
scattered among the royal guard, and they have proofs which
are not able to be denied." Indeed the exploit could not be
defended in court on account of the law being so clear. When,
after lengthy discussion, no defense appeared reliable to them,   205
the alchemist, who needed money immediately, says, "We, Balbinus, have been slow in our deliberations; nevertheless the
thing demands an immediate remedy. I think that those who
will drag me off into harmful circumstances are about to come
here directly." Now indeed when nothing occurs to Balbinus,   210
the alchemist says at last, "Neither has anything come into my
thoughts nor do I see anything to be left except that I may perish
courageously. Unless by chance this is agreeable to you: one
alternative remains, more serviceable than honorable. To use
someone's poverty as a weapon against him is unfeeling, but you   215
know that these kinds of men are greedy for money. On that
account they are able more easily to be corrupted so that they
may be silenced—although it may be hard to give those gallows-
birds what they most certainly will squander. Yet, as things now
stand, I see nothing better." It seemed the same to Balbinus who   220
counted out thirty gold coins so that he might procure silence.
PHILECOUS. The liberality of Balbinus is astonishing.
LALUS. Yes, you might have more quickly forced a tooth from him
     than a coin in an honest matter. Thus, protection has been
     purchased for the alchemist, for whom there was no danger,   225
     except that he needed something to give his mistress.
PHILECOUS. I wonder that Balbinus fails to show good sense in all
     this.
LALUS. Here his good sense is very greatly lacking, but he is most
     sagacious in the rest. Once more the furnace is set up with new 230
     money, but beforehand a little prayer has been dispatched to
     the Virgin Mother that she might be favorable to the undertak-
     ing. Now a whole year has come to an end with the alchemist
     pleading now this thing, now that, while the labor was lost and
     the outlay vanishes. In the meantime, a certain event exciting   235
     laughter has come to light.

The alchemist has had a secret intimacy with the wife of a
courtier, and the husband, whose mistrust has been aroused, has
begun to watch the man. At last, when he learned that the priest
was in the bedroom, he returned home, contrary to expecta-   240
tions, and knocked on the door.

PHILECOUS. What was he going to do to the man?

LALUS. What? Nothing pleasant. He was either about to kill him
or about to castrate him. When the persistent husband threatened that he himself was about to break open the door by force   245
unless the wife might open it, the lovers become exceedingly
agitated, and some kind of stratagem is sought for on the spot.
Nor was there any other remedy than what the situation itself
kept suggesting. He threw down his tunic and lowered himself
through the narrow window not without danger and not without   250
injury and ran away. You know how such stories are spread
around immediately; and so this one flowed on toward Balbinus,
as the alchemist had guessed that it would.

PHILECOUS. Here, therefore, he is caught in the middle.

LALUS. He has slipped away from this matter luckier than from the 255
bedroom. Hear the cunning trick of the man. Balbinus kept
demanding nothing, but he was betraying by his gloomy countenance that he himself was not ignorant of what was being
spread abroad by the crowd. That one knew that Balbinus was
a pious man—I might almost have said superstitious in some   260
things—and those who are such easily forgive someone who
makes humble entreaty for a sin exceedingly great. Therefore,
he lets drop a word concerning the advance of their business in
proportion to the trouble having been expended, complaining
volubly that it does not prosper as he might be accustomed or   265
might wish. Thereupon, Balbinus, who seemed otherwise to
have intended silence, has had his tongue loosened by the favorable moment, and he was someone who might easily be so
moved. "It is not unknown," he says, "what may hinder. Sins
hinder anything that turns out to be less than a success   270
because—and this is appropriate—it has not been managed
purely by the pure." At this utterance, the alchemist sinks down
on his knees, from time to time beating his breast; and with
woeful face and voice, says, "You have spoken very truly, Balbinus. Sins, I say, hinder; but my sins, not yours. I am not   275
ashamed to confess my infamy before you, just as before a most
holy priest. Weakness of the flesh had overcome me. Satan had
enticed me into his snares, and Oh, wretched me! Formerly I
was a priest; now I am an adulterer. Yet that gift, which we sent
to the Virgin Mary, has not been entirely lost. I would certainly 280
have perished if Our Lady had not assisted me. Just now a hus-

band was breaking open the folding doors, and the window was narrower than what I might be able to slip through in such an instant of danger, the idea of helping me occurs to the Most Holy Virgin. I have fallen forward onto my knees, imploring 285 that, if the gift was agreeable, she would assist me. And indeed there is no delay. I go again to the window (for thus need kept pressing me) and I discover it to have become wide enough for my flight.

PHILECOUS. Has Balbinus placed confidence in these words of his? 290

LALUS. He has believed them! Nay rather he has forgiven him indeed and has advised him scrupulously that he might not show himself unthankful to the Most Blessed Virgin. Once more money has been counted out to the fellow, who also promises that hereafter he will manage this holy matter purely. 295

PHILECOUS. What at last is the end of all this?

LALUS. The narrative is lasting a long time, but I may finish in a few words. When he had played the man a long time with contrivances of this kind and had extorted an immoderate quantity of money from him, at last there came one who had knowledge 300 of the good-for-nothing fellow from boyhood. He easily guesses that that man has set in motion the same thing with Balbinus, which he had set in motion elsewhere. He goes to Balbinus secretly and explains what kind of a contriver he had been fostering at his home. He recommends that he send the man away 305 as soon as possible, unless he prefers to see him take flight on some occasion with the contents of his chests.

PHILECOUS. What did Balbinus do at this point? Clearly he has taken care to throw the man into prison.

LALUS. Into prison! Nay, rather, he has counted out money for a 310 journey, beseeching earnestly by all things holy that the fellow might not blab out what had happened. In my opinion Balbinus has for certain acted discreetly, for he has chosen this rather than to be the common talk of feasts and of the marketplace, and afterwards he would be in danger of having his property 315 confiscated. For indeed there was no danger to the impostor. He understood no more of the method than an ass, and imposture in this sort of thing is viewed leniently. But if he had threatened him with the crime of theft, his anointing to the priesthood would have kept him safe from a hanging; and no one willingly 320 supports such a man in prison for free.

PHILECOUS. I am sorry for Balbinus, unless it is that he himself took pleasure in being deluded.

LALUS. I must hasten into the court now. At another time, I may relate things even more foolish by far than these. 325

PHILECOUS. When there shall be leisure, I shall both listen willingly and repay you story with story.

STANTON J. LINDEN

[Alchemy: Definitions and Background]†

* * * [H]istorians often distinguish between practical or exoteric alchemy[1] and a second type of esoteric, spiritual, or philosophical alchemy. Although these two traditions are often intermingled in the
writings of the alchemists themselves, the distinction between them is
important when examining the portrayals of alchemy and alchemists in
medieval and Renaissance literature. Central to this second type is
knowledge of the secrets of nature, not for the purpose of achieving
dominion over nature, as with the philosopher's stone or a magical
elixir, but rather a disinterested, unpragmatic knowledge of the origin,
composition, and secret operations of all aspects of creation. * * *

More important than knowledge of the natural world is esoteric alchemy's concentration on spiritual and philosophical values and ideals,
especially as they impinge on the inner life of the individual adept. For
E.J. Holmyard, this type with its strong religious and mystical overtones
has its origins in the exoteric alchemist's recognition that divine grace
is requisite to obtaining the philosopher's stone; this in turn, "gradually
developed into a devotional system where the mundane transmutation
of metals became merely symbolic of the transformation of sinful man
into a perfect being through prayer and submission to the will of God.
The two kinds of alchemy were often inextricably mixed; however, in
some of the mystical treatises it is clear that the authors are not concerned with material substances but are employing the language of
exoteric alchemy for the sole purpose of expressing theological, philosophical, or mystical beliefs and aspirations."[2] * * *

* * *

For mystically minded adepts, the purely chemical operations and
reactions occurring within their vessels symbolized deeper spiritual
meanings. Imperfect substances used as the proximate ingredients of
the stone were thought, for example, to undergo death and corruption

---

† From Stanton J. Linden, *Darke Hierogliphicks: Alchemy in English Literature from Chaucer
to the Restoration* (Lexington: University of Kentucky Press, 1996), pp. 7–11, 16–20, 23–24.
Copyright 1996. Reproduced by permission of The University Press of Kentucky. The author's
notes have been abridged.
1. The changing of supposedly inferior metals, such as lead, into more precious ones, such as
gold [*Editor*].
2. E. J. Holmyard, *Alchemy* (Harmondsworth, Middlesex: Penguin, 1957), p 16.

in the initial stage of the alchemical process. But following the blackness and death of this *putrefactio* (and continuing the analogy with Christ's death, resurrection, and man's salvation), these base materials later appeared to be "reborn" in the form of perfect, pure, and incorruptible gold. The progress from decay to growth, from death to resurrection, might be seen, furthermore, as a confirmation of the biblical commonplace: "Verily, verily, I say unto you, except a corn of wheat fall into the ground and die, it abideth alone: but if it die, it bringeth forth much fruit" (John 12:24).

*   *   *

Given the problematics of definition, it is useful to think of alchemy as pluralistic rather than singular, as "alchemies" rather than "alchemy." If the latter, it must be recognized that along the continuum bounded by the poles "exoteric" and "esoteric" there are many intermediate points and permutations. For example, as Robert Schuler has shown, a large number of distinguishable "spiritual alchemies" coexisted in the seventeenth century alone, each having its foundation in various theological doctrines or political ideologies rather than in alchemical theories as such.[3]

Complicating problems of definition is the fact that alchemical processes and techniques were often put to service in diverse ways by members of other occupational groups, such as physicians and apothecaries. These groups might be further subdivided according to their allegiance to either Galen[4] or Paracelsus with their corresponding prescriptions of either herbal or chemical medications. The literary consequences of such divisions are seen * * * in the many poetic references to "potable gold" or *aurum potabile*.[5] In a more generalized sense, alchemists often referred to themselves as physicians, restoring health to diseased, "leprous" base metals. Thus, the link between alchemy and medicine was close in the writings of alchemists, surgeons, apothecaries, and poet-physicians like Henry Vaughan.[6]

If, in the final analysis, a comprehensive definition of alchemy is deemed necessary, it is useful to bear in mind one recently proposed by H. J. Sheppard and grounded in the notion that alchemists thought of themselves as making conscious "alterations of duration in some linear time scale," either shortening it (in the case of the artificial pro-

---

3. "Some Spiritual Alchemies of Seventeenth-Century England," *JHI* 41 (April–June 1980): 293–318.
4. Influential Greek writer on medicine of the second century C.E.; Paracelsus (1493–1541) rejected Galen's views on medicine and exerted great influence on subsequent medical and chemical thought in Europe [*Editor*].
5. The nature and efficacy of "drinkable" gold, a popular Paracelsian medication, is clarified in the title of a work by Francis Anthonie: *The Apologie, or Defence of . . . Aurum Potabile, that is, the pure substance of Gold, prepared, and made Potable and Medicinable without corrosives, helpfully given for the health of Man in most Diseases, but especially available for the strengthening and comforting of the Heart and vitall Spirits the performers of health* (London, 1616).
6. Mystical English poet of the seventeenth century [*Editor*].

duction of metals), lengthening it (in the case of life-prolonging elixirs), or, in the case of redemption, removing the subject from time's sway entirely. He states "Alchemy is the art of liberating parts of the Cosmos from temporal existence and achieving perfection which, for metals is gold, and for man, longevity, then immortality and, finally, redemption. Material perfection was sought through the action of a preparation (Philosopher's Stone for metals; Elixir of Life for humans), while spiritual ennoblement resulted from some form of inner revelation or other enlightenment (Gnosis, for example, in Hellenistic and western practices)."[7]

* * *

In the Middle Ages and Renaissance, alchemy in England, though controversial, was popular and thriving. It was borne on a tide of Continental writings, both ancient and contemporary, which lent their respectability, and was also enhanced by a relatively small but important group of native authorities, which included Roger Bacon, Thomas Norton, and George Ripley. But more critical to alchemy's continuing vitality was the fact that the "old" philosophy still held sway and had not yet been "called in doubt" by the new, for it was the traditional medieval and Renaissance worldview that the theory and practice of alchemy depended upon for plausibility and perpetuation. This dependency was grounded in such widely held doctrines as the four elements theory, the sulphur-mercury theory, correspondences between macrocosm and microcosm, and the unity of matter, to each of which I will give brief attention. With the weakening and eventual disappearance of these beliefs in the seventeenth century, alchemy necessarily lost its basis for survival.

Generally associated with Aristotle, although clearly traceable in earlier writers such as Empedocles[8] and Plato, the theory of the four elements (earth, air, water, and fire), the opposing qualities that comprise them, and their relative positions in the universe, constitute the foundation of medieval and Renaissance physics, metaphysics, medicine, and psychology. These principles play an equally vital role in alchemy and the "hermetic" worldview. In contrast to Robert Boyle's[9] modern conception of the elements as primary and discrete nonreducible substances, the four elements theory regarded them as different "appearances" or forms of the underlying matter or *prima materia* from which all visible, material objects are derived, each composed of a different combination of hotness, dryness, coldness, and moistness. Boyle's notion of chemical elements precluded the possibility of transmutation by

7. "European Alchemy in the Context of a Universal Definition," in *Die Alchimie in der europäischen Kultur- und Wissenschaftsgeschichte*, ed. Christoph Meinel, Wolfenbütteler Forschungen, vol. 32 (Wiesbaden: Otto Harrassowitz, 1986), 16–17.
8. Greek Presocratic philosopher (c. 495–435 B.C.E.); Plato lived from 427 to 347 B.C.E. [*Editor*].
9. English chemist (1627–1691) [*Editor*].

definition: they are "certain Primitive and simple, or perfectly unmingled bodies; which not being made of any other bodies, or of one another, are the Ingredients of which all those call'd perfectly mixt Bodies are immediately compounded, and into which they are ultimately resolved."[1]

In contrast, the idea of alchemical transmutation is implicit in the four elements theory because of the "convertibility" of the elements that comprise all substances: earth could be changed to water if its characteristic "dryness" were replaced by "wetness" and "coldness" remained a constant; similarly air would become fire if "dryness" came to replace "wetness." * * * [I]n the following quotation from Plato's *Timaeus*, 49, c, each of the elements is conceived as merely a form or changing manifestation of an underlying prima materia: "In the first place, we see that what we just now called water, by condensation, . . . becomes stone and earth; and this same element, when melted and dispersed, passes into vapour and air. Air, again, when inflamed, becomes fire; and again fire, when condensed and extinguished, passes once more into the form of air; and once more, air, when collected and condensed, produces cloud and mist; and from these, when still more compressed, comes flowing water, and from water comes earth and stones once more; and thus generation appears to be transmitted from one to the other in a circle."[2] Alchemists patterned their cyclical transmutation process upon this platonic model, referring to it as the philosophical circle or wheel. Thus the view of unceasing terrestrial transformation provided, by analogy, sanction for the possibility of transmutation of one metal into another.

* * *

The sulphur-mercury theory also derives from aspects of the old worldview and is the basis for Renaissance notions of the natural formation of metals and minerals in the earth and their artificial production through alchemy. If all sublunary substances are in a state of flux as the result of the imposition of different forms upon prime matter, it follows that metals, too, could be changed through recombining or altering the proportion of the elements that comprise them. The sulphur-mercury theory also draws on the idea of primary opposition inherent in the Aristotelian view: "sulphur" is identified with fire and possesses the qualities of hotness and dryness; "mercury," identified with water, possesses coldness and moistness. These two principles interact in the form of subterranean vapors or exhalations (the former "male," the latter "female"), and if the conjunction occurs under

1. From *The Sceptical Chymist by the Hon. Robert Boyle*, with an introduction by M. M. Pattison Muir (London: J. M. Dent, n.d.), 187.
2. *Timaeus*, in *The Dialogues of Plato*, trans. B. Jowett, 4th ed., 4 vols. (Oxford: Clarendon Press, 1953), 3:736.

proper conditions—the degree of heat is especially crucial—new metals are produced within the womb of the earth. * * *

For the alchemists, two extremely important corollaries developed from the four elements theory. Because in alchemy manipulation of the elements is conducted by human agents rather than nature, they came to consider their art as an imitation of nature, an artificial duplication of the subterranean processes that cause the conception and growth of metals. Second, because these artificial efforts were thought to produce gold more rapidly than the natural processes, alchemists continually described themselves as improvers or perfecters of nature, able to accomplish in a few weeks or months what nature had taken centuries to produce. Elias Ashmole, for example, states that "As *Nature* in her work below used two hot *Workmen* so will I; and because we cannot tarry her leisure, and long time she taketh to that purpose, we will match and countervail her little *Heats* with proportions answerable and meet for our time, that we may do that in fourty dayes which she doth in as many years."[3] For this reason, as noted earlier, H. J. Sheppard sees alchemy as effecting "alterations of duration in some linear time scale." Thus, alchemy was an important manifestation of the Renaissance debate on the relative powers of "art" versus "nature" although it has not generally been considered in this context.

Another alchemical doctrine that was wholly compatible, in fact synonymous, with the medieval-Renaissance worldview was that of the macrocosm and microcosm and the complex system of correspondences and "sympathies" that link them. The primacy of this relationship in alchemy, however, is much less familiar than its presence in Renaissance and seventeenth-century literature. As previously mentioned, the possibility of transmutation was predicated on the idea that underlying all "forms" in which substances appear there is only one prima materia. The macrocosm-microcosm idea is an extension of this theory and of equally ancient origin. "The One is All"—and its visual counterpart, the *ouroboros*[4]—is one of the oldest motifs in alchemy, pervading the *Tabula Smaragdina* or *Emerald Table of Hermes*, which according to two different versions was either found in the tomb of Hermes Trismegistus[5] by Alexander the Great or else "taken from the hands of the dead Hermes in a cave near Hebron, some ages after the Flood, by Sarah the wife of Abraham."[6] Its supposed antiquity and semidivine authorship caused it to be regarded as the most sacred book of alchemy, revealing cryptically the means of producing the philoso-

3. *The Way to Bliss* (London, 1658), 134.
4. A picture of a snake swallowing its tail, a symbol of infinity [*Editor*].
5. Name given to the Egyptian god Thoth—synonymous with the Greek god Hermes—who was the supposed author of ancient philosophical and occult writings [*Editor*].
6. John Read, *Through Alchemy to Chemistry* (New York: Harper and Row, 1963), 22.

pher's stone. Its opening precepts emphasize the correspondences between the greater world and the lesser: "That which is beneath is like
that which is above: & that which is above, is like that which is beneath,
to worke the miracles of one thing. And as all things have proceeded
from one, by the meditation of one, so all things have sprung from this
one thing by adaptation."[7] Explicit in this passage is the idea of resemblance and analogy between the celestial and sublunary spheres and
their creation by a single divine being or principle acting upon a common underlying substance and for a single purpose.

*   *   *

Alchemy also relied on animistic[8] ideas, often combined with anthropomorphism, in a variety of ways. They are basic to the notion that
both natural and artificially produced metals possess sex, soul, and feeling. Sulphur and mercury are the sexually differentiated "parents"
whose union produces offspring, which are other metals. Their birth
from the womb of Mother Earth (or analogically from the "womb" of
the alchemists' alembics) results after "gestation," which follows the
impregnation or *conjunction,* has run its course. * * * Lead and iron
are base metals because their "maturation" is incomplete; gold and
silver are purer because they have "grown ripe" over a prolonged period. An important axiom of alchemy and pre–seventeenth century natural history is that nature always "strives" to make gold, and the "souls"
of base metals continually aspire to this state of perfection. Further, the
volatility of substances within the alchemists' vessels is seen as evidence
of the "spirits" desire to escape the torture of the furnace. Such terms
and concepts, often reminiscent of primitive myth and folklore, are
commonplaces of alchemical animism and anthropomorphism and appear frequently in literary and visual representations of the art. In short,
animism and hylozoism,[9] together with the theories of the four elements, universal correspondences, and the unity of matter, were the
links that securely bound alchemical theory to the common worldview
of the Middle Ages and Renaissance.

Literary authors of the late Middle Ages and early modern period were
usually more interested in the distinctly human aspects of alchemy than
in its theory and history. While isolated theoretical and historical details
appear frequently enough in literary treatments—as a basis for imagery,
simile, or metaphor; to lend an element of concreteness and realism;
to create an aura of "learnedness" or its opposite—such details are most

---

7. From *The Smaragdine Table of Hermes Trismegistus of Alchimy,* in *The Mirror of Alchimy
   Composed by the Thrice-Famous and Learned Fryer, Roger Bacon,* ed. Stanton J. Linden,
   English Renaissance Hermeticism (New York and London: Garland Publishing, 1992), 16.
8. Linden said earlier that animism "posited a universe filled with life and sentiency"; "anthropomorphism" is giving human characteristics to what is not human [*Editor*].
9. The belief that all matter has life [*Editor*].

often subordinated to the overall demands of portrayal of character and distinctly human situations. At its most successful, literary alchemy has the human condition as its prime concern, but it is the human condition as touched, or "worked upon," by recognizable aspects of the theory and practice of the art. Chaucer, Erasmus, Jonson, and Samuel Butler, to name only four, used alchemy to represent the flawed nature of mankind, creating characters corrupted less because of their involvement in alchemical matters than by the presence of deeper evils that have led them to this involvement. For example, in Chaucer's Canon's Yeoman,[1] in Jonson's Face and Subtle and their victims, or in Butler's Hudibras and Ralph, alchemy may be both a cause and an effect of human corruption, but it is more frequently a means of objectifying the *consequences* of original sin than of representing the evil itself. Alchemy is splendidly equipped to represent moral transformation and transmutation, sometimes from evil to good, but also, in works belonging to the satirical tradition, from good or potential good to evil.

* * *

1. Chaucer's "Canon Yeoman's Tale" from *The Canterbury Tales* is a story of alchemy; Face and Subtle are main characters in *The Alchemist*; Hudibras and Ralph are characters used to mock both scientific and occult learning in Samuel Butler's narrative poem *Hudibras*, which appeared between 1662 and 1680.

CRITICISM

JONAS A. BARISH

The Double Plot in *Volpone*[†]

For more than two centuries literary critics have been satisfied to dismiss the subplot of *Volpone* as irrelevant and discordant, because of its lack of overt connection with the main plot. Jonson's most sympathetic admirers have been unable to account for the presence of Sir Politic Would-be, Lady Would-be, and Peregrine any more satisfactorily than by styling them a "makeweight" or a kind of comic relief to offset the "sustained gloom" of the chief action. Without questioning the orthodox opinion that the links of intrigue between the two plots are frail, one may nevertheless protest against a view of drama which criticizes a play exclusively in terms of physical action. What appears peripheral on the level of intrigue may conceal other kinds of relevance. And it is on the thematic level that the presence of the Would-be's can be justified and their peculiar antics related to the major motifs of the play.

John D. Rea, in his edition of *Volpone*, seems to have been the first to notice that Sir Politic Would-be, like the characters of the main plot, has his niche in the common beast fable:[1] he is Sir Pol, the chattering poll parrot, and his wife is a deadlier specimen of the same species. Rea's accurate insistence on the loquaciousness of the parrot, however, must be supplemented by recalling that parrots not only habitually chatter, they mimic. This banal but important little item of bird lore offers a thread whereby we may find our way through the complex thematic structure of the play. For Sir Politic and Lady Would-be function to a large extent precisely as mimics. They imitate their environment, and without knowing it they travesty the actions of the main characters. In so doing, they perform the function of burlesque traditional to comic subplots in English drama, and they make possible the added density and complexity of vision to which the device of the burlesque subplot lends itself.

His effort to Italianize himself takes the form, with Sir Politic, of an obsession with plots, secrets of state, and Machiavellian intrigue. His wife, on the other hand, apes the local styles in dress and cosmetics, reads the Italian poets, and tries to rival the lascivious Venetians in their own game of seduction.

[†] From *Modern Philology* 51 (1953), pp. 83–92. The author's notes have been abridged. References to *Volpone* have been made by act and scene in the present edition, though actual quotations are from the old-spelling text of Herford and Simpson (Oxford: Clarendon Press, 1925–52).

1. (New Haven, 1919), p. xxxiii.

Further, and more specifically, however, Sir Politic and Lady Would-be caricature the actors of the main plot. Sir Pol figures as a comic distortion of Volpone. As his name implies, he is the would-be politician, the speculator *manqué*, the unsuccessful enterpriser. Volpone, by contrast, is the real politician, the successful enterpriser, whose every stratagem succeeds almost beyond expectation. Sir Pol, like Volpone, is infatuated with his own ingenuity, and like Volpone he nurses his get-rich-quick schemes; but none of these ever progresses beyond the talking stage. While Volpone continues to load his coffers with the treasures that pour in from his dupes, Sir Pol continues to haggle over vegetables in the market and to annotate the purchase of toothpicks.

Lady Would-be, for her part, joins the dizzy game of legacy-hunting. Her antics caricature the more sinister gestures of Corvino, Voltore, and Corbaccio. She is jealous, like Corvino, as meaninglessly and perversely erudite as Voltore, and like Corbaccio, she makes compromising proposals to Mosca which leave her at the mercy of his blackmail. But, like her husband, Lady Would-be is incapable of doing anything to the purpose, and when she plays into Mosca's hands in the fourth act, she becomes the most egregious of the dupes because she is the blindest.

We do not learn of the existence of the Would-be's until the close of the first act,[2] and then only in a scrap of dialogue between Mosca and Volpone. Mosca's panegyric on Celia, following his sarcasms about Lady Would-be, serves to initiate a contrast which prevails throughout the play, between the households of Corvino and Sir Politic. If Corvino's besetting vice is jealousy, that of Sir Pol is uxoriousness, and the contrast enlarges itself into a difference between the brutal, obsessive passions of Italy and the milder eccentricities, the acquired follies or humors, of England. The contrast continues to unfold in the opening scene of Act II, where Sir Politic talks to his new acquaintance, Peregrine. Peregrine, it should be mentioned, probably belongs to the beast fable himself, as the pilgrim falcon. A case for this possibility would have to be based on the habits of hawks, commonly trained to hunt other birds. One then might find propriety in the fact of the falcon's hunting the parrot in the play. In Jonson's Epigram LXXXV (Herford and Simpson, VIII, 55), the hawk is described as a bird sacred to Apollo, since it pursues the truth, strikes at ignorance, and makes the fool its quarry. All these activities are performed by Peregrine vis-à-vis Sir Politic.

---

2. For the sake of brevity, this discussion will confine itself as closely as possible to the scenes actually involving the Would-be's. Jonson's sources, which are legion for this play, have been assembled both by Rea and by Herford and Simpson in their editions but will not be considered here.

In the initial scene between them, three chief ideas are developed, all of cardinal importance to the play and all interrelated. The first is the notion of monstrosity. Monstrosity has already made its spectacular appearance in the person of Androgyno and in the passage on Volpone's misbegotten offspring. We are, thereby, already familiar with the moral abnormality of Venice and its inhabitants. The present passage, with its reports of strange marvels sighted in England—a lion whelping in the Tower, a whale discovered in the Thames, porpoises above the bridge —introduces us to an order of monsters more comic than those to be met with in Venice, but to monsters nonetheless, in the proper sense of the word. Sir Pol's prodigies are distant echoes of the moral earth-quake rocking Venice, a looking glass for England whereby that country is warned to heed the lesson of the Italian state lest its own follies turn to vices and destroy it.

The enactment of the interlude in the first act, by placing the soul of the fool in the body of the hermaphrodite, has already established an identification between folly and monstrosity. Appropriately enough, then, having discussed monsters, Peregrine and Sir Pol turn to speak of the death of a famous fool, thus reinforcing the link between the two ideas. Sir Pol's excessive reaction to the event prompts Peregrine to inquire maliciously into a possible parentage between the two, and his companion innocently to deny it. The joke here, that Sir Pol is kin to the dead fool through their mutual folly if not through family, merges into a larger reflection on the ubiquity of folly, picking up that sugges-tion by ricochet, as it were, from the interlude in Act I. When Peregrine asks, "I hope / You thought him not immortall?" (Act II, scene 1, lines 55–56), the question implies its own Jonsonian answer: Master Stone, the fool, is not immortal, but his folly lives on incarnate in hundreds of fools like Sir Politic, much as the soul of Pythagoras, in the interlude, invested the body of one fool after another for thousands of years, only to reach its final and most fitting avatar in the person of Androgyno.

The colloquy concerning the Mamuluchi introduces the third chief motif of the scene, that of mimicry. This passage, where baboons are described in various quasi-human postures,[3] acquires added irony from the fact that it is recited by the parrot, the imitative animal par excel-lence, and also from the fact that the activities of the baboons, like those of Master Stone, the fool, consist chiefly of spying and intriguing and therefore differ so little from the way Sir Pol himself attempts to imitate the Italians.

3. Rea quotes from Edward Topsel's chapter "Of the Cynocephale, or Baboun" in *The Historie of Four-footed Beastes* (1607): "It is the error of vulgar people to think that Babouns are men, differing only in the face or visage. . . . They will imitate all humane actions, loving won-derfully to wear garments . . . they are as lustful and venerous as Goats, attempting to defile all sorts of women" (Rea, p. 178).

The arrival of Volpone disguised as a mountebank produces the expected confrontation between the archknave and the complete gull, the latter hopelessly hypnotized by the eloquence of the former. Volpone commences by disdaining certain imputations that have been cast on him by professional rivals. By way of counterattack, he accuses them of not knowing their trade, of being mere "*ground* Ciarlitani," or spurious mountebanks. If there is any doubt about the application of the passage to Sir Politic, it is settled by that individual's cry of admiration: "Note but his bearing, and contempt of these" (II, 2). Sir Politic thus plays charlatan to Volpone's mountebank as, within the larger frame of the play, he plays parrot to Volpone's fox. But Volpone has brought along his own misshapen child, the dwarf Nano, as an accredited imitator. Nano, who fills the role of Zan Fritada, the zany, is the domesticated mimic, the conscious mimic, as Androgyno is the conscious fool, while Sir Pol remains the unconscious mimic and the unconscious fool.

Volpone, pursuing his attack on imitators, assails them for trying to copy his elixir: "*Indeed, very many have assay'd, like apes in imitation of that, which is really and essentially in mee, to make of this oyle*" (II, 2). What is "really and essentially" in Volpone we know already to be monstrosity, so that to imitate Volpone (as Sir Politic does) is to imitate the unnatural, and therefore, in a sense, to place one's self at two removes from nature. But Volpone believes himself, not without justification, to be inimitable. The wretched practitioners who try to duplicate his ointment end in disaster. "*Poore wretches!*" he concludes, "*I rather pittie their folly, and indiscreation, then their losse of time, and money; for those may be recovered by industrie: but to bee a foole borne, is a disease incurable*" (II, 2). At this moment all that would be needed to drive home the application of Volpone's *sententia*[4] would be a pause on his part, followed by a significant look from Peregrine to Sir Pol.[5] But the situation conceals a further irony. Volpone's aphorism applies to himself. Before long, he, the archknave, will have proved the greatest fool, and this despite the versatility which enables him to transcend for the moment his own preferences, in order to cater to the prejudices of the public. Paradoxically, in this scene, speaking out of character, Volpone utters truths which reverse the premises of his former behavior. In Act I, gold, the great goddess, served him as sovereign remedy and omnipotent healer. For the saltimbanco Scoto of Mantua, peddling his fraudulent elixir, newer and relatively truer axioms celebrate the treasure of health: "*O, health! health! the blessing of the rich! the riches of*

---

4. Aphorism [*Editor*].
5. A proper staging of the scene would involve, I think, placing Sir Pol fairly close to Volpone, so that the two stare each other in the face, the one collecting with ardor every flower of rhetoric that falls from the other. At this moment, Volpone himself might stop to gaze into the infatuated countenance before him: by now Sir Pol's credulity is as apparent to him as it is to Peregrine.

the poore!" (II, 2). But with the application of this facile maxim, error descends again. The new truth proves to be only a distorted half-truth. In place of gold, Volpone offers only his humbug ointment as the *"most soueraigne, and approued remedie"* (II, 2). The real point, and he has made it himself, escapes him: to be a fool born is a disease incurable, and it is this disease to which he himself is destined to succumb.

The *"little remembrance"* which Volpone now presents to Celia proves to be a cosmetic powder with virtues more miraculous than those of the *oglio* itself. It is the powder *"That made* VENVS *a goddesse (given her by* APOLLO) *that kept her perpetually yong, clear'd her wrincles, firm'd her gummes, fill'd her skin, colour'd her haire; from her, deriu'd to* HELEN, *and at the sack of* Troy *(unfortunately) lost: till now, in this our age, it was as happily recouer'd, by a studious Antiquarie . . . who sent a moyetie of it, to the court of* France . . . *wherewith the ladies there, now, colour theire haire"* (II, 2). Thus the history of the powder parallels the metempsychoses of Pythagoras. Like Pythagoras' soul, the powder began its career as a gift from Apollo, and in its transmigrations through the goddess of love, the whore of Sparta, and the court ladies of France, it serves to underline the ancient lineage of vanity as a special case of the folly rehearsed in the interlude.

Mosca's opening soliloquy in Act III shows that this excellent counterfeiter is himself, like his master, obsessed by the notion of imitators. His contempt for ordinary parasites suggests that there is a hierarchy of counterfeits, ranging from those who are deeply and essentially false (like himself) to those who practice falsity out of mere affectation, who are, so to speak, falsely false and therefore, again, at two removes from nature. The shift of scene back to Volpone's house produces still another variation on the theme of mimicry. In order to beguile their master from his boredom, the trio of grotesques stage an impromptu interlude, dominated by Nano, who claims that the dwarf can please a rich man better than the eunuch or the hermaphrodite. The dwarf, explains Nano, is little, and pretty:

> *Else, why doe men say to a creature of my shape,*
> *So soone as they see him, it's a pritty little ape?*
> *And, why a pritty ape? but for pleasing imitation*
> *Of greater mens action, in a ridiculous fashion?*
> [III, 3, 11–14]

The first interlude, it may be recalled again, established an identification between folly and the unnatural. The present fragment confirms a further identity between mimicry and deformity, already hinted at in the mountebank scene where Nano appeared as the zany, or mimic, to Volpone's Scoto. At this point one may represent some of the relationships in the play diagrammatically as follows:

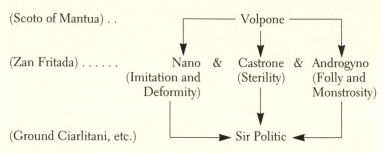

(Scoto of Mantua) . .   Volpone

(Zan Fritada) . . . . . .   Nano   &   Castrone   &   Androgyno
                              (Imitation and   (Sterility)   (Folly and
                                 Deformity)   Monstrosity)

(Ground Ciarlitani, etc.)   Sir Politic

Since Volpone has (presumptively at least) sired both Nano and Androgyno, and since Sir Pol combines the chief attributes of both, one
may, with the aid of the diagram, infer what is already emerging plainly
in context, that mimicry itself is something monstrous and abnormal.
It is unnatural for baboons and apes and parrots to counterfeit human
behavior. It is equally unnatural for men to imitate beasts. It argues a
perversion of their essential humanity. It is not for nothing, then, that
the chief characters of the play fit into one zoölogical classification or
another. As men, they duplicate the habits of beasts; as beasts, they
brutishly travesty humanity. They belong to the genus *monster*—half
man, half brute—that order of fabulous creatures whose common de-
nominator is their unnaturalness, their lack of adherence to whatever
category of being nature has assigned them.

The arrival of Lady Would-be, fuming and fussing over her toilet,
and snapping at her servingwomen, provides still a further object-lesson
in falsity. Here, as so often in Jonson, face physic symbolizes the painted
surface hiding the rotten inside; the cosmetic care of the face signifies
the neglect of the soul. It signifies equally an attachment to appearances, an incapacity to look beyond the superficies of life or truth. The
powder which Volpone offered to Celia and which Celia did not need,
since her beauty was of the platonic sort that revealed the purity of her
soul, might with more justice have been given to Lady Would-be, and
it is Lady Would-be who deserves the epithet of "lady *vanitie*" (II, 5,
21) with which Corvino, in his jealous tantrum, has stigmatized Celia.

The scene between Lady Would-be and Volpone serves partly as a
burlesque of the parallel scenes in Act I between Volpone and the other
captatores.[6] All the essential ingredients of those scenes reappear, but
scrambled and topsy-turvy. Once again Volpone feigns sickness, but this
time it is in self-defense against the terrible oratory of Lady Would-be.
Once again remedies are prescribed, but these are neither Corbaccio's
deadly opiate nor his *aurum palpabile* offered as pump-priming, but
the fantastic assortment of old wives' restoratives dredged up from Lady

6. Legacy-hunters [*Editor*].

Would-be's infernal memory. She rains down the hailstones of her learning on the helpless Volpone, until the arch-rogue, anticipating the judgment to be rendered on him in Act V, cries out in despair: "Before I fayned diseases, now I haue one" (III, 4, 62). The whole episode is a rich application of the principle of comic justice. If in the final denouement Volpone suffers the penalty of vice, here he reaps the more ludicrous reward of his own folly. Trapped by Lady Would-be's rhetoric, itself a consequence of his own scheming, he is finally driven to pronounce himself cured. But the talking machine grinds on, and only Mosca's happy notion of exciting her jealousy, as he has previously aroused Corvino's, and for the same purpose, succeeds in getting rid of her. As her contribution to Volpone's coffers, she leaves behind a wrought cap of her own making; this forms a suitably ridiculous contrast to the treasures earlier offered by Corvino, Corbaccio, and Voltore.

The same scene serves as introduction and comic distortion of the scene immediately to follow between Volpone and Celia. Celia's unearthly purity is made to seem even more unearthly by its contrast to Lady Would-be's lecherousness, this latter apparent in the lady's addiction to cosmetics, in her slips of the tongue, and in her barely disguised sexual overtures. Lady Would-be's attempted seduction of Volpone having been thwarted, the stage is set for Volpone's attempted seduction of Celia. Volpone commences his wooing with a characteristic boast: "I, before / I would haue left my practice, for thy loue," he swears, "In varying figures, I would haue contended / With the blue PROTEVS, or the horned *Floud*" (III, 7, 150–53). Justifiably proud of his powers of disguise, Volpone emphasizes them further by citing a past occasion on which he masqueraded in the ambiguous role of Antinous, Hadrian's favorite. Embarking on an enumeration of the exotic splendors in store for Celia, he reserves as his final inducement the promise that she will participate, with him, in transmutations without end: "Whil'st we, in changed shapes, act OVIDS tales" (the *Metamorphoses*, of course),

> Thou, like EVROPA now, and I like IOVE,
> Then I like MARS, and thou like ERYCINE,
> So, of the rest, till we haue quite run through
> And weary'd all the fables of the gods.
> Then will I haue thee in more moderne formes,
> Attired like some sprightly dame of *France*,
> Braue *Tuscan* lady, or proud *Spanish* beauty.
>   [III, 7, 221–28]

We have already witnessed, in the first interlude, the metempsychosis of folly and, in the powder offered to Celia in Act II, the transmigrations of vanity. Now, as a climax to his eloquence, Volpone rehearses the metamorphoses of lust. Jonson thus endows his central themes with vertical depth in time as well as horizontal extension in space. Folly, vanity, lust, have been, are, will be. At any given moment their prac- titioners are legion, and often interchangeable.

It is at this point that Celia's refusal crystallizes into a repudiation of folly, vanity, and lust combined and that her behavior contrasts most sharply with that of Lady Would-be. The recollection of Lady Would- be lacquering her face and making indecent advances to Volpone brings into sharper focus Celia's sudden horror at her own beauty, and her plea that her face be flayed or smeared with poison, in order to undo the lust she has aroused. If, for Lady Would-be, the cosmetic art is a necessary preliminary to sexual conquest, its opposite, the disfig- urement of the face, becomes for Celia the badge of chastity. Where Lady Would-be strives to adopt Italian vices for her own, Celia's ges- tures as well as her name demonstrate her alienation from the moral and spiritual province of Venice.

Act IV carries us back into the open street, where Sir Pol, ignorant of the plot developing at Volpone's house, continues babbling of plots in terms which ordinarily have one meaning for him and another for the audience. After a patronizing recital of "instructions" to Peregrine on methods of deportment in Venice, he confides suddenly that his money-making projects need only the assistance of one trusty hench- man in order to be put into instant execution. Evidently he is hinting that Peregrine undertake that assignment and thus play Mosca to his Volpone. But Peregrine contents himself with inquiring into the par- ticulars of the plots. The most elaborate of these proves to be a way to protect Venice from the plague by using onions as an index to the state of infection on ships entering the harbor. This mad scheme, with its echo of Volpone's claim to have distributed his *oglio* under official patent to all the commonwealths of Christendom, serves chiefly to re- mind us again of the moral plague prevailing in Venice and of the incomprehension of that fact on the part of those characters who prattle most about disease and cure.

The ensuing scene parodies the episode in Act II where Corvino discovers his wife in conversation with the mountebank. Just as Corvino interrupts Volpone while the latter is advertising his medicine, so Lady Would-be bursts in on Sir Politic as the knight is dilating on his schemes and projects. As Corvino babbles jealously of lechers and sa- tyrs, so Lady Would-be jabbers of land sirens, lewd harlots, and frica- trices. Corvino beats away the mountebank. Lady Would-be rails at Peregrine. Both harp on "honor," and both discard that term as soon as it becomes an inconvenience, Corvino when it becomes an obstacle to his plan of inheritance, Lady Would-be when she discovers that Peregrine is no harlot in disguise, but a young gentleman. As for Sir Politic, though he too plays his part in the little impromptu from the *commedia dell' arte*, he remains, unlike Volpone, quite oblivious to the fact. Actually, Sir Pol reenacts not the role of "Signior FLAMINIO," the lover in disguise—that part, however reluctantly assumed, belongs to Peregrine—but the female role, the "FRANCISCINA," guarded by a jealous "PANTALONE *di besogniosi*" (II, 3, 3–8). The confusion of sexes symbolized in Androgyno, in the indiscriminate journeyings of the soul of Pythagoras, in Volpone's masquerade as Antinous, in Lady Would-be's error, as well as in the reversed masculine-feminine roles of Sir Pol and Lady Would-be, contributes its own kind of abnormality to the deformity of the moral atmosphere chiefly figured by the metamorphoses of beasts into men. And if one regards Sir Politic's uxoriousness as a kind of metaphoric emasculation, one may then equate him with Castrone, as he has already been equated with Nano and Androgyno, to make the pattern of mimicry complete.[7]

The fourth-act trial starts with justice and concludes with a perversion of it. The monsters begotten by Volpone, the prodigies and portents that exercised such a hypnotic effect on Sir Pol, now make a lavish and climactic reappearance in the language of the scene. First they designate their proper objects. But as Voltore begins to exercise his baleful rhetoric, the parlance of unnaturalness, appropriate to the guilty, begins to turn against the innocent. Corbaccio disavows his son for "the meere portent of nature"; he is "an vtter stranger" to his loins, a "Monster of men, swine, goate, wolfe, parricide" (IV, 5, 108–11). Finally Lady Would-be arrives, the eternal parrot, to give testimony which virtually clinches the case against Celia:

> Out, thou *chameleon* harlot; now, thine eies
> Vie teares with the *hyaena*.   [IV, 6, 2–3]

The beast characters in the play display an unerring faculty for describing the innocent as beasts. Corvino has already called Celia a crocodile, referring to that animal's notorious ability to imitate human tears, and Lady Would-be, though she has her unnatural natural history somewhat confused, invokes another creature famous for its powers of mimicry, the hyena, as well as the even more versatile chameleon.

The juxtaposition of the hyena and the chameleon reminds one that there is a point at which the ideas of metamorphosis and mimicry coalesce. The chameleon, shifting its colors to blend itself with its environment, indulges in a highly developed form of protective mimicry. Volpone carries the principle a step further. He goes through his restless series of transformations not as a shield but in order to prey on his own kind, to satisfy something in his unnatural nature which demands in-

---

7. Actually, Florio's *Worlde of Wordes* (1598) defines *Castrone* not only as "a gelded man," but as "a noddie, a meacocke, a cuckold, a ninnie, a gull" (quoted in Rea, p. 144). Any of these will serve as accurate epithets for Sir Pol, with the possible exception of "cuckold," and if that designation does not fit it is not owing to any lack of effort on Lady Would-be's part. [Florio's *Worlde of Words* is an Italian-English dictionary. "Noddie," "meacocke," "ninnie," and "gull" are all variant ways of calling a man a fool.—*Editor*]

cessant changing of shape and form. But knavery and credulity, mimicry and metamorphosis, alike reflect aspects of one basic folly: the folly of becoming, or trying to become, what one is not, the cardinal sin of losing one's nature. Only Bonario and Celia, of all the creatures in the play, never ape others, never change their shapes, never act contrary to their essential natures. And in the unnatural state of Venice it is chiefly they, the unchanging ones, who are attacked as hyenas and chameleons.

Volpone, in short, may be read as a comic restatement of a theme familiar in Shakespeare's plays of the same period, the theme of disorder. Order figures here not as social balance or political hierarchy, but as a principle of differentiation in nature whereby each species, each sex, maintains its separate identity. With the loss of clear-cut divisions between man and beast, between beast and beast, between male and female, all creatures become monsters. The basic structure of nature is violated. The astronomical portents discussed earlier by Sir Pol and Peregrine in connection with animal prodigies reflect the upheaval of the cosmos itself following the degeneracy of man.

But by this time, justice has become as monstrous as its participants, and the *avocatori* close the session piously intoning their horror at the unnaturalness of Celia and Bonario. Volpone's last and greatest hoax is destined to set the balance of nature right again. It starts, however, with one more act of unnaturalness. Volpone, a monster, who therefore occupies no fixed place in the order of created beings, feigns death and thus symbolically demonstrates his lack of status. One by one the inheritors file in for the legacy, only to find that they have been duped by Mosca.

The first to receive her dismissal is Lady Would-be. Having made overtures to both Mosca and Volpone, she is in a position to be summarily blackmailed. "Goe home," advises Mosca, "and vse the poore sir POL, your knight, well; / For feare I tell some riddles; go, be melancholique" (V, 3, 44–45). Thus the learned lady who knew so many bizarre ways of curing Volpone's melancholy now has the opportunity to treat herself for the same ailment, and so do her colleagues. The value of this scene consists partly in its inflicting comic justice on the legacy-hunters before the *avocatori* render their sterner legal judgments, just as Volpone has already, in Lady Would-be, met a comic foretaste of the retribution which overtakes him at the *Scrutineo*. But since the parrot, for all its shrillness, remains less venal than the crow or vulture, the untrussing of Lady Would-be goes no further. In the realm of the severer truths, vice and folly may appear as different aspects of a similar spiritual malaise. In the realm of poetic justice, however, a distinction continues to be practiced. Vice, which is criminal and attacks others, must suffer public correction, whereas folly, a disease essentially self-destructive, may be dealt with in private and without the assistance of constituted authority. For Lady Would-be it is sufficient that, awakened to some sense of her own folly, she vows to quit Venice and take to sea "for physick."

And so with her preposterous knight, Sir Politic, whom we now encounter for the last time, the victim of a private plot which performs the same service of mortification for him that the final trial scene does for Volpone. The *mercatori* enlisted by Peregrine perform the office of the *avocatori* who pronounce sentence on Volpone, and the divulging of the pathetic notebook, with its scraps from playbooks, becomes the burlesque substitute for the exposure of Volpone's will, in bringing on the disaster. Peregrine, echoing Voltore's suggestion that Volpone be tested on the strappado, warns Sir Pol that his persecutors will put him to the rack. Whereupon the knight remembers an "engine" he has designed against just such emergencies, a tortoise shell. And to the disgust of three hundred years of literary critics he climbs into the ungainly object, playing possum after the fashion of his model, Volpone, who has feigned death in the foregoing scene. The arrival of the merchants brings on the catastrophe:

> MER. 1: What
> Are you, sir? PER: I' am a merchant, that came heere
> To looke vpon this tortoyse. MER. 3: How? MER. 1: St. MARKE!
> What beast is this? PER: It is a fish. MER. 2: Come out, here.
> PER: Nay, you may strike him, sir, and tread vpon him:
> Hee'll beare a cart.
>
> [V, 4, 62–67]

Eventually, by stamping and poking, they goad Sir Politic out of his exoskeleton. The scene thus rephrases in a vein of broadest tomfoolery the essential question of the play: "What kind of creatures are these?" Throughout the action one has seen beasts aping men and men imitating beasts on the moral and psychological levels. Here the theme of mimicry reaches its literal climax in an episode of farce, where the most imitative of the characters puts on the physical integument of an animal and the hired pranksters stand about debating its probable zoölogical classification. The final unshelling of the tortoise, a parallel to the uncasing of the fox in the last scene, arouses further comment from the merchants:

> MER. 1: 'Twere a rare motion, to be seene, in *Fleet-street*!
> MER. 2: I, i'the terme. MER. 1. Or *Smithfield*, in the faire.
> [V, 4, 77–78]

Sir Politic, thus, so inquisitive about prodigies, has finally become one himself, a specimen fit to be housed among the freaks of Smithfield or amid the half-natural, half-artificial curiosities of Fleet Street. With the knowledge that he is destined to become a victim of the kind of curiosity he himself has exhibited, his disillusionment is complete and his chastisement effected. He and Lady Would-be, the only survivors, in this play, of Jonson's earlier humor characters, are now "out of their humor," purged of their imitative folly by the strong medicine of ridicule.[8]

Public punishment, however, awaits the actors of the main plot. Jonson is not sporting here with human follies like those of the Would-be's, but dealing grimly with inhuman crimes. The names of fabulous monsters, basilisks and chimeras, continue to echo in our ears as the catastrophe approaches, fastening themselves at last onto their proper objects, the conspirators in the game of *captatio*. Voltore's spurious fit spells out in concrete theatrical terms his unnatural status and the lesson pointed by the *avocatori*: "These possesse wealth, as sicke men possesse feuers, / Which, trulyer, may be said to possesse them" (V, 12, 101–2). The delivery of Volpone's substance to the *Incurabili* places a final and proper valuation on the medicinal powers of gold. The imprisonment of Volpone is specifically designed to give him the opportunity to acquire in reality the diseases he has mimicked and the leisure to ponder the accuracy of his own text: to be a fool born is a disease incurable. Voltore and Corbaccio are henceforth to be secluded from their fellow-men like the unnatural specimens they are, while Corvino's animality is to be the object of a public display more devastating than Sir Politic's brief masquerade as a tortoise.

Thus on successive levels of low comedy and high justice, the monsters of folly and the monsters of vice suffer purgation, exposed as the sort of misshapen marvels they themselves have chattered about so freely. The relative harmlessness of Sir Pol's downfall serves to differentiate his folly from the viciousness of the Venetians, but the many parallels between his catastrophe and theirs warn us that his kind of folly is sufficiently virulent after all, is closely related to graver sins, and if it persists in imitating them, must ultimately fall under the same condemnation.

If these observations are accurate, it should be clear in what sense the subplot of the Would-be's is relevant to the total structure of *Volpone*. Starting from a contrast between Italian vice and English folly, Jonson personifies the latter in two brainless English travelers, makes their folly consist chiefly in mimicry of Italian vice, and Italian vice itself, in its purest form, consist of the more comprehensive form of mimicry we have termed "metamorphosis," thus bringing the two aspects of evil together into the same moral universe and under a common moral judgment; with the use of the beast fable he binds the two together dramatically, and by the distribution of poetic justice he pre-

---

8. Several of Jonson's early plays involve purging characters of their "humors," i.e., correcting an imbalance of their basic dispositions [*Editor*].

serves the distinction between them. Each of the episodes involving the Would-be's, including the much despised incident of the tortoise, thus serves a definite dramatic purpose, and one may conclude, then, that the subplot adds a fresh dimension and a profounder insight without which *Volpone*, though it might be a neater play, would also be a poorer and a thinner one.

ROBERT C. EVANS

Thomas Sutton: Jonson's Volpone?[†]

Jonson's involvement in the poetomachia,[1] and the savage assault on him in *Satiromastix*, both indicate how easily the theater could serve as an arena for personal combat and micropolitical maneuvers. In the case of plays like *Poetaster* or *Satiromastix*, such motives are blatantly obvious, but new evidence suggests that personal satire may also have helped shape the play that remains Jonson's masterwork—*Volpone*. This evidence supports the notion that Thomas Sutton, the founder of London's Charterhouse hospital and the richest commoner in Jacobean England, may have been the model for the play's title character. In the years and decades following the work's first production, this possibility was widely discussed and widely accepted, but more modern commentators have generally dismissed the idea, and most recent editions fail even to mention it. However, several previously unnoted documents throw new light on this old issue, and while they hardly establish that Sutton was Jonson's intended target, they do provide fascinating and valuable evidence about the contemporary context in which his play was written and received and about the whole issue of personal satire on the English Renaissance stage. The documents help illuminate the importance of personal politics for Jonson and his milieu, and they also help to explain why many of the playwright's contemporaries and their immediate descendants believed that Sutton was the object of his satire; why Jonson himself might reasonably have assumed his audience could draw such a conclusion; and how this knowledge may have affected the defensive tone of his play's printed dedication.

It is easy to see why so many commentators have so strongly resisted the notion that Jonson satirized Sutton. During the decades and centuries since his death in 1611, Sutton has been remembered and revered primarily as the pious founder of Charterhouse, one of England's

---

† From Robert C. Evans, *Jonson and the Contexts of His Time* (Lewisburg: Bucknell University Press, 1994), pp. 45–61. Copyright 1994. Reprinted by permission of the Associated University Presses. The author's notes have been abridged.

1. "War of the Poets." Jonson was attacked by Thomas Dekker in his play *Satiromastix* (1601), preceded by Jonson's own attack on Dekker in *Poetaster* (1601) [*Editor*].

greatest charitable institutions, a residential "hospital" designed to provide lodging, sustenance, and education to needy men and boys. English Protestants hailed Sutton and his hospital as sterling examples of
the good men and good works produced by the reformed religion; Sutton was cited repeatedly as a model of Protestant benefaction, useful as
ammunition in propaganda wars with Catholics. Until recently, much
of the biographical commentary on Sutton had an almost hagiographic
tone, and indeed some of the earliest legends verged on the miraculous—such as the amusing claim that his enormous wealth derived from
"faery gold" found as he strolled along a beach. Appropriately enough,
the first published account of his life (and a source for many subsequent
writers) was a commemorative sermon.[2]

A more balanced tone emerges in an important but relatively obscure
1948 article by the historian Hugh Trevor-Roper, himself a product of
the Charterhouse school. Although obviously grateful to Sutton, Trevor-
Roper provides significant correctives to earlier treatments of "the
founder's" life, dismissing most previous accounts as "mythological"
and "fabulous."[3] Unfortunately, his own article, while based on archival
research, is not specifically documented, which makes it difficult for
interested readers to pin down the sources of many of his confident
assertions. Nonetheless, his piece is the starting point for any serious
investigation of Sutton's life; in fact, Neal R. Shipley, another historian,
cautions that "Accounts of Sutton written before the 1940s are, as a
rule, wildly inaccurate."[4] For this reason it may be worth quoting ex-
tensively from Trevor-Roper's article to establish the basic shape of Sutton's career. Once this has been done, we can better appreciate the
significance of the new evidence already mentioned and its relevance
to Jonson's play.

Trevor-Roper begins by remarking that "even in his own lifetime
Sutton's origins, owing to his own silence, were something of a mystery,
which his executors had no sure means of solving. . . . The plain fact
is that there is no evidence of any value at all about Sutton before
1569," when he was pensioned by Ambrose Dudley, the Earl of War-
wick. Sutton was a dependent of the earl's family: "The Dudleys made
his career and fortune, or at least the beginning of it; they provided
him with jobs and influence and a wife; and the only family connexions
which he seems ever to have had were with them and their circle."
Through them he obtained a position by which he acquired the lease
of two estates "which he kept till his death [and which] were the solid

---

2. Perci Burrell, *Sutton's Synagogue or, The English Centurion* (London, 1629). Although not
   printed until later, the sermon was actually delivered in 1614, three years after Sutton's death.
3. "Thomas Sutton," *Carthusiana* 20, no. 1 (October 1948): 2–8; for the quoted passage, see
   p. 2.
4. See "Thomas Sutton: Tudor-Stuart Moneylender," *Business History Review* 50 (1976); 456–
   76; for the quoted passage, see p. 458n.

basis of his fortune." Apparently it was "Ambrose Dudley who had arranged the deal." Dudley also nominated Sutton to the important position of "Master of the Ordnance in the North Parts." During his "period in the North (from 1569 to 1582), . . . he made the first half of his fortune by speculating in coal"; later, while living in the South from 1582 until 1611, "he multiplied it to gigantic proportions by marriage and money-lending."[5]

Trevor-Roper provides a fascinating account of Sutton's struggle for control of the northern coalfields, but it is on the latter part of his life—when, his fortune established, he moved to London and became a notorious money-lender—that we must focus here. He married the rich widow of John Dudley and bought himself

> a house at Broken Wharf in London, and another at Hackney. His illegitimate son, Roger Sutton (now in the army), came frequently to live with him, and so with his wife's daughter, Anne Dudley, and her husband (the son of an immensely rich judge, Chief Justice Popham) he experienced a certain family life; but after his wife's death in 1602 he became more and more a recluse, chiefly concerned with the ultimate fate of his now colossal fortune.[6]

Sutton had boosted that fortune "in the simplest way, by lending it on mortgage." His days as a money-lender coincided with a time of great inflation, when wealthy families were scrambling for the cash they needed for conspicuous consumption or merely to keep themselves afloat. Sutton numbered among his debtors many of the kingdom's most powerful men, including the Earl of Essex; Lord Darcy; Lord Mounteagle; the Earl of Sussex; the Earl of Oxford; the Earl of Suffolk, and many, many others. Some of these people were his friends, and many felt grateful to him; but his enormous wealth (and concomitant power) earned him envy and resentment as well. His scrupulous financial records, many of which survive, provide exceptionally detailed evidence of his activities. Trevor-Roper estimates that "In one form of lending alone, of which we have the records, he lent, in the last sixteen years of his life, £ 220,000 . . . , sometimes lending as much as £ 37,000 in a single year; and at his death, £ 44,891 was still owing to him." Debtors who could not repay their loans often sacrificed their property; land acquired in this way brought Sutton still further sources of wealth. "It seemed that he had only to sit still and let his money multiply. He was known everywhere as 'rich Sutton,' 'Dives[7] Sutton,' 'the English Crassus,' 'the richest gentleman in England.' " Jealousy prompted unfair talk that he was a miserly usurer, but Trevor-Roper comments, somewhat reassuringly, that "his contemporaries never taxed him with ex-

5. All quotations in this paragraph are from Trevor-Roper, pp. 2–3.
6. Trevor-Roper, p. 4.
7. Latin for "rich"; "Crassus": a rich Roman of the first century B.C.E. [Editor].

tortion; and the inventories of his personal effects—his plate and rich clothes and fine services and damask hangings—prove that he was not a miser in the traditional sense." He was kind to his servants and considerate of the poor. Nonetheless, "in his old age, Sutton became increasingly unsocial, increasingly solitary."[8] One researcher remarks that John Lawe, his chief financial assistant, "was the closest that Sutton ever came to having an intimate friend. . . . Sutton was reclusive and needed the sort of information that Lawe, a born gossip, had in great store."[9]

Strained relations with his son (whom he eventually disinherited) and with other relatives spurred speculation about the eventual fate of his gigantic wealth, and in the decade before his death—when Jonson's play was written—rumors were rife, and schemes and proposals abounded. Everyone wondered what would become of the old man's incredible fortune. Sutton seems to have been attracted at an early stage to the idea of endowing a charity of some sort, but "In the last sixteen years of his life he drafted a new will every six months. Throughout he showed an extreme suspicion. He did not trust his relatives; he feared that his foundation would be dissolved by powerful interests at his death"; in general, "he kept very quiet about his intentions." But if Sutton was not entirely sure how he should dispose of his money, others had more definite ideas. Sir John Harington, the courtier and poet, took an active interest. Although Trevor-Roper asserts, on the basis of published evidence, that Harington came into contact with Sutton in 1607, documents from the Charterhouse records show that their relationship began much earlier. It was in 1607, however, that Harington proposed a plan by which he hoped to benefit Sutton, the King, Prince Charles, and (not incidentally) himself. "Harington's scheme was simple. Sutton was to be persuaded by him to declare Prince Charles his heir. In return Sutton, through the intercession of Harington, was to be honoured by the King with a peerage. Harington, as the skilful broker, would receive a rake-off from both sides."[1]

Harington had not counted, however, on Sutton's determination to be his own financial planner. The old man took offense at the scheme and addressed indignant letters to the Lord Chancellor and Lord Treasurer disavowing it. Moreover,

> To Harington Sutton wrote characteristically protesting that the rumour of the proposal had damaged his money-lending business, since everyone now thought his land was so encumbered that no one would take up leases or borrow money from him. Relations

8. All preceding quotations in this paragraph are from Trevor-Roper, pp. 4–5.
9. Shipley, p. 463.
1. All quotations in this paragraph are from Trevor-Roper, pp. 6–7.

between Harington and Sutton continued after the unfortunate end of this project (in which other members of the court were involved), for Harington was irrepressible.[2]

Further evidence suggests that Harington's scheme was only one of many self-serving proposals outsiders concocted for disposing of Sutton's fortune; indeed, the old man's admirers later applauded his skills at turning the tables on would-be manipulators. Of course, not everyone was self-interested: Joseph Hall wrote a long letter endorsing Sutton's charitable impulses and urging him to act on them without delay. Yet even in the final years of his life, no one could be quite sure what would happen to his money, despite the fact that Sutton by this time had definitely settled on a plan to endow a charitable hospital. After his death in 1611, relatives (spurred on by courtiers, including Sir Francis Bacon)[3] challenged his will, but the document was upheld and the future of Charterhouse finally seemed assured. In the ensuing decades Sutton's fame as a philanthropist grew; any subtler shadings tended to fade from published accounts of his life. In the words of Shipley, the most careful and thorough recent investigator of Sutton's career,

> Secretive and colorless, he provided none of the more obvious virtues upon which an admiring posterity might fasten, so a fictitious life began to evolve immediately upon his death. Sutton's reputation was, in particular, the province of his trustees at Charterhouse and their successors, amongst whom a critical spirit was hardly to be expected, especially as these men were attempting to counter a popular tradition that viewed him as a scoundrel and a miser. Succeeding generations of writers and preachers from Charterhouse gradually elaborated the theme of his sagacity and benevolence, calling into the service of the legend any stray facts or accomplishments not definitely claimed elsewhere. Significantly, one of the first facts to be jettisoned in this refurbishment of his reputation was that he had been a money-lender. Sutton's heirs appear to have been embarrassed by the fact that the wealth they had inherited had been earned in the money market. . . . The definitive formulation was made by Samuel Herne in 1677. According to that version, Sutton combined a variety of government positions with one of the most successful and versatile mercantile careers of the early modern era. Subsequent writers drew on Herne's account for their basic narrative, slowly discarding his more egregious inaccuracies, but as late as the 1920's it was still hotly denied that Sutton had ever been induced to accept interest on his loans.[4]

2. Trevor-Roper, p. 7.
3. English statesman and philosopher (1561–1626) [Editor].
4. Shipley, p. 462.

As Shipley indicates, the importance of Samuel Herne's *Domus Car-thusiana: or an Account of the Most Noble Foundation of the Charter-House . . .* is difficult to overestimate. Although many later writers have been at pains to correct various errors in Herne's account, his book has been the basis of most subsequent versions of Sutton's life. Herne himself claimed to be correcting earlier authors; he emphasizes his reliance on careful investigation, although admitting that "The helps I found in the composure of *Sutton's life* were many of them scatter'd here and there, laid hold on rather by chance than direction . . ." (sig. a3ᵛ). Herne's sources included not only "the *Records* of the House" as well as "some Remarks whereof I had from creditable and worthy men, bred in this Foundation long ago" (sig. a4ᵛ), but also the early commemorative sermon, *Sutton's Synagogue.*

Herne's most important source, however, was "an Anonymous and Imperfect MS. left, not long since, in the Booksellers hands, which did me very good service" (sig. a4ᵛ). This last remark is a bit disingenuous, since the manuscript in question is actually the basis for most of Herne's account of Sutton's life; much of his phrasing follows the manuscript verbatim, but Herne's alterations and deletions are even more interesting than his inclusions. The manuscript, Lansdowne 1198, has been housed in the British Library for many years, although few writers on Sutton seem to have consulted it. Comparing the manuscript with Herne's redaction shows how Herne chose to highlight certain aspects of Sutton's career (and the legends associated with it) while downplaying or ignoring others. The manuscript deals much more forthrightly and at greater length with various controversial aspects of Sutton's life than does Herne. Perhaps this is partly because Herne, in addition to dealing with the Founder's life, was also greatly concerned with the institutional history of the hospital itself; he may have felt that any in-depth treatment of Sutton the man was uncalled for. For whatever reasons, however, the manuscript gives a much fuller and more complex sense of Sutton's life, personality, and times than Herne presents; a full comparison of the two accounts would show exactly how Herne tailored the available data to fit the image of Sutton he tried to construct.

A few examples must suffice. Herne only briefly mentions, for instance, a charge the manuscript dwells on—the allegation that part of Sutton's fortune had been won through piracy (40). The manuscript gives a much fuller sense of the kinds of rumors that swirled around the Founder's reputation; whatever the facts of this particular case, the manuscript provides a far clearer picture of the suspicions and innuendoes that dogged Sutton's fame. The manuscript confronts the charge of piracy head-on and at length:

> If it be objected as it hath beene by some that then it seemes
> he bestowed that *well*, which he got *ill*, that he maintained charity

with *Pyracy*; and relieved his own countrymen with what he had taken from strangers, com[m]uting for Robbery with Liberality—

It is answered—that if master Sutton got some part of that [estate] by the *warre* which he bestowed soe well in time of *peace*, he did noe more than Abraham the father of the faithful did who hath Lazarus [the poor] now in his bosome—XXX for Abraham tooke of the Spoyles of his enemies and offered the *Tenth* of them to god Heb: 7.4 and master Sutton it may be took some XXX and justly too [since all we take in warres XXX is ours by the highest law in the world] and gave all unto god[5]

The manuscript's tactic here—defending Sutton by citing Biblical precedent and scholarly theory—is typical of its larger strategy. Nowhere is this clearer than in its later discussion of the charge that Sutton was not merely a money-lender but also a usurer, an issue Herne touches on more briefly and with far less self-assurance (41; 48–49). As part of its attempt to explain "how master Sutton got his vast estate," the manuscript argues that

and as many merchants cannot trade, soe more gentlemen cannot live without money upon use for want whereof their estates will be swallowed up by mortgages and underrate sales which have been p[re]served by easy borrowing upon interest—whereupon my Lord Bacon say[th] that he Remembred a cruell=monied man in the countrey that would say—"the Devill take this usury. it keepes us from forfeitures of mortgages and bonds.["] and truely considering that it is as lawfull to take use for money; as to take money for the use of any thing bought for money "all states and governem[en]ts have judged it better to mitigate usury by *declaration*, than to suffer it to rage and *bite* by *connivance*["]—allowing the lender an ae-quitable consideration 1. for the gain he might have made of his money since he lent it, and 2 the benefit the borrower made of it since he had it and .3. for the losse the lender sustaineth in the want of it either after or before the day of payment—I have heard say that master Sutton would never take use for money that was for victualls or other necessaries spent by the borrower in the use .1. because it was not only uncharitable but unreasonable to design gain in lending that whereby the borrower relieved only his ne-cessity and intended noe gain in borrowing; therefore in that case

5. British Library (hereafter BL) Lansdowne MS. 1198, fol. 1ᵛ. The identity of the manuscript's author is unknown, although a reference on fol. 5ᵛ to "us his relations" implies that the author may have had some familial connection to Sutton.

Brackets and parentheses appear in the original manuscript; any insertions or emendations of mine are indicated by [ ] marks, except where I have silently expanded contractions. XXX marks indicate portions of the manuscript which have been heavily inked over. When a word or phrase is overscored but is still legible, I have reproduced this effect by marking a line through it.

Hebrews 7.4 deals with Melchizedek, a "priest of the Most High God," to whom Abraham gave "the tenth of the spoils."

he Lent [as our Saviour commanded and all good men advised]
looking for nothing again.[6]

* * *

Although the manuscript makes clear that many of those who envied
Sutton were other (if poorer) commoners, it is not difficult to believe
that he must also have been resented by many of his social "superiors,"
especially those who found themselves in his debt. Sutton had to walk
a careful line; he could easily arouse both the jealousy of his inferiors
and the indignation of men who had more rank than cash. Given his
circumstances—his extreme but somewhat mysterious wealth, his isolation, his dependence on a garrulous factotum, the resentment his
position bred—it hardly seems surprising that many spectators of Volpone assumed that Sutton was Jonson's target. Other similarities between Volpone's and Sutton's circumstances could only have reinforced
this assumption, and many members of the play's audience must have
relished the thought of Sutton as an object of satire. The manuscript's
discussion of this issue—in a long passage that should be of great interest to Jonson scholars and other students of Renaissance literature—
is curiously ambivalent. On the one hand the passage dismisses the
possibility that Jonson targeted Sutton; on the other hand it condemns
and mocks him for attacking so worthy a figure:

> a particular pique against him was thought to be maintained
> against him by five sorts of persons whom he used to forebode to
> misery and poverty viz: concelers, promoters, chemists, monopo-
> lists; and poets the last of whom being commonly poore themselves
> addresse themselves to the rich first by Panegyrickes, and flatteries,
> and that not working upon them (who deal too much in things to
> be taken with words) they fall upon them with scoffes and jeares
> to litle purpose when the wealthy laugh at them at home as heart-
> ily as they can laugh at them abroad—

> I must confesse I never heard that any poet had soe litle wit as
> openly to abuse him Master Sutton who had soe much wit as to
> get an estate onely there were severall poems of that time that to
> some app[re]hensions (and fancy hath made actions XX XX and
> persons of a 1000 years standing to poynt at those of our own time
> imagining that the Actions of an old play represented some of their
> new spectators[)] seemed to touch upon those peccadilloes of his
> which thay in their opinion he was thought, rather than in him-
> selfe was really guilty of—and rather expressed their malice towards
> him, than the poets design upon him—and among the rest Ben:
> Johnsons Vulponi is generally reported to be master Suttons
> humor—concerning this I have thus much to offer 1: that though
> nothing can be soe excellent nay nothing so sacred but hath beene

6. BL Lansdowne MS. 1198, fol. 2ʳ.

~~represented~~ exposed as ridiculous (by the power of that faculty that was given us to conceave things aright that we might judge of them; not to represent them foolishly that we might laugh at them) and soe truely we should take as litle notice of these fancifull affronts as he would have done himselfe (who knew that injuries of this nature got advantage by being taken notice of[)] since good men cannot be concerned at those entertai[n]ments in the world wherein they see god himselfe the maker [&] benefactor of it exposed by men that will hazzard the being damned that they may be thought witty—yet *Ben: Johnson* himselfe was so farre from owning that design upon master Sutton that XX often frequenting the Schoole [&] the hall since the foundation of the Charterhouse he expressed his great admiration of him who [he sayd] had erected soe noble a foundation that he wished himselfe (as his friend Broome was) a member of it. Ben understood well enough that his mushrome playes could never disparage or outlast mr Suttons ~~lasting~~ good workes where the oddes is as great as between paper and stone; between pleasure and piety; betweene what at present *Ticklish,* and what is for ever *usefull.*

2. If he had designed the portraicture of Master Sutton in that play [as religious Sir John oldcastle is acted on our Stage as a sot: and the Renowned Sir Jo: Falstaffe as a Buffoone] yet Ben: Johnson lived to correct his mistake of him out of a passage in Cicero twice translated by him [in studio rei amplificandae apparebat, non avaritiae praedam, sed instrumentum bonitati quaeri] in ~~his~~ master Suttons great care for the enlarging of his estate it appeared that [he] sought not soe much a prey for his covetousness to enjoy, as instrument for his goodnesse to bestow; who knew that of great riches there is noe reall use but distribution, the rest is conceit— the personall enjoyment of the wealthiest man living can never reach to feel great riches beyond the imaginary way of the custody or fame of them unlesse it be by the phantasticke pleasure of Lavishing them upon vain followers or the real one of dispensing them among needy and poore men.[7]

Herne also denies that Jonson attacked Sutton, but, like the author of the manuscript, he covers all bases, asserting that if the poet *did* have Sutton in mind, then "he was first of all an ungrateful Wretch, to abuse those hands which afforded him Bread, for he allowed him a constant Pension: And secondly, he disowned his very Handwriting, which he sent to our Founder, in Vindication of himself in this matter" (43). It would be interesting to know Herne's sources for his charges about

---

7. BL Lansdowne MS. 1198, fols. 4ᵛ–5ʳ. The reference to "Broome" is to Richard Brome, Jonson's one-time servant who later became a playwright himself. [Sir John Oldcastle was a supporter of the Lollards, a heretical group of Christians, in the fifteenth century and was portrayed on the English Renaissance stage; he was also thought to be the model for Shakespeare's Sir John Falstaff.—*Editor*]

Jonson's pension and his "Vindication"; since, in these respects, he goes beyond the authority of the manuscript, perhaps his information came from the personal testimony he alludes to in his preface. Yet despite Herne's and the manuscript's best efforts at denigrating the possibility that Sutton was Jonson's target, in the very process of doing so they offer evidence which makes it easier to understand why so many in the play's contemporary audiences jumped to this conclusion. Particularly fascinating are their discussions of how Sutton tricked persons who tried to manipulate him into making them his heirs. Neither the manuscript nor Herne denies that Sutton took advantage of such people; instead, both applaud his cleverness and imply that any such operators got what they deserved. * * *

*   *   *

Certainly Jonson could not have been surprised to learn that others spotted a connection. There is no way to know, of course, whether he deliberately intended any personal satire, and there is even less evidence about his more precise motives even if such satire *was* intended. However, the standard assumption of earlier scholars—that Jonson could not possibly have aimed at Sutton—seems less convincing than it once did. After all, their picture of Sutton—a picture stressing his piety and exemplary character—has been drawn largely from the very sources that sought to whitewash his contemporary reputation. Yet even those sources (especially the unnoted manuscript) offer evidence that many people of Sutton's time viewed him far less benignly than subsequent generations have done.

The fact that the resemblances between Sutton and Volpone are not even more striking does not necessarily prove that no satire was intended. Indeed, if the playwright *had* wanted to mock Sutton, he would have had to guard against mocking him too obviously, lest he be charged with personal libel. Moreover, in deciding about charges of personal satire on the English Renaissance stage, textual evidence alone can never be entirely conclusive; much would have depended on how the actor playing Volpone chose to move or to speak his lines. However, Jonson's intentions or even those of the actors are less important than the interpretations his audience could reasonably have made of his play. What seems clear from a fuller investigation of Sutton's life is that, given the old man's circumstances, Jonson would have had few grounds to complain if Sutton, his friends, or his enemies detected some personal application in the work. The play's subplot, with its English characters and its many references to contemporary English events, would have given comfort to any spectator who wanted to view the main plot in similar terms. The Venetian setting distances the work only partially from relevance to life in London. Whether by accident or design, *Volpone* treats a subject that was highly topical at the time the work was written. The extraordinary speed with which Jonson penned his masterpiece—he claimed to have composed it in five weeks—can reasonably cause one to wonder if something other than his reading alone may have jogged his imagination. In any case, and for whatever reasons, he hit upon a subject that must have struck many auditors as especially timely and pertinent.

* * *

ANNE BARTON

[Names in Jonson's Comedies][†]

* * *

Naming in *Volpone* is as homogeneous in its own way as that in *Cynthia's Revels*,[1] but far more sensitive and complex in what it reveals about characters and their relationships. Volpone the Fox and Mosca the Fly are detached by their names from everyone else in the comedy, but also locked in an uneasy and potentially hostile relationship with each other. Among the birds, the three carrion eaters—Voltore, Corbaccio and Corvino—are automatically linked, and the vulture established as the largest and most formidable of the three, even before they appear in Volpone's sick-room. Sir Pol and Lady Would-be, the male and female parrot, are clearly distinguished from them by breed, as they will be in the plot, but they are also, as harmless seed-eaters, no match for the free-ranging, carnivorous Peregrine with which they imprudently become entangled. A nobler bird than the vulture, the raven, the crow or the parrots, the falcon is nonetheless single-minded, savage, and not notably intelligent, whatever its efficiency as a predator. Jonson had been highly selective when he pillaged from Florio[2] in *Every Man Out of His Humour*. But he takes far greater creative liberties with the Italian names in *Volpone*. They constitute a special dramatic shorthand, articulating not only character but the very structure of the comedy.

Significantly, Volpone and Mosca are the only characters to be aware throughout of the meaning of almost everyone else's name. It is true that they are not perceptive about 'Celia' and 'Bonario': the 'heavenly' and 'the good'. The connotations of 'Celia' should have warned the Fox that, despite her husband's greed and ill-treatment, she could not be seduced. Mosca makes a similar mistake when he supposes that a man called 'Bonario' will turn on his own father even when he knows

---

† From *Ben Jonson: Dramatist* (Cambridge: Cambridge University Press, 1984), pp. 185–93. Copyright © 1984. Reprinted with the permission of Cambridge University Press. The author's notes have been edited.

1. Jonson's play of 1600 [*Editor*].
2. John Florio published an English and Italian dictionary in 1598. Jonson's play *Every Man Out of His Humor* was first acted in 1599 [*Editor*].

that father plans to disinherit him. Their blindness here suggests an inability to credit the existence of disinterested good. It is made all the more striking by contrast with the accuracy with which they perceive the vices of their clients, and decipher their tell-tale names: 'vulture, kite, / Raven, and gor-crow, all my birds of prey, / That thinke me turning carcasse' (I. 2. 88–90). When speaking to each other, or in asides, they frequently reduce 'Corvino', 'Corbaccio' and 'Voltore' to their uncomplimentary English equivalents: 'The vulture's gone, and the old raven's come' (I. 3. 81), or 'Rooke goe with you, raven' (I. 4. 124). The birds themselves give no sign of any similar understanding, nor do they find anything to warn them in the name 'Volpone'. Celia and Bonario are equally obtuse.

In the sub-plot, Peregrine does construe 'Politic Would-be' correctly. 'O, that speaks him', he exclaims as soon as Sir Pol has formally introduced himself (II. 1. 25). He means that, new though he is to Venice and its gossip, word of the absurdities of the English knight and his lady has already reached his ears—but also that the name itself is self-explanatory. Unfortunately, he comes to believe later that Sir Pol has a second, and even more accurate, name: 'Sir POLITIQUE WOULD-BEE? no, sir POLITIQUE bawd! / To bring me, thus, acquainted with his wife' (IV. 3. 20–1). Peregrine is wrong here. Mosca is entirely responsible for Lady Would-be's embarrassing behaviour when she meets Peregrine on the Rialto, not her husband. Hawkish and cruel, Peregrine goes on to humiliate a harmless and basically well-meaning eccentric as the result of a misapprehension. Just like the man whose follies he has undertaken to punish, he imagines a sinister plot where there is none. As for Sir Politic himself, it is only after all his pretensions have been shattered that he arrives at a more sober understanding of at least part of his name. He will flee Venice, and henceforth 'thinke it well, / To shrinke my poore head, in my politique shell' (V. 4. 88–9). His aspirations to be thought 'politique' in the sense of 'shrewd or cunning in affairs of state' have reduced themselves to what can be subsumed under the definition 'prudent'. Peregrine, arguably, never arrives at even this limited comprehension of his own name—a name never actually spoken in the play.

In sharp distinction from Peregrine and the other birds, Volpone never for an instant loses touch with his own name. Throughout the comedy, from his invocation of the beast fable at the beginning to his assertion that 'This is call'd mortifying of a FOXE' at the end (V. 12. 125), he plays delightedly with the word and the morally ambiguous qualities associated with it. Mosca's situation is different. Apart from Voltore, who experiences a belated moment of clairvoyance in which he flings the epithet 'flesh-flie' at the man who has deceived him (V. 9. 1), no one—including Volpone and Mosca himself—ever delves into the etymology of the name. On the other hand, they all think of him as 'the parasite', a designation Mosca himself is entirely happy to accept. In the final court scene, the Avocatori find themselves seriously embarrassed that they do not, in fact, know the proper name of the man who, now that he is rich and a good marriage prospect for their daughters, can no longer be referred to without indecorum simply as 'the parasite'. 'Mosca' is, of course, only another way of saying the same thing, but for most people in Venice, the significance of proper names seems to be invisible. In this respect, the Fox and his accomplice emerge not only as more alert than the other characters, but as men gifted with something of that ability to distinguish the truth of names that Socrates identified specifically with poets.

Epicoene, Jonson's next comedy, is far more diffuse and loosely woven than *Volpone*. This loosening of structure is reflected in a greater heterogeneity of names. The guests who arrive to celebrate Morose's wedding are a scrambled and cacophonous collection, representative of the jumble and disorder of London society in their appellations as in their behaviour. The collegiate lady Mavis ('an ill face') derives once again from Florio.[3] Sir John Daw is a lesser relative of Corvino, humanized somewhat perilously by the addition of a Christian name which can easily be reduced to 'Jack'. Like the tame jackdaw to which the wits compare him, he prattles on tirelessly without understanding his borrowed language. Captain Otter, a mammal even more ambiguous than the fox, but without its intelligence or charisma, is amphibious because he has had command both by land and sea. His domineering wife, who shares his surname, discovers different implications in it. Falstaff, in *I Henry IV*, had insulted Mistress Quickly by calling her 'an otter', a beast 'neither fish nor flesh' (III. 3. 125, 127), and so by implication a sexual anomaly. Mistress Otter is a creature of this kind, as is Madame Centaure, another composite being, specifically associated by her name with lust. The barber Cutberd takes his name from his profession, Morose, Madame Haughty and Sir Amorous La-Foole from engrained social habits.

As might be expected, the power to divine character through an understanding of proper names is vested, in this comedy, in the young men at its centre. Their own names—Dauphine Eugenie, the well-born heir, Clerimont the bright and Truewit—are less telling and weighty than had been usual for main characters in Jonson. Like the gallants who answer to them, they are amoral and, if they make it clear that [with the possible exception of Truewit] their owners are devoid of humours or affectations, they also seem calculatedly external, or even trivial. Dauphine, Clerimont and Truewit do not play on these names, nor does anyone else in the comedy. Morose objects to Dauphine's

---

3. E. B. Partridge makes this point in his edition of *Epicoene* (The Yale Ben Jonson, New Haven and London, 1971), p. 174.

purchased knighthood, but not to the way his name advertises his position as potential inheritor. All three of the young men ignore the etymology of their own names, while being quick to pounce on the connotations of 'Daw', 'Otter' and 'La-Foole'. They turn Daw's arms into wings and mock his birdlike, derivative speech, nail Otter as 'animal amphibium', and craftily lead La-Foole into an unconscious anatomization of his title. La-Foole expatiates happily on the size of his family, the La-Fooles of north, south, east and west, without realizing that he has been encouraged to talk about the ubiquity of folly, and display a fool's pride in his ancestry. Otter is equally imperceptive. Sir John Daw does, on one occasion, claim that he is 'a rooke' if he has any knowledge of Epicoene's proposed marriage to Morose (III. 3. 2), but he seems to be unconscious of his own play on words. Conspicuously shaky where proper names are concerned, Daw cannot even be depended on to distinguish the titles of books from their authors. Some of his favourite writers, much preferred to Homer, Virgil and Horace, turn out to be 'Syntagma', 'Corpus juris civilis' and 'the King of Spain's Bible'. Dauphine and Clerimont try wickedly to encourage him by suggesting that both the 'Corpusses' were Dutchmen, and 'very corpulent authors' (II. 3. 87–9), but Daw is so clueless about etymology that he misses the joke.

The Otters, by contrast, confuse names with essences in a way that almost seems to parody Plato. Having christened his greater drinking cups 'bull', 'bear' and 'horse', both Otter and his wife persistently regard 'the witty denomination' (II. 6. 62) as something which actually introduces these animals into a room. Mrs Otter bans the cups called 'bear' and 'bull' because their scent will pollute the house when it is prepared to receive great ladies. The horse she allows, because courtiers 'love to bee well hors'd, I know. I love it my selfe' (III. 1. 22–3). In Act Four, Otter actually stages a mimic bear-bull-and-horse baiting with the help of cups which, in his imagination, have become the things they name. Dauphine, Clerimont and Truewit are contemptuous onlookers at the sport. Yet their superiority is by no means unqualified. They are far less adept than Volpone and Mosca, let alone Criticus and Horace,[4] at the right interpretation of names. Dauphine can fall in love with all three of the collegiate ladies, despite the fact that 'Mavis', 'Centaure' and 'Haughty' clearly indicate that these women are not worth pursuit. It takes him a long time to discover what the names should have told him from the start. As for Clerimont and Truewit, they are as impervious as Morose to the fact that Epicoene's name—the witty invention of Dauphine—virtually guarantees 'her' eventual discovery as a boy. At the first performance, the theatre audience too would have been challenged

---

4. Characters from Jonson's plays *Cynthia's Revels* and *Poetaster*, respectively [*Editor*].

to interpret 'Epicoene' correctly, a judgement made more difficult by the fact that at Whitefriars[5] all the parts were played by boys.

In its naming as in other respects *The Alchemist* is both more generous and more elusive than *Volpone* or *Epicoene*. It is in keeping with the greater naturalism of this play, its concern with the minutiae of ordinary urban lives, and Jonson's interest in the transformations effected by words, that names should become less fixed and absolute. All are speaking, but what they tell is often riddling, peripheral, or even untrue. At the centre of the comedy, Subtle's name provokes a deliberately mixed response, balanced between the positive and the negative, reminiscent of the fruitful ambiguities generated by 'Volpone'. 'Subtle', however, although it may stir memories of the serpent in Genesis, 'more subtil than any beast of the field', has no marked animal affiliations. Apart from 'Kastril', the small angry falcon, this is true of all the names in *The Alchemist*. With Captain Face, Subtle's confederate, the situation is especially complicated. The name is not his own, but something fabricated by Subtle. According to Subtle, if it had not been for his assistance, Face had 'had no name' (I. 1. 81). Subtle is thinking of 'name' here primarily in the sense 'reputation'; but the fact is that he found a man called 'Jeremy'—an entirely neutral and uncommunicative praenomen—and turned him into 'Face', a name which is 'true' only in the sense that it points to its own falsehood.

'Dol Common' is similarly unstable. Like 'Dol Tearsheet' and 'Kate Common', both invoked by Morose in *Epicoene* (II. 5. 129–30), this is a type name for a whore. Yet Dol cannot be contained within its essentially dismissive and generalized terms. Not only is she a brilliant actress, able to put on a convincing performance as a great lady, both sane and mad, and impersonate the Fairy Queen; other characters are constantly blurring and dissolving the sordid identity to which she is limited by her name. They invent other names for her, epithets, descriptive phrases and fanciful forms of address which come to surround her with a haze of illusory qualities. She is not just 'Dol Common', but 'Dol Proper', 'Dol Singular', 'Mistress Dorothy', 'God's gift', 'dainty Dolkin', 'Sanguine', 'Claridiana', 'Bradamante', 'our cinque-port', 'our Dover pier', 'my guinea-bird', 'sweet honorable lady', 'glory of her sex', 'Lord What'shum's sister', 'my fine flitter-mouse', 'smock rampant', 'bird o' the night', 'Her Grace the Fairy Queen' and 'Madame Suppository'. These are not random and predominantly meaningless appellations like the ones scattered abroad so indiscriminately by Captain Tucca.[6] In the course of the play, Dol can be seen to be all these diverse things. As a result, she escapes the limitations of her own name. This is partly be-

5. London theater [*Editor*].
6. A foolish military man in *Poetaster* [*Editor*].

cause of her skill at play-acting, at assuming a dazzling series of different identities, but also because the woman who adopts these roles is, despite her sexual promiscuity, too much of an individual—in a sense, too rare—truly to be defined as 'Common'.

Among the dupes, Sir Epicure Mammon and Pertinax Surly do entirely validate their names. Not even Surly's Spanish disguise can transform his nature, in the way that Dol is temporarily transformed when she adopts the dress and manners of an aristocrat. The case of Abel Drugger is different. As with Cutberd in *Epicoene*, his surname reflects his occupation. It matters, however, that 'Drugger' should seem like a perfectly naturalistic surname—in Camden's terms—where 'Cutberd' is palpably a fictional invention. Drugger's Christian name, too, not only seems plausible as 'Epicure' or 'Pertinax' do not, it surrounds him with Biblical associations of vulnerability and innocence. (Camden had glossed 'Abel' as 'just'.[7]) By customarily reducing 'Abel' to the nickname 'Nab', Face makes Drugger seem even more homely. In *Remains*, Camden had dealt somewhat sardonically with rebuses and anagrams as alternative forms of naming. He was more respectful, as might be expected from the Clarenceux King of Arms, about armorial bearings, if also professionally discriminating. Jonson's early plays are savage about the coats of arms devised for would-be gentlemen. In *Every Man Out of His Humour*, the heralds maliciously present the hoggish Sogliardo with a scutcheon[8] displaying 'A swine without a head, without braine, wit, any thing indeed, ramping to gentilitie' (III. 4. 64–6). It is, as Puntarvolo observes, 'the most vile, foolish, absurd, palpable, & ridiculous escutcheon, that ever this eye survis'd' (71–2), but the comment it makes on Sogliardo's pretensions goes unperceived by the proud owner. Crispinus, in *Poetaster*, is also inordinately proud of his tell-tale coat of arms, while Sir Amorous La-Foole in *Epicoene* remains blind to the fact that the 'very noted coate' of his family, yellow, checkered azure, gules and 'some three or foure colours more' (I. 4. 40–4) is in fact fool's motley. When Drugger asks Subtle to invent a sign for his shop, and the alchemist announces portentously that he will 'have his name / Form'd in some mystick character' (II. 6. 14–15), some such witty and derogatory device seems inevitable: a visual equivalent for censure to be discovered in the name. In fact, the sign Drugger is given—a bell, Dr Dee standing beside it in a rug gown, and a dog snarling 'Er'—while silly enough, is entirely un-pejorative. The images into which Subtle translates 'Drugger' are no more valuable as a comment on the man whose name this is than most of the rebuses described

---

7. William Camden, *Remains concerning Britain*, intro. Leslie Dunkling (Wakefield, 1974), p. 66. [This work was originally published in 1605.—*Editor*]
8. A heraldic badge [*Editor*].

by Camden. They come close to reducing the assumptions of the *Cratylus*[9] to a joke.

The secret of Abel Drugger's being is not to be deduced from his name, any more than Dol Common's is from hers, or that of Jeremy from either his false title or his true. 'Lovewit' activates the unstable connotations of 'wit' even more ambiguously than 'Truewit' had in *Epicoene*. It is deliberately of no help at all in suggesting how this man, and his behaviour at the end of the play, are to be judged. 'Dapper' too, a name already employed by Dekker and Middleton in *The Roaring Girl* (?1608), conjures up the spruceness and little vanities of the clerk's personal appearance without pretending to pluck out the heart of his mystery: the frustrations and thwarted ambitions that make him easy game for Face and Subtle, and leave him the only customer still undeceived at the end. Drugger's sign is far from being the only hint in this play that Jonson was beginning to distrust, even to mock, the idea of revelatory names.

Kastril's sister, for instance, remains anonymous until the moment, late in Act Four, when she is handed over to Surly in his Spanish disguise:

Sub.	'Pray god, your sister prove but pliant.
Kas.	Why,
	Her name is so; by her other husband.
Sub.	How!
Kas.	The widdow PLIANT. Knew you not that?
Sub.	No faith, sir.
	Yet, by erection of her *figure*, I gest it. (IV. 4. 89–92)

Subtle, of course, had no idea that Kastril's sister was called 'Pliant'. He is obliged hastily to 'remember' that he guessed it from a combination of casting her horoscope and looking at her drooping form. This might have been, but in context is not, a Jonsonian version of Spenser's delayed naming. Subtle stumbles upon Dame Pliant's name purely by chance. It is, as it happens, a 'true' name: passive adaptability characterizes her throughout. Yet Kastril stresses the fact that she acquired this surname through the accident of marriage; it was not hers from birth. In his earlier plays, Jonson had dealt with the minor problem raised by the naming of married women in one of two ways. Either he used their own given names to designate them throughout ('Biancha', 'Tib', 'Fallace', 'Chloe', 'Celia'), or else, as with Lady Would-be and Mrs Otter, the name they took over from their husbands is shown to fit them differently but sufficiently well as to suggest that marriages,

---

9. A dialogue of Plato [*Editor*]. ("Socrates' argument in this dialogue [is] that words are the 'images' of things, possessing a real as opposed to a merely arbitrary connection with what they signify."—Barton, p. 170)

like christenings, are ordered by destiny. In *Epicoene*, where the es-
tranged husbands of Mavis, Haughty and Centaure neither appear nor
are ever described, Jonson is able to proceed on the assumption that
the surnames 'Haughty' and 'Centaure', which describe the two women
so accurately, are equally applicable to the men from whom they took
them, without needing to give the matter any attention. But the striking
thing about 'Pliant' is the way Jonson makes it clear that the temperament it defines is the natural result of the way this woman has been
treated, not necessarily innate. As dim-witted as his sister, Kastril nonetheless uses his male prerogative to bully and threaten her throughout
the play. After years of association with a brother who proposes to
'thumpe' her (V. 5. 45), 'thrust a pinne i' your buttocks' (IV. 4. 75), or
merely give her a good kick or a mauling (IV. 4. 34–7) when she
displays the slightest sign of independence, it is scarcely surprising that
she has become 'pliant'. It matters, too, that both Kastril and Subtle
should regard the correspondence between her disposition and the
name she picked up from her deceased husband as somehow freakish
and surprising.

Belief in the mysterious significance of names is something Subtle
professes at his convenience, as he does here in the matter of Dame
Pliant's horoscope, or when devising for Drugger a sign which 'Striking
the senses of the passers by, / Shall, by a vertuall influence, breed
affections, / That may result upon the partie ownes it' (II. 6. 16–18).
When he wants to rid himself of Ananias, he simulates shock at discovering that his visitor has the name of the man who 'cossend the
Apostles'. 'Had your *holy Consistorie* / No name to send me, of another
sound, / Then wicked ANANIAS?' (II. 5. 74–6). 'Ananias' is possible
as a baptismal name in the period. Camden's first editor observed with
disgust, in 1674, that he had actually known a man whose parents
lumbered him with this ill-omened name.[1] 'Tribulation Wholesome',
on the other hand, like 'Zeal-of-the-Land Busy' later, obviously represents a Puritan christening. Subtle thinks no better of it than Camden
had. When attacking the practices of the exiled saints in Act Three, he
dismisses it, along with 'PERSECUTION, RESTRAINT, LONG-
PATIENCE, and such like', as a name affected 'Onely for glorie, and
to catch the eare / Of the *Disciple*' (2. 92–7). Tribulation himself
meekly acquiesces. Once in possession of the philosopher's stone, the
godly brethren will be able to abandon such practices. Meanwhile,
Subtle has drawn attention to the fact that one of the most outlandish
of all the speaking names in this comedy was not only common among
sectaries, but is patently false. 'Epicure Mammon', 'Kastril', 'Pliant' and
'Surly' set aside, there is not much of real importance that Criticus
could read in the names of *The Alchemist*. In this respect, as in so many

1. *Remains*, p. 56.

others, the play marks a turning point in Jonson's work. When he returned to comedy with *Bartholomew Fair*, after the interval of *Catiline*, the attitude he adopted towards characters and their names was essentially the one initiated in *The Alchemist*.

JOHN DRYDEN

Examen of *The Silent Woman*†

To begin first[1] with the length of the action, it is so far from exceeding the compass of a natural day that it takes not up an artificial one.[2] 'Tis all included in the limits of three hours and an half, which is no more than is required for the presentment on the stage. A beauty perhaps not much observed; if it had, we should not have looked on the Spanish translation of *Five Hours* with so much wonder.[3] The scene of it is laid in London; the latitude of place is almost as little as you can imagine: for it lies all within the compass of two houses, and after the first act in one. The continuity of scenes is observed more than in any of our plays, excepting his own *Fox* and *Alchemist*. They are not broken above twice or thrice at most in the whole comedy;[4] and in the two best of Corneille's plays, the *Cid* and *Cinna*, they are interrupted once apiece. The action of the play is entirely one; the end or aim of which is the settling Morose's estate on Dauphine. The intrigue of it is the greatest and most noble of any pure unmixed comedy in any language; you see in it many persons of various characters and humors, and all delightful: as first, Morose, or an old man, to whom all noise but his own talking is offensive. Some who would be thought critics say this humor of his is forced: but to remove that objection, we may consider

---

† From *Essay on Dramatic Poesy* (1668). All notes are by the editor of this Norton Critical Edition.

1. Dryden (1631–1700) was the most influential poet and critic of the second half of the seventeenth century. Dryden's *Essay* is a four-way dialogue among friends who, as they drift down the Thames in a barge, spend the cool and quiet evening talking about literature. They are gentlemen, not scholars or divines; the literature they discuss is for and about gentlemen, and it is natural that one of them turns his attention to *Epicoene* ("The Silent Woman"). The speaker is called Neander in the dialogue: the name means New Man, and Neander represents Dryden himself. His "Examen" is a casual but incisive account of a play that, though nearly sixty years old and the product of very different circumstances, for its neatness of construction and elegance of wit seemed to Dryden an important precursor of the comedies of his own day.

2. The speaker knows about the doctrine of the "unities" of time, place, and action; though he isn't rigid about them, he does value tight construction.

3. In 1663 Sir Samuel Tuke had adapted from the Spanish of Calderón a play called in English *The Adventures of Five Hours*.

4. "Continuity of scenes" was a structural principle much prized in the seventeenth century; the playwright started a new scene not by introducing a whole new set of characters, but by adding new characters and dismissing old ones to lead into new actions. Jonson is by no means as careful of this principle in *Epicoene* as, for example, in the third act of *The Alchemist*. Corneille (1606–1684) was a French dramatist.

him first to be naturally of a delicate hearing, as many are to whom all
sharp sounds are unpleasant; and secondly, we may attribute much of
it to the peevishness of his age, or the wayward authority of an old man
in his own house, where he may make himself obeyed; and this the
poet seems to allude to in his name *Morose*. Besides this, I am assured
from divers persons that Ben Jonson was actually acquainted with such
a man, one altogether as ridiculous as he is here represented. Others
say it is not enough to find one man of such an humor; it must be
common to more, and the more common the more natural. To prove
this, they instance in the best of comical characters, Falstaff;[5] there are
many men resembling him; old, fat, merry, cowardly, drunken, amorous, vain, and lying. But to convince these people, I need but tell
them that humor is the ridiculous extravagance of conversation,
wherein one man differs from all others. If then it be common, or
communicated, to many, how differs it from other men's? Or what
indeed causes it to be ridiculous so much as the singularity of it? As
for Falstaff, he is not properly one humor, but a miscellany of humors
or images, drawn from so many several men: that wherein he is singular
is his wit, or those things he says *præter expectatum*,[6] unexpected by
the audience; his quick evasions when you imagine him surprised,
which, as they are extremely diverting of themselves, so receive a great
addition from his person; for the very sight of such an unwieldy, old,
debauched fellow is a comedy alone. And here, having a place so
proper for it, I cannot but enlarge somewhat upon this subject of humor
into which I am fallen. The Ancients had little of it in their comedies;
for the τὸ γελοῖον[7] of the Old Comedy, of which Aristophanes was
chief, was not so much to imitate a man as to make the people laugh
at some odd conceit which had commonly somewhat of unnatural or
obscene in it. Thus, when you see Socrates brought upon the stage,[8]
you are not to imagine him made ridiculous by the imitation of his
actions, but rather by making him perform something very unlike himself: something so childish and absurd as, by comparing it with the
gravity of the true Socrates, makes a ridiculous object for the spectators.
In their New Comedy, which succeeded,[9] the poets sought indeed to
express the ἦθος, as in their tragedies the πάθος of mankind. But this
ἦθος contained only the general characters of men and manners; as
old men, lovers, serving-men, courtesans, parasites, and such other persons as we see in their comedies; all which they made alike: that is,

---

5. Shakespeare's fat knight was so popular that he had to be brought back in several different
   plays.
6. Beyond expectation.
7. "The ridiculous" (Aristotle, *Poetics*, chapter 5). Old comedy was invidious and personal.
8. Socrates was ridiculed in Aristophanes' *The Clouds*; it is the same example used by Jonson,
   of the philosopher hoisted aloft in a basket in order to think airy thoughts.
9. I.e., followed. New Comedy dealt with types, not individuals. Dryden's contrast between *ethos*
   and *pathos* is one between "character" and "suffering."

one old man or father, one lover, one courtesan, so like another as if the first of them had begot the rest of every sort: *ex homine hunc natum dicas.*[1] The same custom they observed likewise in their tragedies. As for the French, though they have the word *humeur* among them, yet they have small use of it in their comedies or farces; they being but ill imitations of the *ridiculum,* or that which stirred up laughter in the Old Comedy. But among the English 'tis otherwise: where by humor is meant some extravagant habit, passion, or affection, particular (as I said before) to some one person, by the oddness of which he is immediately distinguished from the rest of men; which being lively and naturally represented, most frequently begets that malicious pleasure in the audience which is testified by laughter; as all things which are deviations from common customs are ever the aptest to produce it: though, by the way, this laughter is only accidental, as the person represented is fantastic or bizarre; but pleasure is essential to it, as the imitation of what is natural. The description of these humors, drawn from the knowledge and observation of particular persons, was the peculiar genius and talent of Ben Jonson; to whose play I now return.

Besides Morose, there are at least nine or ten different characters and humors in *The Silent Woman,* all which persons have several concernments of their own, yet are all used by the poet to the conducting of the main design to perfection. I shall not waste time in commending the writing of this play, but I will give you my opinion that there is more wit and acuteness of fancy in it than in any of Ben Jonson's. Besides, that he has here described the conversation of gentlemen in the persons of True-Wit and his friends, with more gaiety, air, and freedom, than in the rest of his comedies. For the contrivance of the plot, 'tis extreme elaborate, and yet withal easy; for the λύσις,[2] or untying of it, 'tis so admirable that, when it is done, no one of the audience would think the poet could have missed it; and yet it was concealed so much before the last scene that any other way would sooner have entered into your thoughts. But I dare not take upon me to commend the fabric of it, because it is altogether so full of art that I must unravel every scene in it to commend it as I ought. And this excellent contrivance is still the more to be admired because 'tis comedy, where the persons are only of common rank, and their business private, not elevated by passions or high concernments as in serious plays. Here every one is a proper judge of all he sees; nothing is represented but that with which he daily converses: so that by consequence all faults lie open to discovery, and few are pardonable. 'Tis this which Horace has judiciously observed:

1. "You would say this man was born from that": from Terence (second century B.C.E.), *Eunuch,* line 460.
2. The resolution (*lusis*) is the disclosure of Epicoene's true identity.

creditur, ex medio quia res arcessit, habere
sudoris minimum; sed habet Comedia tanto
plus oneris, quanto veniæ minus.[3]

But our poet, who was not ignorant of these difficulties, had prevailed
himself of all advantages; as he who designs a large leap takes his rise
from the highest ground. One of these advantages is that which Corneille has laid down as the greatest which can arrive to any poem, and
which he himself could never compass above thrice in all his plays;
viz. the making choice of some signal and long-expected day, whereon
the action of the play is to depend. This day was that designed by
Dauphine for the settling of his uncle's estate upon him; which to
compass, he contrives to marry him. That the marriage had been plotted by him long beforehand is made evident by what he tells True-Wit
in the second act, that in one moment he had destroyed what he had
been raising many months.

There is another artifice of the poet which I cannot here omit, because by the frequent practice of it in his comedies he has left it to us
almost as a rule: that is, when he has any character or humor wherein
he would show a *coup de maistre*,[4] for his highest skill, he recommends
it to your observation by a pleasant description of it before the person
first appears. Thus, in *Bartholomew Fair* he gives you the pictures of
Numps and Cokes, and in this those of Daw, Lafoole, Morose, and the
Collegiate Ladies; all which you hear described before you see them.
So that before they come upon the stage you have a longing expectation
of them, which prepares you to receive them favorably; and when they
are there, even from their first appearance you are so far acquainted
with them that nothing of their humor is lost to you.

I will observe yet one thing further of this admirable plot: the business of it rises in every act.[5] The second is greater than the first, the
third than the second, and so forward to the fifth. There too you see,
till the very last scene, new difficulties arising to obstruct the action of
the play; and when the audience is brought into despair that the business can naturally be effected, then, and not before, the discovery is
made. But that the poet might entertain you with more variety all this
while, he reserves some new characters to show you, which he opens
not till the second and third act. In the second, Morose, Daw, the
Barber, and Otter; in the third, the Collegiate Ladies: all which he
moves afterwards in by-walks, or under-plots, as diversions to the main
design, lest it should grow tedious, though they are still naturally joined
with it, and somewhere or other subservient to it. Thus, like a skilful

---

3. "Comedy's easy, people say; its actions flow / From common life. It's harder, though; / You
　get no breaks from viewers" (Horace, *Epistles*, 2.1.168–70; tr. Robert M. Adams).
4. Master-stroke.
5. I.e., the tension continually increases.

chess-player, by little and little he draws out his men, and makes his pawns of use to his greater persons.

If this comedy, and some others, of his were translated into French prose (which would now be no wonder to them, since Molière has lately given them plays out of verse which have not displeased them[6]), I believe the controversy would soon be decided betwixt the two nations, even making them the judges. But we need not call our heroes to our aid; be it spoken to the honor of the English, our nation can never want in any age such who are able to dispute the empire of wit with any people in the universe. And though the fury of a civil war, and power for twenty years together abandoned to a barbarous race of men, enemies of all good learning, had buried the Muses under the ruins of monarchy; yet, with the restoration of our happiness, we see revived poesy lifting up its head, and already shaking off the rubbish which lay so heavy on it. We have seen since his Majesty's return[7] many dramatic poems which yield not to those of any foreign nation, and which deserve all laurels but the English. I will set aside flattery and envy: it cannot be denied but we have had some little blemish either in the plot or writing of all those plays which have been made within these seven years (and perhaps there is no nation in the world so quick to discern them, or so difficult to pardon them, as ours): yet if we can persuade ourselves to use the candor of that poet who (though the most severe of critics) has left us this caution by which to moderate our censures:

> ubi plura nitent in carmine, non ego paucis
> offendar maculis;[8]

if, in consideration of their many and great beauties, we can wink at some slight and little imperfections; if we, I say, can be thus equal to ourselves, I ask no favor from the French. And if I do not venture upon any particular judgment of our late plays, 'tis out of the consideration which an ancient writer gives me: *vivorum, ut magna admiratio, ita censura difficilis:*[9] betwixt the extremes of admiration and malice, 'tis hard to judge uprightly of the living. Only I think it may be permitted me to say that as it is no lessening to us to yield to some plays, and those not many, of our own nation in the last age, so can it be no addition to pronounce of our present poets that they have far surpassed all the Ancients, and the modern writers of other countries.

---

6. One of the famous seventeenth-century French dramatist Molière's first and greatest successes, *Les Précieuses Ridicules*, was in prose; Dryden's implication that in 1668 this was a recent innovation is quite wrong.
7. I.e., since the restoration of Charles II in 1660.
8. "When, in a poem, beauty's everywhere, I do not mind a few spots here and there" (Horace, *Art of Poetry*, line 351; tr. Robert M. Adams).
9. Dryden translates the Latin immediately in the text; his source is the Roman historian Velleius Paterculus, who lived under Tiberius, emperor of Rome 14–37 c.e. (*Historia romana* II.36).

ROBERT WATSON

Epicoene†

Epicoene, or The Silent Woman (1609) consists essentially of a series of plots subsuming each other. The three most skillful plotters, however, finally agree to share the authorial "garland" (if a little unevenly) (5.4.199–203), and in so doing they replace formulaic and potentially grim models of satire with a more modern, pleasant, and sophisticated sort of comic improvisation. The play subordinates the relentless bitterness of formal verse satire, embodied by Morose, to the energy of abusive farce, stage-managed by Truewit, which yields in turn to the witty coup contrived by Dauphine. Morose thinks of himself as a sort of lonely satiric Diogenes,[1] searching the folly-ridden world, not for a single honest man, but rather for a single silent woman. But because there is no such thing (in the play's conventional sexist joke) as a silent woman, Morose's plot is superseded by other plots that humor his fantasy toward their own ends.

No audience, of course, is likely to be deluded into believing that Morose is the authorial spokesman, though some critics have argued that he does speak for an important aspect of Jonson's own intolerant psyche. But an audience could easily mistake the farceur Truewit for that spokesman, a misprision shared not only by a number of critics, but also by Truewit himself. Just when the audience begins to feel complacent in its recognition of the plot as a series of cruelly humorous punishments of folly, with Truewit as master of ceremonies, Jonson shifts his ground yet again. Through Dauphine, and through Dauphine's delicate plot to assure his inheritance, Jonson asserts the infinite adaptability of the dramatic illusion and the ultimate sovereignty of the witty illusionist. Dauphine takes control of his financial legacy in a way that asserts Jonson's analogous seizure of control over his dramatic legacy: *Epicoene* is a theatrical trick of transformation that takes the literary riches of Jonson's satiric ancestors and spends them on his own cavalier pleasures.

In an influential study Barish has argued that *Epicoene* is compromised by the conflicting nature of its literary allusions. He sees the play as Jonson's effort to write a pleasant Ovidian story, a conscious project repeatedly undermined by Jonson's subconscious affinity for the harsher Juvenalian viewpoint. More recently, John Ferns has shown that neither

---

† From *Ben Jonson's Parodic Strategy: Literary Imperialism in the Comedies* (Cambridge: Harvard University Press, 1987), pp. 98–109. Copyright © 1987 by the President and Fellows of Harvard College. Reprinted by permission of Harvard University Press. The author's notes have been abridged.
1. Greek Cynic philosopher, c. 400–325 B.C.E. [*Editor*].

the Ovidian nor the Juvenalian[2] viewpoint is privileged in *Epicoene*, and that neither viewpoint is consistently associated with a single character. What unifies the allusions is the ironic distance the gallants always maintain from their sources, expanding the passages from Juvenal and compressing those from Ovid in equally comic ways. This squares very well with my own theory that what matters in Jonsonian comedy is less the nature of a character's literary sources than that character's ability consciously to manipulate those sources, rather than subconsciously to be manipulated by them. So the playful detachment with which the gallants in *Epicoene* echo the ancients is precisely what marks them as the heroes of the play, and what allows them to exploit those for whom literature is an absolute script for life, as Juvenalian satire seems to be for Morose.

Nonetheless, each of the gallants does have a specific plot in mind, and until those plots are reconciled into the play that is *Epicoene*, they repeatedly discomfit each other. At first Truewit focuses overconfidently on a straightforward plot to save Dauphine's inheritance: he will frighten Morose out of marriage by paraphrasing Juvenal's warning from the *Sixth Satire*. When he boasts to Dauphine and Clerimont about how eloquently he has dissuaded Morose, Truewit is surprised that they do not "applaud" him for performing so well on their behalf (2.4.15). They are unenthusiastic simply because they have other plays in mind. Dauphine has let Clerimont in on enough of his secret that Clerimont supposes the play will culminate in a standard *charivari*—a raucous ritual that sometimes made its way onto the medieval stage, consisting (according to Cotgrave's 1632 dictionary) of "an infamous (or infaming) ballade sung, by an armed troup, under the window of an old dotard married, the day before, unto a young wanton, in mockery of them both." When he learns a little more about the plot, Truewit concurs with Clerimont's belief that their enforcement of such conventional boisterous mockery on Morose will be "a jest to posterity, sirs, this day's mirth" (2.6.25). The echo of the title of Chapman's *Humorous Day's Mirth* could be inadvertent on Jonson's part, but more likely it is a sort of Freudian slip Jonson imposes on Truewit to reveal the derivative theatrical character of his expectations. The jest of *Epicoene* will indeed live to posterity, but only because it insists on going a step beyond the popular entertainment that Truewit envisions.

Jonson's audience is invited to share Truewit's and Clerimont's half-informed deduction about the nature of the play, to believe that Jonson is content to create his dramatic legacy by repeating old comic forms. Only by revealing Epicoene's transsexual disguise at the end does Dau-

---

2. Juvenal was the greatest of the Roman satirists whose work was at its height in the early second century C.E.; Ovid, also a Roman poet and most famously the author of the *Metamorphoses*, lived from 43 B.C.E. to 17 C.E. [*Editor*].

phine reveal that he has been one level deeper into plot and theatrical
artifice than the rest of them; Jonson, by the same device, has been
one step ahead of *his* audience. Because of the Elizabethan traditions
of transvestite disguise on the stage, the audience would presumably
have ignored the fact that the actor playing Epicoene was a boy.
Throughout his comedies Jonson teaches his audience to mistrust theatrical conventions, by betraying those conventions and the characters
who rely on them. Epicoene's disguise, impenetrable precisely because
of the conventions of its context, adds a new dimension to that tactic.
This silent woman is both the device and the emblem of the invisible
plot, which turns out to be the masterplot of *Epicoene, or The Silent
Woman.* The crude pleasure of punishing and humiliating a stock target
yields to a more modern—that is, Augustan—sort of delight in the witty
conquest of an inheritance. Dauphine's particular technique may be
another literary inheritance, derived from Aretino's *Il Marescalco* and
perhaps from Plautus' *Casina*,[3] but its purpose within the play looks
ahead to the next generation of comedy, that of the Restoration.

Jonson thus uses the process of his plot to unsettle the inert literary
heritage of his audience; he "refunctions" the convention of transsexual
casting and the motifs of earlier literature. As Dauphine's revelations
alter the context, the audience learns not to lean too heavily on literary
monuments in the future, because they are not the stable supports they
might appear to be. Barton observes that "in *Epicoene*, far more than
in either of its two predecessors, these memories [of the noble past] are
literary. The comedy is riddled with the names of long-dead classical
writers: Homer, Pindar and Plato, Aristotle, Thucydides, Anacreon, Plutarch, Livy, Virgil, Ovid, Catullus, Juvenal, Horace, Martial, Tacitus,
Seneca and many more. They are talismanic names, even though irrelevant and degraded in context."[4] That is a significant "even though";
the problem again is that characters misapply established literature to
contemporary reality. Barton argues that the gallants are harshly judged
by this mass of moral literature; my qualification is that they, and others,
are condemned only when they fail to bring a modern alertness to bear
on their reading of the ancients. To live one's life in utter obeisance
to this literature would be typical Jonsonian folly, not glorious virtue.
When Truewit (playfully?) reproves Clerimont for his luxurious idle-
ness, Clerimont dismisses the criticisms, not by refuting them, but by
describing them as merely a hollow bit of literary quotation: "Foh!
Thou hast read Plutarch's *Morals* now, or some such tedious fellow,
and it shows so vilely with thee, 'fore God, 'twill spoil thy wit utterly"

3. O. J. Campbell, "The Relation of *Epicoene* to Aretino's *Il Marescalco*," *PMLA*, 46 (1931),
752–762; also Daniel Boughner, "Clizia and *Epicoene*," *Philological Quarterly*, 19 (1940),
89–91.
4. Anne Barton, *Ben Jonson, Dramatist* (New York: Cambridge University Press, 1984), p. 209.

(1.1.56–58). Truewit takes his revenge later by attacking Dauphine for allowing the literature of romance to displace any sexual romance in his real life: "you must leave to live i' your chamber, then, a month together, upon *Amadis de Gaul* or *Don Quixote*, as you are wont, and come abroad where . . . a man shall find whom to love, whom to play with, whom to touch once, whom to hold ever" (4.1.50–56). This would normally be a worthwhile warning. But Dauphine has evidently learned from Cervantes the kind of ironic, parodic distance on literary solemnities that Truewit could never glean from Plutarch, and it is precisely this distance that allows Dauphine's more modern plot to displace Truewit's old-fashioned one.

Truewit advises Dauphine to win a woman by a temporary theatrical indulgence of her self-dramatizing fantasies: "Admire her tires, like her in all fashions, compare her in every habit to some deity, invent excellent dreams to flatter her, and riddles; or, if she be a great one, perform always the second parts to her" (4.1.104–106). Truewit, then, does have much of the arsenal of a Jonsonian coney-catcher; at a number of points in the plot he seems wiser and more humane than Dauphine, who lusts after the horrible Ladies Collegiate and would cut off John Daw's arm for the sake of a jest. The still-unresolved controversy about whether Truewit thus establishes himself as the true hero of *Epicoene* reflects Jonson's strategic manipulation of his authorial power. Jonson grants Truewit attributes that would indeed mark him as the hero of many satiric city-comedies, yet deprives him of the authority that might ordinarily arise from his successful exploits of wit by framing the story around Dauphine's plot instead. Like Mosca before him and Subtle after, Truewit finds himself trapped in a play which adds one more twist to the parodic formula that would normally exalt him as its author-surrogate.

The central struggles of the play all take place in oddly bookish terms that suggest a parodic rewriting of eminently serious works. Allusions to forgery, to false authorship, appear repeatedly and, at first glance, superfluously. Dauphine complains that Morose "will disinherit me" because "he thinks I and my company are authors of all the ridiculous acts and monuments are told of him." Truewit replies with a vengeful plan to "make a false almanac, get it printed, and then ha' him drawn out on a coronation day to the Tower-wharf, and kill him with the noise of the ordnance" (1.2.8–15). Along with the controversial thefts from the classics by Truewit and Dauphine, these references establish deceptive authorship as a major theme of *Epicoene*.

Unhealthy bookishness is most prominent, of course, in the fools. Sir John Daw is introduced as "a fellow that pretends only to learning, buys titles, and nothing else of books in him" (1.2.70–72). The pun on "titles" is significant: Daw is, in other words, a sort of false bookshelf, a hollow box purfled[5] with impressive titles and bindings. When Daw recites his poetry in act 2, scene 3, the witty gentlemen mockingly mistake it for the work of Seneca or Plutarch, and Daw angrily dismisses the writings of nearly all the great classical authors. The only ones Daw will praise are not authors at all, but rather titles he mistakes for the authors' names:

> Dauphine   Why, whom do you account for authors, Sir John Daw?
> Daw   *Syntagma juris civilis, Corpus juris civilis, Corpus juris canonici,* the King of Spain's Bible.
> Dauphine   Is the King of Spain's Bible an author?
> Clerimont   Yes, and *Syntagma.*
> Dauphine   What was that *Syntagma,* sir?
> Daw   A civil lawyer, a Spaniard.
> Dauphine   Sure, *Corpus* was a Dutchman . . . [*Aside.*] 'Fore God, you have a simple learned servant, lady, in titles.
>   (2.3.71–85)

This whole exchange renews the pun on "title" in a way that underscores Daw's tendency to confuse people with literary works. The question of whether Daw will "live by his verses" thus becomes not only a standard piece of commentary on the place of professionalism in the arts, but also another hint that Daw's empty literary pretensions reflect a false literary vision of the course his life will take.

It is intriguing, therefore, that this scene ends with Daw reciting a poem that seems to predict the entire plot of *Epicoene:*

> Silence in woman is like speech in man,
> Deny't who can.
>
> . . . . .
> Nor is't a tale
> That female vice should be a virtue male,
> Or masculine vice, a female virtue be:
> You shall it see
> Proved with increase,
> I know to speak, and she to hold her peace.
>   (2.3.111–119)

Jonson has Daw write these lines without permitting him to understand what they mean in the context of Dauphine's plot; Daw misinterprets them as a narrative of his successful seduction and impregnation of a woman, rather than as a formulation of the central paradoxes that structure *Epicoene.* This typifies his general error, and the errors of so many Jonsonian victims who notice the elements of the plot surrounding

---

5. Ornamented, decorated [*Editor*].

them but misshape them into something that suits their own egotistical
fantasies, leaving themselves unprepared to cope with the master wit's
more ingenious satiric structure. When Daw agrees that kicks can
hardly hurt or humiliate "a man that reads Seneca" (4.5.259–261), and
especially when he volunteers to have his left arm cut off, as long as
he can retain the right one and his life "for writing madrigals" (4.5.109–
110), we get an indication of how far Daw will go in substituting a
literary identity for a real one.

The behavior of Amorous La Foole is similarly suggestive. He is
introduced to us as a man who "does give plays" but has so little comprehension of this fashionable entertainment that he will salute "a lady
when she is dancing in a masque, and put her out" (1.3.30–32). He
is, in other words, a perfect candidate for the role of gull, because (like
Bartholomew Cokes in *Bartholomew Fair*) he involves himself in the
world of playing without any comprehension of the divisions between
theater and real life. Like other Jonsonian gulls, La Foole takes pride
in his name and in his literally foolish costume without recognizing
the degrading implications of either: "I myself am descended lineally
of the French La Fooles—and we do bear for our coat *yellow*, or *or*,
checkered *azure* and *gules*, and some three or four colors more, which
is a very noted coat and has sometimes been solemnly worn by divers
nobility of our house" (1.4.36–40).

La Foole then sets about arranging his grand banquet, which he
envisions as a triumphant affirmation of his nobility, but which, in the
context of the previous speech and of the play in general, undergoes a
generic debasement into an archetypal *festa stultorum*.[6] As Bryant observes, "the banquet that ought to bring these people together comes
at the middle of the play rather than at the end and unites no one."[7]
It is the playwright, of course, who decides what will be a middle incident in his play and what will be the ending; the characters, living
out their own full lives, can only guess whether and where each part
of their experiences will fit into the frame. Jonson, through his on-stage
surrogates, provides conventional signals that provoke and then betray
La Foole's hopes of presiding over the comic resolution.

Clerimont easily draws Daw into his minor role in the plot against
Morose by claiming that Dauphine has "discovered the whole plot" in
which Daw (as Epicoene's slighted lover and La Foole's betrayed
friend) is the noble victim, and by painting a scenario in which Daw
would emerge triumphant (3.3.1–33). A similar theatrical fantasy en-
meshes La Foole, a promise of "a pestling device" that "will pound all
your enemy's practices to powder and blow him up with his own mine,

6. Feast of fools [*Editor*].
7. J. A. Bryant, Jr., *The Compassionate Satirist* (Athens, Ga.: University of Georgia Press, 1972),
   p. 97.

his own train" (3.3.92–94). Both gulls are lured into the overarching scheme of the gallants by the notion that they will themselves be out-plotting a plotter. As Dauphine comments,

> Tut, flatter 'em both, as Truewit says, and you may take their understandings in a purse-net. They'll believe themselves to be just such men as we make 'em, neither more nor less. They have nothing, not the use of their senses, but by tradition.
>
> (3.3.84–87; cf. 4.5.86)

This trait is ultimately what makes Jonsonian gulls vulnerable (Mosca makes the same point in *Volpone*, 5.2.23–28), and they transmit that vulnerability to the literary "traditions" they mistakenly credit. The sort of script the gulls proudly follow as if it were holy scripture is discredited when it cannot defend them from Jonsonian satire.

Truewit's scheme for further humiliating these two fools would have looked oddly familiar to Jonson's audience. "It seems clear," one critic comments, "that Jonson was remembering the mock-combat between Viola and Andrew Aguecheek in *Twelfth Night* when he devised the encounter between Daw and La-Foole in Act Four, each one falsely persuaded through the malice of a third party of the fury and terrifying swordsmanship of his adversary."[8] Perhaps the audience is meant to suspect that Truewit, looking for a showy device to turn these hypocrites against each other, remembers the same literary precedent. Both of the cowards must try to maintain noble postures while undergoing a de-meaning sort of punishment, and then are lured into mutual forgiveness when Truewit offers them the hackneyed model of Damon and Pythias which Jonson would later parody so savagely in *Bartholomew Fair*. They are then finally disgraced, in a less crude but no less effective way, by Dauphine's superplot, because their boasts as seducers are undone when the bride they claim to have enjoyed turns out to be a boy. In other words, they are easily lured into scenarios that they believe will affirm their "manly" poses, and just as easily crushed by a strategic revision of those scripts.

Tom Otter, too, is introduced as a creature living in a world of the-atrical lines, roles, and props:

> An excellent animal, equal with your Daw or La Foole, if not transcendent, and does Latin it as much as your barber. He is his wife's subject; he calls her Princess, and at such times as these follows her up and down the house like a page, with his hat off, partly for heat, partly for reverence. At this instant he is marshalling of his bull, bear, and horse . . . he has been a great man at the Bear Garden in his time, and from that subtle sport has ta'en the witty denomination of his chief carousing cups.   (2.6.48–57)

---

8. Barton, *Dramatist*, p. 125.

His wife, Mistress Otter, actually composed their prenuptial agreement as a script in which her role is regal. When he resists her banishment of his carousing cups, she demands, "Is this according to the instrument when I married you? That I would be Princess and reign in mine own house, and you would be my subject and obey me?" (3.1.27–30). Mistress Otter, like Deliro in *Every Man Out of His Humor,* is determined to impose the clichés of Petrarchan courtship onto the realities of marriage. Clerimont's scheme for convincing her to accept the cups is appropriately literary: he will merely remind her of the grand mythological conjunctions of great women with bulls and bears. This idea pleases Otter so much that he vows to "have these stories painted i' the Bear Garden, *ex Ovidii Metamorphosi*" (3.3.114–115). Life and art seem headed toward an infinite regression of mutual imitations.

In a fit of honesty, Otter points out that his wife is less a unitary person than an assembly of costumes and makeup (4.2.87–96). Like an actress playing a noblewoman, she depends on her "excellent choice phrase" to make her into "the only authentical courtier that is not naturally bred one, in the city," as the gallants sarcastically note (3.2.24–26). She frequently dreams about the Lady Mayoress—uneasy wish-fulfillment dreams, quite possibly derived from the various citizen-comedies (such as *The Shoemakers' Holiday*[9]) in which a citizen's wife achieves that status. She also evidently believes that fantastic desires and classical authors translate into her waking reality: she told the latest such dream to Lady Haughty, who "expounded it out of Artemidorus, and I have found it since very true" (3.2.51–55). The ultimate expression of her narcissistic fantasies occurs when she overhears her husband dispraising her and calls him "Thou Judas, to offer to betray thy Princess!" (4.2.110–111). This blasphemous comparison is really only a logical extension of Mistress Otter's willingness to read herself proudly into any story she knows.

Otter and his wife might have been adequate as characters in one of the humors plays,[1] but Jonson has moved beyond a simple series of attacks on such fragile fantasies. Clerimont is finally "glad we are rid of him," and Truewit agrees that "His humour is as tedious at last, as it was ridiculous at first" (4.2.137–139). The Otters and their absurd marriage remain peripheral to *Epicoene,* never permitted to make a bid for control of its central plot, perhaps because Jonson has decided to focus on the superiority of collaborative male friendship to morose male isolation, rather than focusing again on the follies of ordinary social intercourse.

Female collaborations receive much less sympathetic treatment than male ones. The Ladies Collegiate are no more successful than the

9. Comedy written by Thomas Dekker, first printed in 1600 [*Editor*].
1. Plays based on temperaments—sanguine, phlegmatic, melancholic, choleric—derived from the bodily humors, such as Jonson wrote early in his career (e.g., *Every Man in his Humor*) [*Editor*].

Otters in shaping the play to their wishes and their credit. They envision themselves as something like a female version of Shakespeare's Gentlemen of Navarre,[2] but in this case when sexual desire overshadows academic pretenses, the result is dehumanizing rather than humanizing. These are bad actors, not only in their intellectual pretensions, but even in the cosmetic makeup they wear. Truewit eloquently defends the wearing of such makeup, but as Judd Arnold writes, "the Collegians have all put on their artifices 'the wrong way.' "[3] This embarrassing misuse of cosmetics corresponds to the way the other fools wear their own artifices: they try to play roles which might look impressive on the right person and in the right sort of drama, but here are incongruous, ugly, and degrading.

Morose hardly seems like heroic material for any genre, but in fact many of his assumptions and attitudes would make considerably more sense and carry considerably more moral weight if he inhabited a different sort of literary work. He first appears as a sort of casting director for the play of his life, which he envisions as a dumbshow, with himself as the only speaking chorus:

> Cannot I yet find out a more compendious method than by this trunk to save my servants the labor of speech and mine ears the discord of sounds? Let me see. All discourses but mine own afflict me; they seem harsh, impertinent, and irksome. Is it not possible that thou shouldst answer me by signs, and I apprehend thee, fellow?   (2.1.1–5)

The fact that this servant is called simply "Mute" in the dramatis personae is a latent joke on this suggestion that the play be converted into a dumbshow, a joke brought to life when Truewit addresses him as "Mute" in the following scene.

Several excellent critics have seen Morose in a different light: as a degraded figure of the Jonsonian satirist, full of tirades on the stupid impertinencies of all those around him, hiding in horror from the ways of the world. Delight in silence and withdrawal from society are hardly Jonsonian traits, however. Perhaps, more precisely, Morose represents a verse satirist who has stumbled into the world of Jonsonian comedy. From this perspective Morose's demand for silence appears as egoism of a very particular kind: not fully recognizing the transition from verse satire to satiric drama, he is naturally affronted to hear anyone but himself speak. Jonson may be doing to the figure of the verse satirist what he does to characters from other conventional modes of Eliza-

---

2. Characters in Shakespeare's comedy *Love's Labor's Lost* who abandon love for three years in favor of study [*Editor*].

3. *A Grace Pecular: Ben Jonson's Cavalier Heroes*, Penn State University Studies, 35 (University Park: Pennsylvania State University Press, 1972), p. 49.

bethan literature, lifting them into the noisy chaotic world of realistic
city-comedy, which stubbornly refuses to function in the way they expect, and which thereby exploits, exposes, and punishes their egoism.
In fact, when Morose envisions the ultimate torment, contemporary
plays and playhouses appear prominently (4.4.11–16). Even the loose-
flowing prose of *Epicoene* is an affront, not merely to Morose's inbred
resistance to letting his mind "flow loosely" (5.3.44), but also to the
verse form common to Elizabethan satire.

Epicoene thus serves to defend the territory and the autonomy of
satiric city-comedy against the claims of conventional satire, just as
Every Man In His Humor defended satiric city-comedy on its other
border, against the claims of conventional drama. The entire project of
converting satire from its usual narrative mode to an appealing dramatic
mode poses serious problems, particularly since the satirist is the sole
speaker, and an essentially unattractive one, in the narratives. After years
of trying to eradicate the resulting problems of structure and tone, Jonson may have decided instead to embody them starkly in the person of
Morose, where he could vent his frustration by attacking them directly.
Jonson had, of course, managed at times to create tolerably likeable
satirists who knew how to share the stage with others, but only with
great strain and under special circumstances. What Morose needs to
become a Jonsonian spokesman is an ideal audience such as Crites[4]
found in the divine Cynthia, and Macilente found in Queen Elizabeth.
Perhaps Morose is seeking such a figure in marrying his own ideal
woman, Epicoene, but the joke is that she abruptly refuses to be either
an audience or a positive moral exemplar: she talks instead of listening,
and talks mostly about her own superficial appetites. It is as if Jonson
were describing allegorically, through the progress of the plot, his own
false starts in the struggle to create a healthy satiric drama.

*   *   *

EDWARD B. PARTRIDGE

The Alchemist[†]

A poet re-enacts the roles of God and Adam: he creates a world and
names the animals. The naming of the animals in Jonson's plays is, as

---

4. A judicious and wise courtier to Cynthia (Diana), the queen in Jonson's play *Cynthia's Revels*
   (1601). Macilente is a scholar in *Every Man Out of His Humor* who is afflicted by envy
   [*Editor*].
† From *The Broken Compass* (New York: Columbia University Press, 1958), pp. 114–20,
   139–52, 156–60. Copyright © 1958 by Columbia University Press. Reproduced by permission
   of the publisher. References to plays have been changed to conform with the line numbering
   used in this Norton Critical Edition, and the author's notes have been abridged. Quotations
   are from the Herford and Simpson edition.

anyone can recognize, particularly important. So are the epithets, the
names which the animals give each other. Mammon calls Face,

> [Subtle's] fire-drake,
> His lungs, his *Zephyrus*, he that puffes his coales,
> Till he firke nature vp, in her owne center.
> [II. i. 26–28]

This immense blower of bellows blows so hard on the coals of the plot
that the whole thing explodes in his face. '*Till it* [the stone], *and they,
and all in* fume *are gone.*' The explosion of the furnace in the fourth
act is an objectification of what happens to the plot. More than one
play of Jonson's seems to work on the same principle of an explosion.
Jonson's favorite rhetorical device—hyperbole—radiates into all parts of
his plays so that the dialogue trembles on the edge of bombast, the
situations move close to burlesque or mock-heroic, the characters become grotesques, and the plot explodes.

This inflation and explosion of the plot is apparent in the way epithets are used throughout *The Alchemist*. In the first scene two motifs
are developed side by side; both help to establish the atmosphere of
the play. One is the motif of abusive epithets which Subtle, Face, and
Dol fling at each other. They call each other rogue, slave, cheater, cut-
purse, bawd, and witch. That is all very well; at least all of these fine
fellows are human beings. But the vehicles have a wider reference.[1]
The impostors are compared to mongrels, scarabs, vermin, curs. These,
in their several ways, suggest animals which live in a lower plane than
men, or insects which prey on other beings. The dog imagery recurs
most often. Dol is a bitch, and Face and Subtle are mastiffs. In short,
we are among the snarling animals that live on other beings or each
other. We are in that world which Jonson creates so authoritatively—
that ambiguous world between the animal and the human.

The second motif in the first scene is developed by Dol's euphemistic
epithets for her partners. They are 'gentlemen' (Subtle has just said, 'I
fart at thee') and 'masters' who, according to her, ought to have more
regard for their reputations. Dol addresses Face, who is in a captain's
uniform, as 'Generall', and Subtle as 'Soueraigne'. At the end of the
quarrel they are 'My noble Soueraigne, and worthy Generall' (I. i. 172).
These royal and martial allusions are absurdly high-flown and comically
inappropriate when applied to the impostors and their thievery. After
Dol advises them to avoid Don Provost, the hangman, Subtle hails her
as 'Royall DOL! / Spoken like CLARIDIANA, and thy selfe!' (I.i. 174–75).
The quarrel to Dol is a major historical event: 'Will you vn-doe your
selues with ciuill warre?' (I. i. 82). And Dol has grandiose ideas about

---

1. By "vehicle" Partridge means the imagistic form through which the content ("tenor") of a
metaphor is conveyed [*Editor*].

herself: 'Haue yet, some care of me, o' your *republique*—' (I. i. 110).
This republic becomes aristocratic again in the hands of Mammon who
compares Dol to 'One o' the *Austriack* princes' (IV. i. 56).

After the first scene and until the next to the last scene almost all of the
epithets are inflated. The grandeur of their political and martial references works itself into even casual remarks. Subtle says to himself that 'we
must keepe FACE in awe' or he will overlook us 'like a tyranne' (IV. iii.
18–19). Which is more pretentious here—that Face could overlook like
a tyrant or that Subtle, even using the royal 'we', could keep anyone in
awe? But from the first Subtle has thought of himself as awful.

> No, you *scarabe*,
> I'll thunder you, in peeces. I will teach you
> How to beware, to tempt a *furie*'againe
> That carries tempest in his hand, and voice.
>   [I. i. 59–62]

Subtle oscillates somewhere between 'the father of hunger' and a Fury,
a bawd and a learned doctor, until he and his '*republique*' escape over
the back wall.

Before the whole plot blows up in their faces, this royal trio have
almost convinced themselves and certainly convinced others of their
importance. To others Face and Subtle are 'your worship'. To Subtle,
Face is 'so famous, the precious king / Of present wits' (V. iv. 13–14).
Dol, who has been the 'Queene of Faery' to Dapper, becomes 'Queene
Dol' to Face (V. iv. 65). She is in line for a promotion, too, because
Face has exacted from Mammon a promise that he will 'make her
royall, with the *stone*, / An Empresse' (II. iii. 319–20). When Face plans
to marry Dame Pliant, Dol, with fine perception, notes that " 'Tis direct
/ Against our articles' (V. iv. 71–72). Each of the distinct points of a
treaty was called an 'article'; 'articles' in the plural meant a 'formal
agreement' (*OED*[2]). The word scarcely seems appropriate for the usual
agreement between thieves. Subtle, too, is righteously indignant because such a marriage was 'Against the instrument, that was drawne
between vs' (V. iv. 81). An 'instrument' was 'a formal legal document
whereby a right is created or confirmed, or a fact recorded; a formal
writing of any kind, as an agreement, deed, charter, or record, drawn
up and executed in technical form so as to be of legal validity' (*OED*).
When the word is defined in these high-sounding terms, the pretentiousness of Subtle's language is thrown into relief. Three cozeners
agree to rob as many fools as possible; they call this 'drawing up an
instrument'. They are thieves, but they throw a specious air of legality
over their activities by euphemistic terms, believing in the common
fallacy that, if one refers to low things in high words, one raises them

2. Oxford English Dictionary [*Editor*].

legally and aesthetically. In short, Dol, Subtle, and Face speak as
though they had set up a commonwealth ('confederacie' to Surly
[V. iii. 23]), with an instrument and articles, a King and a Queen, and
a whole world of subjects.

Then, suddenly, the bubble bursts. 'Lungs' has blown so hard that
he blows the confederacy and himself right out of existence. Dol, inflated to the 'Queene of Faerie', shrinks to 'my smock-rampant' (V. iv.
126), whom Face will be glad to recommend to 'mistris AMO' or 'madame *Caesarean*', brothel-keepers. Subtle, who thought of Face as 'the
precious king / Of present wits' now finds him a 'precious fiend'
(V. iv. 138). As for himself, he is no longer a Fury 'That carries tempest
in his hand, and voice', but one who will 'hang my selfe' (V. iv. 146).
Subtle has already admitted that he has fallen from his majesty. When
Face asked him if he heard the disturbance at the door, he answered,
'Yes, and I dwindled with it' (V. iv. 15). This movement from dogs up
to kings, queens, and Furies, and back to rogues and whores reminds
one of the final lines of *Volpone* where a similar swelling and bursting
of the beasts occur. The circular effect of the epithets is completed,
not so much by another quarrel between Face and Subtle (neither has
time for a quarrel) as by the chorus of fools who thunder on the door
of Love-Wit's house.

> MAM. Where is this Colliar?
> SVR.   And my Captaine FACE?
> MAM. These day-Owles.
> SVR.   That are birding in mens purses.
> MAM. Madame *Suppository*.
> KAS.   *Doxey*, my suster.
> ANA.   Locusts
>   Of the foule pit.
> TRI.   Profane as BEL, and the *Dragon*.
> ANA. Worse then the Grass-hoppers, or the Lice of *Egypt*.
> MAM. The *Chymicall* cousoner.
> SVR.   And the Captaine *Pandar*.
> KAS. The *Nun*, my suster.
> MAM.   Madame *Rabbi*.
> ANA.   Scorpions.
>   [V. v. 11 ff.]

If anything, the quack, the rascal, and the whore have descended even
lower than the level of the curs in the opening scene. Now they have
become hawk-owls, locusts, scorpions, and caterpillars: that is, parasites
which live on higher beings. Furthermore, Ananias's Biblical allusions
make them appear as plagues.

Mammon's language shows the same deflation. Gone are the classical allusions which had characterized his speech when he was under

the spell of the elixir. Zephyrus, Jove's shower, the boon of Midas, and all the gods have been blown up, along with his hopes. Mammon himself, who was to have been 'King of Bantam', now has humbler plans: he will mount a turnip-cart and preach the end of the world (V. v. 81–82). The picture of the gluttonous Mammon, who wanted shrimps 'In a rare butter, made of dolphins milke' and his 'beds blowne vp; not stuft', so deflated that he takes to a turnip-cart, is a magnificent absurdity.

In one sense Face alone remains what he was—that is, nothing in himself, but living only in the disguises or 'faces' which he assumes: Jeremy, the butler; Captain Face, the pander; Lungs and Zephyrus, the blower; the Spanish count; and always the 'king' of a commonwealth of fools.[3] His kingdom includes even Love-Wit, who says, 'I will be rul'd by thee in any thing, IEREMIE' (V. v. 143) and who, just before, called Face 'my braine'. Surly suggests the variety of Face when, confronted by the smooth Jeremy, he mutters, 'This's a new FACE?' (V. iii. 21). But in another sense Face has blown himself out of existence. He too has come down from a Captain to a butler and is aware that his part fell a little in the final scene (V. v. 158).

Actually, of course, these two motifs of abuse and pretension exist side by side throughout the play. Thus at the very time that Mammon addresses Dol as 'Right noble madame', Face in an aside calls her 'my Guiny-bird', a slang term for a prostitute (IV. i. 38). But, normally, now one, now the other of these strains is dominant. In the first act and in the last two scenes of the final act the abusive epithets are dominant, while during most of the rest of the play the pretentious epithets are dominant. But at both times the subordinate strain remains as counterpoint to the principal melody, contrasting with it for an ironic effect.

Furthermore, both the abusive and the euphemistic names are perfectly characteristic of the speakers because they are typical of thieves' cant. Such cant was originally a peculiar slang devised for secrecy. For example, a brothel was called variously an Academy, Corinth, school of Venus, vaulting school, smuggling ken, pushing school.[4] The same impulse which caused thieves to invent such slang makes Face refer to Dol as 'my smock-rampant' or Dol call Face 'Soueraigne'. The pretentious epithets, then, as well as the abusive, are not mere rhetorical flourishes, but names which, while serving a poetic purpose, remain true to the impulse behind thieves' cant.

3. The OED defines face as "command of countenance, especially with reference to freedom from indication of shame; a bold front; impudence, effrontery, 'cheek.' " There is some hint that Face is really only the clothes he has on. During his quarrel with Face, Subtle threatens to mar "All that the taylor has made" (1.1.9–10). Note also his remark at 1.1.63. In his dedication to Lady Mary Wroth Jonson commented on "the ambitious Faces of the time: who, the more they paint are the lesse themselves."
4. Francis Grose, A Classical Dictionary of the Vulgar Tongue (London, 1785).

One of the poetic purposes of these epithets is to show Subtle, Face, and Dol on more than one level. On one level we see them as the rogues they are; on another, we see them as the insects or animals they are compared to; on still another, we see them as the higher beings that they and others think they are. The simultaneous existence of multiple levels helps create some of the humour and much of the irony which gather about a whore who thinks of herself as a *'republique'*, a quack who will 'thunder' a man in pieces, and a pander who wears a uniform and calls himself 'Captaine'.

* * *

Even as the imagery is instrumental in relating alchemy to religion, medicine, and sex, so also does it suggest a relationship between all of these and business. This connection strikes one on hearing in 'The Argument' that *'A cheater, and his punque'*;

> *Leaving their narrow practise, were become*
> *Cos'ners at large: and, onely wanting some*
> *House to set up, with him they here contract,*
> *Each for a share, and all begin to act.*
> *Much company they draw, and much abuse,*
> *In casting figures, telling fortunes, newes,*
> *Selling of flyes, flat bawdry, with the* stone:
> *Till it, and they, and all in* fume *are gone.*

The commercial implications, latent in the central situation of cheating and prostitution, come out in such words as *'practise'*, *'House to set vp'*, *'contract'*, *'share'*, *'company they draw'*, *'selling'*. Each of these alone might not attract attention to its commercial sense, but, when these words are used together in the same passage, the commercial sense tends to rise above the other senses. The final impression is that Subtle, Dol, and Face have gone into business, with a contract, shares, and an expanding practice—all somewhat dubious, perhaps, but still flourishing. The complexity of this business can be noted in one line, *'Selling of flyes, flat bawdry, with the* stone' where religion, sex, and gold all come together.

Such commercial terms are used throughout the play. Even in the midst of the opening quarrel Face speaks as a business partner who has drawn 'customers' to Subtle for his 'dosen of trades', given him 'credit' for his 'coales' and a 'house to practise in' where he has 'studied the more thriuing skill of bawdrie, since' (I. i. 40–49). Dol reminds them of their business obligations when she breaks up their quarrel by denouncing Subtle for claiming

> a primacie, in the divisions?
> You must be chiefe? as if you, onely, had
> The poulder to project with? and the worke
> Were not begun out of equalitie?

The venter *tripartite*? All things in common?
Without prioritie?

[I. i. 131–136]

From one point of view such a passage is only another example of Dol's pretentious language. But what strikes one about it is that this whore describes their catch-as-catch-can agreement as a 'venter *tripartite*', 'worke,' 'begun out of equalitie,' 'without prioritie'. 'Venter *tripartite*' is the most interesting phrase in the passage, partly because it is echoed in several places later. In this context 'venter' (or venture) principally means a commercial speculation. Later, just before the partnership breaks up, Face uses this meaning of the word when he calls Subtle and Dol 'venturers'. A 'venturer' in the early seventeenth century meant either an adventurer or 'one who undertakes or shares in a commercial or trading venture, especially by sending goods or ships beyond seas' (*OED*). It was used particularly of the trading companies such as the Merchant Venturers of Bristol. 'All things in common!' Dol cries, damning herself in doing so, for the line, read in one way, means all things in Common: that is, a three-fold commercial speculation in Common stock without priority. Dol really is a republic to these speculators, a 'common-wealth', indeed. But no matter how the passage is read, it seems to imply commercial dealings on a high plane.

The high plane is kept right to the end. Just as they are dissolving the company, Face formally ends the '*indenture tripartite*' (V. iv. 130–132). Figuratively, '*indenture*' meant contract or mutual engagement. Literally, an indenture was 'a deed between two or more parties with mutual covenants, executed in two or more copies' (*OED*). There are legal and aristocratic dimensions to the term, as well as commercial, for kings and king-makers have used it. In *Henry IV, Part I*, for instance, when Hotspur, Worcester, Mortimer, and Glendower are dividing up England, Mortimer says that their 'indentures tripartite' are drawn (III. i. 80–82). Seen through the lens of such a definition and such a use as this, Face's use of the phrase is comic, as he may mean it to be, because he is at that moment able to stand back and laugh at their absurd pretension to legality and high finance.

Between the time Dol calls it a 'venter *tripartite*' and Face, an '*indenture tripartite*', commercial terms are frequently used to refer to sex or cheating or the religion of the elixir. Dol settles the quarrel between Subtle and Face by making Subtle swear to leave his 'faction' 'And labour, kindly, in the commune worke' (I. i. 156). She really means that they should cheat fools cheerfully and cooperatively. But, since such a naked way of looking at reality offends her pretentious nature, she generally uses martial or commercial terms to disguise what is called, in plain speech, cheating and whoring. The result is that, when she and others use words like 'worke', 'labour', 'venter', and 'venturers' to refer to activities that, for one thing, are generally not thought of as commercial speculations and, for another, are not legal, then the identification of a tenor (such as whoring) and a vehicle (such as 'venter') appears indecorous and ludicrous, yet illuminating. We are asked to consider to what extent prostitution or cheating can be called a business venture (and possibly even to what extent a business venture involves some kind of prostitution or cheating). The degree to which we can equate business and cheating or business and prostitution or business and religion, as well as the degree to which such tenors and vehicles resist identification, provides some of the humour and meaning of the play.

Let us observe how the imagery suggests connections between business and sex. We have already seen that, in Mammon's world, money and sex are assumed to be monstrous twins of the same bitch goddess. Once money and sex are brought as close together as this, many connections between business (whose blood is money) and sex spring up. Some of these only depend on the nature of things in a world in which some people take money in exchange for sexual experience. The Queen of Mammon's world is, after all, a prostitute whose business is sex. Other connections only capitalize on the ambiguity of many words which have one reference to business and pick up another reference to sex. For instance, both 'venter' and 'venturer' mean 'prostitute' as well as, respectively, 'commercial speculation' and 'commercial speculator' (*OED*). But many of the connections are made simply by the force of the imagery in which commercial vehicles are related to tenors dealing with sex.

Note how commercial vehicles are used in referring to Dame Pliant and Dol. Face and Subtle speak of Dame Pliant in these extraordinary terms:

> FAC. A wife, a wife, for one on'vs, my deare SVBTLE:
>   Wee'll eene draw lots, and he, that failes, shall haue
>   The more in goods, the other has in taile.
> SVD. Rather the lesse. For shee may be so light
>   Shee may want graines.
>   [II. vi. 85–89]

Drawing lots seems to be their normal way of determining the fate of women, for that, one supposes, is what Face referred to in a previous speech: 'the longest cut, at night, / Shall draw thee for his DOL Particular' (I. i. 178–79). There is a certain gay detachment about Face's method of settling erotic problems; getting a wife and sleeping with a whore can be settled in the same simple way—just draw lots. But the interesting aspect of this passage is the compensation suggested: if you miss the wife, you get the goods. 'In taile' is a play on the legal word 'tail', which referred to limiting the inheritance of an estate to descendants in a particular line, and on the obscene word 'tail' which meant then as now—the posterior, or the female pudend. This witty union of sex and inheritance is extended by the assertion that whatever one gets 'in taile', the other ought to get in goods. Money or property, then, becomes a possible substitution for a wife or rather for the sexual experience of having a wife.

This same substitution is emphasized later in a somewhat different way. When Surly, disguised as a Spaniard, enters, Face and Subtle forget their quarrel over marrying Dame Pliant and decide to put the Dame to more useful work.

> FAC.   'Slid, SVBTLE, he puts me in minde o'the widow,
> What dost thou say to draw her to it? ha?
> And tell her, it is her fortune. All our venter
> Now lies vpon't. It is but one man more,
> Which on's chance to haue her: . . .
> The credit of our house too is engag'd.
> SVB. You made me an offer for my share e're while.
> What wilt thou gi' me, i-faith?
> FAC.   O, by that light,
> Ile not buy now . . .
> E'en take your lot, obey your chance, sir; winne her,
> And weare her, out for me.
> SVB.   'Slight. I'll not worke her then.
> FAC. It is the common cause.
> > [IV. iii. 63 ff.]

Face has the spirit of the true capitalist—business before pleasure. Or, perhaps, a better way of putting it is to say—pleasure and business together—because Face's chief pleasure is evidently not sex, but alchemizing people; sex is only one of his many ways of doing so. There is a business terminology in this exchange pretentious enough for even Dol: 'The credit of our house too is engag'd'; 'an offer for my share': 'the common cause'. When the situation is explained in terms as high flown as these, who can blame them for putting that glorious adventure, commerce, before that mean duty, marriage? The burden of the whole passage is, as Face later puts it, that Dame Pliant is to be 'used' (IV. iv. 79) even as Dol is 'emploi'd' (IV. iii. 51). As sexual beings, they both are commodities to be bought, sold, used, worn, and worked.

One scene especially reveals how Dol is to be used—the third scene in the third act, where Dol's profession and Subtle's fraud are thought of in terms of warfare. Face announces the arrival of 'A noble *Count*, a *Don of Spaine*', who has brought his 'munition' with him and is ready

> too make his battry
> Vpon our DOL, our Castle, our *cinque*-Port,

Our *Douer* pire, our what thou wilt. Where is shee?
Shee must prepare perfumes, delicate linnen,
The bath in chiefe, a banquet and her wit,
For shee must milke his *Epididimis*
Where is the *Doxie?*

[III. iii. 17–23]

Face's speech might be the type of the whole play: both begin in abuse, inflate by pretension, and sink into obscenity. The martial imagery, which is quite in keeping with Dol's previous 'Soueraigne' and 'Generall', moves in a kind of graduated expansion from Dol (the tenor) to 'our Castle' (one vehicle); then to '*cinque-* Port' and '*Douer* pire'; and finally, blown apart entirely, to 'what thou wilt'. Face may be making fun of their own tendency (necessary in the profession of passing a whore off as a noble lady) to think of Dol in pretentious terms. Whether he is or not, there is extravagant humour in picturing Dol first as a castle, then as Dover or Sandwich or what you will—'This fortress built by Nature for herself / Against infection and the hand of war'—Dol, ready to receive the battery of that Spanish Armada which has

brought munition with him, sixe great slopps,
Bigger then three *Dutch* hoighs, beside round trunkes,
Furnish'd with pistolets, and pieces of eight.

[III. iii. 13–15]

The munition is money, the danger is infection, England will fall. The ludicrous end of the whole passage is that Dol, the doxy, 'must milke his *Epididimis*'.[5]

Once Face has introduced the theme that sexual aggression is a kind of warfare, he proceeds to vary it in another involved figure, which has a movement similar to the one just analysed. With her customary ceremony Dol asks him (and ludicrously echoes the King's opening question in *The Spanish Tragedy*),[6]

lord *Generall*, how fares our campe?
FAC. As, with the few, that had entrench'd themselues
Safe by their discipline, against a world, DOL:
And laugh'd, within those trenches, and grew fat
With thinking on the booties, DOL, brought in
Daily, by their small parties. This deare houre,
A doughtie *Don* is taken, with my DOL;
And thou maist make his ransome, what thou wilt,
My *Dousabell*: He shall be brought here, fetter'd

---

5. The epididymis is an organ at the back of the testicles. "Milke," as a vulgar term, also meant extract all possible profit from someone by illicit means. This sense appears later in Face's declaration that the don will be "milked" by them (4.3.45).
6. In the opening line of Kyd's *Spanish Tragedy* (1592) the Spanish King asks resonantly "Now say, Lord General, how fares our camp?" [*Editor*].

With thy faire lookes, before he sees thee; and throwne
In a downe-bed, as darke as any dungeon;
Where thou shalt keepe him waking, with thy drum;
Thy drum, my DOL; thy drum; till he be tame
As the poore black-birds were i' the great frost,
Or bees are with a bason: and so hiue him
I'the swan-skin couerlid, and cambrick sheets,
Till he worke honey, and waxe, my little Gods-*guift*.

[III. iii. 33–49]

Here Face extends the martial imagery to include more than sex. The impostors, it appears, are at war with the world and have fortified themselves in their castle, from which, daily, they send out small sorties. Any enemies captured are held for ransom and possibly tortured into submission by Dol's drum. This sardonic picture of economic survival of the fittest which brings together sex, business, and warfare ends with a figure as outrageous as milking the epididymis. Dol's bed first becomes a dungeon and then a beehive in which the 'doughtie *Don*' produces honey. 'Honey' obviously has a sexual meaning and partly from its colour and partly from the context acquires the meaning of gold.

Face is undeniably a virtuoso in erotic imagery. Sexual intercourse has been compared, in succession, to a battery on a castle and seaports, to milking, to keeping awake with a drum, and to extracting honey from a bee. His final erotic image in this passage follows the musical motif suggested by 'drum'.

Sweet DOL,
You must goe tune your virginall, no loosing
O' the least time. And, doe you heare? good action.
Firke, like a flounder; kisse, like a scallop, close:
And tickle him with thy mother-tongue.

[III. iii. 66–70]

This cluster of violently indecorous images is about as absurd as any in the play. The name, 'virginall', applied to a whore, has its ironic humour, which is doubled when she is advised to keep it in tune lest she waste time. Face, as a bawd, has a twentieth century sense of efficiency. Though 'firke' has alchemic (see II. i. 28) and financial connotations, it seems primarily to echo Face's previous remark about Dol: 'A wench is a rare bait, with which a man / No sooner's taken, but he straight firkes mad' (II. iv. 4–5). The obvious erotic allusion in both places may be reinforced by the pronunciation of 'firke'. 'Tickle him with thy mother-tongue' is one of the wittiest images in the whole passage. 'Mother' could then mean 'womb'. 'Mother-tongue' means either one's native language or an original language from which others spring (*OED*). Besides the obvious erotic innuendo, Face may be suggesting that sex is that universal language which even the Spanish don, who knows not a word of English, can understand. Mammon unconsciously takes up this image later when he says he will 'talke to her, all in gold' (IV. i. 25). Poor Mammon had no way of knowing what an expert conversationalist he was going to talk to.

Such obscenity is very far from being aphrodisiac because the ludicrousness and lack of taste both within the images themselves and in the relationship of the images to each other neutralize any possible pornography. That Dol should 'Firke, like a flounder' and 'kisse, like a scallop' does not make her particularly seductive. Such an indecorous mixture of vehicles applied to the same tenor helps maintain a continuous comic tone so that never for a moment do we feel close to the characters. The distance between the tenor and vehicle tends to keep us at a distance. Seen through the eyes of Mammon or Dapper, Dol is a heroine and, like the prostitutes in Plautus's plays,[7] can seem a heroine—of a sort—even to us. But she is not romanticized. The exaggerated absurdity of Dol as a Dover pier makes her whoredom ludicrous, not erotically attractive, nor even pitiful.

Martial imagery throws a cloak of authority and high matters of state over other scenes than this one. When the furnace explodes and Subtle swoons, Face says, 'Coldnesse and death inuades him' (IV. v. 63). Supposing that Mammon is about to assault her virtue, Dol, with her high sense of honour, says, 'You meane no treason, sir!' (IV. i. 118). Love-Wit's house is a 'fort' to Face (V. ii. 29), a *'Citadell'* to Surly (IV. vi. 9), and a 'castle' to Kastril (V. iii. 36). This martial pretentiousness in part explains why Face calls himself 'Captaine' as well as why Dol constantly promotes him to 'Generall'. A Captaine in the seventeenth century was a commander of a body of troops or of a fortress or castle. The exact function of a Captain in this war with the world can be inferred from the dialogue between Subtle, who announces the arrival of Dame Pliant and Kastril, and Face:

> FAC. I must to my Captaine-ship againe, then.
> SVB. Stay, bring 'hem in, first.
> FAC.   So I meant.
>
> [IV. ii 3–4]

A captain is one who brings the customers in. Business is a war, and Face is an Intelligence officer in active service.

Mammon's language is, aside from Face's, the best example of how thoroughly the implications of the imagery relate business, religion, and sex. His name is an example of this. According to the *OED*, Mammon,

---

7. The Roman comic poet Plautus has in his plays quite a number of girls, politely called "courtesans" in the old translations, who are both clever and sympathetic [*Editor*].

the Aramaic word for 'riches', was taken by medieval writers as the proper name of the devil of covetousness. Even in the Elizabethan age Thomas Lodge in *Wits Miserie, or the Worlds Madnesse* (1596) used Mammon as the devil incarnate who tempted man by avarice. After the sixteenth century it was current as a term of opprobrium for wealth regarded as an idol or evil influence. Loosely, 'Epicure' meant 'one who disbelieves in the divine government, and in a future life'. More particularly, it came to mean one who gives himself up to sensual pleasure, especially eating. This idea of a refined taste for the pleasures of the table began as early as 1586 (*OED*). Some sense of what Epicure meant by the time of *The Alchemist* can be gained from the *Nosce Teipsum* (1599) of Sir John Davies. In the passage on the immortality of the soul Davies describes those 'light and vicious persons' who claim that the soul is 'but a smoke or airy blast' and who say, 'Come, let us eat and drink' before we die.

> Therefore no heretics desire to spread
> Their light opinions like these Epicures;[8]

In short, Epicure carries with it a sense of atheism and materialism, just as Mammon symbolized covetousness, riches, and worldliness. 'Epicure,' which comes from Greek, and 'Mammon', which is exclusively a Christian term unite to form a name which is at once a humanistic and Christian comment on impious wealth and immorality.

The geographical allusions of this immense symbol of worldliness and sensuality reveal him to be a more romantic merchant venturer than Face.

> Now, you set your foot on shore
> In *nouo orbe*; Here's the rich *Peru*:
> And there within, sir, are the golden mines,
> Great SALOMON's *Ophir*! He was sayling to't,
> Three yeeres, but we haue reach'd it in ten months.
>   [II. i. 1–5]

Mammon is not merely the explorer setting his foot on the shore of the New World—not even primarily the explorer—but essentially the merchant venturer. His primary interest is in the 'golden mines' within which shall make him rich. Not the least of many ironies in this scene is that Face has been thinking of Mammon himself as a 'vein' to be mined (I. iii. 106). This idea of exploiting distant lands is brought even closer home when Mammon declares that he will purchase Devonshire and Cornwall and make them 'perfect *Indies*' (II. i. 35–36). These counties were noted for tin and copper mines, which Mammon would transmute into 'golden mines'. The commercial note which opens the

8. Part Two, "The Soul of Man," lines 1083–84.

scene is brought in most emphatically in his lines on Subtle who makes the stone, 'But I buy it. / My venter brings it me' (II. ii. 100–101). The use of the commercial terms—'buy' and 'venter'—in reference to the stone shows how intimate is the connection between religion and business in Mammon's world. Mammon can buy his god, the elixir. Divinity and immortality can be bargained for. There is a certain justice, as Mammon himself admits, in the fate to which this business venture in religion comes. The sensual dreams which had drawn him on and his pursuit of Dol are said by Subtle to be the cause of the bursting of the glass and the failure of all his hopes. He cries, 'O my voluptuous mind! I am justly punish'd' (IV. v. 74). It is characteristic of Mammon that he should consider the loss of the power of making gold a just punishment for a voluptuous mind.

Mammon's psychic sensuality is its own best criticism. As L. C. Knights says, each of his speeches 'implicitly refers to a traditional conception of the Mean'.[9] The images he uses more than once betray the essential meanness of his vision. Not simply their constant extravagance—though that is one way of indicating hollowness—but also the action within the image itself shows this. For instance:

> My mists
> I'le haue of perfume, vapor'd 'bout the roome,
> To loose our selues in; and my baths, like pits
> To fall into
>
> [II. ii. 48–51]

Other associations with losing one's self or falling into pits suddenly betray such lines, suggesting that Mammon may have lost himself already and calling up memories of an Inferno where sinners have fallen into pits of fire. Or the dramatic irony implicit in the imagery he uses may reveal him. Thus he explains to Surly that, once his friends are rich, they shall not have to deal with 'the hollow die' or 'the fraile card', nor keep a 'liuery-punke', nor worship 'the golden calfe', nor 'Commit idolatrie with wine, and trumpets' (II. i. 9 ff.). But we know, from the previous act, that the dice are loaded, that Dol is a punk, that Mammon is worshipping a golden calf and committing idolatry with words if not wine. Or when Mammon, to convince Surly of the authenticity of the elixir, alludes to a classical myth, the myth itself betrays him.

> SISIPHVS was damn'd
> To roule the ceaslesse stone, onely, because
> He would haue made ours common.[1]
>
> [II. iii. 208–10]

---

9. *Drama and Society in the Age of Jonson* (London, 1937), p. 190.
1. The stage direction may be important here: "Dol is seene," exactly on the word "common." Is this another way to suggest an equation between the stone and Dol Common?

Sisyphus was punished for his fraud and avarice. Mammon, who is avaricious, if not fraudulent, suddenly turns into Sisyphus, rolling the ceaseless stone of alchemy.

*   *   *

The imagery of *The Alchemist* is perfectly functional in several ways. First, it develops, as alchemy develops, beginning with base metals, such as a whore, a pander, and a quack, which it tries grandiloquently to transmute into finer beings—a Faery Queen, a precious king of present wits, and a divine instructor—finally ending, as the dream of the philosopher's stone ends, in a return to the state of base metals. The various vehicles which alchemize the base situation—the inflated epithets, the erotic allusions, the religious and commercial terms—ultimately show how thoroughly mean the situation is by bringing into the context the very standards by which it could be measured: the Christian and humanistic civilization of rational men. Against the immense background the three impostors and their commonwealth of fools play out their mock-heroic life, their violent little actions contrasting sharply with the permanent values suggested by the imagery. When Subtle is compared to a priest, the comparison itself shows how much he disappoints the ideal. When Dol calls herself Queen of Faeries, we see how far she really is from the Faery Queen.

The imagery is functional in another way. The images work on the same principle that the play as a whole and usually each scene work. They are extravagant, inflated, and ludicrous, because the tenors (gold, Dol, Mammon) are related to great vehicles (god, Queen, Jove). The monstrous gap that opens between the tenor that we know to be mean and the vehicle that we assume to be great, and the demand that we find some similarities between them to bridge that gap, outrages our sense of decency and decorum. That outrage, within the imagery, produces part of the comic tone of the play.

A third function of the imagery is to extend and develop the multiple references that alchemy had in actual life—especially the religious, medical, and commercial references. The alchemic process in this play has religious implications because the desire for gold is thought of as a religion; it has medical implications because the elixir is thought of as a sovereign remedy; it has sexual implications because the elixir is thought to have a sexual power; it has commercial implications because business terms are used in reference to the whole fraudulent practice. When gold or the power of producing gold is spoken of as one normally speaks of a deity, we are expected to question whether this has any connections with reality. Do some people make gold their god? What is the sense in saying that man's nature can be alchemized? Is money in any sense the great healing power of the world? Does the great god, gold, have a sexual power? What is the relation of business to this religion of gold? Is sex to some people a business? Is religion? And so on. In other words, the imagery suggests that, in the Alchemist's world, the acquisition of gold is a religion, a cure-all, a sexual experience, and a commercial enterprise. The world that opens before us, once we understand these multiple references of alchemy, is outrageously obscene, crude in metaphysic and vulgar in emotion. Since this world is, in part, a caricature of the real world, one can make numerous connections between its crudity and obscenity and the crudity and obscenity latent in human experience. But as a universe of discourse, it exists in its own right, comic because it is a caricature, solid and substantial because it has a religion, an ethic, a government, and a flourishing business.

The imagery also suggests that the various peoples whose lives are dedicated to the acquisition of gold—whether they be in secular or religious life, in prostitution or other kinds of business—bear some relation to the alchemists of old. Dol Common is metaphorically an alchemist because she, too, is trying to turn base metals into gold. Mammon's cook is an alchemist in the same way; the reward of all his cooking is the accolade—'there's gold, / Goe forth and be a knight'. Perhaps the true philosopher's stone is not the stone itself; but simply business—that is, selling the public the things it wants. Face's threatening of Subtle is pertinent:

> I will haue
> A booke, but barely reckoning thy impostures,
> Shall proue a true *philosophers stone*, to printers.
> [I. i. 100–102]

The Golden Age comes when you find that you have what someone else wants—a sensational book or a new medicine, a shiny gadget or an old fraud. The true alchemist may be Face, that 'parcell-broker, and whole-bawd' who always has something someone wants and who perpetually finds the elixir of life in Drugger, Mammon, Dame Pliant, Subtle, Dol, and finally Love-Wit. Face may be the face of the future, the prophetic vision of the super-salesman who can sell anything to anyone. All that he needs to work on is man—man who, himself another Face, will sell even things he needs in order to buy things he wants. With naked impudence he expresses his philosophy early in the game.

> You [Subtle] must have stuffe, brought home to you, to worke on?
> And, yet, you thinke, I am at no expence,
> In searching out these veines, then following 'hem,
> Then trying 'hem out. 'Fore god, my intelligence
> Costs me more money, then my share oft comes too,
> In these rare workes.
> [I. iii. 104–109]

That little world, man, contains the base metals on which an alchemist can work. The seams or lodes may lie deep, but they can be searched out and followed. The 'golden mines' of Mammon, his *'nouo orbe'* and 'rich *Peru'* are only new names for this old world of man—new names, ironically, for Sir Epicure Mammon. Though alchemy itself is a fraud, Subtle, Dol, and Face are successful alchemists in that they have found this golden secret. All who discover this secret—all whores like Dol, all quacks like Subtle, all shrewd rascals like Face, all unscrupulous opportunists like Love-Wit—these are the true alchemists.

This conviction that in man's nature lie the base metals of alchemy appears in a different form in an image that Face uses in speaking of his futile search for Surly.

> 'Slight would you haue me stalke like a mill-iade,
> All day, for one, that will not yeeld vs. graines?
> [III. iii. 5–6]

Man could be harvested as well as transmuted. Once ground down in the mill, he could yield 'graines.' This kind of gain was the 'common way' which Volpone avoided: '[I] have no mills for yron, / Oyle, corne, or men, to grinde 'hem into poulder' (I. i. 35–36). But the final source of money for Face is the final source of food for Volpone—man.

IAN DONALDSON

[Jonson's Magic House]†

The action of *The Alchemist* is played out within strict limits both of time and space. Though modern editions of the play sometimes obscure this fact, the entire action, apart from the scenes in Act V in the lane outside, takes place within a single room of Lovewit's house. There are rooms opening off this area—most notably, Subtle's laboratory, which (significantly and suggestively) is never fully revealed—and there are rooms to which Mammon and the Spanish Count are permitted to retire for their amorous engagements. Somewhere 'within', too, is the privy where the luckless Dapper is hurriedly stowed at a critical moment of the play, there to be forgotten. The acting area itself, however, is confined: no use is made of the inner rooms or upper stage for acting purposes, allowing for a concentration of effect which, as E. K. Chambers observed many years ago, is quite unprecedented in the English theatre.[1]

† From *Jonson's Magic Houses: Essays In Interpretation* (Oxford: Oxford University Press, 1997), pp. 74–84. Copyright © 1997 by Ian Donaldson. Reproduced by permission of Oxford University Press. The author's notes have been abridged.
1. *The Elizabethan Stage*, 4 vols. (Oxford: Oxford Univ. Press, 1923), iii. 123.

This sense of enclosure is important to the total effect of the play, stimulating for audience and characters alike various sensations of curiosity, nervousness, and claustrophobia. Lovewit's house in Blackfriars, like Volpone's house in Venice, serves as a 'honeypot', a 'center attractive', a powerful magnet to draw the curious and unwary; what goes on within the house is a constant source of speculation and fascination. The house itself serves as a trap: a trap that may also be sprung on the tricksters themselves, who (unlike Volpone and Mosca) have no legitimate claim to occupy the house and use it in the way they do. The house is set in a neighbourhood, and there is the constant risk that the activities of Dol, Subtle, and Face and their victims will be overheard or overlooked. The conspirators are nervous on this matter right from the start of the play, and in their more reckless and rebellious moments choose to provoke each other by raising their voices.

> DOL   Will you have
> The neighbours heare you? Will you betray all? . . .
> FACE   Will you be so lowd? . . .
> SUBTLE I wish, you could advance your voice, a little. . . .
> FACE You might talke softlier, raskall.
> SUBTLE   No, you *scarabe*,
> I'll thunder you, in peeces.
> (I. i. 7–8, 18, 32, 59–60)

Within the house, there is a similar fear of being overheard; it is as though the walls were paper-thin. When Sir Epicure Mammon is given his opportunity to court Dol Common, Face tells him that his wooing is all too audible in the next room.

> FACE Sir, you are too loud. I heare you, every word,
> Into the laboratory. Some fitter place,
> The garden, or great chamber above.
> (IV. i. 170–2)

During a later quarrel with Subtle, Face threatens to call out 'And loose the hinges' (IV. iii. 82) so Dol can know that Subtle, contrary to the terms of the alliance, has designs upon Dame Pliant. A single cry might suffice to destroy the conspiracy. At the beginning of Act V, a confused neighbour is to tell Lovewit that three weeks earlier he heard 'a dolefull cry' emanating from the house while he sat up mending his wife's stockings: 'like unto a man / That had beene strangled an houre, and could not speake' (V. i. 33, 36–7). Not long afterwards, *Dapper cryes out within* (V. iii. 63, s.d.), shattering the fiction which Face has hastily devised to explain for Lovewit's benefit what has been occurring in the house while he has been away.

The constant knocking at the door of the house heightens the sense of nervous apprehension; it is not always at first clear whether a new caller is friend or foe. 'Is he the Constable?' asks Kastril suspiciously after the entrance of Ananias at IV. vii. 44. In Act V, the master himself is seen knocking repeatedly at the door of his own house. After his admission the knocking continues, for later in the act Mammon, Tribulation, Ananias, Surly, and Kastril return to the house with Officers, noisily demanding entry. 'Harke you, thunder', says Face to Subtle, coolly offering to him and to Dol a means of escape from the trap that has now closed upon them:

> All I can doe
> Is to helpe you over the wall, o' the back-side;
> Or lend you a sheet, to save your velvet gowne, DOL.
> (V. iv. 132–4)

By a variety of small touches, Jonson thus makes us acutely aware of Lovewit's house as a potentially confining place: as a box or prison within which the action of the comedy is played out. Dol spies from the windows of the house, as from a loop-hole, into the lane outside, and communicates with unwanted callers by means of a speaking tube: 'Thorough the trunke, like one of your *familiars*' (I. iv. 5). At moments of high excitement, Face and Subtle rebound within the house like balls within an enclosed court:

> FACE Let us be light, though.
> SUBTLE   I, as balls, and bound
> And hit our heads against the roofe for joy:
> There's so much of our care now cast away.
> (IV. v. 98–100)

The supposed Spanish don is lured, as though to a prison: fettered by Dol's fair looks, he is to be 'throwne / In a downe-bed, as darke as any dungeon' (III. iii. 41–3).

The fixed setting of *The Alchemist* also creates an air of mystery. What cannot be seen from outside the house or from the single room to which most of the visitors gain access is darkly guessed at. The house is constantly spoken of as something more than a house. Mammon fancifully pictures it as '*novo orbe*', 'the rich *Peru*', 'a meere *Chancell*' for Subtle's high art (II. i. 2, V. iii. 2). His companion, Surly, sceptically convinced that the place is nothing but a bawdy house, nevertheless aggrandizes it in his sterner denunciations, speaking gravely of 'The subtilties of this darke *labyrinth*' and of 'the knaveries of this *Citadell*' (II. iii. 308, IV. vi. 9). For other visitors, the house is the residence of a 'cunning man' (I. ii. 8) who can advise them on many matters, a centre of social, religious, and alchemical mysteries. Abel Drugger, an ardent believer in the mystical significance of the art of building, visits the house in Blackfriars in order to consult with Subtle on the construction and disposition of the tobacconist's shop which he is about to erect for himself. Subtle solemnly advises him of the most auspicious orientation for the shop, and urges him to bury a lodestone beneath its threshold, 'To draw in gallants, that weare spurres: The rest, / They'll seeme to follow' (I. iii. 70–I)—advice that humorously reminds us of the magnetic effect that the house in which Subtle himself operates appears to exercise on those who visit it (Drugger himself has been drawn in, as if by the heels). The neighbours with whom Lovewit talks in the lane at the beginning of the fifth act cannot confidently say what has been going on within the house: whether and how it has been used, whether and by whom it has been visited, whether 'open house' has been maintained, or (as Face asserts) the doors have been securely locked for the past three weeks. 'We were deceiv'd, he sayes', admits one neighbour, lamely (V. i. 42). The house in Blackfriars is capable of being whatever people most want it to be: it is a shell within which their fantasies may be projected, a sounding-board for the imagination. When Lovewit finally enters the house, he finds it strangely desolate and abandoned:

> Here, I find
> The emptie walls, worse then I left 'hem, smok'd,
> A few crack'd pots, and glasses, and a fornace,
> The seeling fill'd with *poesies* of the candle:
> And MADAME, with a *Dildo*, writ o' the walls.
> (V. v. 38–42)

For Ananias, on the other hand, this is not just an empty house: it is 'a cage of uncleane birds', 'this den of theeves' (V. iii, 47, V. v. 93). Even as he denounces the place, Ananias, like Surly, makes it sound grander, more mysterious, more compelling, than Lovewit's sober account has suggested. Ananias will go to Amsterdam:

> I will pray there,
> Against thy house: may dogs defile thy walls,
> And waspes, and hornets breed beneath thy roofe,
> This seat of false-hood, and this cave of cos'nage.
> (V. v. 112–15)

'Cage', 'den', 'seat', 'cave': this is no ordinary house, but a magical place, a centre of spiritual enchantment.

The 'house' against which Ananias determines to direct his vengeful prayers is the physical edifice in Blackfriars whose inner rooms he and his companions have now at last penetrated; it is also the entire dynasty and household of Lovewit, which Ananias believes to be responsible for the downfall and humiliation of the Brethren. The 'house' of Lovewit at present comprises exactly three people, Lovewit himself, his new wife Dame Pliant, and his servant Jeremy, alias Face; Ananias's terrible curse aggrandizes the strength of this house even as it threatens its destruction. The imagination that can convert a common London dwelling-house into a Spenserian 'cave of cos'nage' can equally convert three people into an Old Testament dynasty.

The comedy is much concerned with the creation of such imaginary dynastic 'houses'. Sir Epicure Mammon, after catching a subliminal glimpse of Dol Common, is easily persuaded that she is 'A lords sister' (II. iii. 221) and scholar of divinity, now crazed in her wits. When Surly expresses some scepticism about the circumstances of this supposed lady, Sir Epicure at once protests that he knows her family well: her brother is 'one I honour, and my noble friend, / And I respect his house' (II. iii. 277–8). Having so swiftly persuaded himself of his familiarity with this house, Mammon has no difficulty in complying with Face's stipulation before his eventual meeting with the lady.

> FACE And you must praise her house, remember that,
>   And her nobilitie.
> MAMMON   Let me, alone:
>   No *Herald*, no nor *Antiquarie*, Lungs,
>   Shall doe it better.
>   (IV. i. 19–22)

Left alone with Dol, Mammon praises the 'strange nobilitie' of her eye, her lip, her chin:

>   Me thinkes you doe resemble
>   One of the *Austriack* princes.
> FACE   Very like,
>   Her father was an *Irish* costar-monger.
> MAMMON The house of *Valois*, just, had such a nose.
>   And such a fore-head, yet, the *Medici*
>   Of *Florence* boast.
>   (IV. i. 54–60)

Such a lady, he believes, ought rightfully to live not in 'This nooke, here, of the *Friers*', but rather should 'come forth, / And tast the aire of palaces' (IV. i. 131, 134–5): her aristocratic house deserves a grander physical house to set off its dignities and beauties.

In preparing Mammon for this encounter, Face has warned him that he must make no mention of divinity to the lady, 'For feare of putting her in rage'.

> MAMMON   I warrant thee.
> FACE Sixe men will not hold her downe. And then,
>   If the old man should heare, or see you—
> MAMMON   Feare not.
> FACE The very house, sir, would runne mad.
>   (IV. i. 10–13)

'The very house': Face is conjuring up another household to rival that
of the supposedly aristocratic lady whom Mammon is about to meet;
this 'house' consists of Subtle, its apparent master, and his mysterious
retinue (none other than Face and Dol, in their many guises). But
Face's words also contain the further humorous suggestion that the
building which they now inhabit would itself be affected by so grave a
transgression as the mention of scriptural controversy. In his meeting
with Dol, Mammon contrives to break not only Face's prohibition but
also that of Subtle, who has told him that if the elixir is to come to
perfection, he must practice perfect chastity, paying no regard to the
opposite sex. Face has warned Mammon that once the lady falls into
her fit, she

>   will discourse
>   So learned of *genealogies*,
>   As you would runne mad, too, to heare her, sir.
>   (II. iii. 240–2)

And it is of genealogies—of the rise and fall of ancient families—that
Dol indeed discourses in her '*fit of talking*', prompted by Mammon's
indiscreet mention of his wish to establish a fifth monarchy.

> DOL And so we may arrive by *Talmud* skill,
>   And profane *greeke*, to raise the building up
>   Of HELENS house, against the Ismaelite,
>   King of *Thogarma*, and his *Habergions*
>   Brimstony, blew, and fiery; and the force
>   Of King ABADDON, and the Beast of *Cittim*:
>   Which *Rabbi* DAVID KIMCHI, ONKELOS,
>   And ABEN-EZRA doe interpret *Rome*.
>   (IV. v. 25–32)

The pandemonium climaxes with the entrance of Subtle and '*A great
crack and noise within*'. It is indeed as though the very house has now
run mad, the edifice itself responding to Mammon's folly.

> SUBTLE   Hangs my roofe
>   Over us still, and will not fall, o justice,
>   Upon us, for this wicked man!
>   (IV. v. 78–80)

Meanwhile, in another part of the house, Surly is at large, disguised
as a Spanish Count. Almost the first words which Surly utters in this
role concern the nature of the house:

> SURLY *Por dios, Sennores, muy linda casa!*
> SUBTLE What sayes he?
> FACE   Praises the house, I thinke,

    I know no more but's action.
SUBTLE   Yes, the *Casa*,
    My precious DIEGO, will prove faire inough,
To cossen you in. Doe you marke? you shall
Be cossened, DIEGO.
FACE   Cossened, doe you see?
    My worthy DONZEL, cossened.
SURLY   *Entiendo*.
                        (IV. iii. 34–40)

'*Entiendo*', 'I understand'—as Surly indeed does understand, more thoroughly than either Face or Subtle realizes. Surly professes to praise the
house as a *brothel*, which is indeed what he privately believes it to be;
it is an assignation that he is seemingly after, and he pretends to a
certain connoisseurship in the necessary arrangements surrounding
these matters. When Surly arrives, however, the only available lady of
the house, Dol Common, is busy with Sir Epicure, and Face proposes
to Subtle that they must persuade Dame Pliant to stand in for Dol:

FACE What dost thou thinke on't, SUBTLE?
SUBTLE   Who, I? Why—
FACE The credit of our house too is engag'd.
                        (IV. iii. 69–70)

Face makes their enterprise sound like that of a firm of international
bankers, and it is especially revealing that the two of them should adopt
such language in private conversation. 'The credit of our house': 'credit'
means both credibility, the primary meaning of the word, and financial
solvency. For Face and Subtle, the two things are closely connected,
for people put their money where their beliefs are, and it is thus upon
belief that they constantly endeavour to play. But how are Dame Pliant
and her brother Kastril to be persuaded to accept this substitution? The
argument which convinces them both is that of social advancement:
the Spanish Count (they are told) is keen to marry the widow, and, as
Kastril contentedly remarks, 'This match will advance the house of the
KASTRILS' (IV. iv. 88).
    Kastril's phrase confers upon an obscure country family the pomp
and status of a noble European dynasty. The advancement of the house
of the Kastrils is to proceed more modestly than Kastril himself anticipates. The aristocratic claims of the supposed Spanish Count, like
those of the supposed lady whom Mammon ardently pursues, are to
prove wholly fraudulent. The 'houses' to which these characters seemingly belong exist merely in the imagination. So too does the commercial house which Subtle and Face profess to operate, and the house
of retainers which Face pretends Subtle has in his employ. Both in the
literal and the metaphorical senses of the phrase, the three confidence

workers have *no house* to support their enterprises. In the opening scene
of the play Face cuttingly reminds Subtle that he is in fact a houseless
person, a vagabond, and that it is he, Face, who has provided him with
the house in which he now operates—a house, as Subtle is quick to
respond, which does not belong to Face, either.

FACE I ga' you countenance, credit for your coales,
  Your stills, your glasses, your *materialls*,
  Built you a fornace, drew you customers,
  Advanc'd all your black arts; lent you, beside,
  A house to practise in—
SUBTLE   Your masters house?
FACE Where you have studied the more thriving skill
  Of bawdrie, since.
SUBTLE   Yes, in your masters house.
                                            (I. i. 43–9)

The alliance between Subtle, Face, and Dol is as temporary and uncertain as their period of occupancy of Lovewit's premises; theirs is a
house in which little credit can be placed.

The various houses thus far described in *The Alchemist* are 'magic'
in the sense that they lack a basis in reality, existing principally in the
hopes and fantasies and perceptions of the characters themselves. The
almost empty house in Blackfriars is capable of becoming whatever its
occupants and visitors most wish it to become: closely inspected after
the event, it proves to be an almost empty house in Blackfriars. Lovewit's house (in short) is irresistibly like that other house—situated, in
all probability, in Blackfriars too—where this very play was first presented in 1610 by the King's Men. These two houses of illusion are in
fact *the same house*, and the charlatans who arouse and exploit the
fantasies of their victims are (when all is said and done) members of
the company of the King's Men, who use similar arts to somewhat
similar ends. For the playhouse is, *par excellence*, a magic house, a
wooden frame animated and transformed by the skills of the actors,
men who pretend to be what they are not, playing in a house that
seems to be what it is not: closely inspected after the event, it is merely
a wooden frame, an almost empty house in Blackfriars. 'Good faith, sir,
I beleve, / There's no such thing' says Face to his master Lovewit
in the last act of the play, coolly dismissing the confused gossip of
the neighbours: ''Tis all *deceptio visus*' (V. iii. 61–2). What has been
glimpsed in and around Lovewit's house is simply an optical illusion,
deceptio visus, lacking any basis in reality. And, in a double sense, this
might be regarded as true: for the confidence tricksters have indeed
traded in deception, not substance, and (moreover) they themselves
have been impersonated by a group of actors, whose business is likewise
to deceive. Lovewit's house is thus a powerful analogue and symbol of

the playhouse itself, with which it is in a sense coterminous. The charlatan's art is not unlike that of the dramatist and his actors, and there
is thus a further uncomfortable resemblance between the audience who
are currently enjoying this comedy and the gulls whom the charlatans
are currently exploiting. Both groups of people have wandered expec-
tantly into a house in Blackfriars where their fantasies are entertained;
both groups have been gently relieved of their cash. *Caveat spectator.*

Though the warning note is there, it would be a mistake (I believe)
to regard *The Alchemist* merely as a parable on the perils of theatre-
going, or as a costive diatribe against 'the loathed stage'. Jonson certainly
exhibits from time to time what Jonas Barish has called the 'antitheatrical prejudice',[2] but it is impossible to ignore the zest and high
spirits with which the illusory arts are planned and executed. For the
theatre, as the play reminds us, is a magic house in a pleasurable as
well as a delusive sense, and the playwright's and actors' aim is not to
drive their customers from the doors, but instead 'To feast you often,
and invite new ghests' (V. v. 165). The play is (so to speak) its own
lodestone, placed beneath the threshold to draw in visitors to the theatre. The London theatres were in fact closed for substantial periods
around the time of the first performance of *The Alchemist*, on account
of the plague; if there was a risk of contagion in such public congre-
gations as the play now attracted, there must also now have been a
particular pleasure for actors and audience alike in seeing the playhouse
open and full of life. The plague is an important background to the
play itself: it is on account of the plague that Lovewit has shut up his
London house and gone off to tend his hop-fields in the healthier air
of Kent. Like the authorities responsible for the closure of the playhouses, Lovewit is watching the weekly mortality figures in London in
order to decide when to reopen his house. When he returns earlier
than Face, Subtle, and Dol have calculated, Face hastily concocts a
story that the house has been infected by plague during Lovewit's absence: the cat that kept the buttery had the disease a week before Face
noticed it, and so (Face continues) he locked the house up prudently
for a month,

> Purposing then, sir,
> T'have burnt rose-vinegar, triackle, and tarre,
> And, ha' made it sweet, that you should ne'er ha' knowne it.
> (V. ii. 11–13)

Though the story is a fabrication, there is another, deeper, sense in
which Face—as Lovewit himself is soon to recognize—has sweetened
and revived his master's house. For this house has never been, in the

---

2. "Jonson and the Loathed Stage," in id., *The Antitheatrical Prejudice* (Berkeley: Univ. of California Press, 1981).

fullest sense, a *house* since the death of Lovewit's first wife, as Subtle's contemptuous attack upon Face in the opening scene of the play indirectly reveals.

> You, and the rats, here, kept possession.
> Make it not strange. I know, yo'were one, could keepe
> The buttry-hatch still lock'd, and save the chippings,
> Sell the dole-beere to *agua-vitae-men*,
> The which, together with your *christ-masse* vailes,
> At *post and paire*, your letting out of counters,
> Made you a pretty stock, some twentie markes,
> And gave you credit, to converse with cob-webs,
> Here, since your mistris death hath broke up house.
> (I. i. 50–8)

Into this cobwebby house, 'broke up' and run down since the death of his late mistress, Face brings new life and energy—and, for his master, a new wife, Dame Pliant, who 'Will make you seven yeeres yonger, and a rich one' (V. iii. 86). This is not illusion: it is flesh and blood, solid cash and solid 'happinesse' (V. v. 147). A real magic has been worked within the near-dead house, and a new and living one established.

RICHARD HARP

Ben Jonson's Comic Apocalypse[†]

The intense study of the biblical apocalypse in the sixteenth and early seventeenth centuries had a considerable influence on the plot of Ben Jonson's *The Alchemist*. While Jonson as both poet and playwright was sturdily a man of the world and of society, albeit a deeply religious one, and spoke with disdain of literature's presentation of "fools and devils" and "other ridiculous and exploded follies," his plays could make good use of the public's familiarity with such devices. For in *The Alchemist* Jonson gave point and comic force to his theme of greed and trickery by connecting his plot to the Book of Revelation and to some apocalyptic parables in the Gospels.

The early seventeenth century was notable for those writers who associated alchemy with the apocalypse and also for those who made literal applications from the Book of Revelation to history. Thomas Tymme was an outstanding member of the first group. "It may seeme . . . an admirable and new Paradox, that Halchymie should have con-

† From *Cithara* 34 (1994): 34–43. Copyright © 1994. Reproduced by permission of *Cithara*. The author's notes have been abridged.

currence and antiquity with Theologie," wrote Tymme in 1605, but nevertheless such was the case: creation itself was only an "Halchymical Extraction, Separation, Sublimation, and Coniunction," by means of which the four elements were separated out from an "indigested chaos." Similarly, Tymme continued, at the end of the world, a "refining fire" shall by means of "Gods Halchymie" cause the metamorphosis of all things so that there should be a new Heaven and Earth (Dedication A3r).[1]

Those writers who made literal applications of Revelation to history were of course doing nothing new, but, as Katharine Firth says, during the first decades of the seventeenth century there was "a new spirit of millenarianism" (204).[2] Most orthodox commentators had opposed such a spirit; St. Augustine, for example, said that the idea of a thousand-year reign of resurrected saints with Christ could be allowed "if it proposed only spiritual delights unto the saints during this space"; the alternative, that "the saints after this resurrection shall do nothing but revel in fleshly banquets" was "gross, and fit for none but carnal men to believe" (xx. vii.).[3] But this revelling in fleshly banquets is precisely what Sir Epicure Mammon does hope to receive in *The Alchemist* by means of the philosopher's stone, and as I shall try to point out, he does this in a millennarian context.

One of the sections of Revelation besides the millennial descriptions most susceptible to literal historical application was chapters two and three in which the prophet writes letters to the angels of the seven churches. Thomas Brightman's *A Revelation of Revelation* says that each of these churches represents the whole church at a particular point in history: ". . . these seaven contayne the universal condition of the Church among the Gentiles." Ephesus, for example, the first church to receive the prophet's message, a church which "hast tried them which say they are apostles, and are not, and hast found them liars" (Rev. 2.2); had a "counter copie," says Brightman, in the "first Christian Church" which lasted until the time of Constantine (35).[4] Hugh Broughton's 1610 work *A Revelation of the Holy Apocalyps* adopts a similar method. For example, Broughton, Dol Common's favorite theologian, says that the church at "Pergamus heareth of idolatrie and fornication. Rome and Venice be deaf" (2).

The notions, then, that alchemical processes could be involved in producing the mighty changes of the apocalypse and that the pictures of the last times as given in Revelation have literal application to history

1. *The Practice of Chymicall, and Hermeticall Physicke* by Josephus Quersitanus. London, 1605.
2. *The Apocalyptic Tradition in Reformation Britain 1530–1645* (Oxford: Oxford Univ. Press, 1979). "Millenarianism": the belief, from Revelation, ch. 20, that Christ will reign on the earth for 1000 years at the end of history.
3. *The City of God*, trans. John Healey (London: Dent, 1945).
4. The first edition of this book was published in Latin in Frankfurt in 1609; all subsequent editions were in English.

in the early 1600's were highly current ones, and it is these two notions which I think are important to the comedy of Jonson's play. *"The Alchemist,"* observes Peter Bement, presents "the fascinating but perverse decorum of a world that is falling apart" (168).[5] What makes this disintegration comic rather than tragic is that it is not nature itself which is decaying, as those would hold who thought that the end of the world was imminent. Rather, what is decaying are the fantasies of those who seek through alchemy the perfection of nature in a millenarian paradise of voluptuous pleasure or business success or religious fervor. Much of the comedy of the play, that is, results from the mistaking of the spiritual for the physical, of a spiritual reign of the saints, which authorities such as St. Augustine said had begun in fact with the incarnation of Christ and would continue until the end of time (*City of God*, xx. vii.), for the physical indulgence and ease such as Sir Epicure Mammon hopes for with a willing mistress or for a luxurious theocratic state such as the Anabaptists seek. Such a misappropriation of the spiritual by the physical justifies calling the play a comic apocalypse.

There are a number of references to Revelation in the play. These include Ananias' comment that Subtle "bears / The visible mark of the Beast in his forehead" (3.1.7–8); Tribulation Wholesome's response that allowance should be made for the sweaty environment in which Subtle works, whose heat may one day turn into "a zeal . . . / Against the menstruous cloth and rag of Rome" (3.1.31–33); Ananias's comment to the disguised Surly that he "look'st like Antichrist in that lewd hat" (4.7.54); Ananias's millennial reference to "The year of the last patience of the Saints / Six hundred and ten" (4.5.103–04), echoing another millennial reference earlier in the play to the "Fifth Monarchy" by Dol Common (4.4.26); and a few other such commonly glossed allusions.

But there are also a number of other references to or echoes of Revelation in the play not pointed out or commented upon by editors or critics. It is quite possible, for example, that Jonson parodied Brightman and Broughton by making some of his characters "counter copies" to the churches in Revelation. The Church at Ephesus, for instance, in addition to trying them "which say they are apostles," was also criticized "because thou hast left thy first love" (Rev. 2.2–4). In the play Surly does continuously try to expose the fraud of the rogues, is opposed by the false apostles Ananias and Tribulation Wholesome, and does withdraw from his "first love," Dame Pliant, so that she may consider his worthiness. Or the church at Thyatira is told: "I have a few things against thee, because thou suffrest that woman Jezebel, which calleth herself a prophetess, to teach and to seduce my servants to commit fornication, and to eat things sacrificed to idols" (Rev. 2.20). Dol Com-

5. *The Alchemist* (London: Methuen, 1987).

mon does pretend to be a prophetess when she is seducing Mammon and also forces Dapper to stuff his mouth full of gingerbread as a sacrifice to her when she is impersonating the Queen of the Fairies. And then there is the church of the Laodiceans who say that they are "rich, and increased with goods, and have need of nothing" but who are counselled "to buy of me gold tried in the fire, that thou mayest be rich" (Rev. 3.17–18). The parody here is of Mammon, who does indeed desire to be rich by metals "tried in the fire" and who thinks that to be "increased with goods" is to have "need of nothing."

One of the most interesting references to Revelation, though, concerns the date of the play's action. Editors have noted that this is November 1st, and one of the best of them, Ian Donaldson, says that this "creates a minor problem." Stating that the play was performed in Oxford in September and that "it is likely that the original London performance took place before [the] July closure" of the playhouses for the plague, Donaldson asks: "Why should a play so full of contemporary references be seemingly set not in the present but several months in the future" (628)?[6] November 1st, though, is the celebration of All Saints' Day and several comments in the play indicate that its characters are aware of the fact. Face laments at one point that the townsmen that he is trying to fleece are too slow in arriving at Lovewit's house and ascribes their delay to the date: "Such stinkards / Would not be seen upon these festival days" (3.3.54). When Mammon tries to get his money back from the crooks in the last act but cannot get into their house, his friend Surly remarks, "Aye, now 'tis holiday with them" (5.3.9). And when the alchemist Subtle pretends to Mammon that his furnace has exploded, Mammon invokes the patrons of the day by exclaiming, "God, and all saints be good to us" (4.5.56).

The Epistle appointed for All Saints' Day in both the Roman Missal and the Anglican Book of Common Prayer is from Revelation, chapter 7, where a great multitude stands before the throne of God with the divine seal on their foreheads that exempts them from the destruction which angels are about to visit upon the earth (Rev. 7.2–3). Also described there is a throng of persons from all nations standing before the Lamb of God; these have survived great persecution and their robes have been made white in the "blood of the lamb" (Rev. 7.14). As they stand before the divine throne, the prophet comments that these martyrs "shall hunger no more, neither thirst any more. . . . For the Lamb which is in the midst of the throne shall feed them, and shall lead them unto living waters" (Rev. 7.16–17).

In the play Mammon, according to Subtle and Face (who obviously know their victims extremely well), claims that he will inaugurate just such a golden age through possession of the philosopher's stone. Subtle,

6. *Ben Jonson* (Oxford: Oxford Univ. Press, 1985).

waiting for Mammon's arrival for the attempt at projection, says the
knight might be

> Searching the spital to make old bawds young,
> And the highways for beggars to make rich
> ....
> If his dream last, he'll turn the age to gold.
>   (1.4.23–24, 29)

Near the end of the play Mammon says that it is the commonwealth
that will suffer from his ultimate failure to get the stone; he imagines,
says Face, that

> . . . he would ha' built
> The city new, and made a ditch about it
> Of silver, should have run with cream from Hogsden,
> That every Sunday in Moorfields the younkers
> And tits and tomboys should have fed on, gratis.
>   (5.5.76–80)

But these are only the fictions by which Mammon justifies his pursuit
of measureless wealth; his real motivations are recorded in his memo-
rable speeches to both Surly and Face of the luxurious life that he
would lead with the stone's help. Far from hungering and thirsting like
the redeemed in Revelation, Mammon intends to indulge both these
appetites and many more to the maximum degree:

> I will have all my beds blown up, not stuffed;
> Down is too hard . . .
> ....
> . . . My mists
> I'll have of perfume, vapoured 'bout the room
> To lose ourselves [Mammon and his mistresses] in; and my
>   baths like pits
> To fall into; from whence we will come forth
> And roll us dry in gossamer and roses.
>   (2.41–42, 48–52)

On the day of All Saints', then, Mammon is pursuing a heavenly
kingdom much different from that portrayed in Revelation but which
employs similar imagery and themes. One further example: just before
he goes into the raptures cited above, Mammon asks Face, who is then
masquerading as Lungs, if the metals have reached the final stage in
the process of transmutation, the color red, signified by "the flower, the
sanguis agni" (2.2.27). Thus, the spiritual vision of the "blood of the
lamb" ["*sanguis agni*"] is proclaimed by the prophet of Revelation and
heard by those in church on All Saints' Day while Mammon covets

the physical aspects alone of this same image in the alchemist's furnace.

Associations and verbal echoes of this sort between alchemy, biblical imagery, and the Lamb of God were not rare in alchemical literature, and some particularly striking ones were made around the time that Jonson wrote the play. Jacob Boehme's *Aurora* (1613) came close "to blasphemy in openly associating the stone with Jesus" (Rosenberg 573).[7] In a work entitled "An Explanation of the Natural Philosopher's Tincture of Theophrastus Paracelsus," written by Alexander von Suchten and originally published in German in 1608, the redness of metals during projection was said to signify the "Incorruptibility and complete digestion" of the alchemical process. Just so, von Suchten claimed, "Christ became more than perfect in the highest exaltation of His humanity through His rosy blood, in obedience, in fulfilling and satisfying the Law, and in love towards God" (243). This work is another one which also makes eschatological claims for alchemy with imagery taken from Revelation. Once the alchemist's furnace has burned away all the metals' impurities there will be a "New Earth and New Heaven (the old earth and Heaven having been destroyed by fire, together with their works) [and] you will have a New World" (251).

Deluded exaltations like Mammon's over the "blood of the lamb" as signifying the change of ordinary metals into gold rather than imaging the redemptive sacrifice of Christ which changes men's sorrows into the spiritual joys described in Revelation of course afflict all the dupes in the play. This apocalyptic parody is especially noticeable, however, in the two Anabaptist customers of the alchemist, Ananias and Tribulation Wholesome. Subtle refers to them at one point as "my brace of little John Leydens" (3.3.24), alluding to the leader of the branch of Anabaptists who "interpreted their sufferings in apocalyptic terms, as the last great onslaught of Satan and Antichrist against the Saints, as those 'messianic woes' which were to usher in the Millennium" (Cohn 275). The Anabaptists did establish a short-lived messianic kingdom in Munster in 1534 where John of Leyden proclaimed himself a "messiah of the Last Days" (Cohn 295),[8] a kingdom which allowed riches for its leaders. True to this millennial type of Anabaptist, Jonson's own pair also seek great riches at Lovewit's house. Ananias and Tribulation, it will be recalled, frequently resort to apocalyptic imagery through which Jonson reveals their particular greed, which appropriates timeless spiritual realities for current material gain. After Ananias comments on how Surly looks like Antichrist in his Spanish disguise, he goes on to say that the

---

7. Bruce Rosenberg, "Swindling Alchemist, Antichrist." *The Centennial Review* 6 (1962), 566–580.

8. Norman Cohn, *The Pursuit of the Millennium*, 2nd ed. (New York: Harper Torchbooks, 1961).

> . . . ruff of pride
> About thy neck betrays thee, and is the same
> With that which the unclean birds, in seventy-seven,
> Were seen to prank it with on divers coasts.
>
> (4.7.51–54)

This reference to Revelation 18.2 where an angel cries out that "Babylon the great is fallen, is fallen," and is become "a cage of every unclean and hateful bird" is an example of Ananias' expert finding of "countercopies" to events in Revelation. Ananias is especially contemptuous towards Mammon at the end of the play when they both still hope to regain some of the goods which they had given to the crooks for projection, and he says to Lovewit that Mammon is of no account against those "That have the seal" (5.5.100). All the wealth of the house, he claims, belongs to the brethern of his own community in what is "The year of the last patience of the Saints / Six hundred and ten" (5.5.104–05), which as noted earlier is a reference to a contemporary millennial kingdom made possible by the success of alchemy. Thus, in his belief in a too-literal millennium Ananias also believes in the too-literal presence in London in 1610 of the beast and the Antichrist and of some of the other plagues described in Revelation. As a consequence he is blind to his own folly in giving to thieves his wealth.

One of the most pointed scenes in the play where apocalyptic material is used from the Bible for comic purposes occurs when Mammon courts Dol Common. Dol's affectation of talking (at times uncontrollably) about interpretations of the Bible is apt in a play that makes use of material about the Last Things. It is to Dol that Mammon mentions the "fifth monarchy" that he would create with the stone. The "fifth monarchy," of course, refers to the stone in Daniel which is "cut out without hands" (Dan.2.33) and which "shall break in pieces and consume" all other kingdoms "and shall stand for ever" (Dan. 2.44).

Thus, given Mammon's view of the nature of the "fifth monarchy" as one of voluptuous pleasure, there is a comic contrast between what his stone would do—create a kingdom of sensual delights—and that which God's stone does in Daniel, which is to destroy all such earthly kingdoms in order to establish an everlasting spiritual one. And it is in this scene, too, that Mammon discovers that his hopes of great wealth through alchemy are finished when "A great crack and noise within" is heard and Face gives him the (false) news that the alchemical furnace had exploded, "as if a bolt / Of thunder had been driven through the house!" (4.5.59–60). Mammon exclaims, "Oh, my voluptuous mind! I am justly punished." Face replies, "And so am I, sire" (4.5.74–75). Here, again, is a comic catastrophe—the ruin of "hopes" which Mammon never really possessed—and it is also a contrast to the real catastrophes accompanied by thunder in Revelation.[9] For it is Subtle and Face and Dol themselves who contrive for the dupes both millenarian dreams of great wealth and pleasure and who then destroy those dreams, Jonson wittily having Dol use interpretations of apocalyptic visions to frustrate Mammon's design of seducing her. And there is irony, too, in Face's saying to Mammon that his own hopes were also ruined. He did not mean it when he said it, but the thieves soon find out that their connivances were indeed to be destroyed by the return of Lovewit.

The apocalyptic elements of the last act of the play are striking, as Lovewit, the master of the house, returns home at an unexpected time and distributes rewards and punishments for the liberties taken with his house while he was away. There are clear biblical parallels to the action in this part of the play and equally clear inversions of those parallels. For example, Face, though in many ways the master schemer, is unpunished and is received back into the joy of his master, a seeming violation of justice. But Lovewit remarks that he loves a "teeming wit," a faculty Face possesses in abundance, and he also confesses that he is an indulgent master (5.1.16; 5.3.77). Thus, like the industrious servants in the biblical parable of the Talents, Face had increased substantially the wealth that his master had left with him, even though being a good steward was the farthest thing from his mind. To paraphrase the words of Shakespeare's Autolycus, though Face was not naturally a good steward of his master's possessions, he was sometimes so by chance. This is a comic inversion of the apocalyptic parable in the Bible;[1] for the master in the parable makes clear that he is a demanding, not indulgent, master, and his servants, unlike Face, have all at least been conscious of trying to please him.

Or there is the parable of the Unjust Steward in Luke 16, too little discussed as an important source for this play. In the parable, it will be recalled, a rich man's steward wastes his lord's goods and is made to give an accounting of them. He eventually decides to go to his lord's debtors and remit part of what they owe, so that when he is "put out of the stewardship, they may receive me into their houses" (16.4). The lord commends the unjust steward, saying he had "done wisely: for the children of this world are in their generation wiser than the children of light" (16.8), a statement paraphrased in the play by Tribulation

9. At the opening of the first of the seven seals by the heavenly Lamb, the prophet says, "I heard, as it were the noise of thunder, [and] one of the four beasts saying, 'Come and see'" (Rev. 6.2). In the medieval play *Ludus de Antichristo* (1160), just as the Antichrist is declaring his omnipotence in front of all the kings of the world, "thunder crashes over his head, he collapses, and all his followers flee" (Karl Young, *The Drama of the Medieval Church* [Oxford: Oxford Univ. Press, 1967], II, 390). Vendice says in Middleton's *The Revenger's Tragedy* (1607), "When thunder claps heaven likes the tragedy" (5.3.46).
1. The Parable of the Talents is placed in the middle of a number of Jesus's apocalyptic sayings in Matthew, chs. 24–25.

Wholesome when speaking about Subtle ("The children of perdition are oft-times / Made instruments even of the greatest works" [3.1.16–17]). Christ points out the lessons of this parable in some detail, advising his hearers to "Make to yourselves friends of the mammon of unrighteousness; that, when ye fail, they may receive you into everlasting habitations" (16.9), and also using the story to illustrate two famous morals: "No servant can serve two masters" and "Ye cannot serve God and mammon" (16.13).

Now Face is nothing if not an unjust steward, using Lovewit's house and furnishings for his own profit and neglecting to distribute its excess provisions to the poor (1.1.51–58). He also makes friends with (Sir Epicure) Mammon and many others of unrighteousness, "friends" who ultimately fail him and cause him to be readmitted into Lovewit's household. As a child of "darkness" himself, he is indeed shrewd and cunning, but he finally fails because of his attachment to riches, and takes an initiative which restores him to his master's good graces. The comic twisting of the parable is in this final act. For it is no "everlasting habitation" that Face is received into, my argument being that Jonson continually in this play contrives apocalyptic situations that he then comically renders mundane. In Lovewit's very earthly house the existence of wealth is of great value, a point underscored when Face makes the ambiguous promise to the audience in the final words of the play to in the future hold many feasts and to "invite new guests" (5.5.165).

Throughout the play, then, Jonson highlights the greed and trickery of almost every one of his characters by comic allusions to a number of (usually) apocalyptic biblical scenes. As a final example, Ananias and Tribulation Wholesome should be considered. The analogue here is the Ananias who "laid at the apostles' feet" only part of the proceeds of a sale he and his wife had made and as a result was struck dead (Acts 5. 1–5). The greed of Ananias in the play is even more extreme, and comically inverted. He holds nothing back from the alchemist; indeed he brings to him everything that he can get his hands on. The problem is that none of it is his but rather belongs to his "brethern." And there is, again, a "counter copy" to Ananias and Tribulation in the letter to the churches in Revelation. To the church at Smyrna the Prophet writes that "I know thy works, and tribulation, and poverty, (but thou art rich) . . . " (Rev. 2.9–10). The irony here, of course, is that Tribulation and Ananias are not "rich" in the spiritual way meant by the Bible but are so materially—they have, boasts Tribulation, grown "soon and profitably famous" (3.2.101).

For most of *The Alchemist* the world does indeed seem to be falling apart through avarice and deceit, but in the end it is providentially reinvigorated by justice and mercy—not through a world-shattering catastrophe but through the free actions of its characters acting in their own best interests. Lovewit's gain is brought about by his lightheartedness, which disposes him to enter into and order the confusion which he finds on his doorstep, rather than to demand ill-temperedly possessions like Mammon and the others. His unexpected return to his home comes at just the right moment to punish the greed of all those seeking the stone and to forgive the conniving of his unjust steward Face, who had served his master better than he knew.

D. J. GORDON

[The Imagery of *The Masque of Blackness*]†

The scheme of the *Masque of Blacknesse* is very simple. Oceanus, guardian of the realm of Albion, is approached by Niger, "in forme and colour of an *Æthiope*." Niger is followed by the twelve masquers, the queen and eleven other ladies, in the guise of his daughters, Æthiopian nymphs. The masquers enter in a great shell accompanied by their light-bearers, the Oceaniæ, seated on sea-monsters swimming round it. Niger explains to Oceanus why they have left their home. After reading what poets have written about foreign beauties his daughters became sadly dissatisfied with their dark skins; eventually they saw reflected in the lake, whence they took their birth, a face glowing with light and inscribed with the words of an oracle: to find a remedy the nymphs must seek a land the name of which, in its Greek form, ends in TANIA, and which is lit by another and greater light than that Sun which darkened their skins. It is in search of this land that they have come so far West. Niger appeals to Oceanus to reveal the name of this country they have now found. Oceanus does so, and suddenly Æthiopia, the moon, appears and tells Niger that the quest is over: it was her own face that his daughters saw reflected in the lake, and this is the land they have been seeking. This island has now recovered for herself the name BRITANIA, and is

> Rul'd by a SVNNE . . .
> Whose beames shine day, and night, and are of force
> To blanch an ÆTHIOPE, and reuiue a *Cor's*.
> (ll. 253–5) [224–26]

The masquers land from their shell and go through their dances. Æthiopia finally interrupts them, with the promise that if they fulfil certain rites which she prescribes, their complexions will become fair.

---

† From *The Renaissance Imagination: Essays and Lectures by D. J. Gordon*, collected and edited by Stephen Orgel (Berkeley: University of California Press, 1975) pp. 136–41. Copyright © 1975. Reprinted by courtesy of Stephen Orgel. The author's notes have been abridged. Line numbers corresponding to this Norton Critical Edition appear in brackets after the author's original citations.

The nymphs re-enter their great shell and it moves out to the sound of a song.

An "artificiall sea" forms the background to the masque. In front of it are six Tritons "in mouing, and sprightly actions, their vpper parts humane, saue that their haires were blue, as partaking of the sea-colour: their desinent parts, fish, mounted aboue their heads, and all varied in disposition. From their backs were borne out certaine light pieces of taffata, as if carryed by the winde, and their musique made out of wreathed shells" (ll. 30–6) [25–30].

* * * Jonson presents Oceanus as 'horned,' justifying himself by saying in a note that the ancients always gave Oceanus a bull's head and adding an explanation of this in Latin. He also quotes Euripides as calling Oceanus ταυρόκρανος, having the head of a bull, and lists several Latin sources in which the epithet is applied to rivers. Jonson's Latin is a quotation from Conti,[1] who has also supplied the reference to Euripides. In the song that opens the masque, Niger is hailed as "sonne to great OCEANVS," because, as Jonson explains in another note, the ancients believed that rivers and fountains have their origin in the vapours drawn up out of the ocean by the heat of the sun. Conti has also supplied the material for this note with its Latin phrases and references to Homer and the Orphic hymns.

Conti has also influenced the plot of the masque. The nymphs set out on their journey because of the oracle they see inscribed on a glowing face in the lake. Æthiopia, the moon,[2] when she appears, explains:

> I was that bright face
> Reflected by the *Lake*, in which thy *Race*
> Read mysticke lines; (which skill PYTHAGORAS
> First taught to men, by a reuerberate glasse.)
> (ll. 234–7) [205–08]

Whalley[3] noted in his edition of this masque that this is an allusion to a comment by the scholiast on a passage in the *Clouds* of Aristophanes: Pythagoras discovered a way of writing with blood on a mirror so that if the mirror were held opposite the moon, the writing would be reflected and appear to be written on the moon's orb. But all this is to be found in Conti. Conti is discussing the belief that the moon can be charmed from the sky, quoting two verses from the *Clouds* to illustrate

---

1. Author of an influential sixteenth-century manual of mythology [*Editor*].
2. Jonson (VII, p. 176) explains why he calls the moon Aethiopia: "The Aethiopians worshipd the Moone by that surname." [The author's references to Jonson are from the Herford and Simpson edition.—*Editor*]
3. Peter Whalley published an edition of Jonson's works in 1756; "scholiast": an ancient commentator on a classical writer. *The Clouds* was Aristophanes' satire against Socrates and other philosophers who he considered to have inspired absurd ideas. It was performed in Athens in 423 B.C.E. Jonson has been frequently compared to Aristophanes [*Editor*].

the belief that the women of Thessaly were particularly skilled in this art, and goes on to tell this story about Pythagoras.

The twelve Æthiopian nymphs advanced to the dance two by two, *"euery couple . . . seuerally presenting their fans: in one of which were inscribed their mixt* Names, *in the other a mute* Hieroglyphick, *expressing their mixed qualities."* "Which *manner of* Symbole," Jonson continues, "I *rather chose, then* Imprese,[4] *as well for strangenesse, as relishing of antiquitie, and more applying to that originall doctrine of sculpture, which the* Ægyptians *are said, first, to haue brought from the* Æthiopians."

The nymphs, then, arc arranged in pairs. Each pair is distinguished by a "Hieroglyphick": the mute image is represented (painted, presumably) on the fan held by one of the nymphs, while the names of both nymphs are inscribed on the fan held by the other. These names are Greek and of Jonson's own invention (except in one case), and taken together they express the meaning of the "Hieroglyphick"; they give the mute image a tongue to tell us what each pair of nymphs symbolizes.

Several of the six "Hieroglyphicks" were taken from the most obvious source, Valeriano's *Hieroglyphica.*[5] The second pair of nymphs present "The figure *Icosaedron* of crystall." Valeriano tells us that the isocaedrum, which is according to Euclid a solid figure contained by twenty equal equilateral triangles, signifies water, because of the extreme mobility and divisibility of this element. The reading *Isocaedron* is that given in the 1608 quarto of the masque, and in the 1616 and 1640 folios. The Oxford editors adopt Gifford's (1816) reading: *Icosaedron.* This is certainly the correct Euclidean name. Valeriano was wrong— though the name is given correctly in the index—and if the reading given in the quarto and the folios represents correctly what Jonson wrote, then Jonson had been misled by his source.

These two nymphs are called *Diaphane* and *Eucampse.* Taken together these names express the qualities of water. *Diaphane* is derived from διαφανής, transparent or translucent; *Eucampse* has behind it εὐκαμψια, flexibility—strictly, flexibility of the body. The relation of this to the passage from Valeriano is clear. That the *Icosaedron* in question is of crystal reinforces the symbolism.

The third pair of nymphs, *Ocyte* and *Kathare* present on one fan "A payre of naked feet, in a riuer," an image, which, Valeriano tells us, means "the purifier." Valeriano also says that the image comes from Horus Apollo, for whom it means "the fuller," whose business was cleansing. So we can follow this image back beyond Valeriano to the pages of that strange book which the humanists found so exciting: the

---

4. A symbolic picture with a motto attached to it [*Editor*].
5. The standard encyclopedia of hieroglyphs—symbolic pictures—first published by Giovanni Pierio Valeriano in 1556 [*Editor*].

Hieroglyphica of Horus Apollo.[6] That this is the meaning Jonson intended his "Hieroglyphick" to carry is borne out by the names of these nymphs: *Ocyte* from ὠκύς, quick, swift: *Kathare* from καθαρός, pure.

The nymphs *Notis* and *Psychrote* come next with "The Salamander simple." *Notis* is from νότος, the South Wind, a word associated with ideas of dampness and moisture: *Psychrote* from ψυχος, cold. Valeriano, when writing of the meanings of the Salamander, gives one of these as *Amoris Nutrimentum*, in connection with which he says that it is a creature so cold and damp that it can extinguish fire by touch. And in speaking of the first meaning which he gives to this marvellous creature, the Salamander, Valeriano had said:

> . . . tantus enim illi rigor, vt ignes tactu extinguat, non alio modo, quam glacies.[7]

Glycyte and *Malacia* follow with "A clowd full of raine, dropping." *Glycte* is from γλυκύς, sweet, or γλυκύτης, sweetness, pleasantness; *Malacia* from μαλακός, soft, gentle, mild. Valeriano took this image over from Horus Apollo who gives it as dew falling, and heads it πῶς παιδείαν. Valeriano retains this meaning of education or instruction, which he extends and elaborates. He distinguishes between profane learning (*Doctrina gentium*) which is like bitter waters that bring forth no fruit, and heavenly learning (*Doctrina coelestis*) which brings forth much fruit. It was prophesied, he says, that the Apostles should go through the earth changing the *bitter* waters into *sweet* waters. The dew and rain falling from heaven is a particularly suitable symbol of celestial wisdom fertilizing the soul, and is so used by Moses. That Jonson uses the Greek words meaning "sweet" and "soft" in connection with the hieroglyph of the cloud dropping rain suggests that he may have had the meanings given by Valeriano in mind.

The last pair of nymphs, *Baryte* and *Periphere* present "an vrne, spheard with wine." *Baryte* is from βαρύς, heavy, or βαρύτης, heaviness or weight: *Periphere* from περιφερής, rounded or curving, or, when applied to bodies, spherical or globular: taken together, the names suggest earth. The hieroglyph of the urn encircled by a vine is not to be found in Valeriano and Jonson may have taken it from some other source. In Ripa,[8] *Terra* is represented as:

> Donna a giacere in terra, meza nuda, come cosa stabile, con vn braccio appoggiato sopra d'vn vaso, dal quale esce vna vite. . . .
> [a lady half nude, recumbent, as if immobile, with one arm resting upon a vase out of which a vine grows.]

---

6. On the importance and influence of this book see Mario Praz, *Studies in Seventeenth Century Imagery* (London, 1939), pp. 19–20.
7. "Such is its coldness that it needs no other means than its icy touch to extinguish fire" [*Editor*].
8. Cesare Ripa was another Renaissance interpreter of mythology. Editions of his *Iconologia* appeared in 1593, 1603, and 1605 [*Editor*].

This gives a combination of "urn" and "vine" representing earth, but the image is not identical with the one used by Jonson, which cannot be regarded as fully explained. For the general connection with the preceding image Jonson might have had in mind Valeriano's treatment of "Fontes" which he describes as waters springing from earth as compared with waters descending from heaven as rain or dew.

We now return to the first pair of nymphs, *Euphoris* and *Aglaia*, who present "A golden tree, laden with fruit." The queen herself impersonated one of these nymphs. *Euphoris* is derived from εὔφορος, fertile. In the case of *Aglaia*, Jonson has refrained from inventing a name and has used a direct mythological reference. Aglaia was the first of the three Graces, who are associated with fertility and the productiveness of the earth. Giraldi interprets her name as

> ἀγλαιά una, quae nobis dici potest Maiestas, seu venustas, honestasve. . . .[9]

In Ficino's[1] symbolism Aglaia represents "splendour" or beauty of the spirit. Her appearance here, with *Euphoris*, might thus suggest a royal and spiritual beauty fertilizing the earth.

The meaning which the hieroglyph of the golden tree may have had for Jonson is suggested by his use of it in the dispute he wrote for the "Barriers" that followed his masque *Hymenaei*, where Truth says that:

> The golden tree of *marriage* began
> In *paradise*, and bore the fruit of *man*. . . .[2]

The golden tree is not to be found in Valeriano, though he gives the palm as the symbol of marriage. In the lines quoted above Jonson seems to equate the fruitful tree of gold with the Tree of Life in paradise. Such a meaning would connect it with the prevailing theme of the other hieroglyphs. The Water of Life springs near the roots of the Tree of Life and afterwards divides into the four rivers of paradise,[3] which, in one of their interpretations, represent the four elements. The icosaedron and the pair of feet in a river, which in Jonson's scheme follow the golden tree, symbolize water and its purifying qualities. Fire is alluded to through the salamander; air through the cloud; and earth in the last image. And if the waters are the waters of paradise, the connection of the water imagery with "celestial doctrine" becomes less difficult to understand. These are the cooling and cleansing waters in which the nymphs are to bathe and become fair.

The scheme is thus a highly recondite one, and there is much in it

---

9. "Aglaia was the first, which to us could be said to be Majesty or beauty or integrity" [*Editor*]. Lilius Gregorius Giraldi, *De Deis Gentium Libri siue Syntagmata XVII* (Lyons, 1565), p. 357.
1. A fifteenth-century Neo-Platonist [*Editor*].
2. Jonson, *Works*, VII, 234, ll. 727–28. [Jonson wrote the speeches for Prince Henry's Barriers in 1610; *Hymenaei* was performed in 1606.—*Editor*]
3. Genesis 2.9–14.

which awaits fuller explanation.[4] There is obviously also a local application to the watery character of England's situation, cool both in climate and in the temperament of its inhabitants. The hieroglyphs
emphasize a tempering of heat by cold. Fire is tempered by the coldness and dampness of the salamander, and the symbol of air is introduced through the cloud suggesting cooling rain. The blackness of the
nymphs has been caused by the fiery power of the Ethiopian sun. This
blackness, due to an over-enthusiastic heat, is to be cured by the cooler,
damper air of Britain where the "sunne is temperate and refines all
things." It is possible that this is how these hieroglyphs stand in relation
to the theme of the masque.

STEPHEN ORGEL

[The Masque of Blackness][†]

*   *   *

The title itself is paradoxical, for blackness is a quality antithetical to
the court, symbolic source of light and beauty, and to the courtly
masquers. The ultimate resolution is achieved only in a sequel, *The
Masque of Beautie*. If we think of these two works as standing to each
other as antimasque to masque, we shall see that, while Jonson did
think in terms of the traditions and conventions of the form, he was
nevertheless willing from the outset to go very far afield from the practice of his predecessors.

The world of *Blacknesse* is not, like that of *Oberon*,[1] a place large
enough to contain both antimasquers and masquers, satyrs and fairies.
That setting is almost a dramatic landscape, but blackness is a symbol,
and so is its milieu: a court that is an idealized England, allowing no
conflict and no misrule, and where no antimasquers may be admitted.
The masquers provide their own antimasque. The conflict of the paradoxical title is carried out in the work not through their actions, but
through their mere appearance: the embodiments of beauty are characterized by that quality which to the Elizabethans was a synonym for
ugliness. And to a spectator, the action of this Twelfth-Night masque
is precisely a series of epiphanies or revelations. It is only necessary
that the "twelve *Nymphs*, *Negro's*" be revealed—that we *see* them—for
the "antimasque" to have taken place. Between this revelation and the

---

4. For example, the names of the twelve Oceaniae who accompany the twelve nymphs as light-
    bearers have not been taken into account.
† From *The Jonsonian Masque* (Cambridge: Harvard University Press, 1965), pp. 120–28. Copy-
    right © 1965. Reproduced by permission. Line numbers corresponding to this Norton Critical
    Edition appear in brackets after the author's original citations.
1. A masque by Jonson, performed in 1611 [*Editor*].

masque dances and revels, which are still the substance of the entertainment, falls the shadow of the text, which is properly not action but
an explanation of the ladies' presence and an analysis of their peculiar
problem. We may dwell on this at some length, since it illustrates a
method of thinking that is essential to the Jonsonian masque.

Oceanus and Niger, mounted, like Proteus at Kenilworth[2] on sea-
horses, lead in the masquers. They are Niger's daughters and appear
"in a great concave shell, like mother of pearle," and are welcomed—
like Davison's masquers ten years earlier[3]—by the music of tritons and
sea maids:

> Sound, sound aloud
> The welcome of the *Orient* floud,
> Into the *West*;
> Fayre NIGER, sonne to great OCEANUS
> Now honord, thus,
> With all his beautious race:
> Who, though but blacke in face,
> Yet, are they bright,
> And full of life, and light.
> To prove that beauty best,
> Which not the colour, but the feature
> Assures unto the creature.
>   (172:97–108)[4] [77–88]

They are simply, it seems, too much in the sun. Nevertheless, to any
Renaissance aesthetician, color was not essential but merely accidental;
and accidents may be disregarded precisely because, by a curiously
persistent tautology, they *will* happen. The feature, or form, was of the
essence: "For of the soul the body form doth take: / For soule is form,
and doth the body make,"[5] wrote Spenser when he wished to define
beauty. The tritons, good Spenserians, treat the nymphs' blackness as
trivial. Niger, on the other hand, when questioned by Oceanus about
his presence on "these calme, and blessed shores," asserts the positive
values of his daughters' complexions. Pleading his case, Niger sounds
very much like Davison's sea god: both believe what they say, and their
conviction is based solidly on everything they know of their worlds.
Similarly, both figures have the same central dramatic significance; for
it is their world views that the masques must repudiate by realizing
poetically valid alternatives—ideal worlds where, for example, blackness

2. In *The Princelye pleasures at the Courte at Kenelwoorth* when Queen Elizabeth visited Kenilworth Castle in 1575 [*Editor*].
3. Francis Davison wrote *The Mask of Proteus and the Adamantine Rock* for presentation at
Gray's Inn in 1595 [*Editor*].
4. References to the masque are to volume 7 of the Herford and Simpson edition of *Ben Jonson*
[*Editor*].
5. *Hymn in Honour of Beautie*, lines 132–33.

is not admirable or mutability is not a virtue. But Jonson's sea god is not a villain. He is merely the weary representative of the older generation who never can keep up with his daughters' new fads and is willing to try anything for peace in the household.

Niger's defense of blackness has both logic and the force of a consistent though limited view of nature. He urges first that his daughters' color is evidence of the sun's "fervent'st love,"

> and thereby shewes
> That, in their black, the perfectst beauty growes;
> Since the fix't colour of their curled haire,
> (Which is the highest grace of dames most faire)
> No cares, no age can change; or there display
> The fearfull tincture of abhorred *Gray*;
> Since *Death* her selfe (her selfe being pale and blue)
> Can never alter their most faithfull hiew;
> All which are arguments, to prove, how far
> Their beauties conquer, in great beauties warre;
> And more, how neere *Divinitie* they be,
> That stand from passion, or decay so free.
>   (173–174:143–154) [195–130]

The argument is neat, and the tone of the verse supplies a conviction of a sort that was lacking in the last sea god to visit Whitehall. Yet something is wrong. We perceive that Niger must be an antimasque character merely because he is not aware of the paradoxical element in his assumption that blackness is beautiful. Simply, there is something he does not know about his world, and it is expressed by the riddle that has sent the nymphs all over the map and whose solution can turn the antimasquers to masquers:

> That they a Land must forthwith seeke,
> Whose termination (of the *Greeke*)
> Sounds TANIA; where bright *Sol*, that heat
> Their blouds, doth never rise, or set,
> But in his Journey passeth by,
> And leaves that *Clymat* of the sky,
> To comfort of a greater *Light*,
> Who formes all beauty, with his sight.
>   (175:188–195) [164–171]

To say that Niger cannot answer this riddle is as much as to say that he does not know where he is. We may recall again that this was precisely Proteus' difficulty, and it is one that tends to distinguish antimasquers from masquers. For Davison, once the explanations have been accomplished, the antimasque is over and the triumph of the masque world is at hand. Jonson's imagination is more theatrical, but his device is essentially the same. Here a scenic revelation precedes and parallels the verbal one. Aethiopia, the moon goddess, "was discovered in the upper part of the house," and she serves to conclude the exposition:

> Niger, be glad: Resume thy native cheare.
> Thy *Daughters* labors have their period here,
> And so thy errors.
> (176:232–234) [203–205]

Britannia is the land. The nymphs have come to the right place, for it is "Rul'd by a SUNNE"

> Whose beames shine day, and night, and are of force
> To blanch an AETHIOPE, and revive a *Cor's*.[6]
> His light scientiall is, and (past mere nature)
> Can salve the rude defects of every creature.
> (177:254–257) [225–228]

What had seemed to Niger evidence of the sun's "fervent'st love" is ultimately a rude defect. The fact is presumably self-evident, for the goddess does not find it necessary to convince Niger of his error and makes her point simply by adducing the remarkable light to which the sun cedes his dominion. The masque world, in fact, is a world of self-evident truths, such as that whiteness is better than blackness or good better than evil. It is only the figures of the antimasque to whom these are not obvious facts; and we—the audience—are on the side of the masquers, even as we acknowledge in consenting to dance with them that they are our equals.

Aethiopia must of course, in the speech just cited, gesture toward the throne. But we shall be doing Jonson some injustice if we identify the "light scientiall" simply with King James. A trope may be perfectly unexceptionable so long as it is a manner of speaking. If we force it into visual or literal terms—take it, that is, as a manner of thinking or acting—we are in danger of arriving at some such ludicrous formula as "Negroes become white in the presence of the king." The masque, that poetic world, always ran the risk of becoming merely an actualized metaphor, and this problem is in certain ways a particularly Jonsonian one * * * it is significant that the identification of the symbolic figure with the character who physically represents it is never made in the world of *Blacknesse*. The monarch in 1605 is carefully left as an abstract concept: in a kingdom such as the masque postulates, the reigning power may be said to possess all the qualities that are here claimed for it. It is only a paradoxical light that can resolve the paradox of the title. On the other hand, if we wish to be literalistic, we may remark that the sun will bleach as well as burn. This light is not King James; it is,

---

6. Corpse [*Editor*].

at most, that figure which James, as the center of both the fictive and the actual court, represents. If this seems like a mere dodge on the poet's part, we should recall that the failure to merge the "light scientiall" with the spectator-king is one aspect of a structural problem central to the form, and one that we have already seen Jonson failing to solve six years later in the far more adequately realized world of *Oberon*.

But once the king is identified and the riddle answered, once the nymphs know where they are, the antimasque has given way to the masque. So the revels begin. The moon presents her invitation to the dance, and the ladies descend from the stage to the dancing floor:

> *Here the* Tritons *sounded, and they danced on shore, every couple (as they advanced) severally presenting their fans; in one of which were inscribed their mixt* Names, *in the other a mute* Hieroglyphick, *expressing their mixed qualities.*
>
> (177:266–269) [237–240]

As the dramatic action yields to the dance, so does the text, which at this point pauses to give the names of the masquers and to enumerate their symbols. For while the drama of the masque properly employs the devices of theater as a means of expression, Jonson has yet found no way to unite the text with the choreography, and thus to make the verse underlie the revels as it had the spectacle. Such unity implies a more complex idea of form than we find in *Blacknesse*; but it is a complexity that Jonson rapidly moves toward, and he achieves it most completely in *Pleasure Reconcild to Vertue* (1618)—a masque explicitly about dancing. In *Blacknesse*, however, the gap between verse and dance is bridged by music that we, to whom the masque is a poem, cannot hear. Instead of the formal activity of the choreography, we find a static list of the masquers and a description of the "mute Hieroglyphick" each presented. For a moment (and let us remember that it is the climactic moment of the masque), this work, which has been developing and analyzing a poetical symbol, renounces the methods of poetry and drama and takes on the aspect of an emblem book.[7] Not until the dance is over can the emblems again become figures in a world we recognize. That world is the world of the theater, which the nymphs have left in order to perform their dance. It is, therefore, significant but not surprising that the music concluding the dance—this time we can hear it, since Jonson has provided a text to go with it—comes from the stage and recalls the dancers to it:

---

7. Popular in the Renaissance, an emblem consisted of a symbolic picture, a motto, and a group of verses that commented upon the picture [*Editor*].

Their owne single dance *ended, as they were about to make choice*
of their men: one, from the sea, was heard to call 'hem with this
charme, *sung by* a tenor *voyce.*

SONG.

Come away, come away,
We grow jealous of your stay:
If you doe not stop your eare,
We shall have more cause to feare
Syrens of the land, then they
To doubt the *Syrens* of the sea.
(178:291–300) [259–267]

To the masque, it is the real world of the audience that contains the
sirens and the rocks on which the fiction may founder; and the song
urges the nymphs to return to the safety of the stage and the theatrical
illusion. The nymphs, however, not only remain on the floor, but initiate the revels proper:

> *Here they danc'd with their men, severall* measures, *and* corranto's.
> *All which ended, they were againe accited to sea, with a song of*
> *two* trebles, *whose cadences were iterated by a double* eccho, *from*
> *severall parts of the land.*
>
> (178:301–304) [268–271]

It takes, in fact, not only the combined forces of these two trebles with
their double echoes, but another twenty-five-line harangue from Aethiopia to get the nymphs back to their natural habitat. The goddess
concludes her appeal with charms and instructions for the coming year,

So that, this night, the yeare gone round,
You doe againe salute this ground;
And, in the beames of yond' bright *Sunne,*
Your faces dry, and all is done.
(180:347–350) [315–318]

What she is saying is that there can be no unmasking yet. This may
come as a surprise to the nymphs; certainly for us it is well worth
considering carefully.

The dancing section, from the descent of the masquers to their return
"to the Sea, where they tooke their Shell," constitutes the theatrical
climax of the masque. It has been made possible by the solution of
Aethiopia's riddle. And it is interesting that so much has been made of
recalling the masquers to the stage, to the fictive world, because we are
in danger of believing that with this climax an unmasking *is* possible
and that the point of the masque has been reached. But a reader will
be aware, more perhaps than a spectator, that answering the riddle does
not at all solve the problems the masque has presented. We must re-

alize, that is, that the theatrical climax does not coincide with the poetic or literary one. There are two distinct movements in the masque. One is toward the resolution of the conflict embodied in the unsolved riddle, which stands as a verbal acknowledgment of the fact that the nymphs do not know where they are and that they still belong, therefore, to the world of the antimasque. The proper conclusion of this is the descent, the revels, the shift from antimasque to masque, by which we are to understand that Oceanus has come to the right place at last. The other movement is a more complex one and requires a metamorphosis capable of removing the ladies' blackness, the source of the paradox that has constituted the antimasque. For, again, although through the dances the antimasque world has been left behind, resolving the riddle does not turn the nymphs white, and it is a transformation from blackness to beauty that the text demands. The first movement I have described, then, is theatrical; the second, the metamorphosis, is not.

We have seen here, as always in the masque, that the function of the dialogue is to set things up so that the one significant action constituting the "point" of the masque—and, presumably, its climax—can occur. This action in *Blacknesse*, has split into two clearly defined parts. It is a measure of the immaturity of the work that the two parts do not coincide and that, in fact, there is no stage action corresponding to the real point of the masque. At the theatrical climax of *Blacknesse*, nothing really happens; and the significant action, the metamorphosis of blackness to beauty, takes place *between* the masque and its sequel, *The Masque of Beautie* (1608), in which the nymphs are already white when they appear. Indeed, if we recall that not only three years but two other Twelfth-Night masques intervened between the productions of *Blacknesse* and *Beautie*, we shall perceive that the only place these two bear the proper relationship to each other is in the printed text, where they stand side by side and appear at last as antimasque and masque. Only as literature, that is, do these works achieve their full intended meaning.

We could ask for no better illustration of the basic disparity between the text and the production, poetry and theater, in the Jonsonian masque than *The Masque of Blacknesse*. The poet's problem was to turn this disparity to creative use, to make of it a tension integral to the art form, rather than a threat to its coherence.

JOHN MULRYAN

Mythic Interpretations of Ideas in Jonson's
Pleasure Reconciled to Virtue†

Jonson's own insistence that the masques are primarily poetry, not spectacles, encourages us to look beneath the pictorial surface of his mythological characters to their inner meaning, perhaps to hazard a
comparison of these major and minor deities with the nature of language itself. Skimming through (and sometimes ignoring) centuries of
learned commentary on classical mythology, critics of Jonson's masques
either view this mythology as primarily decorative (the "puppet gods"
of Dundas, 176) or else gathered piecemeal from a variety of different
sources (Gilbert, Wheeler), or sometimes even from a single type of
source (Starnes and Talbert).[1] Without denying these studies their
value, I want to set aside the questions of spectacle and derivation to
focus on the cognitive content of the classical myths, and to explore
how Jonson might have applied that content to the thematic develop-
ment of his masque, *Pleasure Reconciled to Virtue*.

While the influence of Vincenzo Cartari and Natale Conti[2] on the
masques of Ben Jonson is well established, both by critics and (in the
case of Conti) by Jonson's own annotations, most of the commentaries
have dealt with surface influence and have failed (or refused) to search
for thematic influence. All of the emphasis has been on the pictorial,
and the view that Jonson's masques are themselves superficial compositions, mere spectacle and "occasional" literature, has further impeded
any serious research into Jonson's creative use of sources. While Peterson, for example, can write eloquently of Jonson's "art of imitation" in
the poetry,[3] and others have performed a similar service for the plays,
the masques are regarded as journeyman work, which Jonson performed unwillingly and (for the most part) superficially.

---

† From *Ben Jonson Journal* 1 (1994): 63–76. Copyright © 1994. Reproduced by permission of
  the *Ben Jonson Journal*. The author's notes have been abridged and line numbers have been
  changed to correspond to this Norton Critical Edition.
1. See Judith Dundas, " 'Those Beautiful Characters of Sense!' Classical Deities and the Court
   Masque," *Comparative Drama* 16.2 (Summer 1982): 166–79; Allan H. Gilbert, *The Symbolic
   Persons in the Masques of Ben Jonson* (Durham: Duke Univ. Press, 1948); C. F. Wheeler,
   Classical Mythology in the Plays, Masques, and Poems of Ben Jonson (Princeton, N.J.: Princeton Univ. Press, 1938); DeWitt T. Starnes and Ernest William Talbert, *Classical Myth and
   Legend in Renaissance Dictionaries: A Study of Renaissance Dictionaries in their Relation to
   the Classical Learning of Contemporary English Writers* (Chapel Hill: North Carolina Univ.
   Press, 1955).
2. Influential Renaissance interpreters of classical mythology [*Editor*].
3. Richard S. Petersen, *Imitation and Praise in the Poems of Ben Jonson* (New Haven, Conn.:
   Yale Univ. Press, 1981).

Rather than rehearse the oft-told tale of Jonson's borrowings from the mythographers, I would prefer to focus on one masque, *Pleasure Reconciled to Virtue* (hereafter *PRV*),[4] and to explore how Jonson's interpretation of the philosophical problem posed in the title might have been influenced by Cartari's *Imagini* (1556, expanded 1571) and Conti's *Mythologiae* (1567, expanded 1581). Or, to put it another way, I want to use the *Imagini* and the *Mythologiae* as proof texts in delineating and defining a sixteenth-century approach to the apparently irreconcilable pursuits of virtue and pleasure. I shall also complement the discussion of Jonson and these mythographers with a single reference to the emblem tradition, for the full import of the tableau of Hercules at the Crossroads cannot be understood without it.

Despite the brevity of *PRV*, five mythological figures whose exploits bear directly on the relationship of Pleasure to Virtue are given extensive treatment: one god (Mercury), three demigods (Atlas, Hercules, Comus), and one mortal man, Daedalus. In one way or another, all of these figures are involved in the struggle between Pleasure and Virtue. Pleasure is represented by unrestrained appetite: drunkenness, gluttony, and libidinous sexuality; virtue is keyed to difficult choices, restraint, and the power (*virtus*) the virtuous person gains through knowledge, intelligence, and personal integrity (the wholeness of one whose body and soul are under complete control). Above all one must choose the right *path*: the path from the mountain which leads to the baffling labyrinth of Daedalus. Ultimately, the reconcilement of Pleasure and Virtue is attained through art. Just as Horace saw poetry as combining the useful (virtue) and the sweet (pleasure), so the artist Daedalus takes over the leadership of the parade of masquers from the pleasure-loving Comus and the laboring "virtuoso" Hercules.

Jonson seems to associate the mountain Atlas with both learning and virtue. It is no accident that the drunken Comus and his attendant are marching *away* from the mountain. Natale Conti sheds some light on this subject. According to the mythographer, Atlas was really an intellectual who dabbled in astronomy and used to ascend the mountain that received his name in order to get a better look at the orbit of the stars:

> They thought that Atlas had an understanding of the celestial and subterranean phenomena; that is, those who named the axis of the world, as the name itself means. In fact it was named *Atlas* after the particle *tlemi*, "I endure," and "I bear," because the axis never wearies of holding up the engine of the world. Some thought that these [the Hyades and Pleiades] were named after the daughters of the Tibyan Atlas, who was very skilled in astronomy; he gave

---

4. [Quotations] are [from] the seventh volume of the Herford and Simpson edition.

the stars the names of his daughters to perpetuate his own memory. (4.7.335)[5]

Conti also provides the tale of how the earth-bearing, much-enduring Atlas became the mountain depicted in the masque. However, because the account makes the god look like a fool, Conti, after reporting on the circumstances of the transformation, does an immediate about-face and refocuses the myth on Atlas as a stargazing intellectual. Atlas, being warned that he will lose his kingdom to a son of Jupiter, denies hospitality to Perseus, who immediately turns the mountainous man into a man-mountain:

> " 'Well, since so small a favour you will not grant to me, let me give you a boon'; and, himself turning his back, he held out from his left hand the ghastly Medusa-head. Straightway Atlas became a mountain huge as the giant had been." [Conti's citation from Ovid's *Metamorphoses* 4.654–57, Loeb transl.]

Some said that Atlas was a Libyan who used to climb that mountain in order to get a better look at the orbit of the stars; and afterwards, Atlas accidentally fell into the nearby sea, and the mountain was named after him. (4.7.332)

Since Atlas was the victim of trickery, Conti's counteremphasis on his intellectual side could be a means of justifying Mercury's description of Atlas turned mountain as "the *hill of knowledge*" (PRV, 187).

As if in mockery of Hercules, one of Comus's followers carries the strong man's cup or bowl in the procession across the stage. Hercules is outraged at this cavalier treatment of his sacred cup, and bitterly reviles the drunken assembly: ". . . and my cup / brought in to fill your druncken *Orgies* up? / & have abusd? . . ." (86–88). This appropriation of Hercules's "bowl," a vessel so large that Hercules used it as a boat when he voyaged by sea, could be interpreted as a desecration of the virtuous god's personal dishware. Still, Cartari's reports of the bowl's absurd size, coupled with legendary accounts of Hercules's prodigious drinking and gluttonous eating habits, suggest that it is the appropriate emblem for the drunken Comus as he and his troops weave their way away from "the *hill of knowledge*":

> The fables also mention that the Sun gave Hercules a huge drinking cup, which he used to sit in and float around in the sea, as Athenaeus tells it. Macrobius sees it as a kind of ship called a Skiff, which was the same name used for the drinking cup. The name is analogous to our terms for a Skiff or Boat, which explains

---

5. All translations from Conti's *Mythologiae* are based on the Frankfurt 1581 edition and are taken from the unpublished translation by John Mulryan and Steven Brown. Numbers refer to book, chapter, and page.

why they never used any other kind of cup in their sacrifices. Vergil, in that section of his work where he has Aeneas come upon Evandrus while he is sacrificing to Hercules, says that the Sacred Skiff weighed down the hands of Evandrus himself. This shows how huge that drinking cup was. Sometimes likenesses of Hercules were fashioned with the cup in hand, an idea taken from the fable I just finished talking about, or else to show that Hercules was a great drinker, as Athenaeus observes. (Mercury, 345)[6]

The same cup, Cartari continues, could become a deadly weapon if someone failed to treat Hercules with the proper respect:

> The Corinthian people who fashioned a young man offering a drink to Hercules in the god's own chapel were probably trying to communicate the same notions about him. But Pausanias writes that once, while Hercules was dining in that area of Corinth with one of his fathers-in-law, a young man named Ciato was pouring a drink into his cup; then Hercules took that drinking cup (just like the one we have been describing) and gave Ciato such a violent crack on the head with it that it killed him. For Hercules thought that Ciato was a discourteous cupbearer; and the Corinthians made sure people would remember the incident by making statues like that. (Mercury, 345, 347)

In addition to his wild drinking habits, Hercules was equally famous for his "amazing gluttony" (Conti, 7.1.703), as Cartari establishes in elaborate detail:

> There are also stories in Apollodorus, Athenaeus, and other writers about Hercules's huge appetite. It was so excessive that he often ate a huge ox all by himself. That's why the bird we call the *Coot* and the Greeks the *Laro* was dedicated to Hercules; as Suidas also informs us, it was a naturally greedy, gluttonous bird.
>
> This same greed of his was also the source of some of his sacrifices, when no one was permitted to say a single decent word. For as Lactantius informs us (it's also in Apollodorus), one day Hercules got very hungry while he was passing through the island of Rhodes. So he took two oxen by force from a farmer who didn't want to sell them, and who needed them to plough his fields; then Hercules and his companions gobbled them up. Then the poor man, who was frantic over the loss of his oxen, and was incapable of taking a proper vengeance on the thieves, turned around and started cursing and blaspheming Hercules, and saying every nasty thing he could think of to Hercules and his men. (Mercury, 347)

6. This and all other references to Cartari are taken from the Venice 1571 (Vincentio Valgrisi) edition; translations are my own, and the numbers refer to the pages of the Venice edition.

Hercules was also an inveterate womanizer. He deflowered the fifty daughters of Thespius, King of Boeotia, in one night, but he also became the sexual slave of Omphale, dressed in female garb and carding wool under her watchful eye as she threatened him with her whip (Ovid, as cited in Conti, 7.1.699).

Obviously, Hercules carries a lot of excess and suspicious baggage with him, and is hardly in a position to lecture Comus and his followers about their duties to virtue "(help Vertue) theis are Sponges, & not men" [PRV, 83]). At the same time, however, Hercules, in the words of Conti, "means nothing other than modesty and fortitude, and outstanding strength, first of the rational soul and then even of the body, which repels and drives out of the mind all defects" (7.1.707).

Some justification for this sumptuous praise can be found in the accounts of the Gallic Hercules, first glossed by Lucian[7] and picked up by both Conti and Cartari. This Hercules is sometimes identified with Mercury, as Cartari reminds us in his account of the god:

> As for Hercules, although he wasn't specifically identified with Mercury, there was no real difference between those two. Lucian tells us that the French worshiped Hercules as the god of prudence and eloquence and crafted an image of him. It was of a very old man in the decrepitude of age, completely bald except for a few strands of hair on his head, with a shadowy face and a rough, wrinkled skin. He wore a lion's pelt, held a club in his right hand and a bow in his left, and bore a quiver on his shoulders. He had a lot of chains attached to the tip of his tongue; they were made of very thin strands of gold and silver. These chains yanked a great crowd of people along by their ears toward Hercules; even so, they were still his willing followers.
>
> This image obviously symbolizes the power of eloquence, which the French credit to Hercules, because, as the same Lucian tells us, Hercules was supposed to be much stronger and more dynamic than Mercury. And they made Hercules old, because the old are often more gifted in eloquence than the young. Homer illustrates this through Nestor, for when he spoke, his mouth seemed to exude the exquisite sweetness of the finest fruits. (Mercury, 339–40)

A second virtuous Hercules emerges from the famous tableau of the Choice of Hercules, where in a dream he is accosted by two women. The one (*Voluptas*), half-clothed, is ready to lead him through "the primrose way to the everlasting bonfire," while the other (*Virtus*) sees

---

7. A Greek born in Syria in the second century C.E., he was the author of 80 works of prose [*Editor*].

him through the rocky road to virtue.[8] Cartari provides both the details
and the sources:

> The philosopher Prodicus (as one reads in Xenophon and as Mar-
> cus Tullius relates) imagined that when Hercules was a young
> man, he came some way or other into a deserted place where he
> found two paths that veered off in different directions. Not know-
> ing which path he should take, and while he was still in doubt
> and thinking hard about the problem, two women appeared to
> him. One of them was Delight, very beautiful to look upon, ex-
> tremely sensuous, and rather attractively decked out with cunning
> ornaments. She induced him to walk through pleasure's path,
> which was very broad, level, and smooth where it started, full of
> green herbs and colored flowers; but it gets narrow toward the end,
> full of stones and very sharp thorns. The other woman had a much
> harsher appearance and was very simply dressed; this was Virtue.
> The beginning of her path was narrow, steep, and difficult, but it
> eventually led into a flowered meadow, and very pleasant fields
> full of exquisitely sweet fruit. This was the path that Hercules took,
> and that's why he had such a glorious reputation. (Minerva, 370).

*   *   *

Thus while Jonson's Hercules self-righteously destroys the grove of
Comus and his followers in PRV ("Sinck Groue, or vanish into clowd,"
103), he is not fit to reconcile the apparent discord between the ideas
of Pleasure and Virtue. The one myth where he piously chooses Lady
Virtue over Lady Pleasure cannot override the many spectacular accounts of his gluttony, lechery, and drunkenness. Even the Gallic Hercules is as much as trickster (the smooth-talking version of the
libidinous strong man) as a moral exemplum. Still, Hercules has not
fully abandoned the struggle against vice, and his own earnest struggles
with his sensual temperament indicate the need to reconcile pleasure
with virtue. On balance, his struggle to achieve self-restraint wins high
marks from Cartari:

> Since the vices of the soul are much more brutal and terrifying
> than any monster, and much crueller to men than any dictator
> could be, some commentators claimed that Hercules's power was

8. Hercules at the Crossroads is taken from the fable of Prodicus, reproduced in Xenophon,
Memorabilia 1.2. The terms Virtus and Voluptas are chosen by Cicero in his recounting of
the fable (De officiis 1.32.118), although only Virtus (for Arete) is an accurate translation of
the Xenophon original. The lady of the pleasant path actually provides two different names
for herself: " 'My friends call me Happiness [Eudaemonia],' she said, 'but among those who
hate me I am nicknamed Vice [Kakia]' " (2.1.27). Jonson's "Pleasure" and "Virtue" are exact
translations of Cicero's Voluptas and Virtus. I am grateful to both Steven Brown and Jeffrey
White of the St. Bonaventure University classics department for verifying these distinctions.
For discussions of the impact of this tale on the Renaissance, see Theodor E. Mommsen,
"Petrarch and the Story of the Choice of Hercules," Journal of the Warburg and Courtauld
Institutes, 15 (1952), 178–92, and also E. Tietze-Conrad, "Notes on 'Hercules at the
Crossroads,' " Journal of the Warburg and Courtauld Institutes, 13 (1950), 305–09.

really in the soul, not the body. And through the soul's power Hercules overcame all of his chaotic appetites, which are like fierce monsters rebelling against reason: they are a constant source of anxiety and pain. (Mercury, 349)

Although Jonson provides us with very few details about Comus—"a Groue of Ivy . . . a wild Musique of *Cimbals Flutes, & Tabers*, is brought forth Comus, the god of *cheere*, or the *belly*, riding in tryumph his head crowned with roses, & other flowres; his haire curld," Cartari's description of the god in his *Imagini* is close enough (in both spirit and detail) to Jonson's to suggest imitation:

> Comus, the god of feasts, . . . was also supposed to be a young man whose beard was just beginning to sprout. Philostratus describes him in that way in a tableau that he made just for him. He puts him outside the door of a room where a fine and joyous banquet had been held in honor of a married couple who had since gone to bed to enjoy the fruits of love together. Comus was weak, with a flabby, ruddy face from excessive drinking. He was too intoxicated to keep his eyes open, so he slept on his feet, letting his flushed face sink to his chest. His left hand, which was propped up by a spear, seemed to be about to slip, just as he seemed to be dropping the burning torch he was holding with his right hand. And it would have singed his leg, if he had been leaning over in a different direction. Everything in that place was full of flowers, and the god himself also had a garland of flowers on his head, for flowers are signs of joy and carelessness, so to speak. That's why the ancients had them at banquets, where men were supposed to be joyful and emptyheaded. And they made garlands not only for themselves, but also for the receptacles they used for drinking. (Bacchus, 414–15)

Just as Comus is displaced by the "virtuous" Hercules, who has in a sense displaced the dehumanized Atlas, so Hercules is displaced by the more sophisticated Mercury, who uses his own brand of smooth talk to flatter and pacify the indignant Hercules: "Rest still, thou active frend of *Vertue*" (PRV, 151).

The interrelation of the various gods is interesting. Atlas obtains the golden apples of the Hesperides for Hercules, who in exchange takes up Atlas's burden until he returns with the coveted fruit: "Prometheus told Hercules that he should send Atlas for the apples instead of going there himself, and that he himself should hold up the sky, for as long as it took Atlas to return" (Conti, 7.1.691). Then he dupes him and leaves him with his burden once again. Hercules is conflated with Mercury in the Gallic Hercules story, but at the same time is inferior to him in other accounts:

It is said that after Hercules defeated the Giants, he gave his club in homage to Mercury (surnamed Polygius). They say that the club was fashioned from a wild olive tree, which sprouted back to life, and after its roots were driven deep into the earth, it grew into a very fine tree. (Conti, 7.1.694)

Conti associates the Gallic Hercules with Mercury, but also supplies the evidence for Mercury's superior rhetorical skill, a skill he uses in *PRV* to displace Hercules:

> Thus he was supposed to draw men wherever it pleased him, with their ears fastened to that golden chain . . . Since all richness and amplitude of speech flows from an ingenious talent, like water from an overflowing fountain, they thought that Mercury himself was the god of eloquence. They also imputed power over storms to him, for just as the sea gods were supposed to calm storms at sea, so the power of rhetoric used to calm the disputes and the arguments of the most boisterous of cities. That was the reasoning behind the dedication of tongues to Mercury, as to that god who had first discovered rhetorical embellishment and craftsmanship in speaking. For it is said that he first taught letters and the track of the stars to men, and gave them laws which shaped their civilization. He gave names to things, invented musical instruments, and discovered all those things which have to do with learning and scholarship. (5.5.449–450)

In *PRV* Mercury treats Hercules with respect—"Rest still, thou active frend of *Vertue*"—but he also reminds him of his debt to the learned Atlas, who "taught thee all the learning of the Sphere, / & how, like him, thou mightst the heaven vp-beare" (161–62). Mercury also (with Conti) identifies Atlas as the brother of Hesperus, the star that will usher in the new age of a reconciled pleasure and virtue:

> there should be a cessation of all iars
> 'twixt Vertue, & hir noted opposite,
> Pleasure; yet both should meet here, in the sight
> of Hesperus, the glory of the West,
> the brightest star, that from his burning Crest
> lights all. . . .
> . . . .
> . . . It is not with his Brother
> bearing the world, but ruling such another
> is his renowne. *Pleasure*, for his delight
> is reconcild to *Vertue*
>
> (PRV, 172–77, 181–84)

Some also gave him another brother, after whom Hesperia was named. When he had climbed up his brother's mountain, to look at the stars, and did not appear again, he was thought to have been changed into a very bright star of his own name. (Conti, 4.7.334)

Mercury, who ultimately reconciles pleasure and virtue, is also the peacemaker ("judge and innovator of peace and war," Conti, 5.5.447), and his caduceus, which he exchanged with Apollo for the lyre, is an instrument of reconciliation and peace: "After Apollo had taken the lyre, he later gave a staff to Mercury, as we said, which had the power easily to bring peace between any two at all, once the staff had been placed between them" (5.5.444). And Cartari: "The Latins called this wand the Caduceus, because they thought it eliminated disagreements, and was therefore the emblem of peace. That is why their ambassadors for peace carried it, and they themselves were called Caduceatores" (Mercury, 313).

It is fitting that the god Mercury and the mortal man Daedalus should have the concluding speeches in the masque, since Mercury represents the language and Daedalus the spectacle of the genre. Mercury, the god of rhetoric and persuasive speech, as well as the peacemaker, represents the healing power of words that bring together Pleasure and Virtue. Daedalus (as Herford and Simpson pointed out, 9.590) echoes Conti's analysis of the labyrinth as an image of the frenzied and confused direction of human existence: *"all actions of mankind / are but a Laborinth, or maze"* (261–62). "Through that labyrinth, they wanted to signify nothing other than the numerous difficulties and perplexities that always entangle human life. For some problems just create other, more serious problems, and no one can extricate himself from those, unless he is exceptionally prudent and courageous" (7.9.743). But Daedalus, who is for Conti the founder of painting and sculpture, not only creates the labyrinth but also physical representations of nature that are so true to form that they make it possible for us to interpret the world that we inhabit:

> Indeed painting is the one art, which does not differ significantly from the disciplines called liberal. Who dares to separate the very art of painting, the mother of the liberal arts, and the imitator (as I would say) of nature, from those disciplines? For this painting is one craft, which like a mute history, portrays accomplishments, and the appearances and colors of the body, but much more painstakingly than a speech can express it, and it puts them in the hands of posterity. (7.16.785)

In fact as Daedalus the artist tracks the persons of the masque through the labyrinth he himself has created, he likens the images of the dancers to the images of painters and artists, ritual "compositions," men and women who are works of art in themselves:

againe yourselves compose,
and now put all the aptnes on
of figure, that proportion
or colour can disclose.
That if those silent arts were lost,
Designe, & Picture: they might boast
from you a newer ground;
instructed to the height(n)ing sence
of dignitie, and reuerence,
in your true motions found:
(PRV, 250–59)

The masque concludes as the participants return to the mountain of contemplation, preparing to ascend it like Conti's Atlas in search of wisdom and knowledge. The artist Daedalus has taught them to journey down life's labyrinth accompanied by both pleasure and virtue, but Mercury has warned them *"to walke with Pleasure, not to dwell."* While Daedalus only recommends that they linger at the fork in the road where Hercules chose between Virtue and Pleasure (*"First, figure out the doubtfull way / at which, a while all youth should stay, / where she and Vertue did contend / which should have Hercules to frend"*[230–33]), Mercury counsels taking the hard, upward path to Virtue, which shines all the brighter in the dark, murky world of Vice:

You must returne unto the Hill,
and there aduaunce
with labour, and inhabit still
that height, and crowne,
from whence you euer may looke downe
upon triumphed Chaunce.
She, she it is, in darkness shines.
'tis she that still hir-self refines,
by hir owne light, to euerie eye,
more seene, more knowne, when Vice stands by.
And though a stranger here on earth,
in heauen she hath her right of birth.
There, there is Vertues seat.
(302–14)

The masque closes with the revellers' return to the mountain: "After which, They daunce their *last Daunce*, and returne into the Scene: which closeth, and is a Mountaine againe, as before" (318–19). Thus Comus's escape from "the *hill of knowledge*," the confrontation with Hercules, the reconcilement with Mercury, and the journey down the labyrinthine ways of Daedalus have only led back to the rugged truth of intellectual and virtuous endeavor. Or as Donne put it in *Satyre III*, "on a huge hill, / Cragged, and steep, Truth stands, and hee that will / Reach her, about must, and about must goe" (79–81).

LEAH S. MARCUS

Pleasure and Virtue Reconciled†

* * *

* * * James drew up the document which came to be known as the *Book of Sports*, a royal declaration which attempted to impose order and uniformity upon the whole confused subject of country pastimes by defining their proper limits within the Anglican community. * * * [I]t shows the king in the process of reconciling pleasure with virtue, of establishing the standard of mediation between traditional pastimes and religious duties which Ben Jonson was to celebrate in *Pleasure Reconciled to Virtue*. The declaration was issued locally in Lancashire in 1617 and published nationally on 24 May 1618. * * *

James I's *Book of Sports* aroused an immediate furor among Puritans. In Lancashire, where it was commanded to be read in churches in place of the earlier antisport ordinances, several ministers were reported for failing to comply and justifying their action on the grounds of Calvinist principle. The declaration became known among its enemies as the "dancing Book," a Churchmen's "*Maskaradoe*" in the "Dances that these Times were guilty of."[1] King James, with a caution his son Charles I was not to share when the *Book of Sports* was reissued in 1633, did not seek to enforce the declaration nationally but did see to it that some of the offending ministers were called in for questioning. As usual, his chief concern was with the maintenance of order. The old pastimes were not only acceptable in themselves and an important symbol of royal authority, they were a crucial means of "keeping up" the Anglican Church.

While the king was in Scotland in 1617, it was remarked about London that Ben Jonson had vowed, no doubt out of zealous emulation of his chief patron but also for his "profit," to retrace James's journey, though Jonson humbly proposed to travel on foot. He did in fact walk to Scotland in the summer of 1618, with the king's approval. But before Jonson set off in imitation of James's stately progress, he wrote a masque commemorating its major policy achievements and depicting emblem-

---

† From *The Politics of Mirth* (Chicago: University of Chicago Press, 1986), pp. 111–20. Copyright © 1986. Reproduced by permission. The author's footnotes have been abridged, and line numbers to the masque have been changed to correspond to this Norton Critical Edition.
1. Arthur Wilson, *The History of Great Britain, Being the Life and Reign of King James the First* (London, 1653), pp. 105–06. ["Maskaradoe": masquerade.—*Editor*]

atically the Lancashire events which had moved the king to formulate the *Book of Sports*. Ben Jonson himself had recently been "reconciled" to Anglicanism. *Pleasure Reconciled to Virtue* is his tribute to the comely *via media*[2] of the Anglican Church and the king's attempts to preserve it against the extremes of Popery and Puritanism.

Pleasure Reconciled to Virtue opens with the mountain Atlas, a hoary old man who suggests the mountainous northern reaches of Scotland and Lancashire from which the king had returned less than four months before the masque was presented. In Lancashire, the king had been forced to conquer two opposite evils which had arisen to plague him, first the licentious, popish prosporters who disrupted Anglican services, then the presumptuous Puritans who had challenged royal authority by railing against all sports. Hercules in the antimasques represents King James in action, first curbing those who carry sport too far, then stifling those who refuse to allow it altogether. Hercules was an appropriate figure for the king on several grounds. As contemporaries were well aware, he was believed to have founded the Olympic Games and was therefore associated with the promotion of state pastimes. Through his labors he was also associated with the dividing of vice from virtue, himself given to excess, according to the Ovidian tradition, but capable of triumphing over it. He was, according to one tract, the "type of a good king, who ought to subdue all monsters, cruelty, disorder, and oppression in his kingdom, who should support the heaven of the Church."[3] Like James in Lancashire, Hercules in the masque operates dialectically, defining his own position by setting limits on one, then another extreme.

As the masque opens, Comus, *"god of cheer, of the belly,"*[4] rides onto the scene in triumph amidst his raucous crew. Just as the Lancashire prosport demonstrators drowned out Sunday services with their dancing and rowdiness, so Comus and his followers make a "hymn" and religion of their debauched pleasures, refusing to recognize any higher obligations. Their cry, "Room, room, make room," the traditional opening line of English mummers' plays, was also used by morris dancers about to perform, and suggests the pushy intrusiveness of the Lancashire morris men. Significantly, one of Comus's drunken retinue carries Hercules' bowl and claims to serve him, just as the Lancashire promoters of "public mirth" claimed the king's support for old pastimes as justification for their brawling. As James I reproved this disruptive faction in Lancashire, so Hercules appears on the scene and condemns Comus and his followers with fine scorn:

---

2. "Middle way" [*Editor*].
3. Quoted from Alexander Ross, *Mystagogus Poeticus* (London, 1647), in Earl Miner, *The Cavalier Mode from Jonson to Cotton* (Princeton: Princeton Univ. Press, 1971), p. 29.
4. Quotations from the masque are from the edition of Stephen Orgel [*Editor*].

What rites are these? Breeds earth more monsters yet?
Antaeus scarce is cold: what can beget
This store?—and stay! such contraries upon her?
Is earth so fruitful of her own dishonor?
Or 'cause his vice was inhumanity,
Hopes she by vicious hospitality
To work an expiation first? and then
(Help, Virtue!) these are sponges, and not men.
Bottles? mere vessels? half a tun of paunch?
How? and the other half thrust forth in haunch?
Whose feast? the belly's? Comus'? and my cup
Brought in to fill the drunken orgies up?
And here abused? that was the crowned reward
Of thirsty heroës after labor hard?

(76–89)

The *Book of Sports* allowed the traditional sports only after church on Sunday and only for those who had demonstrated their loyalty to the king by attending the Anglican liturgy. Hercules, similarly, protests that the rites of hospitality and good cheer are deserved only after they have been earned. Comus and his crew have done just what the king's declaration warned against—they have neglected the practice of arms and similar active sports and "in place thereof set vp filthy tiplings and drunkennesse." The first antimasque, appropriately, is a dance *"by men dressed as bottles and a cask."* Jonson's first antimasque does dwell on gluttony more than would be necessary to suggest the license of the rioting Lancashire Catholics; the poet does that, I think, to make a specific point about the court which will be taken up later in the discussion.

Once Hercules has performed the labor of banishing Comus and his rioters, Atlas undergoes a transformation; Comus's grove of revelry disappears and the *"whole music"* is discovered *"sitting at the foot of the mountain, with Pleasure and Virtue seated above them."* The Choir invites Hercules to rest. But his task is not yet complete: no sooner is excess banished than death and parsimony appear on the hillside. On the level of political allegory, Antaeus and his pygmy "brothers" represent the proud, inhospitable spirit of Puritanism as encountered by King James in Scotland and then in Lancashire. The mythic giant Antaeus refused hospitality and tried to destroy those who came in search of it, just as the proud Scotch Presbyterians scorned to make their own king welcome and attempted even to turn him from his Anglican "errors." At the beginning of the masque, Hercules had just destroyed Antaeus ("Antaeus scarce is cold"), as James had "vanquished" the inhospitable Scots. But after the defeat of Comus, Antaeus' brothers rise up to do battle, just as Lancashire Sabbatarians[5]

5. Those who strictly observe the Sabbath [*Editor*].

had. The pygmies correspond closely to James's habitual characteriza-
tion of the Puritans as mean men, a "sect rather then Religion," who
acted not out of principle but rebellious self-interest and a desire to
topple those in authority.[6] Their size is small, but their rhetoric is lofty
and their ambitions are grandiose:

> Antaeus dead! and Hercules yet live!
> Where is this Hercules? What would I give
> To meet him now? Meet him? nay three such other,
> If they had hand in murder of our brother?
> With three? with four? with ten? nay, with as many
> As the name yields? Pray anger there be any
> Whereon to feed my just revenge, and soon:
> How shall I kill him? Hurl him 'gainst the moon,
> And break him in small portions? Give to Greece
> His brain, and every tract of earth a piece?
>
> (121–30)

The resemblance between their rhetoric and that of contemporary Puritans is admittedly oblique, perhaps for "reasons of state." If Jonson
had made the identification too obvious, he would have touched off
dangerous speculation among the foreign diplomats present for the performance of the masque. James may have hated the Puritans at home,
but he supported the Huguenots in France. When English Puritans
were "openly flowted and abused" in court entertainments, some found
it "unseemly and unseasonable, specially as matters stand now with
those of the religion in Fraunce." Earlier masques that *had* "abused"
the Puritans—like *Christmas* and *Love Restored*—were almost certainly
performed without foreign dignitaries present.

   Jonson's text does not make clear who actually banishes the pygmies,
Hercules himself or the Choir. The poet probably wanted to suggest
that the two act in close conjunction and harmony. Merely to notice
the pygmies is to destroy them: they are not real adversaries, but dream-
ing dwarfs who scurry into holes after their first encounter with real
power and authority. Once he has vanquished both disordered extremes
which have impeded the reconciliation of Pleasure and Virtue, Hercules is rewarded with a crown of poplar and finally allowed to rest.
The mountain undergoes a further transformation from inhospitable
crag to a peaceful, more pleasant landscape. Orazio Busino, chaplain
to the Venetian embassy in London, reported that after the pygmies
had scurried off, Atlas "opened by the turning of two doors, and from
behind the low hills of a distant landscape one saw day break, some
gilded columns being placed along the sides to make the distance seem

6. "The 1603 Speech before Parliament," *The Political Works of James I*, ed. C. H. McIlwain
(Cambridge, Mass.: Harvard Univ. Press, 1918), 274.

greater."[7] At this point the masque's symbolic embodiment of royal power shifts from Hercules, "the active friend of Virtue," to Hesperus, a force of nature who stands outside time and circumstance as Hercules does not. Hesperus is, of course, another representation of King James. Given the recent events in Lancashire, the extreme west of England, it is particularly appropriate that King James should be depicted as Hesperus, the western star. According to Busino, the king was symbolically linked to the world of the masque by a green carpet which extended from his throne at the front of the audience up to the proscenium.

Jonson's distinction between the king as actor in the realm of events (Hercules) and as a force of nature (Hesperus) is very close to the standard seventeenth-century concept of the king's two bodies: one a "body natural," mortal and dependent upon contingency like the struggling Hercules; the other a "body politic," immortal and unchanging like God himself. The promulgation of the *Book of Sports* in Lancashire had grown out of the king's mastery of a series of difficult situations, like the labors of Hercules. Antaeus was "suffocated" and Comus "beat from his grove" (*Marques*, 270). But on a higher level, the royal edict was preordained, part of a grand scheme for order which the king in his immortal body as Hesperus could effect through his mere presence. A climactic speech by Mercury, the son of Maia and therefore associated with Maying pastimes himself, celebrates the *Book of Sports* as a manifestation of universal law. As the western star presides serenely over the reconciliation of the quarrelling Pleasure and Virtue in the Land of the Hesperides, so James has presided over a similar reconciliation in the "other world" of Britain:

> But now
> The time's arrived that Atlas told thee of: how
> By unaltered law, and working of the stars,
> There should be a cessation of all jars
> 'Twixt Virtue and her noted opposite
> Pleasure; that both should meet here in the sight
> Of Hesperus, the glory of the west,
> The brightest star, that from his burning crest
> Lights all on this side the Atlantic seas
> As far as to thy pillars, Hercules.
> See where he shines: Justice and Wisdom placed
> About his throne, and those with Honor graced,
> Beauty and Love. It is not with his brother
> Bearing the world, but ruling such another
> Is his renown.

(169–83)

As Richard Peterson has pointed out in his detailed study of the masque's classical backgrounds, Jonson makes clever use of the two rival traditions of an inhospitable and a hospitable Atlas.[8] The north country of Britain has been transfigured from icy wilderness to an inviting and sunny prospect through the power of James I.

It would be a mistake to argue [that] Mercury's speech commemorates *only* the *Book of Sports*; by alluding to that declaration, Mercury praises James I for a favorite role which the king played particularly well on the occasion of its formulation, his role of peacemaker and mediator. James himself claimed, "I am euer for the *Medium* in euery thing. Betweene foolish rashnesse and extreame length, there is a middle way."[9] In Lancashire, he had negotiated a middle way between pleasure which had degenerated into license and a virtue so stern and inhospitable that it no longer deserved the name. As the masque is being performed, the royal *via media* acts upon the court itself, which, illuminated by the shining light of Hesperus, becomes a Hesperidean garden, a place for virtuous pleasures. The main masque's "distant landscape" of pastoral felicity is brought home to Whitehall and made a living reality. The twelve masquing courtiers, chief among them Prince Charles, the son of Hesperus, are called forth from Mount Atlas to demonstrate their own mastery of the king's *via media* in the reconciliation of Pleasure and Virtue.

Critics have frequently noted the prominence of rituals in Jonson's masques, rituals which sometimes seem to assume a liturgical form and significance. In *Pleasure Reconciled to Virtue*, the twelve princes descend from the hill to the music of a hymnlike song by the Choir. As Orgel has perceptively noted, the masque from this point on "moves almost ritualistically through a series of invocations, ceremonies, and what, if we were speaking in religious terms, we would have to call benedictions."[1] The masquers were apparently led down to the masquing floor by both Virtue and Daedalus, the prototypical artisan who symbolizes the arts in *Pleasure Reconciled to Virtue*. What Busino saw at this point in the masque is quite interesting: "then came a musician with a guitar dressed in a long robe, who played and sang some trills, implying that he was some deity; and then came a number of musicians dressed in the long red robes of high priests, with golden mitres, and in their midst was a goddess in a long white costume." The first musician was undoubtedly Daedalus and the goddess in white, Virtue. The mitred priests accompanying Virtue do not appear in Jonson's text, but on the level of political allegory they were certainly intended to rep-

---

8. "The Iconography of Jonson's *Pleasure Reconciled to Virtue*," *The Journal of Medieval and Renaissance Studies* 5 (1975), 123–51.
9. "The 1607 Speech before Parliament" [*Political Works of James I*], p. 291.
1. Stephen Orgel, *The Jonsonian Masque* (Cambridge: Harvard Univ. Press, 1965), p. 175.

resent Anglican bishops, who did in fact wear red robes for processionals on at least some occasions.

Modern readers have been uncomfortable with the idea that the Stuart court masque could be used to celebrate Anglican religious usage, but that is precisely what Jonson meant the ritualistic final portion of *Pleasure Reconciled to Virtue* to do. By the Caroline period, such "daring" condensation of state and ecclesiastical ritual would become common place, with King Charles himself leading the rites. As the victories of the antimasques in *Pleasure Reconciled to Virtue* emblematize the king's victories in Lancashire, so the patterned order of the main masque's songs and dances commemorate the king's "showcase" of Anglican comeliness in Edinburgh. The language of the songs reinforces the liturgical feeling of the final portion of the masque: Daedalus has composed his dances according to the laws of sacred harmony. It is significant that as the dances are about to begin, Hercules reawakens to question Daedalus, assures himself of the divine origin of the artist's precepts, and then places his benediction upon the dances. So King James himself, when he assumed the English crown, had tested and placed his approval upon the "beauty in holiness" of Anglicanism, a uniform set of ritual practices embellished by human arts. Hercules has banished the "false rites" of Comus and Popery, with their misused artifice and excessive appeals to the senses. The Choir in this particular masque seems to embody the function of music in Anglican rite; Hercules and the Choir together defeat the base pygmies who can boast no rites and no art at all. Finally, as King James tried to bring Anglicanism to Edinburgh and the Scots, Daedalus and Virtue together create a patterned ritual harmony that shuns dangerous extremes and serves as a secure guide through the complex "labyrinth or maze" of life.

In Scotland, the king's decorated chapel furnishings, organ, choristers, and the Anglican liturgy itself had been widely rejected as popish abominations and remnants of pagan idolatry. English Puritans and Scotch Presbyterians tended to condemn all dancing—to call the *Book of Sports* the "dancing Book" was no compliment. Echoing Calvin's condemnation of the Catholic mass, they scorned Anglican bowing, kneeling, and moving ceremoniously before the altar of God as a particularly idolatrous form of dance. The king's use of religious images, similarly, was a worship of idols. Jonson designed the songs of Daedalus to support James's position toward the place of the arts in religious worship and symbolically restore the respect they had lost in Scotland. What the Anglican chapel services at Holyrood House had failed to teach the Scots, Jonson teaches his audience through the masque, a form itself created, in the poet's view, to impart virtue through the arts of poetry, dance, and picture. If contemporary Puritans called the pro-

sport bishops dancers in the "*Maskaradoes*" of the times, Jonson felt no
breach of decorum in using mitred masquers to symbolize bishops.
Daedalus defends the dance in his first song as "an exercise / Not only
shows the mover's wit, / But maketh the beholder wise, / As he hath
power to rise to it" (242–45). He implies that if contemporary Puritans
inveigh against dancing, their hostility merely demonstrates their own
incapacity for wisdom and virtue. The actual dancing that follows his
speech proves his proposition for those who *are* capable of "wit." The
first dance "figures" Hercules' (and James's) dialectical negotiation of
the *via media*, with the dancers appearing to double back on themselves
as they traverse the maze, while in actuality they are defining a path of
measure and wisdom.

Daedalus' second long song defends the pictorial arts as King James,
in yet another manifestation of his role as mediator between extremes,
had recently been forced to defend them in Edinburgh:

> And now put all the aptness on
>   Of figure, that proportion
>   Or color can disclose.
> That if those silent arts were lost,
>   Design and picture, they might boast
>   From you a newer ground,
> Instructed to the height'ning sense
>   Of dignity and reverence
>   In your true motions found.
>   (251–59)

Through observation of the dancers, the viewers will not commit idolatry but will learn the power of "Design and picture" to teach virtue.
The songs of Daedalus and the dances over which he presides demonstrate the value of Anglican ritual in itself, but they also "show" how
its beauty in holiness can order the conduct of all of life. Jonson's
message was emphasized through costume. Red in the masque is the
color of Pleasure—Comus's cupbearer wore red. White is the color of
Virtue. When Virtue in her white robe appears between the bishops in
red to escort the princes down the hill, together they symbolize the
Anglican *via media*. The costumes of the twelve princes carry out the
same symbolic motif: they wore mingled crimson and white. In the last
part of the second song and in the third song about love, Jonson skill-
fully turns his subject back to the motif of the court as Hesperidean
Garden and provides a proper mythic context for the inclusion of court
ladies in the dances. If the princes have learned the proper balance
between the red of Pleasure and the white of Virtue, they can negotiate
even the labyrinth of love without danger. James's negotiation of the
labyrinth of British church politics has provided a pattern by which
they may tread their mazes successfully. The princes, as the concluding

song by Mercury admonishes, must always remember the place of art and Pleasure in the larger scheme of things and keep them reconciled to Virtue. Mercury warns them that this task will not be easy. As the masque's night of revelry draws to an end, the place of the princes is similar to Hercules' at its beginning. They reascend the hill, it closes, and Atlas is once again the forbidding wilderness of the masque's first scene, ready to try the strength and talents of a new set of Herculean heroes.

* * *

Ben Jonson: A Chronology

Jonson was such an active man, so deeply engaged with life on such a variety of fronts, that it has seemed best to present a schematic outline of his career in three parallel columns, representing the events of his life, his plays, and his major masques, arranged in order of time.

Year	Life	Plays
1572	Born, probably in Westminster, of North Country parents.	
1591–92	Soldiering in Holland and Belgium.	
1594	Married to Anne Lewis.	
1597	Acting for Philip Henslowe's company, with some writing.	
1598	Kills Gabriel Spenser in a duel; jailed, branded, and (while in jail) converted to Roman Catholicism.	*Every Man in his Humor* *The Case Is Altered*
1599		*Every Man Out of His Humor*
1600		*Cynthia's Revels*
1601	"War of the Theatres," with Dekker and Marston.	*Poetaster*

Year	Life	Plays	Masques and Entertainments
1603	Elizabeth dies, James succeeds; Jonson's oldest son dies of the plague.	*Sejanus*	*The Satyr, also known as The Entertainment at Althorpe*
1605	Imprisoned for slurs on the Scots in *Eastward Ho*; helps government investigate the Gunpowder Plot.	*Eastward Ho* (with Marston and Chapman)	*The Masque of Blackness*
1606		*Volpone*	*Hymenaei*
1608			*The Masque of Beauty*
1609	Returns to Church of England.	*Epicoene*	*The Masque of Queens*
1610		*The Alchemist*	
1611		*Catiline*	*Oberon, the Faery Prince* / *Love Freed from Ignorance and Folly*
1612–13	Travels to France as tutor to Sir Walter Raleigh's son.		
1613			*The Irish Masque*
1614		*Bartholomew Fair*	
1615			*Mercury Vindicated from the Alchemists* / *The Golden Age Restored*
1616	Granted a 100-mark pension by the King; publishes his *Works* in folio.	*The Devil Is an Ass*	*Christmas his Masque*
1617			*The Vision of Delight*
1618	Walking trip to Scotland, conversations with Drummond.		*Pleasure Reconciled to Virtue*
1619	Honorary degree from Oxford.		

Year	Events	Plays	Masques & Entertainments
1621			News from the New World; The Gypsies Metamorphosed
1622	His personal library and manuscripts destroyed by fire.		The Masque of Augurs
1623			Time Vindicated
1624			Neptune's Triumph
1625		The Staple of News	The Fortunate Isles
1628	Appointed city chronologer; suffers paralytic stroke.		
1629		The New Inn	
1631			Chloridia
1632		The Magnetic Lady	
1633		A Tale of a Tub	The King's Entertainment at Welbeck
1634			Love's Welcome at Bolsover
1637	Dies and is buried in Westminster Abbey.	The Sad Shepherd; The Fall of Mortimer	
1640	Second edition of the Works, including one posthumous fragment, and a few lines of another play.		

Selected Bibliography

• indicates items included or excerpted in this Norton Critical Edition.

JONSON'S WORKS

Ben Jonson. Ed. C. H. Herford and Percy and Evelyn Simpson. 11 vols. Oxford: Clarendon Press, 1925–52. [One of the great editions in modern scholarship. Vols. 1 and 2 contain a Life of Jonson and introductions to each of his works. A new edition of Jonson's works, the *Cambridge Ben Jonson,* will present modernized English versions of Jonson's texts and will apply the scholarship of the past fifty years to Jonson's works.]

Ben Jonson; Four Comedies. Ed. Helen Ostovich. London: Longman, 1997. [Contains *Volpone, Epicoene, The Alchemist,* and *Bartholomew Fair* in the Longman Annotated Texts series.]

The Complete Masques. Ed. Stephen Orgel. New Haven: Yale UP, 1969. [Has modernized texts of the masques with judicious notes.]

The Complete Plays of Ben Jonson. Ed. G. A. Wilkes. 4 vols. Oxford: Clarendon Press, 1981–82. [Based on the Herford and Simpson edition, but with modernized texts and notes on same page as the text.]

Volpone. Ed. Brian Parker and David Bevington. Manchester: Manchester UP, 1999. [A Revels Student Edition; has full notes and introduction.]

JOURNAL

Ben Jonson Journal. Ed. Richard Harp, Stanley Stewart, and Robert C. Evans. West Cornwall, CT: Locust Hill Press, 1994–. [Annual publication.]

RESEARCH RESOURCES

Brock, D. Heyward. *A Ben Jonson Companion.* Bloomington: Indiana UP, 1983. [An excellent resource with detailed information about Jonson's life, works, friends, and colleagues.]

Craig, D. H. *Ben Jonson: The Critical Heritage.* London: Routledge, 1990. [Collection of primary sources of critical opinions about Jonson from his own day until 1798.]

Evans, Robert C. *Ben Jonson's Major Plays: Summaries of Modern Monographs.* Westport, CT: Locust Hill P, 2000.

Harp, Richard, and Stanley Stewart, eds. *The Cambridge Companion to Ben Jonson.* Cambridge: Cambridge UP, 2000. [Contains fourteen essays on all aspects of Jonson's life and works.]

Lehrman, Walter D., Delores J. Sarafinski, and Elizabeth Savage, eds. *The Plays of Ben Jonson: A Reference Guide.* Boston: G. K. Hall, 1980.

Magaw, Katie J. "Modern Books on Ben Jonson: A General Topical Index." *Ben Jonson Journal* 5 (1998): 201–47. [Lists hundreds of topics relevant to Jonson and where information can be found about them in over 100 modern books.]

Probst, Neil. "A Topical Index to Jonson's Discoveries." *Ben Jonson Journal* 3 (1996):153–77. [Highly useful guide to Jonson's unorganized commonplace book.]

BIOGRAPHY

Kay, David. *Ben Jonson: A Literary Life.* New York: St. Martin's Press, 1995. [Incisive and well informed, with many good insights into Jonson's literary materials and his transformation of them.]

Miles, Rosalind. *Ben Jonson: His Life and Work.* London: Routledge and Kegan Paul, 1986.

Riggs, David. *Ben Jonson: A Life.* Cambridge, MA: Harvard UP, 1989.

Summers, Claude J., and Ted-Larry Pebworth. *Ben Jonson.* Twayne's English Authors Series. Boston: Twayne, 1999. [Excellent critical biography.]

CULTURAL AND HISTORICAL BACKGROUND

Braunmuller, A. R., and Michael Hattaway. *The Cambridge Companion to English Renaissance Drama.* Cambridge: Cambridge UP, 1990.

Evans, Robert C. *Habits of Mind: Evidence and Effects of Ben Jonson's Reading.* Lewisburg, PA: Bucknell UP, 1995. [Examines Jonson's underlinings and marginal markings of a number of texts that were influential upon his work; careful and interesting study.]

Gurr, Andrew. *Playgoing in Shakespeare's London.* 2nd edition. Cambridge: Cambridge UP, 1996.

Haynes, Jonathan. *The Social Relations of Jonson's Theater.* Cambridge: Cambridge UP, 1992.

Orgel, Stephen. *The Illusion of Power.* Berkeley: U of California P, 1975.

Parry, Graham. *The Golden Age Restor'd: The Culture of the Stuart Court, 1603–42.* New York: St. Martin's Press, 1981. [Contains informative essays on the masques and on Jonson's role at court.]

Paster, Gail K. *The Idea of the City in the Age of Shakespeare.* Athens, GA: U of Georgia P, 1985.

DRAMA AND MASQUES

Barish, Jonas A. *Ben Jonson and the Language of Prose Comedy.* Cambridge, MA: Harvard UP, 1967.

• ——. "The Double Plot in *Volpone.*" *Modern Philology* 51 (1953):83–92.

• Barton, Anne. *Ben Jonson, dramatist.* Cambridge: Cambridge UP, 1984.

Behunin, Robert. "Classical Wonder in Jonson's Masques." *Ben Jonson Journal* 3 (1996): 39–57.

Bryant, J. A., Jr. *The Compassionate Satirist: Ben Jonson and His Imperfect World.* Athens, GA: U of Georgia P, 1972.

Butler, Martin, ed. *Re-Presenting Ben Jonson: Text, Performance, History.* London: Macmillan, 1999.

Cave, Richard Allen. *Ben Jonson.* New York: St. Martin's Press, 1991.

• Donaldson, Ian. *Jonson's Magic Houses.* Oxford: Clarendon Press, 1997.

——. ed. *Jonson and Shakespeare.* Atlantic Highlands, NJ: Humanities Press, 1983.

Dutton, Richard. *Ben Jonson: To the First Folio.* Cambridge: Cambridge University Press, 1983.

Enck, John J. *Jonson and the Comic Truth.* Madison: U of Wisconsin P, 1957.

• Evans, Robert C. "Thomas Sutton: Jonson's Volpone?" In *Jonson and the Contexts of His Time.* Lewisburg: Bucknell UP, 1994.

Gilbert, Allan. *The Symbolic Persons in the Masques of Ben Jonson.* Durham, NC: Duke UP, 1948.

• Gordon, D. J. *The Renaissance Imagination.* Coll. and ed. Stephen Orgel. Berkeley: U of California P, 1975.

• Harp, Richard. "Ben Jonson's Comic Apocalypse." *Cithara* 34 (1994):34–41.

Hawkins, Harriett. "Folly, Incurable Disease, and *Volpone.*" *Studies in English Literature 1500–1900* 8 (1968):335–48.

Haynes, Jonathan. *The Social Relations of Jonson's Theatre.* Cambridge: Cambridge UP, 1992.

Hinchliffe, Arnold P. *Volpone: Text and Performance.* London: Macmillan, 1985.

Hirsh, James. *New Perspectives on Ben Jonson.* Madison, NJ: Fairleigh Dickinson UP, 1997.

Hyland, Peter. *Disguise and Role-Playing in Ben Jonson's Drama.* Salzburg, Austria: Institut für Englische Sprache und Literatur, 1977.

Jackson, Gabriele Bernhard. *Vision and Judgment in Ben Jonson's Drama.* New Haven: Yale UP, 1968.

Knights, L. C. *Drama and Society in the Age of Jonson*. London: Chatto & Windus, 1937.

Knoll, Robert E. *Ben Jonson's Plays: An Introduction*. Lincoln: U of Nebraska P, 1964.

McDonald, Russ. *Shakespeare and Jonson/Jonson and Shakespeare*. Lincoln: U of Nebraska P, 1988.

McPherson, David. *Shakespeare, Jonson, and the Myth of Venice*. Newark: U of Delaware P, 1990.

• Marcus, Leah S. "*Pleasure and Virtue Reconciled*: Jonson's Celebration of the *Book of Sports*, 1618 and 1633." In *The Politics of Mirth: Jonson, Herrick, Milton, Marvell, and the Defense of Old Holiday Pastimes*. Chicago: U of Chicago P, 1986.

Meagher, John C. *Method and Meaning in Jonson's Masques*. Notre Dame, IN: U of Notre Dame P, 1966.

Mickel, Leslie. *Ben Jonson's Antimasques: A History of Growth and Decline*. Aldershot and Brookfield: Ashgate Publishing Company, 1999.

• Mulryan, John. "Mythic Interpretations of Ideas in Jonson's *Pleasure Reconciled to Virtue*," *Ben Jonson Journal* 1 (1994):63–76.

Orgel, Stephen, and Roy Strong. *Inigo Jones: The Theater of the Stuart Court*. 2 vols. Berkeley: U of California P, 1973. [A sumptuous book, containing many illustrations of Jones's designs for costumes for Jonson's masques as well as much basic information and interpretation about the masques themselves.]

• Orgel, Stephen. *The Jonsonian Masque*. Cambridge, MA: Harvard UP, 1965.

• Partridge, Edward. *The Broken Compass*. New York: Columbia UP, 1958.

Peterson, Richard S. "The Iconography of Jonson's *Pleasure Reconciled to Virtue*." *Journal of Medieval and Renaissance Studies* 5 (1975): 123–53.

Rowe, George. *Distinguishing Jonson: Imitation, Rivalry, and the Direction of a Dramatic Career*. Lincoln: U of Nebraska P, 1988.

Salinger, L. G. "Farce and Fashion in *The Silent Woman*." *Essays and Studies* 20 (1967): 29–46.

Shapiro, James. *Rival Playwrights: Marlowe, Jonson, Shakespeare*. New York: Columbia UP, 1991.

Slights, William W. E. *Ben Jonson and the Arts of Secrecy*. Toronto: U of Toronto P, 1994.

Sweeney, John Gordon. *Jonson and the Psychology of Public Theater*. Princeton: Princeton UP, 1985.

Thayer, C. G. *Ben Jonson: Studies in the Plays*. Norman: U of Oklahoma P, 1963.

• Watson, Robert N. *Ben Jonson's Parodic Strategy*. Cambridge, MA: Harvard UP, 1987.

Wheeler, C. F. *Classical Mythology in the Plays, Masques, and Poems of Jonson*. Princeton: Princeton UP, 1938.